web design

W9-DCA-007

web design

a complete introduction

nigel chapman and jenny chapman

John Wiley & Sons, Ltd

Copyright © 2006   Nigel Chapman and Jenny Chapman
Published by   John Wiley & Sons Ltd, The Atrium, Southern Gate, Chichester,
                    West Sussex PO19 8SQ, England

                    Telephone   (+44) 1243 779777

Email (for orders and customer service enquiries): cs-books@wiley.co.uk
Visit our Home Page on www.wiley.com

Cover illustration: Paul Klee, 'Senecio' 1922, 181 © DACS 2005
All figures © 2006 MacAvon Media Productions.

All Rights Reserved. No part of this publication may be reproduced, stored in a retrieval system or transmitted in
any form or by any means, electronic, mechanical, photocopying, recording, scanning or otherwise, except under
the terms of the Copyright, Designs and Patents Act 1988 or under the terms of a licence issued by the Copyright
Licensing Agency Ltd, 90 Tottenham Court Road, London W1T 4LP, UK, without the permission in writing of the
Publisher. Requests to the Publisher should be addressed to the Permissions Department, John Wiley & Sons Ltd,
The Atrium, Southern Gate, Chichester, West Sussex PO19 8SQ, England, or emailed to permreq@wiley.co.uk, or
faxed to (+44) 1243 770620.

Designations used by companies to distinguish their products are often claimed as trademarks. All brand names and
product names used in this book are trade names, service marks, trademarks or registered trademarks of their respective owners. The Publisher is not associated with any product or vendor mentioned in this book.

This publication is designed to provide accurate and authoritative information in regard to the subject matter
covered. It is sold on the understanding that the Publisher is not engaged in rendering professional services. If
professional advice or other expert assistance is required, the services of a competent professional should be sought.

Nigel Chapman and Jenny Chapman have asserted their right under the Copyright, Designs and Patents Act 1988
to be identified as the authors of this work.

Other Wiley Editorial Offices

John Wiley & Sons Inc., 111 River Street, Hoboken, NJ 07030, USA

Jossey-Bass, 989 Market Street, San Francisco, CA 94103-1741, USA

Wiley-VCH Verlag GmbH, Boschstr. 12, D-69469 Weinheim, Germany

John Wiley & Sons Australia Ltd, 33 Park Road, Milton, Queensland 4064, Australia

John Wiley & Sons (Asia) Pte Ltd, 2 Clementi Loop #02-01, Jin Xing Distripark, Singapore 129809

John Wiley & Sons Canada Ltd, 6045 Freemont Blvd, Mississauga, ONT, L5R 4J3

Wiley also publishes its books in a variety of electronic formats. Some content that appears in print may not be
available in electronic books.

British Library Cataloguing in Publication Data

A catalogue record for this book is available from the British Library

ISBN-13 978-0-470-06089-6 (PB)
ISBN-10 0-470-06089-1 (PB)

Produced from the authors' own PDF files
Printed and bound in Italy by Rotolito Lombarda SpA
This book is printed on acid-free paper responsibly manufactured from sustainable forestry
in which at least two trees are planted for each one used for paper production.

Contents

Welcome

This book provides a broad and thorough introduction to Web design. It is intended primarily as a core text for use in courses in universities, colleges and other tertiary-level educational institutions. It presents a systematic account of the World Wide Web, which will serve as a foundation for students or anyone setting out on a career as a professional Web designer. Some chapters require a basic understanding of computer programming, but no prior knowledge or experience of Web design, digital media or graphic design is necessary. We do assume that all readers are Web users.

For the purposes of this book, the term Web design encompasses all aspects of creating Web sites, from the structure of Web pages and the markup which controls it, through scripts that add interactivity and generate pages dynamically, to issues of accessibility, usability and visual communication. We appreciate that some readers may become specialists in particular areas of Web design, but we take the approach that a general knowledge of the fundamentals of the whole field is an essential pre-requisite to further specialization. This book is not a collection of hints and tips, nor the presentation of a method to follow step-by-step, nor a tutorial introduction to any Web site creation program.

About The Book

We begin with the digital technology without which the World Wide Web could not exist. We then look at markup, the bones which support Web pages, whose appearance is shaped by stylesheets. Graphics and time-based media enrich contemporary Web pages, which are enlivened by scripting. We describe each of these components in its turn, and explain how programs can draw information from databases in response to input from users, and present it on pages. Once we have conveyed this picture of the basic means by which Web pages are constructed, transmitted and displayed in a browser, we are able to turn our attention to the serious issues of how to design pages that are accessible to all users, and which convey their content effectively. Throughout the book, we emphasize the importance of standards, and, as far as possible in such a rapidly changing subject, we look to the future.

You may be puzzled to find that the illustrations throughout the book do not necessarily seem to be of the best in Web design. We have designed working Web page examples and illustrations specifically to demonstrate technical points in the text as simply as possible, and this often means a compromise of style, or even the choice of a deliberately poor design. Limitations of the colour printing process mean that the colours in the illustrations are often not as you would see them on a computer screen. Accurate versions can be found in the slides on the book's supporting Web site.

Teaching and Learning Features

- To aid revision, key points are presented in a section at the end of each chapter, divided into topics. These key points are also available on fully illustrated slides which you may download from the supporting Web site.
- Important terms, marked in **bold italics** on their first occurrence in the text, are defined in a glossary, which can also be found on the supporting Web site.
- Distinctive boxes, headed by a pale blue bar, are used throughout the text to set aside special topics. These include longer explanations of difficult or important terms, descriptions of emerging technology which we expect to become more important in the next few years, notes on significant browser quirks, and extra detail on some subjects for the benefit of technically inclined readers.
- Every chapter ends with a collection of exercises, divided into three sets. First are routine test questions, which assess understanding of the text. Next, we offer some discussion topics, which require more thought and some additional research. These could be suitable as essay titles, or the basis of class discussions. Finally, we suggest some practical tasks. These are the most important exercises, which require readers to exercise their skill and apply their knowledge of Web design. The proportion of these three types of exercise varies according to the subject of each chapter.

Supporting Web Site

Additional support for teaching and learning can be found at the book's own Web site, `www.webdesignbook.org`. Here you will find a wide range of material, including full code and working versions of the examples in the book, slides of the key points, teaching notes, the interactive glossary, links to reference material and useful Web sites, and corrections to any errors we discover after the book goes to print.

Web Experiences

1

Most of the time, you can use the World Wide Web without having a very clear idea of what it is or how it works; it's just a bunch of Web sites scattered around the Internet. When you want to visit a Web site, you enter its address in your Web browser, or choose it from your collection of bookmarks, and the site's home page will be displayed. You can follow links from the home page to other pages in the site, and then move around the site by following links between pages. Many sites also provide links to other sites, which you can follow in the same way, so that sites are connected in a web-like structure.

Although it is nothing like a full or accurate explanation of what's going on, this simple model provides a useful starting point for thinking about how its users experience the Web.

Web Pages and Sites

Pages

The basic element of the Web – the smallest unit you can display in a browser – is a **Web page**. Conceptually, a Web page resembles a page in a book or magazine, in that it consists of some text and usually images, which are laid out in two dimensions for reading. There are, however, some important differences between Web pages and printed pages that affect the way you must approach them as a designer.

The fundamental difference is that a Web page is not a physical object. As we will see in later chapters, a page is a collection of data in a form that can be stored in a computer and transmitted over the Internet. In order to display this data on your screen as a page of text and images, you need a computer or other device connected to the Internet and running a program which fetches the page from wherever it is stored and then interprets the data and renders the page on the screen. This is the function of the familiar **Web browser**, such as Firefox, Internet Explorer, Opera or Safari.

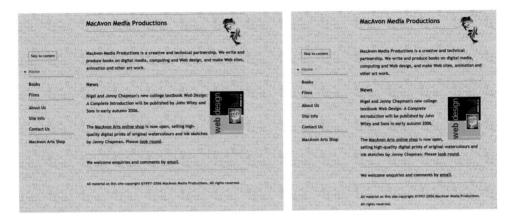

Figure 1.1 Text reflows when the window is resized

A Web page is thus not constrained by the physical limits of a sheet of paper: it has no fixed size and the text may **reflow**. That is, the lines may change length and break in different places when the window in which it is displayed is resized, as Figure 1.1 demonstrates. A Web page can be of any length or width, with scroll bars in the browser being used when it overflows the window. It can use a wider range of colours than is available in most inexpensive printing processes.

Conversely, a Web page does not have the advantages of printed material. It requires additional hardware and software before you can read it. It must be displayed at the low resolutions typical of computer monitors, and cannot, in general, make use of all the facilities for page layout and typography available to print-based designers. In fact, the layout and typography are not fixed when the page is created: most browsers allow the user to change the size of the font used to display text, for instance, which can cause text to reflow; sophisticated users can change almost all aspects of the display. Sadly, it remains the case that browsers may sometimes fail to render pages correctly.

Secondly, a Web page can include elements which cannot be incorporated into a printed page. **Time-based media**, such as sound, video and animation, can be embedded in the page.

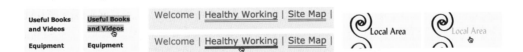

Figure 1.2 Rollovers

A Web page can also be *interactive*: it can respond in a variety of ways to the user's input. A familiar example is the *rollover*, an image or piece of text which changes its appearance when the cursor is moved over it, as shown in Figure 1.2. Clearly, such effects are not possible in printed matter, where the content is fixed once and for all when the ink is applied to the paper. Web pages that incorporate data entry forms, such as the one shown in Figure 1.3, can accept input from users and then pass that data to programs running on a remote computer. This means that a Web page can serve as the user interface to a **Web application**, which may provide a range of complex functions, including database access and processing of commercial transactions such as purchases made with a credit card. Here, we are clearly a long way from a traditional printed page, which is a purely inert object.

A third important difference between Web pages and printed pages arises from the variety of devices and software that may be used to display a Web page, which results in Web users experiencing the same page in different ways. It is probably true that the vast majority of people access the Web using one of the major browsers on a desktop or laptop computer

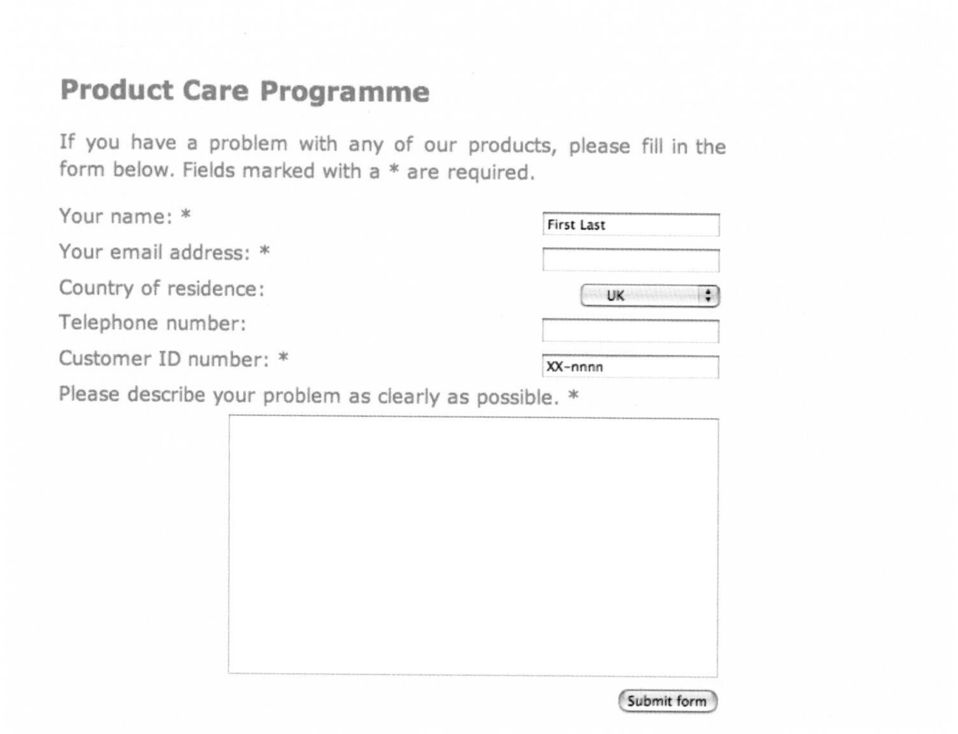

Product Care Programme

If you have a problem with any of our products, please fill in the form below. Fields marked with a * are required.

Your name: *

First Last

Your email address: *

Country of residence:

UK

Telephone number:

Customer ID number: *

XX-nnnn

Please describe your problem as clearly as possible. *

Submit form

Figure 1.3 A form on a Web page

running Windows, MacOS X or some other variety of Unix. Although progress has been made and continues to be made in standardization, it remains the fact that different browsers (or the same browser running on different platforms) sometimes render the same page in different ways. The differences may be minor and cosmetic, but, particularly in the area of interactivity, significant differences between browsers and platforms may be encountered, which can mean that a page only works as intended on certain combinations of browser and platform.

Finally, unlike printed material, Web pages may be linked together so that you can move directly from one to another with a single click of the mouse. A link is simply an element of a Web page – an image (or part of one) or a string of text – which has the Web address of another page associated with it, in a way that we will describe in later chapters. This is what gives the Web its name: it is a web-like network of pages that its users can traverse by following the links. Printed pages may have cross-references, but following these means turning pages, looking at the page numbers. A reference to another book could mean a delay of weeks if you need to buy or borrow a copy and wait for it to be delivered. As an experience, following cross-references in print lacks the immediacy of Web traversal, which can take you from document to document as fast as your network connection allows.

When text is augmented by traversable links it becomes **hypertext**. In the World Wide Web, pages may include embedded images and time-based media, so this network of linked pages is referred to as **hypermedia**.

Web Sites

In general, a **Web site** (or just **site**) comprises a collection of Web pages, which are related conceptually and connected together by links. Each site has a **home page**, which you reach when you type the site's address in your browser. The home page usually provides some introduction to the site and, unless the site is an unusual one, contains links to the other pages of the site.

Sites are a significant part of the Web experience. Although the basic elements which are linked together to form the Web are pages, the site is a focus of navigation, forming an important conceptual element in itself. Since any page is part of a site, at any time you can think of yourself as being at a particular site, and the act of moving to another page within the same site is conceptually different from that of moving to a page in another site.

Personal sites	Usually consist of a few pages reflecting some personal interest of the owner, often giving biographical information and illustrated with photographs. Some personal sites become genuinely useful repositories of specialized information, or individual accounts of experiences, such as coping with diseases, which can be inspiring or helpful to others.
Blogs	(Short for 'weblogs'). A frequently updated collection of short *entries*, usually arranged chronologically. Most blogs are maintained by a single person (blogger), and are organized around some theme, such as politics, films, sport, technology, or just the blogger's personal life. Blogs usually provide an RSS feed and may allow visitors to add comments to entries. Blogs are increasingly superseding personal sites.
Forums	Collections of threaded discussions around a theme. Registered users may post and reply to articles via the forum pages. Usually, discussions are moderated. Forums are often used as an informal support mechanism for hardware and software.
Art and entertainment	Web equivalents of some established forms of entertainment, including cartoons, fiction, horoscopes and pornography. Supplements to established media, in the form of movie trailers, gossip columns, reviews. Online galleries and some novel attempts at online art (installations). Dissemination of entertainment destined to be enjoyed in other forms: music and video downloads, etc.
Information	News, reference works, technical information and reference material (e.g. standards), railway and airline timetables, TV and radio listings, weather and stock reports… In fact, just about any form of information that can be presented on a Web site will be.
Online shops	Direct buying from bricks-and-mortar retailers or Web-only sellers. For digital products, direct download is possible. Online auction sites, providing a venue for users to buy and sell to each other.
Directories and search engines	Classified directories and searchable indexes of Web pages. See main text.

Portals	Mostly evolved from directories, with the addition of news pages, celebrity gossip, small ads, dating services, horoscopes…. Often host forums and provide real-time chat facilities. Facilities can be customized by registered users.
Online services	Online banking (24 hours a day). Share trading. Insurance quotations. Payment services. Employment and recruitment agencies. Travel and holiday booking agencies. Dating agencies. Remote services (e.g. printing). Contact points for design agencies and other services. Internet Service Providers: sign-up and hosting management.
Enterprise sites	The home sites of corporate enterprises, performing multiple functions, which may include information dissemination, product support, direct selling and branding (the dissemination and reinforcement of corporate identity). May be extremely large, with hundreds or thousands of pages.

Table 1.1 Some common types of Web site

The conceptual unity of a Web site is almost always reflected in a unified design for the site's pages. Often, a logo or some other element that identifies the organization whose site this is will also appear in a prominent position on each page, to remind you of whose site you are visiting (although it is surprising how often sites omit such an identifier). Most sites also attempt to maintain a uniform visual style, using the same colour scheme throughout, similar layout, the same fonts, and so on. For commercial and institutional sites, the design may serve a branding function. Where it is appropriate, branding elements already used in other media may be used on the Web site. For instance, a company will almost certainly use its logo on its Web site, and may base the colour scheme on distinctive packaging employed for its products.

For all but the smallest sites, it is customary to provide every page with a set of links to the most important pages of the site. These major links are usually grouped together into a *navigation bar* (*navbar* for short), which is placed in a distinctive position, often across the top or down one side, of every page in a site. Consistency in the style and position of the navbar contributes further to the visual unity of the site.

Every Web site is unique, and some are so quirky that they defy categorization, but it is possible to identify some broad categories into which many sites may be divided. Table 1.1 offers an informal taxonomy of Web sites, based on the experience they offer to visitors. We expect most readers will be familiar with sites in the majority of categories.

Using the Web

Much early writing about the World Wide Web concentrated on its nature as hypermedia, and on the links between Web pages. This led to an emphasis on connections between documents, and a mode of exploration based on following links – what became known as 'Web surfing'. It is true that much of the novelty of the Web lies in this linkage between documents, but the notion that users' primary activity is following links is not true. In fact, if your only way of finding information on the Web was by following links, it is unlikely that you would get very far. Most people's use of the Web consists of a mixture of activities, of which following links is only one. The others include: going directly to sites using addresses obtained from elsewhere (e.g. print advertising), revisiting known sites (probably stored as bookmarks) and searching.

Web Browsers

Most Web browsers provide identical facilities. The differences between them lie in their user interfaces, efficiency, security, adherence to Web standards and the presence or absence of bugs. These various differences will have varying importance to different users, so it makes no sense to ask which is the best browser. Few would claim that Microsoft's Internet Explorer is the best in any of these categories, but it has the advantage of being installed by default with the most widely used desktop operating system, and so it is by far the most commonly used of the different browsers available. It would be a gross error, however, to assume that Internet Explorer is the only browser in use. Others include (at the time of writing) Firefox, Mozilla and Netscape, which are products of the Open Source Mozilla project, Safari, which is the default browser on MacOS X, Konqueror, an integrated browser and file manager for the KDE desktop environment under Unix, and Opera. It should never be forgotten that there are also text-only browsers (such as Lynx), and that blind and partially sighted users may have to browse the Web with non-visual user agents, such as screen readers. Most browsers are available free of charge, although some display advertisements unless you pay a fee to prevent this.

It is important for Web designers to remember that users' experiences of the facilities offered by browsers lead them to have certain expectations about what they can do and how, and it is important not to frustrate these expectations. In particular, the **back button** and **history list**

Terminology

User Agents
Graphical Web browsers are not the only programs that are used to interpret Web pages. Among the others are non-visual browsers, such as screen readers, and the robots used to create indexes for search engines. All such programs are known as user agents; Web browsers are the most important type of user agent.

permit backtracking, an essential part of the activity of exploring the Web by following links. Since the text of a link provides at best a minimum of information about the page that the link points to, it is inevitable that following a link may lead to disappointment: on looking at the destination page, you find that it isn't interesting after all, so you need to go back. Perhaps you might follow a chain of links, only to discover that they lead nowhere interesting, so you need to go back to a known worthwhile page you have visited recently, which the history list enables you to do. Figure 1.4 illustrates this pattern of browsing – the blue arrows represent links between pages, the orange arrows show the user's path through the site, with the dashed arrows indicating backtracking.

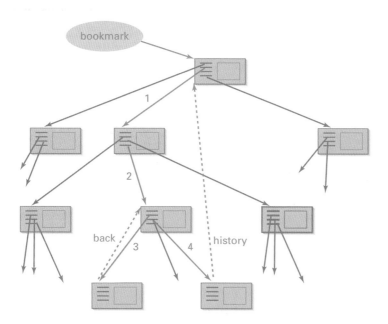

Figure 1.4 Browsing and backtracking

Browser Quirks

Quirky Browsers

In an ideal world, all browsers would implement the relevant standards correctly, and they would all display every Web page identically. This is not what happens. Awareness of the benefits of Web standards has increased dramatically in recent years, but for a long time major browser makers preferred innovation to compliance with standards. In some cases, browsers' innovations were later turned into standards, but often the standards had to effect a compromise between incompatible features invented for and already implemented in different browsers. Additionally, browsers are quite often released with bugs in. Consequently, over the years, there have been many browsers in use that do not implement the standards correctly or completely.

As a result, Web designers have often been forced to use incorrect coding to work round certain browsers' quirks, with the result that browsers released later have had to emulate their predecessors' quirks in order not to break existing pages. The situation is far from satisfactory.

The worst offendors have been Netscape Navigator 4 and Internet Explorer 5 for Windows. Use of these two browsers is now declining, and it is therefore probably safe to stick with the standards – doing so will encourage browser manufacturers to continue supporting standards. There are, however, a few places where Internet Explorer 6 for Windows, which is still widely used, diverges from the standards, and we will note the worst of these, and describe ways of coping with them.

Since experienced users come to depend on the behaviour of these features, it is unwise to interfere with them by, for example, using scripts that load pages without adding them to the history list.

All but the most primitive browsers provide some way of permanently recording the addresses of sites you have visited, by creating **bookmarks** (or *favourites*). Bookmarking an interesting site means that you no longer have to follow a trail of links to reach it, you can always go to it directly. You can consider bookmarks as a way of recording what you have learned from your experience of browsing. A number of sites allow you to maintain and publish a collection of bookmarks so that they can be shared with other users, thereby making this experience available to a wider community.

Searching

There are so many pages in the Web that it is impossible to know whereabouts any particular piece of information you might be interested in can be found. Certainly, there are some cases where it will be obvious where to look: if you want to know who was the cinematographer on a film you have just seen, the Internet Movie Database (IMDb) will probably tell you. But what if you didn't know IMDb existed? Or you were looking for something more obscure that, it turned out, was only described on somebody's personal Web site? Somehow, it is necessary that people be able to find sites that they don't already know about. Two solutions are offered.

Directories are classified listings of Web sites. The classification schemes used by Web directories are invariably hierarchical. At the top of the hierarchy are broad categories. For example, the Open Directory project at `dmoz.org` divides sites into the following top-level categories: arts, business, computers, games, health, home, kids and teens, news, recreation, reference, regional, science, shopping, society, sports and world. As you can see, the classification scheme is somewhat arbitrary. Some sub-categories are listed beneath each top-level category on the directory's front page, which provides some extra indication of what sort of site is contained within the category.

If you are looking for pages on a particular subject, you can work your way down through the hierarchy to progressively more specific topics. Thus, if you were looking for pages related to experimental film festivals, you would choose `arts` from the front page (noting that `movies` is listed among its sub-categories), then `movies`, `film festivals` and finally `experimental`. On the page you ultimately reached, you would find links to pages related to the topic.

Directories stored on computer systems have an advantage over card-based catalogues, such as you might find in a reference library, in that a sub-topic can be filed under more than one topic. For instance, in the Open Directory, experimental film festivals can be reached under `film festivals`, as we noted just now, but also under `experimental` within the `filmmaking` sub-category of `movies`.

Directories are maintained by teams of people, who decide on the classification of pages. Sites may be submitted by their owners or developers, with a suggestion of the appropriate category, but the ultimate decision rests on the judgment of the people maintaining the site.

This makes directories very labour-intensive, and it means that months may elapse between a site's being submitted for inclusion in a directory and its appearing there. Some directories take advantage of this by charging fees for guaranteeing fast inclusion.

Search engines take a different approach. Instead of offering a hierarchical set of categories so that users can find a page on the basis of its possible description in terms of the classification system, search engines allow users to enter some keywords which describe what they are looking for, and then return a list of pages that match those keywords in some sense. In other words, directories require users to navigate their classification, while search engines allow users to specify their goal in their own terms. The lists of results are ordered according to some criteria used by the search engine to judge the relevance of each page in the list to the original search query. If the search engine is a good one, the first few pages in the list will very likely be the sort of thing the user is looking for.

Search engines work by creating huge databases that describe pages on the Web – in principle, all of the pages on the Web. Major search engines use thousands of servers working in parallel, and vast arrays of disks, to process the millions of search requests that are made every day. They obtain their data using programs called *robots, spiders* or *Web crawlers*, which follow links from page to page and from site to site, thereby traversing the whole Web. The precise information gleaned by each engine's robots and the way in which it is used vary, and in some cases the details are surrounded by secrecy. This is because a search engine is judged by the usefulness of the list of results it returns, and this depends on the algorithms and data employed in the searching process.

Early search engines simply used any text that appeared on a page, together with metadata supplied by the page's author to describe the page, and searched for the appearance of keywords in the search query in this text. The results of such a naive approach tended to be somewhat hit and miss. More recently, some engines have incorporated techniques of artificial intelligence to attempt to extract more meaning from pages, and thus to obtain better matches for users' queries.

The major breakthrough in Web searching, however, came with the launch of Google. The innovative idea behind the Google search engine was that the links in the Web itself can be used to deduce the relative importance of pages returned by search queries. Put crudely, if a lot of other sites have found it worth linking to a particular page on a topic, it is probably the case that that page is worth looking at. Therefore, when Google returns a list of pages in response to a search query, it uses the number of other sites with links to that page as part of its weighting that determines the order in which the search results are displayed. The intuition behind this approach has been justified by the perception among users that Google tends to return more relevant results than search engines based on other algorithms.

Closely related to the problem of finding sites on the Web is that of finding information within a site. If, for example, you have gone to Apple's site looking for information about the latest security update to MacOS X, you won't find it on the home page. The site is large, and it would not be practical to visit every page to see whether it told you what you wanted to know. Here again, it is necessary to be able to find pages that satisfy certain criteria.

One way of providing a means of searching within a site is simply to offload the search to one of the major search engines, a method which is becoming increasingly popular. The big search engines make this easy, by providing code fragments which can be incorporated into any Web page to display a text box into which search terms can be entered and sent to the search engine. The query is restricted to pages within the site that sends it, and the results are displayed in the normal way. One of the interesting things about this arrangement is the way in which it demonstrates that there are no really hard boundaries to a Web site: some of its functions may be performed elsewhere. Nevertheless, it may well be the case that a hand-crafted search facility for a particular site will provide better results for the queries typically made by its visitors, especially when the pages are created dynamically from a database.

Searching is such a popular way of finding Web pages that most browsers now incorporate a search box in their user interfaces. Users can type keywords into the box without actually going to the search engine site. The browser passes the query to the search engine, and then goes directly to the page of results.

Web Feeds

Many of the most interesting and useful Web pages are updated, often frequently. News sites and blogs are obvious examples, but others abound. Job vacancies, product announcements, ISPs' system status announcements, software, DVD and CD releases, film reviews and announcements of special offers at online shops are all examples of information that is necessarily updated from time to time. In some cases, updates may occur every few minutes; in others they may be months apart. A user who wishes to ensure that they see any updates that interest them might have to keep returning to the page containing the information in order to check whether there is anything new there. To avoid this time-consuming repeated checking, sites can provide a **Web feed**, which is a summary of their content in a format that can be read by certain sorts of program. In particular, feed readers can read Web feeds and display a short summary of recent updates. Users of such a program can subscribe to the feeds

Terminology

RSS

Web feeds are often referred to as *RSS feeds*. RSS refers to the format used for feed data. More accurately, RSS is a family of formats, with an involved history that has led to several different incompatible versions. The different versions even ascribe different meanings to the initials RSS: they have stood for Rich Site Summary, RDF Site Summary and Really Simple Syndication, in different versions of RSS.

No version of RSS has ever been any sort of official standard. The IETF has defined a standard format, closely related to RSS, called Atom. The name RSS is used loosely to include Atom as well as all versions of RSS itself. Fortunately, almost all systems that handle RSS at all can handle all versions of it, and Atom.

of sites that provide them, usually simply by clicking on a special link displayed on the site. A feed reader will periodically check all its subscribed feeds for any updates. Most modern browsers also incorporate basic feed reading functions.

Web feeds were originally devised for news sites, to make it possible to check the headlines of news items as they were posted. They have achieved greater popularity in conjunction with blogs, allowing their readers to see when new articles have been posted. The format used for feeds allows for the inclusion of files with the feed data. This facility is the basis of **podcasts**, which are basically Web feeds that carry an audio file. Podcasts have achieved great popularity as a way of disseminating the equivalent of radio programs over the Web.

As well as being read with a feed reader, Web feeds can also be incorporated into other Web pages. In fact, this was the purpose for which they were originally devised. The terms **content aggregation** and **syndication** are used to describe this practice, which is often found among the customization options offered by portal sites. The general idea is the same as that behind feed readers: the feeds of interesting sites can be subscribed. Instead of being checked by a reader, though, subscriptions are checked by a program running on some server, which then creates a Web page from the information in the feed. Content aggregation like this is sometimes used by bloggers to add a list of updates from like-minded blogs to their own.

The Web Community

When considering the technology beneath the World Wide Web, and the design challenge of producing exciting and useful Web sites, it is sometimes possible to lose sight of the fact that the most important aspect of the Web is its community of users, in other words, the people who visit Web sites. Without them, the entire exercise would be completely without point.

It is estimated that in early 2006 there were just over a billion people with access to the Internet. This is a large number of people, but it is important to remember that the figure represents less than a sixth of the world's population. The Web community remains an élite minority on a global scale. In a world where huge numbers of people cannot rely on clean drinking water, never mind continuous electricity supplies or telecommunications, it is absurd to suppose, as some commentators apparently do, that the Internet represents a worldwide revolution that will transform everyone's lives within a few years. Compared to the real issues faced by the majority of the world's population, the impact of the Internet and World Wide Web is insignificant.

For those who do have Internet access and the lifestyle to benefit from it, though, the Web has become an important factor. This community is not a homogeneous mass of identical people, with identical abilities, needs and expectations. It exhibits wide diversity in several respects – there is no such thing as an average user. There is just too much diversity, along too many different axes, for average values to be of any use. (What is the gender of the average Web user?) Therefore, trying to aim Web sites at the 'ordinary person' is a pointless exercise. Instead, we need to embrace diversity.

Personal Diversity

We all know that every individual is unique, but when designing Web sites it is very easy to forget this, and to assume that everybody is just like us. For a large number of Web designers, this means relatively young, affluent (certainly by global standards), well educated, able-bodied, male and a native English speaker. After all, if everybody was like that, designing sites for them would be relatively straightforward, because we'd know roughly how they would respond to our designs and how easy they would find it to use our sites. Indeed, some commercially successful sites have recently been designed on this basis, providing services to a user community of Web designers and other technologically sophisticated people. It isn't generally that simple, though, and it is essential for Web designers who cannot afford to restrict their services to a small coterie of like-minded customers to be aware of the need to cater for people who are different from themselves and their immediate circle.

From a social point of view, the most important source of personal diversity is in the area of physical and mental ability. Many people are limited in some way in their interactions with computer systems. They may be blind or partially sighted, in which case they will not be able to use sites that rely solely on graphics for presenting information and performing interactions. They may be unable to use a mouse, owing to illness or injuries, both severe and minor, so that all their interactions must be performed using the keyboard, or in severe cases, through voice input or specialized devices such as breath-activated switches. These people cannot click on anything, so sites whose only form of interaction is point-and-click will be unusable for them. Other people have cognitive difficulties that make it hard for them to understand complex interactions or densely written text.

The list of problems that may interfere with a person's ability to use a Web site goes on. Typically, these problems affect other areas of their lives too, and may make it difficult for them to get around or to find employment. Computers in general, and the Web in particular, can play a big part in making their lives easier, for instance, by removing the need to travel, by allowing them to shop online, or by enabling them to work from home using specialized equipment that would not normally be available in the workplace. However, it takes work on the part of Web designers to make Web sites accessible to everybody, and without this work sites can become another source of frustration and a further barrier to a full life.

People differ in other ways, besides their physical and mental abilities. There is a wide range of educational achievement in most countries. Even in developed countries, although a significant proportion of the population goes to university, many leave school, out of choice or necessity, at the earliest opportunity and without any qualifications. Illiteracy rates vary widely in different countries, ranging from 1% to around 80%.

Even among people with similar levels of education, there is a range of technological sophistication. Elderly people are often lacking in confidence when dealing with computers; teenagers are often not as smart about these things as they like to think. People educated in the arts and humanities sometimes (though by no means always) find it difficult to read manuals and come to terms with the way of thinking required by complex software systems. People with extensive experience of programming and using command-line tools are more used to thinking symbolically than visually, so they can be surprisingly inept at using a graphical user interface.

Experience plays a large part in how effectively users can interact with the Web. As we will see in later chapters, conventions are widely used to indicate the function of different elements. These conventions are essentially arbitrary, so people coming to the Web for the first time will have to learn them. The current high rate of growth of the Web community is a commonplace, but the implication – that many of the people using the Web have very little experience of it – is easily overlooked, especially by Web designers, who are likely to have considerable familiarity with the conventions used on Web sites.

None of this is to suggest that all sites should be designed for some lowest common denominator of users. It is important to bear in mind that there are wide personal variations of ability among the potential visitors to a site, and to do what you can to accommodate them. As we will show in detail in Chapter 9, the standard Web technologies provide many ways of making sites accessible to a wide range of people, without compromising their appearance or function. It takes extra work and thought from Web designers, but the results can be worthwhile to many people who would otherwise be excluded.

Technological Diversity

The World Wide Web was designed from the beginning to be independent of any particular computer hardware or operating system. The Internet is a heterogeneous system: all sorts of computer systems can be connected to it. Web browsers are just computer programs, and any Web page should display and behave correctly in any properly written browser. Nevertheless, some Web designers continue to rely on features that are only supported by some platforms or browsers.

Usually, this means relying on features unique to Microsoft Internet Explorer on Windows. The excuse offered for doing so is always that over 90% of all desktop computers run Windows, so the effort required to make Web sites that work for the remaining few percent is not worthwhile. The statistic is misleading, because it includes many machines used in the business environment, which will not be used for Web browsing. The percentage of other platforms, particularly MacOS X, in some sectors, such as graphic design, and in domestic use is much higher. Nevertheless, even if the raw figures for the number of computers sold is taken at face value, the approximately 3.5% of Internet users who may be using MacOS X still amounts to roughly thirty-five million. That is a lot of people to lock out of your site.

Sites that conform to Web standards (see below) should work on all platforms and browsers. Standard features provide for the full range of Web experience, including complex page formatting and layout, interactivity and embedded media, such as animation. The additional features, such as certain media types and mechanisms for interaction with the user or the operating system, which become possible by using system-dependent features rarely, if ever, justify excluding users on minority platforms.

As well as the mainstream browsers on conventional platforms, a significant number of other types of device are also in use. Although the capabilities of hand-held devices, including Personal Digital Assistants (PDAs) and third generation mobile (cellular) phones, have improved recently, their small screens make conventional rendering of pages designed for a normal monitor screen impossible. Set-top boxes which allow a television set to be used to display Web pages are available. Television screens are of lower resolution than computer monitors, which affects the quality of the display. Where a set-top box and television are used, conventional input devices such as the mouse and keyboard may not be available, or may not provide all the facilities of the equivalent computer peripherals.

There are also significant differences in the **data rate** (speed) of connections which people use to access the Internet. Many people who use the Internet from home or from a small office will connect over the telephone lines using a modem. The fastest modems provide a theoretical speed of up to 56kbps (56 kilobits per second – we will explain this more fully in Chapter 2) although modem connection speeds vary according to the quality of the line (and even the weather) and in practice, speeds are more likely to be in the range 30 to 50kbps. Users with older equipment may still be connecting at half this speed, or even less. At the same time, **broadband** services are available in most developed countries and, as shared resources, in some third world countries. The most common forms of broadband technology are **ADSL** (Asymmetrical Digital Subscriber Line) and **cable**, which provide a guaranteed connection speed many times faster than modems. 256kbps is the minimum offered under the name of broadband (though it's stretching the definition), with higher speeds being available at a premium: 2Mbps (megabits per second, where a megabit is a thousand kilobits) is presently a common speed for domestic broadband. The extent to which broadband is available and its rate of adoption by consumers vary widely from country to country, but two things are clear. Broadband is becoming steadily more common, and it has a long way to go before it entirely supersedes dial-up access. Both classes of connection must therefore be taken into account by Web designers.

Thus, considering only domestic Internet connections, there may be a factor of forty or so between the slowest and fastest connections. This is a sufficient gap to mean that certain things, such as streaming video, which are possible on the fastest connections cannot be done over the slowest. When we also consider the truly high-speed connections available at the institutional level, this qualitative difference in possibilities becomes even more marked. More subtly, the speed of connections may dramatically alter the perception of a page. What a broadband user sees as a responsive and attractive graphically rich interface to an online shop may be perceived as hopelessly slow and full of useless ornamentation by a user with a much slower connection, who is consequently likely to take his or her business elsewhere.

It should be remembered that the Internet only became a significant cultural phenomenon when it became possible for domestic users to make connections to it. Because of the economics, domestic connections will almost invariably be the slowest available at any time, compared to the dedicated lines provided by institutions such as universities or major businesses. Designers must, therefore, resist the temptation to cater only for the fastest connections, even if they themselves have access to them, or they risk alienating the very people on whom the Web depends for its character.

As well as being faster, broadband differs from dial-up access in being a permanent connection. A modem needs to establish a connection to the Internet before it can transfer any data; it literally makes a phone call to the ISP, tying up the telephone line while it is connected. ADSL and other broadband connections do not do this: data can always be transmitted and received, and the telephone line can be used normally at the same time. Because the connection to the Internet is permanent, the Web becomes an extension of the desktop. Looking at a Web page is not much different from looking at a file on the local disk. In contrast, for the dial-up user, looking at a Web page requires the time-consuming establishment of a connection: the Web is clearly somewhere else. With broadband, looking something up on the Web is a casual operation; with dial-up, it is a chore. This means that with broadband, the Web can be more tightly integrated with other applications. For instance, if the help files for a program are only available on the developer's Web site, with broadband they can be consulted just by opening a Web browser window, whereas with dial-up they are unavailable most of the time.

Geographical Diversity

The name World Wide Web is somewhat grandiose for a system that, as we mentioned earlier, is only accessible to about 16% of the world's population. Nevertheless, its reach is global, even if the percentage of the population with access to the Web in some countries is much lower than in others. Table 1.2 summarizes some statistics published on the *Internet World Stats* Web site, in early 2006. You will see that an estimated 68% of the population of North America had Internet access, compared with about 36% in Europe, 10% in Asia and just over 2% in Africa. However, because the total population of Asia is so large, nearly 36% of all Internet users lived on that continent, compared to only about 29% and 22% in Europe and North America, respectively.

You have no way of knowing where a visitor to your site might be in the physical world. To reach all of its potential global audience, a Web site must take account of the different languages spoken around the world (or at least the different degrees of competence in

Region	Population Internet Users (millions, approx)		Internet Users (% Population)	Internet Users (% World Users)
Africa	915	23	2.5	2.2
Asia	3,667	364	9.9	35.7
Europe	807	290	35.9	28.5
Middle East	190	18	9.6	1.8
North America	331	226	68.1	22.2
Latin America & Caribbean	554	79	14.3	7.8
Oceania & Australia	34	18	52.9	1.8
World	6,500	1,018	15.7	100

Source: Internet World Stats, `www.internetworldstats.com`

Table 1.2 Worldwide Internet Access (early 2006)

English), and the cultural differences among societies. Geography also imposes physical limits. E-commerce sites must make it clear which parts of the world they will deliver to, as well as what currencies they will accept payment in. Times need to specify a time zone to be meaningful.

The only really satisfactory way of dealing with geographical diversity is **localization**: the creation of different versions of a site tailored for different regions. Some large corporations do this, providing sites in different languages, possibly with different designs to appeal to regional aesthetic senses. This also enables them to provide e-commerce services on a local basis, with online shops displaying prices in local currency, coordinated with regional ware-housing and delivery, and so on. However, localization is clearly expensive, requiring skilled translators and cultural advisors, duplication of services and careful maintenance to ensure that the sites stay synchronized, and none gets neglected or treated as second-class.

An alternative, less expensive, approach is **internationalization**. This means trying to accom-modate as many different nationalities as possible within a single site. Internationalization includes such things as using flexible input formats for addresses, displaying prices in multiple currencies, specifying distances, temperatures and other values in multiple units, using a limited vocabulary, avoiding complex grammatical constructions, colloquialisms and specific cultural references, and so on. This is easy to say, but effective internationalization requires considerable skill and understanding, and is a serious challenge to Web designers wishing to address the whole world.

Web Design Principles

If you feel the need of such things, you can find Web design guidelines by the hundred on Web sites and in books devoted to the subject. We only wish to offer two:

Get it right

Make it nice

Getting it right means making sure that your sites work properly, delivering their information and services to all visitors. Making it nice means ensuring that the experience of visiting your sites is a pleasant and rewarding one.

Standards

Standards are a key component in getting things right. Within their scope, standards define what is right – or at least they should do. Most standards have no legal status; they are just agreements between interested parties that specify in detail the characteristics of components and processes, with the intention of ensuring that products which conform to standards should be interchangeable. In the case of the World Wide Web, standards specify the precise syntax and semantics of the various languages used to create Web pages, and the protocols (rules governing the way computers exchange data over the Internet) used to retrieve pages. By conforming to standards, Web designers should be able to ensure that their pages will display and behave correctly in all browsers. By implementing the standards, browser developers should be able to ensure that their browsers will be able to display all Web pages correctly.

In reality, matters are not quite so rosy. During the 1990s, the makers of the two most widely used browsers, Microsoft and Netscape, tried to compete to establish a monopoly. They did this by adding proprietary features to their browsers, deliberately making them incompatible. Only towards the end of the 1990s did the stupidity of this approach become evident, but since then progress towards the universal acceptance of standards has been substantial, to the extent that all Web designers should now be creating pages according to the standards, and not trying to cope with the quirks of older browsers that do not implement standards correctly.

Several different bodies create standards concerning the World Wide Web. The most important is the **World Wide Web Consortium**, usually abbreviated **W3C**. W3C standards (officially called Recommendations, but increasingly referred to less diffidently as standards) specify several languages of importance on the Web. Chief among them are XML, XHTML and CSS, all of which will be described in later chapters. The W3C also specifies a Document Object Model (DOM), which provides a means for programs to interact with the components of Web pages, as we will describe in Chapter 7, although the standard for the scripting language most often used in conjunction with the W3C DOM is, JavaScript, somewhat anomalously, the responsibility of the European Computer Manufacturers' Association (ECMA).

The Internet Engineering Task Force defines standards that affect the entire Internet, not just the Web. Several key components of the Web, which we will describe in Chapter 2, are defined by IETF standards. The International Organization for Standards (ISO – it's not an acronym) is partly responsible for some of the standards concerning images and other media formats used on the Web.

Usability

Getting it right, that is, making a site that works – in the sense that it displays and behaves correctly, conforms to standards and is accessible to everybody – is only a beginning. Making it nice begins with ensuring that the site is usable by people who visit it. That is to say, when somebody reaches the site, it must be clear what it offers, how it's organized and what actions, if any, they have to take. These matters are not amenable to standards, since they are subjective and dependent on a host of factors that cannot easily be quantified. Some usability experts publish lengthy lists of guidelines, but these are no substitute for an understanding of how people approach Web sites and how they behave when interacting with them. Above all, making usable Web sites depends on making their potential users the focus of the design – in other words, treating your visitors considerately.

Examples of the sort of usability problems that result from failing to consider the needs of site visitors include inconsistently laid out pages, poorly organized navbars, cluttered layouts, excessively long forms, search boxes and other controls that are hard to find, obscurely labelled buttons that fail to convey their function, unhelpful or incomprehensible error pages and sites whose very purpose is hard to discern.

Few people would deliberately design a site that was not usable, but sometimes it is hard for designers to appreciate how other people approach the Web, what they find obvious and what they find hard. For example, if something goes wrong – perhaps a visitor fills in a form field incorrectly, causing a database query to return no data – it is tempting for the designer to generate an error message explaining what happened when the database query was attempted. The visitor probably doesn't even know a database is involved, they just need to be told what they did wrong and what they need to do to put it right.

Unless you are gifted with an exceptional talent for empathizing with other people's experience, you will not be able to rely on your own intuition for determining whether your site design is usable or not. You must carry out some usability testing. This can be as simple as asking a few potential users to try to carry out some simple tasks, such as finding out how to contact the site's owners, or, in the case of an online shop, finding the price of some item, and observing how they go about it. The test users should be encouraged to think out loud so that you can determine what they take notice of on the screen, what they fail to see, where they encounter difficulties, and so on. When you identify a problem, you should correct it and then test again.

You will appreciate that such small-scale testing is not an infallible guide to users' behaviour. Most usability experts advise that as few as five subjects is adequate to find most problems. This may seem bizarre, given the vastly greater number of people with access to the Web, and statistically, tests using such small samples have no significance, but experience suggests that there is little to be gained from testing on more users. It is impractical to recruit a test sample sufficiently large and diverse to satisfy a statistician that it is representative of the range of abilities found among the population of Web users, so the possibility that the tests will fail to find some problems can never be ruled out. (For the same reason, studies that claim to predict universal usability properties and produce guidelines based on them should be treated with suspicion.) On the other hand, if a small test finds a problem, you can be confident that the problem exists and should be corrected.

Visual Design

It is sometimes assumed that the visual design of Web sites is concerned only with making sites more attractive to users, or with adequately displaying or illustrating the products, services or information that the site offers – or even simply with the exhibition of the graphic designer's skills. This assumption leads to the conclusion that consideration of visual design can be left to graphic designers or other artists as a sort of icing on the cake – the finishing touches that are there for the sole purpose of making a site look pretty. This is a fundamental misunderstanding of the function and importance of visual design and communication, and it can lead to poorly designed sites which are not only unattractive but difficult to use or understand, and which will not compete well for the attention of users or fulfil the purpose for which they were intended.

Even though not everyone who has access to Web sites also has good vision, the Web remains primarily a visual medium, with billions of pages which feature material that – for those who do not have impaired vision – will be looked at rather than listened to or read via touch in the form of Braille. The first and most immediate impression which any Web page will make upon a new (sighted) visitor is visual, and first impressions are vitally important. A bad first impression can be enough to drive that visitor elsewhere within seconds. Except in cases where a site offers something so unique or important to the user that they will put up with a bad Web experience to get that thing, there are so many other sites competing for attention that there is no reason for anyone to linger at a site they don't like.

If the first impression is satisfactory, however, the visitor may then try to explore the site further. Once again, visual design is of fundamental importance. It is not adequate that the site functions properly without error and that everything is structurally well-organized; the structure and the way in which the site functions have to be made clear to the user, and revealed in such a way that they will feel confidence in using the site and an inclination to continue doing so. A link hidden in a clutter of unrelated material in the middle of a page might work in exactly the same way as a link carefully designed and placed so that it is both identifiable and noticed at the point when it will be most useful. But the first link will very possibly go unnoticed, whereas you can be reasonably confident that the second will be used, providing the visitor is interested in where it leads, and sometimes even out of curiosity. Even that interest or curiosity can be invited or enhanced by good visual design, which can serve to entice the visitor to explore the site further.

For sites whose primary function is commercial, for example, visual design is of the utmost importance, not because it serves to illustrate the products or services on sale, although that is important too, but because it can determine whether the prospective purchaser will buy or not. Again, there may be a 'buy' button somewhere on the page that functions perfectly, but if the user cannot find it or readily identify it they will not buy. An information site, by contrast, may possibly contain all the information that exists on a certain topic, but if it is not clear to the user where to find that information, or if it is presented in a way too difficult to assimilate, then they will go away from that site uninformed.

In order for a Web site to function at its maximum potential, it is essential that visual design is considered hand-in-hand with the technical and functional aspects of its design, and this cannot happen unless Web designers of every kind have an understanding of the basic principles of visual design. Although not all of the principles developed over the years for use in print media are of the same value when designing Web pages, many can be adapted to the new medium. In particular, the use of grids for layout design, combined with a well-informed approach to typography, contrast and colour, can make a site more usable, more accessible and more attractive. An understanding of visual hierarchies will help the designer convey a Web page's content more effectively, and some knowledge of interface design principles is necessary for the design of any site. We look at design principles in greater depth in Chapter 10.

New Developments

The World Wide Web does not stand still. Technological advances and an increasingly sophisticated Web community that is quick to take advantage of them mean that the Web is continually becoming capable of new things. Often, the changes that occur are unexpected, as people take new ideas in unforeseen directions. This makes predicting the Web's future a hazardous business. Two current trends seem likely to influence development in the coming years, but it would be foolish to predict the precise way in which they will change the Web experience.

The Semantic Web

The Web as we presently know it consists of linked pages intended to be read by people. In other words, it is a web of documents. Underneath many of these documents is data, in a form that cannot be read by people. For example, an online banking service will display a list of your recent transactions as a document, but this document will have been derived from data in the bank's computer systems; an online shop will display a list of items and their prices in a document built from their catalogue database, and so on. Suppose you want to combine the information in these documents from the bank and the shop, to find out whether you can afford to buy some shiny gadget that is on offer. You would have to look at both documents to find your bank balance and the price, and do some sums in your head to see if the item was affordable. But it's easy to conceive of a computer application that could examine the two sets of data and tell you what the effect of the purchase on your bank balance would be – provided both sets of data were accessible and in a format that the program could decipher.

The intention behind the W3C's Semantic Web Activity is to create a web of data, analogous to the web of documents we already have. This would be a web that was intended to be processed by programs. It should be possible for a program to combine data from disparate sources that are connected by the Semantic Web.

This requires two things. First, it requires a format that allows data to be interchanged between systems. XML (see Chapter 3) can be used to organize data using a common syntax, but this is not sufficient. If a program is to be able to use data it needs some way of determining what it means. Simply knowing that a `record` consists of three fields called `number`, `amount` and `total` doesn't tell you (still less, a program) that the record is a line in an invoice, with `number` being a catalogue number, `amount` representing the quantity supplied and `total` being the total price. Some other invoicing system might use a different structure, or refer to the fields by different names – `catno`, `quantity` and `amount`, for instance. A program that needs to collate the data in invoices from two different suppliers (for example, to determine which charged less for a certain item) needs some way of relating the names and record structures used in data from different sources.

The World Wide Web Consortium has produced specifications of a language called **RDF (Resource Description Framework)** that is intended to allow **metadata** – data about data – to be specified in a standard manner. The intention is that programs should analyze the metadata to determine the meaning of the actual data. On the basis of this they are able to process the real data, irrespective of where it came from.

On top of this, a true Semantic Web needs some way of indicating how the data relates to real world objects, in order to provide the meaning for metadata. This requires a way of representing the meanings of words. An **ontology** is a system for doing this, which also models relationships between the objects that words represent, so that it can be used as a basis for reasoning about these objects. Usually, an ontology is restricted to a specific area of knowledge (or 'domain'), since words are typically used with specific meanings within a domain. The W3C has defined a **Web Ontology Language OWL** for defining ontologies in a form that can be processed by computer programs.

Although it relies on the same basic technology for requesting and transferring data, the Semantic Web will be a quite different sort of system from the familiar World Wide Web. It will make it possible to combine the data behind Web pages in new ways, effectively turning the Web into a huge relational database, but it won't supersede the existing Web, which serves a different purpose: presenting information to people.

It will be some time before tangible benefits from the Semantic Web appear. In the meantime, search engines are becoming more adept at extracting information from human-readable Web pages, and developers are taking the existing Web technologies in new directions. It may be that, in the medium term at least, these developments are more significant than the W3C-sanctioned Semantic Web.

Web 2.0

During the year 2005, the term **Web 2.0** came to be used to signify a collection of developments that, some commentators claimed, will change the way we use the Web and the things that we use it for. These developments are exemplified by a handful of innovative sites that have attracted a disproportionate amount of attention. These include the photo-sharing service Flickr, the Web-based project management system Basecamp, the social bookmarking site del.icio.us and the interactive maps offered by Google Maps, as well as a new class of sites, called mash-ups, based on combining data from other sites in new ways. Some earlier phenomena, especially blogging and the collaborative encyclopedia Wikipedia, are also sometimes included as part of Web 2.0.

Web 2.0 is an amorphous concept that is difficult to define precisely. Cynics may claim that it is simply a term devised for marketing purposes, and it is true that its first public use was as the title of a conference. There are, however, certain features shared by sites that fall into the Web 2.0 category which distinguish them from more traditional sites, and which may represent a significant step in the Web's evolution.

First among these is the idea of delivering applications over the Web, with the sort of rich user interfaces we are familiar with on desktop computers. Instead of installing a program on your own computer and storing all your data locally, you use programs that run on a machine somewhere else on the Internet and store your data remotely. This means that you can access your documents from any machine, and you never need to install any software other than a Web browser. This is sometimes described by the catch-phrase 'the Web as platform', or more evocatively as 'taking the desktop to the Web'.

For Web applications of this sort to be acceptable to users, they must provide the familiar interface components of desktop applications, such as drag and drop, drop-down menus, sortable lists, and so on, and avoid the frequent loading of new pages that has characterized interactivity on most Web sites. A collection of scripting techniques, known as AJAX, has been developed for this purpose. In principle, there is nothing about AJAX that could not have been done several years earlier, but standardization and improved scripting implementations in browsers were necessary before it could become a reality. The wider spread of broadband was also required before Web applications could be sufficiently responsive to be usable.

A second important component of Web 2.0 is participation. Flickr, del.icio.us and a host of imitators depend on their users to provide their content and, more significantly, to organize it. These sites allow users to attach *tags* to items posted there, and then to search for items with particular tags attached. A tag is just a word or phrase which the user thinks apt for describing the item. This contrasts with most conventional approaches to classification, which emphasize controlled vocabularies, to ensure that the same concept is always given the same name, and pre-defined hierarchies of concepts. A tagging system works on the assumption that letting people use their own vocabulary will lead to things being tagged with words that make sense to the community of users. Things will then tend to fall into a natural classification based on users' perception of how they can best be tagged. A classification built in this way is sometimes called a *folksonomy*.

Underlying tagging and folksonomies is the notion of 'the wisdom of crowds', the idea that the collective knowledge of a large community is at least as good as the specialized knowledge of experts. The same idea is used by Wikipedia: articles in this online encyclopedia may be altered by anybody, so users can correct the mistakes of others. Over time, a definitive version of an article should emerge, where all misapprehensions have been corrected. A single user may not know all about a topic, or may be mistaken about some details, but the knowledge of several people taken together will converge on a full and accurate account. Of course, the theory is dubious, and the mechanisms provided for participation are subject to abuse – there are, for instance, many instances of entries in Wikipedia being altered for personal or political reasons – but Web applications that use tagging are becoming increasingly popular as a way of allowing users to participate in organizing large masses of information that defy conventional classification techniques.

The third distinctive aspect of Web 2.0 applications concerns the sharing of data. Instead of simply presenting information in a single form on a page, Web 2.0 sites provide APIs (Application Programming Interfaces) which enable other sites to access their data. As soon as there is more than one site with such an API, the possibility arises of combining information on a third site. Mash-ups are pages that do exactly this. Many are based on maps, since Google Maps was one of the first well-documented APIs. Mapping mash-ups are able to superimpose other data, derived from other sites, onto maps pulled from Google using their API.

There is clearly some similarity between mash-ups and the Semantic Web, which we described earlier. However, mash-ups are much more of an *ad hoc* mechanism for combining data from different sources. For the most part, the data is not self-describing, and each API is documented separately, so that there is no possibility of writing programs that can interpret and combine data from an arbitrary collection of resources, which is the aim of the Semantic Web.

Key Points

Web Pages and Sites

A Web page is the basic element of the Web.

A Web page is not a physical object, but a collection of data that can be transmitted over the Internet and is displayed by a user agent, such as a Web browser.

Web pages are not constrained by physical limitations in the same way as paper. They can contain time-based and interactive elements, but are subject to limitations imposed by maximum data rates and the diversity of hardware and software.

Links connect Web pages into a network of hypermedia.

A Web site is a set of conceptually related Web pages, connected by links.

Typing a Web site's address takes you to its home page, which usually provides an introduction to the site and links to other pages.

The pages making up a site usually exhibit a unified style and layout.

Using The Web

Certain features common to browsers facilitate a pattern of browsing with backtracking.

The back and forward buttons and the history list permit navigation among recently visited pages.

Bookmarks provide a persistent record of the addresses of pages so that they can easily be revisited.

Searching supports a different mode of finding pages, based on how well their content matches a set of keywords.

Directories and search engines provide entry points to the Web.

Web feeds provide an alternative to browsing, by automatically listing updates to sites, which can be checked with a feed reader or aggregated into pages.

The Web Community

The Web community comprises about 16% of the world's population.

It is a diverse community; there is no such thing as an average Web user. Web designers must cater for diversity.

Many people experience physical or mental difficulties which affect the ways in which they can interact with websites.

Education, technological sophistication and past experience all affect the ease with which people can use the Web.

The Internet is a heterogeneous network, connecting different computing platforms (hardware and operating systems), and the Web is accessed using a range of user agents.

There are significant differences in the data rates of connections to the Internet offered to domestic users:

Dial-up via modems at a maximum of 56kbps;

Broadband at between 256kbps and 2Mbs (or higher).

Web users are located throughout the world, with the majority in Asia.

English is presently the dominant language of the Web, but it is not the first language of most Web users.

Localization and internationalization are strategies for coping with geographical, linguistic and cultural differences.

Web Design Principles

Get it right.

Make it nice.

Web standards are created by the World Wide Web Consortium and other bodies, and provide specifications of languages and other key components of the Web.

Usability and accessibility are major factors in improving the quality of the Web experience for all users.

The Web is primarily a visual medium and good visual design is essential for sites to convey information and perform their function effectively.

New Developments

The Web's future is unpredictable and may hold surprises.

The Semantic Web will be a web of data, intended to be processed by programs, that combines information from disparate sources.

RDF is intended to allow metadata to be specified in a standard manner.

OWL can be used to define ontologies in a form that can be processed by computer programs.

Web 2.0 is an amorphous concept, including several features shared by a collection of influential and innovative Web sites.

The Web as platform – delivering applications over the Web.

AJAX.

Participation – tagging, folksonomy and social computing.

Mash-ups and sharing data through Web APIs.

Exercises

Test Questions

1. List four ways in which a Web page differs from a printed page and give three examples of elements that can be included in a Web page but not on a printed page.

2. Give an example of a Web site you have visited that falls into each of the categories listed in Table 1.1. If you have never visited any site in some of the categories, use a directory to find one.

3. In which categories do you find Web sites that would *not* benefit from an RSS feed?

4. What kinds of problems may people experience that would make it difficult for them to use Web sites that have *not* been designed with accessibility in mind?

5. Should sites be designed so that they work best for people using the most popular sort of browser?

6. What are the slowest and fastest connection speeds you would need to take into consideration when designing Web pages?

7. If you ask five people to test your Web site, and none of them encounters any problems, what can you deduce about its usability?

8. What role does visual design play in the design of Web sites?

9. How do Web 2.0 sites differ from other Web sites?

Discussion Topics

1. Suppose you are searching the Web for some information, such as the best treatment for a sprained ankle or an illness. If a search engine returns many results, how do you determine which of the sites to trust?

2. Standards are not laws. Should you always follow standards, even if there is a better way of doing something?

3. In what ways are Web sites that encourage user participation vulnerable to abuse? How can the administrators of such sites protect themselves and their users? To what extent do you think that administrators should interfere, and why?

4. Assume that you are designing a new Web site for a client in your own country. What language do you think the textual content of the site should be written in and why? What provision do you think you might make for users who come from a different part of the world?

5. What factors might prevent the development of the Semantic Web?

Practical Tasks

1. Keep a diary for a week recording your Web browsing: record the address of each page you visit, and each time you visit a page, note whether you got there from one of your bookmarks, using a search box in the browser, using the history list, using the back or forward button, following a link within a site, following a link from a page on another site or following a link from a search page. At the end of the week, create a table and chart in an appropriate format, summarizing your pattern of Web use for the week. Are you a surfer or a searcher? Do you use the Web mainly as a consumer (just looking, buying, etc.), as a contributor (posting to blogs, social networking sites, etc.), or both? Do you feel that there is a significant difference between these types of uses?

2. Using a small number of keywords relating to some topic that you know about, carry out a Web search on each of the major search engines and compare the results. Do you find any search engines' results to be superior or inferior to the rest? Where search engines show sponsored results, are these relevant? Are any sites that you would expect to see listed missing from the results? Can you explain any anomalies in the results you see?

3. Select some sites that you use habitually, and visit them using a text-only browser, such as Lynx. What difficulties, if any, do you encounter trying to use the sites to do the things you normally do there?

4. Search the Web for sites whose content is written in a language foreign to you and visit a selection of sites from different countries. Note how much of each site you can understand (if anything). Can you navigagte around the site, identify what the content is about, find something you might be looking for? What features help you find your way around a site written in a foreign language?

Web Technology

2

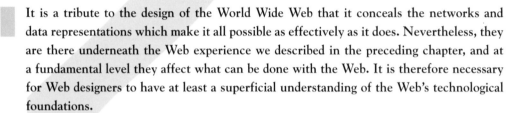

It is a tribute to the design of the World Wide Web that it conceals the networks and data representations which make it all possible as effectively as it does. Nevertheless, they are there underneath the Web experience we described in the preceding chapter, and at a fundamental level they affect what can be done with the Web. It is therefore necessary for Web designers to have at least a superficial understanding of the Web's technological foundations.

It is important to distinguish between the World Wide Web and the Internet. The Internet is a publicly accessible global network of computer networks, communicating via a standard set of *protocols* – rules governing the exchange of data – loosely referred to collectively as **TCP/ IP**. The Internet provides the supporting structure for many different services, including email, file transfer, chat rooms, instant messaging and podcasts, as well as the World Wide Web. Indeed, Web pages can be accessed over any network that uses TCP/IP. Many enterprises run such networks, called *intranets*, to provide services exclusively to their employees. A great many Web sites are developed for intranets and are never seen by the public.

Web Pages

At the beginning of the previous chapter we described a Web page as a collection of data in a form that can be stored in a computer and transmitted over the Internet. This description conceals a lot of detail and begs several questions. How can what we see in a browser window be a collection of data? And how can data be stored in a computer? How is the Internet organized, and how can data be transmitted over it?

URLs

The ability to identify any page uniquely is one of the most basic requirements of the World Wide Web. Without a universal addressing mechanism, it would be impossible to navigate to

Terminology

Universal Resource Identifiers (URIs)

If you read any of the World Wide Web Consortium Recommendations (standards) to which we will refer throughout this book, you will see references to URIs in many places where we use URLs. URIs are a more general way of referring to resources on the Internet. Every URL is a URI, but URIs can also be Uniform Resource Names (URNs), which can be used to identify certain resources in a way that is independent of their location. This is often expressed in the 'equation' URI = URL + URN. Since every Web page must be identified by a URL, we prefer to ignore the possibility of URNs, and so we never refer to URIs.

a site, and the linkage between pages, which is fundamental to the Web, would not be feasible; search engines and directories could not identify pages; you could not save bookmarks or maintain a history list in your browser.

Each page's unique identification is provided by what we have so far been calling its Web address, which is more properly known as its **Uniform Resource Locator (URL)**. A URL has three components. The first is a *prefix*, which, for Web pages, is usually `http://`. This is followed by a **host name**, such as `www.desperatesw.co.uk`, which, to a first approximation, identifies a computer somewhere on the Internet. This computer will be a Web *server*, a machine on which Web pages are stored for retrieval. The third component of the URL is a **path**, such as `/Products/index.html`, which identifies a file within a hierarchical directory structure on the server identified by the host name. By combining these three components we get a complete URL, such as `http://www.desperatesw.co.uk/Products/index.html`.

For most sites, the conceptual relationship between their constituent pages that we described in Chapter 1 is reflected in the organization of their URLs: all the site's pages have the same host name component. You can therefore think of the whole site as being identified by a URL, usually comprising just the host name, such as `www.desperatesw.co.uk`. Typing the site's URL into your browser takes you to its **home page.**[†]

As we will explain later, URLs are always unique, so they can be used to identify Web pages. But what exactly is it that a URL identifies? In other words, what is a Web page?

[†]If you really type www.desperatesw.co.uk into your browser, however, you will be redirected to the support site for this book, since Desperate Software is a little fiction we made up for some of our examples.

Markup

Consider the basic Web page shown in Figure 2.1. (It is not an example of fine Web design, but is representative of a certain style of home-made page that is sometimes favoured by small software companies.) Suppose that this page could be accessed using the URL http://www.desperatesw.co.uk/index.html. If you were able to obtain a copy of the file index.html from Desperate Software and, instead of opening it in your Web browser, you opened it with a text editor, you would see the following:

```
<!DOCTYPE html PUBLIC "-//W3C//DTD XHTML 1.0 Strict//EN"
  "http://www.w3.org/TR/xhtml1/DTD/xhtml1-strict.dtd">
<html xmlns="http://www.w3.org/1999/xhtml" xml:lang="en" lang="en">
<head>
   <meta http-equiv="content-type" content="text/html; charset=utf-8"
/>
   <title>Desperate Software Home</title>
<link rel="stylesheet" href="styles.css" type="text/css"
media="screen" />
</head>
<body>
<div>
<img src="DSlogo.gif" alt="company logo" width="87" height="222" />
</div>
<h1>Desperate Software</h1>
<p>
Purveyors of fine computer programs to the gentry.
</p>
<h2>Our Products</h2>
<p>
Click on a link below for feature lists, download links, and more.
</p>
<ul>
   <li><a href="fridge/index.html">textFridge</a></li>
   <li><a href="magnet/index.html">ScreenMagnet</a></li>
   <li><a href="freezer/index.html">Widget Freezer X</a></li>
</ul>
<h2>Contact Us</h2>
<p>
If you have questions that aren't answered here, do not hesitate to
get in touch using our <a href="feedback.php">feedback form</a>.
</p>
</body>
</html>
```

Desperate Software

Purveyors of fine computer programs to the gentry.

Our Products

Click on a link below for feature lists, download links, and more.

textFridge
ScreenMagnet
Widget Freezer X

Contact Us

If you have questions that aren't answered here, do not hesitate to get in touch using our feedback form.

Figure 2.1 A simple Web page

Technical Detail

URL Encoding

Only certain characters are allowed in URLs: upper and lower case letters, decimal digits and the characters -, _, ., !, ~, *, ', (and). Other characters — ;, /, ?, :, @, &, =, +, $ and , can appear in a URL, but they may have a special meaning when they do so. There is therefore a problem if these, or other excluded characters are needed. (Since file paths on most systems can include other characters, it is highly likely that this situation will arise within the path name component.) Characters other than those just listed must be escaped in order to be included in a URL. This means that they are replaced by a sequence of characters, consisting of a % followed by two hexadecimal digits representing the code for that character in the US-ASCII character set. In particular, a space, the most commonly encountered character requiring escaping in URLs, is represented by %20, while % itself is %25. Thus, a file called contact details.html, at www.desperatesw.co.uk, would have the URL http://www.desperatesw.co.uk/contact%20details.html. Most browsers would allow you to type the URL with the space, and perform the replacement for you. Strings that contain only legal URL characters and escape sequences are said to be *URL-encoded*.

As you can see, all the text of the page appears somewhere in this file, but it is augmented with a lot of other matter. The text that appears in angle brackets, such as <h1> and </h1>, does not appear on the screen when the page is displayed by a browser. It is **markup** information, which enables browsers to break the page up into its structural elements, such as headings, paragraphs and lists, so that it can determine how each part of the page should be displayed: headings are shown in a bigger font than other paragraphs, for instance, while the items in the list of products are indented.

The markup in this file is written using the language **XHTML**, which defines a set of tags (the text in angle brackets) corresponding to a collection of types of element that are allowed in Web pages. The intimidating lines at the beginning of the file are necessary administrative rubric, which indicate that this is indeed an XHTML document. We will describe XHTML fully in Chapter 3.

Most Web browsers provide a command that lets you look at the current Web page in the form of marked-up text, like the example we have just given, which is referred to, by analogy with programs, as the **source code** of the page. In Firefox, for example, the Page Source command on the View menu opens a new window that exhibits the markup. You might be tempted to say that the XHTML source code is what a Web page really is, but this would not be quite adequate.

The source file includes all the text and delineates its structure, but there is no data in this file corresponding to the image that appears at the left of the page. This is actually produced by the tenth line:

```
<img src="DSlogo.gif" alt="company logo" width="87" height="222" />
```

Again, we will explain this fully in later chapters, but you can see that it includes part of a URL, gradient.gif, and this, in fact, identifies the location of an image file, where the data for the design is held.

Stylesheets

The image's markup is not the only place a URL occurs in this page's source. The line

```
<link rel="stylesheet" href="styles.css" type="text/css"
  media="screen" />
```

Desperate Software

Purveyors of fine computer programs to the gentry.

Our Products

Click on a link below for feature lists, download links, and more.

- textFridge
- ScreenMagnet
- Widget Freezer X

Contact Us

If you have questions that aren't answered here, do not hesitate to get in touch using our feedback form.

Figure 2.2 A simple Web page displayed without a stylesheet

also points to a file (`styles.css`). In this case, it contains a *stylesheet*, which is a set of rules telling the Web browser how each of the elements of the page should be laid out. By default, a browser uses some very basic rules to determine how headings, paragraphs, and so on, should be displayed. Web designers create stylesheets to modify (and hopefully improve) pages' appearance. Figure 2.2 shows what our example page would look like if the stylesheet was removed.

Most stylesheets presently in use on the Web are written in a language called CSS. The CSS stylesheet used to display the Desperate Software page looks in part like this:

```
body {
    padding: 40px;
    background-color: #FFFDF0;
    color: #0099D1;
    font-family: Trebuchet,Verdana,Arial,sans-serif;
    font-size: 16px;
    line-height: 1.4;
}
```

```
h1 {
    font-size: 1.35em;
}

h2 {
    font-size: 1.1em;
}
```

We have shown three rules here. Each is labelled with the name of an XHTML tag, and it describes how elements marked up with that tag should be displayed. For each tag, values are provided for properties which control the appearance of corresponding elements. For instance, the rules for h1 and h2 set the size of type to be used to display level 1 and level 2 headings. The rule for body sets values used for the whole page, including the colours of the text and background and the default type size. We will explain the meaning of these and many other properties which can be used in rules when we describe CSS in detail in Chapter 4.

What all this tells us is that a Web page is not just a file of text and XHTML; it may be made up of several files, which must be combined by the browser to produce the page you see displayed. Some pages require even more files: they may include embedded time-based media (animation, video or sound), or make use of scripts, which are small programs that are run in the browser in response to user input. Like stylesheets, scripts are often contained in external files which are referred to from the main XHTML document.

Dynamically Generated Pages

This is still not the full story. Suppose you click on the link labelled feedback form. A new page will be displayed, looking like Figure 2.3. If your browser provides a way of viewing the page's source and you were to use it, you would see something like this (we have omitted some details):

```
<!DOCTYPE html PUBLIC "-//W3C//DTD XHTML 1.0 Strict//EN"
  "http://www.w3.org/TR/xhtml1/DTD/xhtml1-strict.dtd">
<html xmlns="http://www.w3.org/1999/xhtml" xml:lang="en" lang="en">
<head>
    much as before
</head>
<body>
<div>
<img src="DSlogo.gif" alt="company logo" width="87" height="222" />
```

Desperate Software

Purveyors of fine computer programs to the gentry.

Feedback Form

Please fill in all the fields below and click the Send button.

┌─Your Details──┐
│ Name: [_____]   Email Address: [_____] │
└──┘
┌─Your Message──┐
│ ┌──────────────────────────────────────┐   │
│ │   │   │
│ │   │   │
│ │   │   │
│ │   │   │
│ │   │   │
│ └──────────────────────────────────────┘   │
└──┘
(Send)

Figure 2.3 A simple Web form

```
</div>
<h1>Desperate Software</h1>
<p>Purveyors of fine computer programs to the gentry.</p>
<h2>Feedback Form</h2>
<p>Please fill in all the fields below and click the Send button.</p>
<div id="form">
   more marked-up text for the form itself
</div>
</body>
</html>
```

If you checked the URL in the address bar, you would see that it had changed to
http://www.desperatesw.co.uk/feedback.php. If you were able to obtain a copy
of the file feedback.php itself, and open it in a text editor, you would see something
quite different:

```php
<?php
function check_email($email)
{
  return preg_match('/^[a-zA-Z0-9._-]+@[a-zA-Z0-9_-]+\.[a-zA-Z]+(\.[a-zA-Z]+)?$/', $email);
}


$cmd = $_POST['Submit'];
if ($cmd == 'Send') {
   $sending = true;
   more similar lines
}
else $sending = false;
?>
<!DOCTYPE html PUBLIC "-//W3C//DTD XHTML 1.0 Strict//EN"
 "http://www.w3.org/TR/xhtml1/DTD/xhtml1-strict.dtd">
<html xmlns="http://www.w3.org/1999/xhtml" xml:lang="en" lang="en">
<head>
   same as before
   ...
<h2>Feedback Form</h2>

<?php
if ($sending)
   echo("<p>Thank you for your message. We will get back to you
soon.</p>");
else {
?>
<p>Please fill in all the fields below and click the Send button.</p>

   markup for the form
}
<?php
}
?>
</body>
</html>
```

Again, we have left out much of the detail, but you should be able to see from the outline that remains that this file does have the text and markup for the page embedded in it, but it is surrounded by what look like commands in some sort of programming language.

This file does indeed contain a program, written in a slightly unconventional programming language, called PHP. (PHP is often called a scripting language, rather than a programming language, but the distinction is poorly defined and not particularly useful. We will, however, usually follow convention and refer to 'scripts' rather than 'programs' when describing Web applications that use PHP.) If you have ever done any programming, you will probably recognize some familiar features: the lines beginning with if are carrying out tests, so that later code will only be done if a certain condition holds; the = operator is being used to assign a new value to a variable (even though you might be confused to find that the variable's name begins with a $ sign if you haven't used scripting languages before); echo is a function that writes its argument, and so on. One of the things that is special about PHP is that the explicit code is intermingled with XHTML markup. The special sequences <?php and ?> delimit a block of PHP code (shown highlighted here) that will be executed. Everything else is output as it is.

It does not matter at this stage if you don't see how the script works or understand the notation. What is important to recognize is that it is a program that must be run in order to generate the XHTML of the Web page: what is displayed as the source of this page is the output of this PHP script. The page is generated dynamically as a result of the execution of the script.

When a script such as this is run, it may be passed data that was typed into a form on a Web page, and the output it produces may be modified on the basis of that data. For instance, if you filled in the feedback form and then pressed the send button, a brief acknowledgement would be displayed in your browser, as shown in Figure 2.4. However, the URL in the

Desperate Software

Purveyors of fine computer programs to the gentry.

Feedback Form

Thank you for your message. We will get back to you soon.

Figure 2.4 The dynamically generated response

address bar would not change: the new page is created by the same script as the form itself. The script can determine whether or not it was called in response to the send button, and produce different output accordingly.

What this example illustrates is that a Web page cannot be equated with any collection of files, even though its URL does point to a single file on a server. The page source may never reside in a file, but may instead be created as a result of the execution of a script, and data from other files may need to be incorporated to produce the page as displayed. We must conclude that what we see as a Web page is, in fact, a collection of **resources** of various types, including static or dynamically generated marked-up text, stylesheets and images, which are assembled and displayed by a Web browser.

Fetching Pages

The resources making up a Web page will not usually reside on the computer which a visitor to the page is using to run their Web browser. It is evidently essential that resources be fetched from the remote machines on which they are stored or generated. Given the huge number of computers connected by the Internet, their different architectures and operating systems, the variety of networks used to connect machines and the bewildering topology of the interconnections between networks, it is a cause for wonder that this can be done at all.

A large part of the success of this engineering feat is due to the use of abstraction in the design of the Internet. Very briefly, the architecture of the Internet consists of a series of

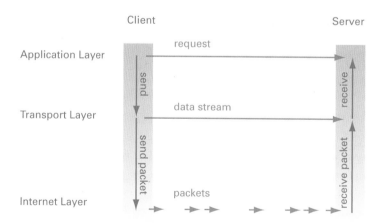

Figure 2.5 Protocol layers

layers, some in hardware and others in software. Each layer provides a set of *services* that can be used by the level above. These services encapsulate sequences of operations that the layer performs, usually by calling on services provided by a lower layer. (Not always, since there is a lowest layer, essentially composed of wires and switches, which provides the raw physical data transmission operations.)

For instance, one of the lower layers in the Internet is itself referred to as the **Internet Layer**. What this layer does is transmit data in the form of *packets* (sequences of bits with a simple structure) from one *host* (as computers connected to the Internet are often called) to another. The services it provides are the sending of a packet and the receiving of a packet. It doesn't maintain any relationship between individual packets (such as their being part of the same file), and doesn't even guarantee to get them to their destination intact. The layer above, known as the **Transport Layer**, uses the Internet Layer's services to implement its own higher-level services, which allow for the sending and receipt of a stream of data (see Figure 2.5). Although this stream must be broken up into packets in order to be passed down to the Internet Layer, these packets are invisible to any layers above the Transport Layer, which can implement any services they wish to provide in terms of the Transport Layer's data streams, without worrying about how streams are built out of packets. The Transport Layer makes up for the failings of the Internet Layer by making sure that separate packets from the same stream are recombined in the correct order, checking whether all packets that are sent arrive safely and resending any that do not.

The highest layer in the Internet is called the **Application Layer**, and it provides relatively high level services to application programs, such as Web browsers and email clients. Because of the use of layered abstractions, these applications do not need to take much account of the details of the data communication that is going on over the network – nor do we. We can imagine a browser simply asking for the resources needed to display a Web page. The fact that its requests must ultimately be translated into signals passing over wires should not be forgotten, but the details of how that happens are, for the most part, of no concern.

A little reflection should convince you that there must be some program responding to the browser's requests, finding the necessary resources and sending them back to the browser. Networked applications which are constructed in this general way, with one program sending requests to which another responds, are called client/server systems; the program that sends the requests is the *client*, the one that responds is the *server*; messages from the client to the server are called *requests*, those from the server to the client are called *responses*.

An analogy might be found in a sandwich shop: the workers or students on their lunch break would be the clients. They send requests, such as 'One Brie and salad baguette, please', to which the person behind the counter (the server) hands over a response in the form of a sandwich. In the case of the World Wide Web, the clients are usually Web browsers, the servers are special programs whose sole purpose is to deliver resources to Web clients. Web servers don't do anything until they are asked to, they just listen, waiting for a request to arrive from some client. Usually, Web servers run on dedicated hosts, which are themselves often referred to loosely as servers, too.

HTTP

We can imagine the interaction between a Web browser and server as a little conversation. The browser attracts the attention of the server and asks it for the resource identified by a URL. The server finds the corresponding file or runs the corresponding script and sends the data back to the browser. On examining this data, the browser may find that it needs another resource (an image or a stylesheet, for example), so it attracts the server's attention again, and asks for this new resource, and so on. However, this conversation is not taking place between people, the way a conversation in a sandwich shop does, but between computer programs. There is no room for banter or gratuitous remarks about the weather, and no flexibility in the permitted phrasing of requests; the interaction must correspond precisely to some set of rules that have been written in to the two programs. Such a set of rules is called a **protocol**. Protocols govern the interaction between programs on networks at all levels. There is an **Internet Protocol (IP)** for the Internet Layer, and two transport protocols, the **Transmission Control Protocol (TCP)** and the **User Datagram Protocol (UDP)**, at the Transport Layer. Interactions between Web clients and servers obey a simple application-level protocol called the **Hypertext Transfer Protocol**, abbreviated **HTTP**. HTTP defines the set of requests that a client may make and their format, and the appropriate response for the server to return to each request under all possible circumstances. (For example, the protocol specifies what a server should return in response to a request for a resource not only if that resource is found, but also if it cannot be found, or if the server does not have sufficient privileges to read it, and so on.)

HTTP makes use of the services provided by TCP to open connections between clients and servers and to pass the requests and responses between them. Thus, when a user clicks on a link or bookmark, or types a URL in their browser's address bar, the first thing that happens is that a TCP connection is opened between the browser and the Web server running on the computer identified by the host name part of the URL. (TCP connects running programs, not just machines.) Data can then be passed between the client and server as long as the connection is kept open – a TCP connection is similar to a telephone connection in this respect.

HTTP is a *stateless* protocol. What this means is that each request is dealt with in isolation, and once the server has sent its response it forgets everything about the request. (In early versions of HTTP, it would close the connection as soon as it had sent the response. The current version, HTTP/1.1, allows the connection to be kept open, but this is the only concession it makes to the possibility that a client may need to make a series of requests.) This is in contrast to the situation in most sandwich shops. There, having given you your lunch, the person behind the counter is quite likely to tell you how much it cost, so that you can pay for it. With HTTP, there is no equivalent of the recognition that a request for a sandwich might imply a subsequent payment. HTTP provides no way for a server to recognize that two requests are being made by the same client. It is as if, having got your sandwich, you then had to present it at the counter again and ask how much you should pay. This lack of continuity between separate interactions can be a major headache: for example, in an ecommerce application, remembering the contents of a particular user's shopping basket is something that must be done by the shopping basket script sending data to the client, which the client must send back in order to be recognized as the basket's owner. Statelessness is, however, a much more efficient arrangement for the server, since it does not have to keep new clients waiting while it makes sure that it has finished dealing with the current one.

Domain Names and DNS

It is not quite true that the first thing that happens when a user clicks on a link is that a TCP connection is opened. URLs identify servers by names, such as `www.desperatesw.co.uk`, but TCP does not work with these names. Instead, it makes connections between entities called *sockets*, which consist of two components: an **IP address** and a **port number**. An IP address is just a number that uniquely identifies a host on the Internet. It is attached to packets so that they can be routed to their correct destination. In the version of IP currently used for most of the Internet (IPv4), addresses are 32 bits long, and are usually written as four numbers (each less than 256) separated by dots, for instance, 213.171.218.204. Any host name can be translated into an IP address: essentially, it can just be looked up in a database, rather like looking up a number in the phone book. Port numbers identify a communication channel on which servers listen for incoming packets. By default, HTTP servers listen on port 80, so in order to open a connection for HTTP, the host name must first be translated into an IP address, and then this must be combined with a port number. (In fact, port numbers can be explicitly appended to the host part of a URL, following a colon, and you may occasionally see URLs that include them. Numerical IP addresses are also permitted instead of host names in URLs, but their use is discouraged.) The hard part is ensuring that the translation from host name to IP address can be performed efficiently. This is the function of the **Domain Name System (DNS)**. The organization of the DNS is bound up with the structure of host names, so a quick review of how these are constructed is in order.

The host name part of a URL has a hierarchical structure, just as the path does (although the components are nested in the opposite direction). The final component of the name identifies a top-level domain, which will be one of two types: either a **country domain**, identified by a two-letter country code, such as .uk, .fr, .za, .jp or .au, or a **generic top-level domain (gTLD)**. Originally there were seven of these: .com, .edu, .gov, .int, .mil, .net and .org. Since 2000, some more generic domains have been added to the list, but they have not proved very popular as yet. Although some generic domains are restricted to use in the United States (.edu, .gov and .mil are explicitly for use by the US educational sector, federal government and armed forces, respectively), others are used internationally; .com in particular is often used by commercial organizations not wishing to appear to belong to a single country. (The .int domain is reserved for official intergovernmental organizations, such as the World Health Organization.) Although the .us top-level country domain does exist, it is rarely used, except for punning domains such as del.icio.us, and the default assumption, for fairly obvious reasons, is that generic domains belong to the US. Some other countries add a second level within their national domains (in the UK, for instance, the domains .co.uk, .ac.uk, .gov.uk and .org.uk exist, among others, mimicking some of the generic domains), but others do not.

Top-level domains are administered centrally, by an organization known as the **Internet Corporation for Assigned Names and Numbers (ICANN)**; countries that have second level domains have a central authority for managing these. Domains at lower levels can be assigned to individuals and organizations, and the administration of these assignments is usually delegated to commercial organizations, which assign names on a first-come, first-served basis. The registration process ensures that domain names are unique – the same name can never be assigned to more than one individual or organization (except in error). This means that the owner of a domain name can create sub-domains within it for their hosts, knowing that they can never conflict with any other. (This has led to the use of domain names for purposes other than identifying hosts on the Internet; they are also used for generating unique identifiers for quite unrelated functions. Appendix B includes an example.)

Hence, the host name www.desperatesw.co.uk can be read from right to left: the top-level domain is .uk, showing that Desperate Software registered its domain name in the UK and is therefore probably (though not certainly) a British entity. Within UK domain names, .co is the sub-domain used for commercial enterprises, so Desperate Software is almost certainly a business of some sort. The `desperatesw` component is their chosen name for their own domain: `desperatesw.co.uk` is the company's domain name, within which they are able to create their own sub-domains. This they have done, following convention by using `www` to identify their Web server, giving the full host name `www.desperatesw.co.uk`.

It is important that the translation process from `www.desperatesw.co.uk` to 213.171.218.204 be efficient and reliable. To ensure this, the DNS is implemented using a distributed hierarchical database. Without going into precise details, the essence of the arrangement is that every top-level domain has a name server with a database that records the address of a name server for every second-level domain within it. Similarly, at the second level there are name servers which record the addresses of third-level name servers, and so on. When a browser needs to find the IP address corresponding to a host name, it could send a query to the name server for the top-level domain in the name. This server would then pass the query down to the name server for the second-level component, which would pass it further down until a name server was contacted that had a record giving the required IP address.

For instance, to look up `www.desperatesw.co.uk`, a request could be sent to the `.uk` name server. This would forward it down to the `.co.uk` server. The latter would know where to look for IP addresses for hosts in the `desperatesw.co.uk` domain – probably a name server at the ISP used by Desperate Software. (There are not necessarily distinct name servers for every domain.) This could then return the IP address.

This is not exactly what happens, though, because the lookup is made more efficient by the use of caching. When the response to a DNS query is received, a copy of the DNS record is saved in every name server used in the query, so in future the IP address can be returned from one of the intermediate servers, instead of going through the whole chain. The record is even cached on the machine that made the original query, so in future a query for the same name can be resolved just by looking in the local cache, without having to communicate with any remote name servers. If the required information is not available locally, a query is first sent from a host to the name server that holds its own record, in case it is cached there. Only if this fails is the query sent up to the top level. (A slight complication is that the IP address corresponding to a host name might change at some time, so it is necessary to ensure that cached records are discarded if there is any risk of their being out of date. This is just a minor technical problem and the current DNS solves it.)

Because it would be unacceptably inconvenient to have to use numerical IP addresses all the time, the DNS is vital to the functioning of the World Wide Web, and also to email and other Internet services. Once a host name has been successfully converted to an IP address after a DNS lookup, it can be combined with the port number to get a socket address, which is then used to open a TCP connection that can carry the actual communication needed to fetch the resources making up a Web page. This is the function of HTTP itself.

HTTP Messages

HTTP requests and responses are collectively known as **messages**. Both consist of a string of 8-bit characters, so they can be treated as text by browsers and Web servers (and can be read by humans if they have a program that can eavesdrop on HTTP). Messages conform to a simple rigid structure. They are made up of lines, which are terminated by a pair of characters comprising a carriage return followed by a line feed. Each message begins with an initial line, called the **request line** for a request, or the **status line** for a response, containing the essential message. This line is followed by one or more **headers**, containing various parameters and modifiers. These may be followed by the **message body**, which contains data, such as the contents of a file being sent by the server, if there is any. Headers are separated from the data by a blank line.

A request line comprises three elements: the **method**, **identifier** and **version**. The method is a name identifying the service being requested. The most commonly used methods are GET, which is used to request a file or other resource, and POST, which is used to send data from a form to a script running on the server. The identifier comes next, and tells the server which resource is being requested, for example by giving the path name of a file or script. Finally, the HTTP version indicates which protocol version the client is using.

For example, if a user typed the URL http://www.desperatesw.co.uk into the address bar of their Web browser, it would look up www.desperatesw.co.uk using the DNS and then connect to the Web server at port 80 on the host with that name. It would then send an HTTP request, whose request line was:

```
GET / HTTP/1.1
```

Since there was no path component, the browser would infer that it should just be /, and use that as the identifier for this request. Some headers will follow this request line, each taking the form of a header name followed by a colon and some arguments. We will ignore all but one of them, the Host header, for now. Including the host name in the request may seem redundant, but the same server may actually be used for several hosts, so it is necessary for the request to specify which host it is directed at. This line, therefore, follows the request line in our example:

```
Host: www.desperatesw.co.uk
```

Since a GET request does not send any data, its body is empty – the message consists only of the message line and headers, and is terminated with a blank line.

The first line of an HTTP server's response is the **status line**, indicating how it coped with the request. This line begins with the protocol version, telling the client which HTTP version the server is using. Next comes a numerical status code, whose meaning is defined by the HTTP standard, followed by a short phrase, explaining to human readers what the code means. If all goes well, the code will be 200, which means OK, as shown:

```
HTTP/1.1 200 OK
```

Typically, a server's response does contain some data. In the case of a successful response to a GET request for a static document, this will be the contents of the file that was requested. In this example request, however, the identifier identifies a directory (folder). Under these circumstances the server will look in the directory for files with certain names. The actual set of names can be configured at the server, but invariably index.html is among them. Therefore, the body of the response will contain the contents of /index.html from the Web document directory on www.desperatesw.co.uk, which will be the XHTML source we showed you earlier.

When it analyzes the data it receives, the browser will encounter the link to the stylesheet styles.css. To obtain the stylesheet itself, it must send out another HTTP GET request, which will have the following request line:

```
GET /styles.css HTTP/1.1
```

Similarly, when it encounters the reference to the image, it will send a third request:

```
GET /gradient.gif HTTP/1.1
```

If nothing goes wrong, the server will send back the contents of these two files, each wrapped up in an HTTP response, with the status line

```
HTTP/1.1 200 OK
```

Figure 2.6 summarizes this interaction. (Time increases downwards in this diagram.)

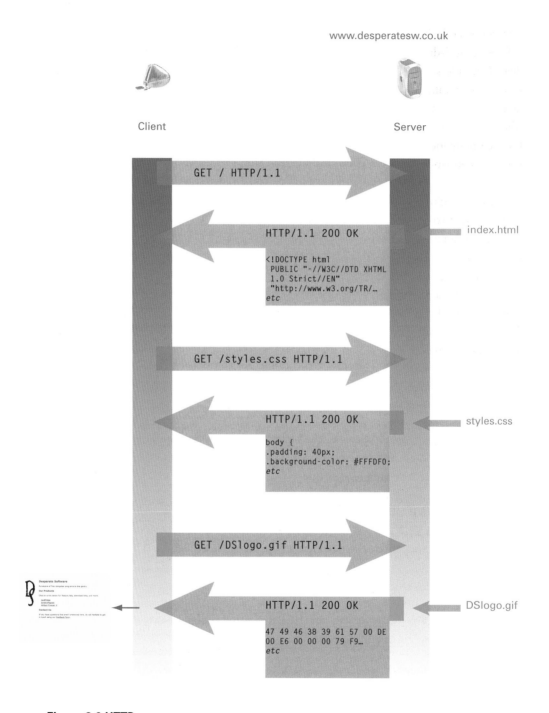

Figure 2.6 HTTP messages

The status code in a response is not always 200, unfortunately. The HTTP 1.1 standard defines many 3-digit return codes. These are divided into groups, distinguished by their first digit. Codes less than 200 are informative; for example, code 101 is sent when the server switches to a different protocol, for example to stream some real-time data. Codes in the range 200–299 indicate success of one sort or another. Those in the three hundreds are used when the server must redirect the request to a different URL. For example, a code of 301 ('moved permanently') indicates that the resource identified by the URL in a GET request has been permanently moved to a new location.

Codes that begin with a 4 or a 5 represent errors, by the client and server, respectively. Probably the two most commonly encountered error codes are 400 and 404. 400 means 'bad request' – the request was malformed in some way. This error usually occurs when requests are manufactured by programs other than Web browsers. Error code 404 is 'not found' – the URL in a GET request does not correspond to any resource on the server. This is the code that results from broken links. Other error codes in this range correspond to requests for services that are denied by the server, such as attempts to access protected files. Server errors include 500 ('internal server error'), which should never happen, and 501 ('not implemented'), which is sent when the server does not know how to implement a requested method.

Media Types

Each of the three responses in the previous example contains different sorts of data: text marked up with XHTML tags, a CSS stylesheet and an image. Each must be dealt with differently by the browser, so it is necessary that the response include some indication of the type of data.

You may think that this information is already there, in the form of the extensions on the files' names: .html might indicate an XHTML file, files ending .css and .gif would be CSS stylesheets and GIF images, respectively. However, although nowadays most operating systems use filename extensions to indicate the type of data in the file, the convention is not universal, and there are no standards for determining which extensions should be used for each possible kind of data. More fundamentally, these extensions are a property of the file stored on the server machine, they are not part of the HTTP response. In the case of dynamically generated responses, there is not any named file on disk containing the data in the response; there is just a script whose name might indicate what language it is written in, but which gives no indication of what kind of data it might produce as its output. Hence, some other mechanism is required.

Technical Detail

The User-Agent and Server Headers

When a user agent such as a Web browser sends a request to a server, it includes a header, called User-Agent, identifying itself and the platform it is running on. For example, this is the header sent by Firefox from a machine running MacOS X:

```
User-Agent: Mozilla/5.0 (Macintosh; U; PPC Mac OS X
Mach-O; en-US; rv:1.7.8) Gecko/20050511 Firefox/1.0.4
```

while this is what Safari sends from the same machine:

```
User-Agent: Mozilla/5.0 (Macintosh; U; PPC Mac OS X;
en-us) AppleWebKit/312.1 (KHTML, like Gecko) Safari/312
```

You can probably see what the Firefox/1.0.4 and Safari/312 parts mean, and the specification of the OS is quite clear (if excessively detailed in the case of Firefox), but what of the rest?

The intention behind this header is that the server, or some script that generates a dynamic response, may modify its behaviour according to the capabilities of the user agent. The content of this header is also made available to scripts running in the client (see Chapter 7), and has been commonly used by such scripts to determine which scripting features the client supports. The use of 'browser-sniffing' code that analyzes the user agent's identifying string has had some unforeseen consequences.

Whenever a new browser is introduced, it must be able to display most, if not all, existing Web pages. If a page has some browser-sniffing code that only allows it to work with certain browsers that it knows support the scripting features it uses, it will inevitably reject requests by browsers that did not exist when the code was written. Thus, newer browsers tend to include identifiers for older browsers with which they are compatible. Modern browsers fall into families based on common rendering engines, such as Gecko or KHTML. Different browser-sniffing scripts may look for more or less specific types of browser, so `User-Agent` headers must include an indication of the generic browser as well as the actual program.

As you can see from the examples above, things have got somewhat out of hand. To make matters more ridiculous, most Web browsers allow users to change the user agent string, so that they can pretend to be some other browser.

All of this provides a good reason to stick to standards and not use browser-dependent tricks on your Web pages.

The server returns the compliment by including a `Server` header in its response, with a similar indication of its identity, for example:

```
Server: Apache/1.3.33 (Darwin) PHP/4.3.10
```

This is much less elaborate than the browsers' `User-Agent` headers, and less subject to abuse. Here it simply indicates the server's name (Apache) and version number, together with an indication of the operating system it is running on, and the name and version number of an important module it is using, in this case, the module that processes PHP scripts.

We mentioned earlier that HTTP requests and responses include headers after the request or status line, and showed an example of the `Host` header. Another such header is used to declare the type of data in the body of a response. Its name is `Content-Type`; its argument is a two-part specification of the data type of the response's body. The first part is a generic type (`image`, `text`, etc.); the second part is a specific sub-type, such as `gif` or `css`. These two parts are separated by a slash character, as in `text/css`. So the HTTP response in which the stylesheet for the Desperate Software home page is sent includes the header

```
Content-Type: text/css
```

Two-part type specifications of this sort are called **Internet Media Types**, although you will sometimes see the older name **MIME Types** used instead. Types and sub-types are registered with the **Internet Assigned Number Authority** (**IANA**), so that there is a *de facto* standard collection of types, which should always be used. There are eight types: `application`, `audio`, `image`, `message`, `model`, `multipart`, `text` and `video`. Half of these names – `audio`,

Data	Media Type
XHTML document	`text/html` or `application/xhtml+xml`
CSS stylesheet	`text/css`
JavaScript script	`text/javascript`
JPEG image	`image/jpeg`
GIF image	`image/gif`
PNG image	`image/PNG`
MPEG video	`video/mpeg`
QuickTime video	`video/quicktime`
Form data	`application/x-www-form-urlencoded`
Uploaded file	`multipart/form-data`

Table 2.1 Some commonly used Internet Media Types

`image`, `text` and `video` – should be self-explanatory, though the others may be more enigmatic. Sub-types of `model` are intended for 3-D model data, such as VRML, although such data is rarely encountered on the Web at the moment. The `application` type is used not to denote executable code, as you might think, but data in a format that must be processed by some application program. Many file formats thus end up belonging to this type; `pdf`, for instance, is not a sub-type of `text` but of `application`, since it must be displayed by the Adobe Reader or some other software.

The MIME in the older name MIME Types stands for Multipurpose Internet Mail Extensions, a scheme to allow mail to support richer types of data than pure text. Internet Media Types have their origin in this scheme, and the remaining types, `message` and `multipart`, derive from this origin. The former is used for various sorts of email and newsgroup messages, so it is not really relevant to Web designers. The `multipart` type is used, as its name implies, for data streams that include data of more than one type. On the Web, the most important application of this type is for uploading files, which is an option provided by some data entry forms (see Chapters 3 and 8).

Table 2.1 summarizes the media types most commonly used on the Web. (We will have more to say about the multiple possibilities for XHTML in Chapter 3.) The type used for form data, `application/x-www-form-urlencoded`, is an example of an experimental sub-type; these all begin with `x-`, and do not appear in the official list of Internet Media Types maintained by IANA. However, the use of this particular sub-type is now so well established that it is effectively a standard.

Content Negotiation

A URL, as we have tried to show, does not identify a file, but a resource, which is an abstract entity that may originate in various ways. An abstract resource may be available in different representations. For instance, a page of text may be available in several languages, an image may be available in several different formats. When this is the case, a user may wish to express a preference about which representation of the resource should be sent when it is requested. Several HTTP headers can be used for this purpose.

The main vehicle for expressing preferences about representations is the Accept header, which specifies a list of media types that the browser is willing to accept as a response to a request. For instance,

```
Accept: text/xml,application/xml,application/xhtml+xml,text/html
```

shows that the browser will accept any of the media types for XHTML data.

The ordering of media types is not significant. If it is necessary to specify some preference among types, they may be followed by a quality setting, of the form ;q=n, where n is between 0 and 1. Lower values mean less acceptable types. For instance,

```
Accept: text/xml,application/xml,application/xhtml+xml,
text/html;q=0.9,*/*;q=0.5
```

specifies that the specific XML and XHTML types are entirely acceptable (if q is omitted it is taken to be 1), that text/html (which might be an older version of HTML) is only 90% acceptable, while any other type is only half as good. Note here the use of wildcard * characters to indicate any type or sub-type.

A Web server will use the specifications and quality values to choose the representation that is most acceptable to the client. Each representation will probably be a separate file, and the server will use some implementation-dependant way of mapping URLs and media types to the actual files.

Similar headers, Accept-Charset and Accept-Language, can be used to express preferences between character sets (see later in this chapter) and languages. A standard set of language codes is used for the latter purpose. A two-letter code is used to identify a language (en for English, fr for French, jp for Japanese, and so on). This may be followed by a hyphen and another code specifying a variant, such as en-us for American English.

These headers are automatically generated by the browser. Users may be able to set preferences which influence the headers, for example, by choosing the languages in which they are willing to read pages.

Dynamically Generated Pages

As we explained earlier, the feedback form for our Desperate Software site is different from the home page, because it is generated dynamically by a script. Such a page may be fetched in the same way as a static page, by sending a GET HTTP request. The server will recognize that a dynamic page has been requested, because the identifier refers to a location within a particular designated script directory (often /cgi-bin) or because it identifies a file with a distinctive extension, such as .php, .jsp or .asp, or because the request is sent to a specific port on the server. Using some appropriate mechanism, whose precise nature will depend on the particular server and the type of script, it will cause the script to be executed, and return its output. At the risk of stretching the analogy too far, this is like the person behind the counter in the sandwich shop going into the back to make your sandwich instead of handing you one already made from the counter.

Things are a bit different if the script requires input data from a form on a Web page. Consider once again Desperate Software's feedback form, for example. There is little point in somebody filling in their name and email address and leaving a message unless that information gets passed on to somebody in the company. The only way this can happen is by the data that has been entered in the various fields of the form being sent to the server, which can then pass it to a script that deals with it – sending an email or filing it in a database, for example. Most, if not all, Web applications have such a requirement for sending data from a page to a script running on a remote machine. Clicking on a submit button (a special type of button, which is often labelled submit, but does not need to be – see Chapter 3) normally causes a request containing the data to be sent to the server. (Sometimes, a script will be executed in the browser first, a possibility we will ignore until Chapter 7.)

Sending Form Data

As we will see in Chapter 3, each field in a form has a name associated with it – you can think of this as a variable. When a user clicks the submit button on a form, each of the values in the fields is assigned to the associated variable, so the data can be considered to exist as a collection of pairs, consisting of a name and a value. This association is handled by the browser, so HTTP just has to provide mechanisms for sending the name/value pairs in a message. It provides two ways of doing this.

The first way uses a GET request, such as the ones we have considered so far. The data is simply added to the end of the identifier on the request line, in the form of a *query string*. This begins with a question mark, which is followed by a sequence of strings of the form *name=value*, separated by ampersands. Any spaces in the name or value are replaced by + signs, and then the query string is URL-encoded. Using this method, when the user submits the feedback form, a request with a request line such as the following would be sent to the Web server on www.desperatesw.co.uk:

```
GET /feedback.php?Name=Zachary+Fisk&Email=zf%40fisk.com&Message=
Your+software+is+wonderful.+I+want+to+produce+it+on+Broadway.&
Submit=Send HTTP/1.1
```

We have had to split this to fit the page, but it would actually be sent as a single long line. As you may guess, there are practical limits on how long such a line can be (although the HTTP standard decrees that there should not be any limit), and this method cannot reliably be used for extensive amounts of data.

A request like this would also be generated if a user clicked on a link with a URL that had the same query string attached to it, so the GET method provides a way of passing data to a server-side script without using a form, for circumstances where it is not necessary to obtain the input from a user. Such a URL can also be bookmarked.

The second way of sending data is in the body of a request. The POST method is provided for this purpose. The request line has the same components as for a GET request, except that the method is POST. Most of the headers are also the same, but since the message's body includes some data, a Content-Type header is required, together with a Content-Length header, giving the number of bytes in the data. As we mentioned when describing Internet Media Types, the type of data is application/x-www-form-urlencoded; this just means that the data must be encoded in the same way as a query string, as a set of URL-encoded name/value pairs separated by ampersands, with spaces replaced by + signs. Thus, if the data from the feedback form was sent using POST, the request would look like this:

```
POST /feedback.php HTTP/1.1
Host: www.desperatesw.co.uk
```

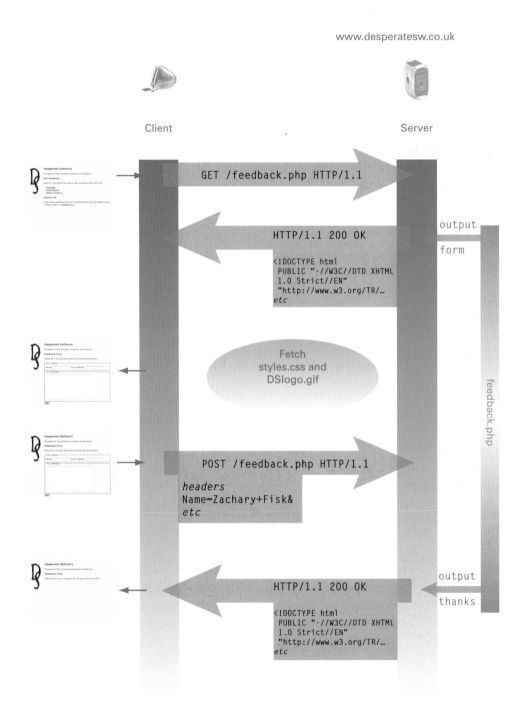

Figure 2.7 Posting form data

```
Other headers
Content-Type: application/x-www-form-urlencoded
Content-Length: 119

Name=Zachary+Fisk&Email=zf%40fisk.com&Message=Your+software+is
+wonderful.+I+want+to+produce+it+on+Broadway.&Submit=Send
```

Note the blank line separating the headers from the message body.

A POST request can never result from simply clicking on a link. It is normally only sent by a browser when a user clicks a submit button on a form, although of course other programs can build requests internally and send them explicitly. There are effectively no limits on the amount of data that can be posted, and posted data is marginally more secure than data in a query string (since the latter is visible in the address bar).

It is fairly common for the same script to be run to generate a form and to handle the data sent from it. This means that a script may be invoked in response to both GET and POST requests. This is the case with our hypothetical feedback form. Figure 2.7 illustrates the sequence of HTTP messages used in fetching the form and returning data from it.

The final link in the chain between a user filling in a form on a Web page and a script processing it on a remote machine is the passing of data between the Web server and the script. Remember that the GET or POST request is sent over a TCP connection between the browser and the server, so the server has to find the script, start it running and pass any relevant data from the request to it. There are now several mechanisms available for doing this, depending on the particular server software and the type of script.

For practical purposes, the precise mechanism can be regarded as an implementation detail. The oldest way of doing it uses an interface called the **Common Gateway Interface (CGI)**. This is somewhat over-specified, in that it stipulates that some values should be passed in environment variables, others as command line arguments and still others through the script's standard input – all system-dependent concepts. Although the CGI specification does not stipulate any language, many CGI scripts are written in Perl, and there are Perl modules that hide the implementation details of CGI and present the CGI data simply as an associative array, mapping names to the values associated with them in the request.

This is the approach taken by most other server-side scripting systems, such as PHP and JSP: request data is presented to the script in the form of one or more aggregate data structures

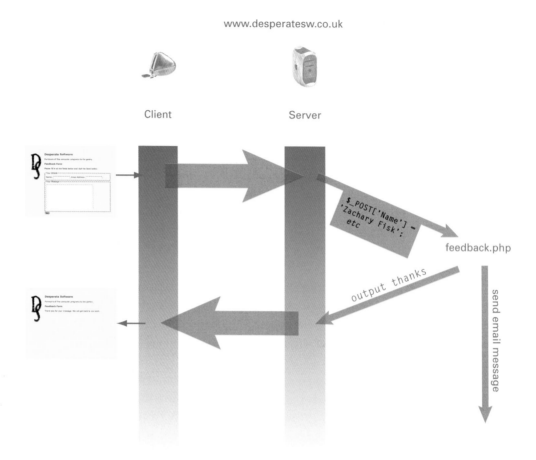

www.desperatesw.co.uk

Client   Server

$_POST['Name'] = 'Zachary Fisk'; etc

feedback.php

output thanks

send email message

Figure 2.8 Data flow at the server

from which it can easily be extracted using the normal operations of the language. This data structure invariably includes the name/value pairs from the query string of a GET request or the body of a POST, as well as information extracted from the request headers, such as the URL and method, the browser's identifying string from the User-Agent header, the date and time at which the request was sent, and many other more or less useful pieces of information that the script can use to create its response. We will look further into how this is done in Chapter 8.

Scripts usually produce some output that must be sent back to the user. (Generally, they will also perform some operations such as updating a database on the remote machine or sending an email message.) This output may go back to the server to be passed on to the client as part of a response, or the script may create the entire response and send it directly to the client. The former option is easier and more reliable, since the server adds all the necessary headers – a job it is already well equipped to perform. Again, the precise mechanism whereby the output is sent is an implementation detail. Essentially, it is arranged that when the script writes its output in the normal way, as if it was writing to a standard output stream, it is sent to the server. Some technologies, such as JSP, hide the writing of the output behind elaborate syntactical mechanisms, which make it look as if the script's logic is embedded in the page source, but underneath, all that is happening is that the output is being merged with some static text in a transparent way. Figure 2.8 shows the flow of data at the server end during processing of our example feedback form.

Cookies

We mentioned earlier that, because HTTP is stateless, it provides no way for the server, and hence for a script running on the server machine, to recognize that two requests come from the same source, even though, from the user's point of view, they are part of the same interaction. A familiar example of a related sequence of requests is a purchase from an online shopping site. Typically, you place one or more items in a shopping basket and then proceed to a checkout page to pay for them. It is of the essence of the interaction that the contents of your shopping basket be remembered between the adding of an item (which will cause one request to a script) and the start of the payment procedure (which will be a separate request). In the case of sites that allow you to accumulate a collection of items in the shopping basket, all the requests by a single user during a shopping session must be related to the same basket.

An extension to HTTP (originally a Netscape proposal, but now widely implemented) is used to permit server-side scripts to keep track of users, with the assistance of pieces of information in the form of short strings of text, known as **cookies**. A cookie can be sent as part of an HTTP response, using the Set-Cookie header. Whenever a request is sent to the server that sent the cookie, the client should send the cookie back, using the Cookie header. This implies that the cookie must be stored on the user's machine, a fact which causes some people concern. However, cookies are just data, and cannot be used to plant viruses or other malicious programs – they are never executed. Cookies should not, however, be used to store sensitive data, because it is possible that security holes may allow unauthorized agents to gain access to the cookies on a machine. (This shouldn't be possible, but it has happened.) The worst thing that cookies are normally likely to do is allow marketing companies to track your online behaviour to some extent, without your knowledge. Browsers usually allow you to refuse to accept cookies, which prevents any possible abuse, but it also means that many sites will not work properly. A more useful option is refusing cookies from any site that you do not explicitly navigate to. This will exclude cookies that have been embedded in advertisements, or even in invisible images, by third parties, which is the most common means adopted by companies to keep track of you.

The value sent in a Set-Cookie header may have several components, separated by semi-colons. The first has the form *name=value*; it gives the cookie a name and sets its value. Following this, the second component has the form expires=*date*. If this component is omitted, cookies are discarded when the user next quits the browser, but if it is present, cookies are preserved on disk until the expiry date specified. There are therefore two different types of cookie: *session cookies*, which only last until the browser is quitted, need never be written to disk, they can be kept in memory by the browser; *persistent cookies*, which may, in principle, last for years, must be stored in a file somewhere on the user's computer. The former are adequate for most shopping basket applications, but the latter are needed for such tasks as remembering a user's preferences for sites that can be customized.

The next two components specify the domain and path for which the cookie is valid. A client will only send a cookie as part of a request that is directed to the domain, and requests a resource whose path begins with the specified path. If the domain is omitted, the host that sent the cookie originally is used. The final component, if it is present, consists of the word secure, and specifies that the cookie should only be sent in a request over a secure connection.

The simplest case, therefore, is a session cookie, which is valid for all resources within a single domain. The server would set such a cookie by including a header like the following in a response:

```
Set-Cookie: PHPSESSID=0a5da990f2eef7b5dd2c0948d0dc9d5e; path=/
```

Here, the name of the cookie is PHPSESSID, and its value is a random string of characters. This is one of the most common cases: the value will presumably be used as a way of identifying the user who receives it, in the event of their sending further requests. If such a request is sent, it will include the header:

```
Cookie: PHPSESSID=0a5da990f2eef7b5dd2c0948d0dc9d5e
```

Cookies are made available to scripts on the server in the same way as other values sent in an HTTP request, so a script can discover whether it has been sent a cookie and, if so, retrieve its value and use it to find information, such as a shopping basket's contents, belonging to the user whose browser sent the cookie.

There are some limitations concerning cookies. Each cookie must be at most 4kB in size, and each domain may only send up to twenty cookies. These limitations mean that cookies cannot be used for storing extensive data, hence the more normal usage of just storing an identifier in the cookie, and keeping the actual data on the server. (This is more secure, anyway, since cookies are usually transmitted in a readable form.)

The account we have just given is based on the original Netscape proposal for cookies. A more official IETF proposal also exists, which uses a Set-Cookie2 header, with slightly different format, but it is rarely used. In any case, the precise syntax used in sending the cookie is transparent to scripts, which can always access the values they need in the same way.

Caching

If every resource required by every Web page were fetched using HTTP in the way we have described every time somebody wanted to view that page, an immense number of requests and responses would be generated. Many of these can potentially be eliminated by using caching. This means keeping a copy of each response on the client machine (the machine running the Web browser), and using this copy if the same resource is ever requested again, instead of sending for the identical data all over again. That way, many requests can be satisfied without any data being sent over the network at all. As the HTTP specification puts it: 'The goal of caching in HTTP/1.1 is to eliminate the need to send requests in many cases, and to eliminate the need to send full responses in many other cases.' Not in all cases, of course. A resource must be fetched at least once.

The trouble with caching is that a version of the requested resource that is newer than the version in the cache might have appeared on the server subsequently. In that case, the new version should be retrieved, and the old one in the cache should be discarded. The difficulty lies in determining whether this is the case for any particular request.

The simplest way for the client to find out is by asking. It may do so by sending an If-Modified-Since header as part of a GET request, giving the date and time of its cached copy (which it knows from the Date header, which is included in the response to its original request). The server only sends the requested page if the page has been modified since the date specified in the header. If it has, the server sends a response containing the modified page, as before. If not, it sends a response with status code 304, which means 'not modified'. On receiving this code, the browser displays the page from its cache.

A second mechanism is also used, in case the server does not keep track of when resources are modified. Each response may include a string called an entity tag, which is a unique identifier for the resource at the time it was sent. This string is sent as the value of the ETag header. When a client sends a request for a resource that it has a copy of in its cache, it can include the entity tag in a header with the name If-None-Match. The meaning is that the server need only return a full response if the entity tag sent in the request does not match that of the response that would be sent.

Suppose, for instance, that every page in the Desperate Sofware site uses styles.css as a stylesheet. The first time a browser sends for a page from the site, the stylesheet will be fetched as we described above. The response will include an Etag header, which will be stored in the cache, together with the time and date the file was received and its contents. Next time a page from the same site is requested and received, the browser will determine that it needs styles.css and discover that it has a copy of it in the cache. It needs to know whether it is all right to use this cached copy, so it sends a request including an If-Modified-Since and an If-None-Match header, like this:

```
GET /styles.css HTTP/1.1
Host: www.desperatesw.co.uk
Other headers
If-Modified-Since: Fri, 20 May 2005 12:22:11 GMT
If-None-Match: "aac2c-18d-428dd673"
```

On the basis of one or other of these headers, the server determines that the cached resource is no different from what it would return, so it sends a response, in effect telling the browser that it is OK to use the cached stylesheet:

```
HTTP/1.1 304 Not Modified
Other headers
ETag: "aac2c-18d-428dd673"
```

Requests of this sort eliminate the need for servers to send complete responses in all cases. A further facility potentially eliminates the need for servers to send any response at all, by eliminating the need for clients to send requests. A server can include an Expires header in its response to a GET request, indicating the date and time after which the data it returns should no longer be considered up-to-date. Until that time, the client is free to use a cached copy of the data to satisfy any subsequent requests for the same resource. Thus no network activity at all is required to obtain the same page until it reaches its expiry date.

While this mechanism is sound, it begs the question of how servers are to assign expiry dates to arbitrary pages. Most of them appear not to try, although one can imagine tightly controlled environments in which it would be known how long a page would remain valid. (In practice, it appears to be the case that Expires headers are more commonly used to force browsers to always fetch a new copy of a resource, by the server's specifying an expiry date in the past.)

In addition to these basic facilities, HTTP/1.1 specifies additional headers concerned with caching, which allow servers and clients to exert fine control over the way in which caches operate. These details are of little interest to Web designers, however.

So far, we have assumed that a cache is maintained on a user's machine. There are other places that data can be cached, though, sometimes more effectively. In particular, **Web proxies** usually maintain large caches. A proxy is a machine that handles requests directed to some other server. So when a client that is configured to use a proxy sends a request, the request is sent to the proxy, which then forwards it to its designated destination, receives the response and passes it back to the client. This apparently pointless exercise is often needed when clients are operating behind a **firewall** – a specially modified router that filters packets to provide additional security. Firewalls prevent users inside them from making HTTP requests, so a proxy is used, which has access to the outside world and the protected machines. Security can be added to the proxy to prevent unauthorized access across the firewall, in either direction. This implies that all responses to requests sent by any machine inside the firewall pass through the proxy, which means that a cache on the proxy will end up holding a pool of data that is of interest to people in the organization maintaining the firewall. This is likely to mean that many requests can be met from the proxy's cache.

Proxies can provide effective caches whenever they are placed somewhere that many requests pass through. ISPs, in particular, can employ proxies with extremely large caches to intercept a high proportion of their customers' requests.

Caches cannot help with pages that are dynamically generated, nor do they help users who never visit the same page twice unless it has been updated. And caches are finite, so that, sooner or later, cached copies of pages must be discarded, and retrieved again if they are requested subsequently. Nevertheless, they are widely considered to be making a useful contribution to keeping network traffic within bounds.

From the designer's point of view, the main relevance of caching is that if the same resource (stylesheet, image, etc.) is used several times within a site, then users who make requests for several pages in a short period of time, or who visit the site repeatedly, will only need to retrieve those resources once. This means that although they may experience a delay when a background image, a logo or a set of button images on a navbar is retrieved the first time, subsequently these items will appear almost instantly, provided that each occurrence on the site points to the same file on the server. If every page uses an identical background image, but there is a different copy of it for each page, the advantages of caching will be lost. The practice of keeping all images and stylesheets in a single `Resources` directory within a site is helpful in ensuring that no such duplication occurs.

Data Representations

The preceding section will have explained how Web pages are fetched over the Internet when you click on a link, provided that you are happy to accept that text, such as that making up HTTP messages, stylesheets and XHTML documents, is something that can be transmitted over a network and stored on a computer system. Since networks are just wires (or their equivalent) carrying electrical signals, this is far from self-evident. Hence, to provide a full picture of what is going on, we need to look at how text and other types of data that we encounter on the Web can be represented in digital form, and how digital data can be transmitted over networks.

Digital Values

A really full picture of what happens when you click on a link would require us to describe the underlying physics and electrical engineering that makes it possible to build computers and networks. We do not intend to do this here, but ask you to take it on trust that it is possible to construct computers and storage and transmission devices such as hard disks and ethernets out of devices with the property that they can be in only one of two distinct and well-defined states at a time. For example, an electronic device might have a voltage of either 0V or 3.3V at its output, but never any other. (This can only ever be approximately true, but the time during which the voltage has any other value can be made negligibly short.) These two voltages correspond to the two states of the device.

Two is the smallest number of states that can be distinguished, so if we consider our devices as holding information, the amount of information they store is the smallest unit of information there can be. It is called a *bit*. We could call the two states on and off, + and −, this and that or 1 and 0. An important insight comes from the last option, namely that groups of bits can be considered to be numbers, written in base 2 notation. This is probably a familiar idea, but we will review it briefly in case you have never encountered it before.

Numbers

The numbers we use in everyday life, such as 4598, are written in a positional notation, where the value of the number is obtained by multiplying each digit by a power of ten, according to how far from the right hand end it is. Thus, 4598 is equivalent to $4 \times 1000 + 5 \times 100 + 9 \times 10 + 8$, or, using a more perspicuous notation, $4 \times 10^3 + 5 \times 10^2 + 9 \times 10^1 + 8 \times 10^0$. Although there may be sound cultural and physical reasons for using it, mathematically, the number 10 as used in this notation is no better or worse than any other. The idea of positional notation can be generalized to encompass numbers written to any *base*, as the number whose powers we multiply by is called. For example, for reasons we will come to shortly, 16 is a popular number base in computer applications. Using 16 as the base, 4598 is equivalent to $4 \times 16^3 + 5 \times 16^2 + 9 \times 16^1 + 8 \times 16^0$, which is equal to 17816 in decimal (base 10).

Whatever base is chosen, the digits used to write a number must each be less than the base. In decimal numbers, every digit is less than 10; in *octal* (base 8), they must each be less than 8. In *hexadecimal*, as the base 16 notation is called, we need sixteen digits, representing the decimal numbers 0 to 15; the letters A to F are co-opted for the extra numbers, 10 to 15, which cannot be represented by a single decimal digit. The hexadecimal number 3FF is $3 \times 16 \times 16 + 15 \times 16 + 15$, that is, 1023. We will meet hexadecimal notation again, later.

If the number base is 2, then only two digits, 0 and 1, are needed. In other words, a single bit can represent a *binary* (base 2) digit. (In this context, the word 'bit' is a contraction of 'binary digit.') A group of bits can be used to represent any number in binary notation. Furthermore, the rules of arithmetic for binary numbers are so simple that it is relatively easy to construct electronic devices that perform arithmetic operations on groups of bits. Thus, the 2-state devices that are used to build computer processors and memories can store and manipulate numbers in the binary system.

Normally, we don't impose any limits on how many digits a number can have. It may be impractical to write down more than twenty or so digits on paper, and long numbers are hard to read (hence the use of scientific notation for very large and very small numbers), but there is no mathematical reason to restrict the number of digits in a number, and hence the magnitude of the numbers that can be represented using conventional positional decimal notation. (Quite the contrary, in fact.) Computers, however, only work efficiently if they can operate on quantities that occupy a fixed number of bits. A group of eight bits is normally called a **byte**. On conventional computers, memory is organized as a sequence of bytes. Each individual byte can be accessed by its number in the sequence, known as its address. The contents of each byte can be read or changed; values can be taken from memory, subjected to arithmetic and other operations, and then stored back into memory. All of this can take place under the control of a program, which is itself nothing more than a sequence of bytes stored in memory. (Space and the subject matter of this book do not permit us to expand on this last point, but any introductory computing text ought to provide a full explanation.)

A byte can only store 256 different values in its eight bits. (Note that an eight-bit value can be written as a two-digit hexadecimal number.) This isn't enough for most purposes. Bytes are therefore normally combined into larger units of storage, in order to accommodate larger values. The most common arrangement is to group together four bytes into a 32-bit **word**. This is sufficient for most purposes, but double-length words of 64 bits are sometimes used when a high degree of precision is needed in numerical calculations, or to address very large memories.

Text

The foregoing outline showed that computers built from devices with two distinct states are capable of storing numbers and carrying out arithmetic, but Web designers are rarely concerned with numbers and arithmetic. Web pages, stylesheets and, as we saw in the previous section, HTTP messages are composed of text. Web pages also use still and moving images, and sound. We depend on being able to use numbers to represent text, images and sounds for the Web to be possible. That is, we are concerned with **digital** representations of these types of data. We will describe how images can be stored in digital form in Chapter 5. Here we will consider the digital representation of text.

Character Sets

We must first distinguish between a character and the way it is written down. Figure 2.9 shows twenty-one different upper-case letter As. The differences between some, such as the

Figure 2.9 Upper-case Letter A

first two, are subtle, while others, such as the one in the middle of the bottom row, are markedly different from the rest. Nevertheless, most people would recognize all these shapes as being the same letter. They can be considered as different graphic renditions of the abstract character A that is the first letter of the Latin alphabet and the indefinite article in English. It is the character that carries information, its different renditions simply alter its appearance, which may be important for readability or aesthetics, but do not change the character itself: an A is an A, and you can use three of them to write the English word AARDVARK, no matter what style the letter is drawn in.

When text is stored digitally, characters and their appearance are kept separate. This is necessary if text is to be processed in any way that involves comparisons of characters; it is also much more efficient. It is only when the text comes to be displayed or printed that characters need to be dressed up, as it were, in some specific shape. This can be done by keeping a collection of shapes, one for each character, in the form of small images, and retrieving the appropriate image to display for each character in a string of text. These shapes might be stored in the hardware of an output device, but are more often found in font files on disk. We will look at this aspect of text in detail in Chapter 4. At the moment we are concerned with the more fundamental issue of representing (abstract) characters digitally.

We already know how to represent numbers digitally, so the problem of representing characters digitally becomes that of representing characters by numbers. Conceptually, this is trivial: assign a different number to each character. Making sure that the right number is stored in response to the pressing of a particular key on a keyboard, and that the right shape is displayed for a particular number, are matters that can be taken care of by the hardware and device drivers.

Although any mapping from characters to numbers would do the job of representing text in digital form, some practical considerations suggest that a mapping should have certain properties. Small numbers should be used in preference to large ones, in order to minimize the amount of storage required by the text. Sorting strings into alphabetical order can be done efficiently if the numbers representing letters ascend through the alphabet (because sorting routines can then make use of the arithmetic comparison operations built into hardware). Likewise, the numbers used to represent digits should form an ordered sequence. Certain operations are simplified if there is a fixed relationship between the numbers used for upper- and lower-case letters, for those alphabets that are bicameral. (That is, the difference between the number used for A and that for a should be the same as the difference between the numbers used for B and b, and so on.) The most straightforward way of doing this is to use a sequential run of numbers for the upper-case letters, another sequential run for lower-

Code	Char	Code	Char	Code	Char	Code	Char
32		56	8	80	P	104	h
33	!	57	9	81	Q	105	i
34	"	58	:	82	R	106	j
35	#	59	;	83	S	107	k
36	$	60	<	84	T	108	l
37	%	61	=	85	U	109	m
38	&	62	>	86	V	110	n
39	'	63	?	87	W	111	o
40	(	64	@	88	X	112	p
41	)	65	A	89	Y	113	q
42	*	66	B	90	Z	114	r
43	+	67	C	91	[	115	s
44	,	68	D	92	\	116	t
45	-	69	E	93	]	117	u
46	.	70	F	94	^	118	v
47	/	71	G	95	_	119	w
48	0	72	H	96	`	120	x
49	1	73	I	97	a	121	y
50	2	74	J	98	b	122	z
51	3	75	K	99	c	123	{
52	4	76	L	100	d	124		
53	5	77	M	101	e	125	}
54	6	78	N	102	f	126	~
55	7	79	O	103	g		

Table 2.2 The ASCII character set

case letters and a third for digits, and to assign arbitrary numbers to any additional symbols, such as punctuation marks.

These constraints by no means lead to a unique way of assigning numbers to characters, and therein lies the source of most of the complexity of text representations. Because there are many possible ways of mapping characters to numbers, standards are needed to ensure

Technical Detail

Newline Characters

If you have ever used a manual typewriter, you will remember that in order to move on to a new line, you press a lever at the left hand end of the carriage. This moves a ratchet that engages with a toothed wheel that causes the carriage to rotate, moving the paper up a line. At the same time, a locking mechanism disengages allowing the carriage to move all the way back to the right, so that the next time you press a key the character will appear at the beginning of a new line on the paper, as intended. This idea that moving to a new line is a two-stage process involving a line feed and carriage return appears in the corresponding ASCII control characters. If you are more interested in breaking a text file into lines, two characters is one too many: what you want is a 'newline' character that gets mapped to whatever is necessary to make a new line appear on any output device.

Different systems have adopted different conventions for newlines. Unix uses carriage return; MacOS prefers line feed; Windows sticks with the carriage return/line feed combination. The result can be chaotic when files are transferred from one system to another. Fortunately, most text files used on the Web are not broken into lines in this way. As we will see in later chapters, formatting is applied explicitly, and carriage return and line feed are both treated as white space. The exception is HTTP requests, which, as we mentioned earlier, are divided into lines. Here, a carriage return followed by a line feed marks a new line.

that text can be transmitted between different systems. Standards are always contentious, but standards for characters are more complicated than might at first sight appear necessary, because they must accommodate all the different writing systems that are in use all over the world.

A mapping between characters and numbers is called, not very logically, a **character set**. If you are not comfortable with the idea of a mapping, you can think of a character set as a table, such as the one in Table 2.2, which allows you to look up the number for any character or the character for any number. The number which a character set assigns to a character is called its **character code** in that character set. In the character set shown in Table 2.2, the character code for A is 65, that for a is 97 and that for a space is 32.

Code	Char	Code	Char	Code	Char	Code	Char
160		184	₎	208	Ð	232	è
161	¡	185	¹	209	Ñ	233	é
162	¢	186	º	210	Ò	234	ê
163	£	187	»	211	Ó	235	ë
164	¤	188	¼	212	Ô	236	ì
165	¥	189	½	213	Õ	237	í
166	¦	190	¾	214	Ö	238	î
167	§	191	¿	215	×	239	ï
168	¨	192	À	216	Ø	240	ð
169	©	193	Á	217	Ù	241	ñ
170	ª	194	Â	218	Ú	242	ò
171	«	195	Ã	219	Û	243	ó
172	¬	196	Ä	220	Ü	244	ô
173	-	197	Å	221	Ý	245	õ
174	®	198	Æ	222	Þ	246	ö
175	¯	199	Ç	223	ß	247	÷
176	°	200	È	224	à	248	ø
177	±	201	É	225	á	249	ù
178	²	202	Ê	226	â	250	ú
179	³	203	Ë	227	ã	251	û
180	´	204	Ì	228	ä	252	ü
181	µ	205	Í	229	å	253	ý
182	¶	206	Î	230	æ	254	þ
183	·	207	Ï	231	ç	255	ÿ

Table 2.3 The upper part of the ISO 8859-1 character set

The collection of characters to which a character set assigns codes is its **alphabet**, even though it typically includes characters, such as digits and punctuation marks, which are not usually considered alphabetical.

The character set we have shown here is the American Standard Code for Information Interchange, or **ASCII** as it is usually abbreviated. The table only shows the 95 printable

Terminology

ASCII, US-ASCII and ISO646-US

These are all the same thing. Because countries outside the US needed characters that were not available in ASCII, national variants of the character set were developed. For instance, in Britain, the # sign is rarely used, but £ is frequently required, so the ASCII code for # was used for £. In other countries, other substitutions were made. To distinguish the original ASCII code, it is often called US-ASCII, and this is the character code used by Internet protocols and for URLs.

The major national variants of ASCII were standardized as a multi-part standard, ISO 646. These character sets were never satisfactory, though, because some characters were always missing, hence the development of ISO 8859 and Unicode.

ASCII characters; the codes 0 to 31 and 127, which we have not included, correspond to characters that cannot be printed, but may affect the output on certain sorts of device in other ways. For example, 12 is the character code for 'form feed', which causes some types of printer to throw a new page; 10 and 13 are 'line feed' and 'carriage return', respectively, which between them would make a new line on a teletype; 127 is the code for 'delete'; other control characters are defined to perform more esoteric functions, related to data transmission. These control characters are a legacy from ASCII's origins in earlier character sets used for telegraphy; apart from carriage return, line feed and tab, they are now pretty much irrelevant.

Because computers can process bytes efficiently, there is much to be said in favour of character sets whose codes fit into eight bits. ASCII's 128 values only use seven bits. This is another hangover from ASCII's origins in telegraphy: the eighth bit was intended to provide simple error checking when characters were transmitted over unreliable connections. Modern networks provide better means of error detection, so it is possible to support character sets that use all the bits in a byte to represent up to 256 different characters.

This is just as well, because there are few languages other than American English that can be adequately written down using ASCII. Many languages' writing systems can be accommodated within an eight-bit character set, with its 256 possible character codes, though. For instance, adding all the national currency symbols and accented letters used in Western

European languages does not exceed the capacity of character codes that will fit into a single byte. The Cyrillic alphabet can also be accommodated with fewer than 256 character codes, as can the Hebrew and modern Greek alphabets. Each of these alphabets needs its own character set, though. Using a single byte it is not possible to accommodate all of them at once, for multi-lingual documents.

Eight-bit character sets were standardized in the 1980s as **ISO 8859**, a multi-part ISO international standard, which defines character sets for various alphabets. The **ISO 8859-1** character set contains the characters required for most Western European languages. It is often referred to as **ISO Latin1**. Its lower half is identical to ASCII, which ensures compatibility for such things as computer programs, which are often written using pure ASCII. Table 2.3 shows the characters in the upper range. (The values in the gap from 128 to 159 are either unused or used for isolated diacritical marks, which may be used for building up additional accented characters. The code 160 corresponds to a non-breaking space.)

Other ISO 8859 character sets include ISO 8859-2 or Latin2, for use with Eastern European languages, including Czech, Slovak and Croatian; ISO 8859-5, for languages, including Russian, that use the Cyrillic alphabet; ISO 8859-6, ISO 8859-7 and ISO 8859-8, for Arabic, modern Greek and Hebrew, respectively. There is a total of 10 parts to ISO 8859, with more projected. However, no eight-bit character set is going to be adequate for the Japanese, Korean or Chinese alphabets, which each have thousands of characters. More bytes are required.

The ultimate multi-byte character set is **ISO 10646**, which uses 32-bit (4-byte) character codes, potentially allowing more than four billion characters to be represented. This is a generous allowance, and, provided a linguistically dubious device of using the same code for two characters that look the same, even if they belong to different languages and are, in fact, different, is employed, all the major contemporary languages can be accommodated using 2-byte character codes within a single character set. Codes are allocated in ISO 10646 in such a way that all the characters in these languages have zeros in their top two bytes, so these can be dropped and a 2-byte subset of ISO 10646, called **Unicode**, results. Furthermore, all the ISO 8859-1 character codes appear in ISO 10646 with the top three bytes all zeros, so it is easy to translate an 8859-1 character code to its 10646 equivalent.

Unicode is inefficient in its use of storage and bandwidth for documents that can be written using ISO 8859-1 or ASCII, and, for economic and historical reasons, there are very many such documents in existence, including many Web pages. Unicode incorporates a mechanism of transformation formats that re-encode the two bytes of a character code into a different format, which is more efficient for the codes which are currently the most common – those that correspond to ASCII codes. In particular, the transformation known as **UTF-8** encodes Unicode values so that if their high-order byte is zero and the low-order byte is less than 128, the value is encoded as the single low-order byte. That is, ASCII characters are sent as themselves. Otherwise, the two-byte value is encoded using up to six bytes, with the highest bit of each byte set to 1 to indicate it is part of an encoded string and not an ASCII character. (Strictly speaking, Unicode is another transformation format from the 32-bit ISO 10646 values, called UTF-16.)

With so many character sets in use (we have barely scratched the surface here), it would not be practical for a single one to be mandated for use on the Web. Instead, the Web has to be capable of dealing with different character sets. IANA maintains a register of character sets that may be used on the Internet, and defines names for each type. These names may be used in several contexts; we will see in Chapter 3 how and why they might be incorporated into XHTML documents, for instance. Character set names may also be appended to media types that are a sub-type of `text`. The syntax used for this purpose is exemplified by the following HTTP header:

```
Content-Type: text/html; charset=iso-8859-1
```

The character set specification is separated from the media type by a semicolon, and the keyword `charset` is used to identify the parameter as a character set's identifier. Commonly used identifiers for pages that use Latin alphabets are `iso-8859-1`, `utf-8` and `us-ascii`. These identifiers are also used by the `Accept-Charset` headers, to indicate to the server which character sets a user agent can process.

Transmission of Digital Data

We have shown that Web resources consist of text and other media (we will consider images and time-based media in later chapters), and that text can be represented digitally and stored in devices that have two states. We have also shown that the fetching of resources consists of the exchange of HTTP messages, which are also text. These in turn can be represented digitally. To complete the picture, therefore, we need to look briefly at how digital data can be transmitted over networks.

The wires, optical fibres and radio links that make up the physical Internet are not inherently digital. They all transmit information by varying some physical property. For example, if a voltage is applied to one end of a perfectly conducting wire, the same voltage will appear

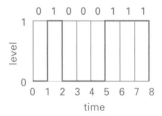

Figure 2.10 Digital data as a train of pulses

at the other end (if both ends have a common earth). A change in the voltage at one end over time will be reflected by a matching change at the other end, so the wire serves as a *transmission medium*, transmitting a time-varying signal, in the form of voltage, from one end to the other.

To transmit digital data over such a medium, it is necessary to construct a signal that encodes information represented by zeros and ones. There are several possible ways of doing this. The basic method used in computer networks is illustrated in Figure 2.10. Time is divided up into equal-sized intervals. (These will usually be very short.) During any interval, the signal is set to one of two possible values, representing 0 or 1. A group of bits, such as the value stored in a byte, is thus represented by a sequence of pulses sent down the transmission medium one after the other. For instance, the character G would be stored in a byte as the eight bits 01000111, which is the binary representation of the decimal number 71, its character code in ISO 8859-1. The character could be transmitted one bit at a time, from left to right (from the most significant to the least significant bit) as the signal shown in Figure 2.10: for the first interval the value is set to 0, then it changes to 1, returns to 0 where it stays for three intervals, then goes up to 1 again for the remaining three. Taking a stored value and turning it into such a signal is a relatively easy piece of electronic engineering, as is the inverse operation of taking a sequence of pulses and storing them in a byte.

If wires, fibres and radio links all behaved as perfect transmission media that would be the end of the story, for once we can transmit bytes, we can build up the higher level conversations necessary for retrieving pages using HTTP. However, there is no such thing in the physical world as a perfect transmission medium, which faithfully transmits a signal from one end to the other. In practice, there is always some degradation of the signal, owing to inherent physical limitations and to the presence of thermal noise. The important practical implication of these imperfections is that there is a limit to how fast any medium can transmit data, that is, how many bits it can transmit in a second.

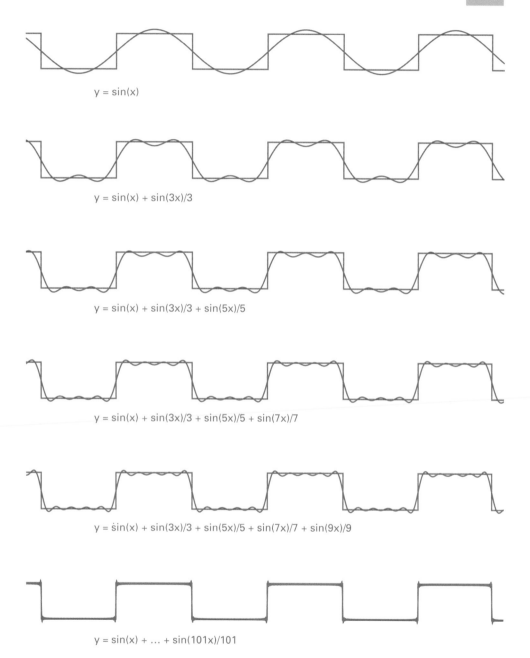

Figure 2.11 Harmonic composition of a square wave

Bandwidth

You probably know that a note produced on a musical instrument consists of a mixture of tones of different frequencies, combined in differing proportions. As well as the fundamental, which is the tone corresponding to the pitch of the note, there is a set of harmonics, whose presence contributes the distinctive timbre of the note as it is played or sung. In physical terms, the fundamental and each of the harmonics is a pure sine wave; the frequencies of the harmonics are multiples of the frequency of the fundamental. The amplitude of each of the harmonics is always less than that of the fundamental.

Any signal that varies over time can be analyzed into a collection of sine waves in a similar way. Figure 2.11 shows, as an example, how a square wave can be built up by adding harmonic components to a sine wave of the same frequency. Actually, the figure shows how better and better approximations to the square wave can be built up in this way. To construct an exact square wave by adding sine waves, we would need an infinite series of harmonics with arbitrarily high frequencies, and this is not physically possible.

The relevance of this to data transmission lies in the physical limitations of transmission media, to which we alluded earlier. It is impossible for a signal to be transmitted over any medium without losing some energy in the process – the laws of thermodynamics would not permit it. In other words, a signal will be attenuated during transmission. In itself, this is not necessarily a problem, since the signal could be amplified; however, the attenuation is not uniform at all frequencies. All of the media used for data transmission attenuate higher frequencies more than low frequencies. There is a frequency below which, to all intents and purposes, the signal is transmitted unaltered, but above this frequency, the loss increases rapidly. The range of frequencies over which a medium transmits signals with less than half the energy being lost is called its **bandwidth**.

Looking back at Figure 2.11, you can see that if the higher frequency components of the square wave are not transmitted, what appears at the receiving end will be a distorted version of the signal, corresponding to one of the earlier waveforms illustrated. Notice that as higher frequency harmonics are lost, it is the steep edges of the waveform that are worst affected. However, as long as it was possible to determine where the edges should be, it would be possible to reconstruct the original sequence of bits that had been transmitted. Digital signals are much more robust in this sense than analogue signals, which once distorted can never be reliably recovered. However, evidently there must come a point where the lowest frequency component of the signal is not transmitted, so that the signal is lost. In other words, the bandwidth of the transmission medium imposes a definite limit on the rate at which bits can

Terminology

Kilo- and Mega-

In most contexts, the prefix *kilo-* (abbreviated k) means one thousand: a kilometre is a thousand metres, a kilogram is a thousand grams, and so on. Similarly, *mega-* (M) means one million, as in megaherz and megawatts. In computing, with its physical basis in binary devices, a thousand and a million are not particularly significant numbers. It is the powers of two that have significance, since they correspond to the number of values that can be stored in a particular number of bits. (For example, 32 is 2^5, so you can store thirty two different values in five bits.)

It so happens that 2^{10} is equal to 1024, which is close to 1000. When talking about memory sizes, it is customary to use kilo- to mean this value. Thus, a kilobyte (kB) is 1024 bytes. Similarly, mega- is used to mean 1024^2, so a megabyte (MB) is 1048576 bytes. (Although sometimes hard disk manufacturers use megabyte to mean a million bytes, to make their disks appear to hold more megabytes than they do.)

In data communications, however, the conventional meaning is used for these prefixes. A bit rate of 8 kilobits per second means 8000 bits per second, not 8192. Thus, a connection with that speed would take more than a second to transmit a kilobyte of data.

be transmitted. The maximum rate at which a medium can transmit digital data is sometimes called its **bit rate**, which is quoted in bits per second.

Transmission Media in the Internet

Several different communication technologies are used in the Internet, some for the high-speed interconnections between major installations, others for connecting individual users to the network. The structure can accommodate many different sorts of links. It has already evolved to include new developments in telecommunications, and will without doubt continue to do so.

Dial-up Connections and ADSL

Many domestic users connect to the Internet by using the telephone system to transmit data between their computers and an Internet Service Provider's equipment. The bit rate of such a connection is limited by the bandwidth of the **local loop**, the two-way link between the residence and the local telephone exchange (the 'end office', in American terminology). The long-distance trunk lines between exchanges have a much higher bandwidth, but data rates must always be slow enough for the local loop, or 'the last mile', as it is often called (even though the actual distance may be more or less than a mile).

Signals traverse the local loop on insulated copper wires twisted together to form a so-called *twisted pair*. (The twists serve to prevent the wires operating as an antenna and radiating energy.) The bandwidth of twisted pairs depends on their construction and length, but for typical distances between homes and exchanges, a data rate of several megabits per second can be achieved.

For traditional voice communication, though, the bandwidth of the local loop is artificially restricted at the exchange to approximately 4kHz. This is adequate to transmit speech at a comprehensible quality, while restricting the amount of noise on the line, but it would be hopeless for sending bits as data pulses in the way we described above. By using clever encodings that allow more than two levels, and more sophisticated techniques for carrying the digital data on an analogue signal, however, it has been possible to stretch the data rate to 56 kilobits per second (kbps), the rate achieved by modems conforming to the V.90 and V.92 standards. (This data rate is only achieved in the 'downstream' direction, from the network to the computer. The upstream rate is lower: 33.6 kbps for V.90, 48 kbps for V.92.)

To get higher rates from copper wires, it is necessary to remove the artificial bandwidth restriction, and this is what *Asymmetric Digital Subscriber Line (ADSL)* does. By installing different equipment at the exchange, the full bandwidth of the line becomes potentially available. Digital data can be sent using the higher frequencies which were previously filtered out, while voice traffic can still be sent using the lower part of the available frequency spectrum. As well as being significantly faster than a dial-up connection, ADSL services have the advantages of being always connected, without the need to establish a connection every time something is needed from the Internet, and not tying up the voice line.

ADSL is asymmetric in that the upstream data rate is usually less than the downstream rate. This makes a lot of sense for typical domestic and small business users, who will normally spend most of their time downloading Web pages and other files over the network, and relatively little time, if any, uploading anything other than email attachments and updates to their Web sites. Other DSL technologies, including Symmetric DSL (SDSL), provide higher upstream data rates, and are becoming more widely available.

As we mentioned earlier, the bandwidth of a twisted pair depends on its length: it decreases as the length increases. The consequence is that the data rates that can be achieved by an ADSL connection depend on the distance between the exchange and the user's computer: the further away from the exchange you are, the slower the data rate will be. Telecommunication service providers usually offer a range of ADSL packages with different data rates through ISPs. Higher rate packages may only be available to users who are close to the exchange.

The precise combinations of upstream and downstream data rates on offer varies around the world, and changes all the time as the market for broadband access develops. 512kbps is currently a popular downstream rate for domestic users, which is often available for little more than the cost of a dial-up connection; in some countries, though, 2Mbps is considered the norm for domestic connections, whereas in some other countries most access is still via a 56kbps dial-up connection. Upstream rates vary from 64kbps to 512kbps. Higher downstream rates of 8Mbps or higher are increasingly available to premises close enough to an exchange. The cost of these packages increases with the data rate, which probably seems reasonable to the telecomms companies.

Just as clever encoding schemes allowed the speed of dial-up connections to increase from 14.4kbps to 56kbps, so refined versions of ADSL are being developed, which provide higher data rates or increased 'reach' (the maximum distance from the exchange at which a given rate can be reliably achieved.)

Cable

In places where cable TV is available, the coaxial cables used to distribute television broadcasts can also be used to provide high-speed Internet access. Coax, as it is widely known (when pronounced as two syllables), has substantially higher bandwidth than twisted pair cables, so it can support higher bit rates when it is used to carry digital traffic. Just as ADSL employs the unused bandwidth of the telephone system to carry data traffic, Internet traffic on the cable network is carried using the high frequencies above those used for television, and the low frequencies below them. There is more free bandwidth above the TV frequencies than there is below; the high frequencies are used for downstream traffic, the low for upstream, so, as with ADSL, there is an asymmetry between the downstream and upstream data rates, which fits well with the expected pattern of use. (Since businesses rarely subscribe to cable TV, cable is really only an option for domestic users.) Like ADSL, cable provides a connection that is 'always on'.

There are some similarities between the way cable TV networks and the telephone networks are organized. In particular, both use high-speed fibre-optic links for long-distance connections, interfacing to lower-speed local links, which determine the maximum data rate: twisted pairs for the local loop in the telephone system, coax cables leading to homes for cable TV. There is an important difference, though, which has major implications for these two systems' use for providing Internet access. Whereas each individual telephone line has its own local loop, a single coax cable may provide many households with their television signals. When Internet access is provided over this cable, the bandwidth must be shared between all those households which are accessing the network at any time. Some of the time, when only a few people are using the Internet, high speeds may be achieved, whereas at other times, when there are many users, the speed will be much lower. It is not, therefore, possible to give a figure for the data rate of cable: it will vary. What cable service providers do in practice is cap the data rates of users' connections to values that ought to be achievable most of the time. Typical values are comparable to those for ADSL: 512kbps as an entry-level rate, rising to 4Mbps or higher.

Internet access over cable has its drawbacks. The sharing of the cable creates security and privacy problems, since anybody with suitable equipment can eavesdrop on the data being sent by other users. This means that data must be encrypted by the cable system, which complicates the system and makes it less robust; equipment failures can lead to the loss of their connections for many users at a time. And, of course, cable access is only possible where cables are installed. This means that it is restricted for the most part to urban locations in developed countries, where it is economically worthwhile for companies to install the infrastructure and there is already a demand for many TV channels.

Wireless Connections

Radio and microwave connections are used in three distinct ways to connect users to the Internet. First, the mobile (cellular) phone networks can be used to connect various mobile devices to the Internet. Second, wireless local area networks in public places are used to provide access points for people with portable computers. Third, satellites are used to provide access in areas that are not served by other communication networks.

A great deal of fuss has been made about the potential of mobile Web access by means of hand-held devices, whether these are mobile phones enhanced with computing capabilities, PDAs with communications abilities, or a new generation of devices combining the features of both. In fact, people seem to prefer to use their phones for texting and sending each other photographs, rather than for reading Web pages. On the other hand, people who take their

Terminology

IEEE 802.11 and WiFi

The IEEE has produced a series of standards for wireless local area networks, all of which have numbers beginning 802.11. The original specification was not widely used. The first wireless Internet access points were based on 802.11b, an improved specification giving data rates up to 11Mbps (on the local network – data rates on the Internet will depend on the broadband link to which it is attached). Subsequently, networks based on 802.11g have appeared, which can give rates up to 54Mbps.

The name WiFi is commonly used to describe any 802.11 network; the shorthand 802.11x is also used to indicate any of the 802.11 family. Apple Computer's 802.11b and 802.11g implementations are marketed under the names Airport and Airport Extreme, respectively.

laptops on the road a lot find it helpful to be able to use their mobile phones to connect to the Internet over the mobile network in the same way as they use fixed telephone lines to connect their desktop machines. Second generation (2G) mobile phones (the first type to support digital voice transmission) are not, however, very suitable for this purpose. To make best use of the radio frequencies allocated to mobile telephony, they perform advanced compression and encoding of voice data before it is transmitted, with the result that the bit rate of a digitized conversation is much lower than that required by fixed telephones, so it requires less bandwidth. This is extremely clever, but somewhat unhelpful if what you want to send is raw digital data, such as an HTTP response, since this will have to go at the reduced rate needed for voice. As a result, using a modem with a 2G phone only provides around 9.6kbps, which is no use for anything except reading email.

Data rates comparable to those of an ordinary dial-up connection (i.e. around 56kbps) are possible using a system called **GPRS (General Packet Radio Service)**. This is sometimes referred to as a 2.5G system, to indicate that it is a transition between second and third generations. It is an IP network built on top of the voice network, rather than a system designed specifically for data. To use GPRS to access the Internet, a telephone with GPRS capabilities that can be connected to a computer or a PCMCIA card that fits into a laptop computer is required.

Third generation (3G) phones are intended to provide a system designed for both voice and data from the start. Originally, the International Telecommunications Union specified a system called International Mobile Telecommunications (IMT2000), which was supposed to provide a global 3G standard. In practice, six different variants have been developed in different parts of the world, but all offer bit rates for data just under 2Mbps, which means 3G mobile phones can be used for broadband access. There are some practical difficulties associated with 3G, however, not least the fact that it is not clear that there is much demand for it among consumers, even though the phone companies have paid enormous amounts of money to governments for licences to operate 3G services. Many pundits have predicted that a new generation of mobile devices based on the 3G network will emerge and that mobile Web browsing would be one of their main uses. If this happens, Web designers will need to be aware that their pages might be viewed on such devices, which will almost certainly have relatively small screens.

Since 2G, 2.5G and 3G phones may all be in use for an extended period while the 3G infra-structure is built and consumers are persuaded to buy new handsets, it will be the case that Internet access from mobile devices will take place at a wide a range of different speeds.

Meanwhile, an alternative way of accessing the Web while away from home or out of the office is becoming popular. Wireless local area networks based on some version of the IEEE 802.11 standard are being installed in public places, such as coffee shops, airports, hotels and even parks. Anyone with a laptop equipped with an 802.11 card can bring it along to one of these *access points* and connect to the Internet through this network, which will itself have some sort of broadband connection. Since many new laptops are supplied with such a card installed, no extra equipment is needed, and many access points come with the bonus of a congenial location and decent espresso. The bandwidth of both the local area network and its Internet connection are shared between customers, but at most times of day only a few people are likely to be browsing the Web from any access point, so they will typically experience data rates comparable to those they would get from an ADSL or cable connection at home.

Wireless access points are mostly only to be found in urban areas, which have the requisite coffee shops and so on, as well as some form of broadband to connect the wireless network to the Internet. In remote rural areas, they are not often found.

In some parts of the world, wireless networks with a longer range are used to provide broadband access. These are based on a different IEEE wireless network standard, 802.16. Essentially, the local loop is replaced by a radio connection. Larger antennas are required;

at the exchange end, these will be sited on towers, consumers may need to fix an antenna to their roof. Networks covering a range of several kilometres are sometimes called Metropolitan Area Networks (MANs), and it is in cities that wireless MANs replacing the local loop are most common. In some parts of the world, the same technology is used to provide access in rural areas, where dwellings are too far from the exchange for ADSL. Radio links require a clear line of sight between antennas, though, and this cannot always be achieved where hills and trees may obscure the signal.

In remote areas where wireless links are not practical, distances from telephone exchanges are too long for ADSL, and cable operators never tread, the only possibility for broadband Internet access at present lies in communication satellites. There are plans to use satellites in low orbits for this purpose, but at the moment, services depend on the use of satellites in geostationary orbits above the equator. This means that the height of the satellite above ground is such that it takes twenty-four hours to complete a single orbit, so that it appears to be stationary over the same point on the Earth. Thus, a fixed dish antenna can be permanently pointed at the satellite. This is the principle used for satellite television. Signals can reach any point on the Earth, provided there is a clear line of sight in the direction of the equator. This can almost always be provided.

Satellite access has the overwhelming advantage of not requiring any extensive infrastructure in the form of cables or microwave towers. All that is needed is a relatively small dish antenna (typically 75cm in diameter), connected to a suitable modem. This makes it eminently suitable for remote areas and especially for developing countries, which do not have an existing telephone network to support ADSL. Service providers offer connections with downstream data rates of roughly 512kbps or, for a premium, 2Mbps, making satellite comparable in speed to the other broadband technologies we have described. However, satellite does have considerable disadvantages.

First, it takes a noticable time for signals, even those travelling at the speed of light, to travel from the Earth's surface up to the satellite and back down again. Geostationary satellites orbit at an altitude of roughly 35,800km. The time for a round trip depends on the latitude of the the sending and receiving computers, but it is usually quoted as being between 250 and 350 milliseconds. Thus, if a user agent sends an HTTP request, there will be a delay of over half a second before the response starts to arrive (discounting the time it takes the server to process the request and generate the response). This makes satellite links useless for applications requiring real-time interaction, although it should not affect Web browsing too badly, except inasmuch as the speed of response may not be much faster than that of a dial-up connection for small pages.

A second disadvantage is that signals in the frequencies allocated for satellite communication are absorbed by water, so the connection may be lost during heavy rain or in dense fog. The signal will also be lost if the satellite dish is knocked out of position so that it no longer points directly at the satellite. A less frequent problem with the connection is that twice a year, at the equinoxes, the satellite must pass directly between the Sun and the Earth, which will cause a loss of the signal for several minutes.

Satellites can provide two-way communication, but the small dishes installed at users' premises cannot transmit a very powerful signal, so the data rate in the upstream direction is much lower than that in the downstream direction – a familiar situation. Some service providers go so far as offering one-way satellite links, where the downstream data comes via a satellite, but the upstream data is sent over a dial-up connection. This would seem to offer the worst of both worlds.

Leased Lines and Fibre Optics

None of the broadband technologies we have described so far provides adequate data rates for medium-sized or large businesses, or for organizations wishing to run their own servers, in the expectation of having to deal with a lot of traffic. The customary solution for organizations in this position is to lease a dedicated trunk line. Trunk lines are normally used to connect telephone exchanges to each other; in that case, each line carries many simultaneous calls, using a technique known as multiplexing. If a trunk line is leased to an organization, it can be dedicated to carrying all its data traffic. This gives high data rates in both directions. Since the detailed engineering of trunk lines is done differently around the world, the possible data rates vary. In North America, the slowest leased lines are called T1 lines, and have a capacity of just over 1.5Mbps; in the rest of the world, the equivalent lines are classed as E1, which gives 2Mbps. Higher speed leased lines give speeds of 44Mbps and higher. However, these data rates will usually be shared among several (possibly many) users, so it is unlikely that any single user will have access to data rates that high.

Conventional copper trunk lines are ultimately limited in their carrying capacity to data rates around 500Mbps (half a gigabit per second). Increasingly, long-distance high-speed trunks are being replaced by fibre optic links, which have much higher bandwidth than copper. Optical fibres are just very thin strands of glass, and data is carried down them in the form of pulses of light. Because of the high bandwidth, correspondingly high data rates can be achieved. In theory, an optical link can carry data at over 50,000Gbps: 100,000 times as fast as copper wire. In practice, the data rate is limited to around 10Gbps at present, but the limiting factor is the speed at which data can be converted between optical and

Connection Type		Speed	Text-only 20kB	Light Graphics 100kB	Rich Media 2MB
Dial-up (V90)		56kbps	2.9s	14.6s	5min
ADSL	typical	512kbps	320ms	1.6s	32.8s
	premium	2Mbps	82ms	410ms	8.4s
Cable	typical	512kbps	320ms	1.6s	32.8s
	premium	2Mbps	82ms	410ms	8.4s
Satellite		512kbps	860ms	2.1s	33.3s
Leased line	T1	1.5Mbps	109ms	546ms	11.2s
	T3	44Mbps	3.7ms	19ms	381ms
Abilene		100Mbps	1.6ms	8.2ms	168ms

Table 2.4 Approximate typical download times

electrical forms. It is confidently expected that further research will extend the possible speed of fibre links, to the point at which data can be carried over the network faster than it can be produced by computers.

Wide area internetworking based on fibre is being tested in the form of a network called Abilene, which connects major universities across the United States. (Abilene is sometimes referred to as Internet2, but Internet2 is actually an organization which is coordinating research into a high-speed successor to today's Internet.) Abilene uses cross-country links running at 10Gbps, and the intention is that it should provide 100Mbps between every computer attached to the network. At present, these speeds are only available to American universities, and the financial difficulty of replacing all the copper wire in local loops makes it unlikely that a comparable network will be available to the population at large very soon. Nevertheless, barring natural or man-made catastrophes, it seems inevitable that one day the Internet will operate at these rates, which will have a dramatic effect on the kinds of services that can be made available over it. Possibly, such a high-speed Internet will spell the end of the World Wide Web as we know it.

Performance Comparison

Table 2.4 is an attempt to put the raw bit rate figures into perspective, by demonstrating roughly how long it would take to download different sorts of Web page over the different types of link we have described. There is no such thing as a typical Web page; the page sizes we have chosen correspond to a page roughly the size of a screen, consisting of text and fairly dense markup, without any images; a page with some text, a couple of images roughly a quarter of the size of the screen, and a collection of rollover images and icons; and a page with a short video clip and some images.

The figures should not be taken too seriously as an accurate prediction of download times. We have assumed, somewhat unrealistically, that all connections are operating at their maximum speed, without considering the effect of contention for connections such as cable, whose speed depends on the number of simultaneous users. (We have, however, added a typical value of 270ms for latency in the case of satellite.) Also, we have taken no account of possible delays at the server, or congestion that can occur in the network, and we have not attempted to model the dynamics of the data flow – TCP connections don't just start at their final speed instantaneously, for example, but we have worked out the times as if they did. Nevertheless, the relative values of the numbers provide an indication of the qualitative differences between the different sorts of Internet connection that people might use to view your Web pages.

Several points emerge from the comparison. First, there is a clear divide into three categories: dial-up, broadband and high-speed connections. Using rich media such as video over dial-up is more or less infeasible – few users will wait five minutes for a short video clip to download; even broadband users will require good motivation to wait for the same clip. If you want users with all sorts of connection to view your pages reasonably quickly, a relatively light use of graphics and avoidance of rich media is indicated.

For the moment, dial-up, ADSL and cable are the most widespread forms of access for domestic consumers and small businesses, with some significant use of satellites in remote areas. Other forms of broadband are being developed, including the delivery of data over power cables, and the use of tethered balloons and unmanned light aircraft as wireless relay stations. It remains to be seen whether any of these will be commercially viable.

Key Points

Web Pages

Uniform Resource Locators (URLs) are used to identify Web pages.

A URL consists of a prefix (usually `http://` for Web pages), a host name and a path, which together identify a file on a computer connected to the Internet.

XHTML is a markup language, used to define the structure and content of documents, using tags to delimit logical elements.

CSS is a stylesheet language, used to define the appearance of XHTML documents by defining rules that describe how elements of each type should appear.

A Web page comprises several files, including an XHTML document, containing the marked-up text, a stylesheet and possibly some images or other media. These are combined by a Web browser when it displays the page.

Styesheets and images reside in external files, which are referred to from the XHTML document.

Pages may be created dynamically as the output of scripts, which may use data from other files and databases.

Fetching Pages

Architecturally, the Internet consists of a collection of layers, each one providing services for the one above it.

The Internet Layer gets packets to their destinations; the Transport Layer sends streams of data; the Application Layer provides high-level services to applications such as Web browsers.

The Web is a client/server application: Web browsers are clients which send requests to Web servers, which send responses back.

Interactions between Web clients and servers obey a simple application-level protocol called the Hypertext Transfer Protocol (HTTP).

The Domain Name System (DNS) translates host names into IP addresses, which can be used by TCP to establish connections between HTTP clients and servers.

Domain names have a hierarchical structure and are administered in such a way that they are guaranteed to be unique.

HTTP messages (request and responses) consist of a request or status line, followed by some headers and then the body of the message.

The request line specifies a method, usually GET or POST, and the resource being requested.

The status line of a response indicates whether it was successful; any returned data is contained in the body of the response.

The content-type header indicates what sort of data is contained in the reponse, using a two-part Internet Media Type.

For dynamically generated pages, the server will cause the appropriate script to be executed and return its output in the body of the response.

Data from forms are sent as name/value pairs, which can be passed to the script by the server.

These name/value pairs may be appended to a GET request as a query string, or sent in the body of a POST request.

Cookies are used to keep track of related requests.

HTTP's caching mechanism helps reduce network traffic.

Data Representations

Computers, storage devices and networks are built from devices that can only be in one of two states at a time.

A device with two states can hold one bit of information.

If bits are interpreted as 0 or 1, groups of bits can be treated as numbers to base 2.

A byte is eight bits, so it can store 256 values. Four bytes are often grouped into a word of 32 bits.

Abstract characters can be represented simply by assigning numbers to them.

A character set is a mapping between the characters of an alphabet and numbers (character codes).

ASCII uses seven bits per character code, but only 95 ASCII characters are printable.

ISO 8859 defines a family of eight-bit characters sets for various alphabets.

ISO 8859-1 (ISO Latin1) contains the characters for most West European languages, including English.

ISO 10646 is a four-byte character set, which can accommodate all written alphabets.

Unicode is a two-byte subset of ISO 10646, which can accommodate all major contemporary languages.

UTF-8 is an efficient encoding of Unicode, which only uses a single byte for ASCII characters.

Character set specifications may be appended to Internet Media Types that are a sub-type of text, to specify the character set in a document.

Transmission of Digital Data

Media such as copper wires and optical fibres transmit time-varying signals; digital information must be encoded for transmission.

A group of bits (e.g. a character) can be transmitted as a sequence of pulses, where the signal is set to 0 or 1 for the duration of each pulse.

There is always a limit to how many bits per second can be sent over any physical medium.

The range of frequencies over which a medium transmits signals with less than half the energy being lost is called its bandwidth.

The bandwidth determines the maximum bit rate.

The bandwidth of the local loop is restricted to optimize speech transmission, so even with clever encoding of digital signals, modems can only achieve 56kpbs for dial-up connections.

ADSL removes the artificial bandwidth restriction and provides speeds of 512kbps to 8Mbps or higher in the downstream direction over the telephone network.

Internet access over the cable TV networks provides similar speeds to ADSL, but bandwidth is shared between households.

GPRS telephones can provide a similar bit rate to dial-up connections.

3G mobile phones offer access at nearly 2Mbps.

Wireless access points allow users of laptops equipped with IEEE 802.11 cards to connect to the Internet in cafés, airports, hotels, etc.

Wireless networks and satellites are used to provide access in remote rural areas.

Fibre optic links provide virtually unlimited bandwidth.

Exercises

Test Questions

1. Must the host name of a Web server begin with www?

2. Explain the purpose of the Domain Name System. Could the World Wide Web exist without the DNS?

3. What are the two types of HTTP message? Describe the structure of each and give examples.

4. Describe what normally happens when a user clicks on a submit button after filling in a web form.

5. What components might the value sent in a Set-Cookie header have, and what is their role? Which components would you use in a shopping basket application for an online store?

6. Which Internet Media Types are most commonly encountered on Web pages?

7. What problems might arise with the use of caching in HTTP and how are they dealt with? What are the advantages of caching?

8. Explain the purpose and any benefits of using Web proxies.

9. Describe how text is represented digitally.

10. Is ADSL a suitable technology for connecting Web servers to the Internet?

11. Describe the advantages and disadvantages of using satellites for Internet access.

Discussion Topics

1. Why is HTTP a stateless protocol? What advantages and disadvantages would there be in allowing HTTP to maintain state information (i.e. to remember previous requests made from the same client)?

2. Do Internet Media Types provide an adequate mechanism for describing the type of all resources that might be incorporated in Web pages?

3. Would it be desirable to extend the syntax of URLs to allow arbitrary Unicode characters to be used in any component? What would be the technical implications of such a change?

4. Suppose you were making a round-the-world trip. Would it be possible for you to access the Web throughout your journey? What facilities could you use, and what access technologies would you be likely to encounter?

5. When domestic connections with data rates in excess of 8Mbps become common, services such as video-on-demand and interactive TV will become feasible over the Internet. Will the World Wide Web then become redundant?

Practical Tasks

1. Use a traffic watching utility to observe the requests and responses that occur when you type www.desperatesw.co.uk into your browser's address bar. Explain what is happening.

2. In your Web browser preferences or Internet options change the settings for cookies to ensure that you are asked every time a request to set a cookie reaches your browser. (Note that some browsers do not have this option; if yours doesn't, try using Firefox or Opera.) Navigate to a number of different types of Web site, including e-commerce sites, and note which ones want to set cookies. Try refusing cookies and see whether it makes any difference to the behaviour of the site. Look at the list of all the cookies that have been stored on your computer over time. What do you think they were being used for? Do you think that all the sites using cookies were justified in doing so?

Markup

3

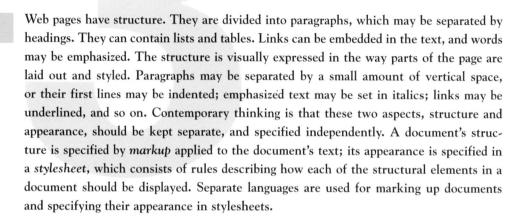

Web pages have **structure**. They are divided into paragraphs, which may be separated by headings. They can contain **lists** and **tables**. Links can be embedded in the text, and words may be emphasized. The **structure** is visually expressed in the way parts of the page are laid out and styled. Paragraphs may be separated by a small amount of vertical space, or their **first** lines may be indented; emphasized text may be set in italics; links may be underlined, and so on. Contemporary thinking is that these two aspects, structure and appearance, should be kept separate, and specified independently. A document's structure is specified by *markup* applied to the document's text; its appearance is specified in a *stylesheet*, which consists of rules describing how each of the structural elements in a document should be displayed. Separate languages are used for marking up documents and specifying their appearance in stylesheets.

This principle of separation between structure and appearance has not always been followed on the Web. Originally, documents were marked up in **HTML** (the Hypertext Markup Language). The earliest version of this language had no provision for controlling appearance, and all documents were, in effect, styled using a default stylesheet programmed into the browser. As HTML developed through subsequent versions, facilities were added to it to control appearance. By the time HTML 4 was defined in 1998, though, it was recognized that this was not a satisfactory way of proceeding. A separate stylesheet language, **CSS (Cascading Stylesheets)**, was designed, and facilities were added to HTML to allow a stylesheet to be associated with a document. However, in the interests of backward compatibility, styling facilities were retained in HTML, leading to a confused situation where the same effect could be achieved in two different ways.

At about the same time, it was also recognized that a markup language with a fixed repertoire of structures, such as HTML, could not accommodate all imaginable documents that might appear on the Web and represent their structure accurately. It was necessary to have a language that allowed users to define their own types of structure. **XML** (the Extensible Markup Language) was developed for this purpose. In XML, you can define a set of elements, corresponding to the structural components of a particular sort of document, and some rules about how these may be combined. In effect, this defines a special-purpose markup language for documents of that type, so XML can be thought of as a markup *metalanguage*: a language for defining other markup languages. HTML is a markup language, so the logical thing to do was to redefine HTML using XML. (HTML and XML have a common ancestry, so this was not a radical operation.) The result was **XHTML**, the currently preferred markup language for Web pages. XML has also been used to define other markup languages – such as SVG, XForms, RDF, MathML and SMIL – that are coming into use on the Web for more specialized purposes.

XML

The Web designer's main concern is with XHTML. It would be possible to describe XHTML in isolation, as a self-contained markup language, but it is more informative and accurate to describe it in terms of XML, which is how it is defined. In the absence of any knowledge about XML, certain features of XHTML would appear to be mere unnecessary red tape. Additionally, other markup languages defined in XML will become increasingly important on the Web, so Web designers need to have a basic understanding of XML. First, though, you need to understand how markup is used to define a document's structure.

Markup

For most people, the visual appearance of text indicates its structure. Computer programs need a more explicit, consistent and unambiguous indication of where paragraphs, headings and so on begin and end than is provided by the various typographic and layout conventions found in printed documents. This can be done by adding special markers, known as *tags*, to the actual textual content, which serve to delineate the structural components.

For instance, the line containing the single word 'Markup' in blue, above the preceding paragraph, is a sub-heading. It is followed by a paragraph of text, which ends before the extra vertical space. Within the paragraph, the word 'tags' is set in a special font, because it is a word that appears in the online glossary. We could dispense with the typography and spacing, and show this structure explicitly using tags like this:

```
<subheading>Markup</subheading><paragraph>For most people, the
visual appearance of text indicates its structure. Computer programs
```

```
need a more explicit, consistent and unambiguous indication of
where paragraphs or headings begin and end than the various
typographic and layout conventions found in printed documents
provide. This can be done by adding special markers, known as
<glossaryitem>tags</glossaryitem>, to the actual textual content,
which serve to delineate the structural components.</paragraph>
```

Here, the highlighted strings are the tags. We have adopted the convention used in XML that tags are names enclosed in angle brackets (that is, between a 'less than' sign <, and a 'greater than' sign, >). The tags come in pairs, one at the beginning and one at the end of each piece of text we want to identify as a structural unit. The tag at the end is identical to the one at the beginning, except that a slash, /, follows the opening <, so the tags at the start and end of the paragraph are `<paragraph>` and `</paragraph>`. As the example demonstrates, other tags may appear between the start and end tag, as well as text. Here we have `<glossaryitem>` and `</glossaryitem>` between `<paragraph>` and `</paragraph>`.

As well as marking the beginning and end of a unit, tags also classify them. The name in the tag identifies a type of construct that can appear in the document: subheading, paragraph, and so on. The tagging of a document assigns types to each of the pieces that the tags delimit. These pieces are called *elements*.

There is no indication in the marked-up text of how subheadings and paragraphs are to be laid out. Some additional specification of its appearance, in the form of a stylesheet, will be required before the text can be displayed, but this means that the appearance is not fixed, and can easily be changed or adapted. In fact, the structural information embodied in the markup is not just applicable to a visual rendering. It could also be used, in conjunction with a suitable stylesheet language, by text reading software, to control intonation, pauses and other verbal indications of the structure. The tags can also be used by computer programs for automatic processing of the text. For instance, it would be relatively simple to write a program to extract all the glossary terms from a document that had been marked up using the tags in our little example.

Elements and Tags

XML provides a standard syntax for writing marked-up documents, which is inherited by all languages, including XHTML, that are defined using XML. A document is made up of elements; an element consists of a start tag, some text, other elements or a mixture of both, and a matching end tag. The text and elements between the start and end tags are called the element's *content*. Thus, if an element is called e1, it will look like:

```
<el>content</el>
```

If the content of an element includes other elements, they are called its **child elements** or **children**. Some elements have no content; these are called **empty elements**. (You will see some examples when we describe XHTML.) In these cases, the start and end tags may be combined into a special form where a / immediately precedes the closing >. If eel was an empty element, its tag would be <eel/>. (You will often see a space written before the / in such tags. This is not required, but makes it easier for older browsers to cope with XHTML tags.)

Element names are subject to some restrictions. They must begin with a letter or underline character, which may be followed by any number of letters, digits, underlines, hyphens or full stops. (For most purposes it is wise to stick with these, although – since XML is written using Unicode characters – a wider range of characters is permitted in names. Note that letters are not restricted to the Latin alphabet, however.) Colons have a special significance in the context of names, which is described in Appendix B. A name may not begin with the three-letter sequence xml (in any mixture of upper and lower case), because such names are used for special purposes within XML. An element name may not contain any spaces, so you can't use something like list item as an element name. You have to run such compound names together. To do this you can use hyphens or underscores, or mixed-case conventions to improve readability: listitem, list-item, list_item or ListItem are possible element names. Names are case-sensitive, that is, upper- and lower-case versions of the same letter are considered to be different, so ListItem is a different name from listItem. The names in the start and end tags of an element must match exactly.

The < sign at the beginning of a tag shows where it starts. There is therefore a problem if you wish to use this character for any other purpose within the text of a document. Whenever you wish to do so, you must use the sequence < instead. (The semicolon at the end is part of the sequence.) Astute or experienced readers will recognize that this only defers the problem. What if you want to use an ampersand in the text? A similar expedient is adopted: you write &. This does not introduce any more problematical characters. Any other character may be used as itself.

The syntax for these sequences probably looks excessively complicated for the purpose. Why not just use something simple like &< and &&? The reason is that < and & are examples of a more general mechanism for providing special names for various sorts of things in XML. If you are mainly going to work with XHTML documents, you need not worry about the details. In XML, five such **entity references**, as these constructs beginning with & and ending with ; are called, are predefined. In addition to the two we have seen, > is used for >, and ' and " for a single quote (apostrophe) and double quote, respectively. You can also use related constructs called *character references*, of the form &#d; or &#xh; to refer to Unicode characters by their decimal or hexadecimal character codes. For instance, the pilcrow, or paragraph sign, ¶ has Unicode value 182, which is B6 in hexadecimal. It can therefore be written as ¶ or ¶.

A fundamental restriction that XML imposes on the structure of documents is that elements must be properly nested. That is, if an element's start tag appears within the content of another element, its end tag must also lie within that element's content. For instance, if paragraph elements denote paragraphs and emphasis elements are used for emphasized text, the following is illegal:

```
<paragraph>This paragraph ends with some <emphasis>emphasized
text...</paragraph>
<paragraph>...which goes on</emphasis> into the next
paragraph.</paragraph>
```

Instead, you would have to write this:

```
<paragraph>This paragraph ends with some <emphasis>emphasized
text...</emphasis></paragraph>
<paragraph><emphasis>...which goes on</emphasis> into the next
paragraph.</paragraph>
```

An XML document must have a 'top level' *root element*, which contains all the other elements in the document. Because of the requirement for proper nesting, this means that the elements of a document have a hierarchical structure, which may be represented as a tree in which all the other elements are descendants of the root element. As we will see later, there may be some parts of an XML document that lie outside the root element.

Attributes

Attributes are named properties of elements; each element type has its own collection of attributes. Attributes are given values within the element's start tag. For example, a paragraph of text will be written in some natural language. It would be helpful to programs processing the text (for example, search engines) if it included some indication of what language was being used. This can be done by associating a language code with each paragraph element, using an attribute, which we could call lang. To assign a value to an attribute, we write the attribute's name, followed by an = sign, and then the value, enclosed in single or double quote marks. Thus, if a paragraph was written in French, its start tag could be `<paragraph lang="fr">`. You can't use the quote marks surrounding the value within it (for reasons that should be obvious), so you must use the appropriate entity reference if you need to do this. You must also use the entity reference for < within attribute values, to avoid confusing software that reads XML.

XML actually allows several different sorts of value to be used for attributes, but Web designers using XHTML need only be concerned with strings. Note that, even if an attribute has a value that you might naturally think of as a number or a Boolean, you must assign a string. So, if you wanted to assign a level of importance to each paragraph using an attribute `level`, you would have to write tags such as `<paragraph level="2">` and not `<paragraph level=2>`. The convention for Boolean values is counter-intuitive: if you want to set an attribute's value to true (or on, if you prefer to think of it that way), you must assign its own name to it. For instance, if an attribute `changed` indicated whether a paragraph had been edited recently, edited paragraphs would begin `<paragraph changed="changed">`, while paragraphs that had not been edited would just have the attribute omitted from their start tags.

Any number of attributes may be assigned values within an element's start tag, but the same attribute may only occur once. Multiple assignments are separated by white space. A level 2 paragraph written in French that had been changed could be indicated with the start tag `<paragraph level="2" changed="changed" lang="fr">`

Strictly speaking, there is one additional type of value that you will encounter. Attributes of type `ID` take strings as their values, but are subject to an additional constraint: each value may occur only once in a document. Attributes of this type (which usually have names like `id`) are used to provide unique identifiers for individual elements. One use of such attributes is to allow special styling to be applied to a particular element, instead of the default styling for elements of its type.

Document Type Definitions and Schemas

XML documents as described in the previous section are said to be **well-formed**. In summary, this means that they satisfy a few simple rules. Every element that is not empty must be delimited by matching start and end tags. An element that is empty may consist of a special start tag, with a / before the closing > to indicate that there is no end tag. Elements must be properly nested. All attribute values must be enclosed in matching quote marks.

The symbols < and & must not appear, except at the beginning of a tag or a character or entity reference, respectively.

If a document is well-formed, a program can analyse it to determine its structure – how elements are combined into a hierarchy and how attribute values are associated with each element. Well-formed documents can use any elements (provided their names are of the legal form). This makes XML a very flexible format – in effect, you can make up your own elements for any sort of structured document you need.

If a well-formed document is combined with some specification of which element names may be used in it, which attributes each element type is allowed, and what context they may occur in, then programs can perform more rigorous checking, and having done so, can perform additional processing. Web pages, for example, may have headers, paragraphs, lists containing list elements, tables containing rows of data, and so on. A different class of document would have different features: a business invoice could have an invoice number, a customer's name and address, a list of items supplied, and so on. A Web browser that knows how to display elements of the various types allowed in a Web page can display any legal page; an accounting application that knows which elements of an invoice contain relevant financial data can extract that data and store it in a database.

You can think of a specification of the type we have just described as providing a definition of a class or type of document, by listing the different features (elements) that documents of that type may have. Equivalently, you can think of it as defining a language with which documents of that type may be marked up. This language will inherit the rules for well-formedness from XML; the additional specification will define a vocabulary of tags and attributes that may be used in documents of the corresponding type. We call markup languages defined in this way *XML-based languages*. (Strictly speaking, using the terminology of SGML, they are 'XML applications', but this term is confusing for most people, who are more used to applications being programs.) XML-based languages used on the Web include XHTML, SVG (for vector graphics), MathML (for mathematics) and XForms (for data entry).

There are two mechanisms used for creating such definitions in XML. The older, known as a *Document Type Definition* (*DTD*) is inherited from SGML. It is presently the more commonly used for defining Web markup languages. A DTD consists of declarations of elements and attributes, written using a special syntax. In contrast, the newer form of definition, an XML *Schema*, is itself an ordinary XML document, which uses a set of elements that can contain declarations. Schemas are written in a schema definition language, which is itself an

Technical Detail

CDATA Sections

Sometimes, it is necessary to include marked-up text – or text that looks as if it is marked up – within an XML document, without the tags being treated as markup. The classic example of such a situation occurs if you wish to include examples of XML syntax within an XML document. We will see in later chapters, that it is sometimes necessary to include scripts that use the < and & characters inside an XHTML document. In both cases, it is tedious to have to replace all <s and &s with entity references. XML allows you to mark parts of a document as *character data*, which is just treated as literal text, whether it contains XML tags or not. A section of character data (a CDATA section) is enclosed between the delimiters <![CDATA[at the beginning, and]]> at the end. Any characters may appear between these two delimiters, except for the string]]>. (This gives rise to another rule for well-formed XML:]]> may only be used to mark the end of a CDATA section.) Note that this mechanism can only be used to include literal character data (arbitrary text). It cannot be used for binary data.

XML-based language. This is a more elegant approach, and one which permits more powerful syntactic restrictions to be expressed.

If an XML document is well-formed and it conforms to the rules expressed in an associated DTD or schema, it is said to be **valid**.

For the most part, Web designers do not need to know how to write DTDs or schemas. The languages used to mark up Web pages are defined by DTDs, and increasingly by schemas, but the defining standards also provide a description in English, which can be read without understanding the more formal DTD or schema. It is, however, necessary to understand how a DTD can be associated with a document, since the current standards require that this be done. (Some emerging standards will also require a schema to be associated with documents, which is a bit more complicated.)

The DTDs for the XML-based languages used on the Web are resources, whose URLs are published as part of the standard defining the language. The standards also define something called a 'public identifier' for these DTDs, which is an alternative way of referring to it without reference to a specific location. If a document is marked up using a language defined by a DTD, it must include a ***document type declaration***, which identifies the DTD by its URL and its public identifier. (So the document type *declaration* tells you or a program where to find the document type *definition*.) The declaration also specifies the name to be used as the root element.

The form of a document type declaration is exemplified by the following, which could be used for XHTML documents:

```
<!DOCTYPE html
    PUBLIC "-//W3C//DTD XHTML 1.0 Strict//EN"
    "http://www.w3.org/TR/xhtml1/DTD/xhtml1-strict.dtd">
```

The ! after the opening < distinguishes the declaration from the start tag of an element. The name immediately following the DOCTYPE keyword identifies the root element. Here it is html: all the elements of an XHTML document are enclosed in an html element. The public identifier for the DTD comes after the keyword PUBLIC. Its form is inherited from SGML; Web designers do not need to enquire into the internal structure of these identifiers. Finally comes the DTD's URL. Although this really does identify a file that is available over the Internet, there is no suggestion that a program reading the XML document will necessarily go and download it. Most modern Web browsers have the XHTML DTD incorporated into their code, for example.

Technical Detail

XML Versions

Version 1.0 of XML was adopted as a W3C Recommendation in February 1998. Minor corrections have been made to the specification since, but it was only in 2004 that a new version, XML 1.1, was defined. The changes made at that point are, in fact, very minor and mostly only concern some technical details of character sets. However, these are enough to introduce minor incompatibilities with XML 1.0, hence the changed version number.

If an XML declaration is omitted from a document, it is assumed that the version is 1.0. For documents that do not need the new features added in XML 1.1, it is advised that the XML declaration specifies version 1.0, since this may be accepted by more XML-processing programs than 1.1.

The document type declaration must come before the start tag of the root element. It is recommended (but not required) that it be preceded by an **XML declaration**, which serves to identify the document as XML. It may also indicate the version of the language being used, and the character encoding. A typical XML declaration is:

```
<?xml version="1.0" encoding="UTF-8"?>
```

Notice that in this case the < is followed by a ?, and the > is preceded by one. (The parts of XML outside the actual markup tags – the declarations in a DTD, in particular – make use of a variety of punctuation characters in this way to distinguish different constructs. One of the attractions of schemas is that they do not rely on such unattractive syntactic devices.) If it appears, the XML declaration must be the very first thing in the document. The XML and document type declarations constitute the document's prologue.

Technical Detail

SGML, XML, HTML and XHTML

The relationship between Web markup languages is rather convoluted. They all share a common ancestor in SGML (the Standard Generalized Markup Language), which, like XML, is a metalanguage used for defining specialized markup languages for particular types of document. It has been widely used in the publishing industry. When the World Wide Web was first designed, SGML was used to define the markup language HTML, which continued to be defined in this way. As the limitations of HTML's fixed repertoire of tags grew more apparent, it became clear that something akin to SGML was needed to allow new markup languages to be defined for the Web. For technical reasons, SGML itself was considered unsuitable for use on the Web, so a subset of it was defined for this purpose. This simplified version is XML, which is now used to define the Web's increasing number of markup languages, including XHTML, a slightly modified version of HTML 4. The relationships between these languages can be shown diagramatically as shown. The orange lines indicate which metalanguage was used to define each language, the blue lines show the ancestry of the languages and metalanguages.

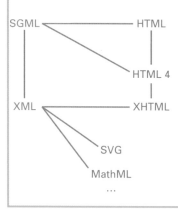

XHTML

Introduction

All these details about XML syntax, DTDs and schemas may seem a long way removed from creating Web pages. However, modern Web pages are marked up using XHTML, which is an XML-based language. Consequently, the description of XML has already told you a lot about XHTML: what elements and attributes are, what tags look like, how entity and character references are used, the criteria for being well-formed and what DTDs are. You should therefore be able to understand many things about the following simple XHTML document:

```
<!DOCTYPE html PUBLIC "-//W3C//DTD XHTML 1.0 Strict//EN"
    "http://www.w3.org/TR/xhtml1/DTD/xhtml1-strict.dtd">
<html xmlns="http://www.w3.org/1999/xhtml" xml:lang="en" lang="en">
<head>
  <title>A Simple Page</title>
</head>
<body>
<h1>Simplicity</h1>
<p>This is not <em>quite</em> the simplest Web page imaginable, but
it comes pretty close.</p>
</body>
</html>
```

The document begins with a document type declaration, which is necessary for it to be validated. The public identifier and URL shown here are only one of three possibilities for XHTML 1.0. They identify the *strict* DTD. This, as its name implies, forbids the use of certain attributes and elements which are permitted by the more lax *transitional* DTD. These are concerned with appearance, which should ideally be separated from the structure specified by markup, hence their omission from the strict DTD. The third, *frameset*, DTD adds additional facilities for breaking a page into independent frames. We will have more to say about frames later, but note for the present that their use is not encouraged. You should use

DTD	Public Identifier	URL
Strict	-//W3C//DTD XHTML 1.0 Strict//EN	http://www.w3.org/TR/xhtml1/ DTD/xhtml1-strict.dtd
Transitional	-//W3C//DTD XHTML 1.0 Transitional//EN	http://www.w3.org/TR/xhtml1/ DTD/xhtml1-transitional.dtd
Frameset	-//W3C//DTD XHTML 1.0 Frameset//EN	http://www.w3.org/TR/xhtml1/ DTD/xhtml1-frameset.dtd

Table 3.1 XHTML 1.0 DTDs

the strict DTD unless you have good reason for doing otherwise. The public identifiers and URLs for these DTDs are listed in Table 3.1.

The document type declaration declares html to be the root element. This must always be the case, no matter which XHTML DTD you use. The start tag for this element has three attributes, which serve special purposes. The xmlns attribute is used to declare a default *namespace* for the document. This tells any program processing it that the names of elements and attributes belong to the XHTML language. The value of the attribute is a URL uniquely associated with XHTML names. The purpose of namespaces is to avoid potential nameclashes when different markup languages are combined in a single document. The mechanism is described more fully in Appendix B. For now, you can safely regard the xmlns attribute as some necessary red tape that should appear in every document. (Its value would be the same whichever DTD was used.)

In addition, two attributes are used to set the default language for the document's content. The xml:lang attribute does this for XML documents; lang does the same job for HTML. By specifying both (as recommended by the XHTML 1.0 standard), you ensure that browsers that treat XHTML as XML and those that treat it as HTML will both recognize the language specification. Here, we have set the language to English.

Emerging Technology

XHTML 2

XHTML 1 was simply a reformulation of HTML 4 using XML as meta-language instead of SGML. Apart from imposing stricter requirements on well-formed documents, the new language made no changes, and most XHTML documents can be treated as HTML. XHTML 2, in contrast, does introduce some incompatibilities. The main thrust of the revisions has been to remove all presentational features from the language, so that true separation of content and appearance can be achieved. This will make many existing HTML documents illegal as XHTML 2. In addition, significant changes have been made to the way links and images are incorporated.

At the time this book was written, the XHTML 2.0 standard was only a draft, so although we will briefly describe some of its innovations, the details may change by the time the Recommendation is formally adopted.

Browser Quirks

DTD Switching

Early versions of Internet Explorer, Netscape and other browsers implemented some features incorrectly, or in ways that were subsequently invalidated by later standards. Web designers had to build sites that worked with these browsers nevertheless. When new versions of these browsers that implemented the standards (more or less) correctly appeared, some mechanism was required to ensure that old sites, built to work with incorrect browsers, still worked. The solution that was hit upon was this: when a Web page includes a DTD, the browser will work in 'strict mode', doing its best to conform to standards. If no DTD is present, the browser switches to 'quirks mode' and faithfully imitates the bugs in its predecessors.

You should routinely include a DTD in your XHTML documents, so they will always be interpreted in strict mode.

There is one refinement to the use of quirks mode. If a document has a DTD but it also has an XML declaration, Internet Explorer 6 will switch to quirks mode. This is for people who want to be able to validate their pages while having them displayed incorrectly. Hence, although the W3C recommends including an XML declaration, there is a good practical reason for leaving it out.

You will notice that there is no XML declaration. Although one is preferred by the W3C, its presence can cause problems with older browsers. Some will reject documents that are served as HTML if they include an XML declaration; others will use it as a signal to switch to quirks mode. Since the declaration is optional, there is no harm in leaving it out.

At the syntactic level, XHTML differs from XML in having a large number of entity references predefined, in addition to the five built in to XML. (This isn't exactly a difference, inasmuch as XML provides a mechanism for defining entity references in the DTD.) These include entities for mathematical and other symbols, punctuation and Greek and accented letters. One of the most commonly used is , which creates a non-breakable space (i.e. it connects two words so that they cannot be split across two lines).

Everything we have described so far is common to all XHTML documents, and would normally be inserted automatically whenever a document is created. It is the content of the html element which characterizes each individual document.

Simplicity

This is not *quite* the simplest Web page imaginable, but it comes pretty close.

Figure 3.1 A simple Web page

At the next structural level below the root, our document contains two elements: head and body. Every XHTML document that is valid with respect to the strict DTD must have these two elements. The head contains information that is not actually part of the document's contents, but may be used by software that processes the document. This includes search engines as well as browsers. Much of the information in the head element can be described as **metadata**, that is, information about the document. In this example, we have only included a title element within the head. This element is required. Its content is usually displayed by browsers in the title bar of the document window; the title is also displayed in history lists and bookmarks. It is not, however, displayed as part of the page within the window.

The elements that constitute the page proper – what you see displayed in the browser window – make up the content of the body element. In our simple example, this consists of an h1 element followed by a p element. Both of these elements contain text in their content; the p element also has an em element among the text. This markup could just be XML; the fact that this document is XHTML gives some meaning to these elements, though, and enables a Web browser to display them. Figure 3.1 shows the default display of this page by a Web browser.

Possibly, the visual clues provided by this rendering of the page allow you to deduce the meaning of the elements in the page's body. The h1 element is a heading. The text below the heading consists of a single paragraph, which is what a p element is. The text within the em element contained in the paragraph is emphasized; by default, this browser (and most others) displays it in italics.

We stress that the markup applied to this document does nothing more than indicate its structure. It does not control the display of the elements. It is the browser that determines what size type headers should be displayed in, what colour background is used behind the page, and so on. The browser user can set preferences for these aspects of the display, overriding the browser's defaults. Most Web designers will want to specify at least some aspects of their documents' appearance, but this cannot be done using XHTML markup – except crudely,

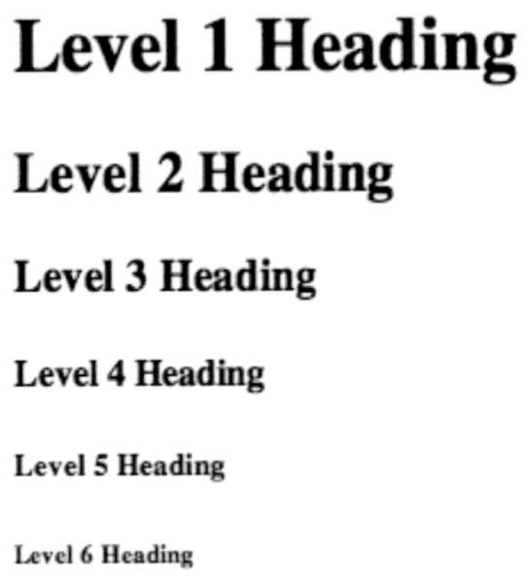

Level 1 Heading

Level 2 Heading

Level 3 Heading

Level 4 Heading

Level 5 Heading

Level 6 Heading

Figure 3.2 XHTML headings

using **deprecated** language features. Specifying appearance is the job of stylesheets; XHTML markup should only be used to specify structure.

Text Elements

HTML was originally devised for marking up the scientific research papers that the Web was invented for sharing, and its repertoire of textual elements betrays this origin. Headings, sub-headings, sub-sub-headings, numbered lists, definitions, tables, citations and program code are among the structures for which elements are defined. Many Web pages that are not scientific papers can make do with just paragraphs, marked up as p elements, with different formatting applied using stylesheets.

Headings can be useful for marking the division of a page into sections, just as they are used in books. XHTML supports up to six levels of heading, using the elements h1, h2,...,h6 (which seems like a lot). Figure 3.2 shows the default rendering of the six levels. To show the structure of a hierarchically organized document effectively, it is necessary to nest sections headed by the different levels of heading in order, with h3 below h2 below h1, and so on. You should resist the temptation to choose a heading level on the basis of the size you want the heading to appear. This should be controlled by a stylesheet, and the heading level should only be used to indicate the level within the document's hierarchy.

Text elements in XHTML can be broadly divided into two categories. **Block elements** are those, like h1 and p, which are normally displayed as separate blocks of text with line breaks before and after them. **Inline elements** are displayed within blocks. Whereas block elements

Emerging Technology

Sections in XHTML 2

Headings are used to demarcate sections of a document, so the use of heading elements in XHTML 1 is not very satisfactory: a heading is used to start a section, but there is no element corresponding to the section as a unit. This has been rectified in XHTML 2, where the `section` element is used in the way its name indicates. Within a section, h elements (with no level number suffix) are used for headings. Sections may be nested, giving subsections and so on. The headings contained in nested sections naturally form a corresponding hierarchy of subheadings: heading levels are implicit. A stylesheet may be used to apply suitable formatting to each level, or even to generate section numbers automatically.

may contain inline elements, inline elements may not contain block elements, though they may contain other inline elements. An example of an inline element is em, which is used for emphasized text, as in the simple example above. Another inline element, `strong`, can be used for more strongly emphasized text. Unless you are writing technical documents, the remaining textual inline elements (otherwise known as phrase elements) are unlikely to be of much use to you. They are summarized in Table 3.2.

XHTML retains some inline elements which control the physical appearance of the text, such as i, for italic text (as opposed to em, which *may* be set in italics, but denotes emphasis) and tt, for fixed-width 'teletype' text. The use of such elements is generally discouraged,

Element	Meaning	Element	Meaning
em	emphasis	var	a program variable
strong	stronger emphasis	abbr	an abbreviation
cite	citation or reference	acronym	an acronym
dfn	definition	sub	subscript
code	program fragment	sup	superscript
samp	sample output from a program etc	q	short quotation
kbd	text to be entered by a user		

Table 3.2 Phrase elements

The next paragraph is a **block quotation**

> Lorem ipsum dolor sit amet, consectetur adipisicing elit, sed do eiusmod tempor incididunt ut labore et dolore magna aliqua. Ut enim ad minim veniam, quis nostrud exercitation ullamco laboris nisi ut aliquip ex ea commodo consequat. Duis aute irure dolor in reprehenderit in voluptate velit esse cillum dolore eu fugiat nulla pariatur. Excepteur sint occaecat cupidatat non proident, sunt in culpa qui officia deserunt mollit anim id est laborum.

Contact email: webmaster@desperatesw.co.uk

Figure 3.3 Block elements

so we will not describe them any further. The font element, which you may see being used in older HTML documents to select a font, is deprecated in XHTML and should not, therefore, be used at all.

A slightly anomalous inline element is br, which is an empty element, whose name stands for break, and forces a line break. It is treated as if it were a special character, by analogy with the way line breaks are represented in text files. Although it forces a line break, it does not end a block, so it may appear inside a p element (and usually does).

A few special types of block are given their own element types. Lengthy quotations, which will normally be set as indented paragraphs, are contained in blockquote elements. The content of a blockquote consists of other block elements – you cannot put bare text inside a blockquote. An author's contact details can be placed in an address element, allowing the contact information to be extracted easily. An unusual kind of block contains no text at all, just a horizontal rule (straight line). This is generated by an hr element, which is empty. Rules are used as separators. A common idiom is the use of a rule followed by an address element at the bottom of a page, as shown in Figure 3.3, which also illustrates some of the other block and phrase elements we have described so far. It was produced from a document with the following body:

```
<body>
<p>The next paragraph is a <strong>block quotation</strong></p>
<blockquote><p>Lorem ipsum dolor
 etc.</p>
</blockquote>
<hr/>
<address>Contact email: <a href="#">webmaster@desperatesw.co.uk</a>
```

```
</address>
</body>
```

Occasionally, it may be necessary to include text in a page without the browser applying its default formatting to it. The `pre` (pre-formatted) element type is used for this purpose. Spaces and line breaks in the content of a `pre` element are respected, and the text is set in a special font and does not reflow if the window size is altered. A fixed-width 'teletype' font is usually employed, because the most common use of pre-formatted text is for displaying the source code of computer programs in Web pages. Embedded phrase elements are displayed in the usual way. Pre-formatted text is still subject to the rules for well-formed XML, so literal < signs and &s should be replaced by `&lt;` and `&amp;`. (You might get away with not doing, but that is only because of present-day browsers' lax behaviour, and cannot be relied on.) Do not use `pre` elements as a way of laying out text by hand, for example, in two columns. The result will almost always be poor, and there are better ways of controlling layout.

Because XHTML's repertoire of elements is fixed and limited, there will be occasions when you need to identify part of a document as a unit (usually so that you can apply special styling to it), but none of the block and phrase elements is appropriate. For those occasions, XHTML provides two elements, `div` and `span`, which just serve as generic containers; `div` is a block element and `span` is inline. We will see examples of their use in Chapter 4.

Most of these textual elements share a small set of common attributes, the majority of which are not directly concerned with the markup itself. Any element may have an `id` attribute, whose value is an identifier for that element. (This attribute is of type ID, so as we explained earlier, the values must be unique.) It may also have a `class` attribute, which assigns it to one or more subsets of elements of the same type, for the purpose of applying special formatting with a stylesheet, as we will describe in Chapter 4. The `title` attribute (not to be confused with the `title` element) can be used to provide a short descriptive name for any element. Graphical browsers often display them as a 'tool tip' when the cursor is over the element; non-visual user agents may read them out. Their usefulness varies according to the element. For instance, if a meaningful title is provided for a link (see below), it could help a user decide whether it is worth following.

Other common attributes are concerned with internationalization. Like `body`, any block or inline textual element can have a value assigned to the attributes `xml:lang` and `lang`, to indicate the language in which the text is written. The language of any element is taken, by default, to be the same as that of its enclosing element, so for documents written in a single language, it is sufficient to use these attributes on the `body`. It is only if a document

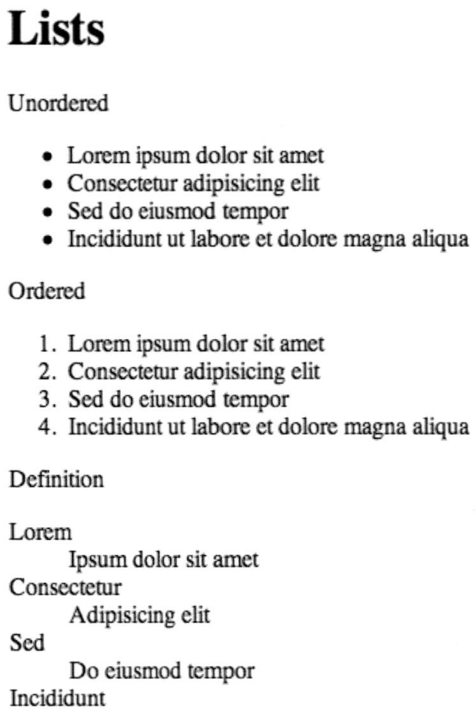

Lists

Unordered

- Lorem ipsum dolor sit amet
- Consectetur adipisicing elit
- Sed do eiusmod tempor
- Incididunt ut labore et dolore magna aliqua

Ordered

1. Lorem ipsum dolor sit amet
2. Consectetur adipisicing elit
3. Sed do eiusmod tempor
4. Incididunt ut labore et dolore magna aliqua

Definition

Lorem
    Ipsum dolor sit amet
Consectetur
    Adipisicing elit
Sed
    Do eiusmod tempor
Incididunt

Figure 3.4 Lists

contains paragraphs or fragments in a different language that they should be used on an enclosed element. The attribute `dir` may also be used to indicate the direction in which text is to be written (`dir="ltr"` for left-to-right, `dir="rtl"` for right-to-left). Most of the time, however, the browser will deduce this correctly from the `lang` attributes. The remaining common attributes may be used for adding interactivity, but there are better mechanisms for this, as we will explain in detail in Chapter 7.

Lists

Bullet lists, as beloved of academics and marketing executives giving presentations, can be added to XHTML documents in the form of `ul` (unordered list) elements. The individual items (bullet points) are represented as `li` (list item) elements in the content of the `ul`. Lists of this sort can be an effective way of presenting a collection of short pieces of information in a compact layout. In more formal contexts, it may be appropriate to number the items in the list. This is done very simply, by using an `ol` (ordered list) element, instead of a `ul` element.

The items are represented as li elements in the same way; the item numbers are generated automatically. Figure 3.4 illustrates these types of list.

At the bottom of Figure 3.4 is an example of the third type of list available in XHTML. It is referred to in the standard as a definition list, and it may be used for glossaries, as this suggests, but it has wider application. The element for a definition list is dl; within it may appear dt and dd elements. Where a dl actually is a list of definitions, its dt children are the terms being defined, and the dd elements are the definitions. Normally, therefore, dt and dd elements occur in pairs, but this is not a requirement. (The same term may have more than one meaning, for example.) Generally, dt is used as a label, and dd for the text that goes with it. The default display of definition lists is illustrated in Figure 3.4.

The markup that produced this display was as follows:

```
<body>
<h1>Lists</h1>
<p>Unordered</p>
<ul>
   <li>Lorem ipsum dolor sit amet</li>
   <li>Consectetur adipisicing elit</li>
   <li>Sed do eiusmod tempor</li>
   <li>Incididunt ut labore et dolore magna aliqua</li>
</ul>
<p>Ordered</p>
<ol>
   <li>Lorem ipsum dolor sit amet</li>
   <li>Consectetur adipisicing elit</li>
   <li>Sed do eiusmod tempor</li>
   <li>Incididunt ut labore et dolore magna aliqua</li>
</ol>
<p>Definition</p>
<dl>
   <dt>Lorem</dt><dd>Ipsum dolor sit amet</dd>
   <dt>Consectetur</dt><dd>Adipisicing elit</dd>
   <dt>Sed</dt><dd>Do eiusmod tempor</dd>
   <dt>Incididunt</dt><dd>Ut labore et dolore magna aliqua</dd>
</dl>
</body>
```

Tables

Tables are among XHTML's most complicated features. They are intended to provide a way of presenting tabular data on a Web page. This is a fairly common requirement for many types of page, but the elements for building tables are used much more widely than the amount of tabulated information you see on the Web might lead you to believe. This is because tables have been pressed into service for the purpose of controlling the position of text and images within a page. This can no longer be considered good practice. From the point of view of structural markup, a table should be a collection of information organized in rows and columns that display a relationship between the tabulated items. As well as being an abuse of markup, organizing text on the page using a table may interfere with the ability of screen-reading programs to speak the text for the benefit of blind users: they may read paragraphs in the wrong order, or, in extreme cases, read lines straight across the rows of the table. Furthermore, since there are now facilities for positioning text blocks and images using stylesheets, as we will describe in Chapter 4, the use of tables for this purpose is redundant. These are forceful objections, and you should use stylesheets instead of tables to control layout. There remains tabular data, for which tables are the correct means of presentation.

The basic model used for creating tables is simple: a table consists of one or more rows, each of which consists of one or more cells; the arrangement into columns is implicit. The XHTML elements `table`, `tr` (table row) and `td` (table data) are used for the table, its rows and the cells, respectively, and are nested so that a `table` element contains one or more `tr` elements each containing one or more `td` elements, in correspondence with the table's structure.

Here is an example of a simple table built out of these elements:

```
<table>
  <tr>
    <td></td>
    <td>kbps (theoretical)</td>
    <td>6kB text page</td>
    <td>100 kB text page</td>
    <td>4 MB movie</td>
  </tr>
  <tr>
    <td>Modem</td>
    <td>56</td>
    <td>1 sec</td>
    <td>15 secs</td>
```

	kbps (theoretical)	6kB text page	100 kB text page	4 MB movie
Modem	56	1 sec	15 secs	10 mins
ADSL (typical)	512	0.1 sec	2 secs	1 min

Figure 3.5 A simple table

```
      <td>10 mins</td>
   </tr>
   <tr>
      <td>ADSL (typical)</td>
      <td>512</td>
      <td>0.1 sec</td>
      <td>2 secs</td>
      <td>1 min</td>
   </tr>
</table>
```

Figure 3.5 shows its default rendering in a browser. As you can see, by default, tables look awful. In Chapter 4, we will demonstrate how stylesheets can be used to improve their appearance dramatically. In this chapter, though, we are solely concerned with their structure, and the structure of this example is not adequate. If you compare this table with Table 2.4 in Chapter 2, which displays similar data, you will see that in the original the top row and leftmost column are distinguished as column and row headings, since they describe the data in the cells. This is an important *structural* distinction (expressed visually in this book by the distinctive colouring and font of the headings), which should be expressed in the markup. XHTML provides the th element for table headings. The original table also has a caption, which briefly describes the data presented in the table. In XHTML, the caption element can be used to provide a caption. If it is used, the caption must appear immediately after the start tag of the table. Figure 3.6 shows how the browser renders headings in a distinguishable style. It also illustrates the default display of a caption. To produce this display, the markup is modified as follows:

	Approximate Download Times			
	kbps (theoretical)	**6kB text page**	**100 kB text page**	**4 MB movie**
Modem	56	1 sec	15 secs	10 mins
ADSL (typical)	512	0.1 sec	2 secs	1 min

Figure 3.6 A table with caption and headings

```
<table>
   <caption>
      Approximate Download Times
   </caption>
   <tr>
      <td></td>
      <th>kbps (theoretical)</th>
      <th>6kB text page</th>
      <th>100 kB text page</th>
      <th>4 MB movie</th>
   </tr>
   <tr>
      <th>Modem</th>
      td elements are before
   </tr>
   <tr>
      <th>ADSL (typical)</th>
      td elements are before
   </tr>
</table>
```

A further refinement of XHTML tables is illustrated in Figure 3.7. Sometimes, a heading may need to span several rows or columns. In this example, we have shown two typical cases. First, we have added a row to the table for satellite, but we don't want to duplicate the download times, which will be the same as those for ADSL. Hence, the last set of values has been placed in cells which span two rows; by default, the values are centred vertically, so it is clear that both the row headings apply to these values. (Again, using stylesheets, we will be able to improve on the default rendering of the table to make this clearer.) To specify that a td or th element spans more than one row, the rowspan attribute is used, with a value equal to the number of spanned rows, in this case, 2. When this is done, the corresponding td elements must be omitted from the following row. Hence, the markup for the bottom two rows of the table is as follows:

	Approximate Download Times			
	kbps	text page		4 MB movie
	(theoretical)	6kB	100 kB	
Modem	56	1 sec	15 secs	10 mins
ADSL (typical)	512	0.1 sec	2 secs	1 min
Satellite				

Figure 3.7 Spanning rows and columns

```
<tr>
    <th>ADSL (typical)</th>
    <td rowspan="2">512</td>
    <td rowspan="2">0.1 sec</td>
    <td rowspan="2">2 secs</td>
    <td rowspan="2">1 min</td>
</tr>
<tr>
    <th>Satellite</th>
</tr>
```

In a similar way, the colspan attribute can be used to make a td or th element span several columns. We have used this to consolidate the headings for the text page columns. The heading text page now spans two columns, with the two different sizes of text page below it, each heading its own column. In this case, a th element is omitted from the tr element, to make the number of columns add up correctly. The markup for the top row of the table now looks like this:

```
<tr>
    <td></td>
    <th>kbps</th>
    <th colspan="2">text page</th>
    <th>4 MB movie</th>
</tr>
```

Most tables can be created from these elements. XHTML provides additional features for making tables accessible to disabled users, and for providing extra hooks for styling. We will describe both these sets of features in a more appropriate place.

Links

The ability to link pages together is fundamental to the World Wide Web. XHTML implements links in a very simple way, which has nevertheless proved powerful enough to create the richly interconnected network of pages that make up the Web today.

The ends of links are called *anchors*, which are implemented using elements of type a. A link goes from its *source anchor* to its *destination anchor*. An a element that serves as the source anchor of a link has an href attribute, the value of which is a URL. The content of the element will typically be a short piece of text or an image. It is this content that the user sees displayed in a distinctive fashion and clicks on to follow the link. Thus, a typical element used for the

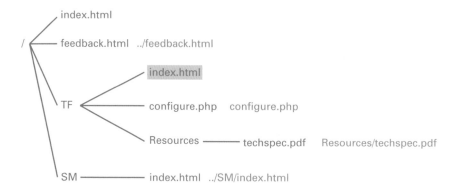

Figure 3.8 Relative URLs

source anchor of a link would be `<a href="../feedback.html">our feedback page</a>`. By default, textual links are displayed in blue and underlined, but as with everything else, stylesheets can be used to change their appearance.

The value of the `href` attribute in our example link doesn't look like a URL as we described it in Chapter 2. It is an example of a **relative URL**. As the name suggests, relative URLs identify resources relative to the location of the document they appear in. A complete URL of the form we described previously identifies the location absolutely: no matter which document it appears in, it refers to the same location. In contrast, a relative URL's meaning depends on the location of the document containing it. The URL only specifies the difference between the current document's location and that of the document referred to.

You will recall from Chapter 2 that the path component of a URL defines the location of a document within a hierarchy (which may well be a sub-hierarchy of the file system of the server, but doesn't have to be). It consists of a sequence of **path segments**, separated by / characters, each one identifying a directory or, in the case of the final segment only, a document. For any document in the hierarchy, it is possible to identify its parent, which is the element that contains it. (In terms of file systems, a file or directory's parent is the directory it is stored in.) If a URL does not begin with a prefix, such as `http://`, or a /, then the location it refers to is the same as that referred to by the current document's parent with a / and the partial URL added to the end. This may sound complicated, but it is actually very simple. Consider Figure 3.8, which shows a small part of the hierarchy of a fictional Web site at `www.desperatesw.co.uk`. The highlighted file `index.html` within the TF sub-directory has URL `http://www.desperatesw.co.uk/TF/index.html`. Its parent is the directory with URL `http://www.desperatesw.co.uk/TF`. This is the URL

> ## Emerging Technology
>
> ### Links in XHTML 2.0
> In XHTML 2, any element can serve as the source anchor for a link, because any element can have an `href` attribute. This removes the need to wrap an `a` element around any image, heading or other element that you wish to attach a link to. Simple runs of text can be made into links using a `span` element with an `href` attribute. Nevertheless, the `a` element type has been retained, presumably out of feelings of nostalgia.

that is placed in front of any relative URLs in `index.html`. Thus, any document – such as `configure.php` – with the same parent can be referred to in a relative URL just by its name. The relative URL `configure.php` expands, with the addition of the parent's URL, to `http://www.desperatesw.co.uk/TF/configure.php`, which is the correct absolute URL of this document. The same interpretation is applied to relative URLs with more than one path segment, so, as shown, the PDF file within the `Resources` sub-directory of the TF directory can be referred to by the relative URL `Resources/techspec.pdf`.

By convention (and inconsistently), an empty URL refers to the document is appears in. We will see shortly why such a URL is not useless.

This mechanism allows you to write relative URLs for documents within the same directory or within its sub-directories, to an arbitrary depth, but it doesn't provide a way of referring to documents higher in the hierarchy, or in separate sub-directory branches. To accomplish this, two dots, `..`, can be used within a path to refer to the parent's parent. In our example, `..` refers to the parent of `TF`, which is the root of the hierarchy, denoted by `/`. Using this notation, the relative URLs `../feedback.html` and `../SM/index.html` can be used to refer to the documents indicated on the diagram. When creating an absolute URL from a relative one containing `..` segments, all you need to do is apply the procedure outlined above, and wherever a segment is followed by `../`, remove both of them. Thus, in our example, the relative URL `../feedback.html` becomes `http://www.desperatesw.co.uk/TF/../feedback.html` when the parent's URL is inserted in front of it. 'Cancelling out' the `../` with the `TF/` then gives the expected absolute URL `http://www.desperatesw.co.uk/feedback.html`. A relative URL can refer as far up the hierarchy as necessary, using an appropriate number of `..`s. Note, however, that in this example, `../..` would refer to a non-existent (or at least inaccessible) document above the root, which would result in an error.

The main purpose of relative URLs is to allow a hierarchy of documents to be moved to a different location; cross-reference links within the hierarchy will remain valid when this is done. Since Web sites almost always form a self-contained hierarchy of documents on the same host, using relative URLs for links within a site makes it easy to move the site to a different host machine. In particular, a site can be developed on a Web designer's machine and then uploaded to a server, without any relative URLs being changed.

It is also permissible in a URL to omit the prefix and hostname components, and just write a complete path, beginning with a /. Thus, we could use /TF/configure.php as another way of referring to the configuration document. This may be more manageable than using strings of ../s in a deep hierarchy. It still makes it possible to move the site to a different host without changing the URLs on links.

URLs refer to entire documents. A link whose href attribute is a full or relative URL of the kind described is considered to point to the beginning of the body of the document identified by the URL. In other words, there is an implicit destination anchor at the beginning of every document. Sometimes, though, links are required to point to locations within a document – often the same document that contains the link. For this purpose, a *fragment identifier* can be added to the end of any (relative or absolute) URL. A fragment identifier consists of a # character immediately followed by a name. It points to the element in the document referred to by the URL, with an id attribute whose value is equal to the name contained in the fragment, if such an element exists. (If it does exist, it must be unique, because id attributes are of type ID.) So, if the feedback.html document included a heading <h1 id="Comments">Your Comments</h1>, then this heading could serve as a destination anchor for links. Within TF/index.html, the element <a href="../feedback.html#Comments">Send a comment</a> would be the source anchor of a link that pointed to it. If a user clicked on this link, feedback.html would be displayed in their browser, which would scroll if necessary so that the heading Your Comments was at the top of the browser window.

As we noted earlier, an empty URL is taken to refer to the document it occurs in, so a URL consisting of nothing but a fragment identifier points to a location within the same document. URLs like this are typically used for creating links from sections within a long document back to the top of the document, or from a table of contents to the start of the sections of such a document.

In early versions of HTML, elements did not have id attributes. Destination anchors could only be implemented as a elements with a name attribute, either as well as or, more often, instead of an `href` attribute. Such elements are called **named anchors**. Although it is now redundant, the `name` attribute is still available for a elements in XHTML (although it will probably be dropped from XHTML 2), and named anchors are still often generated by HTML editors. While the source anchors of links are usually displayed with some distinctive styling to indicate their nature, their destination anchors are not.

Forms

Forms are used on Web pages to allow visitors to enter data that will be processed by applications running on the server or by scripts. They are a vital component in interactive Web applications. Forms are used for entering address and credit card details in e-commerce sites, for entering search terms, for gathering data in surveys, for typing messages to be sent to help desks, and for a host of other purposes when a user has to submit some input. In this chapter, we will not be concerned with what happens to the data entered into a form, but we will describe the markup available for creating forms and the various types of control that can be used within them.

Figure 3.9 shows a simple survey form. Once again, we have shown the browser's default styling of the form, although normally a stylesheet would be used to improve its appearance. Several types of **control** – the interface elements used to enter data – can be seen. In the *Course Details* section at the top are three single-line **text input fields**, into which site visitors can type short pieces of text. The next section of the form uses **pop-up menus**, from which a single answer to the question can be chosen. The *Upgrading* question uses **radio buttons**; again, only one option can be chosen, this time by clicking on the button. The next section uses **check boxes**, which are similar, except that more than one box in the group can be checked. The *Other Comments* section provides a **text area**, which allows comments occupying more than one line to be typed in. Finally, at the bottom, there are two **buttons**, one for submitting the form, the other for resetting it to its original state.

Controls can appear anywhere in a document, but if they are being used in the conventional way for accepting input to be passed to a program on the server, they must appear among the content of a `form` element. This element has two attributes which determine what happens to the data when the form is submitted. The value of the `action` attribute is the URL (which may be absolute or relative) of the program which will process the data. The `method` attribute determines how the data is sent to the server. The form data is always included in an HTTP request. If the method is `get`, it is appended to the URL; if `post`, it is included in the body of the request, as described in Chapter 2. As a broad guideline, the XHTML standard advises that `get` should be used when the processing of the data has no side-effects

Please help us to plan supplements and possible future editions of *Digital Media Tools* so that we can try to meet your needs better.

```
┌─ Course Details ──────────────────────────────────────────────────────────┐
│                                                                            │
│   Institution: [_____]                                          │
│   Country: [_____]                                              │
│   Approximate number of students using media tools software on your course:│
│                                                                      [____] │
│                                                                            │
└────────────────────────────────────────────────────────────────────────────┘
```

```
┌─ Use of Media Tools Software ─────────────────────────────────────────────┐
│                                                                            │
│   If your course uses any of the following tools, please select the        │
│   versions you are currently using from the pop-up menus.                  │
│                                                                            │
│   Photoshop: [ Not used     ▼ ]                                            │
│   ImageReady: [ Not used    ▼ ]                                            │
│   Flash: [ Not used    ▼ ]                                                 │
│   Dreamweaver [ Not used   ▼ ]                                            │
│                                                                            │
└────────────────────────────────────────────────────────────────────────────┘
```

```
┌─ Upgrading ───────────────────────────────────────────────────────────────┐
│                                                                            │
│   How often do you upgrade the media tools software used on your course?   │
│   ○ Shortly after the release of each new version                          │
│   ○ Within one year of the release of each new version                     │
│   ○ At irregular intervals                                                 │
│   ○ Only when it becomes impossible to continue with the present versions  │
│   ○ Different patterns for the different tools                             │
│                                                                            │
└────────────────────────────────────────────────────────────────────────────┘
```

```
┌─ Platforms ───────────────────────────────────────────────────────────────┐
│                                                                            │
│   Which operating systems does the course make significant use of? (Check  │
│   any boxes that apply.)                                                    │
│                                                                            │
│   Windows ☐                                                                │
│   MacOS 9 or earlier ☐                                                     │
│   MacOS X ☐                                                                │
│   Linux ☐                                                                  │
│   Other Unix ☐                                                             │
│                                                                            │
└────────────────────────────────────────────────────────────────────────────┘
```

```
┌─ Other Comments ──────────────────────────────────────────────────────────┐
│                                                                            │
│   If you have any other comments about your use of media tools software,   │
│   which you think might be helpful to us in planning future supplements    │
│   and new editions, please enter them here.                                │
│                                                                            │
│   ┌────────────────────────────────────────────────────┐                  │
│   │                                                    │                  │
│   │                                                    │                  │
│   │                                                    │                  │
│   └────────────────────────────────────────────────────┘                  │
│                                                                            │
└────────────────────────────────────────────────────────────────────────────┘
```

(Clear form) (Submit Form)

Figure 3.9 A survey form

(for example, it performs a database query and returns the result), and post should be used if there are side-effects (for example, a database is updated). We will expand on the way form data is sent to programs on the server in Chapter 8, where we will also consider factors that might determine your choice of method.

The survey form has the following skeleton structure:

```
<form action="survey-script.php" method="post">
  controls and other elements appearing in the form
</form>
```

The controls are intermixed with ordinary text elements, including headers and paragraphs, in the body of the form element. The only type of block element that may not appear inside a form is form itself.

Each of the controls is implemented as an XHTML element in the document containing the form. All control elements have a name attribute. Both radio buttons and checkboxes are usually organized in groups, as in our survey example. In this case, all of the controls in the group have the same name. In the case of radio buttons, the browser will ensure that only one button in a group can be selected at a time. When the form is submitted, the form data is sent to the server as a set of pairs, comprising a name and a value. For each control in the form, the name attribute is used to provide the name. The corresponding value is obtained in different ways for different controls, as we will describe as we look at each control element type. Note that, since several check boxes may have the same name, and more than one of them may be selected, several pairs with the same name may be sent in the form data.

Many of the kinds of control available in XHTML are implemented as input elements, whose type attribute is used to distinguish different sorts of control. For example, the tag <input type="text" name="Country"/> produces a text input field, whereas <input type="submit" name="Submit" value="Submit Form"/> produces a submit button. Table 3.3 lists the possible values for the type attribute, and the kind of control each produces. If the type attribute is omitted, its value is taken to be text, so an input element defaults to being a text input field.

Every input element may have a value attribute, although it is only compulsory for check boxes and radio buttons. For these, the attribute is used to provide the value sent to the server if the control is selected when the form is submitted. For all other types of input element, it provides a default value, which is displayed initially and whenever the form is reset.

type Attribute	Control	Type-specific Attributes
text	text input field	maxlength
password	obscured text input field	
checkbox	check box	checked, value
radio	radio button	
submit	submit button	
image	submit button with image	src, alt
reset	reset button	
button	push button	
hidden	not displayed	
file	file selector	

Table 3.3 Types of input **element**

Every input element may also have a size attribute, which determines the width of the displayed control. Normally, you would use a stylesheet to set the size of form controls, but it is worth using the size attribute too, to ensure that user agents that do not obey stylesheets will know how wide each control should be – styling of form elements is one of the areas in which browsers' stylesheet support is least satisfactory. The width is given in pixels, except for text and password types (see below), for which it is given as a number of characters.

Most types of input element provide a straightforward way of creating a control, simply by setting the the type attribute appropriately, and providing a name and value. Only a few require additional attribute values to be specified. Some types do not correspond to any of the controls in our survey example, and a couple require a little additional description.

A password field (type="password") is just like a text field, except that asterisks or bullets are displayed in the field when the user types in it, to conceal sensitive data such as passwords. If a value attribute is defined, it will not be displayed visibly, but it will be sent as the value of the control if the user does not enter any text in the field, so it functions as a default. For both password and text types, it is possible to specify a maximum length, in characters, for the string that may be typed into the field, using the maxlength attribute. This provides a small measure of validation for the user's input in those cases where there is a known limit on the length of allowable values.

For check boxes and radio buttons, as we noted earlier, the value attribute must be provided. These types of control may also use the Boolean attribute checked. If this is set (checked="checked"), the control will be initially selected, otherwise it will not. For a group of radio buttons, this attribute should be set for one of the buttons; the behaviour of the browser if none of the radio buttons is checked is undefined.

The implementation of buttons as input elements is a little messy. If the type is submit, then clicking the button will always cause the form data to be sent to the server; similarly if the type is reset, clicking will always cause the fields to be cleared and reset to their default values. By default, these buttons are labelled Submit or Reset, respectively, when they are displayed by the browser. If you want to use a more specific label, as in our example, you can assign it to the value attribute. This value will also be sent as part of the form data, in the usual way, which allows the server script to determine which of several buttons has been pressed, provided each has a different value.

As an alternative for a submit button, you can set the type of the input element to img, and specify the location of an image file (see Chapter 5) by assigning its URL to the src attribute. This allows you to use iconic buttons, although you have to be careful that their meaning is clear to the user – the default style of submit button will be immediately recognizable to experienced Web users. If you use an image as a button, you should also provide a textual alternative using the alt attribute, for the benefit of users with non-visual browsers and users with visual impairments.

If the type is set to button, a push-button control with a label provided by the value attribute is created. It doesn't do anything. That is, it doesn't do anything, unless a script activated by mouse clicks is attached to it. (See Chapter 7.) This means that the button will not do anything on a browser that does not support scripting, or for which the user has disabled scripting. The use of such buttons cannot, therefore, be encouraged.

A hidden control may seem useless, and, indeed, input elements with type set to hidden are not used for accepting input from the user, as other controls are. Instead, they provide a way for information that is not explicitly entered by the user to be included among the data sent to the server when the form is submitted. Figure 3.10 shows a typical situation that requires hidden input elements. When the user clicks on the submit button labelled Add To Basket, the name of the product they want to add has to be sent to the server. It would be silly to ask the user to select the name from a pop-up menu or otherwise enter it, because, from their point of view, they have selected the product by coming to its page. By adding a hidden input element, whose value attribute holds the appropriate data,

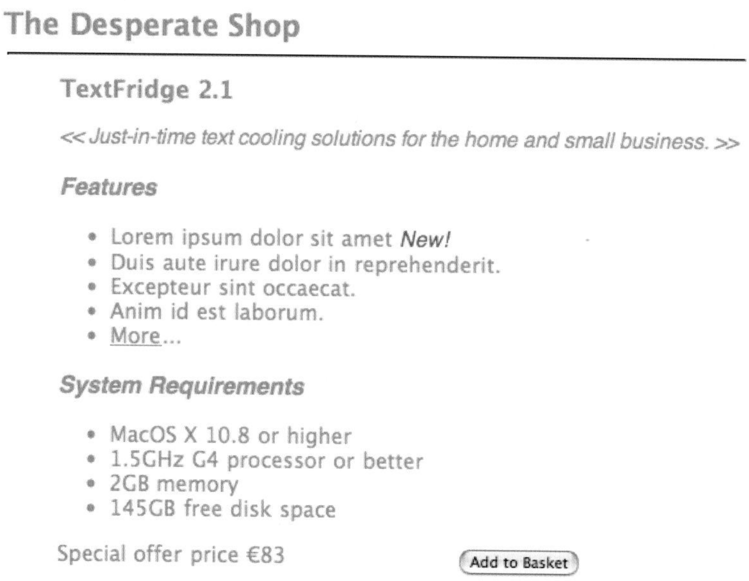

The Desperate Shop

TextFridge 2.1

<< Just-in-time text cooling solutions for the home and small business. >>

Features

- Lorem ipsum dolor sit amet *New!*
- Duis aute irure dolor in reprehenderit.
- Excepteur sint occaecat.
- Anim id est laborum.
- More...

System Requirements

- MacOS X 10.8 or higher
- 1.5GHz G4 processor or better
- 2GB memory
- 145GB free disk space

Special offer price €83   (Add to Basket)

Figure 3.10 A situation that requires a hidden input field

this can be avoided. (It would also be possible to make the button into a link to a server script, and add the data to the URL that is its `href` attribute, but this would make the data visible, which might be considered a security risk. If the information is included in the form data, it can be sent with a `post` request, so that it will not be casually disclosed.)

Hidden input elements are also used to allow the server to save data in the page when it sends it, so that it can be sent back when a form is submitted. One application of this technique is to allow the server to keep track of users during a session, a task which, because of the stateless nature of the HTTP protocol, is otherwise difficult.

The final option for the `type` attribute of an `input` element is `file`. This causes the browser to display a control that can be used to select a file on the user's computer. This usually takes the form of a button that opens a system file navigation dialogue. The contents of the chosen file will be sent with the data from the other controls when the form is submitted. This facility might be used on a software manufacturer's bug-reporting page, for example, to allow users to upload a system log file when reporting a bug.

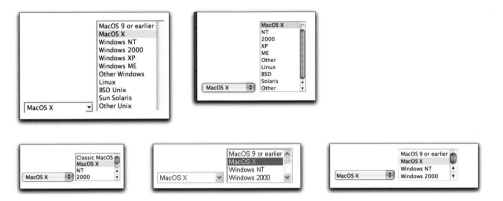

Figure 3.11 Different browsers' display of select elements

The remaining kinds of form control are implemented using two other element types. A textarea element, not surprisingly, is used to create a text area. Besides the common attributes for all elements, and those for controls, it has two attributes which define the size of the box displayed on the page for text entry. These are cols (columns) and rows, which define the width and height in units of characters and lines respectively. Since users may need to enter text that exceeds the bounds of this box, user agents are expected to provide scroll bars and to wrap overlong lines.

The final element type, select, is somewhat more complex. It is used for any control that presents several options to the user, from which one or more may be chosen. The presentation of a select element may take the form of a pop-up menu or a list. The user agent is free to choose the form of presentation, and different browsers may present the same select element in different ways. The size attribute of a select element specifies the number of lines of a list that should be displayed, if the element is presented in that form. The Boolean attribute multiple, if set, specifies that more than one item may be chosen. (This almost certainly means that the element will be displayed as a list.) Figure 3.11 shows the display in several browsers of a simple select, with and without the multiple attribute set.

Where do the individual items to be selected come from? A select element must contain at least one option element. Usually, of course, it contains more than one. Each option element has a value attribute; if that option is selected, this attribute provides the value to be sent with the name of the select element in the form data. The content of each option may be used as the text for the corresponding menu entry. Alternatively, a label attribute may be used for this purpose. (The standard recommends that the label value be used in preference, but, as Figure 3.11 shows, different browsers make different choices.)

Finally, the Boolean `selected` attribute is used to indicate a default selection. The XHTML code for the menus shown in Figure 3.11 is as follows:

```
<select id="ch" multiple="multiple" >
<option label="Classic MacOS" value="classic">MacOS 9 or earlier
</option>
<option label="MacOS X" value="osx" selected="selected">MacOS X
</option>
<option label="NT" value="winnt">Windows NT</option>
<option label="2000" value="win2k">Windows 2000</option>
<option label="XP" value="winxp">Windows XP</option>
<option label="ME" value="winme">Windows ME</option>
<option label="Other" value="winoth">Other Windows</option>
<option label="Linux" value="linux">Linux</option>
<option label="BSD" value="bsd">BSD Unix</option>
<option label="Solaris" value="solaris">Sun Solaris</option>
<option label="Other" value="othux">Other Unix</option>
</select>
```

This is the version which allows multiple selections, and is displayed by all our browsers as a list. (The control on the right of each pair in Figure 3.11.) We have omitted the `size` attribute so a default, which varies between the browsers, has been used.

Options within a select may be grouped using the `optgroup` element. This is intended to break up long menus into more easily understandable pieces. The `optgroup` elements each have a `label` attribute, which serves as a heading for the group. (These elements cannot be nested, so you can't have sub-groups within groups.) We could usefully break up our example menu into three groups, for the three platforms represented, like this:

```
<select id="ch" multiple="multiple" >
<optgroup label="Macintosh">
   <option label="Classic MacOS" value="classic">MacOS 9 or earlier
</option>
   <option label="MacOS X" value="osx" selected="selected">MacOS X
</option>
</optgroup>
<optgroup label="Windows">
   <option label="NT" value="winnt">Windows NT</option>
   options for other versions of Windows
</optgroup>
<optgroup label="Unix">
   <option label="Other" value="winoth">Other Windows</option>
```

```
    options for other flavours of Unix
  </optgroup>
  </select>
```

Browsers display optgroups in different ways. All manage to show the group labels as more or less distinguishable headers in lists, but their treatment of groups in pop-up menus varies from ignoring them to displaying them as cascading hierarchical menus.

Most form controls have some text near them, which serves as a label, indicating to the person filling in the form what each choice or field represents. Since input, textarea and select elements can be mixed with text and almost any other element that can appear in the document body, it would be simple to include some label text wherever you want. The association between the control and its label is purely visual, based on proximity. The principle of structural markup suggests that the labels ought to be marked as such, according to their logical function in the document. This would make it easy for non-visual user agents to associate the label with the field it referred to. The label element type is provided for just this purpose. It has an attribute called for, whose value is the id of the form control element to which the label is logically attached. Hence, if label elements are to be used, every input, textarea and select element must have a defined id attribute. For example, the label Windows is attached to the first check box on the survey form as follows:

```
  <label for="win"> Windows </label>
  <input type="checkbox" name="Windows" id="win" />
```

In a similar spirit, the grouping of controls within the form ought also to be expressed in the markup. Radio buttons and checkboxes always come in groups; more generally, the information that is to be entered into a form can be broken down into categories. Many printed forms are laid out in sections, with headings, and the same approach can be used in XHTML, with h1, h2, ... elements, but a more explicit way of expressing the structure of a form is provided by the fieldset element, which is used as a container for a collection of elements within a form which are to be considered as a logical sub-unit. This element has no attributes, beyond the common collection that all elements can have; its start and end tags delimit a field set, which should be displayed in a way that expresses the structure. You can see the default display in Figure 3.9: the boxes surround field sets. The titles for each field set, displayed by default as insets in the box borders, are provided as the content of a legend element contained within the fieldset. For instance, the three questions concerning course details are marked up as follows:

Emerging Technology

XForms

HTML forms have certain shortcomings. In particular, the same elements are used to specify the layout of the form and the structure of the data it sends to the server. If these two aspects of the form can be separated, it will be easier to re-use one or the other for different purposes, or to change them independently. XForms is an XML-based language that provides form definitions and controls, in which separation of the layout and the data is possible. It also provides for validation of form data in the browser without using scripting, and uses a more logical collection of element types for form controls.

Using XForms, a form consists of a section called a model, which specifies what the form does – in particular, the model includes the outline of an XML document that describes the data that will be collected from the form – and a separate section containing control elements, similar to those provided by HTML forms. A specification of how the two are bound together is also required.

XForms is intended to be integrated as a module with other XML-based markup languages. It will provide the form elements in XHTML 2.

```
<fieldset>
    <legend>Course Details</legend>
    <p>
      <label for="inst"> Institution: </label>
      <input name="Institution" type="text" id="inst" /><br />
      input elements for the other questions
    </p>
</fieldset>
```

All of these controls are inline elements, so they must appear within some block element, usually a paragraph. CSS provides various means of positioning and aligning them, which are more elegant and powerful than the simple line breaks we have used here.

The Document Head

As we remarked earlier, the document head contains information about the document that is not considered part of its contents. This being so, the content of the head element is not rendered by browsers in the document window. The content of the `title` element is displayed in various ways, as we explained previously, but never within the browser window itself. While the `title` is the only compulsory element in the head, several other element types may appear there. In particular, the `style` and `script` elements may be used to include stylesheets and scripts within a document, as we will describe in Chapters 4 and 7.

The `meta` element provides a general-purpose mechanism for including any kind of metadata (data about the document). It is an empty element, and when used for metadata it has two attributes, `name` and `content`. The name is used to identify some property of the document, while the content is the value of that property. For instance

```
<meta name="author" content="Hugo Z Hackenbush"/>
```

might be used to identify a page's author, by specifying the value of the property called `author` as the string `Hugo Z Hackenbush`. We say *might be* used to identify the page's author, because the semantics of any property name is not defined by the XHTML specification. There are some conventions and standards concerning certain property names and metadata, but the XHTML standard does not include any formal list of names and their meanings, and imposes no obligation on user agents to do anything at all with `meta` elements.

Perhaps the most common use of `meta` elements is to provide data for search engines, in the form of keywords and a short description of the page's content. Conventionally, the names `keywords` and `description` are used for these properties. The `content` attribute of a `meta` element whose `name` is keywords consists of a list of key words and phrases, which might be appropriate search terms for the page, separated by commas. For instance, the home page of the support site for this book might include the following:

```
<meta name="keywords" content="Web design, Web development,
    Web standards, college textbook, XHTML, CSS, accessibility"/>
```

Note, though, that some important search engines do not look at `meta` elements whose `name` attribute is `keywords`, but analyse the page's contents instead. (This is partly a response to the abuse of the `keywords` property by Web masters trying to improve their pages' search ratings by using inappropriate key words.)

If the name is `description`, the content should just be a short piece of text, succinctly describing the page and its purpose, such as:

Keyword	Meaning
index	This document may be indexed.
noindex	This document may be not indexed.
follow	Links from this document may be followed.
nofollow	Links from this document may not be followed.
all	This document may be indexed and links from it may be followed.
none	This document may not be indexed and links from it may not be followed.

Table 3.4 Keywords for the robots property in meta elements

```
<meta name="description" content="The support site for the textbook
Web Design by Nigel and Jenny Chapman"/>
```

When a page is among the list of those returned by a search query, some search engines will use the description as the text it displays alongside the URL. The lang attribute may be used in a meta element to identify the language in which a description or a set of keywords are written.

Also in the context of search engines, meta elements can be used to control access to pages by robots and spiders. If the name attribute is set to robots, the content can consist of one or more of the directives listed in Table 3.4. Hence, to tell robots that they should index the current document, but not follow any links from it, the following could be included in the document head:

```
<meta name="robots" content="index,nofollow"/>
```

HTML editors sometimes use meta elements to give themselves credit, as in:

```
<meta name="generator" content="BBEdit 8.0"/>
```

Another common use of meta elements is somewhat different. Instead of using the name attribute, you can set the http-equiv attribute to the name of an HTTP response header. In this case, the content attribute gives the string to be used as the rest of the header. Web servers may extract these elements and actually use them to create HTTP headers, but more commonly, user agents examine them and modify their behaviour as if the corresponding header had been sent. One way in which such elements are used is to allow the expiry date of a document to be embedded in the XHTML itself, in the following way:

```
<meta http-equiv="expires" content="Fri, 23 Apr 2010 23:00:00 GMT"/>
```

It is common practice to use an element of this sort to extend the `content-type` header, by adding a specification of the character set. Whereas Web servers can map filename extensions to media types in order to create the `content-type` header, they may not have any mechanism for determining character sets. Hence, it is recommended that all documents have some element such as

```
<meta http-equiv="content-type" content="text/html; charset=utf-8"/>
```

in their head.

As well as metadata, the document head may contain stylesheet definitions and scripts, using the `style` and `script` elements. We will describe these elements in Chapters 4 and 7, respectively. It may also include a `base` element, which has a single attribute `href`, whose value is a URL. If a `base` is present, the URL will be used instead of the document's own URL when resolving relative URLs. There are several scenarios where this can be useful. Suppose, for instance, you have copied the file `index.html` from `www.desperatesw.co.uk` to some other server, to make some changes to it. Then, unless you also copy the rest of the site, any relative URLs will not be correctly resolved, unless you add a `base` element to the document head, setting the base URL to the file's original location, thus: `<base href="http://www.desperatesw.co.uk/index.html"/>`.

Technical Detail

Media Types for XHTML Documents

Since XHTML is also XML, a question arises of what media type should be used for XHTML documents. The same question will arise for any XML-based language, so the IETF has extended the notation for media types to include a suffix `+xml`, at the end of the sub-type, to accommodate such languages. The recommended media type for XHTML documents is `application/xhtml+xml`. For XHTML documents (the majority) that are compatible with HTML 4, the established content type `text/html` may also be used, and many Web servers are configured to do this. The media type `application/xml` may also be used for XHTML documents, but this means that user agents will treat the document as XML, which will rarely be the appropriate thing in the case of a Web page. A final possibility, which is even less often likely to be appropriate, is `text/xml`, which should cause the XML source to be displayed in the browser.

The last type of element that may appear in the document head is link. This is rarely used for its intended purpose, which is to express semantic relationships between documents, such as 'this document is the sequel to that document' or 'this document is a Polish translation of that document'. Instead, its most common use is to point to a stylesheet that is held in a file external to the document. In its general form, the link element uses an href attribute whose value is a URL to point to the linked document; a type attribute, whose value is a media type to indicate its type; and a rel attribute to describe the relationship that the link embodies. Thus, in the particular common case, a CSS stylesheet is usually associated with a document by placing a link in the head whose rel value is stylesheet:

```
<link href="Resources/styles.css"
 rel="stylesheet" type="text/css"/>
```

Frames

If, instead of following our advice and using the strict XHTML DTD, you use the frameset DTD, a new possibility arises. Instead of a body element, a document's head may be followed by a frameset element. The purpose of this is to partition the page area into a *frameset*, a collection of independently updated sub-pages, called *frames*. Each frame has an XHTML document associated with it; the contents of each frame may be updated independently of the others. For example, when a link is followed, the linked page may be loaded into the frame containing the link, while the other frames are left alone, or it may be loaded into one of the other frames instead of the one the link is in.

Figure 3.12 shows a typical use of a frameset. The page is divided into three frames: one holds the navbar, another a banner identifying the site, while the third, main, frame holds the contents of the page. (We have used the thin orange outline to indicate where the individual frames are.) This arrangement means that the site banner and navbar can always be visible, if only the main frame is updated when links are followed or selections are made from the navbar.

Frames may seem like a useful innovation, and when they were first introduced they were received enthusiastically by Web designers, not only because they allowed independent updating of parts of the page, but because they provided a ready means of implementing grid-based layouts for Web pages. However, years of experience with frames has shown that they have considerable disadvantages in the areas of usability and accessibility. CSS now provides an alternative means of defining grid layouts with independently scrolled areas, and JavaScript can be used to update elements of a page independently. The use of frames should, therefore, be avoided.

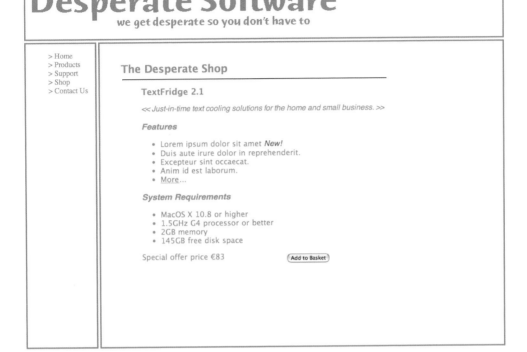

Figure 3.12 A frameset

To appreciate the practical drawbacks of frames, it is necessary to understand how `frameset` elements define a collection of frames. The element has two attributes, `rows` and `cols`, which allow you to define a grid of frames. The size of the rows and columns may be specified in various way, but we will only consider the simplest case, where the value of the attribute is a list of percentages, separated by commas, indicating the proportion of the available vertical and horizontal space each row or column of the grid occupies. For instance:

```
<frameset cols="50%,50%" rows="50%,50%">
content of the frameset
</frameset>
```

would divide the page into equal quarters, like a Battenberg cake, while

```
<frameset rows="25%,75%">
content of the frameset
</frameset>
```

Emerging Technology

XFrames

The W3C is developing a replacement for HTML frames, in the form of XFrames. This proposal differs from the existing facilities for using frames in several ways. Most importantly, it attempts to overcome the usability problems of frames by using a new form of URL, which incorporates information about the contents of each frame. This is intended to make it possible to bookmark framesets correctly. At the time of writing, XFrames is only a Working Draft and there is no support for it in any browser.

would divide it into two horizontal strips, the top one occupying a quarter of the page, the bottom one the remaining three quarters. As this second example shows, one or other of rows and cols may be omitted, when it defaults to 100%.

Within the frameset element, a collection of frame elements specifies the contents of each frame. Frames are filled from left to right, top to bottom, using frame elements in the order they appear within the frameset. The most important attribute of a frame, which is an empty element, is src, which holds the URL of the document that is loaded into the frame when the frameset is first displayed. Other attributes, which we will not describe, are used to specify whether the frame should be displayed with a border and scrollbars. To create layouts more complex than a simple grid, framesets may be nested within framesets. Frames must always be rectangular and there must always be enough to fill the page without leaving gaps, but within those constraints, arbitrary layouts are, in principle, possible. The popular three-frame layout illustrated in Figure 3.12 could be created in the following way:

```
<frameset rows="17%,83%">
  <frame name="topFrame" src="top.html"/>
  <frameset cols="15%,85%" >
    <frame name="leftFrame" src="left.html"/>
    <frame name="mainFrame" src="main.html"/>
  </frameset>
</frameset>
```

Where frames are being used, by default a click on a link causes a new page to be loaded into the frame containing the link. For navbars this is not usually appropriate: it is more likely that you will want to load a new page into the main frame. An a element may have an attribute called target, whose value may be the name of a frame into which the linked page should be loaded. With the frameset layout above, links in the navbar, contained in the frame called `leftFrame` would be of the form

```
<a target="mainFrame" href="contact.html">Contact Us</a>
```

and so on.

The fundamental problem with using frames is that there is no longer a one-to-one mapping between the page displayed in a user's browser and a URL. This may sound like an esoteric objection, but it has important practical consequences. Once again, take as an example the three-frame layout of Figure 3.12. The document containing the frameset has its own URL, and this is the address which will be typed in the address bar or used in a link to cause the three frames, each of which has its own URL, to be displayed. If a user clicks on a link in the navbar, a new page will be loaded into the main frame from another URL, but since the document being displayed is still the same frameset, the URL in the browser's address bar will be unchanged, even though one of the frames has been updated. This means that it is impossible to bookmark the updated frameset. If you wanted to be able to return to the contacts page by typing its URL, you could only do so by returning to the frameset in its original configuration and following a link again.

Every time the main frame is updated a new entry will be created in the history list, but each new entry will point to the same URL – that of the frameset. The browser may be sufficiently sophisticated to take you back to an appropriate state of the frameset when you select an entry from the history list, or it may not – in some early browsers that implemented frames, the back button did not even take you back to the previous state.

These may seem like small imperfections, but given the importance of bookmarks and history lists in most users' browsing patterns, they can seriously impair their Web experience.

Conversely, every document that is loaded into a frame within a frameset must have its own URL. That means that it is possible to access the document on its own, without the surrounding frameset. Stripped of its intended context, the document may lose some of its meaning. Looking again at Figure 3.12, you can see that if the main frame is displayed on its own it will lose all the links in the navbar, and also the banner which helpfully informs the user which site they have arrived at. Users will therefore be disoriented and unable to move about within the site as intended. It is not unusual to find that a frame is be displayed in this way. If a search engine's robot visits the site, it may index every document it finds, not just the framesets, with the consequence that the URL of any single document may be returned among the results of a search query. Therefore, to be safe, it is necessary to include the site identification and navigational links in every document, which rather defeats the object of separating them into their own frames.

Finally, the possibility of user agents' not supporting frames must be considered. All mainstream graphical browsers for desktop machines will display frames correctly, unless their user has disabled the facility – an option which exists on some browsers, and which some users will inevitably avail themselves of. Unconventional user agents, such as speech-based or text-only browsers, or browsers for handheld devices with a limited screen area, may not be able to cope with frames, however. For such agents, the noframes element is provided. This is the only element that may appear at the top level besides head and frameset within the html element of a document containing framesets. If a user agent cannot or will not display frames, it displays the content of the noframes element instead. But what should you put in this element? A popular choice is a message informing the user that their browser does not support frames and suggesting that they get a better one. This is more or less useless, and ignores the possibility that the user may not actually have a choice. The alternative is to provide a version of the page that does not depend on frames – but if you can do that, why not do it anyway and forget about the frames? Given the objections to their use, this is the preferred approach, and accordingly we will not describe frames any further.

Key Points

XML

The structure and appearance of Web pages should be specified independently.

Structure is specified by markup; appearance is specified by stylesheets.

Separate languages are used for markup and stylesheets.

XML is a markup metalanguage.

Tags are used to delimit the structural elements of a document.

XML tags are names enclosed in angle brackets. End tags have a slash before the name.

An element has the form `<el>` content `</el>`. Empty elements have the form `<eel />`.

XML defines five entity references: `&amp;`, `&lt;`, `&gt;`, `&apos` and `&quot`.

Character references of the form `&#d;` or `&#xd;` are used to refer to Unicode characters by their decimal or hexadecimal character codes.

Elements must be properly nested.

Attributes are named properties of elements.

Attributes are assigned values in elements' start tags, using an = sign. String values must be enclosed in quotes.

XML documents that satisfy the structural rules are well-formed.

DTDs and schemas are used to specify a collection of allowable elements, with their attributes and some contextual restrictions.

A well-formed XML document that conforms to the rules expressed in a DTD or schema is valid.

A document type declaration associates a DTD with an XML document

XHTML

XHTML is an XML-based language, defined by a DTD.

The root element is html, which contains the head and body elements.

The document head contains metadata about the document; the content of the document is in its body.

Paragraphs, headings, lists, definitions, tables, citations and program code are among the structures for which XHTML elements are defined.

Text elements may be block level (like p and h1) or inline (like em).

div and span can be used as generic block level and inline containers.

Any element may have id, title and lang attributes.

Bullet lists are produced by ul elements, numbered lists by ol elements. Both contain li elements for the list items.

dl, dt and dd elements are used for definition lists.

Tables should only be used to display tabular data.

A table element contains rows (tr) made out of cells (td). Heading cells should be marked up with th, captions attached with caption elements.

A link connects its source anchor to its destination anchor.

An a element has an href element whose value is a URL pointing to the destination. The element's content is displayed as the link.

Relative URLs describe a resource's location relative to the current document. They are useful for links within a site.

Fragment identifiers are used to point to destination anchors within a document. They identify the destination using an element's `id` attribute.

A fragment identifier consists of a # followed by a name, and may be added to the end of a URL.

Forms are used to allow users to enter data values.

Controls – `input`, `textarea` and `select` elements – may appear within `form` elements.

The content of the `head` element is not rendered in the browser window.

The `title` element is compulsory and is displayed in the title bar and elsewhere.

The `meta` element provides a general-purpose mechanism for adding metadata to XHTML documents.

`meta` elements with the names `keywords`, `description` and `robots` are used to provide information to search engines and to control the behaviour of their robots.

`meta` elements with the name `http-equiv` are used to simulate HTTP headers.

`style` and `script` elements may appear in the `head`, to define stylesheets and scripts within a document.

`link` elements may be used to associate external stylesheets with a document.

A document's `head` may be followed by a `frameset` element, which partitions the page area into a *frameset*, defining a collection of *frames*.

Each frame has an XHTML document associated with it; the contents of each frame may be updated independently.

Frames have considerable usability and accessibility disadvantages, and their use should be avoided.

Exercises

Test Questions

1. Explain why it is necessary to use explicit markup to specify the structure of a Web page instead of relying on appearance to identify its structural components.

2. Identify the errors in this fragment of an XML document:

```
<A Head>Elements and Tags</A Head>
<Paragraph>It is important to distinguish between
<emph>elements</emph> and <emph>tags</paragraph ref="2">
<Paragraph id=def>Tags</emph> are written between < and >
signs to delimit elements.<copyright>&169 2006.
</copyright>
```

3. Can a well-formed XML document include a DTD? Must a valid XML document include a DTD?

4. Most XHTML documents begin like this:

```
<!DOCTYPE html PUBLIC "-//W3C//DTD XHTML 1.0 Strict//EN"
        "http://www.w3.org/TR/xhtml1/DTD/xhtml1-strict.
dtd">
<html xmlns="http://www.w3.org/1999/xhtml" xml:lang="en"
lang="en">
<head>
   <meta http-equiv="content-type" content="text/html;
charset=utf-8" />
   <title>Untitled</title>
</head>
```

Explain carefully what each piece of the code does. What might appear before this code, and why is it usually omitted? What will follow this code?

5. What elements must every valid XHTML document include?

6. What is the difference between block elements and inline elements? Give examples of each.

7. Why should you not use `pre` elements to lay out the content of a page with spaces as you would on a typewriter? Give an example of a legitimate use of a `pre` element.

8. What are each of the three types of list element and what are they used for?

9. For each file and directory in Figure 3.8, write down the relative URL that could be used to refer to it from inside the document `index.html` in the SM folder.

10. Why should you avoid using frames on your Web pages?

Discussion Topics

1. Any element in an XHTML document can have a `class` attribute, so we could define a set of classes and some conventions about how to use elements that allowed us to represent specific sorts of structured data, such as personnel records or bibliographic references, consistently in XHTML. Discuss the advantages and disadvantages of such an approach, compared with writing an XML DTD or schema to define a special-purpose markup language for such data.

2. Suppose you were able to define a new version of XHTML without having to worry about backward compatibility with older markup languages. Which elements and attributes from XHTML 1.0 would you leave out? What new ones would you include?

Practical Tasks

1. Create a valid XHTML document that displays as a single Web page containing a brief résumé of your life so far, including your education, qualifications and any jobs you have held, with relevant dates, as well as personal and contact details. Include some information about your interests and spare-time activities. Think of it as a Web version of a CV for a job or college application. Use appropriate markup to delimit the different parts of the page and organize the content. (Don't worry about the page's appearance at this stage.) Add keywords and a summary using `meta` elements in the document head. Use a validator to check the syntax, and test the page in as many browsers as you can.

2. Create a table to display your educational qualifications, showing the school or college and year, subject and grade. Add headings and use spanned rows or columns where appropriate to display the data in a compact and perspicuous way.

3. Create a form for entering the data for a résumé, such as the one you created in the previous exercise. You will need to make some simplifying assumptions at this stage. For example, you will probably have to set a maximum number of schools attended and jobs held. You will also need to use a dummy value for the `action` attribute of the `form` element.

4. Visit several Web pages of different sorts, for example, a blog, an e-commerce site, the home page of your college. For each page, use your browser's facility for viewing the source, or save the source to disk and open it in a text editor. For each page, examine the markup. Is it valid? Does it use tables for layout? Are elements used logically and consistently? Could you improve the code?

Stylesheets

4

As the examples in the previous chapter demonstrate, the default way in which browsers display the elements that make up Web pages varies from the uninspiring to the dreadful. Thanks to the efforts and ingenuity of Web designers, most real Web pages don't look that bad. Stylesheets are the modern tool that allows designers to control the appearance of pages and improve on the browser's default efforts. Other more tortuous methods have been used in the past, and earlier versions of HTML provided some support for styling using attributes. Stylesheets are to be preferred, however, for two reasons. First, they provide more extensive control over all aspects of a page's layout and appearance than HTML's presentational attributes ever did. Second, they allow the specification of appearance to be kept independent of the markup that expresses structure. The structure is always available in the markup, irrespective of what a page looks like. It is also available to user agents that are not concerned with appearance at all, such as search engine spiders or screen readers. The appearance can be altered without affecting the structure. Different stylesheets can be applied to the same document for different purposes, and stylesheets can be used to control presentation in any medium, not just for display on a screen.

In principle, another advantage of separating stylesheets from markup is that any stylesheet language can be used with XHTML. At the present time, however, browers only understand stylesheets written in one of two languages: **CSS** (the Cascading Stylesheets language) and *XSLT* (the Extensible Stylesheet Language for Transformations). CSS provides extensive control over layout, typography and other aspects of the presentation of XML, XHTML and HTML documents in graphical browsers. XSLT is a more powerful language, which can be used for radically restructuring a document for the purposes of presentation. One fairly common use of XSLT is for transforming XML documents into HTML, as a means of preparing them for display in browsers that cannot display XML documents directly. We will not describe XSLT at all, since CSS is more than adequate for most Web designers' needs.

In this chapter, we discuss the mechanics of using stylesheets in conjunction with XHTML markup to control many aspects of the appearance of Web pages. In Chapter 10 we will return to this subject and consider the more important question of how to use these techniques to create usable and good-looking pages.

A minor but important matter is the way in which a stylesheet becomes associated with an XHMTL document. The easiest way is to place the stylesheet in its own file (typically this will have an extension .css), and refer to it from the document using a link element in the head, as described in Chapter 3:

```
<link href="Resources/styles.css" rel="stylesheet" type="text/css"/>
```

This arrangement means that a single stylesheet can be shared by many documents – often an entire Web site – to ensure a consistent style. Changes to the stylesheet will affect all the documents, making maintenance much easier. Occasionally, a stylesheet will only be applicable to a single document. In that case, you might prefer to embed the stylesheet in the document itself. This can be done using the style element, which appears in the head. It has a type attribute, which should be set to text/css. The content of the element consists of the CSS code which would otherwise be in an external file.

```
<style type="text/css">
    stylesheet
</style>
```

Various expedients are commonly used to conceal embedded stylesheets from old browsers that don't understand them, and to avoid the need for entity references within the stylesheet. HTML editors and Web authoring programs will normally insert these automatically. Linking to external stylesheet files is generally trouble-free and is to be preferred.

Rules in CSS

A CSS stylesheet consists of a collection of **rules**, describing how the browser should display elements of an XHTML document. Each rule consists of two parts: a **selector**, which determines which elements the rule applies to, and some **declarations**, which describe how those elements should be displayed. Here is an example of a simple CSS rule:

Technical Detail

The `style` Attribute

There is a third way of adding stylesheet information to a document. Any XHTML element may have a `style` attribute, whose value is a string consisting of a sequence of declarations. The effect is the same as a rule with a selector that matches just that element and a body containing the declarations. For instance, to style a level 1 heading in the same way as it would be using the example rule given in the main text, the following start tag could be used:

```
<h1 style="font-family: 'Lydian MT', Futura, Georgia, serif;
font-size: 200%;text-align: center;">
```

Unlike the stylesheet rule, this attribute would only affect the particular heading to which it was attached.

Although not actually deprecated in XHTML 1 or 2, the use of the `style` attribute is discouraged, because it fails to separate the styling and content cleanly. Web authoring programs routinely generate `style` attributes, though.

```
h1 {
    font-family: "Lydian MT", Futura, Georgia, serif;
    font-size: 200%;
    text-align: center;
}
```

This example shows the general form of a CSS rule. The selector comes first. In this case, it is the element name h1. A selector like this, consisting of an element name, matches all elements of the corresponding type, so the styling specified in the declarations of this rule will be applied to all h1 elements.

The declarations follow the selector; they are enclosed in curly brackets, which mark the extent of this rule. (The delimiters can never be omitted, even if there is only one declaration.) Declarations are separated by a semicolon – almost everyone also adds a semicolon after the last declaration in a rule, although this is optional, because it makes editing easier. Declarations do not need to be written on separate lines, but they often are, to make rules more readable.

Each declaration consists of two parts. First comes a ***property***, which is the name of some aspect of the element's appearance. This is followed by a colon, and then the value for the property. Thus, the second declaration in our example gives the value 200% to the property called font-size. As you see, unlike attribute values in XHTML, most property values in CSS do not have to be enclosed in quotes, unless the value includes a space (or other whitespace character, such as a tab).

More than one hundred different properties are available in CSS2.1, the version we will be concerned with. They are the semantic heart of CSS, since they determine what can be controlled using a stylesheet. The language's syntax is trivial in comparison – we have already described most of it. Much of the remainder is concerned with different forms of selector. In order to provide concrete examples of rules while describing the syntax of selectors, we will use a single property, color[†], which controls the colour of text. It can take values that specify a colour in various ways. We will just use names, which hopefully will be self-explanatory. CSS allows sixteen colours to be named in this way. (In Chapter 5 we will describe how to specify a much wider and more useful range of colours.) A simple example of a rule that sets the color property is:

```
h1 { color: aqua; }
```

which causes all h1 elements to be set in aqua-coloured text.

Selectors

We have illustrated the simplest form of selector, an element name. Rules that use element names as selectors define a consistent appearance for every element with that name in a document. They replace the browser's default rules, but still only allow for as many different styles as there are element types in XHTML, which may not be adequate. It is common practice to format the opening paragraph of an article slightly differently from the rest, for example. Rules which have p as the selector will apply to all paragraphs, though. In XML you could define a separate element – p1, say – for first paragraphs (though you might question whether it would really represent a structural unit), but in XHTML you must stick with the repertoire of available element types. The class attribute provides a way of distinguishing between subsets of an element type.

As we explained in Chapter 3, any element may have a class attribute, whose value is a string consisting of one or more names, separated by spaces. If the same name appears among

---

† North American spelling is always used for property names and keywords.

the class values of two elements, they are considered to belong to the same class, which has that name. For instance, the tag <h1 class="red"> assigns an h1 element to the class red, and <h1 class="red underlined"> assigns it to two classes, red and underlined. The primary purpose of this classification is to support different styling for different classes.

Suppose we assign the value first to the class attribute of the first paragraph of every section of a page, by using the start tag <p class="first"> to open such paragraphs. (There is, of course, no section element in XHTML 1, so suppose that we assign any paragraph that follows an h1 element to this class.) Then the selector p.first will match all first paragraphs, and can be used in a rule to define any special formatting that seems appropriate. To set the opening paragraph in grey, you would use the following rule:

```
p.first { color: gray; }
```

In the general case, a selector consisting of an element type followed by a dot and a name matches all elements in that class (i.e. all elements of that type whose class attribute includes the name). A rule with a selector of this form will take priority over one that selects all elements of a type, so if there is a rule with selector p as well as one with selector p.first, it will be used for all paragraphs, except those with class="first" (or any other value for which there is a specific rule). Thus, if in addition to the rule above, we had

```
p { color: black; }
```

all paragraph text except for paragraphs belonging to the class first would be set in black. Where an element belongs to more than one class, the rules for all of its classes are applied. If this causes a conflict, later rules take precedence over earlier ones. For instance, if a paragraph belongs to two classes, first and changed, and there are two rules:

```
p.first { color: gray; }
p.changed { color: purple; }
```

the last rule will be used: any paragraph with class="first changed" will be set in purple. Conflicts between CSS rules are always resolved in favour of the later rule.

Actually, matters are slightly more complicated – although the complications correspond to what you would probably expect. A rule with a selector for a class within an element type takes precedence over a general rule with a selector for that element type, only in respect of those properties that are explicitly declared in the class's rule. Suppose, for example, we define a rule of the form:

```
p {
    prop1: value1;
    prop2: value2;
    prop3: value3;
    prop4: value4;
    prop5: value5;
}
```

(where *prop1* and so on stand for some CSS property names, and *value1* and so on for appropriate values) and another:

```
p.first {
    prop3: value31;
    prop5: value51;
}
```

Then a paragraph element of class first would have the values *value1*, *value2*, *value31*, *value4* and *value51* for these properties.

The selector * matches any element. Hence, *.c matches any element belonging to the class c. This is a commonly used kind of selector, because classes may be used to apply aspects of styling to several different element types. For instance, you might decide that certain links (a elements), headings (h1, h2,...) and also arbitrary runs of text (span elements) should be purple, so elements of any of these types might be assigned to the class purple. Rather than use separate selectors for all the possible cases, you could simply write a single rule:

```
*.purple { color: purple; }
```

This would allow you to assign other types of element to this class later, without changing the stylesheet. Because this is a common pattern, a shorthand is provided, whereby you may omit the *, so that the selector just comprises a dot followed by a class name, for example,

```
.purple { color: purple; }
```

If you wish to apply special styling to one individual element, you could invent a class and assign just that element to it, but you can also use the value of its id attribute in a selector.

A selector consisting of an element name followed by a # and a name matches the element whose id is equal to the name, so p#summary would match the paragraph with id="summary". So would *#summary, since id values must be unique. As with classes, * can be omitted, giving the shorthand form #summary for selectors based on id values.

Careful assignment of elements to classes can be used to produce any styling scheme you might wish, but some patterns can be dealt with more conveniently using special-purpose *contextual selectors*. These selectors are for using on those occasions when you wish to apply certain formatting to elements of a particular type only when it occurs in a certain context. A good example is provided by li elements. Recall from Chapter 3 that these may appear either inside an ol element, as the items in an ordered list, or a ul element, as those of an unordered (bulleted) list. You might very well want to apply different formatting to the two cases. In reality, it isn't very likely that you would want to set them in different colours, but let's suppose that you do: items in a bullet list will be blue, those in a numbered list grey. If a selector consists of two element names separated by a space, it matches elements with the second name if and only if they are found in the content of an element with the first name. For instance, the selector ul li matches li elements within a ul, so we could achieve our aim of colour-coded list items with these rules:

```
ul li { color: blue; }
ol li { color: grey; }
```

Contextual selectors like this can be used to alter the styling of any element in circumstances where the appearance of a surrounding element makes the usual styling inappropriate. It is not quite adequate for all cases, though. Considering list items again, the following XHTML markup in conjunction with the rules above does not produce the desired result.

```
<ol>
   <li>One</li>
   <li>Two</li>
   <li>
   <ul>
      <li>Un</li>
      <li>Deux</li>
      <li>Trois</li>
   </ul>
   </li>
</ol>
```

Technical Detail

Attribute Selectors

Some additional forms of selector, based on attribute values, are available. These are more useful for stylesheets used with XML documents, and are rarely needed with XHTML. If *E* is an element name, and *a* is an attribute of elements of that type, *E*[*a*] matches all elements of type *E* that have *a* defined, *E*[*a=v*] matches all elements of type *E* whose *a* attribute is equal to *v*, and *E*[*a~=v*] matches all elements of type *E* whose *a* attribute consists of a sequence of names separated by white space, one of which is equal to *v*. You should be able to see that *E.c* is an abbreviation for *E*[class~=c] and *E#i* is an abbreviation for *E*[id=*i*]. The full forms of these selectors are required in XML, because XML documents do not have a fixed repertoire of elements and attributes; in particular, there is no reason to suppose that class and id will be attributes of every element.

A final form of attribute selector is *E*[*a|=v*]. This only matches on elements whose attribute *a* consists of a series of words separated by hyphens, which begins with *v*. To see why this might be useful, consider the form of language codes that might be the value of the xml:lang attribute of any element.

The numbered items in the inner list appear in grey, because they are inside an ol element, and the CSS rule for ol li takes precedence, since it appears later in the stylesheet. Reversing the order of the rules fixes this problem, but will fail if the lists are nested the other way out. To cope with such contingencies, if > replaces the space in a contextual selector, the rule is only applied to elements of the second type if they are children of the first, that is, they are immediately contained in them, as the li elements with French numbers are with respect to the ul element, but not the ol element. If the stylesheet rules are changed to

```
ul>li { color: blue; }
ol>li { color: grey; }
```

all the list items are coloured as intended.

The formatting of an element might depend not just on the element it is contained in, but on the element that precedes it. For instance, we have already noted that the first paragraph following a heading is often given special typographical treatment. We have shown how this can be done using a class, but a more direct way is by using the selector h1 + p, which matches a p element if and only if it follows an h1 element, so the rule with p.first as its selector given previously could be replaced by

```
h1 + p { color: gray; }
```

In this context, an element follows another if it comes right after its end tag; in terms of the document tree, the two elements must be siblings.

A similar special case occurs with elements that are the first child of their parents. For example, the first item in an unordered list would be the first child of the enclosing ul element; if an h1 element was the first thing in a document, it would be the first child of the body element, and so on. Such first children may benefit from special styling. A selector consisting of an element name followed by :first-child matches elements in this position. To set an h1 at the beginning of a document's body in purple, we could use the following rule:

```
h1:first-child { color: purple; }
```

This colon notation is used for selectors that match *pseudo-classes* of element. These are classes that don't depend on the presence of a name in the class attribute, but depend on properties of the document. We will see more examples of pseudo-classes later.

With all the possibilities available for writing selectors, it is quite possible that you will end up writing several rules with different selectors but the same declarations. These can be combined: several selectors, separated by commas may appear in a rule. The single rule behaves as if it was a sequence of rules, one for each of the selectors, with identical declarations. Thus, if you wanted to set headings at all levels in a document in blue, instead of writing six rules for each of the heading element types, you could write a single rule:

```
h1,h2,h3,h4,h5,h6 { color: blue; }
```

(Perl and Awk programmers will probably expect to be able to use regular expressions, such as h[1-6], as selectors, but you can't.)

Inheritance

If a value is assigned to some property for an element in a document, the value is inherited by that element's children, unless a rule causes a different value to be explicitly assigned.

Browser Quirks

CSS Hacks

There are some cases where certain browsers' implementation of some CSS features is so badly flawed that pages using those features will be displayed too poorly to be acceptable. The chief offendors are Internet Explorer 5 (both Windows and Macintosh versions, although they exhibit different problems) and Netscape 4. All of these browsers are now considered obsolete, but they are still in use, especially IE5/Win. For modern browsers, adding a DTD to your documents to force them into strict mode is usually sufficient to get most CSS to display properly.

To work round the problems with defective browsers, certain tricks, which exploit additional bugs, have been developed to allow different CSS rules to be used for different browsers. In particular, IE5 does not implement the `>` operator in selectors, so any rule that uses the selector `html>body`, which should always match, will be ignored. Conversely, `* html` should always fail, since `html` is the root element, but IE5 behaves as if the root was enclosed in some other element, so rules that should only be used for this browser can use this selector.

On the whole, such hacks ought to be avoided, and you should keep an eye on published statistics on browser usage and your site logs to see whether you need to use them.

In other words, the value of a property is applied to the entire contents of an element. For instance, given the rules

```
.red { color:red; }
.purple { color:purple; }
```

and the markup

```
<p class="red">
A paragraph containing some <em>emphasized</em> text.
</p>
```

the word *emphasized* would be set in red, together with whatever styling had been specified for em elements, because the `color` property is inherited from its parent p element. On the other hand, if the markup was

```
<p class="red">
A paragraph containing some <em class="purple">
emphasized</em> text.
</p>
```

emphasized would be in purple, because the explicit assignment of a colour to text of class `purple`, to which this element belongs, overrides the inherited value. This rule is intuitive and usually causes no problems. For some properties whose values are numerical and may depend on context, it is occasionally unclear what the inherited value will be. As a general rule, any computation that is necessary to arrive at a value is performed before inheritance, so any values that are dependent on context will be computed in the context of the parent element. We will see some examples of how this operates later in the chapter.

As a consequence of the way inheritance works, default values of properties that affect an entire document can be set simply by using a rule with selector `body` or `html`. Any properties that are not set in this way will be set to default values, which may be chosen by the user, wired in to the browser, or determined by the CSS standard.

Typography

Typography – the style and appearance of text – is a central concern in design for print-based media. Centuries of experience in typesetting have led to the creation of thousands of type-faces that can be used – in conjunction with design skill and powerful software – to create attractive and effective pages in a huge variety of styles. It would be nice if the expertise of traditional typesetting could be transferred to the Web, but the new medium imposes some constraints which seriously limit the scope for fine typography.

Fonts

A *font* is a collection of character shapes, called **glyphs**, which are used for displaying text. All the glyphs in a font will share certain characteristics that convey an impression of uni-formity. Whenever a character is to be displayed, the corresponding glyph – which is nothing more than a small image – is selected from the font and rendered on the screen. Although glyphs are usually very small, and each glyph for a particular character must be recognizable whatever the font, there is considerable scope for subtle differences in the appearance of the glyphs, with the result that the look of a piece of text can vary greatly, depending on the font in which it has been displayed. The few samples shown in Figure 4.1 are sufficient to give some idea of the variations that are possible within the limits of font design.

Several fonts that share some fundamental characteristics may be grouped into a ***font family***, consisting of several ***variants***, such as a regular version, an italic and a boldface one. These variants will be noticeably different, but the members of the family will have a similar appearance, based on such things as the height of characters, the style of serifs (see below) and the ratio of thick to thin strokes in the glyphs. These similarities will ensure that fonts from the same family look well together on the page, whereas fonts from different families are unlikely to do so. Figure 4.2 shows samples of the members of two contrasting font families. There is no standard specifying how many members there must be in a font family, or what they should be. Some families consist of just a regular and an italic version, while others may have several different boldface versions or boldface italics as well.

The characteristics of fonts can be described in several ways. A fundamental distinction is drawn between ***monospaced*** – or ***fixed width*** – fonts, in which each character occupies exactly the same horizontal space, and ***proportional*** fonts, in which the space occupied depends on the width of the character. In Figure 4.1, Andale Mono and Courier are examples of monospaced fonts, all the rest are proportional. Text in a monospaced font looks as if it had been produced on a typewriter or teletype machine, and is often used for computer program code. On the Web, monospaced fonts are the default choice for `pre` elements.

Another distinction is between ***serifed*** and ***sans serif*** fonts. Serifs are the little decorative strokes on the ends of letters, as shown in Figure 4.3. Glyphs in sans serif fonts lack these. Trebuchet, Arial and Verdana are all sans serif fonts; so is Andale Mono, although Courier has crude serifs. Proportional serifed fonts, such as Times Roman and Georgia, are the traditional choice for setting long passages of continuous text in books and other printed material. They work less well on screen, because the fine detail of the serifs is not rendered accurately at low resolutions. The bolder appearance of sans serif fonts is generally considered more readable on screen. Despite this, the default proportional font on most browsers when they are first installed is usually a serifed font, often Times Roman.

The last three fonts shown in Figure 4.1 are different from the rest. They are examples of what are called ***display fonts***. The majority of existing fonts fall into this general category. They are fonts that are not suitable for continuous text, but have more eye-catching designs, suitable for headlines, advertising and other short pieces of text that need to have a high visual impact. This gives greater scope to the font designer, hence the vast number of display fonts. Some display fonts, such as Brush Script, are loosely based on handwriting styles;

ABCDEFGHIJKLMNOPQRSTUVWXYZ
abcdefghijklmnopqrstuvwxyz
1234567890
The quick brown fox jumps over the
lazy dog
Georgia

ABCDEFGHIJKLMNOPQRSTUVWXYZ
abcdefghijklmnopqrstuvwxyz
1234567890
The quick brown fox jumps
over the lazy dog
Andale Mono

ABCDEFGHIJKLMNOPQRSTUVWXYZ
abcdefghijklmnopqrstuvwxyz
1234567890
The quick brown fox jumps over the lazy
dog
Times New Roman

ABCDEFGHIJKLMNOPQRSTUVWXYZ
abcdefghijklmnopqrstuvwxyz
1234567890
The quick brown fox jumps
over the lazy dog
Courier

ABCDEFGHIJKLMNOPQRSTUVWXYZ
abcdefghijklmnopqrstuvwxyz
1234567890
The quick brown fox jumps over
the lazy dog
Verdana

ABCDEFGHIJKLMNOP2RSTUVWXYZ
abcdefghijklmnopqrstuvwxyz
1234567890
The quick brown fox jumps over the lazy dog

Brush Script

ABCDEFGHIJKLMNOPQRSTUVWXYZ
abcdefghijklmnopqrstuvwxyz
1234567890
The quick brown fox jumps over the
lazy dog
Arial

ABCDEFGHIJKLMNOPQRSTUVWXYZ
abcdefghijklmnopqrstuvwxyz
1234567890
The quick brown fox jumps over the lazy
dog
Impact

ABCDEFGHIJKLMNOPQRSTUVWXYZ
abcdefghijklmnopqrstuvwxyz
1234567890
The quick brown fox jumps over the
lazy dog
Trebuchet

ABCDEFGHIJKLMNOPQRSTUVWXYZ
abcdefghijklmnopqrstuvwxyz
1234567890
The quick brown fox jumps over the
lazy dog
Comic Sans

Figure 4.1 Some common Web fonts

ABCDEFGHIJKLMNOPQRSTUVWXYZ
abcdefghijklmnopqrstuvwxyz
1234567890
The quick brown fox jumps over the lazy
dog
Georgia Regular

ABCDEFGHIJKLMNOPQRSTUVWXYZ
abcdefghijklmnopqrstuvwxyz
1234567890
The quick brown fox jumps over the lazy
dog
Arial Regular

ABCDEFGHIJKLMNOPQRSTUVWXYZ
abcdefghijklmnopqrstuvwxyz
1234567890
*The quick brown fox jumps over the
lazy dog*
Georgia Italic

ABCDEFGHIJKLMNOPQRSTUVWXYZ
abcdefghijklmnopqrstuvwxyz
1234567890
*The quick brown fox jumps over the lazy
dog*
Arial Italic

**ABCDEFGHIJKLMNOPQRSTU-
VWXYZ**
abcdefghijklmnopqrstuvwxyz
1234567890
**The quick brown fox jumps over
the lazy dog**
Georgia Bold

ABCDEFGHIJKLMNOPQRSTUVWXYZ
abcdefghijklmnopqrstuvwxyz
1234567890
**The quick brown fox jumps over the
lazy dog**
Arial Bold

***ABCDEFGHIJKLMNOPQRSTU-
VWXYZ***
abcdefghijklmnopqrstuvwxyz
1234567890
***The quick brown fox jumps over
the lazy dog***
Georgia Bold Italic

ABCDEFGHIJKLMNOPQRSTUVWXYZ
abcdefghijklmnopqrstuvwxyz
1234567890
***The quick brown fox jumps over the
lazy dog***
Arial Bold Italic

Figure 4.2 The members of two font families

Serif

Sans serif

Figure 4.3 Serifed and sans serif fonts

they are generically referred to as **calligraphic** or **cursive** fonts. Fonts which do not fit neatly into any category, are sometimes called **fantasy** fonts. Comic Sans is a fairly restrained example; there are many more fantastic fantasies.

The choice of a font in which to set a page makes a significant difference to its appearance. On the Web, though, you can never know for sure which font will be used to view the text on your pages. As we will explain shortly, CSS provides a way for a designer to *suggest* which fonts should be used for each type of element, but there is no guarantee that they will actually be used, for the simple reason that Web browsers can usually only use fonts that are installed on the system on which they are running, and there is no guarantee that any particular visitor to a page will have the designer's chosen fonts installed on their system. In fact, the fonts shown in Figure 4.1, with the exception of Brush Script, are the only ones likely to be installed on all recent Windows and MacOS X systems. It's particularly unlikely that an average domestic or business user will have the vast array of esoteric fonts that most graphic designers acquire, so there is little point in a designer spending a lot of time choosing the perfect font for a Web page that gives it just the right degree of style and distinction. The chances are that most people will see it in Times Roman.

Even if you choose a font that almost everybody is bound to have, it is still possible that some people will see the page rendered in a different one, because many browsers allow their users to specify a stylesheet of their own, which overrides any referred to in the page. It is probably the case that very few ordinary people do this, and those who do will generally have a good reason – for instance, they may have some vision defect, which makes it necessary to use highly readable fonts and colours. You can't even work backwards, assume that if you don't specify a font the browser's default will be used, and design around that. This is because browsers provide different defaults (some version of Times Roman is a popular choice, but it is not a universal one), and all browsers provide a simple means for the user to change the default. Many people switch to a sans serif font as their default.

Given this situation, no typographical decisions made by a designer can be considered final, but CSS does allow you to specify your preferred fonts, using a collection of font properties. The first of these is `font-family`, which is used to select a font family. You could have guessed that, but perhaps not guessed that its value is a list of names. As our first example of a CSS rule illustrated, the names are separated by commas, and names with spaces in them must be enclosed in quotes. The collection of fonts in the list is called a **font set**. The browser is expected to look for each of the fonts in the set in turn, until it finds one it can use. In other words, the font set consists of those fonts that the designer would find acceptable, in decreasing order of preference. Thus, given the rule:

```
h1 { font-family: "Lydian MT", Futura, Georgia, serif; }
```

the browser would first look for fonts in the Lydian MT family. This is a bit of a long shot, so the search is likely to fail. Next, it would try Futura, which is more commonly found but still not part of most standard installations. If no Futura fonts are found, the browser will try Georgia. This time, it is very likely to succeed, because Georgia is present on most systems. The final name in the list, serif, is provided in case none of the named font families is available. It is one of CSS's *generic font families*. The others are sans-serif (note the hyphen), cursive, fantasy and monospace. Browsers must provide some font for each of these families. It is to be expected that they will correspond to the class of font suggested by each generic family's name, but there is no guarantee of this. Some browsers allow their users to choose the fonts which will be used for some or all of these generic families, so it is quite possible that a rule such as the one above could result in h1 elements being set in Verdana.

The example rule for h1 elements shows a useful pattern for font set values: start with the specific font you would like to use, follow it with more common ones that resemble it, and finish off with a generic font family. It is worth specifying the less common fonts, as long as your design does not depend on them too heavily, because there is no knowing what fonts any user may have: word processors, desktop publishing and vector drawing programs, among others, usually install a wide selection of fonts. It is, however, a good idea to test your page on systems without the fonts you have specified, to see how badly their absence affects its appearance. (Using a font management program to turn off each of the fonts in the set, until only the generic family is left will show you how it degrades. Figure 4.4 shows the effect of turning off each of the fonts in our example set. Notice the change of width, even though these fonts are all nominally the same size.) If a page looks truly awful without your preferred fonts, you should consider redesigning it.

Font Styling

Four other properties may be used to refine the choice of font: font-style, font-variant, font-weight and font-stretch. These set (somewhat arbitrary) independent characteristics, which together are enough to identify a font within a family. The font-style may be normal, italic or oblique. The first two values should be self-explanatory. An oblique font is slanted, as italic fonts invariably are, but does not necessarily have the handwritten quality of italics. Often, oblique fonts are created just by applying a skew transformation to a normal font. If the font-style is italic, but no actual italic font can be found, an oblique font may be substituted.

Technical Detail

Intelligent Font Matching in CSS2

The method described in the main text for choosing a font in response to a font-family declaration is not the full story. It is the method prescribed for CSS1, but CSS2 provides additional facilities which potentially can produce better results. The idea is that, if a browser cannot find a font that matches the name specified for a font-family, it may try to find an alternative that resembles the correct font. If that fails, it may try to download a suitable font from a server. If that also fails, it may synthesize a suitable font. Not all browsers will be capable of all these steps, and in practice most contemporary ones fall back on the CSS1 mechanism.

A CSS2 stylesheet can include font descriptions, which, as the name suggests, provide a description of the characteristics of a font. These descriptions take the form of special 'at-rules', which are a type of CSS rule that do not have a conventional selector, but instead use a keyword, prefixed by an @ character, and perform some function other than specifying the styling of elements of a document. For font descriptions, the rule has the form

```
@font-face { declarations }
```

The declarations set the values of various font-related properties, which provide a description of the font, sufficient for a browser to select a good approximation to a desired font, or to synthesize one.

Most interestingly, one of the properties that can be set in an @font-face rule is src, whose value is a URL from which the font can be obtained. This seems to be the perfect solution to the problems of Web typography: if browsers can download fonts, designers can use any font they wish to. Sadly, this state of affairs has not been achieved. Fonts are valuable intellectual property, and font foundries are reluctant to make them available for download. Until browsers implement a means of downloading fonts without potentially making them available to other applications, which is secure enough to satisfy the owners of font designs, font downloading will not take place. Given this, and the fact that font synthesis and intelligent matching are non-trivial to implement, most browsers simply ignore @font-face rules.

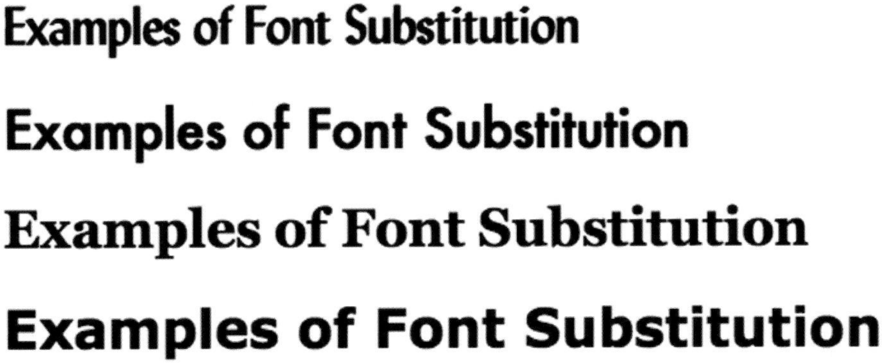

Examples of Font Substitution

Examples of Font Substitution

Examples of Font Substitution

Examples of Font Substitution

Figure 4.4 Font substitution

In CSS terms, the font variants are `normal` and `small-caps`: some font families include a special font that has small versions of upper case letters in place of lower-case, and this will be selected if `font-variant` is set to `small-caps`.

The `font-weight` property is more complicated. It selects the weight, or darkness, of a font. As the samples in Figure 4.2 illustrate, many font families include a boldface version, which is darker than the normal version, by virtue of using thicker strokes for the letter forms. Some font families include several versions with different weights; these are identified by terms such as ultra-light, light, bold, ultra-bold and black, but there is no standard system of terminology. Furthermore, the normal font of one family may actually be darker than the bold version of another, so boldness cannot be an absolute property. (Consider the font Impact in Figure 4.1.)

To accommodate the diversity of font weights, the `font-weight` property may take numerical values between 100 and 900. The value must be divisible by 100 (so it is something of a mystery why the range is not 1 to 9). The only meaning given to the weight values is that if $b > a$, a font with weight b is at least as dark as (i.e. is not lighter than) a font with weight a. The two fonts may, however, be of the same weight. This will often be the case, in fact, since few font families have as many as nine different weights. For convenience, some keywords may be used as values for this property: `normal` is the same as 400, `bold` is the same as 700. The keywords `bolder` and `lighter` can also be used, to specify the weight of a font relative to the weight inherited from an element's parent. The intention is to increase or decrease the weight, but, in view of our earlier remarks, this cannot be guaranteed. The effect of `bolder` is defined as specifying a font that is darker than the inherited one, if it exists; otherwise it adds 100 to the inherited font-weight value. If the inherited value is 900, it has no effect. The meaning of lighter is similar, but changes the weight in the opposite direction.

A similar approach is taken to the font-stretch property. Some fonts come in versions which are spaced out horizontally to a different degree. Fonts which have letters closed up tightly together are called condensed fonts; they are used for setting type in narrow columns (in newspapers, for example). Fonts which have letters stretched wider apart are called expanded fonts. As with weight, the stretch of a font is not an absolute property. Times New Roman Regular, for example, is a condensed font and has no extended version; Univers has extended, condensed and ultra-condensed versions, in different weights. The CSS keywords ultra-condensed, extra-condensed, condensed, semi-condensed, normal, semi-expanded, expanded, extra-expanded and ultra-expanded form a partial ordering from narrowest to widest, like the numerical weight values. The keywords wider and narrower are used to select a font with a different width from the inherited value, in the same way as bolder and lighter are used to select relative weights.

Type Size

Specifying font sizes introduces additional complications. The keywords for the font-size property are xx-small, x-small, small, medium, large, x-large and xx-large. It is recommended that the size corresponding to each of these values should be 1.2 times that corresponding to the previous value, so if medium is 14pt, say, large should be 16.8pt. The keywords larger and smaller can be used to specify size changes relative to an inherited value. Generally, user agents are able to scale fonts to arbitrary sizes, so there is no question of missing sizes, as there is of missing weights. However, the question that does arise is: how big is medium? The answer is that it might be anything. It is the default size set by the user in their browser. This means that, using the size keywords, a designer cannot know exactly how big the text on their Web pages will appear when displayed in a browser.

As an apparent way to control type size, CSS also allows the font-size property to specify the size as an absolute dimension. This may be in any units, but the size of a font is usually given in units of *points*, abbreviated pt; in CSS, 1pt is defined to be exactly equal to 1/72 inch. (And an inch is defined to be 2.54cm.) The font size is a measure of the maximum height occupied by text set in the font; it is not necessarily the height of any particular glyph, although brackets are often exactly equal in height to the font size. Nor is it the case that two fonts that are the same nominal size will have characters that are the same height. The complexities of letter forms mean that one might appear much smaller than the other, hence font substitution can have a marked effect on the apparent size of type, even though the font size is unchanged (as Figure 4.4 demonstrated).

The CSS rule

```
body { font-size:12pt; }
```

should set the default font size in a document to 12pt. However, as with so many aspects of Web page layout, it is the user who has the final say. Browsers provide commands for increasing and decreasing the size of text, and this can override the effect of any font-size declarations in a stylesheet. Sizes will all be increased or decreased by the same factor, though, so the relative sizes of different elements will be maintained.

An alternative to specifying font sizes in points is to specify them in pixels, abbreviated px in CSS. Since, as we will explain in Chapter 5, the resolution of monitors is always taken to be 72 pixels per inch, px would appear to be identical to pt. Matters are more complicated, however, because browsers may use different resolutions for text in order to make type appear to be the same size on different platforms. Specifying sizes in pixels has the advantage that the type will scale appropriately when a page is displayed or printed on a device with a different resolution, so if this is an important consideration, the value for the font-size property should be given in pixels.

Font sizes can also be specified as a percentage of their inherited value. Thus

```
h1 { font-size: 135%; }
```

would cause level 1 headers to be set 1.35 times the default font size, which would be inherited from the enclosing body element. Another way of achieving the same effect, which is based on traditional typesetting practice, is to use units of ems instead of points. An em is a unit that is equal to the font size, so in a 12pt font, 1em equals 12pt, in a 10pt font, 1em equals 10pt, and so on. (The unit's name comes from the fact that in many fonts an upper case M is 1em wide.) When the value of font-size is given in ems, the em unit is inherited, that is, it is equal to the font size in the parent element. Thus, the following rule is equivalent to the previous one:

```
h1 { font-size: 1.35em; }
```

As a general rule, you should use relative units for font sizes, thereby respecting users' preferences. If you find it necessary to fix the size of type in your pages for any reason, it is advisable only to use an absolute size in a rule for the body element, and to set the size of type in any other elements relative to this. In this way, changing a single rule will be sufficient to change the sizes throughout the document, while maintaining their relative proportions.

The font size does not dictate the height of lines of text: extra space (known as leading) can be inserted between lines to produce a more open appearance. Therefore, the line height must be specified separately, and this is done with the line-height property. Like font-size, this can be set in absolute units (usually pt or px), relative units (em), or as a percentage. In the case of line-height, the percentage is relative to the current font size (not any inherited line height). The line height can also be expressed as a number, which is multiplied by the font size. Thus, if the font size has been set to 12pt, the following four rules all have the same effect:

```
body { line-height: 15pt; }
body { line-height: 1.25em; }
body { line-height: 1.25; }
body { line-height: 125%; }
```

Notice, though, that the line height specified by the first of these rules will be the same irrespective of the font size, whereas the others will scale with the font.

Because it is often convenient to set several of the font properties and the line height at once, CSS has a font property to do exactly that. Its value consists of values for any or all of the font style, variant and weight (in any order) separated by spaces, followed by a font size, then optionally a / and a line height, and finally a font set. Defaults are used for any of the omitted values. The notation for the size and height is taken from conventional usage in typesetting, where 12pt text on a 14pt baseline is written 12pt/14pt. A CSS rule to set default font characteristics would be

```
body { font: 12pt/15pt Trebuchet,Verdana,sans-serif; }
```

Here, the style, variant and weight will take their default value. Although the notation for setting size and height is conventionally used for absolutely sized type, it can also be used with relative values. For instance, to set type in a small size with double the default line spacing, the following rule could be used:

```
body { font: small/200% Trebuchet,Verdana,sans-serif; }
```

Note that you cannot omit the size and font family components and have them inherited. If you wanted to set text belonging to the class `emphatic` in bold italics, for instance, you would need to use a rule like the following one:

```
.emphatic { font: italic bold small/200% Trebuchet,Verdana,sans-
serif; }
```

(In fact, it would be easier to use explicit `font-style` and `font-weight` declarations in this case.)

Text Decorations

The font-related properties determine the font from which character glyphs are taken. Other properties can be used to modify the appearance of text. We demonstrated at length in the early part of this chapter how to change the colour of text, using the `color` property. In Chapter 5 we will explain how to access the full range of colours.

Other forms of decoration are possible. The `font-decoration` property may take any of the values `underline`, `overline`, `line-through`, `none` or `blink`. Underlining is used so commonly for links, that it can have few other uses without confusing people. Overlining is rarely used at all. A line through text is sometimes used to indicate changes that have been made to a page. The value `none` is not redundant, since `text-decoration` is inherited, and this value must therefore be used to turn it off. The final value `blink` is something of a curiosity: its intended effect is to make the text disappear and reappear at regular (short) intervals. This mimics the effect of a custom HTML element, `blink`, that was once supported by some browsers. The result is irritating to most people and has the potential to cause seizures in some, so the element fell into disuse. As if ashamed of the presence of the `blink` value for `text-decoration`, the CSS2 standard specifies that '… user agents … are not required to support this value.'

It may seem that the case of letters is not a matter of presentation, but you may reflect that setting a heading in upper-case is often done for visual emphasis, so it can make sense to consider case as a style property, and CSS does so. The relevant property is `text-transform`, with the possible values `none`, `capitalize`, `uppercase` and `lowercase`. In this case, `capitalize` means setting the first letter of each word in upper case. (This style is sometimes called 'title case'.)

Formatting Paragraphs

The contents of block elements – paragraphs in particular – are laid out in lines, in the familiar way. This offers further scope for styling. A line will rarely fit the available width exactly. Extra space can be used to fill up lines in one of four ways. It can be added at the right hand end (for text that is written from right to left), so that the left edge of the paragraph is straight, but the right is ragged. Alternatively, it can be added at the left end, causing the right edge to be straight. A third option is to add an equal amount of space at both ends, so that both edges are ragged and each line is centred in the available width. Finally, the space may be distributed between the words, so that both edges are straight, but the inter-word spacing may not be the same on consecutive lines. Text laid out in this way is said to be *justified*. Figure 4.5 illustrates these four possibilities. The `text-align` property is used to determine which option is used; it takes the values `left`, `right`, `center` or `justify`. In general, left alignment is the best option for extended passages of text. Centred and right-aligned text may be useful for headings, or for certain kinds of list. Justification is the norm for many sorts of printed matter, including books and academic papers, but Web browsers make a poor job of justification compared with the specialized software used for typesetting. Justified text must, therefore, be used judiciously on Web pages.

One of the standard conventions for marking the start of a new paragraph is to indent the first line. To format paragraphs in this way using CSS, use the `text-indent` property, whose value is the length by which you want the first line indented. Relative units, such as ems can be used here, to produce an indent that scales with the font size. Note that it is only the first line's indentation that is controlled by this property. To indent an entire paragraph you must use other properties, which we will describe later. The `text-indent` value can be negative, to 'exdent' the first line, like this:

```
p.exdented { text-indent: -2em;}
```

However, unless there is space to the left of the paragraph, the exdented material will disappear. To produce hanging indentation, the entire paragraph must be indented, in the way we will describe later, and the first line indent set to a negative value.

There is a tradition in certain sorts of printing of giving more elaborate special treatment to the first line of a paragraph, or its first letter. CSS supports these special cases with the pseudo-classes `:first-line` and `:first-letter`, which may be used in selectors. You may sometimes see books in which the first line of certain paragraphs is set in boldface. This effect could be applied to every paragraph on a Web page with the following rule:

Lorem ipsum dolor sit amet, consectetur adipisicing elit, sed do eiusmod tempor incididunt ut labore et dolore magna aliqua. Ut enim ad minim veniam, quis nostrud exercitation ullamco laboris nisi ut aliquip ex ea commodo consequat. Duis aute irure dolor in reprehenderit in voluptate velit esse cillum dolore eu fugiat nulla pariatur. Excepteur sint occaecat cupidatat non proident, sunt in culpa qui officia deserunt mollit anim id est laborum.

left

Lorem ipsum dolor sit amet, consectetur adipisicing elit, sed do eiusmod tempor incididunt ut labore et dolore magna aliqua. Ut enim ad minim veniam, quis nostrud exercitation ullamco laboris nisi ut aliquip ex ea commodo consequat. Duis aute irure dolor in reprehenderit in voluptate velit esse cillum dolore eu fugiat nulla pariatur. Excepteur sint occaecat cupidatat non proident, sunt in culpa qui officia deserunt mollit anim id est laborum.

right

Lorem ipsum dolor sit amet, consectetur adipisicing elit, sed do eiusmod tempor incididunt ut labore et dolore magna aliqua. Ut enim ad minim veniam, quis nostrud exercitation ullamco laboris nisi ut aliquip ex ea commodo consequat. Duis aute irure dolor in reprehenderit in voluptate velit esse cillum dolore eu fugiat nulla pariatur. Excepteur sint occaecat cupidatat non proident, sunt in culpa qui officia deserunt mollit anim id est laborum.

center

Lorem ipsum dolor sit amet, consectetur adipisicing elit, sed do eiusmod tempor incididunt ut labore et dolore magna aliqua. Ut enim ad minim veniam, quis nostrud exercitation ullamco laboris nisi ut aliquip ex ea commodo consequat. Duis aute irure dolor in reprehenderit in voluptate velit esse cillum dolore eu fugiat nulla pariatur. Excepteur sint occaecat cupidatat non proident, sunt in culpa qui officia deserunt mollit anim id est laborum.

justify

Figure 4.5 Alignment of paragraphs

```
p:first-line { font-weight:bold; }
```

The first letter of a paragraph (usually the first paragraph of a chapter) is often set larger than the rest. A simple rule for doing this to every paragraph is

```
p:first-letter { font-size:200%; }
```

Lorem ipsum dolor sit amet, consectetur
adipisicing elit, sed do eiusmod tempor incididunt ut
labore et dolore magna aliqua. Ut enim ad minim
veniam, quis nostrud exercitation ullamco laboris nisi
ut aliquip ex ea commodo consequat. Duis aute irure
dolor in reprehenderit in voluptate velit esse cillum
dolore eu fugiat nulla pariatur. Excepteur sint
occaecat cupidatat non proident, sunt in culpa qui
officia deserunt mollit anim id est laborum.

Figure 4.6 Applying special styling to the first line and letter of a paragraph

Figure 4.6 shows the combined effect of these rules. The large initial letter sticks up above the first line, which is a nice and fairly modern-looking style. More traditionally, large initials are set as 'drop caps', which fall below the line, with later lines wrapping round them. We will explain how to achieve that effect later in the chapter.

Layout

The properties described so far allow you to control the appearance of text to the extent that a basic word processor would support. Achieving more sophisticated results requires an understanding of the 'box model' that is used for controlling the layout of elements within a page.

Every element (including the body) is placed inside a box. As the name suggests, a box is a rectangular area which contains the styled content of the element. Each box is divided into regions, as shown in Figure 4.7. The bounding box of the content forms the innermost region. This is surrounded by some *padding*, which separates it from a *border*. Often, the border has a thickness of zero, because you rarely want to surround elements with visible borders. Outside the border is a transparent *margin* region, which will separate the box from its neighbours when the boxes for the elements on a page are laid out on the screen. As the figure indicates, the padding, border and margin regions do not have to be symmetrical with respect to the content. For instance, the padding below an element may be bigger than the padding above it. Any or all of these regions may have a thickness of zero. The margins' thickness may be negative, in which case the content may extend beyond the box.

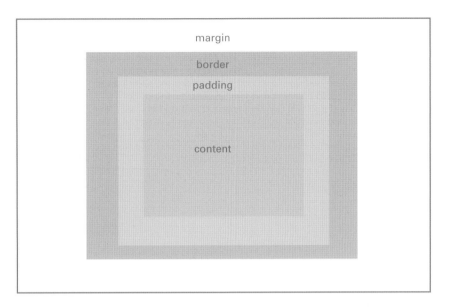

Figure 4.7 The CSS box model

Layout Algorithm for Normal Flow

The boxes containing the contents of the elements making up a page must be placed together in a browser window to display the page to a user. CSS2 has facilities that allow page authors to position the boxes just about wherever they want, relative to the page or relative to each other. If these facilities are not used, though, the browser puts the boxes together so that their content can be read from top to bottom, and in the normal reading direction for the page's language. (We will consistently assume that this is left to right; the necessary adjustments for right to left text should be obvious.) This is said to be the **normal flow** layout.

The essence of the layout algorithm for normal flow is easy to grasp: boxes for inline elements and the textual content of block elements are laid out next to each other, and then 'folded up' to fit inside the content region of the box of the block element that contains them. The boxes for block elements are then placed one above the other in the window. (See Figure 4.8.) The details are slightly complicated, though, especially in respect of the width of block elements' boxes.

Box Widths

Just as every element, except the document root, has an ancestor, every box has a **containing box**, which is the box corresponding to its closest block-level ancestor element.

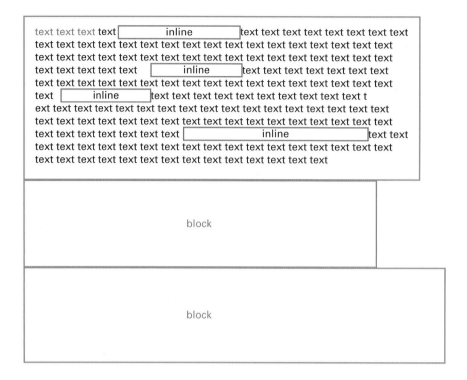

Figure 4.8 Normal flow

The root element's containing box is determined by the browser – in effect, it is the browser window. Thus, given the document body

```
<body>
  <div>
  This <span class="code">div</span> element contains some bare text
  as well as an embedded paragraph.
    <p>
    This paragraph lies <em>within</em> the <span class="xref">
    <span class="code">div</span> element</span>, so it is an example
    of a block element within a block element.
    </p>
  </div>
</body>
```

the containing box of the p element's box is that of the div, as is that of the first occurrence of a span with class="code". The boxes for both the span elements nested inside the paragraph are contained in the p element's box. The second occurrence of a span with class="code" does not have the span with class="xref" as its containing box, because containing boxes must correspond to block elements.

As this little example reminds you, div elements may contain bare text as well as block elements. For the purposes of layout, such text is considered to be in an anonymous box, as if it was the content of some block element. The containing box of the em element is therefore the anonymous box that holds the first sentence inside the div.

Text and inline elements are folded into lines so that they fit within the content area of their containing box. Extra space is added to fill up the width, according to the text-align property. This may entail breaking apart the box for an inline element, and assigning the parts to separate boxes on consecutive lines. Words are never broken using hyphens, though, and the line-breaking algorithms employed by Web browsers are not very sophisticated, so the resulting text is not laid out to the highest standards. After this, the block elements are laid out vertically inside their containing block. If there are nested block elements (divs within divs, for example), this process is repeated.

The main question that remains is: how is the width of each block element's box determined? This is what determines the length of the lines in which the inline elements are arranged.

Conceptually, the simplest case arises if the width is set explicitly to some absolute value. This is done by assigning a value in absolute units, such as pixels, to the width property. For instance

```
p { width: 600px; }
```

would set the content region of all paragraphs to be 600 pixels wide (unless a more specific rule applied). The text of each paragraph would be wrapped to fit into lines of that length. (The width of the padding, border and margin areas can be set independently using other properties, as we will describe later. Since the text only flows inside the content region, these properties have no influence on its layout.) Since px units have been specified, every paragraph to which the rule applied would be the same width. In particular, the paragraphs' width would be independent of the font size.

If, however, the width is specified using ems, like this:

```
p { width: 30em; }
```

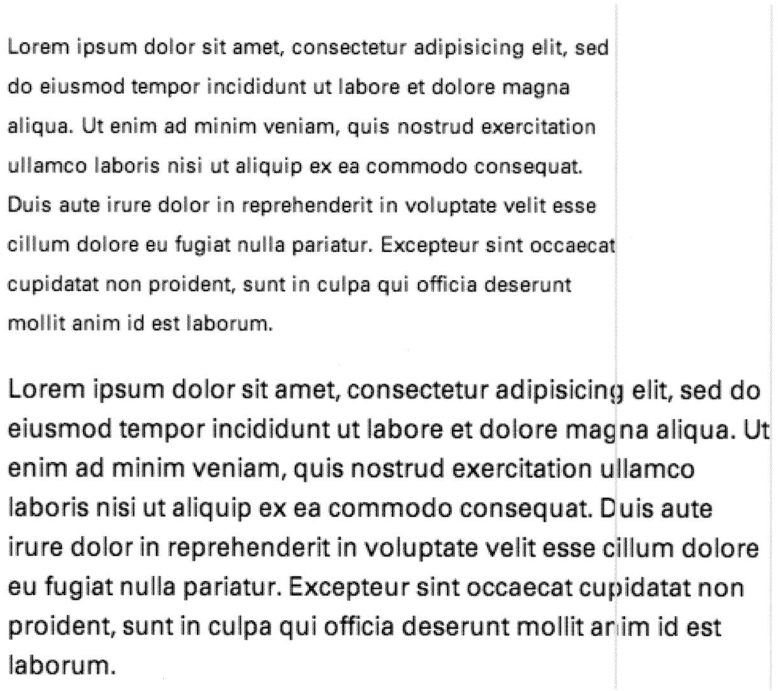

Lorem ipsum dolor sit amet, consectetur adipisicing elit, sed do eiusmod tempor incididunt ut labore et dolore magna aliqua. Ut enim ad minim veniam, quis nostrud exercitation ullamco laboris nisi ut aliquip ex ea commodo consequat. Duis aute irure dolor in reprehenderit in voluptate velit esse cillum dolore eu fugiat nulla pariatur. Excepteur sint occaecat cupidatat non proident, sunt in culpa qui officia deserunt mollit anim id est laborum.

Lorem ipsum dolor sit amet, consectetur adipisicing elit, sed do eiusmod tempor incididunt ut labore et dolore magna aliqua. Ut enim ad minim veniam, quis nostrud exercitation ullamco laboris nisi ut aliquip ex ea commodo consequat. Duis aute irure dolor in reprehenderit in voluptate velit esse cillum dolore eu fugiat nulla pariatur. Excepteur sint occaecat cupidatat non proident, sunt in culpa qui officia deserunt mollit anim id est laborum.

Figure 4.9 Paragraph widths specified in em units

paragraphs set in different-sized type would have different widths, because the em unit relates to the font size within the paragraph (see Figure 4.9).

Furthermore, when paragraph widths are specified in em units, a user who increased the size of the type in their browser would see a 'zooming' effect, as the text and its enclosing boxes became larger. On the other hand, if the paragraph width is specified in pixels or some other absolute unit, the enlarged text would reflow to fit within the specified width when the font size is increased (see Figure 4.10).

A slightly more complex situation arises if the value of width is given as a percentage, for what is it a percentage of? The only sensible answer is that the percentage must refer to the containing box. In fact, it is a percentage of that box's content region. (Usually… we will explain later on how it sometimes includes its padding.) This makes intuitive sense, because that is the region into which enclosed boxes must be fitted. A consequence of this arrangement is that, if the containing box's width is specified in relative units, any enclosed boxes whose widths are percentages will expand along with it.

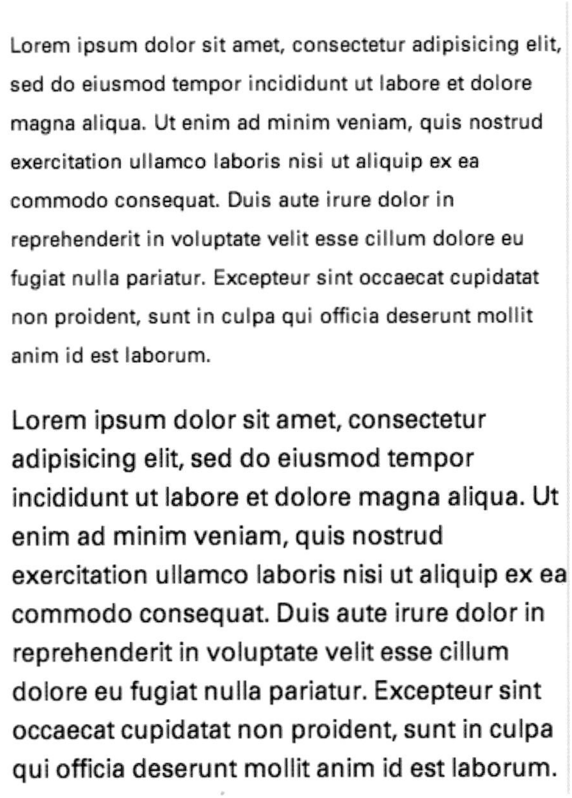

Lorem ipsum dolor sit amet, consectetur adipisicing elit, sed do eiusmod tempor incididunt ut labore et dolore magna aliqua. Ut enim ad minim veniam, quis nostrud exercitation ullamco laboris nisi ut aliquip ex ea commodo consequat. Duis aute irure dolor in reprehenderit in voluptate velit esse cillum dolore eu fugiat nulla pariatur. Excepteur sint occaecat cupidatat non proident, sunt in culpa qui officia deserunt mollit anim id est laborum.

Lorem ipsum dolor sit amet, consectetur adipisicing elit, sed do eiusmod tempor incididunt ut labore et dolore magna aliqua. Ut enim ad minim veniam, quis nostrud exercitation ullamco laboris nisi ut aliquip ex ea commodo consequat. Duis aute irure dolor in reprehenderit in voluptate velit esse cillum dolore eu fugiat nulla pariatur. Excepteur sint occaecat cupidatat non proident, sunt in culpa qui officia deserunt mollit anim id est laborum.

Figure 4.10 Paragraph widths specified in px units

An interesting degenerate case arises when the containing box is the browser window. This will happen to block elements that are not contained in any other element with an explicitly specified width. In that case, as you would expect, the following rule causes all paragraphs to extend half-way across the window:

```
p { width: 50%; }
```

This relationship is maintained no matter what the width of the window, and continues to be maintained if the user resizes the browser window. In that case, the text reflows in order to keep the lines restricted to half the width of the window.

This brings us to the final possibility. What if the width is not specified for a block element? In that case, as you might guess, the width is computed so that the element's box fills the available width. That is, the sum of its left and right margins, borders and padding, together with the width of the content region, must add up to the width of the containing block. We will describe in the next section how to set the widths of the margins and so on, but it will hold few surprises. As long as all the relevant properties have explicit values, the content of the inner box will flow into the available left-over space. The same result is achieved by specifying the width explicitly as auto. In the degenerate case, where the containing block is the window, the text of the page will be broken into lines that fill the available width, reflowing as the window is resized, in the familiar fashion.

Where widths are specified in relative units, it is possible that some combination of font size and window width may lead to impossibly narrow or inconveniently wide text boxes. To avoid this possibility, the properties min-width and max-width can be used to specify a minimum and maximum width. If the computed width is less than the minimum, the minimum is used, and similarly if the computed width is greater than the maximum, the maximum is used. Thus, if you wanted a paragraph to be half the width of its containing box, unless that exceeded 30em in the current font, you could use the following rule:

```
p {
    width: 50%;
    max-width: 30em;
}
```

Box Height and Overflow

Since boxes are rectangles, they have height as well as width; you can specify the height of their content region using the height property. Like width, its value can be a length in absolute units, which does not therefore scale with font size, a length in relative units, such as ems, which does, or a percentage. In this case, this is a percentage of the height of the content region of any enclosing box. In the case that the enclosing box is the browser window, though, using a percentage height is meaningless, since windows are effectively unbounded in height. You can also leave the height unspecified, or set it to auto. If you do so, the box will be made tall enough to accommodate its contents.

There are min-height and max-height properties to set bounds on the height in the same way as min-width and max-width limit the width.

If a box's height is set explicitly, it is possible that the contents will be too tall to fit into it. For instance, given the rule

```
p { height: 6em; line-height: 1.2em; }
```

any paragraph longer than five lines will be taller than its box. What happens to the over-matter (the lines that won't fit) depends on the value of the overflow property.

If overflow is set to hidden, the paragraph is clipped to the box; over-matter disappears. (This can actually be very convenient, as we will demonstrate later.) In contrast, if overflow is set to visible, the over-matter spills out below the box. This may cause it to run into any following text, usually with illegible results. An alternative is to set overflow to scroll. This causes scroll bars to be added to the box, so that over-matter can be brought into view by scrolling. It is difficult to make this look good on a page, and, since scroll bars require a certain amount of vertical space to display their arrows, using this setting with very short boxes may produce peculiar results which can be very frustrating for users. A final possible value for overflow is auto. The effect is browser-dependent, but should cause scroll bars to be provided if they are necessary; the standard does not stipulate whether they should be displayed if there is no over-matter, but a common interpretation of auto is to display scroll bars only when there is over-matter.

The overflow value is inherited. If there is no explicit value available to be inherited, it defaults to visible.

Padding, Borders and Margins

There are CSS properties for controlling the size of each of the padding, border and margin regions. For each of these regions there are five separate properties. We will illustrate the pattern these follow by describing the properties controlling the padding.

To set the thickness of the padding on each of the four sides of the box, you can use the properties padding-top, padding-right, padding-bottom and padding-left, each of which affects the side indicated by the last part of its name. The value may be a length, specified in any unit. You can use px, for instance, to set a padding width that is independent of the font size, or you can use em to get a padding whose width scales up with the font size. You can also specify a percentage. This will be interpreted as a percentage of the width of the containing box (not the box to which the property is being applied). Percentages in this context (unlike the height property) relate to the enclosing box's *width*, even for vertical measurements, such as the thickness of the top and bottom borders.

Values	Effect
v	top = right = bottom = left = v
v1 v2	top = bottom = v1, right = left = v2
v1 v2 v3	top = v1, right = left = v2, bottom = v3
v1 v2 v3 v4	top = v1, right = v2, bottom = v3, left = v4

Table 4.1 Shorthand notation for properties

The padding property is provided as a shorthand for setting the thickness of the padding on all four sides at once. It takes between one and four values (separated by spaces), which are interpreted as shown in Table 4.1.

For example,

```
h1 { padding: 1em 0em 0.5em; }
```

is equivalent to

```
h1 {
    padding-top: 1em;
    padding-right: 0em;
    padding-bottom: 0.5em;
    padding-right: 0em;
}
```

Region	Properties for Individual Sides	Shorthand
padding	padding-top, padding-right, padding-left, padding-bottom	padding
border	border-top-width, border-right-width, border-left-width, border-bottom-width	border-width
	border-top-color, border-right-color, border-left-color, border-bottom-color	border-color
	border-top-style, border-right-style, border-left-style, border-bottom-style	border-style
margin	margin-top, margin-right, margin-left, margin-bottom	margin

Table 4.2 Properties controlling the box regions

You may find it easier to remember how these values work if you bear in mind that the specified values are applied to the sides in clockwise order: the first value is always applied to the top, the second, if present, is always applied to the right, the third to the bottom, the fourth to the left. Missing values are filled in by symmetry.

This pattern of four properties to set the thicknesses of individual sides and a fifth shorthand to set all four at once is used for all the regions of the box whose thickness can be controlled by the stylesheet. The names of the relevant properties are given in Table 4.2. As a special case, the properties for the border widths can also take one of the values `thick`, `medium` and `thin`, which give standard borders; the actual thickness corresponding to these values is browser-dependent. The only guarantee about them is that a thick border will be at least as thick as a medium border, which will be at least as thick as a thin one.

Borders

The table includes some extra properties which control borders. Since these are potentially visible, their appearance may vary as well as their thickness. These properties, too, come in sets of five, which follow the same pattern as `border-width` and its relatives. The colour is controlled by `border-color` and its variants, whose value can be any colour name or a more precise colour specification of the kind we will describe in Chapter 5. The `border-style` properties control the kind of line used for the border. The available set of values is summarized in Table 4.3.

Value	Appearance
none	no border
hidden	no border, and suppress any coincident box's border
dotted	a dotted line
dashed	a dashed line
solid	a solid line
double	two parallel solid lines with a gap between them
groove	a groove carved into the page
ridge	a ridge extruded from the page
inset	a shaded border that makes the box appear to be sunk into the page
outset	a shaded border that makes the box appear to be coming out of the page

Table 4.3 Border styles

Emerging Technology

CSS3 Borders

Some Web designers have expended a great deal of energy and ingenuity creating boxes with rounded corners, using a mixture of tricky XHTML markup, CSS backgrounds and even JavaScript. The CSS3 Backgrounds and Borders Module defines a `border-radius` property, which will make all this effort redundant. It takes two lengths, which define the radii of a quarter-ellipse to be used as the corner of a box border. The radii of the four corners can be defined separately, so for example, tabs with round corners can be produced by setting non-zero radii for the two top corners of a box.

The same module defines a `border-image` property, which allows you to define an image to be used along the border, so that you can have fancy patterned borders, as favoured for intertitles in silent melodramas.

The CSS3 Backgrounds and Borders Module is only a working draft at the time of writing, so the details of this feature may change before it is generally implemented in browsers.

There is still another level of shorthand applicable to borders. The style, width and colour of the border on any side can all be set at the same time, using `border-top`, `border-right`, `border-bottom`, `border-left` and `border`. These take up to three values, specifying the style (as in `border-style`), the width (as in `border-width`) and colour (as in `border-color`), in any order. Thus, the following rule puts elements belonging to the class boxed into a thin red box:

```
.boxed { border: thin red solid; }
```

Omitted values are set to defaults (which usually means that they are inherited). The values specified for the `border` property are applied to the borders on all four sides of the box – you can't specify different values for different sides, the way you can with `padding` and so on.

Despite the wealth of properties for controlling the appearance of borders, you probably won't use them very often.

Collapsing Margins

The values for `margin-top` and `margin-bottom` for vertically adjacent boxes are combined when boxes are placed above each other in the normal flow. The way this is done sounds odd, but it usually produces the expected effect. If the adjacent margins' values are either both positive or both negative, the margins are collapsed and the space between the boxes is set to the value with the larger magnitude. For instance, suppose the following rules apply:

```
p {
    font-size: 14px;
    margin-top: 1em;
    margin-bottom: 6em;
}
h1 {
    font-size: 18px;
    margin-top: 0em;
    margin-bottom: 3em;
}
```

and a document contained a level 1 heading followed by two paragraphs. The distance below the heading would be 54px (3em in the specified font size): the top margin of the paragraph would have been removed. Similarly, the space between paragraphs would be 84px, not 98px, because of the collapsing margins. However, if one of the margins is negative and the other postive, their values are added (i.e. the negative value is taken off the positive one), so if the paragraph rule was changed to

```
p {
    font-size: 14px;
    margin-top: -1em;
    margin-bottom: 6em;
}
```

the negative margin above the paragraphs would be subtracted, giving a distance of just 40px between the heading and the first paragraph.

These rules perhaps appear somewhat arbitrary, but in practice they usually behave so as to honour the designer's likely intent, maintaining important vertical spacing rules and discarding lesser ones where there is potentially a conflict. For straightforward layouts, it may be advisable to use either bottom or top margins consistently for spacing most elements, so that the question of collapsing margins does not arise.

Backgrounds

The background of every element's box can be set independently, either to a colour or to an image. To be precise, the background of the content, padding and border regions can be set to a colour or an image: the margin region is always transparent. Solid borders obscure the background, but if a dashed border is used, the background will show through in the gaps between the dashes.

The case of a plain coloured background is extremely simple: the background-color property has a colour name or specification (see Chapter 5) as its value, so the rule

```
.highlighted { background-color: yellow; }
```

would cause all elements belonging to the class highlighted to appear on a yellow background. To put the entire page on a coloured background, you simply use a rule that sets the background-color for the body element, like this:

```
body { background-color: gray; }
```

The value transparent may also be used, which has the effect of letting whatever is below the element show through. It is the default value for this property so – although backgrounds are not, technically speaking, inherited – the background of an element's parent will, by default, show through behind the element, giving the same effect as if it was inherited.

More elaborate pages can be created by using images as backgrounds. The background-image property is used for this purpose. It is the first example we have seen of a property which has a URL as its value. In such cases, the value is written as url(*the url*). For instance,

```
body { background-image: url(bg.gif); }
```

This rule would place the image found at the URL bg.gif behind the content of the document body. While using an image as the background for the entire page is perhaps the most common use of the background-image property, it can be used in any rule, to apply a background to any element in the document. Applying different backgrounds to div elements can be an effective way of breaking up a page into visually distinct regions.

It is unlikely that any particular image will fit exactly the area occupied by a page or element – especially since pages can be resized by the user. If the image is larger than the box it will be clipped, but what happens if the background image is too small to fill the box it has been

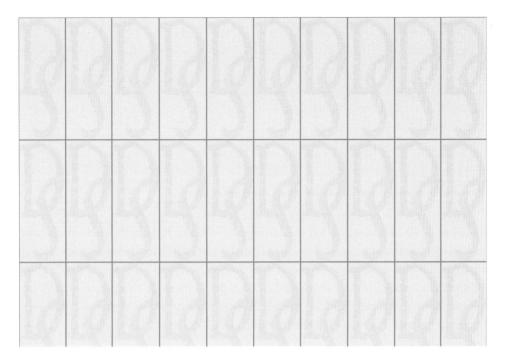

Figure 4.11 A tiled background

applied to? This depends on the value of the background-repeat property. If this is repeat (which it is by default), the image will be tiled, that is copies of it will be placed across and down the box to fill up the available space (see Figure 4.11 – we have added orange lines to show the edges of the tiles). This behaviour is most appropriately used to fill the background with a texture. For this to work, the image must be designed so that copies of it fit together smoothly, or at least in such a way as to create an obviously deliberate pattern.

If you intend to use a single image as a background for all the other content of a page, make sure to set background-repeat to no-repeat. This prevents tiling occurring: a single copy of the background image is used, and if it is too small, the background colour is used for the rest of the box. Failure to prevent a background image repeating in this way leads to pages that look amateur at best.

Between the two extreme options for background-repeat there are two other possibilities: repeat-x and repeat-y cause the image to be repeated horizontally and vertically, respectively. Figure 4.12 shows a possible application of horizontal tiling. The colour at the bottom of the gradient matches the background colour of the page, so no matter how tall

Figure 4.12 A background gradient using horizontal tiling

the window is, the colour at the top will always fade into the body of the page. In all cases where a background texture is produced by tiling, the tiled image itself can be much smaller than the box it fills: the gradient in Figure 4.12 is only two pixels wide, for instance. Thus, the background image will only occupy a small number of bytes. In contrast, an image that is used to provide a background for the whole page must be big enough to fill the page in a typical browser. Using such a background may noticeably increase the time a page takes to download.

One of the more interesting things you can do with a background image on a page that is too long to fit in a browser window is to hold it fixed while the page content scrolls on top of it – this is an effect that has no analogy in printed matter. The relevant CSS property is `background-attachment`. Setting this to `scroll` (its default value) allows the background image to be scrolled along with the rest of the page, but setting it to fixed holds the background, allowing the page content to slide over it as the user scrolls down the page. (Try it.) There isn't much point in fixing a repeated background, but if a single image is used, fixing it in this way should ensure that it is always visible behind the page.

There is a shorthand `background` property, which has as its value a list of values for the background properties. It is not necessary to include values for all of the properties `background-color`, `background-image`, `background-repeat`, `background-attachment` and `background-position` because default values will be used for any that are omitted. For example,

```
body { background: gray url(bg.gif); }
```

would be sufficient to set the background colour to grey, and use the image in `bg.gif` as a tiled scrolling background.

As in this example, it is a good idea to specify a background colour even if a background image is being used, to provide a fallback in case the image is not available owing to server or network errors. If the image has any transparent areas the background colour will show through them, so it is also necessary to provide a colour for such a contingency. (You cannot rely on the browser default for a background colour being set to white; several browsers allow the user to specify a default colour.)

Positioning

The normal flow algorithm produces a single text flow, intended to be read from top to bottom. This is not always what is required. Most monitors are wider than they are tall, which means that they can accommodate relatively short fat windows. There is ample evidence, though, that using long lines of text substantially decreases readability for most people, so if a designer wishes to take advantage of the available width it will be necessary to break the page into regions, none of which is excessively wide. (As a rule of thumb, a line of text is definitely too long if it exceeds seventy characters.) One possibility is to emulate the multi-column layout of newspapers; a more popular alternative is to use a fairly narrow region for the main textual content, and separate regions for auxiliary matter, such as navbars or external references. We will look at layout design in Chapter 10. Here we will describe the various mechanisms provided by CSS for breaking out of the normal flow.

Floats

The longest established way of disrupting the normal flow is by *floating* elements to one side. A floated element is taken from its position in the normal flow and moved as far left or right as possible, to the edge of its containing block. That is, if a box is floated to the left, it is positioned with its left edge coincident with the left edge of its containing box. Meanwhile, the normal flow continues down the right of the floated box (the lines being made shorter to make room for the float), as shown in Figure 4.13, where the coloured background shows the extent of the floated box. The top of the floated box is aligned with the top of the line in which the floated element appears. Once floated, a box becomes a block box, irrespective of the element whose content it contains. The float property controls floated elements. Its possible values are left, right and none, with the obvious meanings.

To force an element past a float and restore the normal flow, use the clear property, which has the possible values left, right and both, specifying which side of the element's box may *not* have a float next to it. For instance, if clear is set to left for a paragraph element, the paragraph will be placed on the first available line that does not have any preceding left-floated element beside it. In other words, it is pushed past any left floats that would have interfered with its normal flow.

Lorem ipsum dolor sit amet, consectetur adipisicing elit. Lorem ipsum dolor sit amet, consectetur adipisicing elit, sed do eiusmod tempor incididunt ut labore et dolore magna aliqua. Ut enim ad minim veniam, quis nostrud exercitation ullamco laboris nisi ut aliquip ex ea commodo consequat. Duis aute irure dolor in reprehenderit in voluptate velit esse cillum dolore eu fugiat nulla pariatur. Excepteur sint occaecat cupidatat non proident, sunt in culpa qui officia deserunt mollit anim id est laborum. Lorem ipsum dolor sit amet, consectetur adipisicing elit, sed do eiusmod tempor incididunt ut labore et dolore magna aliqua. Ut enim ad minim veniam, quis nostrud exercitation ullamco laboris nisi ut aliquip ex ea commodo consequat. Duis aute irure dolor in reprehenderit in voluptate velit esse cillum dolore eu fugiat nulla pariatur. Excepteur sint occaecat cupidatat non proident, sunt in culpa qui officia deserunt mollit anim id est laborum.

Figure 4.13 A left-floated element

Traditionally, floats have been used for wrapping text around images that are too narrow to be sensibly placed on their own, but in conjunction with other CSS features they can be used to produce some attractive and useful text layouts.

Floating provides a way of implementing dropped initials, as illustrated in Figure 4.14. You will recall from earlier in this chapter that the :first-letter pseudo-class lets us apply special formatting to the first letter of a paragraph or other element, but that simply increasing the size of the first letter makes it stick up above the first line, rather than being embedded in the paragraph in the more traditional manner. The required behaviour is precisely that of a float. It is necessary to use a little care and some experimentation in setting the padding, margins and line height to make an initial letter of any given size fit into the paragraph. Figure 4.14 was produced using the following rule:

L orem ipsum dolor sit amet, consectetur adipisicing elit, sed do eiusmod tempor incididunt ut labore et dolore magna aliqua. Ut enim ad minim veniam, quis nostrud exercitation ullamco laboris nisi ut aliquip ex ea commodo consequat. Duis aute irure dolor in reprehenderit in voluptate velit esse cillum dolore eu fugiat nulla pariatur. Excepteur sint occaecat cupidatat non proident, sunt in culpa qui officia deserunt mollit anim id est laborum.

Figure 4.14 A dropped initial letter

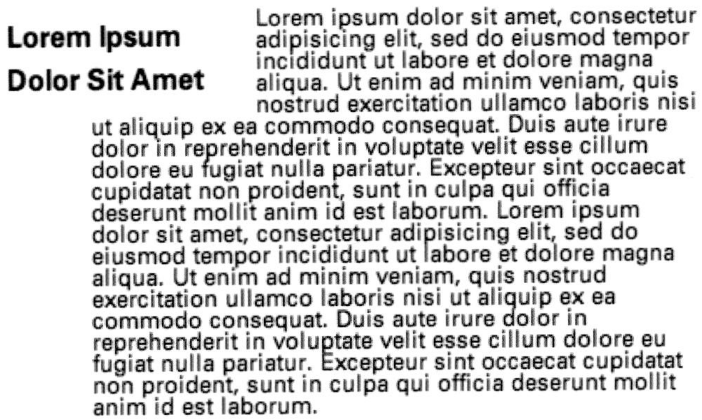

Lorem Ipsum Dolor Sit Amet Lorem ipsum dolor sit amet, consectetur adipisicing elit, sed do eiusmod tempor incididunt ut labore et dolore magna aliqua. Ut enim ad minim veniam, quis nostrud exercitation ullamco laboris nisi ut aliquip ex ea commodo consequat. Duis aute irure dolor in reprehenderit in voluptate velit esse cillum dolore eu fugiat nulla pariatur. Excepteur sint occaecat cupidatat non proident, sunt in culpa qui officia deserunt mollit anim id est laborum. Lorem ipsum dolor sit amet, consectetur adipisicing elit, sed do eiusmod tempor incididunt ut labore et dolore magna aliqua. Ut enim ad minim veniam, quis nostrud exercitation ullamco laboris nisi ut aliquip ex ea commodo consequat. Duis aute irure dolor in reprehenderit in voluptate velit esse cillum dolore eu fugiat nulla pariatur. Excepteur sint occaecat cupidatat non proident, sunt in culpa qui officia deserunt mollit anim id est laborum.

Figure 4.15 A called-out heading

```
p:first-letter {
    width: auto;
    margin: 0em;
    padding:0 0.1em 0 0;
    font-size: 300%;
    line-height:0.733em;
    float: left;
}
```

A more radical use of floated boxes is to provide 'called out' headings, such as the one in Figure 4.15. Here, instead of putting the section heading on a line above the section, in the conventional manner, it has been placed in a box which has been floated to the left. You will notice a significant difference between the placement of the call-out in this example and the dropped initial in the previous one: the call-out box sticks out so that it only partly overlaps the following paragraph. This creates a more effective visual distinction. It is done by adding padding to the left of the paragraph, while placing the h1 element for the call-out before the p element in the XHTML document. Thus, the containing box for the heading is the body's box, and the call-out moves all the way to the left of it. The paragraph shares this containing box, but – because of its left padding – the actual text is indented from the left, allowing room for the call-out to overlap. The relevant CSS rules are as follows:

```
h1 {
    width: 8em;
    float: left;
    color: black;
    font-size: 125%;
```

```
    line-height: 150%;
    padding: 0.25em;
    margin:0 0.5em 0 0;
}
p { padding: 0 0 0 4em; }
```

The XHTML document's body has the following outline:

```
<body>
<h1>Lorem...</h1>
<p>
Lorem ipsum...
</p>
</body>
```

Once again, some care and experimentation is required in setting the exact padding and margin values. Note also that the width of the call-out box has been set explicitly.

The idea of floating a box so that it ends up in the padding area of following paragraphs can be taken further. If the padding is made wider than the floating box, then the latter will end up entirely to the left of any paragraph. It can then be used as a place to put content that is complementary to the main page – a navbar or a collection of links to other sites, for example. This is a commonly employed layout that makes good use of the available space in the window.

Absolute Positioning

Normal flow and floating provide a surprising amount of flexibility for designing page layouts that adapt themselves to different screen and font sizes, but sometimes it will be necessary to exert more explicit control over the positioning of elements on the screen. This can be done by setting the `position` property to `absolute`. If this is done, then some or all of the properties `left`, `right`, `top` and `bottom` can be set in order to determine the position of the four sides of the box. The box will be removed from the normal flow, and placed according to the values of these properties, each of which is a length, measured from the corresponding side of the box's containing box to the edge of the box's margin on that side (see Figure 4.16). As the diagram shows, for absolutely positioned elements, the position is measured relative to the outside of any padding in the containing box, but to the edge of the margin of the absolutely positioned box.

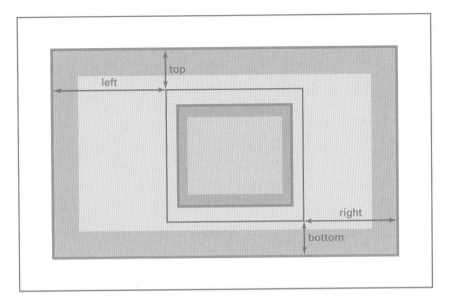

Figure 4.16 Absolute positioning

Effectively, absolute positioning allows you to place an arbitrarily sized box anywhere you want it on a Web page. It would seem, therefore, to be the perfect approach to layout, allowing designers to compose a page from boxes, much as they would when creating page layouts for print in a desktop publishing application such as InDesign. However, the Web is not a print medium, and some consequences of this make absolute positioning slightly less attractive than it might seem at first sight.

There is one technical point that can be easily dismissed. Astute readers will have understood that if `left`, `right` and `width` are all specified, there is a potential for disagreement about how wide the box should be. In such a case, the value of `width` takes precedence: if the language of the page is read from left to right, the value of `right` is ignored; if it is read from right to left, the value of `left` is ignored. Similarly, if the specified values lead to a conflict in determining the box's height, the `height` property is used. Generally, the best way to position a box is using `left` and `top`, essentially providing the coordinates of its top left corner, and then specifying its size, if that is desired, with `width` and `height`.

Thornier issues are raised by the different units in which values for the positions of the box's sides may be specified. These are lengths, so they can be specified in absolute units (such as `px`) or relative units (such as `em`). If absolute units are used, then the position is also absolute, that is, it is independent of any font size. This might seem to be what is required, but if there are several boxes on a page, their interactions need to be taken into account. Consider, for example, the following stylesheet for a two-column page:

```
div {
    position: absolute;
    width: 350px;
    height: 600px;
}
#leftcolumn {
    top: 0px;
    left: 0px;
    background-color: gray;
}
#rightcolumn {
    top: 0px;
    left: 350px;
    background-color: silver;
}
```

The stylesheet could be used in conjunction with an XHTML document with the following structure:

```
<body>
 <div id="leftcolumn">
  contents of the left column
 </div>
 <div id="rightcolumn">
 contents of the right column
 </div>
</body>
```

The result would be a page with two text boxes side by side, each 350px wide. Because of the fixed width, this layout would be vulnerable to changes in font size. If the font size was changed, either by the designer or the user, any text that had been fitted to the two boxes would reflow. Since the height of the boxes is fixed, any overmatter would spill out by default. This can be avoided by changing the height to auto, but this could cause the boxes themselves to grow taller if the font size was increased, which might result in their overlapping any absolutely positioned elements lower down the page.

These problems can be partially avoided by specifying the boxes' dimensions in em units:

```
div {
   position: absolute;
   width: 25em;
   height: 50em;
}
```

Now the boxes will grow to accommodate any increase in the font size, but, because the left side of the right column is positioned absolutely at 350px, the left column will overlap the right if it expands, and if it shrinks a gap will appear between the two. Therefore, the position of the left side of the right column must now also be specified in em units, so that it moves to accommodate any change in the width of the left column. Similar considerations apply to the top of any boxes positioned below these two.

As with box dimensions, positions can also be specified as a percentage. In this context, percentages refer to the corresponding dimension of the containing box, so one way of splitting our page into two columns would be to use the rule

```
div {
   position: absolute;
   width: 50%;
   height: auto;
}
```

with a corresponding change to the left value for the right column. This way, the two columns will expand or contract if the browser window is resized, while maintaining their relationship.

Hopefully, these considerations will seem obvious. However, a common way of using absolutely positioned boxes for layouts consists of drawing the boxes on screen in a visual Web authoring program, so that the designer can position them by eye. Almost without exception, such programs will generate layout rules which combine absolute positioning with absolute units, which will lead to the problems outlined above.

When boxes can be placed anywhere on the page, the possibility of their overlapping arises. (Text does not flow around an absolutely positioned element the way it does around a floated one.) If two boxes overlap, partially or totally, the question arises of which is in front, since whichever it is will obscure the box behind it. The stacking of elements is controlled by the z-index property, which may have any integer as its value. This property only applies to absolutely positioned elements. Although the full details of the stacking algorithm are

Technical Detail

Fixed and Relative Positioning

These two variations on the absolute positioning scheme deserve a brief mention.

If the `position` property is set to fixed, the box is positioned according to `left`, `top` and so on, with respect to the browser window, irrespective of which part of the page is being displayed. In other words, the box for an element whose position is fixed stays still if the content of the window is scrolled, in the same way as a fixed background image does. Fixed positioning can be used to keep an element such as a navbar in a fixed and easily accessible position on the screen as the user scrolls through a long page.

If `position` is `relative`, `left`, `top`, `right` and `bottom` define offsets from the edges of the box that the element would have occupied if it had been set in the normal flow. One possible use of relative positioning is to move elements into sub- and superscript positions below or above the normal baseline. More interestingly, if an absolutely positioned element appears within a relatively positioned element, it will be positioned relative to the containing block of the latter. Since a relatively positioned element moves as text reflows (because it is offset with respect to its position in the normal flow), the enclosed absolutely positioned box will move too. This can be used, for instance, to place images in the margin that stay aligned with some textual element within the text. (If an element is relatively positioned, but all the offsets have value zero, it remains where it would have been in the normal flow, but can be used as the basis for absolute positioning.)

surprisingly complex, in most cases the behaviour is simple: elements are stacked from front to back in increasing order of z-index. The content of the root element effectively has a z-index of zero, so to put a box behind that, its z-index must be negative. The content of boxes behind the frontmost box will show through any transparent areas; setting a background colour or image will conceal any underlying content.

A little thought will show you that, strictly speaking, absolutely positioned elements are actually positioned relatively, since the left and top properties specify distances from the edges of the containing block, which might itself be an absolutely positioned element. Only elements at the outermost level are positioned absolutely with respect to the page.

In case you ever need to specify it explicitly, the normal flow algorithm is used if the `position` property is set to `static`.

Special Cases

Links

The source anchors of links demand special typographic treatment. It is vital that users be able to identify links. The customary way of distinguishing them is by underlining; traditionalists also colour them blue. In XHTML (including XHTML 2), source anchors are always elements with an `href` attribute, so an attribute selector would suffice in a rule that was intended to apply to links. This is not the case in XML, though, so CSS provides a pseudo-class `:link`, which matches any elements that are links. Thus, to enforce traditional link designations in XHTML documents, either of the following rules could be used:

```
:link { color:blue; text-decoration:underlined;}
a:link { color:blue; text-decoration:underlined;}
```

More varied and subtle underlines can be produced by applying a bottom border to linking elements, and using the various possibilities offered by the `border-bottom-style` property. For instance

```
a:link {
   border-bottom: dotted blue 0.15em;
   text-decoration: none;
   color: inherit;
}
```

will cause a subtle blue dotted underline to appear beneath links.

Three other link-related pseudo-classes are also provided; these make possible some effects which cannot be achieved by any other form of selector. The first, `:visited`, matches the source anchors of links that the user has already visited. (The question of how recently a link must have been visited to count as a visited link is an open one. The CSS standard merely notes that after a certain amount of time a user agent may return a visited link to the unvisited state, when it will belong to the pseudo-class `:link` again, not `:visited`.) The following CSS rule causes visited links to be shown in purple, as early browsers always did.

```
a:visited { color:purple; text-decoration:underlined;}
```

(As with :link, the element a in the selector is redundant in XHTML.)

It has become customary to attach rollovers to links. This is often done using scripting (see Chapter 7), but simple rollover effects can be implemented using CSS. (Actually, with a certain amount of ingenuity, quite elaborate rollovers can be implemented purely in CSS.) The pseudo-class :hover matches an element that the cursor is presently over. The standard actually specifies a less specific condition: it matches 'while the user designates an element (with some pointing device), but does not activate it.' To take the simplest possibility, a link could turn silver when the cursor was over it (that is, when a click would activate it), if the following rule was used:

```
a:hover { color:silver; text-decoration:underlined;}
```

A rollover effect that has been widely adopted consists of changing the background colour of the link element. Thus,

```
a:hover { background-color: yellow; }
```

will cause a yellow highlight to appear behind the link when the cursor is over it – an effective but relatively subtle way of signifying that something will happen if the mouse button is clicked.

Finally, the :active pseudo-class matches elements that are in the process of being activated. That is, for graphical browsers and a conventional input device, the element below the cursor is in this state during the time between pressing and releasing the mouse button. Carrying on with the simple expedient of altering the colour, we could make the link turn black while it was being clicked, like this:

```
a:active { color:black; text-decoration:underlined;}
```

If you provide an explicit rule for a:link, it is as well to provide rules for a:visited and a:active as well, otherwise the default appearance will be used for visited and active links. This may look incongruous in conjunction with your custom unvisited links.

Don't be tempted to change the font weight or style in rules for :hover elements. In almost all fonts, this will change the space occupied by the link on the screen, which will usually cause other elements to move in a disturbing fashion when the cursor hovers over the link. This will invariably occur if the link is embedded in some text within a paragraph. Even with isolated links (on navbars and so on) the change in size can be disorienting.

Links that occur within the text will usually need different treatment from links in navbars, since what works in isolation will not necessarily work in context. You may not consider it necessary to distinguish visited links in a navbar, for example. To discriminate between links in different contexts, contextual selectors can be used. A collection of links, such as a navbar, is usually marked up as an unordered list; ul elements with a distinguishing class attribute can be used for any list of links that needs special treatment. Thus, if a navbar is enclosed between <ul class="navbar"> and </ul>, the selector .navbar a:link would match navbar links, while a:link would match any others, and so on, for visited, hovered-over and active links.

Lists

Because of the way they are laid out, with bullets or numbers and so on, lists provide additional opportunities for styling, and several CSS properties apply only to them. Each item in an ordered or unordered list generates two boxes: a principal box, which holds the content of the item, and a marker box, which holds the bullet or item number. (Definition lists are different, and the remarks in this section do not apply to them. The dt and dd elements can be styled separately, like any other elements.)

Type	Value	Marker
Glyph	disc	●
	circle	○
	square	■
Numerical	decimal	1, 2, 3,...
	decimal-leading-zero	01, 02, 03,...
Alphabetical	lower-roman	i, ii, iii,...
	upper-roman	I, II, III,...
	lower-latin	a, b, c,...
	lower-alpha	
	upper-latin	A, B, C,...
	upper-alpha	

Table 4.4 Common list style types

The value of the `list-style-type` property determines what goes into the marker box. The most widely supported possibilities are summarized in Table 4.4. (We have omitted some more esoteric numerical schemes, since these are not implemented in most browsers.) The disc, circle and square options provide for bullet lists; the precise appearance of these glyphs is determined by the browsers. The disc is the familiar circular solid bullet, and this is the default. All the other values for this property produce numbered lists using various different numbering schemes. To create lists with square bullets, the following rule could be used:

```
ul { list-style-type: square; }
```

Any of these values can be used with either `ul` or `ol` elements: as far as CSS is concerned there is no distinction between ordered and unordered lists: either can be displayed with bullets or with numbers. However, there remains a structural distinction, which should be expressed in the XHTML code for the benefit of non-visual user agents, and unless there is a good reason to do otherwise, `ul` elements should be styled with bullets of some sort, and `ol` elements with numbers.

If none of the bullet styles is satisfactory, you can use a small image as the list item marker, by specifying its URL as the value of the `list-style-image` property, like this:

```
ul { list-style-image: url(Tiny-Logo.gif); }
```

This property allows you to use arbitrary bullets, but there are inevitably pitfalls. The image is never scaled, so it must be prepared at the correct size to match the text of the list items before it can be used in this way. If the user changes the font size in the browser, the list item markers will stay the same size, no longer matching the text they accompany.

Tables

Tables offer special formatting opportunities. As we saw in Chapter 3, the default layout of tables is ugly and hard to read. A great deal can be done to improve on it. We will sketch the basics, which should be enough to enable you to produce decent-looking tables for your Web pages.

Each type of element involved in building tables – `table`, `caption`, `tr`, `td` and `th` – generates a box, which can therefore be styled like any other: it can have margins, padding, borders and a background, and the text within it can be aligned and styled. These properties alone can make a big difference to the appearance of tables.

Consider the example in Figure 3.5 from Chapter 3. We can approximate the layout of tables in this book using a few simple rules. To begin with, the text in headers and data cells should be left-aligned:

```
th,td { text-align: left; }
```

Setting the fonts and colours does not introduce any new CSS:

```
th {
    color: navy;
    font: bold 1.1em Univers,Verdana,sans-serif;
}

td {
    color: black;
    font: 1.1 em Goudy,Georgia,serif;
}
```

(Navy isn't the right shade of blue, but it will do until we have described how to choose colours more accurately in Chapter 5.)

Besides controlling the typography of the contents of table cells, CSS rules can be used to provide them with backgrounds, just as they can for other elements. The lines that are often used to separate rows and columns of tables can be created using border properties on the elements making up the table, but their behaviour must be modified slightly to create the layouts usually preferred for tables.

Suppose that, instead of the sparser layout used in this book, you wished to create a table with a complete grid of lines separating each of the rows and columns from its neighbours. A little thought would suggest that you could use the following rule:

```
th,td { border: navy medium solid; }
```

	kbps (theoretical)	6kB text page	100 kB text page	4 MB movie
Modem	56	1 sec	15 secs	10 mins
ADSL (typical)	512	0.1 sec	2 secs	1 min

Figure 4.17 Separated borders

	kbps (theoretical)	6kB text page	100 kB text page	4 MB movie
Modem	56	1 sec	15 secs	10 mins
ADSL (typical)	512	0.1 sec	2 secs	1 min

Figure 4.18 Collapsed borders

The result, shown in Figure 4.17, is probably not what you would expect. The browser has applied CSS's *separated border* model to the table, adding a little space between each cell's box, so that each has its own border. If that is actually what you want to do, the amount of inter-border space can be controlled using the border-spacing property. More often, though, the table should use the collapsing border model, where the borders for adjoining cells are combined into a single separator. The border model is controlled by the border-collapse property, whose value can be separate (the default) or collapse. This property only sensibly applies to an entire table. Adding the rule

```
table { border-collapse: collapse; }
```

would cause the sample table to display as shown in Figure 4.18.

This is not actually what we set out to do: the original intention was to simulate the table layout of the book. This uses no vertical separators, but has thick lines above and below the header and at the very bottom of the table, and thin separators between the rows. Since we are only concerned with separating entire rows, we can use the borders of tr elements as the separators. To distinguish the top and bottom rows, it is necessary to add some id attributes to the XHTML markup.

```
<table>
  <tr id="heading">
  heading cells
  </tr>
  other data rows
  <tr id="bottomrow">
  data cells for last row
  </tr>
</table>
```

In the stylesheet, we must remove the rule we added earlier for the border property with selector th,td. Now we can add rules to create the required separator lines.

	kbps (theoretical)	6kB text page	100 kB text page	4 MB movie
Modem	56	1 sec	15 secs	10 mins
ADSL (typical)	512	0.1 sec	2 secs	1 min

Figure 4.19 Applying borders to rows

	kbps (theoretical)	6kB text page	100 kB text page	4 MB movie
Modem	56	1 sec	15 secs	10 mins
ADSL (typical)	512	0.1 sec	2 secs	1 min

Figure 4.20 Adding extra padding to the cells

```
tr {
   border-color: navy;
   border-width: thin;
   border-style: none none solid none;
}

#bottomrow {
   border-color: navy;
   border-width: medium;
   border-style: none none solid none;
}

#heading {
   border-color: navy;
   border-width: medium;
   border-style: solid none solid none;
}
```

The result is shown in Figure 4.19. The lines and fonts are correct, but as you can see the spacing remains unacceptable. The table cells are just boxes, though, so we can add some padding. The rule

```
th,td { padding: 1em; }
```

is sufficient to produce a readable and fairly attractive table, as shown in Figure 4.20.

Technical Detail

Conflicting Borders

If the collapsing border model is used, most of the horizontal separators can be considered to be both the bottom border of one row and the top border of the one below it. What happens if two different CSS rules apply to these borders? The standard specifies the exact rule for resolving such conflicts. The general idea is that the most eye-catching border is used, so thick borders are used in preference to thinner ones, solid to dashed, and so on. If the only disagreement is between colours, then the colour specified for a cell takes precedence over that for a row. (If two adjoining cells disagree as to the colour of their shared border, the result is undefined.)

Padding is usually a good way to space out tables for readability, but precise control over cells' widths is possible using the width property. The CSS standard allows some latitude in how table widths are calculated. It is safest to assume that the widths of the cells in the first row may be used to set the width of each column and to work out how wide the whole table is, so it is unwise to leave out any cells in that row. If an explicit width is set for all the cells, the table width will be equal to their sum; if a width has also been specified for the whole table, and this is larger than the sum of the cell widths, the extra space will be evenly divided between columns.

The height of each row can also be specified: it will be the maximum of the height of the cells in that row and any explicit height set for the row as a whole.

A table element can include a caption. This can of course be styled like any other element, and it is usual to apply some distinctive typography to captions. It is also possible to control the positioning of the caption with respect to the table, using the caption-side property. This takes the value top or bottom, to place the caption above or below the body of the table, respectively. All the captions in a document could be set in a suitable font and positioned a short way below their tables with the following rule:

```
caption {
    color: black;
    font: italic bold 1.1em Goudy,Georgia,serif;
    padding: 1em 0em;
    text-align: left;
```

```
    caption-side: bottom;
}
```

Forms

XHTML forms are among the most difficult of elements to format satisfactorily, because control elements are often implemented by browsers using the corresponding objects from the host operating system's user interface. These are not amenable to styling. Even browsers which use their own platform-independent controls rarely allow their appearance to be controlled by stylesheets. The 2.1 revision to the CSS specification is explicit about this:

> 'CSS2.1 does not define which properties apply to form controls [...] or how CSS can be used to style them. User agents may apply CSS properties to these elements. Authors are recommended to treat such support as experimental.'

Thus, the Web designer is faced with the problem of incorporating these given elements into a page design. Their positioning offers no special difficulties: controls may be placed in `div` and `span` elements, floated or absolutely positioned. Altering the fonts that they use, or fixing their size or colour, are jobs that cannot be done reliably by CSS. Labels, however, can be treated like any other textual element, and styled and positioned however you like.

A special pseudo-class selector, `:focus`, is available for those browsers that do support styling of form controls. An element belongs to this class when it is being used for input. For example, when the cursor is placed in a text input field, either by moving the mouse or tabbing, that field is said to have the focus. Browsers usually indicate this fact by highlighting the field in some way. If you wish to customize the highlighting, you can do so by using `:focus` as a selector in a rule (on the understanding that it might have no effect on some browsers).

A set of properties that can be profitably used in such rules control the presence and appearance of an outline around an element. An outline is much like a border, except that it is placed over the element, without occupying any space itself. This means that turning an outline on and off does not cause any page content to reflow. Because of the similarity between outlines and borders, the set of properties affecting outlines has the same structure as the border properties we met earlier. The following rule puts a thick red line around the element that has the focus (providing the browser supports it):

```
:focus { outline: thick solid red; }
```

Advanced Features of CSS

Despite the excessive length of this chapter, we have by no means described every feature of CSS. Enough has been said to allow you to control the appearance of Web pages to a considerable extent, and in Chapter 10 we will explore some of the design possibilities that this opens up. A few more CSS features that will be needed therefore require a brief description.

Generated Content

The `content` property creates new text to be displayed on a page. Its value may take several forms, some of which we will describe. Most frequently, it is simply a string (written between double quote marks, with `\"` being used to represent such marks within the string). This property can only be used with any effect in conjunction with the pseudo-elements `:before` and `:after`, whose meaning is best conveyed by a simple example.

The effect of the following rule is to insert the word NEW in red (followed by a space) before every paragraph belonging to the class `new`.

```
p.new:before { content: "NEW "; color: red; }
```

The selector applies the rule to any inserted content that appears before a p element with `class="new"`. The declaration of the `content` property specifies what this generated content should be. Any further declarations in the rule will be applied to this content, so the effect is as originally described. In a similar way, selectors using `:after` apply to generated content placed after any element matched by the rest of the selector; the `content` property must be declared in the rule if there is to be anything to match.

The generation of content by rules such as this takes place after the XHTML has been parsed, so it is not possible to include any markup in the string that is the value of content. For instance,

```
p.new:before { content: "<span class=\"prefix\">NEW </span>"; }
```

doesn't assign the generated content to the class `prefix`, so that you can apply further styling to it; it just inserts the string `<span class="prefix">NEW </span>` verbatim in front of every new paragraph. Any styling that is to be applied to generated content must be declared in the rule that generates the content. Furthermore, the generated content becomes part of the element, so that any rules that apply to that element will also be applied to it.

As a consequence, the :first-letter pseudo-element will match the first letter of any inserted string, not the first letter of the original element.

The content property may also have a URL as its value, which typically will identify an image to be inserted before or after some element. For instance, if the URL icon/new.gif pointed to a small image of an icon used to indicate new items, the following rule could be used to insert it before all new paragraphs:

```
p.new:before { content: url(new.gif); }
```

This property can also be used to insert the values of attributes of the element it applies to, using the form attr(*attribute name*) as its value. Sometimes, Web pages will have links which are simply the text of the URL to which each link points. (Sometimes there really is nothing better.) To avoid the necessity of retyping the URL, and the consequent risk of errors and inconsistency, the following rule could be used to pull the value out of the href attribute of links belonging to the class selfref:

```
a.selfref:before { content: attr(href); }
```

One of the most useful applications of generated content is in the insertion of opening and closing quotation marks around a quotation, marked up as a q or blockquote element. If the quotation marks appear in the marked-up document, the possibility of adopting a convention for displaying quotations that does not use them (for instance, italicizing or setting as an indented block) is no longer available, since CSS provides no way of deleting text from a document. For maximum flexibility, quotation marks should be inserted by a stylesheet. CSS provides some special values for this case: content may be open-quote or close-quote, so a rule for setting inline quotes using conventional punctuation would be:

```
q:before { content: open-quote; }
q:after { content: close-quote; }
```

Actually, this is what browsers do by default, but using the explicit rule provides greater freedom, since additional styling can be applied, as with any other generated content, and the glyphs to be used for opening and closing quotes can be specified using the quotes property. For example, to use single curly quotes instead of the default double straight quotes throughout a document, the following rule could be used:

```
body { quotes: "\002018" "\002019"; }
```

(In a CSS string, a \ followed by a hexadecimal number stands for the character which has that number as its Unicode character code.)

Finally, generated content can include automatically incremented counters, for generating sequential numbers for elements other than list items. A stylesheet may use any number of named counters. For instance, if we wished to add numbered captions to all our tables, we might use a counter called `tablenum`. The expression `counter(tablenum)`, when used as the value of the `content` property, produces the value of this counter. A second argument may be supplied, in the form of any of the possible values for the `list-style-type` property. If such an argument is present, it is used to format the counter. For example, in principle `counter(tablenum, upper-latin)` should produce a Roman numeral corresponding to the counter's value (though no browser available to us at the time of writing managed to do so).

None of this is much use unless the value can be changed. The `counter-increment` property has a name as its value, and increments the corresponding counter. By default, it adds one; if an integer follows the counter name, it is added to the counter. The `counter-reset` property is used similarly to set the counter to an initial value. If no value is given, the counter is set to zero. If a rule uses a counter's value in a declaration for `content`, and also increments it, the increment is performed first, irrespective of the order the declarations appear. Hence, to add numbered captions to the tables on a page, starting at 7 (perhaps the first six were on a previous page), the following rules will suffice:

```
body { counter-reset: tablenum 6; }
caption:before {
    content:  "Table " counter(tablenum) ". ";
    counter-increment: tablenum;
}
```

(This example also illustrates how string values may be concatenated in declarations.)

Specifying Box Types

It is usually clear which XHTML element types should be blocks and which should be inline: p and `blockquote` should obviously generate blocks, em and `strong` elements should be displayed inline. Sometimes, though, it may be desirable to change the default display for certain elements. You might ask, why not use a different element type that displays the way you want it? The answer is that element types should be chosen to reflect the semantic structure of the document, not to specify its appearance, so the choice of element type

Web Design > Accessibility > Graphics > Colour > Colour Blindness

Figure 4.21 Breadcrumbs

comes first, and is dictated by the meaning of its content; the styling comes afterwards. Of course, since XHTML has only a limited repertoire of element types, it is not always clear which one should be used for a specific purpose that is not directly catered for, so although choosing element types to reflect semantics is a good rule, it cannot be an exhaustive guide to marking up a document.

To illustrate both these points, consider the feature known as ***breadcrumbs***. Breadcrumbs provide a display of the route through a hierarchically organized site that leads to the page in the browser window. Figure 4.21 shows a typical style of display for breadcrumbs. What markup should be used? There is no breadcrumb element in XHTML. However, a breadcrumb trail is like a list, itemizing the steps to the current page, so the most apposite markup is an ordered list:

```
<ol>
   <li>Web Design</li>
   <li>Accessibility</li>
   <li>Graphics</li>
   <li>Colour</li>
   <li>Colour Blindness</li>
</ol>
```

(The list items would normally contain links, but we have omitted the anchors in the interests of clarity.) This expresses the structure and will work for non-visual user agents, but displaying the trail as a numbered list is not very perspicuous, and, with each litem on a separate line, occupies more screen space than the feature deserves. To obtain the preferred display of Figure 4.21, the list items must be displayed inline. This can be done using a declaration for the property display. This may have the value inline or block, with the expected effect. The full collection of rules for producing the breadcrumb display as illustrated is as follows:

```
li { display: inline; }
li:before { content: ">"; }
li:first-child:before { content: ""; }
```

The first rule turns the items into inline elements, the second inserts > signs in front of each element, while the last rule suppresses the > before the first item.

As well as `inline` and `block`, `display` can take a range of other values that cause arbitrary elements to be displayed as list items or the various components of tables. These are mostly of little use in the context of XHTML. However, for XML documents, which give no *a priori* meaning to any element type, the use of `display` is vital.

One other value that may be of occasional use is `none`. This causes any elements to which it applies to generate no box at all. The element cannot be seen and it does not affect the layout of the rest of the document. Visually, it is as if it was not there at all, although the markup is still in the document and available to non-visual user agents.

Media-Specific Stylesheets

Most of the time, Web pages are displayed in a graphical Web browser, but not always. Sometimes, visitors to a site will want a hard copy of some page, so they will print it. Formatting that is suitable for display on a screen will not necessarily be appropriate on paper. For instance, type is usually set in a larger size on screen, and sans serif fonts are generally preferred for readability at low resolution, but at higher resolution on paper, a smaller, serifed font may be more readable. A layout that makes good use of screen space may not work well on a sheet of paper, with its different aspect ratio. Page breaks can be profitably used to break up the printed version of an XHTML document at suitable places, whereas the same document will be displayed continuously in a browser window.

Conventional computer screens and print are not the only potential destinations for a document. Other possibilities include Braille devices, speech synthesizers, TV screens, handheld devices with small screens and data projectors. Each has its own distinctive capabilities and limitations. It is unrealistic to expect a single stylesheet to produce a layout that will work for all output devices and media. Instead, if it is important that a document be displayed optimally on several types of device, it is necessary to provide alternative stylesheets. For instance, the following rule will produce nice clear text on a neutral background on a monitor:

```
body {
    background-color: silver;
    color: black;
    font-family: Arial, Verdana, sans-serif;
    font-size: 18px;
```

```
    line-height: 1.6;
}
```

Text styled according to this rule would look too big on paper, and unless the browser was intelligent enough to remove the background when printing (most are) it would waste a tremendous amount of ink.

This rule, on the other hand, would produce compact, but still clean and readable, text on paper:

```
body {
    background-color: white;
    color: black;
    font-family: Times, Georgia, serif;
    font-size: 12px;
    line-height: 1.2;
}
```

What is required is some way of specifying which rule should be applied to which medium. CSS provides one mechanism; XHTML another.

In a CSS stylesheet, rules can be grouped using a special construct, the @media rule. (This is an example of a more general class of CSS construct, the @-rule. We will not describe any others; there are only a few in the current version of CSS, and they are not generally useful.) The keyword @media is followed by a list of media types, separated by commas, and then

all	All devices
braille	Refreshable tactile Braille displays
embossed	Braille printers
handheld	Handheld devices (PDAs etc)
print	Printers
projection	Data projectors
screen	Computer displays
speech	Speech synthesizers
tty	Teletype-like devices, using fixed-width text
tv	Television screens

Table 4.5 Media types

some ordinary CSS rules, enclosed in curly brackets. The implication is that those rules only apply when the document is displayed on the named media. Table 4.5 lists the currently recognized media types. We could create a stylesheet that formatted text differently for screen and print along the following lines:

```
@media screen {
body {
   background-color: silver;
   Other declarations for body on screen
   }
Other rules for screen display
}
@media print {
body {
   background-color: white;
   Other declarations for body on paper
   }
Other rules for printed output
}
Rules for both media
```

This mechanism allows the rules for all media to be kept in a single stylesheet. If you are happy to maintain separate stylesheets for different media, it is possible to use the media attribute of the link element when referencing an external stylesheet, to indicate the media for which it is appropriate. If, for example, the file print-styles.css held a collection of rules for print formatting, and screen-styles.css a collection for on-screen display, they could be referenced in a document as follows:

```
<link rel="stylesheet" href="screen-styles.css" media="screen" />
<link rel="stylesheet" href="print-styles.css" media="print" />
```

The browser would then use the appropriate stylesheet for display and printing.

CSS includes special properties for use in stylesheets for media that break text into pages (print and projectors, for example), that allow the designer to specify page breaks and paper sizes. It also includes an extensive sub-language for aural stylesheets, with properties that control the volume, voice, stress and other properties of spoken text synthesized from the document. Pauses and cues can be inserted, and the position of voices in a 3D surround-sound space can be controlled.

Key Points

Stylesheets are used to specify appearance independently of structure and content.

Rules in CSS

A stylesheet is a set of rules, each consisting of a selector and some declarations. Each declaration sets the value of a property.

The declarations in a rule with an element name (e.g. h1) as the selector are applied to all occurrences of that element.

A selector consisting of an element type followed by a dot and a name (e.g. p.first) matches all elements whose class attribute includes that name.

The selector * matches any element. It can be omitted in selectors of the form *.c, where c is a class name.

A selector consisting of an element name followed by a # (e.g. p#summary) and a name matches the element whose id is equal to the name. The element name can be omitted.

A selector consisting of two element names separated by a space (e.g. ul li), matches elements with the second name in the content of an element with the first name (e.g. li elements inside a ul element).

A selector consisting of two element names separated by a > (e.g. ul>li), matches elements with the second name that are children of an element with the first name (e.g. li elements immediately inside a ul element).

A selector consisting of two element names separated by a + (e.g. h1+h2), matches elements with the second name that follow an element with the first name (e.g. h2 elements after an h1 element).

The pseudo-class :first-child matches the first child of an element.

A rule consisting of a sequence of selectors separated by commas followed by some declarations is equivalent to a sequence of rules, one for each of the selectors, with the same declarations.

A value that is assigned to some property for an element is inherited by that element's children, unless a rule causes a value to be explicitly assigned.

Typography

A font is a collection of character shapes, called glyphs.

The `font-family` property has a list of fonts as its value; the browser will use the first in the list which is installed on the user's system.

> The generic font families `serif`, `sans-serif`, `cursive`, `fantasy` and `monospace` provide fallbacks in case no font named in the list is available.

The `font-style`, `font-variant`, `font-weight` and `font-stretch` properties control other aspects of type's appearance.

> The `font-weight` property may take numerical values between 100 and 900, or the keyword values `normal`, `bold`, `bolder` and `lighter`.

The `font-size` property may take the values `xx-small`, `x-small`, `small`, `medium`, `large`, `x-large`, `xx-large`, `smaller` and `larger`.

> `medium` is the default size set by the user in their browser.

Font size can also be specified in absolute units (including `pt` and `px`) or relative units (`em`, `ex` and `%`).

> Relative units are calculated with respect to the inherited font size.

The `line-height` property is used to specify leading.

Relative units for line-height are calculated with respect to the current font-size value.

The color, font-decoration and text-transform properties modify the appearance of text.

The text-align property takes the values left, right, center or justify to control the alignment of text in paragraphs and other block elements.

The text-indent property controls indentation of the first line of a paragraph. Its value may be negative for exdented first lines.

The pseudo-classes :first-line and :first-letter are used to apply special styling to the first line and letter of a paragraph.

Layout

Every element is placed inside a box.

Each box is divided into content, padding, border and margin regions.

Unless explicit positioning is specified, boxes are laid out using the normal flow algorithm.

Text and inline elements are folded into lines so that they fit within the content area of their containing box.

Box widths can be specified in absolute or relative units with the width property.

em units cause the width to change with font size.

% units refer to the width of the containing box.

Box heights can be set using the height property. The overflow property determines what happens to any over-matter.

The thickness of padding can be set to an absolute or relative length using the `padding-top`, `padding-right`, `padding-bottom` and `padding-left` properties, or the shorthand `padding` property.

Border and margin thicknesses are controlled in a similar way.

> The border thicknesses may use the keyword values `thick`, `medium` and `thin`

Border colour and style may also be specified for each side, using similar properties.

The style, width and colour of the border on any side can all be set at the same time, using `border-top` etc, or the shorthand `border` property.

The top and bottom margins of vertically adjacent boxes are collapsed.

The background of every element's box can be set to a colour or to an image, using the `background-color` and `background-image` properties.

> The value for `background-image` is written as `url(`*the url*`)`.

> Tiling of background images can be specified or prevented using the `background-repeat` property.

Positioning

Setting the `float` property to `left` or `right` causes an element's box to be taken from its position in the normal flow and moved as far left or right as possible.

If the `position` property is set to `absolute`, `left`, `right`, `top` and `bottom` can be set in order to determine the position of the four sides of the box.

> The positions of the sides can be set in absolute or relative units.

> The stacking of overlapping absolutely positioned elements is controlled by the `z-index` property.

Special Cases

The pseudo-class :link matches any elements that are links, in particular, a elements in XHTML documents.

The pseudo-class :visited can be used to style recently visited links.

The pseudo-class :hover matches an element when the cursor is over it. It can be used to implement rollovers in CSS.

The :active pseudo-class matches elements that are in the process of being activated.

The list-style-type property is used to specify markers (bullets or numbers) for list elements.

> The list-style-image property allows you to choose a small image as a list item marker.

The padding, margins and borders of table cells can be specified using the appropriate CSS properties applied to td, th and tr elements.

> The border-collapse property must be set to collapse if spaces between cells are not required.

CSS styling cannot be applied to form control elements reliably.

Advanced Features of CSS

The content property creates new text to be displayed.

The pseudo-elements :before and :after cause generated content to appear before or after a matching element.

The display property can be used to change the type of an element from block to inline or vice-versa.

> Setting display to none causes the element to generate no box.

@media rules allow different rules to be applied to different media.

Exercises

Test Questions

1. Find the syntactic errors in the following stylesheet rule:

   ```
   h1: { color = "red" }
   ```

2. Suppose a stylesheet includes the following rules:

   ```
   .red {color: red;}
   .green {color:green;}
   p,.orange {color:orange;}
   ```

   What colour will the word colour appear in when each of the following is displayed in a browser that correctly interprets the stylesheet?

   ```
   <p>What colour is it?</p>
   <p>What <span class="red">colour</span> is it?</p>
   <p class="red">What colour is it?</p>
   <p>What <span class="orange red">colour</span> is it?</p>
   ```

3. Show how you can use class attributes instead of contextual selectors to make items in an ordered list a different colour from those in an unordered list. Which is better?

4. If the font-weight property has the value bold, will the chosen font be a boldface?

5. Do the following two rules have the same effect?

   ```
   * { font-size: 14px; }
   body { font-size: 14px; }
   ```

6. What is the minimum set of font properties that must be specified in a font declaration?

7. Write a CSS rule that sets the first paragraph after each h1 with its first line in bold and a red double-height initial letter.

8. Why would you not use a rule with a as its selector to style links?

9. If you specify the width of a box in ems, what units should you use for its height?

10. Write a rule or rules to automatically number all the paragraphs in a document, with a prefix of the form Para 23, and so on.

Discussion Topics

1. Adobe's Portable Document Format (PDF) allows any document to be displayed with all its formatting intact, no matter how it was originally created. PDF also supports hypertext links and embedded images and time-based media. Does PDF, therefore, provide a superior alternative to standard Web formats for hypermedia on the Internet?

2. Large CSS stylesheets tend to become disorganized and unwieldy, since the only structuring facility in CSS is the cascade. What conventions could be adopted for keeping stylesheets organized and maintainable? Are there any language features that could be added to CSS to help with organizing stylesheets?

3. Explain why the idea of a WYSIWYG (what you see is what you get) editor for Web pages is misconceived.

Practical Tasks

1. Add a CSS stylesheet to the résumé you created as an XHTML document in Chapter 3, to format it in a neat and attractive way that will impress a prospective employer.

2. Create two alternative stylesheets for the same résumé page, one that would be suitable for reading on screen by people with poor eyesight, the other to present yourself on a social networking site. (If you feel it necessary to suppress some of the information for one or other of these versions, do so using the stylesheet, not by editing the XHTML document.)

3. Rectangles with rounded corners are popular in some forms of graphic design. The top halves of such rectangles are often used as tabs, for example on navbars. Although CSS3 will include support for rounded corners, current Web standards do not. Devise methods of setting blocks of text in rounded rectangles. (You may need to add semantically superfluous markup to achieve the desired result.)

4. The `blockquote` element is used to markup passages that are quoted from some other source. Research different ways block quotes are typeset in books and magazines, and how they are presented on Web pages. Write CSS stylesheets to display `blockquote` elements in many different styles.

Web Graphics

5

There are two types of representation used for storing and displaying graphics on computers: *bitmaps* and *vector graphics*. To understand the difference between the two, we must briefly review the way in which images are stored on computers and displayed on monitors.

Display and Storage of Images

Displays

Computer monitors can be divided into two types: **CRTs**, so called because they use a cathode ray tube, like most televisions, and *flat panel* displays, also often called **LCD** or **TFT** displays, whose screens incorporate liquid crystals and thin-film transistors. From the user's point of view, the most striking difference between these two types of monitor is that, as the name implies, flat panel displays take the form of a flat panel, as little as quarter of an inch thick, while CRT displays are much bulkier in order to accommodate the cathode ray tube. Flat panels are the only option for use in laptop computers, and are becoming more and more popular as desktop displays, not least because of their lower energy consumption.

The precise way in which each of these two types of monitor works is largely irrelevant in the context of Web graphics. All you really need to know is that the image on the screen – whether it's a Web page, a digital photograph, your desktop or the interface to any application program with all its windows – is a rectangular array of small square dots of colour, called *pixels*. The size of the pixels varies; usually, they are between about one hundredth and one seventieth of an inch across, which means that individual pixels cannot be distinguished by the naked eye. When the pixels on the screen are set to suitable colours, the merged pixels produce the image we see, which to all intents and purposes is made up of continuous tones. As Figure 5.1} illustrates, when an image is magnified sufficiently, the pixels become visible.

Figure 5.1 An image is made up of pixels

The task of producing a picture on the screen, or part of the screen, thus becomes one of setting all the pixels within the area it occupies to the correct colours to create the desired image. To do this, a program such as a Web browser needs to have access to some representation of the image that contains the information necessary to determine the colour that each pixel must be. Although other types of program may generate images in different ways, the images embedded in Web pages are displayed using information stored in a file.

Image Files

There are two ways of storing image data in a file.

The first is to store a set of numbers, one for each pixel in the image, which comprises a numerical representation of the colours of the pixels. (See Figure 5.2 – we will explain the hexadecimal notation used for the stored numbers later.) Images stored in this way are called *bitmapped* images. Conceptually, an image of width m pixels and height n pixels is stored in a bitmapped image file as an $m \times n$ array of *colour values*: numbers which are mapped to colours on the screen in a way that we will describe shortly. In fact, more complex structures are usually employed in bitmapped image files, either to reduce the space that they occupy or to store additional information.

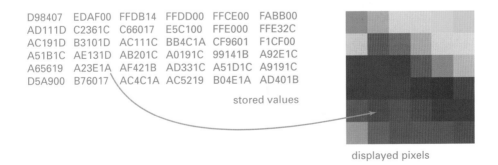

Figure 5.2 Bitmapped image representation

Terminology

Pixmaps

The term bitmapped image is not entirely accurate. Strictly speaking, a bitmap should consist of a single bit for each pixel in the image, which would only allow the pixels to have one of two colours. Usually these would be black and white, and a bitmapped image ought to be purely monochromatic. The term 'pixmapped image' – 'pixmap' being a contraction of 'pixel map' – was coined as a more accurate name for full colour images stored with several bits for each pixel, but it never achieved much currency. Some writers, especially in North America, prefer the name raster graphics, but all modern displays are based on raster scanning, so this is not much clearer.

The alternative to storing the values of all the pixels explicitly is to store a mathematical description of the picture, as a collection of geometrical shapes – ellipses, rectangles, other polygons and paths made up of lines and curves. The description of each shape is stored together with information about how it is to be drawn: what colour its outline (*stroke*) and inside (*fill*) are to be and the width of the stroke. This way of representing images is called *vector graphics*. To display an image stored in a vector graphic file, the browser must interpret the mathematical representation of the shapes, by combining the stored data (e.g. the centre point and radius of a circle) with equations describing the general form of such shapes (e.g. $x^2 + y^2 = r^2$) to deduce which pixels must be set to the stroke and fill colour to produce the shape described (e.g. a red circle with a blue outline). (See Figure 5.3.)

Although vector graphics can, with the use of paths made up of many segments and complex fills and strokes, be used to create more subtle pictures than the preceding description of

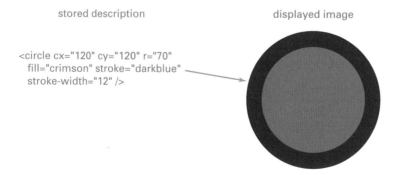

stored description   displayed image

```
<circle cx="120" cy="120" r="70"
    fill="crimson" stroke="darkblue"
    stroke-width="12" />
```

Figure 5.3 Vector graphic representation

simple geometrical shapes may suggest, the form is inherently more limited than bitmapped images, which can effectively store any image with the characteristics of a photograph, that is, with continuously varying tones. Vector graphics are more suitable for diagrams and cartoon-style drawing. For this reason, and because of the lack until recently of any widely used standard for vector graphics on the Web, the bulk of Web graphics takes the form of bitmapped images.

Colour

RGB Colour

We have been too glib in our description of the way colour values are stored and used. We need to explain how a colour can be represented by a number. Before we can do this, we need to look more closely at how displays produce colour. We will consider CRTs, since the mechanics are somewhat simpler, but the same principle applies to flat panel displays.

The face of a colour CRT is coated with three different types of phosphor, which emit light of three different colours when struck by a beam of electrons. The phospors are arranged in groups of three dots, one of each type. Three separate electron guns fire beams of electrons towards them. A thin metal screen with holes in, known as a shadow mask, is positioned just behind the face of the CRT to ensure that, as the beam from each electron gun is scanned over the face of the tube in a series of lines, it only strikes phospor dots of one type. The three colours emitted by the phosphors are specific shades of red, blue and green. The brightness of the light emitted by a phosphor dot depends on the energy of the beam that strikes it; this is controlled by circuitry in the display.

Red, blue and green are called the ***additive primary colours*** because to a first approximation (and it is only an approximation – see Chapter 6 of *Digital Multimedia* for more details) any colour can be produced by combining red, blue and green light in varying proportions. The cone cells of the retina in the eye are divided into three types, which respond (again, approximately speaking) to red, green and blue light. This provides a physiological basis for the theory that any colour can be made up from components of these three primaries. The coloured images on television sets and computer monitors are composites formed from red, blue and green components by the three electron beams, as we just described. Flat panel displays also mix colours from three additive primary components, though the physical mechanism is different. The colour of a pixel on any display is thus made up of proportions of the three additive primaries. Any colour that can be displayed can therefore be represented by three numbers specifying the relative proportions of red, green and blue. This system of storing colour values is known as the ***RGB colour model***, or simply ***RGB colour***.

It is the relative proportions of primaries which specify a colour, not any absolute quantity, so any range can be used for the actual stored values. For people, percentages are familiar (i.e. each of the three components of the colour value is in the range 0 to 100), but for computers it is more convenient to use values that fit neatly into the basic storage unit, the byte. The most common arrangement is to use values in the range 0 to 255, each of which will fit into a single byte. Using this representation, we would write pure red and pure blue as (255, 0, 0) and (0, 0, 255) respectively, listing the red, green and blue components in that order. The value (0, 71, 29) is a dark shade of emerald green, whereas (184, 242, 208) is a much paler green: the higher numbers and the presence of a red component can be interpreted as the addition of white, which, being made up of equal components of the maximum amounts of red, green and blue is (255, 255, 255). Black is the absence of colour, so its RGB value is (0, 0, 0). When one byte is employed for each component like this, a colour value consisting of red, green and blue components needs twenty-four bits. This representation is therefore often called **24-bit colour**; it is capable of storing distinct values for about 16.7 million different colours, which is more than the human eye can distinguish.

Indexed Colour

All colour monitors are physically able to produce millions of shades, but other components of a computer's graphics subsystem, specifically the amount of VRAM, may limit the number of colours that can be displayed simultaneously. This is less of a problem nowadays than it used to be, with most, if not all, computers having the necessary capability for 24-bit colour. However, few images actually contain millions of different colours, so using twenty-four bits for each pixel may be unnecessarily generous. A simple expedient known as **indexed colour** is often used to reduce the space required by images, so that they can be transmitted over networks more efficiently.

By analogy with painting, the set of colours contained in an image is called its colour **palette**. An image's palette will depend on many features of the image, including its subject matter, its origin and, in the case of original artwork, the artist's style. For example, rural landscapes will tend to have many shades of green, seascapes will often be predominantly blue, and so on. Photographs of natural scenes and objects will tend to have many subtly different shades, whereas computer-generated images may have only a few. Figure 5.4 shows some differing images and their palettes.

If the number of colours in a palette is small enough, fewer than 24 bits will be needed to distinguish between them. In particular, if the palette contains 256 or fewer colours, a single byte will be adequate to store a number that uniquely identifies each colour, since a byte's eight bits are adequate for holding numbers in the range 0 to 255. The colour of each pixel in an image can therefore be represented by one byte instead of three. These single-byte

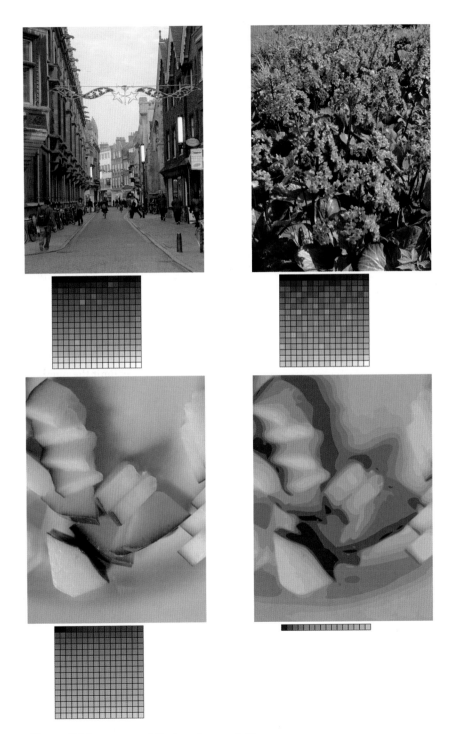

Figure 5.4 Images and their colour palettes

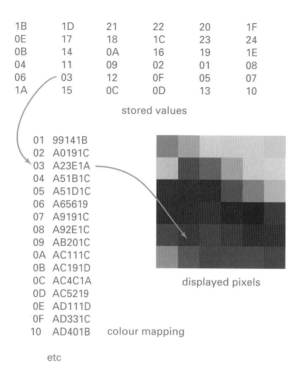

stored values

displayed pixels

colour mapping

etc

Figure 5.5 Indexed colour

values can be arbitrarily assigned to elements of the palette, provided that there is some way of mapping them to the 24-bit numbers which specify the actual red, green and blue proportions of the colour. In other words, we need to associate a **colour mapping** with the image, which translates from the small stored numbers to full colour values. In concrete terms, a colour mapping can simply be an array or table, which is indexed by the stored numbers, as shown in Figure 5.5. Hence, a bitmapped image file using indexed colour will contain a bitmap, comprising small index values instead of 24-bit colour values, together with a table which records the colour mapping. (Indexed colour is rarely used for vector graphics.) Often the distinction between this colour table and the values it contains is elided, and you will see both referred to as the image's palette.

The number 256 is convenient for computers, but there is no particular reason to expect any image to have a palette of that many colours. Artifical or computer-generated images may well have fewer. In that case, it is feasible to use even fewer bits for each stored pixel, although this is not always done even when it is possible, because it is usually most efficient to access entire bytes, and this may be felt to outweigh any savings in memory requirements obtained from using very few bits for each pixel. More often, especially when dealing with photographs or scanned images, the actual palette will contain more than 256 colours. If we still wish to use indexed colour and a single byte for each pixel, what can be done?

Evidently, some colours which are present in the image will have to be left out of the colour table. The least commonly occurring colours are the obvious candidates for omission, although sometimes a more sophisticated consideration based on the significance of each colour may be used. In this case, the table may have to be constructed by hand, whereas a colour table based on the frequency of occurrence of colours in the image can be created automatically by a program. The real question, though, is what should be done with the pixels whose colour has been omitted.

Each missing colour will have to be replaced by one that is in the table. The replacement should be 'close' to the original, but defining closeness between colours is not entirely straightforward. A simple calculation based on the numerical values of the red, green and blue components (such as minimizing the Euclidean distance) does not always correspond to the human visual system's non-linear perception of the nearest colour. Nevertheless, some such simple measure is usually employed by programs which create indexed colour images. Even if a good substitute is found for each missing colour, reducing the number of colours in an image inevitably produces some undesirable artefacts. Suppose, for instance, a small area of a picture which is predominantly made up of shades of green contains a subtle blend of pinks – a flower among some foliage, perhaps. If there is only room for a single pink in the colour table, all these tints will end up the same colour, and instead of a subtle blend there will be an area of one solid colour. Any soft outline the area originally possessed will be replaced by a hard edge. In general, if the number of colours in an image is drastically reduced in order to store it using indexed colour, blends and gradations will be replaced by such hard-edged areas. This usually undesirable effect is known as **posterization**, since the result resembles a cheaply printed poster, as the image in the bottom right if Figure 5.4, with its very limited palette illustrates.

To avoid posterization, a device known as **dithering** may be employed. Instead of replacing the colour of each individual pixel by a different colour, areas of a missing colour are replaced by a mixture of colours. For instance, if an area of four pixels is pink, but there is no pink in the colour table, two of the four pixels may be made red and the other two white. Optical mixing will produce the effect of pink in that area. If we assume that optical mixing works perfectly, then using combinations of 256 colours, a four-pixel area can appear to have any of millions of different colours. In effect, though, we are using pixels four times as big when dithering, so some artefaction of the image may occur. In general, dithered images will

Figure 5.6 Posterization and dithering

appear slightly fuzzy compared with their originals; in extreme cases, dithered areas will have a speckled appearance. This is often less intrusive than posterization, however. Figure 5.6 shows three versions of the same picture. The original on the left is in 24-bit colour. The middle image uses indexed colour and exhibits posterization – note the white area in the right hand petal, for instance. The image on the right uses the same colour table as the one in the middle, but with dithering. Here, you should be able to see the speckling that occurs as a result.

Indexed colour images may be displayed with the assistance of hardware: the colour table stored in the image is loaded into an associative memory, known as a *colour lookup table* **(CLUT)**, so that colours can be looked up rapidly. On most systems, this approach works well to facilitate the efficient display of such images. However, on some older computers, it is not possible to change the palette dynamically, and instead all images will be displayed using the system palette. This may also happen if software has not been correctly written to deal with dynamic palettes. The effect on the image will almost always be disastrous. When it is vital that colours display correctly you should restrict yourself to the set of 216 colours which are common to the system palettes of the major operating systems. This set of colours is called the **Web-safe palette**; it is shown in Figure 5.7. Programs used for preparing images for the Web will allow you to select the Web-safe palette when exporting your image to one of the Web file formats – it is usually necessary to dither if you want to avoid excessive posterization. The use of Web-safe colours is so restrictive that you may well feel that it is better to risk users of older systems seeing an incorrectly coloured version of your page than to confine yourself to such a limited palette.

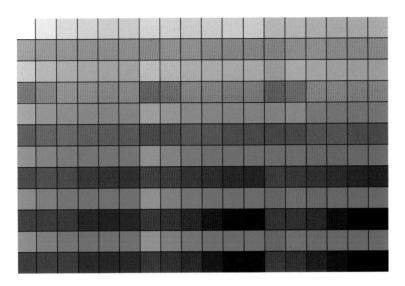

Figure 5.7 The Web-safe palette

Colour Spaces

The RGB model of colour that we have described and used informally is an example of a **colour space**, which is a general mechanism for representing colours numerically as a tuple of n components. (For RGB colour, $n = 3$, and the values are the triples we have seen. Some other colour spaces use a different number of components.) The term 'colour space' arises from the geometrical interpretation of the components of any colour value as coordinates in an n-dimensional space. The RGB colour space can be represented as a cube in the conventional three-dimensional coordinate system, with black at the origin, and the axes labelled with red, green and blue values, as shown in Figure 5.8. The edges of the cube are delimited by the maximum value that can be used for any colour component. As we explained previously, this value is essentially arbitrary; here we have used 255. Any point inside the cube corresponds to a colour that can be represented in the RGB model. (In reality, since values stored in a computer can only be integers in the stored range, there will be infinitely many colours that can't actually be stored. However, to the eye these will be indistinguishable from some colours that can be stored.) The set of all such colours is referred to as the **RGB gamut**. There are visible colours that lie outside the RGB gamut – as we mentioned earlier, the theory that any colour can be represented by its red, green and blue components is only an approximation, owing to the complex way in which the human visual system works.

This is all very neat, but leaves unanswered an important question: What do we mean by red, green and blue? In normal everyday usage these three names are each applied to a wide range

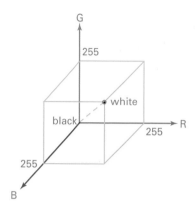

Figure 5.8 The RGB colour space

of colours. If an RGB value is to be interpreted as a specific colour, it is necessary to have a precise specification of *which* red, green and blue are the primary colours. Since we are only interested in displaying images on a computer monitor, it would seem to be the case that we ought to use the colours produced on a CRT when each of the phosphors is excited by the maximum intensity of electron beam, or the equivalent on a flat panel display. This is not an adequate approach for precise colour work, for the simple reason that every display is different; even the colours produced by a single display may change over time as its components age. (In other words, every device has its own colour space.)

In applications where colour fidelity is vital, **colour management systems** are used to ensure that, as far as possible, the colours of an image are reproduced consistently on all output devices. This is done by embedding a description of the colour characteristics of the device on which the image was prepared in the file in which the image is stored. Such a description is called a **colour profile**, and as well as specifying the values of the primaries (using a device-independent standard colour space), it includes numerical values for other features of the device which affect the way it reproduces colour. When the image is to be displayed or printed on some other device, software which understands colour profiles can then combine the embedded colour profile with a profile for the output device, and transform the colour values if necessary to ensure consistency.

Some file formats used for Web graphics do support embedded colour profiles, and some browsers are able to interpret them, but there are several drawbacks to their use on the Web. In the first place, the calculations necessary to transform between colour spaces are complicated and time-consuming, which adds additional overheads to the display of images

Technical Detail

CMYK Colour

All Web images use RGB colour, because they are only intended to be displayed on a monitor. There exist other colour models, however. The most important is CMYK. The CMYK colour space has four dimensions, corresponding to cyan, magenta, yellow and black components. Cyan, magenta and yellow are the so-called subtractive primaries, which serve the same function in mixing ink as the additive primaries do in mixing light. In theory, any colour can be printed by mixing inks of these three primaries in different quantities. (For more information about the theoretical basis of subtractive colour mixing see Chapter 6 of *Digital Multimedia*.) In practice, it is more convenient to add black ink as a fourth component, and most colour printing (including this book) is done using these four inks. The CMYK colour model arises from the need to specify colours for four-colour printing processes.

CMYK should only be a concern to Web designers if they wish to reuse images originally prepared for print on their Web pages. In that case, it will be necessary to transform them to RGB first, otherwise colours will be distorted. Although RGB is capable of representing more colours than CMYK, there are colours in the CMYK gamut that are not in the RGB gamut, so some colour shifts may occur, relative to the printed version. This is unavoidable.

in a browser. Secondly, the success of colour management is dependent on the availability of accurate colour profiles. In the case of monitors, this requires that the device be periodically calibrated. This can only be done properly using a specialized instrument and software; the calibration routines provided by operating systems and image manipulation programs are only approximate, and are very rarely performed by domestic users anyway. Given the enormous number of domestic users on the Web, this consideration alone would make the use of embedded colour profiles for Web graphics pointless. Finally, embedded profiles represent additional data to be transmitted over a network.

An alternative to embedding colour profiles is to transform images to some standard colour space. If this is done, sophisticated browsers can use monitor profiles to transform from the standard colour space to the user's monitor's colour space. If the parameters of the standard colour space are chosen to represent typical monitors, less sophisticated software can simply use the stored colour values as they are, and the result should be more or less all right.

Even if the image does not exactly match its original, all images displayed in this way will be consistent with each other.

The W3C has defined just such a standard colour space, known as **sRGB** (standard RGB). Although the precise values used in sRGB are somewhat controversial, it is gaining acceptance as a colour space for Web graphics, and is the basis of colour specification in CSS. Image preparation tools such as Photoshop allow images to be stored using the sRGB colour space, by using the colour profile of the device on which it was prepared to transform the colour values to their nearest equivalent in sRGB. The resulting file can then be used on a Web page, and should be reproduced consistently by browsers.

Colour and CSS

As we saw in Chapter 4, it is often necessary to specify colours in stylesheets. Examples include the colour of text (`color` property), the background colour to a page or box (`background-color`) and the colour of box outlines (`border-color`, `border-top-color`, etc.). In our examples up until now, we have used the sixteen colour names that CSS recognizes as keywords. When a wider range of colours is desired, colours may be specified numerically as values in the sRGB colour space. Each value therefore consists of three numbers, as we explained earlier in this chapter.

There are several different ways of writing colour values in CSS. The simplest is as a triplet of percentages. The three values must be preceded by the keyword `rgb`, enclosed in brackets and separated by commas, as in `rgb(18%,56%,75%)`. (This is the blue colour used in the running heads of this book.) Alternatively, for a more computer-oriented format, the values can be expressed as integers in the range 0 to 255. The same blue could be written as `rgb(48,142,191)`. Finally, the least readable but most popular format uses hexadecimal (base 16) numbers for values between 0 and 255 (so each value uses two hexadecimal digits) and concatenates the three values to form a string of six digits. In this case, the value is preceded by a single # sign, without the `rgb()`. Our blue is #308EBF in this notation.

One useful property of the hexadecimal colour notation is that the Web-safe colours all consist of three pairs of identical digits: the nearest Web-safe colour to our example is #3399CC. Such colours may be written in an abbreviated form with just three digits, omitting the duplicate in each pair, for example, the same Web-safe colour could be written as #39C.

Bitmapped Images

Bitmapped images are the most common type of image used on the Web. They are the only choice for photographic material, which forms the bulk of the pictorial content of the Web. They are also used as background textures, for rollover buttons and, more dubiously, as a way of including text in specific fonts and styles which cannot be changed by browsers.

Bitmapped images can originate from digital cameras or scanners, or they can be created from the beginning in digital form using a painting program, which allows you to use the digital equivalent of paint and brushes to create an image using cursor movements, usually controlled by a graphics pen and tablet. Bitmapped images can also be created by rendering a vector image, as we will describe later, or a 3-D scene.

It is almost always necessary to perform some operations on an image before it is ready for use on the Web. Pictures uploaded from a digital camera or captured by a scanner will usually need to be downsampled for display on screen (see below). They may also require correction, for example to compensate for poor exposure in the case of a photograph, or to remove a colour cast from a scanned image. Sometimes it may be appropriate to apply special effects to alter an image artificially; in other cases, elements of different images may be combined into a collage or artificial composition. All of these operations can be carried out using image manipulation programs such as Photoshop or The Gimp.

Once an image has been captured or created, corrected and altered, it must be saved in a file format appropriate for the Web. In most cases, this will involve applying some form of compression to the image data; for some formats, the image will be saved using indexed colour, so a suitable palette will have to be chosen, and dithering applied if necessary. In this context, these processes are sometimes referred to collectively as *image optimization*. Photoshop and similar programs provide a built-in interface for optimizing and saving images for the Web, which allow you to select palettes and compression parameters interactively and to preview the effect of different settings on your image's appearance.

Resolution and Resampling

A bitmapped image has no physical dimensions. It is just an array of pixel values. The size at which it appears on any physical device, such as a monitor or a printer, depends on the size of the physical dots used by the device to represent each pixel of the image. Monitors display large pixels compared to printers, so an image that appears at a sensible size, for example

5 by 3 inches, on a monitor, would print as a tiny picture on most printers if the pixel data were simply mapped to printer dots in an obvious way. Conversely, if an image uploaded from a four-megapixel digital camera is displayed at full size on the screen it will be enormous, although it can be printed by a suitable printer on a conventional photocard.

It is usual to describe what is going on here in terms of the device's **resolution**, although this term is used in several confusingly different ways. Originally, it was a measure of a device's ability to distinguish fine detail. In the case of a camera or scanner, this was measured by determining how far apart the lines on a target grid had to be for the device to 'see' every one. For a printer or display, the resolution in this sense would be measured by how closely spaced it could reproduce such a grid. The resolution is quoted as the pitch of the grid, in units of lines per inch (or the metric equivalent). To a first approximation, this is the same as the number of dots in each inch, since a line a single dot wide is the narrowest that can be displayed. This accounts for the more modern (if less exact) use of resolution as a measure of the number of dots per unit length that a device can display or sample – although in the case of capturing devices this may very well not be the same as the resolution in the original sense, because of the effect of the optical components. In English-speaking countries, resolution in this sense is usually quoted in units of **dots per inch**.

To add further confusion, the resolution of some sorts of device – digital still and video cameras and monitors, in particular – is often quoted simply as the pixel dimensions of the biggest image they can capture or display. Thus, a 17-inch widescreen display may be said to have a resolution of 1440 by 900 pixels. A 20-inch display may have the same resolution, but the dots would be bigger, so that images displayed on the larger screen would appear larger. (Just as a small television will show the same picture as a massive plasma screen, but much smaller.)

Although a bitmapped image has no intrinsic resolution, it is often convenient to associate a resolution with it – usually the resolution of the device from which it originated. To emphasize that this stored resolution is a property of the image, it is usually quoted in units of **pixels per inch**. This makes it possible for software to ensure that the image is always reproduced at its natural size, by compensating for the difference between the stored resolution and the resolution of the output device. But how can this be done for monitors? The solution adopted here is to assert that **screen resolution** is always 72 dots per inch, even though nowadays it almost never is. The result is that an image will always occupy the same proportion of any screen with the same resolution (in the sense described above of pixel dimensions), no matter how big or small the screen is physically.

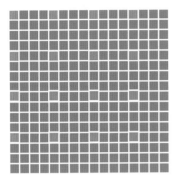

Figure 5.9 Resampling

Consider the case of a 4 by 3 inch image scanned at 288 dots per inch (a figure which is convenient rather than realistic). If we simply displayed the image's pixels on a screen it would be (nominally) 16 inches wide and 12 inches tall. To display this image at its original size at screen resolution, we need to shrink it, so that it is only 288 pixels by 216 pixels, instead of the original 1152 by 864. A simple-minded solution to this problem would be to display only every fourth pixel in every fourth row, as shown in Figure 5.9. In the more usual general case, where the output device's resolution is not an exact multiple of the stored image resolution, matters are more complicated, since pixels do not align on the array of dots of the screen. The colour of a dot must be set according to the value of the pixel that most nearly coincides with it, called its **nearest neighbour**. Simply discarding pixels in this way generally results in a loss of image quality, so more sophisticated algorithms are usually employed, which make use of the information in adjoining stored pixels in order to compute a value for each pixel in the displayed image. The two common algorithms are known as **bilinear interpolation** and **bicubic interpolation**; the latter produces better results but is more computationally expensive.

Notice that we can think about this process of reducing the number of pixels in two ways, either as a reduction in the size of the image, or as a reduction in its resolution. The latter is a more useful way of looking at things when we wish to change the data in a stored image, so that it can be displayed at its natural size on a device with a different resolution without further computation. This is precisely what we often need to do when preparing images for use on the Web, since they originate at high resolution on digital cameras and scanners, but must be displayed on relatively low-resolution monitors. It is possible to use a high-resolution image and specify its desired dimensions in the XHTML code, but apart from the needless use of bandwidth in downloading an image with more data than is required for display,

Web browsers invariably make a poor job of changing resolution, so the task is best done in advance using a specialized tool, such as Photoshop.

The process of changing an image's resolution is called **resampling**. If the resolution is to be decreased, it is **downsampling**; in the less common case of the resolution's being increased, it is **upsampling**. Resampling always potentially involves a loss of image quality, although bicubic downsampling generally produces very good results, within the capabilities of low-resolution output devices.

Image Compression

The obvious way to store a bitmapped image using 24-bit colour is as a rectangular array of 3-byte values (although for some purposes three arrays of single-byte values are preferred). So, if an image is m pixels wide and n pixels high, it will require $3mn$ bytes to hold the image data. Assuming it is stored at screen resolution, an image w inches wide and h inches tall will require $3\times72w\times72h = 15552wh$ bytes, so a 4 by 3 inch image would require 182.25 kilobytes. It is not uncommon to find several such images embedded in a single Web page; it is also fairly common to find pages that use much larger images as their backgrounds, so it seems as though the image content of a single page could easily occupy several hundred kilobytes. As we showed in Chapter 2, this would certainly take an appreciable time to download over a dial-up connection. It is therefore common to apply **compression** to bitmapped images, in order to reduce the amount of storage they require. (Compression is useful even for broadband users, since it allows ever more visual content to be added to Web pages.)

The effectiveness of an algorithm in compressing a file is measured by the **compression ratio** it achieves, which is simply the size of the input (uncompressed) file divided by the size of the output (compressed) file, so an algorithm that managed to squeeze our 4 by 3 inch image down to 9kb would have achieved a compression ratio of just over 20. Note that the compression ratio is dependent on the file being compressed: the effectiveness of a compression algorithm is dependent on the actual data with which it is presented. The same algorithm may give widely differing compression ratios on different files.

Compression algorithms are broadly divided into two categories: **lossless** and **lossy**. Lossless algorithms rearrange the data, representing it in a more efficient way and removing redundancy, but they do not discard any data. That is, if a file is compressed losslessly and then decompressed, the result will be identical to the original file. More formally, if C is a compression algorithm and C′ is the corresponding decompression algorithm, C is lossless if and only if, for any input data i, $C'(C(i)) = i$.

Lossless compression algorithms can be applied to data of any sort, including images, but the degree of compression that can be achieved losslessly is limited. For images, it has been shown in extensive experiments that some data can be discarded without noticeable loss of quality, since it represents information that is not well perceived by the human visual system. Lossy compression algorithms make use of this fact to achieve higher compression ratios by throwing away this relatively unimportant data. C is a lossy compression algorithm if, for any data i, $C'(C(i)) \approx i$. Whether the reconstructed image is a sufficiently good approximation to the original can only be judged subjectively. (The use of indexed colour is sometimes classified as a form of lossy image compression, since by discarding some colour information it reduces the size of the image file by almost two thirds.)

Since the reconstructed image only approximates the original, repeated lossy compression and decompression can cause the image's quality to decay progressively to a point where it becomes noticeable. Therefore, wherever possible, you should only apply lossy compression to an image at the very final stage of processing. Photographs taken on digital cameras are often lossily compressed (to save space on the camera's memory and decrease the time for uploading) so these should be decompressed and saved in uncompressed form during any processing, only being recompressed when they are ready for transferring to the Web server.

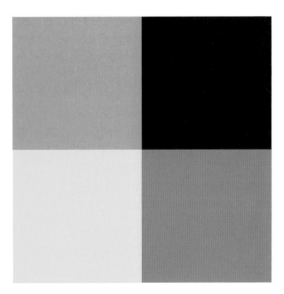

Figure 5.10 An image that can be losslessly compressed effectively

Lossless Compression

Consider the simple image shown in Figure 5.10. It is 256 pixels on each side, with each of the quarters being 128 pixels square. If this image were stored as an array of colour values, the first 128 rows would each consist of 128 identical entries for the orange colour, followed by 128 identical entries for the black. Similarly, the second 128 rows would be identical, with the orange and black values replaced by yellow and blue. Instead of storing each **run** of 128 identical values explicitly, by repeating the same value 128 times, we could save space by storing a repeat count (128) and a single copy of the value. Assuming three-byte colour values are used, an uncompressed bitmap for this image requires $3 \times 256 \times 256 = 196608$ bytes. Using repeat counts, each row would require 2 bytes for the counts and three bytes for each run, a total of 8 bytes per row, or 2048 bytes for the whole file, that is, just a shade over 1% of the space originally required.

The example was contrived, of course, to produce spectacular space savings, but many images, particularly computer-generated ones, contain areas of flat colour, which will give rise to runs of identical pixels in their bitmap representation, so this technique, known as **run-length encoding (RLE)**, may provide some savings in space. However, its main application in image compression is as part of the JPEG algorithm, described below. RLE is lossless, since there is an obvious decompression algorithm which reconstructs all the original runs.

Two other lossless techniques are used in image compression, either as part of JPEG or on their own account. They are **variable-length coding** and **dictionary-based** schemes. They both work by replacing values in the input file with different values, called codes, in such a way that the collection of codes occupies less space than the original data.

The insight behind variable-length coding is that you don't need to use the same number of bits to represent every value. Instead you can assign codes of different lengths to values. If you use codes that occupy a small number of bits for the most common values, and longer codes occupying more bits for the less common values, you should be able to make a net saving in space (although you can't guarantee you always will). For instance, a picture in a popular style for advertisements could feature a model against a plain coloured background. The colour value for the background colour would be the most common value in the image's bitmap, so if this could be stored in a single bit, the image would occupy less space, even if some of the least common colours had to be stored using codes with more than twenty-four bits.

The hard part of variable-length coding is finding an algorithm which assigns codes of optimum length to the original stored values in such a way that the original data can be recovered. The best-known technique for doing this is called **Huffman coding**. It works by constructing a binary tree structure, based on the frequency of occurrence of each value in its input. We will omit the details of the algorithm for constructing the tree here (see Mark Nelson and Jean-Loup Gailly, *The Data Compression Book*, M&T Books, 1996, Chapter 3, for a complete description and sample implementation); the effect is to produce a tree with the values attached to its leaves, such that the distance from the root to a leaf is inversely proportional to the frequency of occurrence of the value at that leaf. That is, the most common values are near the root, the least common values at the greatest distance from it. The two edges leaving any internal node are arbitrarily assigned the bits 0 and 1. The code for a value is obtained by following the unique path from the root to that symbol's leaf, writing down the bit values encountered on the way. (In practice, you would probably work back from the leaf to the root, which would give you the bits in the wrong order, but they are easily reversed.) Conversely, given a code and a copy of the coding tree, you can obtain the corresponding colour value by following a path from the root of the tree, using the next bit of the code to choose between edges, according to their labels. (This means that if you use Huffman coding to compress a file, a copy of the coding tree must be included in the compressed file, but this should not significantly decrease the compression ratio, except for small files.) If you try this, you will realize that no code is a prefix of any other, so that given a stream of bits, you can decode them into a sequence of values just by scanning from left to right; there is no need for any additional information to tell you where each code begins and ends.

Although Huffman coding is well understood and efficient, it doesn't always make optimum use of the regularities found in some kinds of images. Dictionary-based compression works in a completely different way, by building a table of strings (sequences of bytes) that are encountered in the input file. The file is encoded by replacing each occurrence of a string in the dictionary with a code that serves as a pointer to its dictionary entry. Ideally, the strings in the dictionary will be much longer than the length of the codes. You can get an idea of how dictionary-based compression works by imagining that you are trying to compress a file containing English text, rather than an image. A simple approach would be to pre-process the file and construct a list of every word that occurred in it, to serve as the dictionary. The codes would be offsets into this list; two bytes would almost certainly be adequate to index such a list, so the file would be compressed, except in the unlikely event that most of the words in it were two or fewer characters in length.

Image files and other files containing non-textual data do not come conveniently divided into words that can be used as the dictionary entries. Instead, the compression algorithm must segment the stream of bytes into strings on the basis of their distribution in the file. Here the difficulty lies in devising a way of doing this efficiently so that the strings that the algorithm chooses will in fact occur repeatedly in the file. Various algorithms have been devised for constructing dictionaries dynamically, making use of information obtained as the input file is scanned. Again, we will not go into details, but refer you to Chapters 7–9 of *The Data Compression Book*. The algorithms presently in use are derived by work carried out in the late 1970s by Jacob Ziv and Abraham Lempel, who published papers in 1977 and 1978 describing two different methods of constructing a dictionary for compression. These two methods have subsequently become known as LZ77 and LZ78. A refinement to LZ78 was devised by Terry Welch, and is known as LZW. Both LZ77 and LZW compression are used in image file formats for Web graphics, as we will see.

JPEG Compression

By far the most widely used form of lossy compression used for bitmapped images on the Web is that defined by the CCITT/ISO *Joint Photographic Experts Group*, known by the initials of that organization, as **JPEG** (universally pronounced *jay peg*) compression. Because of its importance it is worth looking at how JPEG compression works in some detail, though we will not go far into the mathematics or any details of implementation. (In fact, the JPEG standard leaves some leeway in how the algorithm is implemented, in order to allow vendors to produce competing implementations.)

The effectiveness of lossy image compression relies on identifying information that is not easily perceived by eye, and discarding it. This is easy to say, but it is not at all obvious how a computer program can find such information among an array of pixel values. JPEG compression doesn't try. Instead, it begins by transforming the image data into a different form, in which the perceptual significance of different components is more explicit. To help make this remark less enigmatic, we will return to the image in Figure 5.10.

Imagine repeatedly scanning this image horizontally in the middle of the top pair of squares with a device that measured the intensity of the orange colour. If the output of this device was plotted on a graph, it would look like the top waveform shown in Figure 5.11: at the left edge of the picture the orange immediately rises to its full intensity, and since the square is of a uniform colour, the level stays there until it reaches the middle of the picture where it falls instantaneously to zero, since there is no orange in the black square. At the right edge of the picture, we assume that the reading device immediately returns to the left edge (as though the two edges were in fact joined, making a cylinder of the picture), and the

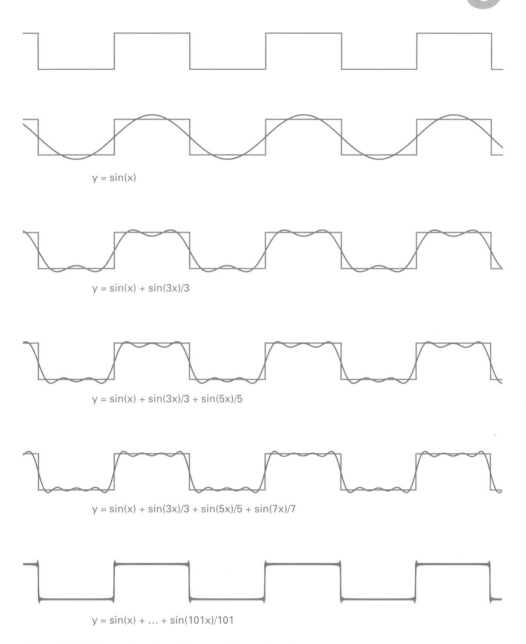

$y = sin(x)$

$y = sin(x) + sin(3x)/3$

$y = sin(x) + sin(3x)/3 + sin(5x)/5$

$y = sin(x) + sin(3x)/3 + sin(5x)/5 + sin(7x)/7$

$y = sin(x) + ... + sin(101x)/101$

Figure 5.11 Approximating the waveform of an image

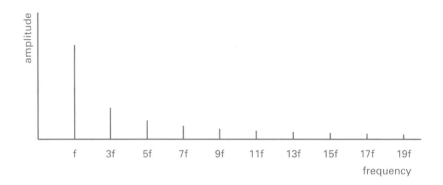

Figure 5.12 Frequency domain representation of a square wave

orange value therefore rises to a maximum again. The supposed output thus follows a square wave, as shown.

As we mentioned in Chapter 2, any periodic waveform can be expressed as a sum of sine waves of different frequencies and amplitudes. The waveforms shown here again in Figure 5.11 demonstrate how this works in the present example. As we also mentioned before, as additional frequency components are added, the resulting waveform becomes a better and better approximation to the original square wave. Instead of plotting the values of the square wave as it changes over time, we could represent the same information by plotting the amplitudes of the different frequency components, as shown in Figure 5.12. We say that these values represent the waveform in the *frequency domain*; the original waveform is said to be in the *time domain*. However, since it arose from the scanning process described above, we can just as well consider it to be a representation of the spatial variation of colour in the image as a periodic waveform.

The addition of high frequences mostly affects the fidelity with which the steep edges are represented. When the waveform represents an image, these edges correspond to abrupt changes in colour. The key experimental observation behind JPEG compression is that the high frequency components associated with such abrupt transitions are not well perceived by people. Therefore, if it were possible to take an image and transform it into the frequency domain, some of the high frequency information that became identifiable in the transformed image could be discarded imperceptibly. In other words, the image quality would not be adversely affected by the loss of this information. This then is the essence of JPEG compression: transform the image into the frequency domain and discard high frequency information. How can this be done?

There is an established method for transforming continuous periodic signals to their frequency domain representation, using an operation known as the Fourier Transform. This is thoroughly understood, and there are well-known computational optimizations that can be used to perform the transformation efficiently. Although the Fourier Transform is almost invariably described in terms of signals that vary over time, it can equally be applied to signals that vary over space – in the abstract mathematics it makes no difference whether a symbol represents time or distance, but if you like, you can consider a time-varying representation of an image being generated by a scanning operation, as we described above. Unfortunately, there are two complications which prevent the classical Fourier Transform being used for JPEG compression. First, an image is two-dimensional, so we have to deal with values that vary in two dimensions. Second, we are going to be working with bitmaps, so instead of a continuously varying (analogue) signal, we must deal with a (digital) sequence of discrete values. These two complications are not intractable, but they mean that instead of the Fourier Transform, JPEG compression uses a related, but less well-known operation, called the **Discrete Cosine Transform (DCT)**.

There is no need to know how the DCT is defined mathematically. It is more important to note the following two facts which its definition implies. First, a DCT operation takes an image's bitmap and produces an array of frequency coefficients which has exactly the same dimensions. This means that the transformation operation does not perform any compression in itself. Second, the transform is a nested sum operation, so that, for a square image of width (and height) N pixels, the time it takes is proportional to N^2. While this is by no means computationally intractable, it nevertheless implies that the time taken to perform the DCT will increase more than linearly with the size of image, and that typical bitmapped images hundreds of pixels square may take an appreciable time to transform. This last point was more of a problem when the JPEG standard was originally devised than it is now, but in order to make JPEG compression feasible on the hardware available at that time, the standard specifies that the DCT should be applied to 8-pixel square blocks of the image, so this is how the procedure is implemented (hence the DCT is usually defined in terms of a square matrix). It has the unfortunate side-effect that at high compression ratios, the edges of these blocks may become visible.

Once the DCT operation has been applied, the image data is in a form in which the perceptually unimportant high frequency components can be identified. Rather than simply throw away coefficients above a certain point, the JPEG algorithm quantizes their values, with differing degrees of coarseness. Suppose, for example, that coefficients are integers between 0 and 99. The coefficients for the lowest frequency components could be allowed to have any of the 100 possible values. Coefficients for less significant frequencies could be constrained to have only values that were divisible by 10, while the highest frequency values could be restricted to be only 0 or 50. This quantization of values can be easily performed by some simple arithmetic operations. For maximum flexibility in controlling the compression, the JPEG algorithm uses an array of quantization values, so that the degree of quantization applied to each of the 64 values in the coefficient matrix produced by the DCT of an 8 by 8 block of pixels can be set individually. Various semi-standard arrays derived from experiments are used to produce the best subjective image quality at different compression ratios. (When you set the 'Quality' value in a JPEG compression program, you are actually adjusting the values in the quantization array.)

The quantization step is where the loss occurs in JPEG compression, but it still does not produce any compression. This comes next. In most images, quantization will cause many coefficients to become zero; others will take on only a few values, so that fewer bits are necessary to represent each one. The zeros are compressed using run-length encoding; other values are usually Huffman encoded. (The JPEG standard allows for another, marginally more efficient lossless compression technique called arithmetic coding to be used instead, but since there are patents applying to arithmetic coding it is rarely used.) An additional saving is obtained by treating the coefficient in the top-left corner in a special way. This coefficient is the amplitude of the component with zero frequency; for historical reasons it is known as the DC component. Informally, it is the average value over the 8 by 8 block to which the DCT has been applied. Generally, the change in the DC component between adjacent blocks is small: photographic images tend to feature gradual tonal changes. Therefore, some space can be saved by storing the difference between the DC component of the current block and that of the preceding block, instead of storing the actual value.

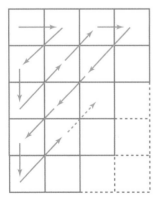

Figure 5.13 The zig-zag sequence

Emerging Technology

JPEG2000

A successor to the JPEG standard has been developed. It was adopted as a standard in 2000, hence it is called JPEG2000. Its aim is to improve on the existing DCT-based JPEG in several areas, including providing better quality at high compression ratios (low bit rates), incorporating lossless compression and alpha channel transparency within the single framework of JPEG2000, 'region of interest' coding, where some parts of the image are compressed with greater fidelity than others, better progressive display and increased robustness in the face of transmission errors. Unlike the original JPEG standard, JPEG2000 also specifies a file format.

The basic structure of the compression is the same. First, the image is divided into rectangular tiles, each of which is compressed separately. JPEG2000 tiles may be any size, up to the size of the entire image, so the artefacts seen in JPEG images at the edges of the 8 by 8 blocks can be reduced or eliminated by using bigger tiles. A transformation is next applied to the data, giving a set of frequency coefficients. However, instead of the DCT a transformation based on completely diffferent principles, known as a Discrete Wavelet Transformation is used in JPEG2000. This transformation may introduce some loss of information. The transformed data are then quantized, and the quantized coefficients are losslessly encoded using arithmetic coding, instead of Huffman coding. It is estimated that decoders for JPEG2000 will be an order of magnitude more complex than those for JPEG. More details of the compression algorithm can be found in: Charilaos Christopoulos, Athanassios Skodras and Touradj Ebrahimi 'The JPEG2000 Still Image Coding System: An Overview' *IEEE Transactions on Consumer Electronics*, Vol. 46, No. 4, pp. 1103-1127, November 2000.

In view of the vast number of JPEG images already available on the Web, the number of tools for creating JPEG images and incorporating them into Web pages, and the extent to which Web designers are familiar with JPEG, it seems likely that adoption of the new standard will be slow, and dependent on support in browsers and other software.

A very useful property of the DCT is that the lowest frequency components are concentrated in the top left corner of the coefficient array; as you move further down and to the right, the frequency increases, and thus the significance of the component diminishes. After quantization, the values towards the bottom right of the array will tend to be zero or heavily quantized. It is possible to take advantage of this structure to maximize the lengths of runs of zeros by traversing the array of coefficients in a *zig-zag sequence*, as illustrated in Figure 5.13.

We have implicitly assumed in the preceding description that the DCT and subsequent processing are applied to the stored colour values of the pixels. In fact, JPEG compression is applied to each of the colour components separately. Thus, for an RGB image, each of the red, green and blue components would be treated as a separate image in 8-bit greyscale. The JPEG standard does not assume that images are in the RGB colour space, and implementations may take advantage of this by transforming them to a different colour space and performing additional preprocessing to save still more space.

Usually, images are transformed to what is known (loosely) as the **YUV colour space**, where Y is a brightness (luminance) component and U and V are two colour differences, $B-Y$ and $R-Y$. (YUV is the colour space used in video.) The RGB values can be recovered from these three components, so there is no loss of information in using YUV. Since people are more sensitive to brightness than to colour, it is possible to compress the colour difference components more aggressively than the brightness component. It is, in fact, possible to discard some of the colour information completely, without seriously altering the perception of the image. It is common practice in video to use only half as many samples in the horizontal direction for the colour difference components as for the brightness. This practice of using fewer samples for colour than for brightness is called **chrominance sub-sampling**; for reasons that are somewhat obscure, discarding half the colour samples horizontally is called 4:2:2 sub-sampling; discarding half the samples in both directions is 4:1:1 sub-sampling. (See Figure 5.14.) Both varieties of chrominance sub-sampling are sometimes used in conjunction with JPEG compression.

Decompressing a JPEG image is done by reversing the Huffman and RLE compression to produce a coefficient array, applying the inverse DCT to recover an array of pixel values, and then, if a colour space transformation and chrominance sub-sampling had been applied, reversing these steps. The information discarded during quantization is gone forever, though, and cannot be recovered, which is why JPEG compression is lossy.

The preceding account describes baseline JPEG compression, the basic algorithm for DCT-based lossy compression of images described in the JPEG standard. The standard also defines

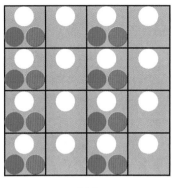 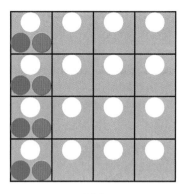

4:2:2   4:1:1

Figure 5.14 Chrominance sub-sampling

a (completely different) lossless compression algorithm, but this is rarely used. The only significant variant of JPEG is progressive encoding, in which the compression is performed in multiple passes over the data, with the result that a decompressor can reconstruct an approximation to the image very quickly from the initial section of the compressed data; this approximation is then refined as more data becomes available.

Bitmapped Image File Formats

Only three bitmapped image file formats are displayed natively by most Web browsers: **GIF**, **JPEG** and **PNG**.

GIF

GIF stands for Graphics Interchange Format, having originally been devised to allow users of CompuServe's bulletin board system to exchange bitmapped images. (Opinion is more or less equally divided about whether GIF should be pronounced *giff* or *jiff*.) There have been two versions of the GIF specification: the original, known as GIF87a, and an extended version, known as GIF89a, published, as you might guess, in 1987 and 1989 respectively. The GIF format provides the ability to include the data for more than one image in a single file. GIF files containing more than one image have been widely used as a means of embedding animations in Web pages, as we will describe in Chapter 6. GIF files are identified by the Internet media type `image/gif`.

GIF images use indexed colour, with 8-bit index values and therefore a maximum of 256 colours in the palette. Programs which create GIF files usually provide facilities for applying dithering and editing the colour table to help overcome the limitations of small palettes.

A useful feature of GIF is that one colour may be specified as representing transparency. When the image is displayed on a Web page, the background colour or image shows through any areas of that colour. This allows you to include images that are apparently not rectangular on a page, and to perform primitive image compositing.

GIFs are compressed losslessly, using LZW compression. Although this does not provide the high compression ratios achievable with JPEG compression on photographic images, it also means that it does not suffer from the artefaction associated with low quality JPEG. In particular, hard edges and straight lines are preserved better in GIFs than in JPEGs. In conjunction with the tendency for posterization to occur when continuous tone images are reduced to indexed colour, this makes GIFs especially suitable for bold drawings and designs, with areas of uniform flat colour, such as might be produced using a drawing package on a computer, for diagrams and for images containing text. GIFs are often used for buttons and rollover elements, logos and tiled background textures. In all these cases, files are usually small and the advantages of lossless compression are particularly appreciated.

JPEG

The JPEG standard does not include the specification of any file format, so strictly speaking 'JPEG file' is a misnomer. However, there is an obvious way of storing the output of a JPEG compressor in a file, and files in this form, with extensions `.jpeg` or `.jpg` are universally recognized, as is the Internet media type `image/jpeg`. So, although technically they are JFIF (JPEG File Interchange Format) files, and only an *ad hoc* standard, it is reasonable in practice to refer to these as JPEG files. (JPEG data can also be stored in graphics files of other types, including TIFF, but these are not displayed natively by Web browsers.)

JPEG files use full 24-bit colour; they do not provide any sort of support for transparency, so the only way to combine a JPEG image with a background is by pre-compositing the two before adding the JPEG to a Web page. JPEG files are, of course, lossily compressed, but except at the highest compression ratios the quality is extremely good. JPEG is the best choice for any colour images with continuous tones, especially photographs.

As we mentioned in our earlier description, JPEG compression and decompression can operate in a progressive mode. To the user, the effect is that a rough version of the image is displayed soon after downloading begins, and becomes clearer and more detailed as it proceeds. This may be considered to provide a better user experience than waiting for all the data to arrive before seeing any image at all, but with broadband connections the advantages are debatable as the waiting time will be short and a very blocky image can be irritating.

Digital cameras often employ a file format called EXIF. This is an extension of the JFIF format, which allows for additional data to be included, such as the date and time at which the photograph was taken. EXIF files can be treated as JPEG files in constructing Web pages.

JPEG2000 has its own file format, with media type `image/jp2`. At the time of writing, these files are rare.

PNG

The PNG (Portable Network Graphics) format was devised to provide a replacement for GIF. The immediate incentive for creating a new format was the decision in 1994 by Unisys, who own a patent on LZW compression, to demand licence fees for any implementation of the LZW algorithm. Since any program that works with GIF files must compress and decompress them, this meant that use of the GIF format was subject to such fees. This was no great hardship for the major browser and image software vendors, but left less wealthy shareware and freeware authors unable to incorporate GIF support into their programs legally. PNG uses a version of LZ77 to perform lossless compression, and is unencumbered by any patents. As a bonus, it is estimated that the PNG compression algorithm typically attains compression ratios between 5% and 25% better than those of GIF. By the time work on defining the PNG format began, GIF was beginning to look rather outdated anyway, and PNG provided an opportunity to improve on GIF at the same time as avoiding the LZW patent.

PNG files may use indexed colour or full 24-bit colour; the two cases are often distinguished by the names PNG-8 (for indexed) and PNG-24, but these are not separate types of file, and PNG implementations should be able to display both PNG-8 and PNG-24. Only a single media type, `image/png`, is defined for PNG images. PNG-8 is in any case a misleading name, since the index values may be 1, 2, 4 or 8 bits wide, and the colour table may contain any number of entries, up to the maximum number of values that can be indexed (2, 4, 16 or 256). PNG images may be interlaced so that they are displayed with increasing resolution as more data becomes available, much like progressive JPEGs.

An outstanding feature of PNG images is their support for **alpha channels**. An alpha channel is an additional component of the colour values stored in an image file, which is used to specify transparency. It is easy to imagine storing an extra bit with every colour value, with the interpretation that if its value was 1 the pixel's colour as specified by the remaining bits should be displayed, but if it was 0, the underlying colour would be displayed instead – the pixel would be transparent. Alpha channels take this idea further by using an entire 8-bit value to specify a degree of transparency, ranging from completely transparent to completely opaque, with a range of partial transparency in between. As well as allowing translucent images, where the background can be seen through the image, alpha channel transparency is used for several well-known visual effects that are difficult to achieve with the other Web graphics formats, such as feathered edges and drop shadows.

PNG is described by a W3C Recommendation and is an ISO standard. Despite this official standing and its inherent technical superiority to GIF as a losslessly compressed bitmapped image format, PNG remains the least used of the three Web graphics file formats, largely because of inertia on the part of developers satisfied with GIF, and poor initial support in mainstream browsers and image manipulation programs. Given this slow adoption, it is possible that the PNG format will eventually fall into disuse unless new Web design idioms that depend on its unique facilities such as alpha channels become popular.

Vector Graphics

If you were asked to look back at Figure 5.10 and describe it, you would probably say that it was four squares, coloured orange, black, yellow and blue, butted together to make a big square, or words to that effect. The design has a simple structure, which is clear to any person looking at it, but in the bitmapped representation this structure is completely lost. The image is represented simply as an array of pixel colour values. Because many of the pixels are the same colour, the image will compress well using lossless methods, but the fact that all the orange pixels are part of a square which is a clearly identifiable shape within the total image is not part of the bitmapped representation. If you wanted to change the colour of the orange square to pink in an image editing program, for example, you could not select the shape, you could only select all the orange pixels.

The squares example is so simple that this would be a feasible way of performing this change, but consider the image on the left of Figure 5.15. Again, this comprises four squares, which you can easily identify, but they are now filled with decorative patterns. Selecting one of these squares from a bitmap and changing the colours in the pattern would not be a trivial exercise. Modifying the sizes of the patterned areas as shown on the right of Figure 5.15 would be quite challenging. Vector graphics offers an alternative way of representing images, which is based on shapes. In a vector graphic version of Figure 5.15, each square would be a distinct object, and it would be simple to select one of them in an image editing program and change the colours of its pattern or increase its height. (Which was exactly how this illustration was created.)

Figure 5.15 Modifying objects within an image

Shapes, lines and curves, and transformations on them, can be described mathematically, using coordinate geometry. This will probably be familiar to most readers, but it is not necessary to understand the mathematics in any detail. The underlying concept is that a point in two-dimensional space can be described by a pair of numbers, its **coordinates**, which give its horizontal and vertical distance from a fixed point in space, called the **origin**. To be more accurate, the two coordinates specify the distance in some arbitrary units from the origin in two directions at right angles to each other. The straight lines in these two directions which intersect at the origin are called the **axes**. Conventionally, they are shown horizontally and vertically, and labelled x and y. The two coordinates are also referred to as the x and y coordinates. Figure 5.16 illustrates these concepts. Notice that we have shown y values increasing downwards. In mathematics, it is conventional to have the y axis pointing upwards, but for vector graphics it is more usual to invert it, as we have shown here.

By using letters to stand for unknown coordinates, we can write down equations which describe, for example, all the points lying along a straight line, or all the points on the circumference of a circle. The equation $(x-c_x)^2 + (y-c_y)^2 = r^2$ is satisfied by the x and y coordinates of the points on the circumference of any circle whose radius is r and whose centre has coordinates (c_x, c_y). (See Figure 5.16; you can derive the equation easily just by using Pythagoras's Theorem.) By plugging in different values of the parameters r, c_x and c_y you obtain the equation of a specific circle, with a given radius and centre point. The circle with radius 10 centred on the origin $(0,0)$, has equation $x^2 + y^2 = 100$, putting $c_x = c_y = 0$ and $r = 10$. In other words, if you know its radius and the coordinates of its centre, you have

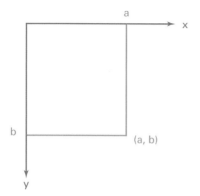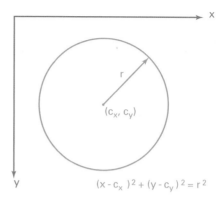

Figure 5.16 Coordinates and equations

enough information to work out where all the points on the circumference of a circle are, knowing the general form of the equation. If you also have a specification of how wide a stroke you want the outline of the circle to be drawn with, and the colours you want to use to draw the outline and to fill in the middle, you have enough information to draw a circle by setting pixels to appropriate colours.

In principle, this is how vector graphics works. Shapes (and other graphic objects,) are stored in the form of a few parameters which can be plugged in to equations describing the general form of each type of shape. For instance, in SVG (which we will describe in more detail shortly), shapes are represented by elements (SVG is derived from XML), whose attributes correspond to the parameters appropriate to the corresponding sort of shape. A circle is described by a `circle` element, with attributes cx, cy and r, which together fully specify the size and whereabouts of the circle, and `fill`, `stroke` and `stroke-width`, which specify how the circle is to be drawn. For example,

```
<circle cx="120" cy="120" r="70" fill="crimson" stroke="darkblue"
   stroke-width="12" />
```

is the part of an SVG document which corresponds to the circle in Figure 5.3.

In general terms, it is fairly obvious how a representation like this can be displayed on the screen, or *rendered*, as the process of converting a vector graphic to pixels is called. The abstract two-dimensional coordinate space in which the equations are defined is similar to the array of pixels on a screen, inasmuch as each pixel can be identified by a pair of numbers, its row and column in the array. So, although the details of doing it efficiently are non-trivial,

Figure 5.17 Anti-aliasing

it should be clear that it is possible to work out, from the equations and the values of the parameters, which pixels should be coloured in to make the shape that the vector object describes. The major practical problem that affects users is that, whereas pixels are discrete objects, whose coordinates are always integers (whole numbers), coordinate geometry is defined using real numbers, which may have fractional parts. For instance, suppose that you wished to render the line of width one pixel defined by the equation $y = x/2$, between the endpoints $(0,0)$ and $(10,5)$. If you went about this in a naive way by stepping the value of x from 0 to 10, computing the corresponding value of y and then setting the pixel in row y and column x to the fill colour, you would rapidly find that half the points you computed fell 'in between' pixels. If you then do the obvious thing and round to the nearest integer, you would end up drawing a sort of staircase, as shown on the left of Figure 5.17, instead of a smooth line. This phenomenon, often called the *jaggies*, is inevitable when drawing on a device with pixels of a finite size. If the pixels are small – in other words, the output device's resolution is high – the jaggies will not be noticeable. On a low-resolution display, though, the pixels are sufficiently large for jaggies to be intrusive. A technique that is often used to mitigate the effect is known as *anti-aliasing*. This is done by colouring pixels around the jagged edge in shades of the stroke colour (for example, shades of grey for a black line), as shown on the right of Figure 5.17. The effect at normal magnifications is to replace the abrupt change of contrast at the edge by a more gradual fading. This is seen as a softening of edges, which conveys a smoother effect; most people find this more acceptable than the jaggies, despite the blurring that occurs.

It should be clear that, for images composed of shapes and curves, vector graphics offers a highly compact alternative to bitmaps: only the values of a few parameters need to be stored, instead of the value of every pixel. Because the objects in the image retain their identities, they can be easily edited and transformed. This makes vector graphics suitable for certain kinds of animation and motion graphics, since applying transformations to parameter values over time can create the illusion of movement. A final advantage of vector graphics is that they are scalable, that is, they can be displayed at different sizes and resolutions without loss of quality. Whereas decreasing the resolution or increasing the size of a bitmapped image may make the pixels visible and introduce artefacts, a vector image can be displayed at different sizes and resolutions without loss of quality (within the capabilities of the output device), since the size of objects can be altered just by changing their stored parameter values.

For these reasons, vector graphics have long been popular for technical drawing and illustration. They have not been much used on the Web, though, except for animation in Flash (which is a vector-based format). One reason for this is the absence until recently of any standard vector graphics file format for the Web, but this has now been supplied in the form of SVG, which we will describe later. Perhaps a more substantial impediment to the wider use of vector graphics on the Web is a perceived lack of any need. Most of the images found on websites are photographic in nature, and not amenable to vector representation. There are some important exceptions, though, including technical diagrams, cartoon-style drawings, and simple geometrical designs, which might be appropriate for buttons. Vector images work well for these purposes, but images created in vector form tend to compress well as GIFs, so it has been usual to export finished artwork in this form, instead of using a vector format.

Vector Drawing

Whereas it remains to be seen whether vector graphics will become a common element of Web pages, images created in vector form already are, even if most of them are converted to GIFs before being added to the page. It is instructive to consider the most common elements of vector images and the way in which they can be created. For a text-based graphic language such as SVG, it is actually possible to make an image by creating a document and entering the necessary elements and attribute values, but few if any people are capable of visualizing anything but a trivial picture in numerical terms. At the very least, it is necessary to make a sketch on squared paper and read off the values of coordinates and dimensions. This would be a time-wasting, error-prone and tedious process. It is much better to draw directly using an interactive program that provides a direct manipulation interface, displays the picture as it is being drawn and allows the user to save it in a file in some suitable format, such as PDF or SVG, or export it in a bitmapped format, such as GIF. The most popular commercial example of such a program is Adobe Illustrator; Flash also provides vector drawing capabilities. Less polished freeware and shareware alternatives abound.

Shapes

The basic drawing shapes are rectangles (with squares as a special case), ellipses (circles may be treated separately or as a special case of ellipses) and polygons, both regular and irregular. A typical vector drawing program provides separate tools for drawing each of these shapes. Tools for drawing additional shapes, such as stars and spirals, may also be provided. These tools all work in the same general way. A tool is selected from a toolbox – a palette of icons representing each tool – and then mouse gestures are used to create the shape. For example, to draw a rectangle in Illustrator, you would select the rectangle tool and drag the cursor diagonally from corner to corner of where you wanted the rectangle to appear. You should be able to appreciate how this mouse gesture effectively sets the coordinates of the top left corner of the rectangle, its height and its width, which are sufficient data to specify the position and size of the rectangle. An alternative way of working with these tools is to click at the point where you want to place the object. A dialogue box then allows you to enter the dimensions numerically. This ability to use numerical values makes it possible to draw with great precision in a vector program.

Lines, Curves and Paths

You can't make a very interesting picture out of rectangles, ellipses and polygons alone. What makes vector graphics more generally useful is the ability to add straight and curved lines, and use these to create freeform shapes. The standard tool for this job is called a pen, although it scarcely resembles a conventional drawing pen. To draw straight line segments, you simply click at the end points. To understand how curves are drawn requires a short digression.

Geometers are familiar with many sorts of curve, but most of them are not suitable for vector drawing, because it is not, in general, possible to join segments smoothly to form longer flowing curves. The pen tool in vector drawing programs produces curves known as **Bézier curves**, for which this is possible, and the pen provides a way of joining them to make **paths**, which are connected sequences of curve and line segments.

We will not go into the mathematical details of how Bézier curves are defined. It is enough to know that a curve can be defined by four points, known as its **control points**. Two of these are the endpoints of the curve, the other two are called its **direction points**. This terminology is explained by Figure 5.18, which shows how the control points define the curve. The lines between the endpoints and direction points (the **direction lines**) are the tangent vectors at the endpoints. What this means is that the curve sets off from the first endpoint heading towards the first direction point, and that it arrives at the other endpoint heading directly

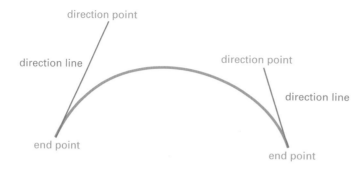

Figure 5.18 A Bézier curve

away from the other direction point. The curve sweeps round smoothly in between the two direction lines; the depth of the curve is controlled by the length of the direction lines. It is as if the curve was the trajectory of a runner, who set off along the first direction line at a speed proportional to its length, but got pulled round by some attractive force from the other endpoint, and ended up running towards it, at a speed that depended on the length of the second direction line. Figure 5.19 shows how the direction and length of the direction lines alters the shape of a Bézier curve.

If you think now about joining two curves at a point, you should be able to see that if the direction lines through the joining point are lined up, and they are the same length on either side of the join, as shown on the left of Figure 5.20, the curves will join up smoothly. (Our runner does not have to alter speed or direction as he passes through the joining point.) Alternatively, if the direction lines are not joined up, the two curve segments will join at a discernible corner as shown on the right of Figure 5.20.

If a path joins up on itself (its first and last points are the same), it is said to be **closed**, and it can be filled with colour, in the same way as a primitive shape can. A path that is not closed is **open**.

Figure 5.19 The effect of changing direction lines

Figure 5.20 Joining two Bézier curves at a point

Stroke and Fill

Notionally, paths and the outlines of shapes have zero width. To make them visible, a stroke of finite width must be applied to them. The stroke is applied symmetrically about the path or outline, which therefore has an effect on the overall size of objects, as you can see in Figure 5.21, where all of the shapes have the same dimensions, as indicated by the thin blue lines. Strokes may be of any colour, and dotted and dashed strokes are commonly provided. Fills can take the form of solid colours, gradients or patterns. The case of a solid colour is simple; as with the stroke colour, the current fill colour is applied to objects as they are drawn, and the fill may be changed subsequently just by selecting the object and choosing a new fill colour.

Gradients are fills composed of several colours, blending into each other. (Gradients cannot be used as strokes.) They are usually of one of two types: linear or radial, as illustrated in Figure 5.22. In either case, to specify a gradient it is necessary to specify the colours and a set of *gradient stops*. When it is applied to an object as a fill, a linear gradient extends right across the object. The gradient stops define points as a proportion of the width of the gradient.

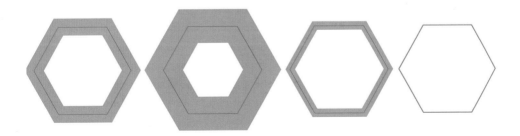

Figure 5.21 Applying different strokes to a shape

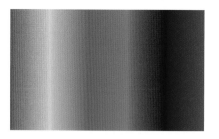 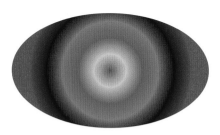

Figure 5.22 Linear and radial gradient fills

At each stop, a colour can be chosen. The gradient is created so that between any two stops there is a smooth blend of the pure colours at the stops. Radial gradients work similarly, but the gradient is defined inside a circle and the stops are defined along its radius. Vector drawing programs allow you to define gradients along a ramp, clicking to set the stops and choosing the colours with a colour picker.

As Figure 5.15 showed, patterns made up of repeated tiles can also be used as fills.

Both stroke and fill can be empty. An object with an empty stroke has no outline, its fill just stops at the edge. An object with an empty fill has a transparent interior. Note that an empty fill or stroke is different from a white fill.

Transformations

The coordinates of its top left corner, its height, width, stroke and fill are sufficient information to enable a program to display a rectangle, provided it is positioned parallel to the axes. What if you want to display a rectangle tilted at 45°? You could accommodate tilted shapes by adding some extra information, in the form of the angle by which they should be rotated from the horizontal, but an easier and more general approach is to allow **transformations** to be applied to shapes after they have been created. Generally, five types of transformation are supported: scaling, rotation, reflection, skewing and displacement. They are illustrated in Figure 5.23. These five transformations all share the property that their effect can be achieved by altering the values of the stored representation of a shape in accordance with simple trigonometrical operations. Clearly, some of these transformations are redundant when applied to a single shape, in that their effect could be produced by changing the positional coordinates, height or width. However, as the illustration shows, transformations can be applied simultaneously to groups of objects, whose position and dimensions are implicitly derived from the objects they comprise.

Figure 5.23 Transformations

Technical Detail

Transformation Matrices

Mathematicians will be aware that any combination of translation, scaling, rotation, reflection and skewing can be expressed in the form of a 3×3 transformation matrix

$$T = \begin{bmatrix} a & c & e \\ b & d & f \\ 0 & 0 & 1 \end{bmatrix}$$

To be able to express any transformation, including translation, as a matrix product, a point $P = (x, y)$ is written as the column vector

$$\begin{bmatrix} x \\ y \\ 1 \end{bmatrix}$$

(P is said to be specified using 'homogeneous coordinates'), and the effect of applying the transformation is given by the product $T \cdot P$. Since the bottom row of the transformation matrix is always the same, just six numbers are required to specify any transformation. This compact representation is often used internally by graphics systems to store transformation information, and can be specified explicitly, for example in SVG.

SVG

Although the bulk of vector graphics on the Web takes the form of animations or still images in SWF (Flash) files, **Scalable Vector Graphics (SVG)** is the World Wide Web Consortium's recommended markup language for vector graphic images. It is defined by an XML DTD, so, like any other language defined in this way, it has a public identifier (`PUBLIC "-//W3C//DTD SVG 1.1//EN"`) and a system identifier (`http://www.w3.org/Graphics/SVG/1.1/DTD/svg11.dtd` for SVG 1.1). There is also an SVG namespace (`http://www.w3.org/2000/svg`), and the document element is `svg`. Hence, every valid SVG document has the following outline structure:

```
<?xml version="1.0" encoding="utf-8"?>
<!DOCTYPE svg PUBLIC "-//W3C//DTD SVG 1.1//EN"
   "http://www.w3.org/Graphics/SVG/1.1/DTD/svg11.dtd">
<svg xmlns="http://www.w3.org/2000/svg">
        content of the document
</svg>
```

And, of course, the document must be well-formed XML.

Shapes

Within the `svg` element are elements which define the objects making up the image. The simplest of these are those which correspond to the basic geometrical shapes. Table 5.1 lists these, and the attributes which are unique to each one. As you will see, these attributes' values will be precisely the information needed to specify the size and position of each shape: the rectangle has its height, width and top left corner coordinates; the circle its centre and radius, and so on. Coordinates and lengths may be specified in any of the units used in CSS. If a unit is not specified, values are interpreted as pixels.

In addition to these shape-specific attributes, all the shape elements share a collection of **presentation attributes**, whose values control the shape's appearance when it is drawn. The most often used of these are `stroke`, and `stroke-width`, which set the colour and width of the object's stroke, and `fill` which specifies a colour, gradient or pattern for its fill.

Fills

If an object is to be filled with a solid colour, the value for the `fill` attribute may be specified in the any of the ways provided for specifying colours in CSS. The attribute may also have the special value `none`, or a URL identifying what the SVG specification calls a paint server, which is a definition of a gradient or pattern. For URL values, the CSS syntax, `url(URL)`,

Element name	Attributes	Notes
rect	x	coordinates of top left corner
	y	
	width	
	height	
	rx	x and y radii of rounded corners
	ry	
circle	cx	coordinates of centre
	cy	
	r	radius
ellipse	cx	coordinates of centre
	cy	
	rx	x and y radii
	ry	
line	x1	coordinates of end points
	y1	
	x2	
	y2	
polyline polygon	points	list of points – see text

Table 5.1 SVG shape elements

is used. Normally, the URL will be a fragment identifier, and the paint server will be an element with an id attribute which it identifies.

Linear and radial gradients are defined by the linearGradient and radialGradient elements, respectively. These elements can have several attributes which permit fine control over the disposition of the gradient, but for most purposes the defaults are adequate and only an id attribute is required, in order for the gradient to be used as a fill. Gradient elements may contain stop elements, which correspond to the gradient stops described earlier. Each has two attributes, offset (which can be specified as a percentage) and stop-color, which has a CSS-style colour specification as its value. (For more esoteric effects, you can also specify a stop-opacity, as a real number between 0 and 1.) You might therefore define the linear rainbow gradient used in Figure 5.22 in the following way:

```
<linearGradient id="rainbow">
        <stop   offset="0" stop-color="#E11B25"/>
        <stop   offset="0.2" stop-color="#FFE800"/>
        <stop   offset="0.4" stop-color="#009140"/>
        <stop   offset="0.6" stop-color="#009ED7"/>
        <stop   offset="0.8" stop-color="#222A82"/>
        <stop   offset="1" stop-color="#E10079"/>
</linearGradient>
```

and use it like this:

```
<rect fill="url(#rainbow)" width="150" height="90"/>
```

Patterns are specified in a similar way, using a `pattern` element containing arbitrary elements, which define the pattern in the same way as elements are used to define a picture. Attributes control the way in which the pattern is tiled to a shape; we will omit the details.

Paths

Paths are specified using a `path` element. The path's control points are contained within a string of data used as the value of the d attribute. This string is, in effect, a small program in a specialized (and very simple) graphics language for creating paths from Bézier curves and straight line segments. It consists of a sequence of commands for controlling a notional pen, which behaves like the pen tool in vector graphics applications, and draws the path in response to these commands. Each command is followed by some values. The pen can be moved to a specific point, made to draw a straight line or a curve or to close an open path.

The path data is written in a concise form, since paths form the bulk of many SVG images. Each instruction has a name, but is identified in the data string by a single letter, and, although values may be separated by spaces and commas, any such delimiters which are not required to separate values unambiguously may be omitted. Where a string contains a sequence of some particular command (for example, a series of curve segments), all but the first command letter may be omitted. We will, however, show path data without these omissions, to make them more readable.

Generally, to begin a path, the pen is moved to its starting point. The `moveto` command is used for this purpose. Like all commands, it comes in two forms: one which uses absolute coordinates, and one which uses coordinates that are relative to the pen's current position. In all cases, an upper case letter (`M` in the case of `moveto`) is used for the absolute form, and the corresponding lower case letter (`m`) for the relative form. Thus `M100,100` would move the pen to the point (100, 100). If that command were followed by m0,100, the pen would move to (100, 200). Here, we have separated the coordinate values by a comma, although we could have used a space instead.

The usefulness of relative coordinates becomes apparent when we consider drawing lines, which is done by the lineto command, written as L for absolute coordinates, or l for relative. The effect of this command is to draw a line from the current point to the point indicated by the following values. If we had moved the pen to (100, 100), the command L 0, 100 would draw a (horizontal) line between (100, 100) and (0, 100), whereas l 0, 100 would draw a (vertical) line between (100, 100) and (100, 200). The special cases of horizontal and vertical lines are optimized using the vertical lineto (V or v) and horizontal lineto (H or h) commands, which omit the redundant value. The two lines in the preceding examples could also have been drawn using the commands H 0 or h -100 and V 200 or v 100.

The commands for drawing curves are the most elaborate, reflecting the more elaborate nature of their construction. (In fact, SVG supports the drawing of more types of curve than we have described, but we will only mention the most important, which is the Bézier curve we described earlier.) The basic command for this purpose is curveto, abbreviated C or c. This is followed by three pairs of values, which are interpreted as the coordinates of the two direction points and the endpoint of a Bézier curve segment; the start point is implicitly taken to be the pen's current position (so normally a curveto command would be preceded by a moveto or some other drawing command). Thus, with the current point at (100, 100), C 200,200 300,200 400,100 would draw a symmetrical curve from (100, 100) to (400, 100) using (200, 200) and (300, 200) as direction points. The same curve could be drawn using c 100,100 100,0 100,-100. (There is no way of mixing absolute and relative coordinates within the same curve.) Although we have used commas to separate the coordinates of each point and spaces to separate the points, this is not required in SVG, it is just a convention that makes paths more readable. In fact, commas and spaces are interchangeable as separators.

To optimize the construction of paths from smoothly joined Bézier curves, the smooth curveto command (S or s) is provided. This is followed by just two pairs of coordinate values, which are the second direction point and the endpoint (in other words, the ends of the second direction line). As before, the start point is taken to be the pen's current location; the first direction point is taken to be the reflection in the start point of the second direction point of an immediately preceding curve segment. You should be able to see how this corresponds with our description of Bézier paths, when symmetrical direction lines are produced where the segments join.

Transform	Effect
`translate(tx,ty)`	Translate (move) element by *tx* units in *x* direction and *ty* in the *y* direction (*ty* = 0 if omitted)
`scale(sx, sy)`	Scale by factor of *sx* in *x* direction, *sy* in *y* direction (*sy* = *sx* if omitted)
`rotate(a, cx, cy)`	Rotate by *a* degrees around the point (*cx*, *cy*) (*cx* = *cy* = 0 if omitted)
`skewX(a)`	Skew by *a* degrees along *x*-axis
`skewY(a)`	Skew by *a* degrees along *y*-axis
`matrix(a, b, c, d, e, f)`	Apply transformation matrix [*a b c d e f*]

Table 5.2 SVG transforms

Transformations

Transformations applied to an object are represented as the value of the `transform` attribute, which is common to all the shape and path elements. Its value is a list of transform definitions, separated by commas or spaces. Each transform definition consists of the name of a transform, followed by some argument values in brackets. Table 5.2 summarizes the possible transform definitions that may be included in this list. For example, an element like this could be used to create an ellipse and rotate it about its centre:

```
<ellipse fill="red" stroke="black" cx="100" cy="100"
  rx="75" ry="45" transform = "rotate(45, 100, 100)"/>
```

Notice that reflection is not available as a primitive definition, but it can be simulated using a matrix: `matrix(-1,0,0,1,0,0)` defines a reflection in the vertical axis, for example.

Groups

The last feature of SVG that we will describe is grouping. In any vector graphics system, objects can be combined into groups which can be transformed and otherwise manipulated as a single entity; groups can themselves be combined into bigger groups. The idea of grouping maps very naturally onto the containment hierarchy of elements in XML (and thus in SVG). A collection of objects can be made into a group by placing the corresponding SVG elements into the content of a g element. The presentation attributes of the group and any transformations from its transform attribute are inherited by the elements contained in it, so, for example, our rainbow gradient fill can be applied to several objects, which are rotated as a unit, in the following way:

```
<g fill="url(#rainbow)" transform="rotate(45, 50,50)">
        <rect x="0" y="0" width="50" height="50"/>
        <ellipse cx="100" cy="50" rx="25" ry="15"/>
        <ellipse cx="150" cy="100" rx="25" ry="15"/>
</g>
```

XHTML Markup for Images

GIF, JPEG and PNG images may be embedded in an XHTML document using the img element. This is an empty element. Its src attribute's value is a URL that points to the file containing the image data in one of these three formats. In case the user's browser cannot display the image, the compulsory alt attribute should be used to provide a short textual alternative. (See Chapter 9 for more details.) Images can be positioned and formatted using CSS rules if a class or id attribute is provided. A typical example is:

```
<img src="Resources/logo.gif" alt="Company logo" class="leftfloating"
/>
```

The img element is an example of a *replaced element*, whose content is some resource separate from the XHTML document in which the element occurs. Since the image is contained in a separate file from the document, the presence of an img element will cause a separate HTTP request to be sent in order to retrieve the image data.

The img element is an inline element, so images should only appear within block elements. Their placement can be controlled using stylesheets. The float property is often used in conjunction with images. If a stylesheet rule causes an image to float to the left or right, nearby text will be wrapped around the edge of the image; images can be placed in the margin using float and wide margins, as we demonstrated for text boxes in Chapter 4. Alternatively, where wrapping of text is not desired, an image can be placed within a paragraph of its own, and aligned left, right or centre. Arbitrarily complex page layouts can be created by placing images within div elements, which can be absolutely positioned. Placing an image in a paragraph of text without floating it usually produces unattractive results, as the image is treated as a (large) character for the purpose of setting the line of text it appears in.

Like any other element, an img can have its height and width set using the corresponding CSS properties, but usually it is not a good idea to do this. If a stylesheet sets a size for the image different from its actual size (as recorded in the image file), resampling will be necessary to scale the image. Browsers do not, in general, make a good job of this. Most likely, they will simply perform nearest neighbour interpolation, since more sophisticated algorithms

Emerging Technology

Images in XHTML 2.0

The img element in HTML has some shortcomings. In particular, if, for whatever reason, it is not possible to display the image it references, the only expedient is to use the text that is the value of the alt attribute in its place. In XHTML 2.0, a fairly radical means has been adopted to overcome this deficiency. The img element has been removed from the language; instead, *any* element may have a src attribute whose value is the URL of an image; it will often be used in conjunction with the type attribute, which specifies the media type of the image. The semantics is that if the image can be displayed it will be and the content of the element will be ignored; if the image cannot be displayed (perhaps because of a network problem, or because the user agent does not support images) the element content is used instead. In the simplest case, the src attribute would be applied to a p element. The text of the paragraph would then serve as a textual alternative to the image. Unlike the value of the alt attribute, this text can be marked up. For example:

```
<p src="Resources/Images/ snowflake.gif" type="image/gif">
 Fractally generated image of a snowflake, reproduced from
 page 108 of <em>Digital Multimedia</em></p>
```

Because the src attribute can be used with any element, including div, the textual alternative to an image can be arbitrarily long or complicated. For example, a table of data values could be used as an alternative to a graph.

take too long. If the stylesheet does not specify any width or height, the image's natural size is used, which will produce the best results. Therefore, images should be sized correctly in Photoshop or some equivalent program before being added to a Web page, and stylesheets should not specify any different size.

The img element has its own width and height attributes, whose values are numbers, which are interpreted as being lengths in pixels. Using these attributes has the same drawbacks as using the CSS properties, with the additional disadvantage that it mixes presentation information with markup, which we always try to avoid. There is a case for using these attributes, though. Many browsers will reserve space for the image when they read the <img> tag, and lay out the rest of the page around it. If the width and height attributes are not present, the text will first be laid out without taking account of the image, and then, when the image data arrives, the page will be relaid to accommodate it. This will cause a shift in the page contents, which can be annoying to somebody who is reading the page's text while waiting for its images to appear. Therefore, it is good practice to set the `height` and `width` attributes of any `img` elements to the actual pixel dimensions of the image. Most Web authoring packages and HTML editors will do this for you automatically.

An SVG image can, in theory, be embedded in an HTML document using an `img` element, in the same way as bitmapped GIF, JPEG and PNG images can. In practice, this method is unreliable, because of poor browser support for SVG. A more reliable way of embedding SVG in a Web page is to use the `object` element. We will describe this fully in Chapter 6, but for now it is enough to know that you can embed an SVG image with a tag such as the following:

```
<object data="Resources/Images/Squares.svg"
  type="image/svg+xml" name="Squares" width="200" height="200">
        Image made up of coloured squares
</object>
```

The URL of the image is the value of the `data` attribute; the media type is given by the value of the `type` attribute (which is why this approach is more reliable than using an `img`, since the browser is explicitly told that it is dealing with an SVG image). Note that the media type is `image/svg+xml`, since SVG is an application of XML. The `width` and `height` attributes' values set the size of the screen area in which the SVG image will be rendered. They should therefore be set to a sufficient size to accommodate the image; omitting these attributes may lead to the images' being clipped.

Note also that the `object` element is not empty. Its content (here, the text `Image made up of coloured squares`) is displayed if, for some reason, the specified data cannot be, so here we are using the element content to provide a textual alternative to the image, in the same way as the `alt` attribute of a more conventional `img` element does.

The `object` element can be used to embed images of other types, such as TIFF, provided a suitable plug-in (see Chapter 6) is installed.

Image Maps

Since `img` is an inline element, images can be placed in the content of anchors, producing graphic links: clicking on the image causes a new page to be fetched and displayed.

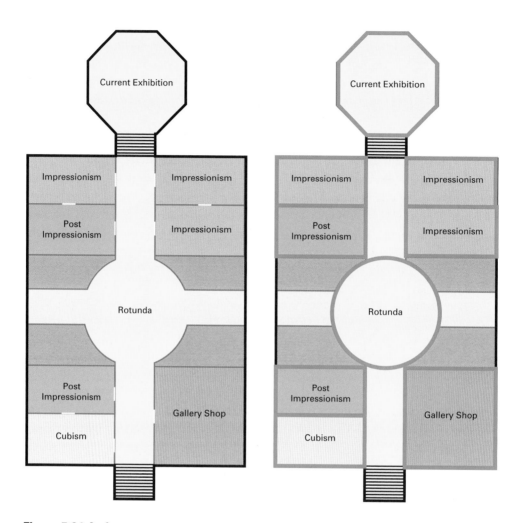

Figure 5.24 An image map

A common idiom is the use of small images as links within navbars; the images can be made to look like buttons, with the use of drop-shadows and other pseudo-3D effects. Scripts are commonly used to apply rollover effects to buttons of this type.

The idea of graphical links is taken a step further with **image maps**. An image map is an image containing **hot spots**, which are regions within the image that act as link anchors. For example, a floorplan of a museum or art gallery could have hot spots for each of the rooms, linked to pages describing the objects on display in that room; clicking in a room on the plan would cause the corresponding page of exhibits to be displayed. Figure 5.24 shows such

Shape	Coordinates	
rect	*left-x, top-y, right-x, bottom-y*	coordinates of top left and bottom right corners of the rectangle
circle	*centre-x, centre-y, radius*	coordinates of the centre and radius of the circle
poly	$x_1, y_1, x_2, y_2, \ldots, x_n, y_n$	coordinates of the polygon's vertices

Table 5.3 Image map areas

an image map: normally, the hotspots are not visible, the image is displayed as it is shown on the left; on the right, we have indicated the hot spots' borders. As you can see, hot spots may be rectangular, polygonal or circular. There is no requirement that they correspond to any features of the image itself, although normally, as in this case, they will.

Several steps are needed to turn an image into an image map. The data that defines the hot spots and associates links with them appears in the content of a map element. This has a name attribute, which is used to identify it. (Like img elements, it may also be identified by its id attribute, but this is less reliable, since not all browsers use name correctly in this context.) The map is linked to the image by way of the usemap attribute which must be added to the img element's tag. Its value is a fragment identifier that matches the name attribute of the map element that is to be used. (Theoretically, the usemap attribute's value may be a URL, so that it can point to a map element in a different document, but this possibility is not widely implemented.) Thus, the markup for the image map in Figure 5.24 has the following form:

```
<img src="images/floorplan.gif" alt="Gallery plan"
usemap="#floorplan_Map" />
    <map name="floorplan_Map">
    content of the map
</map>
```

There are two distinct ways of defining the hot spots within the map element. The older and more widely used method is to use a collection of area elements, one for each hot spot, as the map's content. Each area element has a shape attribute, which may have one of the values rect, circle or poly, specifying that the hot spot is a rectangle, circle or polygon, respectively. The area's geometry is specified by the coords attribute, which provides a list of coordinates, whose meaning depends on the value of shape, as shown in Table 5.3. The destination of the hot spot's link is given by the href attribute, as it is for anchors.

Finally, each area should have an alt attribute, giving a textual alternative, so that non-visual user agents can display the image map's links in a textual form.

If area elements were used for the hot spots, the map for our gallery floorplan would look like this:

```
<map name="floorplan_Map">
        <area shape="poly"
        coords="85,94, 58,67, 58,29, 85,2, 122,2, 149,29,
        149,67, 122,94, 85,94" alt="Current exhibition"
        href="current.html" />
        <area shape="circle" coords="104, 254, 50"
        alt="Sculpture gallery" href="sculpture.html" />
        <area shape="rect" coords="122,158,206,203"
        alt="Impressionists I" href="impressionists1.html" />
        <area shape="rect" coords="122,114,204,158"
        alt="Impressionists II" href="impressionists2.html" />

        area elements for the other hot spots

</map>
```

It isn't usually necessary to measure the coordinates by hand. Most graphics programs that include some Web facilities allow you to draw the hot spot areas on top of an image, and will generate the markup, including the coordinates, automatically. There also exist small utilities dedicated to the same job.

Areas may overlap. If two of them do so, and a user clicks in the overlapping area, the link in the hot spot whose area element appears first in the map will be activated. It is as if hot spots are stacked on top of each other, with later ones below earlier ones. An area element may have a Boolean attribute nohref. If this is set (nohref="nohref"), there is no link associated with the hot spot. This may be used to create dead areas within an underlying hot spot.

The second way of specifying hot spots uses the familiar a element within the map. As well as the attributes we described in Chapter 3, a elements may also have shape and coords attributes, which work just as they do for area elements, to define the geometry of hot spots, if the a element appears inside a map. The difference between this method and the use of area is that a elements are displayed, just as they would be in any other context, as well as serving to define hot spots. This means that a textual alternative to the image map is automatically available, for non-visual user agents and for the benefit of people who prefer that form of navigation.

If a elements are to be used to define the hot spots, the content of the map should consist of block elements. Since the collection of hot spots is essentially a list of links, as a navbar is, logically it makes sense for a map to contain a ul, which contains li elements containing the links. Hence, for our example, using this approach the map would look like this:

```
<map name="floorplan_Map">
<ul>
    <li><a shape="poly" coords="85,94, 58,67, 58,29, 85,2, 122,2,
    149,29, 149,67, 122,94, 85,94" href="current.html" >Current
    Exhibition </a></li>
    <li><a shape="circle" coords="104, 254, 50" href="sculpture.html"
    >Sculpture Gallery</a></li>
    <li><a shape="rect" coords="122,158,206,203"
    href="impressionists1.html" >Impressionists I</a></li>
    <li><a shape="rect" coords="122,114,204,158"
    href="impressionists2.html" >Impressionists II</a></li>

    list elements for the other hot spots

</ul>
</map>
```

With this markup, the image map would be displayed with a conventional list of links below it, which could be styled using a suitable stylesheet.

Since using a elements within the map produces a textual alternative to the hot spots with no additional effort and without interfering with the graphical links, it is generally to be preferred to the use of area elements. Support for this form of map is not, however, universal in browsers – although those that do not implement the shape and coords attributes of a elements correctly do at least fail safely, by displaying the textual links. It is permissible to use both area and a redundantly in the same map. If this is done, browsers that correctly implement both will ignore the area elements. This is therefore the safest approach, but means that two sets of links need to be maintained.

Key Points

There are two types of representation used for computer graphics: bitmaps and vector graphics.

Display and Storage of Images

Any image displayed on a computer screen is a rectangular array of small square dots of colour, called pixels.

A bitmapped image consists of an array of colour values, one for each pixel in the image.

Any image with continuously varying tones (such as a photograph) can be represented by a bitmap.

A vector graphic image consists of a mathematical description of the picture, as a collection of geometrical shapes, together with stroke and fill information.

Vector graphics are generally more suitable for diagrams and cartoon-style drawing.

Colour

The colour of a pixel on any display is made up of proportions of the three additive primaries: red, green and blue.

The RGB colour model is the method of representing any colour by three numbers, specifying the relative proportions of red, green and blue.

With 24-bit colour (one byte for each of R, G and B) about 16.7 million different colours can be represented.

Indexed colour can be used to reduce the space required by images.

If an image's palette (the set of colours it uses) contains 256 or fewer colours, a single byte will be adequate to store a unique number for each colour.

A colour mapping is used to translate from small numbers stored in a bitmap to full 24-bit colour values.

Where colours must be omitted from the colour table, posterization may result. The effects of this may be mitigated by dithering.

The Web-safe palette contains the only 216 colours that can be reliably displayed correctly on both Windows and Mac systems using indexed colour, but it is no longer necessary to restrict colours to these.

Colour spaces are a general mechanism for representing colours as a tuple of numerical values. They depend on the precise values used for red, green and blue.

sRGB is a standard colour space, defined by W3C, which helps ensure that colours are reproduced consistently.

In CSS, colours are commonly represented as six hexadecimal digits (two for each of R, G and B), preceded by a # sign. (e.g. #308EBF).

Bitmapped Images

Image optimization – a process of compression, possibly reduction to indexed colour and dithering, then saving to a suitable file format – is usually required before images can be used on Web pages.

Device resolution is usually quoted in dots per inch, but for cameras and monitors, resolution is often simply the pixel dimensions.

Images for embedding in Web pages should always be saved at screen resolution, which is taken to be 72 dots per inch.

The process of changing an image's resolution is called resampling, and always potentially involves a loss of quality. If the resolution is reduced, the process is called downsampling.

It is common to apply compression to bitmapped images, in order to reduce the amount of storage they require and the time they take to transfer over a network.

Compression algorithms may be lossless or lossy.

Run-length encoding (RLE) can be used to represent areas of flat colour compactly, but is more often used as part of the JPEG algorithm.

Huffman coding is another lossless algorithm sometimes employed as part of JPEG compression.

LZ77, LZ78 and LZW are dictionary-based lossless schemes. LZ77 and LZW are used in some Web image file formats.

The high frequency spatial components that are associated with abrupt transitions in an image are not well perceived by people, so images can be compressed by discarding it without loss of quality.

The Discrete Cosine Tranformation (DCT) produces a representation of an image in the frequency domain, where these components can be identified easily.

The JPEG algorithm quantizes coefficients in the frequency domain, so less significant coefficients can take on fewer values.

Quantized coefficients are then encoded using RLE and Huffman.

Traversing the array of coefficients in a zig-zag sequence maximizes the length of runs of zeros.

Chrominance sub-sampling is used to achieve further compression of colour images.

GIF images use 8-bit indexed colour, for a maximum of 256 colours, and employ lossless LZW compression. One colour may be used to designate transparency.

JPEG images use 24-bit colour and are lossily compressed.

PNG images may use indexed or 24-bit colour. They are losslessly compressed and support alpha channels.

Vector Graphics

Shapes are stored in the form of a few parameters which can be plugged in to equations describing the general form of each type of shape.

Anti-aliasing is used to mitigate the jaggies, which result from rendering vector shapes defined using real numbers to finite pixels.

Vector graphics are compact, scalable, and easily modified or animated.

The basic shapes are rectangles, ellipses and polygons; they may be combined with lines and curves.

Bézier curves are defined by two endpoints and two direction points. They can be joined smoothly to make paths.

Strokes may be of any width and colour, and may be dotted or dashed.

Fills can take the form of solid colours, gradients or patterns.

Both stroke and fill can be empty.

There are five types of transformation: scaling, rotation, reflection, skewing and displacement.

SVG is the W3C's recommended markup language for vector graphics. It is defined in XML.

Shapes are defined by elements, whose attributes' values specify their size and position.

Presentation attributes control appearance, including stroke and fill.

Colours may be specified as in CSS, or with the URL of a paint server, which may be an element defining a gradient or pattern.

Paths are specified using a path element. The d attribute holds a sequence of drawing commands, which implicitly specify control points of Bézier curves and endpoints of straight lines.

Transformations are represented as the value of the transform attribute.

A collection of objects can be combined into a group by placing the corresponding SVG elements into the content of a g element.

XHTML Markup for Images

Images may be embedded in an XHTML document using the empty, inline img element, whose src attribute's value is the URL of a GIF, JPEG or PNG file.

The compulsory alt attribute provides a short textual alternative.

SVG images and other types of bitmapped image can be embedded using the object element.

Images can be placed in the content of a elements, as graphic links.

An image map contains hot spots, which act as link anchors.

Hot spots may be defined by the shape and coords attributes of area or a elements within a map element, referred to by the usemap attribute of the img.

Exercises

Test Questions

1. Is the bitmapped image produced by rendering a vector graphic always less compact than the original vector image?

2. Is the following statement true or false? Any colour can be represented by three numbers specifying the relative proportions of red, green and blue it contains.

3. When would you *not* use dithering when saving an image in a format that used indexed colour?

4. Explain carefully what is meant by the statement that, in CSS, all RGB colours are specified in the sRGB color space.

5. Why is lossy compression more commonly used for Web graphics than lossless?

6. At what point in JPEG compression is information discarded? Is this the point at which the data is compressed?

7. If you wanted to post a copy of a printed document that you had scanned to a Web page, what file format would you use and why?

8. Why are paths in most vector graphics made up of Bézier curves and not, for example, of sections of ellipses?

9. Of the five vector transformations described in this chapter, which are redundant when applied to a rectangle? (That is, which transformations could be produced simply by altering the stored data describing the rectangle?)

10. What attributes must every `img` element have?

Discussion Topics

1. Is the Web-safe colour palette irrelevant to modern Web design?

2. Would it be possible to devise a compression algorithm that was guaranteed to cut down the storage requirement of any arbitrary image? Give a reason for your answer.

3. Many graphics programs allow you to 'slice' an image, that is, divide it into regions which are saved in separate files, together with some XHTML and CSS that assembles them on a page so that they fit together and make up the original image. What purpose might there be in such a facility?

Practical Tasks

1. Use the Save For Web command in Photoshop, or the equivalent in any other image editing program available to you, to export an image as a JPEG, using a medium quality setting. Open the saved image, and then export it again at the same quality. Repeat the exercise until you see a visible deterioration in the image's quality. Now go back to the original image and go through the same sequence of steps, but using the highest quality setting. Finally, do the whole thing again, using the lowest quality setting. What conclusion can you draw about the most suitable setting for exporting a JPEG image for use on a Web page, and for archiving images for additional processing? Do further experiments to determine what effect the visual characteristics of the image have on the results.

2. Choose any bitmapped image in a format suitable for the Web and create an XHTML document that embeds it in a page. Using CSS, set the dimensions of the image to values other than the size at which the file was saved. View the resulting page in a range of browsers, and assess the quality of their image resizing algorithms. Repeat the experiment for a range of sizes. Does it make any difference whether the image is upsampled or downsampled? Are dimensions that are a simple multiple of the original handled better than more awkward values?

Time-Based Media

6

The possibility of including video, animation and sound is one of the most significant ways in which Web pages differ from printed pages. The distinguishing characteristic of these three forms of media is that time is an essential part of what they are. Time does pass when you look at a still image or read a piece of text, of course, but the image and the text do not change in any way during that time. *Time-based media* are those media which themselves exhibit some change over time. Without time, animation, video and sound do not exist.

Video and animation are artificial forms that re-create or simulate the way in which things look in the real world by presenting a sequence of complete still images (called *frames*) in rapid succession. The frames of an animation or video clip must be displayed one after another at a fast enough speed and in the right order for an illusion of motion to occur. Without this sequencing of the frames in time there is no animation or video, just a collection of still images. When we look at the real world we do see movement that is genuinely continuous in time, but in video or animation we see only a series of snapshots, presented quickly enough to trick the brain into believing that it sees continuous movement.

Figure 6.1 shows some successive video frames; the twelve frames in this clip represent approximately half a second of movement (the frames progress down each column in turn). Each frame is a recognizable still image in itself, with a noticeable difference between each image, but when they are played back in quick succession (in this case at a rate of 25 frames per second) we believe that we are seeing continuous flowing movement. If we slowed down the playback of the same clip, however, we would see very jerky movement, and realize that the movie was really just a collection of still photographs. The fact that video is actually a series of photographs – and thus a collection of bitmapped images – is fundamental to the methods we can use to compress it and prepare it for the Web. Animation, on the other hand, may be either bitmapped or vector graphics.

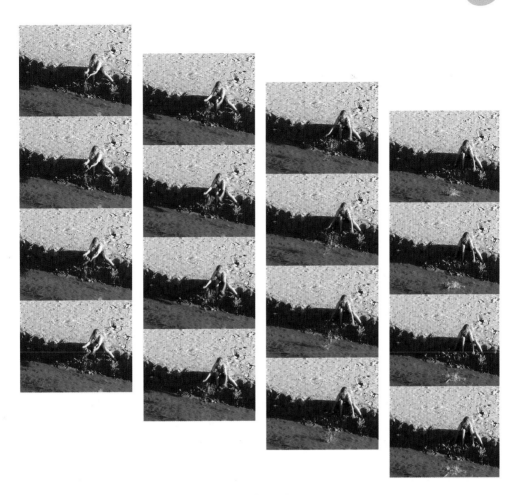

Figure 6.1 Video consists of a sequence of still images

Sound is rather different; it cannot be re-created by presenting a handful of recognizable snapshots played back in sequence. Digital sampling of sound does take a set of snapshots, in a sense, but it requires 44,100 samples per second for CD quality, for example, compared with something between 12 and 30 pictures per second for animation or video. It would be impossible to experience something that has a duration of approximately one forty thousandth of a second – our brains cannot cope with something that short – so we therefore think of recorded sound as continuous in time, as illustrated by the continuously varying waveform in Figure 6.2.

Figure 6.2 Sound varies continuously

Including time-based media in Web pages presents both technical and design difficulties. The former are easy to understand and are amenable to technical solutions. The latter are more challenging. The Web in particular and digital multimedia in general have provided the opportunity of mixing static media, such as images and text, with time-based media. While there is hundreds of years' worth of experience in combining static media in page designs, there is little precedent for adding time-based media to them. The main established precedents come from film and television, but these are themselves time-based forms, which may include text and still images (think of a news bulletin, for instance). Starting from a static page, as we do on the Web, and embedding time-based elements within it, is a new design problem which has not yet been adequately solved.

We have stressed that video, animation and sound are time-based media. A consequence of this is that it is only possible to experience traditional forms of these media as their creators intended if we allow them to play from beginning to end. This means that the user must change from the active role normally played when browsing the Web – reading or skimming text, looking at images, following links – to a passive role – watching an animation or video clip, or listening to an audio clip as it plays. Often, users don't do this, they simply move on as soon as the animation or whatever fails to hold their attention. Subjectively, this seems to be a much less momentous decision than, say, walking out of a cinema or changing channels when a film becomes too tedious. Creators of time-based media for the Web cannot assume that people will necessarily watch or listen. However, if they do choose to do so, their attention will usually be fully engaged, so it is advisable not to add many other elements to a page which presents any time-based media that lasts longer than a few seconds.

Time-based media are quite often found embedded in a Web page without offering the user any form of control. Advertisements, blinking alert signs, background music and Flash introductions to corporate sites are just some examples of this approach, which can frequently cause annoyance and may even result in the user leaving the site. In many cases, therefore, when time-based media are embedded in a page, it is preferable to provide controls for

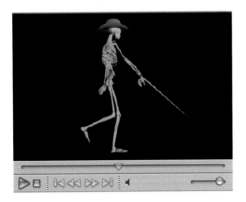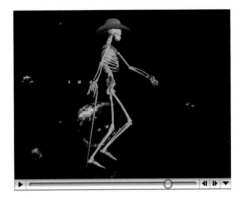

Figure 6.3 Controllers for Windows Media and QuickTime video

starting and stopping, pausing, rewinding and turning sound on or off and changing its volume. (Figure 6.3 shows the standard controllers for some time-based media types.) Web designers often have no way of altering the appearance of these controllers, which makes them difficult to integrate into a page design. (Experts can usually create 'skins' which alter the appearance of media players, but there are few options for creating novel controllers whose operation will still be obvious to users.)

Time-Based Media and Web Pages

Before looking at the different types of time-based media in detail it is useful to consider the mechanisms common to displaying almost all forms of time-based media in Web browsers, and the markup used for embedding them.

Plug-ins and ActiveX Controls

Every graphical Web browser can display formatted text and bitmapped images in two or three different formats, but it would be impractical to expect every browser to be able to cope with data of every media type that designers might want to add to their pages. One response that browsers might make to data they cannot handle is to pass it on to some other program that can. Most browsers allow their users to designate such *helper programs* for each Internet Media Type. With this approach, though, extra types of media, including time-based media, cannot be displayed as part of a page inside the main Web browser window. For example, a PDF document requires the helper program Adobe Reader and cannot be displayed as an integrated part of the design of the Web page which linked to it; the PDF file can only be displayed within a new browser window, or by downloading it and opening it in Adobe Reader. In either case the helper program must be installed on the user's computer.

To allow for the possibility of truly embedding time-based media in pages, browsers use an extensibility mechanism that allows them to call on additional modules – which may be provided by a third parties, such as the creator of a proprietary media format – to handle media types that they cannot display themselves. For example, animations produced by Adobe's Flash program can be viewed using the Flash Player plug-in, which Adobe have made available for free. Users must download this module and install it on their systems if they wish to view pages containing Flash movies. (Some browsers do this automatically the first time they encounter a Flash movie, but this is potentially a security risk.)

For the same module to be used by different browsers, a standard is required. Unfortunately, two completely incompatible *ad hoc* standards are in use, and there is no reason to suppose that an official standard will be developed or would be accepted by all parties if it were. Thus, modules must be created in two forms: a **plug-in** and an **ActiveX control**.

Plug-ins

The plug-in format was devised by Netscape for use with their Navigator browser, and has been adopted by most other browsers, including Safari and Opera, as well as Navigator's successors in the Mozilla family.

Any plug-in will be designed to handle data of one or more Internet Media Types. When an HTTP response includes data of a type that a browser using plug-ins cannot handle itself, it will look for a plug-in that can do so on its behalf. If it finds one, it will load it, reserve some space on the page for the plug-in to display its output, and then pass the data to the plug-in, which will usually display some representation of it on the page.

ActiveX

The alternative mechanism for dealing with data that the browser cannot handle directly is ActiveX, part of Microsoft's Component Object Model (COM), which is a system of reusable software components, used on Windows operating systems. An ActiveX component, known as a control, can be used on that system in much the same way as a plug-in. In practice, ActiveX controls are only used in this way by Microsoft's own Internet Explorer browser (IE). When IE encounters data of a media type that it cannot handle itself, it creates an instance of an appropriate control to deal with it instead.

Although the technical details of how ActiveX controls are written and called differ from the corresponding details of plug-ins, the general scheme is the same: the browser passes data to a dynamically loaded extension that actually displays the media. Both plug-ins and

ActiveX controls are available for all of the time-based media types that we will describe (with one exception, which needs neither).

There is a curious asymmetry in the availability of the two mechanisms. ActiveX controls are only used by one browser on one family of operating systems, while plug-ins are used by all other browsers on all platforms (including Windows). However, that one browser accounts for over 80% of all the browsers in use, so that, while ActiveX is used by a minority of browsers, it is used by a substantial majority of browser users. Hence, neither technology can simply be dismissed by Web designers.

Markup

The most regrettable aspect of the existence of the two separate mechanisms for displaying time-based media in Web browsers is that they require different information to be included in the markup. The fundamental difference is that, with ActiveX, it is the control itself that is considered to be embedded in the page, with the location of the data being passed to it as a parameter, while, where plug-ins are used, it is the data that is considered to be embedded, with the plug-in being called to display it. Both viewpoints are defensible, but they lead to different markup.

In theory, the requirements of both ActiveX controls and plug-ins can be accommodated in XHTML documents with the `object` element. This is a versatile element, which is intended to provide a way of embedding any sort of media (including still images as well as time-based media) or executable code in a page. It is an inline element, so media can be included within paragraphs or absolutely positioned `div` elements, if that is appropriate.

Unlike `img`, which it resembles in some ways, `object` is not an empty element. Its content is displayed if, for some reason, the object itself cannot be. Thus, the content serves an analogous purpose to the `alt` attribute of `img`, but allows for richer alternatives: for example, an image as an alternative to a video clip, or styled text as an alternative to an image. This also makes the alternative available to search engines.

The `object` element has several attributes, which must be used in different combinations to cover different types of media content.

The simplest possibility is a browser that uses plug-ins and a media type for which a plug-in exists. In that case, specifying the media type as the value of the `type` attribute is sufficient for the browser to identify the required plug-in. (In fact, this information should also be available in the HTTP response which contains the data, but specifying it in the `object` element's start tag enables the browser to determine whether a suitable plug-in is available before it starts to download what may be a large file. If it is not, the data need not be downloaded, and the browser should display the element's content.) The location of the data is given by the `data` attribute, which functions in the same way as the `src` attribute of the `img` element: its value is a URL.

Since the browser must reserve space to display the object, it needs to know its dimensions. This is done using the `width` and `height` attributes, whose values are the corresponding lengths, in pixels. (Some browsers are able to discover this information from the data itself, but most set the dimensions to zero if the attributes are omitted, with the result that the object cannot be seen.)

As an illustration of the simple use of `object`, consider embedding a Flash movie in a page. (We will describe Flash movies in detail later in this chapter. They are a form of vector-graphic animation.) The Internet Media Type for Flash movies is `application/x-shockwave-flash` (which we will also explain later). Hence, to include a Flash movie with the relative URL `Explode.swf` in an XHTML document for the benefit of browsers that use the Flash plug-in to play them, the following markup could be used:

```
<object data="Explode.swf" type="application/x-shockwave-flash"
 height="400" width="550">
 content of the object element
</object>
```

As well as elements to be displayed in case the Flash movie cannot be, the content of the `object` element can include `param` elements, which are used to pass additional information to the plug-in. Since there is no way of knowing what parameters might be required by any plug-in that may be written at any time in the future, the mechanism for passing information must be as general as possible. Accordingly, the `param` element has two attributes, `name` and `value`, which are used to specify the name of a parameter which the plug-in understands, and its value. The possible paramater names should be listed in the documentation for any plug-in. For instance, the Flash plug-in has a parameter called `quality`, which may be used to specify how much anti-aliasing is applied to vector objects, and thus how smoothly drawn they will appear. This parameter can be set to `high` with the following element, to force all vector artwork in the movie to be anti-aliased:

```
<param name="quality" value="high" />
```

If there are any `param` elements, they must be the first things in the content of the `object` element.

It may not be possible for a browser to show the specified Flash movie for several reasons: the absence of the plug-in, network or server errors preventing the data being received, or a typographical error in the URL used in the tag, for example. In any of these cases, the browser will display the content of the `object` element. In the case of a Flash movie, a sensible fallback would be to display a still image from the movie. Normally, you would probably use an `img` element to do this, but it is possible to use `object` here, too, at least in theory. Doing so allows you to specify a second level fallback, in the form of some text. Taking this approach, the complete markup for embedding our Flash movie would be as follows:

```
<div>
<object data="Explode.swf" type="application/x-shockwave-flash"
height="400" width="550">
   <param name="quality" value="high" />
   <object data="Explode.jpeg" type="image/jpeg" height="400"
width="550" >
           <p>The exploding text movie</p>
         </object>
</object>
</div>
```

This markup will not work as intended with Internet Explorer for Windows: a blank area will be displayed on the page where the movie should be. For that browser only, `object` must be used with different attributes in order to invoke the Flash ActiveX control to play the movie.

The required information is an identifier for the ActiveX control. This takes the form of a pseudo-URL, beginning with `clsid:`, which serves the same function as `http:` in Web URLs, of identifying the sort of information contained in the rest of the URL. In this case, this information consists of a string of apparent gibberish, known as a Globally Unique Identifier, which is simply a codename for the plug-in, which is guaranteed to be unique. This entire pseudo-URL is the value of the `classid` attribute. As before, the height and width must be specified, so that space for displaying the movie can be reserved on the page. To embed a Flash movie, the following markup is required:

```
<object classid="clsid:D27CDB6E-AE6D-11cf-96B8-444553540000"
 width="550" height="400">
 content of the object element
</object>
```

Most people do not remember the identifier. Markup such as this is usually generated auto-matically by Flash or by Web authoring programs.

As we mentioned earlier, this markup does not really embed the movie, it embeds the ActiveX control, which needs to be told where the movie is. This is done using a `param` ele-ment, with its `name` attribute set to `movie` and its `value` set to the movie's URL. As before, an image could be used as a fallback in case the movie cannot be displayed. This time, for reasons we will explain shortly, we will use an `img` element for this purpose.

```
<div>
<object classid="clsid:D27CDB6E-AE6D-11cf-96B8-444553540000"
 width="550" height="400">
   <param name="movie" value="Explode.swf" />
   <param name="quality" value="high" />
   <img src="Explode.jpeg" alt="The exploding text movie" />
</object>
```

Before looking at ways of reconciling the markup needed by plug-ins and ActiveX controls, we will describe some more aspects of the `object` element.

As well as being used for embedding time-based and other media objects, the `object` ele-ment is intended for including executable content in pages. The most familiar example of such executable content is a Java applet. The mechanism is intended to support other programming languages too, but the choice of attributes and their names shows a bias towards Java.

The `classid` attribute's value is the URL of what the HTML standard calls the object's implementation, in other words, its executable code. If the object was an applet, this might indeed identify a Java class, hence perhaps the attribute's otherwise mysterious name. The `data` attribute, on the other hand, identifies the location of data to be read and used by the object's implementation. An applet might very well need both of these pieces of information. Taking the view that an ActiveX control is a piece of executable content that is embedded in the page, it makes sense to use the `classid` attribute to identify it; from the alternative view that Flash movies and so on are information that is embedded in the page and which happens to need a plug-in to display it, it makes sense to use the `data` attribute.

Since Java applets are often packaged in archives, there is also an `archive` attribute. The `codebase` attribute is intended to provide a base URL, relative to which these other attributes (`classid`, `data` and `archive`) can be resolved. It has, however, been hijacked in practice, to provide a means of automatically finding missing plug-ins and ActiveX controls. The value of `codebase` is often the URL of a page from which the plug-in or control required by the object can be downloaded. Some browsers, notably Internet Explorer on Windows, will proceed to download and install the missing module. While convenient, this has proven to be a security risk.

Your first thought about combining the markup for plug-ins and ActiveX might be that, since the two use separate attributes for the `object` element, you could simply specify `type` and `data` as well as `classid`, and each mechanism could find the information it needed. Unfortunately, this doesn't work, because browsers that do not use ActiveX must still use `classid` to identify the implementation of executable objects, such as Java applets. If a `classid` attribute is present, the browser will attempt to find some executable content. If it does not support ActiveX, this attempt will fail when `classid` has a control's Globally Unique Identifier as its value, so the `type` and `data` attributes will be ignored, and the browser will proceed to display the content of the `object` element.

This suggests a better approach: put the `object` element for the plug-in inside that for the ActiveX control. Internet Explorer for Windows should load the control ansd ignore the content; other browsers will be unable to load the control and so will use the inner `object`, which will invoke the plug-in. In the case of our Flash movie, the markup would look like this:

```
<object classid="clsid:D27CDB6E-AE6D-11cf-96B8-444553540000"
 width="550" height="400">
  <param name="movie" value="Explode.swf" />
  <param name="quality" value="high" />
  <object data="Explode.swf" type="application/x-shockwave-flash"
   height="400" width="550">
    <param name="quality" value="high" />
    <object data="Explode.jpeg" type="image/jpeg" height="400"
    width="550" >
          <p>The exploding text movie</p>
```

Browser Quirks

The embed Element

The nested `object` markup described in the main text is the preferred way to embed objects so that either a plug-in or an ActiveX control can be used to display them, and it will work on any browser that correctly implements the HTML 4 or XHTML 1 standards. If compatibility with older versions of browsers is important, though, a less satisfactory expedient must be employed. This is because versions of Internet Explorer for Windows up to and including IE 6 incorrectly implement nested `object` elements. If the browser has been able to display the object, instead of ignoring the content of the element it tries to display it as well, in the case that it is another `object`. Thus, nested `object` elements do not solve the problem as they should on legacy versions of Internet Explorer. (Also, if you wish to provide an image as a fall-back for an `object`, using `img` is more robust than using an inner `object`.)

When Netscape introduced plug-ins, they also defined a proprietary HTML element, `embed`, for the purpose of including data to be displayed using a plug-in. This element has never been part of any official HTML standard, not even as a deprecated element, and it is certainly not part of XHTML. Nevertheless, all browsers that can presently use plug-ins recognize `embed`. Furthermore, Internet Explorer correctly ignores `embed` elements in the content of `object` elements. Therefore, a working solution to coping with plug-ins and ActiveX controls consists of nesting an `embed` element (for the plug-in) in an `object` (with attributes for the ActiveX control).

The `embed` element is empty. Instead of using `param` elements to pass values to the plug-in, it passes its attributes. Therefore, there is not really a fixed set of attributes for this element, you must use whichever ones the plug-ins require. A few attributes 'belong' to `embed`, notably `src`, which is used as it is with `img` to identify the source of the data for the plug-in, and `type`, which specifies the Internet Media Type. As with `object`, the width and height must also be specified, to enable the browser to reserve space on the page for the embedded content.

The following element can be used to embed our Flash movie:

```
<embed data="Explode.swf"
  type="application/x-shockwave-flash"
  height="400" width="550" quality="high" />
```

Here `quality` is actually a parameter used by the Flash plug-in.

To cope with browsers that use ActiveX as well as those that use plug-ins, this markup must be placed inside an object element with the ActiveX attributes, like this:

```
<object
  classid="clsid:D27CDB6E-AE6D-11cf-96B8-444553540000"
  width="550" height="400" >
    <param name="movie" value="Explode.swf" />
    <param name="quality" value="high" />
    <embed data="Explode.swf"
      type="application/x-shockwave-flash"
      height="400" width="550" quality="high" />
</object>
```

If embed must be used, there is no way of providing some alternative content for occasions when the Flash movie cannot be displayed.

There is something extremely unsatisfactory about a situation whereby it is necessary to use invalid XHTML markup for browsers that do conform to the standard, in order to cope with the shortcomings of a browser that fails to do so. Hopefully, use of early versions of Internet Explorer will decline, so that the standard markup can be used exclusively.

```
      </object>
    </object>
</object>
```

Similar markup can be used to display video or to include audio in a page, with appropriate changes to the `type` and `classid` attributes' values.

To avoid unnecessary repetition, in the remainder of this chapter we will use the term 'plug-in' to include both plug-ins and ActiveX controls, except where it is important to distinguish between the two.

Animation

The movement that we see when watching movies or television is an illusion created by displaying a sequence of still images (*frames*) one after the other at a sufficiently high rate for persistence of vision to cause them to blend into an apparently continuously changing picture. In video and film, these frames are captured by a camera in real time; people, places and events that in reality exist continuously in time are photographed by a camera capable of taking pictures in rapid succession, normally at a speed of between 24 and 30 still images per second. When these still photographs are played back at the same speed we believe that we see continuous movement, but in fact we are only seeing a very large collection of photographs presented one after another, any one of which may be inspected independently. When film was first invented it was quickly realized that if you could convincingly record and replay real-life movement in this way, then you could also create artificial moving creatures and objects and scenes by making your own sequence of still images, recording them one by one with a moving picture camera, and playing back the resulting sequence in the same way as if it had been recorded from the real world. This technique was called animation, because it brought inanimate art work and objects to life. Video thus *records* motion that takes place in the real world; animation *creates* artificial motion, but they both rely on exactly the same means to convince their audience that they are actually seeing something move.

In the context of the Web we need to extend the traditional idea of animation. Animation for distribution on film or TV has a significant extent in time – much longer than just a couple of frames – and it is linear, i.e. the animation is designed to play from start to finish (although the user can control starting, stopping, pausing etc. with video or DVD recorder controls) and passive. Web animation often departs from these constraints, and includes new forms of image changes and user control. Web animation may have only a very few frames, perhaps as few as two, and it may be presented in interactive forms which are non-linear, that is, the animation responds to user input in ways which go well beyond traditional playback control. It is not even necessarily designed to play from a beginning to an end.

These new types of animation include such simple Web page elements as rollover buttons that change appearance in their different states when the cursor is off, over or the mouse is clicked; looping animations of very few frames, such as blinking or moving alert signs, and more sophisticated interactive animations which may respond to such input as cursor position and movement on the screen. Providing an image changes, either independently or in response to user input, and the changing image has been created frame by frame (by animator or by program) and not recorded in real time, we will refer to it as animation. Figure 6.4 shows an example of one of these new types of animation in use on the Web and in other

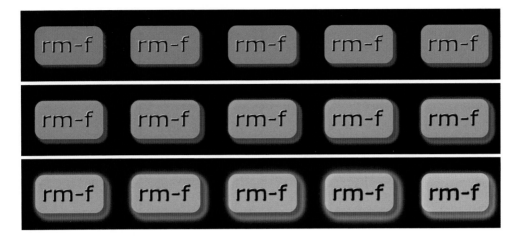

Figure 6.4 An animated button

multimedia environments. This simple animation has fifteen frames and loops continuously in order to give an impression of throbbing. The separate frames are not created individually by the designer, but are generated by Flash according to parameters set at the time the animation was designed. An animation of this kind is typically interactive, so that clicking on it causes something to happen – a feature clearly impossible in traditional animation.

It follows, too, that not all Web animation exploits the phenomenon of persistence of vision in the same way as traditional animation, nor is it limited to a single, pre-defined playback rate; the rate of change of images may be very slow or extremely fast, neither of which will create the normal illusion of realistic movement, and it may be controlled by the user, resulting in a variable playback rate impossible in animation confined to film, video or TV.

There are many different techniques that can be used to create animation. Over the relatively long period of its history, animators have developed a host of methods for creating their work, and most of them can be used or adapted for Web animation, no matter whether just two frames are required or many thousands. Traditional methods can be used for animation that is to be captured into a computer: instead of recording the frames on to the physical media of film or video, they are digitized and converted to a form in which they can be manipulated and displayed by software. Often, frames are captured using a video camera connected to the computer. In this case technical issues connected with broadcast standards and interlacing will arise; these are discussed under *video*, later in this chapter. However, it is possible to use an ordinary digital stills camera instead, providing images are either photographed or downsampled to a suitable size for the Web. This avoids any problems to do with interlacing, creating whole frames well suited to Web animation. Images that have been created on flat media, such as paper, can also be digitized using a scanner, which again will avoid problems connected with interlacing.

Many traditional techniques of drawing or painting a complete frame at a time, or of making successive small alterations to one image, can also be applied to the creation of animation using software. Any graphics program can be used to create individual images, and there are programs that combine a sequence of images into an animation, in one of the formats that we will describe shortly. Many programs, however, provide more elaborate support for the animation process. Some have an 'onion-skinning' facility, which allows the animator to see a dimmed version of the previous frame while working on the current one. (This mimics the technique of using a lightbox when drawing on paper.) Photoshop allows animations in some formats to be created in layers; a set of layers can be associated with each frame. This makes it possible to share parts of the image (for instance, elements of the background) among different frames in a cel-like technique, or to make small changes to several overlaid layers in a way similar to painting on layers of glass.

Vector graphics are well suited to some types of animation, because changes to an image can be made simply by manipulating anchor points. The smooth lines and flat areas of colour typical of vector graphic images can produce an appearance similar to traditional cartoon drawing, so vector graphics can well be used for cartoon-style animations, or *toons*. Flash is a widely used program for creating vector animations. It tries to provide some help with the animation process, in the form of automatic interpolation, which allows the animator to create the frames at the beginning and end of a sequence of movement, and leaves the program to create the frames in between. (This doesn't produce very convincing results, though, except in the case of simple linear movements.)

To many people, computer-generated animation is synonymous with animation made by manipulating three-dimensional models of characters and objects using software packages. The extension of the vector graphics techniques of Chapter 5 by the addition of a third dimension is conceptually straightforward, and mathematically reasonably tractable, but it adds considerable practical difficulties. Animation based on 3-D vector graphics is a direct analogue of traditional 3-D work, except that the models are mathematical descriptions of three-dimensional objects, instead of actual physical models. It is necessary to add simulated lighting and to model its effect on different physical surfaces, as well as modelling the movement of the objects and camera. This sort of animation requires considerable specialized skill and extensive computing power if a convincing result is to be achieved.

Creating good animation by any means is a specialized skill, and in most cases the job is best left to trained animators. The Web designer is more usually concerned with adding the animation to Web pages. An exception to this might be in the case of the most simple forms of Web animation: blinking alerts, rollover buttons that change, and other animated elements that have only two or three different states of a very simple graphic element.

Animation can be used to divert and entertain or to instruct, but it is too frequently used simply to attract attention. For good evolutionary reasons to do with the need to escape predators, people are highly sensitive to motion, especially in the peripheral area of their field of vision. Because of this, if there is a moving element on an otherwise static page, the viewer's attention will be involuntarily drawn to the movement. Crass advertisers know this, and use simple, bold animations in an effort to draw attention to their messages. However, this often produces irritation and resentment. If people's reflexes are stimulated in this way to make them look at something which really holds no interest for them, they will feel put-upon and become annoyed. This holds true not only for animation used in commercial advertising, but also for animation used by Web designers to highlight parts of the page that they think are important, and for any other gratuitous use of animation. It follows, too, that even when the user likes the animation it will necessarily tend to distract that user's attention away from the rest of the content of the page, an effect which will frequently be undesirable. Web designers therefore need to give careful thought to how animation is integrated into any page.

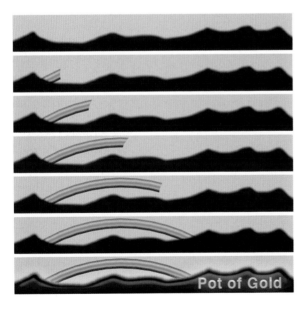

Figure 6.5 A simple GIF animation

Animated GIFs

Despite everything we wrote in the first part of this chapter, there is one popular format in which animation can be added to Web pages that does not require any plug-in: ***animated GIFs***. We mentioned in Chapter 5, when describing the GIF image file format, that it is possible to include the data for more than one image in a single GIF file. In the original GIF87a format, this facility was of little use, but the revised GIF89a format added a means of storing additional information in the file, including a value for a delay time between images. This meant that the file could store an animation consisting of a sequence of frames – the individual images contained in the file – and an indication of the speed at which it should be played back. This is sufficient information for a program, in particular a Web browser, to display the animation at the speed it was designed for.

Like files in any other image format, animated GIFs are usually embedded in a page using img elements. This markup never invokes a plug-in; the browser itself must handle the display of the animation. Most graphical browsers are capable of doing so. It is normal for browsers to provide an option for their users to turn off the playing of animated GIFs, though, since, as we noted earlier, people often find them irritating.

Indeed, animated GIFs have something of a bad reputation. Compared with other Web animation formats, animated GIFs are easy to create and use on the Web. Technically, they are easy to make – all you need is a program that packs up a set of images into a single GIF file, and there are many such programs available for free. They can be added to Web pages just like any other image. This ease of use led to many Web designers, professional and amateur, making animated GIFs and adding them to their pages without paying much attention to the quality of the animation. Advertisers like animated GIFs because they do not require a plug-in, which means there is little risk of users not being able to play them. Consequently, in the popular mind, animated GIFs became associated with intrusive moving advertisements and amateur animations of a kind that can most charitably described as 'cheap and cheerful', such as the example shown in Figure 6.5.

It doesn't have to be this way, though. GIF is a bitmapped format, which means that it is capable of representing the widest range of textures and drawing styles (within a palette of 256 colours). It is quite possible to store visually rich or sophisticated animations in animated GIF files. Figure 6.6 shows a few selected frames from an animated GIF which has a total of 417 frames and a file size of 1.7Mb. When embedded in a Web page it will tend to play jerkily on the first time through, but once it is cached on the user's machine it plays smoothly at the correct frame rate, despite its large size.

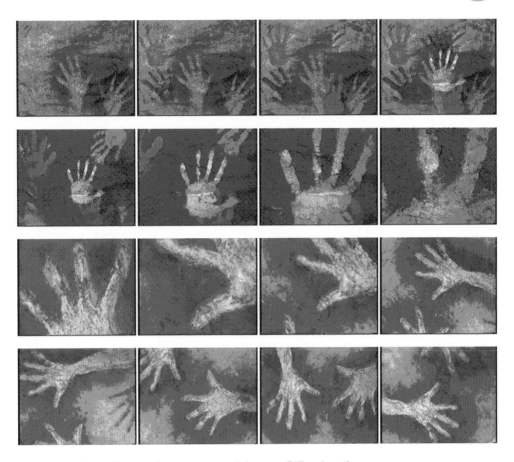

Figure 6.6 Some frames from a more elaborate GIF animation

The fault does not lie with the format, therefore, but only with the way in which it was so often used in the early years of the Web. At present it is common to find a mix of animated GIFs and Flash animations on a site that carries advertisements, and it is often not possible to tell which is which simply by looking at the style and quality of animation (there are good and bad examples in both formats). However, it remains that the GIF is limited to 256 colours, which may be too restrictive for some types of animation.

There are some technical drawbacks to the animated GIF format, though. Firstly, it has no provision for sound, so adding a synchronized soundtrack to an animation is impossible. (Many users will consider this a blessing, though.) Secondly, although it is possible to specify a delay between the frames when the file is created, there is no guarantee that any program playing back the animation will honour this specification. In fact, it is a fairly good bet that it won't: the animated GIF format is designed so that the each frame can be displayed as soon as it has been read, without having to wait for any later frames or other information. Browsers invariably do this, so that the rate at which the frames are displayed is dependent on the rate at which they arrive, which is subject to unpredictable network delays. (This only applies to the first time the animation is displayed. Most animated GIFs loop, and once all the frames have been received, more uniform playback is possible, although there is still no guarantee that the playback rate implied by the interframe delays will be achieved.) Animated GIF is not, therefore, suitable for any animation that depends on precise timing. Attempts to synchronize several animated GIFs on one page also suffer as a result of this problem.

The size of an animated GIF file depends on the images' height and width (which must be the same for all the frames), the number of frames and the visual characteristics of the images. You will recall that GIF images are losslessly compressed. The LZW compression algorithm used for GIFs works better on images with flat areas of colour than on subtle gradations and textures. Toon-style animations will generally result in smaller files than animations in looser styles.

As well as the delay time, which is given in hundredths of a second, some additional information can be stored in an animated GIF. The number of times the animation should play can be specified. If this value is set to zero, the animation will loop indefinitely. (This loop count is actually an extension to the GIF89a format, but is generally understood by browsers.) It is also possible to specify what should be done with the image in a frame after it has been displayed. Normally, each frame is simply replaced by the next one, but you can also specify that it should be overlaid by it (i.e. the frame should be retained and composited with its successor) or that the image should be replaced with a background colour, or by whatever was displayed before it, preparatory to displaying the next frame. Clever use of these disposal options makes it possible to optimize the size of animated GIFs, by only storing the differences between frames instead of the complete frame data. The interframe delay and the disposal method can be specified on an individual basis for each frame.

Note that all these options are part of the image file itself. There are no parameters for controlling the playback of a GIF animation that can be specified in the XHTML markup, which, as we noted before, consists of nothing more than an `img` element whose `src` attribute points to the animated GIF file.

Flash Animation

Animated GIF is a bitmapped format, with all the advantages and disadvantages that implies. As we mentioned earlier, vector graphics is suitable for certain types of animation, because change can be created by moving anchor points, or by altering other elements of the numerical description of the objects comprising the image. This makes it possible for animators to animate using simple vector transformations (or tools that accomplish them); it also means that the animation can be represented in a compact fashion, because instead of recording all the pixel data for each frame, all that needs to be recorded is the vector information for certain frames, called *key frames*, and the transformations applied to them to create the rest. The result is that vector animations can be more compact than bitmapped animations.

Flash movies are the most common type of vector animation on the Web. Flash was originally conceived as a program for creating Web animation, but it has evolved considerably through its associated scripting language, ActionScript, into a much more capable system. Flash movies may have a synchronized soundtrack. They can be fully interactive and can communicate with servers, so that they can be used as a time-based interface to Web applications, providing an alternative to the page-based interfaces based on the Web standards (XHTML and so on). Although Flash itself no longer has a monopoly on the creation of Flash movies – layers of an Illustrator image can be exported as frames of a Flash movie, for example – it remains the canonical environment for their production, particularly where interactivity is required.

Flash animations based on the simple shapes that are easily drawn with vector tools are usually quite crude. To obtain more pleasing or unusual results, animators often resort to other techniques. Some animators draw using Flash's brush tool, which produces more natural-looking marks, but it does this by creating 'strokes' which are actually filled vector shapes (though this is not always apparent to the animator); elaborate drawings created in this way will therefore contain vector objects which require a large number of values to describe them (because of the large number of anchor points on the complex outlines of the brush strokes), with a resulting increase in file size. Bitmapped images may be imported, either for use on background layers that don't change, or sometimes as whole sequences of images to be used as animation. In this latter case two options are possible; even though Flash is a vector graphics format, it can play back bitmapped images without conversion – it simply treats each complete bitmapped image as a single vector object. Alternatively, Flash offers a facility to vectorize bitmaps, with a set of parameters to control the extent to which the result departs visually from the original imported image. All of these techniques, as well as the more obvious method of creating complex shapes by using paths with many control points, lead to larger movie files, and in some cases to very large files indeed.

Flash offers a number of facilities for making savings in the sizes of animation movie files. The most notable of these, besides the vectorization of bitmaps just described, are **_tweening_** and **_symbols_**. ('Tween' is a contraction of 'in-between'.)

A tweened sequence in Flash is one where the animator creates only the first and last frame of a sequence (the **_key frames_**) and instructs Flash to create all the necessary in-between frames by interpolation. This is most frequently done for movement, and it is easy to see how the frames for the different positions of an object between its starting and ending position might be interpolated. The saving in file size is achieved by the fact that the intermediate frames are never stored explicitly; all that is held in the movie are the two key frames and a sequence of transformation matrices that create the tweened motion. Tweening can also be applied to other properties of objects beside motion, including size, orientation, colour and transparency. This means that scaling, rotation and fading, among other effects, can all be achieved by interpolation, thus producing movie files which are much more compact than if each frame had been drawn by hand.

Another way in which significant savings can be made – and animation can be partially automated – is through reusable elements called symbols. These may just be simple graphic objects, or they may be entire animated movies within the main movie. For example, a short looping animation of a boat rocking on the water could be made into a symbol, and then a fleet of such boats at anchor could be created out of copies of the one symbol. In the final movie file, only a single version of the artwork for each symbol is stored; the copies are simply pointers to the original, together with matrices describing any transformations that may have been applied.

Flash movies are displayed by the Flash Player, which is available as both a plug-in and an ActiveX control. We showed the markup required to embed Flash movies in Web pages earlier in this chapter. You will recall that the location of the movie file is given by either the `data` attribute of the `object` element (for the plug-in) or as the value of a `param` element whose `name` is `movie` (for the ActiveX control). In addition to the `quality` parameter mentioned previously, two parameters whose `value` may be `true` or `false` are also available. They are `play`, which determines whether the movie should start playing automatically and `loop`, which specifies whether, when it reaches the end, it should return to the beginning and go on playing indefinitely. The default values of these parameters are both `true`.

The Flash Player plug-in does not provide playback controls. Commands for starting, stopping, rewinding, stepping forwards or backwards and for turning looping on or off are available in a context-sensitive menu, if the parameter menu is set to true (which it is by default). However, having playback controls available only through a context-sensitive menu violates user interface and accessibility guidelines, and for this reason this method should not be depended on. By using Flash's scripting facilites instead, it is possible to provide playback controls within the movie. Recent versions of Flash include pre-built controller elements that can be incorporated into movies for this purpose.

An important characteristic of the Flash Player is that it plays movies in a streamed mode. This means that each frame is displayed as soon as it is received over the network. If the network cannot deliver the data fast enough, playback will stutter. The factor that determines whether this happens is not the total size of the movie file, but its data rate. This will not, in general, be a constant value, since some frames will contain more data than others. To ensure smooth playback, it is necessary that the peak data rate of the movie does not exceed the speed of the user's connection. As we stressed in Chapter 2, there is presently considerable variation in the data rates available to Internet users, so designers and animators must make a decision about whether they wish to support the slowest dial-up connections or just

Terminology

Shockwave Flash

Before the Web became the premier means of delivering multimedia, many multimedia CD-ROMs were created using Macromedia Director. As the Web grew in importance, Macromedia attempted to adapt Director to the new environment, by creating a format called Shockwave, which allowed Director productions to be streamed over the Web; a plug-in was used to play Shockwave in Web browsers.

When Flash first appeared, the format for the movies it created was called Shockwave Flash, presumably in an effort to emphasize Flash's relationship to the better-known Director. A Flash movie was originally the document from which the Shockwave Flash file was created – what is now referred to, in a more natural way, as a Flash project. The term Shockwave Flash has fallen into disuse, but is the source of the Internet Media Type application/x-shockwave-flash, and also of the .swf extension conventionally used for Flash movies, which are therefore sometimes called SWF (often pronounced 'swoof') files.

broadband. The former allows the movie to reach the largest audience, but in practice it imposes constraints which animators might find constricting. Flash includes facilities for estimating the bandwidth requirements of movies.

Other Approaches to Animation

Animated GIFs and Flash account for the majority of animation on Web pages, but they are not the only possibilities. Some other ways of adding animation are sometimes useful.

Programmed Animation

Animation of bitmapped images is achieved by replacing one image with another repeatedly. Animation of vector images is achieved by changing the stored values representing the properties of the shapes in the image. Ultimately, on a Web page, both of these kinds of change are performed by software. One way of animating is by explicitly writing programs or scripts that perform the changes.

The earliest Web animation was done in this way, using Java applets. These are programs, written in the Java language, which can be embedded in Web pages. Simple animation applets work by displaying a succession of bitmapped images to the screen. Others apply filters and effects to a single still image, making it ripple, for example. Animations can be interactive, so that a ripple follows the cursor's motion around the image. Non-programmers can create new animations by providing new sets of images as data for the applet.

Animating by program is flexible and efficient. Its main drawback is that few people are both good animators and good programmers. There appear to be more programmers who think they can animate than animators who think they can write programs, so Java animation is often ingenious, but usually visually crude.

With the development of client-side scripting (which we will describe in Chapter 7), programmed animation became simplified. Using JavaScript, programs can be written which change the elements of a page. In particular, the source of an `img` element can be altered dynamically by a script. By doing this repeatedly, an animation can be displayed. It is also possible for a script to change the coordinates of absolutely positioned elements, making them move about the screen. Other style properties can be changed, so colours, fonts and so on can be made to change. Again, these changes can be triggered by cursor movements or other forms of user input.

The name **Dynamic HTML (DHTML)** is sometimes used for this sort of scripted alteration of a page. DHTML created a lot of excitement when it first appeared, but inspired little work of any merit. It was also plagued by browser incompatibilities and bugs. Its use has become confined to simple effects, such as rollovers and slide shows, and it is unlikely to see a revival for more ambitious animation.

Animation on Video

Although we have drawn a distinction between video and animation, it is quite possible to convert animation (that is, moving pictures made from individually created frames) to one of the video formats that we will describe in the next section. Although these formats are intended for captured video, they are essentially just ways of storing a sequence of frames, and software can arrange images in such a format, whether they originated from a video camera or were created in some other way. It's just a data structure conversion. Once such a conversion has been performed, the video of the animation can be treated like any other video.

Video formats are especially suitable for animations that are short films, as animations in traditional media usually are. A film of this sort may well already exist as video, to be shown on a screen.

Video

Digital video is a field which has advanced rapidly in recent years. Not so long ago, it required high-end computers with amounts of disk storage that were then considered massive, dedicated capture hardware and expensive specialized software. Now, most desktop and portable computers are capable of capturing video from amateur or semi-professional DV equipment through Firewire ports. Rudimentary video editing software, such as iMovie, is available at minimal cost, while the cost of professional editing and post-production software, such as Final Cut Pro, has fallen drastically, putting it well within the budget of independent studios or individuals. The Internet now offers a potential channel for dissemination of video. We will only consider video on the Web, but you should be aware that the Internet can be used for distributing streamed video to dedicated software in ways that by-pass the Web browser and HTTP servers.

As with animation, the creation of video is usually best left to specialists, who understand the requirements of lighting, shooting, editing and post-production, and are familiar with the hardware and software used for these activities. Web designers may, however, be required to convert original footage to a format suitable for use on the Web, and so need to understand some of the technical details.

Technical Detail

Interlacing

It is convenient to think of a movie as a sequence of complete frames, but broadcast video is slightly different. Each frame is divided into two fields, one consisting of the odd-numbered lines, the other of the even-numbered lines. The fields are displayed at twice the nominal frame rate, so in PAL, for example, fields are displayed at a rate of 50 per second. This is because, if a screen is refreshed at fewer than 40 times per second, it will appear to flicker. Transmitting full frames at that rate is not feasible within the bandwidth available for television broadcasts, so this expedient of writing each frame in two pieces was adopted. Video constructed in this way is said to be interlaced.

Video cameras normally produce interlaced output. Most Web video formats are capable of dealing correctly with interlaced video. Sometimes, it is more convenient to combine fields into a single frame, a process called de-interlacing. In video with a lot of movement, de-interlacing can produce visible artefacts, so it is best avoided if possible.

Standards

Video cameras were originally designed to be compatible with broadcast standards. Many of the issues arising from the needs of television are irrelevant on the Web, but they are embodied in the standards and formats used by video hardware. In particular, the frame size and rate at which video can be captured by a typical video camera (camcorder) is determined by television standards. The principle standards in use at present are **PAL**, which is used in most of Western Europe, China, the Indian sub-continent, some South American countries, Africa, Australia and New Zealand, and **NTSC**, which is used in North America, the Caribbean, parts of South America, Japan and some other Far Eastern countries. In France, Russia and most of Eastern Europe, broadcast television uses a standard called SECAM. This standard only deals with details of signal transmission; in other respects, it is identical with PAL.

We will ignore HDTV (high-definition television), since the equipment for this format is still largely confined to professional television. The original PAL and NTSC standards both define a frame size with an aspect ratio (the ratio of the width to height) of 4:3. These standards were devised for analogue devices, with screens that are not divided into discrete pixels.

Instead, an electron beam scans the screen in a series of lines. Within each line, the intensity of the beam may be varied continuously. The standards therefore only define a number of scan lines: for PAL this is 625, for NTSC it is 525. Some of these lines carry control and timing information, leaving 576 lines in PAL and 480 in NTSC for the picture itself.

To create a digital image consistent with the standards, the scan lines naturally translate into rows of pixels. To maintain the aspect ratio, an image size of 768 × 576 pixels for PAL, and 640 × 480 for NTSC, is required, and when analogue video is digitized, these are the sizes obtained. However, nowadays most video originates on digital equipment, and this introduces a new complication. When the standards for digital television were developed, rather than use two different values for the number of pixels in each row, 720 pixels were used in both PAL and NTSC. To maintain the correct aspect ratio of 4:3 using the standard number of scan lines, these pixels cannot be square. They cannot even be the same shape for PAL and NTSC. When video that was captured from a source such as a DV camera, which uses non-square pixels, is displayed on a computer screen with square pixels, some distortion results. The amount is small and is usually considered acceptable, especially in the case of PAL. If necessary, the video can be resampled to 768 or 640 square pixels per line.

The size of a full frame of video is fairly large; it will almost fill many computer screens. Adding video at its full size to a Web page will leave little room for anything else on that page. In the case of smaller monitors, the full frame may not fit, once space has been reserved for playback controls, the menu bar and the browser's window border, address bar and toolbars. As we will demonstrate soon, full frame video also requires a lot of bandwidth. It is therefore common to downsample video to a smaller frame size. Halving both the height and width, to give a quarter-frame picture, is a sensible and popular option.

PAL and NTSC differ in their frame rates as well as their dimensions. PAL frames are shown at a rate of 25 per second, NTSC at 29.97, which is usually taken to be 30. (The different rates arise from the different AC line frequencies used in the countries in which the standards originated. The 0.1% discrepancy in the NTSC frame rate is a technical requirement to prevent interference with the sound in NTSC broadcasts.) Conversion between PAL and NTSC frame rates can only be done satisfactorily using expensive specialized equipment. Software conversions are rarely acceptable. However, for use on the Web, conversion is unnecessary. Computers are able to play video at any frame rate, subject to the limitations of the hardware, so video in either format can be displayed on the Web. (It is important to ensure that the video file prepared for the Web records the correct frame rate. Some video software assumes NTSC as the default.)

Video Compression

Each frame of video is essentially a bitmapped image. Each uncompressed PAL quarter-frame, measuring 360×288 pixels, in 24-bit colour occupies just over 300kB. At a frame rate of 25fps, this means a data rate of just over 60Mbps, which far exceeds the data rate of almost all Internet connections. Obviously, the data must be compressed. Chrominancce sub-sampling, as described in Chapter 5, is always applied to video data, producing an immediate reduction to one half its size, but further compression is still required. Any piece of software or hardware that performs compression and decompression of video is referred to as a video *codec* (short for compressor/decompressor). Using a codec that simply applied JPEG compression to each frame could cut the rate down to about 3Mbps without much loss of quality, but this is still too high for general Internet use. Some additional compression must be obtained.

The key to effective video compression lies in the use of *inter-frame* compression. Put simply, this means that, instead of storing and transmitting all the pixels in each frame, only the difference between successive frames is used. Typically, only some elements in a scene being recorded on video are in motion or changing, so the strategy can potentially make big savings in file sizes. For instance, if a person is recorded being interviewed, their face will move and from time to time they will shift their position, but any inanimate objects in the background – furniture, potted plants, wallpaper, and so on – will stay the same over long periods. (It would not be true to say that they will never change, because the position of shadows might move, the light may alter or the camera may be moved.) Over long sequences of frames, only the parts of each frame that correspond to the moving person need be stored; the information that remains constant can be recorded once, and re-used. Some frames must be stored in their entirety; these will, however, be compressed using some method similar to JPEG. Using the same terminology as we met in connection with motion tweening in Flash, these frames are called key frames. In the MPEG family of standards (see below), compressed key frames are called *I-frames* (the I stands for intra-, since compression is only applied within these frames).

To produce high-quality video at sufficiently low data rates to transmit over the Internet, inter-frame compression that is more sophisticated than simple differencing is required. The way this is done can best be introduced schematically. Consider the two images at the top of Figure 6.7, which might represent the objects in two consecutive frames of a video clip. If the first of these is used as a key frame, the second can be stored as a difference frame, obtained by numerically subtracting the value of each pixel in the key frame from the value of the corresponding pixel in the second frame. This produces the difference frame shown at the

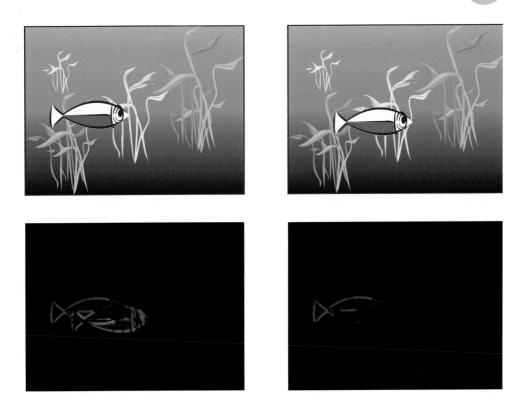

Figure 6.7 Inter-frame compression and motion compensation

bottom left of Figure 6.7 . All the pixels in the black area have the value zero, since the two frames are identical here; only the small coloured area corresponding to the union of the two positions of the fish is different. This difference frame can be compressed much more effectively using any of the image compression algorithms that we described in Chapter 5 than the complete frame, and it is clear that the complete frame can be reconstructed by adding the pixels of the decompressed I-frame produced from the key frame to the corresponding pixels of the decompressed difference frame. However, by making use of the relationship between the two frames, further compression can be achieved.

The fish is identical in both frames, only its position has altered. Therefore, if we were able to record how it had moved, we would not need to store any pixels for the area of the second frame occupied by the fish: these could be obtained from the decompressed I-frame. We would only need to store values for the area, shown in the bottom right of Figure 6.7, that becomes exposed as the fish moves. This technique of incorporating a record of the relative displacement of objects in the difference frames is called **motion compensation**

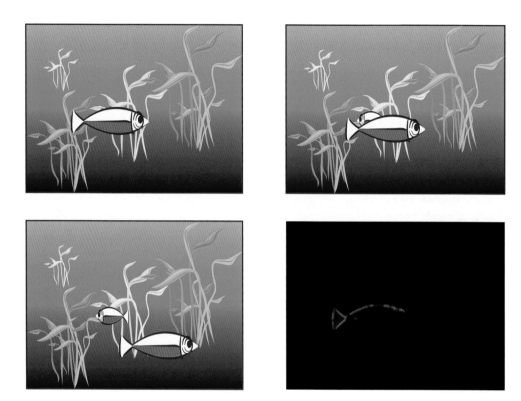

Figure 6.8 Predictive motion compensation

or ***motion estimation***. Of course, it is now necessary to store the displacement as part of the compressed file. This information can be recorded as a ***displacement vector***, giving the number of pixels the object has moved in each direction. Displacement vectors can be stored compactly. A difference frame incorporating displacement vectors is called a predicted frame, or ***P-frame***, in MPEG terminology.

Motion compensation can be taken further. Figure 6.8 shows some more frames of the same sequence. As the big fish moves further, a little fish that was concealed behind it is revealed. If motion compensation is used as just described, a P-frame recording the pixels in the coloured area shown in the bottom right would result for the frame above it. However, all the pixels in this area can be found in the third frame in the figure (which will not necessarily immediately follow the second) where the small fish is entirely visible, so there is no actual need to store them in the P-frame. Motion compensation using key frames that follow the current frame as well as those that precede it can be used instead. A difference frame that uses pixels from both preceding and following I-frames is called a bi-directionally predictive frame, or **B-frame** for short.

If we had some frames of video shot under water showing a real fish swimming among weeds (or a good animation of such a scene) instead of these schematic pictures, the objects and their movements would be less simple than they appear in the illustrations. The fish's body would change shape as it propelled itself, the lighting would alter, the weeds would not stay still. Attempting to identify the objects in a real scene and apply motion compensation to them would not, therefore, work (even if it were practical to identify objects in such a scene). Instead, codecs using motion compensation simply consider the displacement of blocks of pixels, between 4 and 16 pixels square, depending on the codec. For each block in a frame, they search within a restricted region of a key frame for blocks with the same pixel values. If they find one, they record the displacement instead of any pixel difference values for that block. It is likely that the displacement vectors for adjacent blocks will be the same, or differ by only a small amount, so the vectors can be compressed themselves by just storing the difference between them instead of their values.

The preceding account of inter-frame compression is rather glib. Making a practical codec based on these principles is difficult, but much research in the area has yielded some highly effective algorithms. Presently, the most important algorithms are those defined in a series of standards by the **Motion Picture Experts Group (MPEG)**. Some proprietary codecs, which we will mention in the context of Web video formats, are also of practical importance. Although their details are not publicly available, they are known to work on similar principles to MPEG.

The first MPEG standard for digital video is known, appropriately enough, as MPEG-1. It was mostly used with the Video Compact Disk format. Although this format was never widely popular, MPEG-1 is important as the basis of the MPEG family of codecs. All modern codecs used for Web video are based on the same compression principles and can be seen as refinements of the MPEG-1 algorthithm.

MPEG-1 uses motion compensation, with both backward and forward prediction. (That is, based on key frames that precede or follow the difference frame.) P-frames may be based on a preceding I-frame or P-frame; B-frames may be based on the following I- or P-frame as well. (See Figure 6.9.) The standard format of Video CD based on PAL uses a frame 352 pixels wide by 288 pixels high, and a frame rate of 25fps. Video in this format compresses down to a data rate of 1.86Mbps, which is just within the range of higher-speed broadband connections, but it too slow for other Internet connections. Furthermore, the quality of

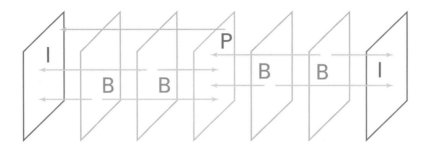

Figure 6.9 Frame dependencies

MPEG-1 video is poor compared to that produced by more recent codecs, so it is not an ideal choice for Web video.

MPEG-2 is a development of MPEG-1 that can be applied to broadcast television. It is used in DVD video and for digital TV. The quality is good, but the data rates it requires make it inappropriate for use on the Internet.

MPEG-4 (there was no MPEG-3) is ostensibly a standard defining a format for three-dimensional scenes incorporating multimedia elements including video and sound. In practice, only its video and audio codecs have received much attention. There are two video codecs. The original MPEG-4 video codec (MPEG-4 Part 2) represents a further refinement of the techniques used in MPEG-1, specifically intended to produce high quality pictures at low bit rates, suitable for the Internet. It augments the basic motion compensation with optimizations for specific idioms, such as panning and zooming. Displacement is recorded to a fraction of a pixel, which prevents errors accumulating and results in better picture quality.

At the time of writing, MPEG-4 Part 10, more often known as H.264, is the MPEG video codec producing the best quality at the lowest bit rate. It is an aggressively optimized version of MPEG-4, which, among other refinements, allows the use of different-sized blocks for motion compensation, so that areas with little change can be encoded efficiently using large blocks (up to 16 × 16 pixels), but areas that do change can be broken into smaller blocks (down to 4 × 4 pixels), which is more likely to result in compression, while preserving the picture quality in fast-moving parts of the frame. Additionally, whereas MPEG-4 Part 2, like MPEG-1, only allows difference frames to depend on at most one preceding and one following frame, H.264 allows data from a stack of frames anywhere in a movie to be used. (The whole movie thus becomes a source of blocks of pixels, which can be reused. This is somewhat similar to the dictionary-based approach to compression found in the LZ algorithms

Terminology

MPEG and H.264

The similarity in names of MPEG and JPEG is not coincidental. Both JPEG and MPEG are committees established jointly by ISO and IEC, and their documents have the status of international standards. MPEG is not the only organization that concerns itself with digital video standards. The International Telecommunications Union (ITU) has also created a series of standards, which include the definition of codecs for still and moving images. These are aimed at applications such as facsimile transmission and video conferencing, which can be said to fall within the area of telecommunications.

The ITU standards have names beginning H., such as H.263, a video conferencing codec. Since the aims of MPEG-4 Part 10, and H.264, the ITU's proposed successor to H.263, are essentially identical, the two organizations cooperated on the definition of the standard which is now known as both MPEG-4 Part 10 and H.264. You may also see it called AVC, or Advanced Video Compression, another term from MPEG-4. Usage seems to have settled on H.264 as the preferred name.

we mentioned in Chapter 5.) B-frames may even depend on other B-frames. H.264 also uses compression algorithms more sophisticated than JPEG for compressing the individual I-, P- and B-frames, and incorporates filters for removing some compression artefacts, which result in better picture quality. It is said that MPEG-4 produces DVD quality video at a third to half the data rate of MPEG-2.

H.264 was designed with the Internet in mind, but it is not just intended for Web video. H.264 is a scalable technology that can be used at different frames sizes and rates on anything from a mobile phone to broadcast television, with the quality and data rate varying from 64kbps to 240Mbps. Near the bottom end of this range, quarter-frame PAL or NTSC at their full frame rate can be compressed to a data rate of 192kbps, at reasonable picture quality. Halving the height, width and frame rate allows the data rate to be reduced to 64kbps.

Even this value is too high for dial-up connections. To reduce video to a low enough data rate for V.90 modems, picture quality, frame size or frame rate must be sacrificed further, and the results are, frankly, not worth the effort. People's expectations of video are based on their experience of television and DVD; a visitor to a Web site may accept a video picture of relatively small size, but no-one is going to be impressed by a blocky, jerky picture which stops and starts, breaks up, and loses synchronization with its soundtrack. Hence, Web video is only an option for users with broadband connections.

Streaming Video

When video was first used on Web pages, browsers and servers treated movies in a similar way to images. A browser would send an HTTP request for the movie file and the server would return a response containing the video data. The browser would wait until the complete response had arrived before displaying the movie (that is, until invoking a plug-in to display it). This makes sense if the data rate of the movie exceeds the maximum data rate of the connection, but it means there is a delay, which might be substantial, between the sending of the request and the playing of the movie. Consider, for instance, a 30 second movie that has been compressed to a data rate of 192kbps. This would take 120 seconds to download over a dial-up connection operating at a realistic 48kbps; that is, the user would have to wait two minutes before seeing any of the movie. In this example the waiting time is four times as long as the movie itself.

It is possible to do a little better than this. After 90 seconds have elapsed, three quarters of the frames will have been received by the browser. If the movie starts playing, by the time these frames have been used up, new ones will have arrived. In fact, since the movie lasts for 30 seconds, and the remaining quarter of it will take that amount of time to arrive, it should be possible to play the entire movie starting from the 90 second point. (See Figure 6.10.) This makes some optimistic assumptions about the consistency of the speed of the connection, but the principle of starting to play the movie while it is still being downloaded is a sound one. The technique is variously known as *progressive download* or *HTTP streaming*. It depends on there being no forward dependencies in the movie data, which means that where compression using B-frames is employed, the data stream must be reorganized so that the B-frames follow any frames they depend on, whether or not they are consecutive in the movie itself. Frames will have to be re-ordered when they arrive in the browser, so some buffering is necessary.

Progressive download is the best that can be achieved if the data rate of the movie exceeds the maximum data rate of the connection, but consider the case of a broadband connection that is capable of transferring data at the rate it is contained in the movie. Suppose in particular, that our movie is arriving over a connection at 192kbps, the same data rate as that at which the movie plays. Then each frame could be played as soon as it arrives; the next frame's data will have arrived by the time it is required. In that case, there is no need to store

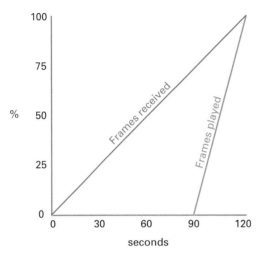

Figure 6.10 Progressive download

the movie data on disk at all, it can be played straight off the server. Video that is played in this way is said to be *streamed*.

Streaming video avoids the delay associated with downloading. Since the movie is never stored, it doesn't use up disk space (with our example, users would end up with over half a megabyte of data in their browser's cache; with a long movie it could be a lot more). More importantly from the copyright owners' point of view, it means that users do not retain a copy of the movie, not even in their browser's cache. Streaming also allows for the possibility of delivering live video over the Internet.

HTTP is not a very suitable protocol for transmitting streamed video. To begin with, as we mentioned in Chapter 2, it uses TCP as a transport protocol. TCP is designed to provide reliable connections; reliability is vital for transferring data such as XHTML documents, where an error in a single byte could invalidate the document. However, in order to guarantee that all packets are received, TCP uses a system of acknowledgements and retransmission, which result in delays if a packet is lost and has to be sent again. For streaming video, however, reliability is less important than efficiency and a consistent data rate. It is more acceptable to drop a frame – many viewers won't even notice – than for the playback to stutter while TCP waits for a packet to arrive then asks for it to be resent when it doesn't. The transport protocol UDP, which we mentioned briefly in Chapter 2 provides a more appropriate vehicle for carrying streamed video, since it does not guarantee that all packets will necessarily arrive, it just does its best to get them to their destination.

On its own, UDP is not adequate, however. Just as HTTP has to operate on top of TCP, so a protocol called the **Real-Time Transport Protocol (RTP)** runs on top of UDP to provide the services of a data stream. These include facilities for synchronizing separate streams, so that, for instance, a movie's soundtrack can be sent separately from its picture, but the two will play back in synch.

If video data is being streamed, any controls provided by a player embedded in a Web page must affect the server. For instance, if there is a pause button, its effect must be to temporarily stop frames being streamed from the server. Thus, yet another protocol is needed to allow the stream to be controlled from the browser. This is the **Real-Time Streaming Protocol (RTSP)**, which is sometimes described as the Internet VCR remote control protocol, because it enables commands to stop, start, pause, rewind and so on, to be sent to a server.

A simple Web server implementing HTTP cannot stream data. A special **streaming server**, which understands RTSP requests and sends data over an RTP stream, is needed for this. Streaming servers usually support the transmission of video in only one of the particular formats we will describe in the following section. Often, non-trivial licence fees are required for the use of a streaming server. If only short movies are to be used on a site, it may well not be worth the money and the additional technical complexity which the use of streaming implies, in which case progressive download will suffice. However, for long movies and live video, a streaming server is required.

Video Formats and Plug-ins

The formats and plug-ins available for Web video present a somewhat confused picture. There are several competing formats, all of which do more or less the same thing, but they are not directly comparable. Each has its own plug-in, but some plug-ins can handle video in more than one format. To add further complexity, some formats can accommodate data compressed by more than one codec but others cannot.

There are four major Web video formats at the time of writing: **Flash Video**, **QuickTime**, **Windows Media** and **RealVideo**. For all of these, the preferred way of embedding movies in a Web page is to use nested object elements, in the way we described in the first part of this chapter. (For backward compatibility, it may be necessary to use an embed element instead of the inner object.) The precise attributes and plug-in parameters differ in detail between the formats.

Terminology

Movies and Clips

A digital video sequence is usually referred to as a movie, although the movies used on the Web are often very short. There is no implication that a movie is anything like as long as a feature film, or that it is structured in the same way. Short movies are sometimes called clips; some video editing applications refer to individual short video sequences as clips, and to the finished whole as a movie.

In Flash, the term movie has long been used in a confusing way. Originally, a Flash movie was the whole Flash project, but the term Flash document is now used in that way. However, a Flash movie is still a whole Flash presentation, which may be highly complex and include still elements as well as moving ones and interactivity – or it may just be a movie in the more normal sense. A movie clip in Flash is specifically a symbol instance, that is, a movie within a movie; it is not just a short sequence. Again, the term movie here does not necessarily refer to a sequence of moving pictures.

With the exception of Flash, video plug-ins are capable of playing video in formats other than their own. MPEG-1 and MPEG-4 have their own formats, for instance. Files in these formats can be played by the QuickTime, RealVideo and Windows Media plug-ins. (If users have several plug-ins, the choice of which one will handle MPEG files will depend on how the browser is configured. There are ways of forcing these files to be handled by a specific plug-in, but it shouldn't matter.) Other video formats that are sometimes encountered, and which can be handled by one or more of these plug-ins include AVI, an older Windows video file format, and DivX, a version of AVI that has been extended to hold MPEG-4 data.

Flash Video

Increasingly, Flash is being used for presenting video on the Web and may become the predominant form of Web video in the immediate future. Flash has long provided some means of incorporating video into movies. This was originally achieved by importing frames of video into Flash, where they were converted to bitmapped images – frame by frame. These could then be combined with drawn elements in the Flash movie. With the release of Flash MX and the accompanying Flash Player 6, a different way of working was provided. Video could be converted to Flash's own Flash Video format, and referenced from within a Flash movie. The difference from the earlier way of working is that the video was still treated as video, and compressed accordingly, using an inter-frame compression scheme, instead of being taken apart and treated as a sequence of distinct bitmapped images.

When the next release of Flash and the Flash Player appeared, video support was improved. It became possible to stream Flash video, using the Flash Communication Server. Alternatively, video can be downloaded using progressive download. Thus, Flash video offers the same possibilities as the other video formats. A Flash Video movie cannot be used on its own, though; it must be referred to from a conventional Flash (SWF) movie. This movie can provide the controls for playing the video, using Flash's facilities for interactivity. (Reusable components for including such controls are available in Flash itself, affording a degree of standardization in the appearance of Flash controllers.) Since this controlling movie is just an ordinary Flash movie, it is embedded in a Web page in exactly the same way as the Flash animations we described earlier in this chapter, using the same object attributes and param elements.

The proprietary codecs used for compressing Flash Video are said to provide excellent quality at low bit rates, but in reality the quality will vary considerably with the nature of the video material. What really distinguishes Flash Video from the other formats is simply that it can be played back in a Web browser by the Flash Player plug-in. It is estimated that over 90% of devices connected to the Internet have the Flash Player installed on them, because it is included in the default installations of most popular browsers and is installed on many mobile phones. Therefore, Flash Video is a format that can fairly certainly be displayed by most users.

QuickTime

Apple's QuickTime is a multimedia architecture. That is, it is a collection of programs (including a stand-alone movie player, a Web browser plug-in and an ActiveX control) and APIs, which provide facilities for capturing, playing, editing and compressing video and other types of media, including images and sound, and for importing and exporting media in many different formats, including QuickTime's own extensible file format. The APIs enable programmers to add QuickTime's facilities to their programs in a standard manner. QuickTime was originally developed for Macintosh systems; it was subsequently ported to Windows.

QuickTime movies can be created using many different video editing applications. When a movie is exported from such a program, a host of options are available for setting its properties. In particular, it is possible to choose between many different codecs, including (in QuickTime 7) MPEG-4 Part 2 and H.264, and to set the desired quality and data rate. It is also possible to prepare the movie for progressive download or true streaming. For the latter, the movie must be served by the QuickTime Streaming Server (or the Open Source Darwin Streaming Server which is based on the same code).

A useful possibility provided by QuickTime for Web video is the use of a 'reference movie', which is essentially a collection of pointers to different versions of the same movie, each optimized for a different connection type. So, for example, a movie might be created in a small, heavily compressed version, for users of dial-up connections, a larger, less compressed version for domestic broadband users, and a full-screen, high quality version for users of higher-speed broadband connections. The object used for embedding the movie points to a reference movie which points to these three versions, and associates a minimum set of system requirements, in particular, a data rate, with each. (QuickTime editing and compression software provides facilities for creating such reference movies and specifying the requirements associated with each referenced movie.) When the QuickTime plug-in reads the reference movie, it selects and plays the appropriate version of the actual movie according to the user's connection speed. (This is not determined empirically, but is based on settings provided by the user.) In the case of streamed QuickTime, it is always necessary to create a small reference movie, which simply contains the URL of the video stream itself. The reference movie is embedded in the page (using the markup shown below) and fetched using HTTP, as all elements of a Web page must be. The information contained in the movie can then be used by the QuickTime plug-in to set up a streaming session using the RTP and RTSP protocols, which the browser itself does not understand.

The typical markup for embedding a QuickTime movie in a page would be as follows:

```
<object classid="clsid:02BF25D5-8C17-4B23-BC80-D3488ABDDC6B"
 width="352" height="304">
  <param name="src" value="birds.mov" />
  <param name="autoplay" value="true" />
  <param name="controller" value="true" />
  <object data="birds.mov" type="video/quicktime" width="352"
   height="304">
    <param name="autoplay" value="true" />
    <param name="controller" value="true" />
    <p>QuickTime is required for playing this movie of birds</p>
  </object>
</object>
```

We have highlighted the distinctive parts of the markup for this media type. The classid for the QuickTime ActiveX control shown must be used for any embedded QuickTime that

Name	Values	Default	Meaning
autoplay	true|false| @hh:mm:ss:ff	Determined by user preferences	Playback starts without user intervention if true; waits for the play button to be pressed if false; or starts when specified frame is received.
bgcolor	#rrggbb| colour name	Page background colour	Sets the colour of any part of the area allocated to the object that is not occupied by the movie.
controller	true|false	true	Display standard movie playback controls if true.
kioskmode	true|false	false	Does not allow the user to save the movie if true.
loop	true|false| palindrome	false	Makes the movie go back to the beginning and play again after finishing if true, not if false. Plays it alternately backwards and forwards if palindrome
scale	tofit|aspect| number	1	Scales the movie if necessary to fit the specified height and width if tofit; scales to fill as much as possible while preserving aspect ratio, if aspect; scales by specified number otherwise.
volume	percent	100	Sets audio volume to the specified percentage of the system volume setting

Table 6.1 Parameters for QuickTime video

is required to play in IE for Windows. The parameter that the ActiveX control uses for identifying the location of the movie has the name src. The Internet Media Type, required in the inner object element is video/quicktime.

There are roughly 30 parameters that can be used to control the QuickTime plug-in, but many of these are irrelevant to video. Because QuickTime is a multimedia architecture, QuickTime movies are capable of storing many things besides video, including interactive

3-D panoramas (somewhat disingenuously referred to as QTVR – QuickTime Virtual Reality – although they fall well short of most people's idea of virtual reality). Many of the parameters are concerned with the display of QTVR and other QuickTime features that are not relevant to playing video. Table 6.1 lists those that are relevant to video. (In the column headed 'Values', the vertical bar separates the possible alternatives.) It is rarely necessary to use any parameters besides the two shown in the example above.

It is important to note that the `height` parameter specifies the height of the area of the browser window that is occupied by the movie together with the playback controls, if the `controller` parameter is set to `true`. In that case, `height` should be set to the height of the actual movie plus 16.

The QuickTime plug-in can be controlled by scripts attached to the Web page containing the embedded movie. This means that, instead of using the default controller that is displayed if the `controller` parameter is `true`, other elements of the page can be used to start and stop the movie in response to user input. For example, a small image could be used as a start button. Other events can also be used to control playback if this approach is taken. For instance, a movie can be made to start playing when the cursor is over it, and stop when it is moved away.

Windows Media

Windows Media is Microsoft's framework for multimedia, including video. It features its own video (and audio) codec, and an elaborate digital rights management system, for the protection of copyright material. The Windows Media Player is bundled with the Windows operating system, which makes it a *de facto* standard (although for the most part, Windows Media ignores official standards). Although the Windows Media Player for MacOS X is no longer supported, a QuickTime component that plays Windows Media is available, so Windows Media files and streams can be played on most machines. Implementation details are scarce, but it appears to be the case that the Windows Media 9 video codec is similar in principle to H.264; Microsoft claim that it achieves better quality at lower data rates. Judgements of video quality are subjective, but the quality is certainly very good. The codec forms the basis of the VC-1 codec, which is being standardized by SMPTE. Like H.264, it is scalable to both high and low data rates.

The following markup can be used to embed a Windows Media movie in a Web page. (For versions of the Media Player plug-in earlier than 7, there are slight differences.)

```
<object classid="clsid:6BF52A52-394A-11d3-B153-00C04F79FAA6"
 width="525" height="640">
  <param name="url" value="demo.wmv" />
  <object data="demo.wmv" type="video/x-ms-wmv" height="640"
   width="525">
       <p>Windows Media Player 7 or higher is needed to view this
   demo.</p>
  </object>
</object>
```

For streaming, an indirect arrangement is required. The movie itself must be uploaded to a host running the Windows Media Server (technically, some version of Microsoft Windows Server incorporating the optional Windows Media Services). A special metafile must then be prepared, which is a small XML file containing an element that points to the URL of the video stream. This is usually the location of the movie file, but instead of beginning with http:// the URL begins with mms://. This prefix identifies the Microsoft Media Services protocol, which is used for streaming Windows Media. The metafile thus serves the same function as a QuickTime reference movie in providing a description of the stream. A simple metafile (whose meaning should be evident) would look like this:

```
<ASX version = "3.0">
<Entry>
    <Ref href = "mms://wms.desperatesw.co.uk/demo.wmv" />
</Entry>
</ASX>
```

In the embedding code, the (HTTP) URL of the metafile is used as the value of the url parameter or the data attribute instead of the actual video file. For the inner object element using data, the type should be set to application/x-mplayer2.

A collection of param elements is available for controlling some aspects of the playback and display of Windows Media files. The principal ones are summarized in Table 6.2. You will notice that, although the names and detailed meanings are different, they control much the same aspects of the display as the parameters for QuickTime do. As is the case with the QuickTime plug-in, scripting can be used to control the player instead of the standard controls.

Name	Values	Default	Meaning
autostart	true|false	true	Playback starts without user intervention if true; waits for the play button to be pressed if false.
playcount	number	1	The number of times the movie should be played.
stretchtofit	true|false	false	Scales the movie if necessary to fit the specified height and width if true.
uimode (ActiveX only)	none|mini| full	full	Determines which player controls are displayed: full shows all controls, mini a reduced subset, none no controls.
showcontrols (Plug-in only)	true|false	true	Show or hide the controls.
volume	percent	Last value used	Sets audio volume to the specified percentage of the system volume setting

Table 6.2 Parameters for Windows Media video

RealVideo

Real Networks produced the first commercial implementation of streamed media for the Internet with RealAudio, which was followed by RealVideo for streaming moving pictures. RealVideo can be embedded in Web pages and played back by a plug-in, like the other video formats we have described, but it is more often played through its own RealPlayer program. (In fact, Real's own documentation discourages embedding in Web pages.) This is not just a simple video player; it can display parallel multimedia streams, including several video and audio streams, text, still images and even HTML pages, whose layout and synchronization are coordinated using the markup language SMIL (which is defined by a W3C Recommendation). The plug-in for Real media has the same capabilities.

RealVideo has been somewhat eclipsed in recent times by the growth of Flash video and Windows Media, so we will deal with it only briefly.

Real Video streams are compressed using a proprietary codec, for which the usual claims concerning quality and data rate are made. Movies must be streamed from Real's Helix server, which uses RTSP. The markup for embedding a movie follows the same pattern of nested object elements that we have used for the other time-based media in this chapter. The classid for the Real ActiveX control is CFCDAA03-8BE4-11cf-B84B-0020AFBBCCFA; the param element that identifies the location of the movie has the name src. As with QuickTime and Windows Media, when a stream is to be embedded in a Web page, the object elements cannot refer to the stream directly, but must point to a small file that contains the stream's actual URL. There are several parameters that control playback and the display of controls. To avoid repetition we will not list them here.

Sound

Sound is a medium that must be handled judiciously on Web pages. Including sounds that play spontaneously when a page is loaded is a dubious practice. For every visitor who is delighted at being greeted by a fanfare, a heavy metal guitar riff or a welcoming speech on arriving at a site, there may be hundreds who hastily leave on hearing the first sound, never to return. At best they may simply turn the volume right down on their computer. Unsolicited sound is annoying to many people, and even more so if it does not play properly: if the user has a low-bandwidth connection and the sound is not very short in duration, playback may stutter badly, with important sound information being lost.

The contemporary world is already full of a cacophany of man-made sounds; in some urban environments people rarely if ever experience silence, and research indicates that this can significantly add to stress. Although we may be used to cameras and telephones bleeping and singing in public places whenever they do anything, many people dislike this (which is why, for example, UK trains provide 'quiet' carriages where equipment that makes noises is not permitted) and resent the intrusion of other people's sounds. So we take the position that adding to noise pollution by making Web browsers clink and whistle whenever a user clicks on a link or visits a particular page is not acceptable, especially when we consider that many users may be browsing in public places such as cafés or offices. Hence, the safe course of action is to refrain from using sound in these ways.

One of the most common legitimate uses of sound is as an accompaniment to video or animation. Most movies have some sort of soundtrack. Music may be used as an anodyne background, or in the case of music videos, it may be at least as important as the pictures. Interviews, lectures, exhortatory speeches and so on require the voice of the participants. Voice-overs are often used to add exposition to visual material. Very few applications of video do not lend themselves to the addition of sound, although to save bandwidth on the Web, designers sometimes use short pieces of text superimposed on the pictures instead.

All of the video formats we described in the previous section support soundtracks. There is no way of adding synchronized sound to an animated GIF, but Flash animations may have sound added to them. Flash distinguishes two different types of sound: stream sounds and event sounds. Stream sounds are synchronized with the animation and streamed in parallel with it. That is, they constitute a conventional soundtrack. Event sounds, on the other hand, are downloaded in their entirety before playing, and play all the way through, independently of what happens to the animation. The playing of such a sound is triggered by some event, such as a mouse click, or simply by the animation's reaching a specified frame.

Except in the case of live video, integration of sound and pictures is carried out in a video editing program (or in Flash) as part of the post-production process, and this will have been done before the video is added to any Web page. For live transmission, sound and picture are captured and transmitted in real time; their coordination is taken care of by the streaming server.

The presence or absence of a soundtrack makes no difference to the markup that is used to incorporate the video in the page, except that it is important to make sure that the correct parameters are used to provide controls for altering the volume of the sound, or muting it entirely. In the case of Flash video, it may be necessary to provide such controls within the controlling movie.

Although sound does not require as much bandwidth as video, there is still a fair amount of data in an audio stream. As you probably know, sound (a continuous analogue phenomenon) is digitized by sampling the waveform at regular intervals, and quantizing the sampled value to one of a several discrete levels. For CD-quality sound, the samples are taken 44,100 times per second, and 65,536 different levels are used. 65,536 is 2^{16}, which means that each sample can be stored or transmitted as 16 bits. A simple calculation shows that a stereo soundtrack consisting of two channels at CD quality will have a data rate of about 1.4Mbps, which is too high to stream over most Internet connections, even before adding it to a video stream.

Audio is therefore compressed for digital transmission. As with images, the most effective forms of compression involve discarding some insignificant information. Since the physics and physiology of hearing are radically different from those of sight, the way in which this is done for sound is different from the way in which we discard information in images, but the result is the same: sound can be dramatically compressed without seriously altering its perceived quality. In the context of audio, compression based on the principle of discarding insignificant information is referred to as *perceptual coding*. (For a more detailed description, consult Chapter 9 of *Digital Multimedia*.)

The best-known method of audio compression is defined in Part 3 of the MPEG-2 standard, and is familiarly known as **MP3**. Although MP3 is most familiar as a file format for downloading music and storing it on portable music players, sound compressed by the MP3 codec can also be added to Flash, QuickTime and other video formats; MP3 is probably the codec most frequently used for Web audio in general. MPEG-4 defines an improved version of MP3, known as *Advanced Audio Coding (AAC)*, which can be used by QuickTime. When sound is compressed using the AAC codec, quality can be traded off against data rate (as it can when compressing images with JPEG).

Sound quality is highly subjective, so claims about the quality of audio at different data rates must be treated with caution. However, it is claimed that 'expert listeners' find AAC sound at 128kbps to be indistinguishable from uncompressed audio, and that the quality at 64kbps is 'excellent'. This would make it a suitable data rate for soundtracks intended for broadband delivery with H.264 video. It follows, though, that if audio is compressed to a rate suitable for transmitting over dial-up connections, the quality will be less than excellent.

As with video, Windows Media and Real Audio employ their own sound codecs in preference to the standards. If you choose to use one or other of these formats for video that has a soundtrack, it makes sense to use the accompanying audio codec.

When video that has a soundtrack is streamed, the picture and sound are sent as separate data streams. These are transmitted over the Internet independently, which means that one of them may be subject to some delay that does not affect the other. If the two streams were just played as they arrive, such asymmetrical delays could result in a loss of synchronization between them. This can have comical or disconcerting results, and is always undesirable. To avoid it, the plug-in must take steps to keep the streams in synch. This is usually done by dropping frames of video, if the sound overtakes the picture, or freezing the picture to let the sound catch up if the sound falls behind. This is because stuttering audio is usually more intrusive than occasional jumps in the picture. Some buffering is normally used to minimize the need for adjustments that are seen by the user. (Nevertheless, if the connection is slow, both sound and picture will stutter.)

There are some occasions when it is appropriate to incorporate sounds without pictures in a Web page. For instance, on a site devoted to ornithology, examples of the songs of different birds would be a useful supplement to textual descriptions. Many sites selling CDs offer tasters of the audio for potential buyers. Educational sites designed for children might usefully have audio to supplement text and images. (Think of the old idea of playing animal sounds to help young children identify either the name or the appearance of an animal).

Another case for using sound independently is when you know that most of a site's visitors will not have sufficiently fast connections to access video. An audio transmission of a lecture, for example, will convey quite a lot of the information that could be given by a video transmission, but at a lower data rate.

In such cases, Flash and the video formats can still be used. It is always possible to create a movie that consists of nothing but a soundtrack. The same markup can be used to embed the movie, but when it is displayed no area is needed to show the picture, since there isn't one. Instead, the player controls alone will be displayed, to allow the user to start and stop the sound and control its volume. This, as we remarked earlier, is always necessary.

If it is not possible to convert a sound recording to Flash or a video format, sounds stored in pure audio formats can be used instead. **AIFF**, **WAVE**, AAC and MP3 files are all used on the Web. The QuickTime and Real plug-ins can be used to play such files, as if they were in the appropriate media format, provided the browser is configured appropriately. In that case, the normal markup for embedded time-based media can be used, with the appropriate media type: `audio/aiff`, `audio/wav`, `audio/x-aac` and `audio/mp3`, respectively, for the file types just mentioned. For example, to play an AIFF audio file using QuickTime, the following markup could be used:

```
<object classid="clsid:02BF25D5-8C17-4B23-BC80-D3488ABDDC6B"
  width="150" height="16">
    <param name="movie" value="boogie.aif" />
    <param name="controller" value="true" />
    <param name="autoplay" value="false" />
    <param name="loop" value="false" />
    <object data="boogie.aif" type="audio/aiff" height="16"
     width="150">
        <param name="controller" value="true" />
        <param name="autoplay" value="false" />
        <param name="loop" value="false" />
          <p>QuickTime is required for this boogie-woogie</p>
    </object>
</object>
```

We have used the `controller` parameter to ensure that controls are displayed to allow the user to start and stop the sound and set its volume. We have also set `autoplay` and `loop` to `false`, to prevent its playing spontaneously or going on forever. The height of a standard controller is 16 pixels, and there is no need to reserve any more space, since no picture will be displayed. The length of the controller is arbitrary, although it is recommended that it

Figure 6.11 A standard audio controller

should be at least 150 pixels, to avoid cramping the controls. Any higher value that fits in better with the page layout may be used.

Figure 6.11 shows what the object for this audio clip would look like in a browser. The QuickTime audio controller is identical to the video controller, but in the absence of an area to hold the picture, it may not be apparent to every user what the controls do. As the screenshot on the right shows, clicking on the loudspeaker icon, which you might expect to cause some sound to play, actually makes a volume slider pop up. You will probably also appreciate that integrating these controls into a page will not always be easy. Quite often, you will see a page containing nothing but an audio controller. This usually results from a Web designer having added a link to an audio file to a page, instead of embedding it using an `object` element. This should be avoided.

Given this, it may be preferable to hide the controller, and provide an alternative means of starting and stopping the sound, in the form of a simple perspicuous icon, such as a loud-speaker or a single play button, or even just a link with a label such `Play boogie-woogie`. To make this work, a script would need to be used to control the player. The controller can be hidden by setting the `controller` parameter to `false`, in which case the height can be set to zero.

Key Points

Animation, video and sound are time-based media: they have an extent in time and time passes when you experience them.

Sound is effectively continuous and you cannot distinguish separate samples, but animation and video are sequences of recognizable still images.

Time-based media should be used with discretion on Web pages; gratuitous use is irritating. Playback controls should be provided unless duration is extremely short.

Time-Based Media and Web Pages

Browsers use additional software modules to display time-based media:

ActiveX controls are used by Internet Explorer on Windows

Plug-ins are used by other browsers on all platforms.

Time-based media can be embedded in an XHTML document using the `object` element.

If the media cannot be displayed, the element's content is used as a fallback.

The `height` and `width` attributes must be used to reserve space in the window for displaying the object.

Within the object, `param` elements can be used to pass values to the plug-in or control.

For plug-ins, the `data` attribute identifies the location of the object, and the `type` attribute identifies its Internet Media Type.

For ActiveX, the `classid` attribute specifies a Globally Unique Identifier for the control, and the location is given by a `param` element with `name` equal to `movie`.

To accommodate both plug-ins and ActiveX controls, an object for the plug-in can be placed inside an object for the ActiveX control.

The embed element may be required for compatibility with older browsers.

The presentation of Web video and Web audio can be controlled by scripting, instead of by the default player controls.

Animation

Animation is created one frame at a time, but this may be done by a computer program.

The concept of animation is extended for the Web to include both extremely short and interactive forms, and it may have a variable playback rate.

The frames may be captured from some external medium, or created inside the computer.

If animation is captured from a video camera then issues of broadcast standards and interlacing will arise.

Animated GIFs consist of a sequence of bitmapped images within a single GIF file. They are limited to 256 colours, but use a custom palette.

They can be played back without the use of any plug-in.

They are embedded using img elements, like any other image.

The GIF file can include a loop count and a specification of the delay time between frames (hence the frame rate).

Browsers dispay each frame of an animated GIF as it arrives; playback can be jerky over low bandwidth connections or if file size is very big.

Vector animation on the Web is usually in the form of a Flash movie.

In Flash, key frames are drawn and stored in their entirety. The position, size and other properties of objects can be tweened (interpolated) for crude animation.

Flash movies can contain many instances of the same symbol, which may be a movie within a movie.

Flash movies are embedded in pages using `object` elements, and displayed by the Flash Player plug-in.

Flash movies are displayed in streamed mode; playback can be jerky over low bandwidth connections.

Animation that is interactive can be created by programming (e.g. Java applets) or scripting (Dynamic HTML or Flash).

Once animation is exported to a video format it is treated like any other video, no matter how it originated.

Video

Video may be captured from DV equipment through a Firewire (IEEE 1394) connection and edited using inexpensive software.

Video equipment must be compatible with broadcast standards (PAL or NTSC).

For digital video, PAL frames are 720 by 576 pixels, NTSC frames are 720 by 640 pixels.

These pixels are not square.

PAL's frame rate is 25 frames per second, NTSC's is just under 30.

The data rate of quarter-frame PAL video is approximately 60Mbps.

Inter-frame compression is used to reduce the data rate.

Motion compensation allows additional data from preceding and following frames to be used to achieve further compression.

Recent codecs used for Web video are based on the MPEG codec family.

In MPEG terms, I-frames are compressed on their own, P-frames use inter-frame compression based on preceding frames, and B-frames use inter-frame compression based on preceding and following frames.

MPEG-4 Part 2 and H.264 are effective video codecs based on inter-frame compression with motion compensation.

Streaming video is played as it arrives, avoiding the delay in download-ing movies and the need for a copy of the movie on the user's disk. It is not suitable for low-bandwidth connections.

Progressive download starts playing video once part of it has arrived, and is useful when the data rate of the movie exceeds the maximum data rate of the connection.

Video is streamed using RTP and controlled using RTSP.

There are four major Web video formats and plug-ins: Flash Video, QuickTime, Windows Media and RealVideo.

The capabilities of all four are comparable: they all support streaming and feature codecs that produce good quality at low data rates.

Nested `object` elements can be used to embed video; the attributes and parameters for each format are different but do roughly the same thing.

Flash video must be referenced from a SWF movie, which can be played by the Flash Player plug-in.

QuickTime is a multimedia architecture that supports a multitude of different media types and video codecs, inclusing H.264.

Windows Media and RealVideo use their own codecs.

Sound

All four video formats also support sound.

Audio can be added as a synchronized soundtrack, or used on its own.

MP3, AAC or the proprietary Windows Media and RealAudio codecs can be used to compress sound.

When video formats are not being used to deliver sound, one of the pure audio formats – AIFF, WAVE, AAC or MP3 – can be used instead.

The QuickTime and Real plug-ins can be used to play these formats.

Exercises

Test Questions

1. By what means can Web browsers display time-based media as an integrated part of a page? What are the disadvantages of embedding media like this? What would be the disadvantages of using a helper program instead?

2. What attributes of the `object` element do you need to use with a plug-in? What attributes of the element do you need to use with ActiveX?

3. In what important ways will the markup used for embedding a movie to be played by an ActiveX control differ from that used for embedding it to be played by a plug-in and why?

4. Describe the characteristics of an animated GIF and explain what information can be stored in the file.

5. The Flash Player plays back Flash movies embedded in Web pages in a streamed mode. What effect will this have on playback and why? What factors will you need to take into consideration when including a Flash animation within a Web page?

6. Describe the different techniques for reducing file size which can be used in inter-frame compression of video, and the specific characteristics of each one. Which, if any, can be used on its own?

7. We stated in this chapter that animated GIF is an animation format; in fact it can also be used to deliver video, in the sense of moving pictures originally captured in real time by a video camera. Desribe how you would do this, and what this method would and would not be suitable for.

8. Explain why HTTP is not a very suitable protocol for transmitting streamed video, what should be used instead, and why.

9. List the names of the `param` elements commonly used within `object` elements used to embed QuickTime video in a Web page, and describe what each one is used for.

10. List the names of the principal `param` elements used within `object` elements for controlling playback and display of Windows Media files, and describe what each one is used for.

Discussion Topics

1. Under what circumstances do you think that it is a good idea to embed animation in Web pages? Try to think of as many examples of pages that really benefit from Web animation (of any kind) as you can, and defend your choices as though you were in a design meeting where other members of the team opposed your ideas.

2. Under what circumstances would you justify the inclusion of a flashing button or alert sign on a Web page and why?

3. Which Web video format would you choose for embedding video in a Web page and why? Would you choose different formats in different circumstances?

4. As broadband gets ever faster and more widely available, video is being used increasingly on Web pages in new ways. For example, it is now

common for software developers to post short tutorial demonstrations as video clips on their support pages. Give other examples of ways in which video may replace traditional hypertext on the Web. Do you think the Web will evolve to become more like television, with content based on moving pictures, or will it retain its textual basis?

5. If you were creating a site for a client who was prepared to allow third-party advertisements on their site, what media and format(s) of advertisement would you recommend that your client permitted, and why?

6. We say that sound is a medium that must be treated judiciously on Web pages. Do you agree with this? Justify your answer.

Practical Tasks

1. Take the résumé you created in Chapter 3 with the stylesheet you used in Chapter 4 to present yourself on a social networking site and add an appropriate video clip to it. This can be a clip of yourself, or something that reflects your interests. Use whatever facilities are available to you (even if it's only a mobile phone and iMovie) to create and, if necessary, edit the clip. Prepare the clip in a suitable format for the Web and try to integrate it with the rest of the page.

2. If you have access to a program (such as Flash or ImageReady) that allows you to create flashing buttons easily, create a simple flashing alert sign to draw attention to one or more parts of your résumé, and insert it in the appropriate place(s) on the page. How does this alter your perception of the page?

3. One of the most common uses of animation on the Web is for advertisements. Visit a few sites that carry animated adverts and save copies of the animations. (This is easiest if they are animated GIFs, but some Flash movies can also be saved.) Try adding an advertisement to the page you just created, in such a way that it does not detract too much from the page's main material, but still serves the advertiser's needs. Try adding more advertisements. Experiment both with placing the ads in conventional positions (a banner across the top, a tall 'skyscraper' down the right, and so on), and in less obvious places on the page.

4. Design a Web page whose sole purpose is to display a short video clip in your chosen format, together with a title and some brief details about the clip. Use appropriate markup and a stylesheet to create a page that enhances the experience of viewing the clip without detracting from it.

5. This exercise requires the use of a DV camera. Shoot a short clip (less than 30 seconds) of a slow moving subject, keeping the camera still. Use a tripod if you have one. Take a second clip of a similar subject, but use a handheld camera and a lot of camera movement, including fast pans and zooms. Compress each of these clips in as many different video formats as you can, to a data rate suitable for Internet streaming. How is the quality of the resulting video affected by the character of the original footage?

DOM Scripting

7

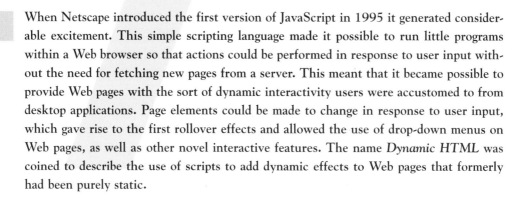

When Netscape introduced the first version of JavaScript in 1995 it generated considerable excitement. This simple scripting language made it possible to run little programs within a Web browser so that actions could be performed in response to user input without the need for fetching new pages from a server. This meant that it became possible to provide Web pages with the sort of dynamic interactivity users were accustomed to from desktop applications. Page elements could be made to change in response to user input, which gave rise to the first rollover effects and allowed the use of drop-down menus on Web pages, as well as other novel interactive features. The name *Dynamic HTML* was coined to describe the use of scripts to add dynamic effects to Web pages that formerly had been purely static.

The initial enthusiasm rapidly turned sour. In practice, many of the things that were commonly done with scripting can be done by some other means, or else are not very useful things to do anyway. Owing to a history of incompatible implementations coupled with the lack of programming experience of enthusiastic early Web designers, scripts have been responsible for more error messages and non-functioning pages than any other feature of the World Wide Web. To make matters worse, scripting has been employed to implement some of the most intrusive forms of Web advertising, specifically pop-up and pop-under adverts, which cause browsers to spawn new windows without any action from the user. It seemed for a while that client-side scripting was one of the Great Bad Ideas of the Web.

Perhaps, though, it would be fairer to say that JavaScript was a good idea that turned out badly. To abandon it because of early mistakes and abuse would be hasty. We now have a better understanding of how to use scripts in sensible ways, and new standards mean that the browser incompatibilities that plagued scripts in the past have been much reduced, if not entirely eliminated.

Some effects can only be achieved using scripting – which means using JavaScript, as there is currently no other universally supported client-side scripting language for the Web. Consider the style of interactive element illustrated in Figure 7.1. You are probably familiar with collapsible lists of this sort. Clicking on one of the top-level categories, like `vegetables`, causes a sub-list to appear. Clicking on it again causes the sub-list to disappear. Collapsible lists of this sort are common in desktop software, but their use on Web pages presents a problem. Using the features we have described so far, the only way that the contents of a browser's window can be changed for longer than the time the cursor is over a rollover is by retrieving a new page. In this case, that would mean that there would have to be separate pages for each of the eight possible combinations of states of the lists, and that the response to clicking on a category would not be instant. Since a new page would have to be loaded, the immediacy of the connection between clicking and seeing the sub-list revealed would be lost, and with it some valuable interface feedback.

As we will show later in this chapter, a script can be used to implement a collapsible list on a Web page so that it behaves the same way as in a program. Generally, scripts allow designers to implement a more fluid style of interactivity on Web pages. Because not all browsers and devices used to access the Web support scripting, and some users (as many as 10% according to some estimates) disable scripting support to avoid the worst abuses it is prone to, it is important that the functioning of a page should not depend entirely on scripting – alternatives must always be provided. As with stylesheets, the absence of scripting may cause the user to experience a less attractive page, but it should never prevent them from seeing any of the page's content or deny them any of its essential functionality. To take an obvious example, a visitor to an e-commerce site should not be prevented from buying something because they have disabled scripts in their browser.

Figure 7.1 A collapsible list

One response to the problems with scripts has been to turn to Flash. Flash, too, has a sophisticated scripting language, called ActionScript, which allows many sorts of interactivity to be implemented inside Flash movies. Flash scripts can also send HTTP requests, and interact with data sources on a server in different ways, so it is possible to create Flash movies that can do everything that a standard Web page can do. Since Flash is a proprietary format, implemented with a plug-in under the control of a single company, there has never been any problem with incompatible implementations.

Designers who rely on Flash often create entire sites as Flash movies, just using HTML to embed them in a Web page. As well as providing interactivity using ActionScript, Flash sites can profit from Flash's vector graphics and animation facilities to create an appearance that is closer to conventional graphic design than standard Web sites. There are drawbacks to this approach, of course, primarily its reliance on a proprietary plug-in instead of Web standards. Flash sites are often inefficient and slow to load and they may present problems to people who need to access the Web using screen readers and other forms of assistive technology. The freedom that Flash allows designers in creating novel types of interactivity and using unconventional controls can make sites hard to use and understand. Many people simply don't like the appearance that Flash encourages.

Despite these drawbacks, developing sites in Flash is popular with designers. However, this kind of development is a different activity from developing sites using Web standards, which is our primary concern in this book, so we will not consider it any further.

Fundamentals

Writing scripts is a form of programming and requires the same skills and attention to detail. Most scripts used on Web pages are simple, though, and a high level of specialized programming knowledge is not required – but if you lack that knowledge, you should not be too ambitious in your scripting. It is necessary to understand some fundamental concepts that underlie modern programming practice, however.

Objects

Object-oriented programming (OOP) is presently the dominant approach to the construction of computer programs. It is based on the notion that a program is a model of some real or abstract system, and can be composed from the interaction of objects which correspond to parts of the system being modelled. Objects can be grouped into classes, all of whose members share certain general characteristics.

That may sound abstruse, but modelling the world in terms of classes and objects is something we do all the time. Consider, for instance, the sandwich shop which we used in Chapter 2 as an analogy of client/server interaction. In such a shop at lunchtime, we would most likely find several people. Each of these people is an object (in our restricted sense for this example, without any disrespect). Some of them will be customers, that is objects belonging to the class of customers. Another will be the assistant behind the counter, an object belonging to the class of assistants. The shop itself is an object; it belongs to the class of sandwich shops. Sandwich shops are only one sort of take-away food shop. Pavement crêpe bars are another. Everything that is true about every take-away food shop is also true of every sandwich shop, but certain things that are true about sandwich shops are not true of other types of take-away food shop. We say that the class of sandwich shops is a sub-class of the class of take-away food shops.

The objects we have described so far are things in the real world (or conceptual analogues of them). If we wished to write a program to model sandwich shops, we would need to create objects in some programming language. Although the word 'object' is used in both cases, the objects in programs are just collections of data whose computational behaviour mimics aspects of the real system we are trying to model.

In a program, an object consists of a set of values, called **properties**, together with a set of operations, called **methods**, which define what an object can do. Methods are just pieces of program; to make an object do something, one of its methods must be executed. Both properties and methods have names, by which they can be referred to. It is customary to describe objects in anthropomorphic terms, by saying that an object knows certain facts about itself – what the values of its properties are; how to do certain things – what methods are defined for it; and that an object will do things when it is asked to – it will execute one of its methods if it is called upon to do so. Crucially, the values of an object's properties can change, usually as a result of a method's being executed.

Consider again the sandwich shop. Suppose that the customers form an orderly queue, and there is just one assistant behind the counter, Charlie, who takes their orders one at a time. Charlie jots down the items in the current customer's order, and then adds up their prices and asks for some money. He then prepares the sandwiches, coffee and so on, and hands the customer their lunch when it is made. Charlie goes on to deal with the next customer, if there is anyone still waiting, otherwise he rests for a while.

Although any real assistant will have many properties, such as their sex, age, the colour of their hair, eyes and skin, height, weight, and so on, only one property is required to model

Charlie's behaviour in this (conveniently over-simplified) scenario: a list of items in the current customer's order. We could write this property as `charlie.order`, using a notation that we will explain further later on. The current customer would be an object that modelled the relevant aspects of a customer, such as what they wanted to eat and how much money they had. The object for the shop itself would include, among other objects, a list of waiting customers and the object representing Charlie.

The methods appropriate to any assistant, and thus to Charlie, would include one for taking an order from the current customer. This would entail getting the order, by using one of the customer's methods (i.e. asking the customer object what it wanted). The entire transaction would be written as `charlie.note_order(customer.give_order())` and would have the effect of setting `charlie.order` to a list of the items ordered. The method thus updates the property. Another method would be used to compute the price of the lunch, which would involve looking up the prices of the items in the order and adding them up. Here the method uses the property (the list of items) to compute a result. When the interaction with the current customer was completed, the assistant would attend to the next, if one was waiting. This would require it to ask the shop object to execute a method that removed the first customer from the front of the queue, and handed them over to the assistant for serving.

As this example shows, the objects in a program interact: objects ask each other to execute methods, and pass information between themselves. We will explain how methods can be executed and perform computations, and how values can be exchanged between objects, later, when we have introduced some programming notation.

Because methods provide a way of asking an object to do something, it is never necessary for other objects to know anything about how a method accomplishes its task. For example, in the sandwich bar, if the object representing Charlie provides a method that prepares a customer's order, this method can be executed, without enquiring whether sandwiches are going to be made freshly or fetched from a refrigerator. This means that if the shop throws out the refrigerator so that it can advertise its sandwiches as being freshly made, the methods called when Charlie deals with customers and the values passed to them are unaffected. In large programs, this isolation of the effects of changes provides a huge benefit in making programs easier to maintain, and errors easier to track down. It is common in large programs for the properties of an object only to be used by its own methods, which are the exclusive means for interacting with other objects.

By using a suitable notation, we can describe the way customers are served in the sandwich shop in a concise and precise way – sufficiently precise for a computer to execute the steps in our description. We will use the language JavaScript for this purpose. First, though, we need to look a little more closely at methods.

Functions and Methods

The object-oriented concept of a method is closely related to an older concept, that of a *function*. Functions pre-date programming; they are used by mathematicians for describing operations which map values, known as the function's arguments, to some new value. An example which will probably be familiar is the sine function, sin(x). This maps angles to numbers between 0 and 1: sin(0°) is equal to 0, sin(90°) is 1, sin(45°) is ½√2, and so on. In mathematics, this relationship between the argument and the value produced by the function just exists, but in computing, functions perform some calculations to turn their arguments into results. In order to make a function perform its computation it must be explicitly called, and the value it computes is said to be returned from the call.

You can think of a function in a program as a sort of black box, into which argument values are placed when it is called. Generally, functions may take several arguments and combine them into a result. Some computation goes on inside the box, but when we use a function we do not need to worry about how it happens. A result comes out of the box, which can then be used. In almost all programming languages, functions are called using the classical mathematical notation: the function name is followed by the values being supplied as arguments in brackets. For example, `average(312,68)` is a function call. If the function `average` was defined to compute the arithmetic mean of its two arguments, this call would produce the value 190.

A method is like a function, in that it takes argument values, does some computation using them, and may generate a result. The difference is that methods are associated with objects and can use the properties of the object they are associated with, as well as the arguments they are passed explicitly, in order to perform their computation. Methods often have side-effects: as well as (or instead of) computing a result, they change the values of some of their object's properties.

If `take_payment` is a method associated with `charlie`, an object from our simulation of a sandwich shop, it can be referred to in a JavaScript program using the notation `charlie.take_payment`, which is simply a short way of saying the `take_payment` method of the `charlie` object. It is called like a function, with argument values in brackets, so for `charlie` to take a payment of £6.50, we would write `charlie.take_payment(6.50)`. Since methods can use the values of properties, they sometimes do not take any arguments at all.

In that case, they are called by writing their name followed by an empty pair of brackets, as for example, `charlie.prepare_lunch()`.

This dot notation is also used to refer to properties. If `the_shop` is the object representing the sandwich shop, and it has a property `prices`, recording the prices of everything on offer, this property would be referred to as `the_shop.prices`.

Programming with Objects

With the aid of a little additional JavaScript notation, we can now write a pseudo-program that simulates our sandwich shop, as we described it earlier. (It isn't a real program because we assume that certain objects already exist, whereas in a real program we would have to define them.) We will begin by showing you the whole program, and then we will explain the details:

```
while (the_shop.is_open()) {
   var customer = the_shop.first_customer();
   if (customer != null) {
      charlie.note_order(customer.give_order());
      var amount = charlie.compute_total(the_shop.prices);
      charlie.take_payment(customer.pay(amount));
      customer.take_lunch(charlie.prepare_lunch());
   }
   else charlie.relax_a_bit();
}
```

In trying to follow what is happening here, you might find it helpful to read a method call such as `charlie.compute_total(the_shop.prices)` as if it was an instruction or request to the object that the method is being called through: 'Charlie, compute the total using the prices from the shop', as it were.

We begin by assuming that two objects, `the_shop` and `charlie` already exist. We also assume that `the_shop` has a method `is_open`, which returns `true` or `false` depending on whether the shop is open or closed. We don't want Charlie to go on serving customers after the shop has closed, so we wrap our little description of his work in a loop. This is introduced by the keyword `while`, which indicates that the code that follows it will be executed repeatedly, as long as the expression in the brackets gives the value `true`. Hence, `while (the_shop.is_open())` makes the loop repeat until the shop closes.

There is a certain arbitrariness about what we put in the loop. We might have written the entire program like this:

```
while (the_shop.is_open()) charlie.serve_customers();
```

and left all the detail to be defined inside the serve_customers method. However, we prefer to elaborate some of the steps in the serving explicitly, so we have used more methods, each of which performs a smaller step in the process.

A JavaScript program is a sequence of statements. There are several different sorts of statement; a while loop is one sort, and a method call that does not use any returned value is another. If there is more than a single statement inside a while loop, the repeated statements must be enclosed in curly brackets. Furthermore, every statement must be terminated by a semi-colon.[†]

Hitherto, we have quietly assumed that objects have names, without enquiring how they get them. For Web scripting, this is often a good assumption, since many of the objects that scripts must manipulate are provided by the browser. Sometimes, however, we need to be able to refer to objects (and other values) by name. To do this, we can use **variables**. Variables are named containers that can hold objects and values. If an object is stored in a variable, its methods and properties can be accessed using the variable's name. An object can be introduced into a script using the keyword var. To store a value in the variable at the same time, its name is followed by an = sign, and then some expression whose value is to be stored.

The first thing that happens in the loop of our program is that the first waiting customer, obtained by calling the_shop's first_customer method, is stored in a variable called customer:

```
var customer = the_shop.first_customer();
```

But there might not be a customer waiting. In that case, the_shop.first_customer() will return a null value. Since Charlie can't serve a null customer, the next thing to do is test whether this happened. A conditional statement begins with they keyword if, which is followed by an expression in brackets. If this expression evaluates to true, the next statements (between the { and }) are executed. Otherwise, the statement following the keyword else

† This isn't actually true, most such semi-colons can be left out, but it's easier to put them all in than to remember the precise rules about which ones are compulsory.

further down the script is executed. Here we test the value of customer to see if it is not null; in JavaScript the operator != is used to mean 'is not equal to'. If customer is null, this test will fail, the next block of statements will be skipped, and Charlie will get to rest:

```
if (customer != null) {
  serve the customer
}
else charlie.relax_a_bit();
```

If customer isn't null, and the test succeeds, then according to our description, Charlie takes their order. This means that the value of the order must be given to Charlie to store. To get the value, the give_order method of customer is called. The result of this is then passed to the note_order method of charlie. As a side-effect of this call, the order will be stored in a property belonging to the object charlie. Observe how the result of calling a method on one object can be passed to a method of another object:

```
charlie.note_order(customer.give_order());
```

In the next two lines, the price of the order is computed. This is done using the stored value of the order and the price list, which we have modelled here as a property of the_shop. We have chosen to store the value temporarily in a variable amount, before passing it to customer.pay, the method that extracts the money from the customer. This variable is redundant, since we could have passed the result of charlie.compute_total straight into customer.pay, in the same way as we pass the result of that call (the amount handed over by the customer) to charlie.take_payment, but using the variable makes the script a little bit more readable:

```
var amount = charlie.compute_total(the_shop.prices);
charlie.take_payment(customer.pay(amount));
```

After the business of payment is finished, all that remains is for the lunch to be prepared and taken by the customer. Both these operations are modelled by simple method calls:

```
customer.take_lunch(charlie.prepare_lunch());
```

Whichever branch of the conditional statement was taken, the loop is then repeated: the test is made to see whether the shop is still open, and if so, the next customer is served.

We have conveniently glossed over a lot of details that would be required to complete this program, not least the definitions of all these methods we have used and the means whereby new customers enter the shop. We will not go into those additional details here, though. Despite appearances, our main concern in this book is not with sandwich shops, but with Web pages, and a different set of objects is needed for modelling those. However, they will still have methods and properties, and will need to be combined in programs making use of variables, loops and conditional statements.

The DOM

There is no unique way of modelling any non-trivial system as a collection of objects. Much of the trouble with scripting on the Web resulted from several distinct models of Web pages being implemented in different browsers. However, there now exists a standard in the form of the W3C *Document Object Model (DOM)*, which should allow scripts to be written that will work in any browser that conforms to the W3C standards.

The DOM is defined by several W3C Recommendations, referred to as DOM Levels 1, 2 and 3. Level 1 defines the basic objects that allow XML and XHTML documents to be manipulated by scripts. Level 2 adds support for event handling and style manipulation. Level 3 goes further, refining the facilities in Levels 1 and 2, and providing a standard way for scripts to access external XML data. Most Web browsers implement Level 1 and parts of Level 2.

The Recommendations actually define two object models. The **Core DOM** is suitable for modelling any XML document, including XHTML documents. The **HTML DOM** adds additional objects, properties and methods, which are specific to HTML and XHTML documents, taking advantage of the fixed set of element types in those languages. Although it is possible to manipulate any XHTML document using the Core DOM objects only, it is often more convenient to use the HTML DOM. In some cases, doing so also enhances compatibility with certain browsers whose implementation of the DOM is not altogether rigorous.

The DOM is defined as a purely abstract model: the Recommendations define 'interfaces', which are methods and properties that must be made available to programs. They do not define these interfaces in terms of any actual scripting or programming language. Instead, they use a specification language (OMG IDL) to provide a definition that can be mapped on to the actual syntax of any language that may be used for writing scripts, or any other program that must manipulate the structure of XML and XHTML documents. The understandable desire to avoid tying the object model to any particular language has the unfortunate effect of making the DOM Recommendations hard to read and difficult to relate to actual scripting practice, since people writing scripts are concerned with concrete objects and their actual properties and methods, and not with abstract interfaces. However, there are specifications of 'language bindings' that show how the abstract interfaces can be mapped into concrete objects. We will describe the JavaScript objects that result from applying the bindings from the DOM Recommendations, and which you can use in your scripts, and leave it to enthusiastic readers to look up the abstract interfaces in the Recommendations themselves.

DOM Objects

The DOM provides a standard way of representing an XHTML document using objects, which can be manipulated in a program, just as we previously represented a sandwich shop using objects. For instance, the following is a simple XHTML document (with an embedded stylesheet):

```
<?xml version="1.0" encoding="utf-8"?>
<!DOCTYPE html PUBLIC "-//W3C//DTD XHTML 1.0 Strict//EN"
        "http://www.w3.org/TR/xhtml1/DTD/xhtml1-strict.dtd">
<html xmlns="http://www.w3.org/1999/xhtml" xml:lang="en" lang="en">
<head>
   <meta http-equiv="content-type" content="text/html; charset=utf-8"
/>
   <title>Desperate Software</title>
<style type="text/css" title="text/css" media="screen">
li.current { color: red; }
li.special { color: green; }
</style>
</head>
<body>
<ul id="navbar"><li>Home</li>
<li>Products</li>
<li>Downloads</li>
<li>Help</li></ul>
  rest of the body content
</body>
</html>
```

Here is a small piece of program that operates on this document to change the class of the first item in the list:

```
var navbar = document.getElementById("navbar");
var first_item = navbar.firstChild;
```

```
if (first_item.className != "special")
    first_item.className = "current";
```

(We will leave the question of how this code might be activated until later.)

You should be able to see that this program is using objects and methods in a way similar to our earlier example, and that some of the same constructs are being used to control their execution. As before, you can read the method calls as instructions to the objects, so – in the first line – we are asking the document object to perform some operation called getElementById using the string "navbar". You can probably guess from the method's name that we are in fact asking the document to get the object corresponding to the element whose id is navbar.

Three objects are used in this script: document represents the entire document; it is built in to the browser and can always be accessed. It has many methods and properties, some of which will be described later in this chapter, but here we just use one of its methods, getElementById. (The peculiar use of upper- and lower-case letters in the name is a convention used for names that are really made up of several words, since names in JavaScript cannot have spaces in them. Using underline characters to stand in for spaces is an alternative, which we use for our own variables, to distinguish them from names belonging to the DOM.) This takes a string and returns the element that has that string as the value of its id attribute. Here, we supply the string "navbar", so we get back a second object, which represents the ul element, and assign it to the variable navbar.

Objects that represent elements also have several methods and properties, including a property called firstChild. You will recall from Chapter 3 that if an element has other elements in its content, they are called its children. The firstChild property of an object representing an element has as its value an object representing the first of these children. Hence, in our program, navbar.firstChild is an object representing the first of the li elements in the list. It gets stored in the variable first_item.

Once this object has been obtained, we use a conditional statement to decide what to do with it. In the condition, the className property is used to find the value of the class attribute of the element. (This property belongs to the HTML DOM, whereas all the other methods and properties we have used here belong to the Core DOM.) Unless the element belongs to the class special (!= is JavaScript's notation for 'not equal to'), an assignment to this property is used to change the class to current. Because of the rule for li.current in the stylesheet, the effect of this change is to turn the list element for Home red. If, however, the markup for the first list element had been:

```
<li class = "special">Home</li>
```

Home would have stayed green, because the test would have failed. (There is no else in this conditional expression, so nothing is done if the tested condition is not true.)

This example is not especially realistic, but we will show later how altering the value of class attributes can be used to achieve useful results. The important point to grasp is that by providing objects with suitable methods and properties, the DOM allows us to write programs that alter XHTML documents and change their appearance in the browser.

DOM Trees

The structure of XML and XHTML documents is hierarchical: elements contain other elements. The DOM models this hierarchy: objects contain other objects. We say that the objects modelling a document form a *tree*. Figure 7.2 shows how the element hierarchy of a simple XHTML document can be displayed as a tree. We are using 'tree' in a technical sense here, to mean a collection of *nodes* connected by *edges*, which connect a node with its *children*. In the diagram, nodes are indicated by the text in blue or orange, and edges by the connecting lines; edges run down and to the right. The node at the top left, which corresponds to the root element of the document, is also the *root* of the tree. With the exception of the root, each node has exactly one parent node. You should be able to see how the tree diagram captures the hierarchy of elements in the XHTML document, and how the relationship between nodes and their children mirrors the relationship between elements and their children, which we described in Chapter 3.

There are two types of node in the tree shown in Figure 7.2: *element nodes*, which we have shown in blue, correspond to the XHTML elements in the document, while *text nodes*, which we have shown in orange, correspond to the text that appears in the content of some elements. (The trees for XML documents may include several other types of node, but we will not be concerned with those.) A noticeable feature of the tree is the large number of text nodes containing a single newline character (written as \n in the diagram, for reasons that will be explained later). Although white space in the document does not affect the appearance in a browser, it does appear in the DOM tree. Forgetting that these nodes will occur is a common source of programming errors in scripts that manipulate the tree. (Observant readers may have wondered why we used unconventional layout for the list in our example in

```
html
├─ head
│   └─ sub-tree for head contents
└─ body
    ├─ text [ \n ]
    ├─ img
    ├─ text [ \n ]
    ├─ h1
    │   └─ text [ Desperate Software ]
    ├─ text [ \n ]
    ├─ p
    │   └─ text node for p contents
    ├─ text [ \n ]
    ├─ h2
    │   └─ text [ Our Products ]
    ├─ text [ \n ]
    ├─ p
    │   └─ text node for p contents
    ├─ text [ \n ]
    ├─ ul
    │   ├─ text [ \n ]
    │   ├─ li
    │   │   └─ a
    │   │       └─ text [ textFridge ]
    │   ├─ text [ \n ]
    │   ├─ li
    │   │   └─ sub-tree for 2nd list item
    │   ├─ text [ \n ]
    │   └─ li
    │       └─ sub-tree for 3rd list item
    ├─ text [ \n ]
    ├─ h2
    │   └─ sub-tree for h2
    └─ and so on...
```

```html
<html xmlns="http://www.w3.org/1999/xhtml"
ml:lang="en" lang="en">
<head>
          ...
</head>
<body>
<img src="gradient.gif" alt="sunburst logo" width="87"
height="222" />
<h1>Desperate Software</h1>
<p>
Purveyors of fine computer programs to the gentry.
</p>
<h2>Our Products</h2>
<p>
Click on a link below for feature lists, download links, and
more.
</p>
<ul>
        <li><a href="fridge.html">textFridge</a></li>
        <li><a href="magnet/index.html">
            ScreenMagnet</a></li>
        <li><a href="freezer/index.html">
            Widget Freezer X</a></li>
</ul>
<h2>Contact Us</h2>
...
</body>
</html>
```

Figure 7.2 The DOM tree for a simple Web page

the preceding section. This was done to avoid introducing the complication of white space text nodes at that stage.)

`Element` objects (that is, the objects that correspond to the elements of the document) are defined in the Core DOM. They have a method called `getAttribute`, which returns the value of an attribute, given its name, and `setAttribute`, which changes the value of a named attribute. They also have properties for accessing the objects corresponding to nearby elements. These include `firstChild`, `lastChild` and `parentNode`, for accessing the nodes below and above, and `previousSibling` and `nextSibling` for accessing those on the same level. For instance, if `li1` was the object corresponding to the first `li` element in the tree shown in Figure 7.2, whose content is the link for the `textFridge` product, then `li1.firstChild` is an `Element` object corresponding to the enclosed a element, and so is `li1.lastChild` (because `li1` only has one child). The `li` element is contained in the `ul` element, so `li1.parentNode` is an object corresponding to the `ul`. Both `li1.previousSibling` and `li1.nextSibling` are text nodes, one for the newline preceding the `li` element and the other for the one following it. Since these properties are themselves `Element` objects, we can call methods through them. For instance, `li1.firstchild.getAttribute("href")` returns the URL attached to the link.

All the properties we have mentioned so far each have a single object as their value. The `childNodes` property of an `Element` object is different: it return a list of objects corresponding to all the element's children. Such a list is itself an object – a `NodeList` object – with a property and a method of its own. The `length` property holds the number of items in the list. For example, `li1.childNodes.length` is equal to 1. The `item` method takes a number (actually, an integer greater than or equal to zero) and returns the object at the corresponding position in the list. These indices begin at 0, not 1, so the only object in the list of children of li1 is `li1.childNodes.item(0)`. One way of accessing the objects for the three `li` elements in the example document is as `li1.parentNode.childNodesitem(1)`, `li1.parentNode.childNodes.item(3)` and `li1.parentNode.childNodes.item(5)`. (Don't forget the text nodes.)

As well as passively traversing the tree, the DOM provides `Element` objects with methods for changing it. The most useful of these is `appendChild`, which takes an `Element` or `Text` object and inserts it as a new child, following any existing children. For instance, if tn is a text object, containing an exclamation mark, `li1.appendChild(tn)` would add it after the node for the `textFridge` link, causing it to be displayed as `textFridge!` (though the ! would not be part of the link). Shortly, we will explain how such a text node would be created.

One remaining object is of fundamental importance. The document object represents the entire document. It has properties corresponding to the DTD and the root element, among others. As we demonstrated in our little example, it also has a method getElementById, which can be used to obtain the object corresponding to any element in the document which has an id attribute. An equally useful method is getElementsByTagName, which takes a string, such as "h1", which is the name of an element type, and returns a NodeList containing objects for all the elements of that type in the document – all the h1 elements, in this case. The document object is also where the methods for creating new nodes are found: the createElement method takes an element type name and returns a brand new object corresponding to an element of that type. For example, document.createElement("h1") would be used to create a new h1 object. Similarly, the createTextNode method is used to wrap up a string as a text node: document.createTextNode("Notes") turns the string "Notes" into a text node. The result of either of these methods would be suitable for appending to the children of some other Element object. For instance, the following code would have the effect of adding a new heading at the end of the page:

```
var h1 = document.createElement("h1");
h1.appendChild(document.createTextNode("Notes"));
var body = document.getElementsByTagName("body").item(0);
body.appendChild(h1);
```

First, we ask document to create the node, and store it in a variable. Next, we tell the newly created node object to add a text node – which document creates from the string – to its children. We then ask document to get all the body objects; there is only one, but we can't access it easily any other way, so we take the first item from the list that is returned, and store that in a variable, too. (Remember, item(0) is the first item.) Finally, we ask this body object to add the node we created and populated with text to its children. This pattern of creating nodes using the document methods and then appending them to Elements is a common one used in scripts that create parts of documents dynamically.

Table 7.1 summarizes the principal Core DOM objects. A few methods which we have not described in detail are included in the table.

The main additional convenience provided by the HTML DOM is the ability to use properties to refer to attributes, instead of having to access them through the getAttribute and setAttribute methods. Almost all of these properties bear the same name as the corresponding attribute. For instance, if the_link is an object corresponding to some link (a element), the_link.href would hold the URL that was the value of its href attribute.

Object	Property or Method	Meaning
document	createElement(n)	Make a new Element object of type n.
	createTextNode(t)	Make a new text node with the text t.
	getElementsByTagName(n)	Find all the Element objects of type n in the document and return them in a NodeList.
Element	getAttribute(n)	Return the string value of this element's attribute with name n.
	setAttribute(n,v)	Set the value of this element's attribute with name n to v.
	getElementsByTagName(n)	Find all the Element objects of type n in this element's children and return them in a NodeList.
	appendChild(e)	Add the Element e to this element's children after all its existing children.
	insertBefore(e,c)	Add the Element e to this element's children, before the child c.
	removeChild(c)	Remove the Element c from among this element's children.
	replaceChild(c, d)	Replace the Element's child d with c.
	firstChild	This element's first child Element.
	lastChild	This element's last child Element.
	previousSibling	The Element to the left of this element in the tree.
	nextSibling	The Element to the right of this element in the tree.
	parentNode	The Element above this element in the tree.
	childNodes	A NodeList containing all this element's children.
	nodeType	Always equal to 1.
NodeList	item(i)	Get the object at position i in the list.
	length	The number of items in the list.
Text	data	The string of text.
	length	The number of characters in the text.
	nodeType	Always equal to 3.

Table 7.1 Principal DOM objects

To change the URL, we would assign a new value to the property. The property for the `class` attribute is an exception to the naming convention: it is called `className`, not `class`. (This is to avoid potential conflicts with the use of the word `class` as a keyword in many programming languages.) We will make free use of these properties in our examples. The HTML DOM also adds extra properties to the `document` object, which hold collections grouping together certain types of element in a document. For instance, `document.forms` holds objects corresponding to all the `form` elements in the document, while `document.images` holds all the `img` elements.

JavaScript

As we have demonstrated, scripts are built by combining the objects of the DOM with JavaScript constructs, which organize the ordering and interaction of method calls. Before we can show you some actual examples of scripts we must be less vague about our programming notation, and describe a few more features of JavaScript which will be needed. We do not have space here to provide anything like a full description of the language or a thorough introduction to programming. We will confine ourselves to those features which we need to demonstrate the principles of scripting for Web pages.

Values, Expressions and Assignment

Although the main business of JavaScript is manipulating host objects, scripts also need to be able to operate on some other sorts of values. In particular, it must be possible to perform arithmetic on numbers, for purposes such as counting, and to manipulate strings of text.

Numbers

Computer programs can perform arithmetic on two sorts of numbers: integers (whole numbers) and floating point numbers, which are finite approximations to real numbers. (Few Web scripts have much use for the latter.) Numbers can be written down using the ordinary decimal notation. They can be assigned to variables, using the syntax we saw before, such as:

```
var i = 0;
```

More interestingly, numbers – and variables storing numbers – can be combined to make new numbers, using an approximation to ordinary arithmetic notation. The operators +, -, * and / are used for addition, subtraction, multiplication and division. If you have not written any programs before, note the use of *: you cannot use implicit multiplication (e.g. 3x) and you cannot use x as a multiplication operator, even though it looks more like one than * does.

Terminology

ECMAScript

The language used for scripting in Netscape 2 was called JavaScript. A distinction was made between core JavaScript, which comprised the programming features, and the objects which served the same function as the DOM does now, but JavaScript referred to the combination of the two. The distinction was and is considered unimportant by most people.

When ECMA (the European Computer Manufacturers' Association) was approached to standardize a Web scripting language, in order to put an end to the incompatibilities between JavaScript and Microsoft's JScript, they chose only to standardize the core language, and called the resulting language, which lacked any DOM objects, *ECMAScript*. The DOM was standardized independently by the W3C.

ECMAScript is not, in itself, capable of doing much that is useful. (In fact, since it has no facilities for performing output, it is debatable whether it can do anything useful at all.) It merely provides a framework for manipulating DOM objects – or any other set of *host objects*, that is, objects that provide an interface to some system. The DOM is the set of host objects that provide an interface to Web pages. ECMAScript is also the basis of ActionScript, the language used for scripting in Flash, and it is commonly used for controlling application programs, such as Photoshop, too.

Because of its familiarity, the name JavaScript is almost always used, as we use it, to refer to the combination of ECMAScript and the DOM. It is also used, where context permits, as a synonym for ECMAScript.

The less familiar, but frequently useful, operation of taking the remainder after division is somewhat arbitrarily denoted by the % operator: 7%5 is equal to 2, for example. Brackets work as expected: 3 * (i + 1) is the same as 3 * i + 3. Arithmetic should hold no surprises, but remember that computers can only deal with finite quantities, so there is a limit to the size of numbers you can deal with. It is unlikely that you will meet this limit when writing typical Web scripts, but if you do perform an operation whose result is too large to store, the special value Infinity will be returned. Remember also that the result of dividing 0 by 0 is undefined;

this will produce another special value, NaN ('not a number'), if you try to do it in a script, as will other operations whose result does not make sense arithmetically.

Numbers and variables are not the only things that may appear in arithmetic expressions. If a function or method returns a numerical value, or if a property of some object holds a number, it may be called anywhere a number is needed. For example, `1+el.childnodes.length` and `2*average(x, y)` are both legal expressions, assuming `el` is an Element object, and `average` is a function that computes the arithmetic mean of its arguments.

Some well-known mathematical constants and functions are built in to JavaScript in the form of the `Math` object. The constants are its properties and the functions its methods. For instance, `Math.PI` is a finite approximation to π; `Math.cos(x)` computes the cosine of x. The object itself only exists to provide a way of grouping the constants and functions together.

Strings

Strings of text are at least as important as numbers in scripts: they enable us to examine and change the text of pages, values of attributes, names of elements and many other quantities. It is sometimes necessary to write strings down literally. We have used the appropriate notation in our examples already: the characters of the string are enclosed in double quote symbols, as in `"Notes"` and `"h1"`. It is also permissible to use single quotes, as in `'h1'`. Most of the time, the difference is cosmetic, but if you need to include a double quote inside a string, you can do so without prematurely terminating the string by using single quotes to enclose it: `'href="../index.html"'`, for example. Conversely, if you need a single quote in a string, enclose the string in double quotes. Alternatively, you can escape the quote symbol by putting a \ in front of it, as in `"href=\"../index.html\""`. This is clumsier, but \ escapes provide a general mechanism for including problematical characters in a string. In particular, \n is a newline, which is otherwise not allowed inside a string, and \\ is used for a single \. (Compare this with the use of character entities in XHTML.)

You can store strings in variables as easily as you can store numbers. You can also add strings together, in the sense of making a new string by adding the characters of one string to the end of another. The operator + is used for this purpose, too. For instance,

```
var web = "Web";
var design = "Design";
var web_design = web + " " + design;
```

is a long-winded way of storing the string "Web Design" in the variable web_design. Notice that the space between the two words must be added explicitly: adding strings does not automatically introduce spaces.

Strings that only consist of digits look like numbers, but they aren't, they are strings: the string "897" is not the same sort of value as the number 897. You quite often need to convert between the two, though. For instance, if a user types something into a text field, you will only be able to access the characters they typed – a string – but you may well want to do arithmetic on the corresponding number. JavaScript converts between the two automatically in some contexts; it is easy to do the conversions explicitly, and it is safer. If s is a string that looks like a number, Number(s) converts it to that number. For instance Number("897") is the number 897. Conversely, String(897) is the string "897".

Strings are actually objects in JavaScript, and have some methods and a property. A string's length property holds the number of characters, so given the assignments above, web_design.length is equal to 10.

The string methods include several different ways of taking strings apart: charAt takes a number and returns the character that it finds at the corresponding position in the string: web_design.charAt(2) is "b". Note that character positions start at 0 for the first character, and that the value returned is itself a string, of length 1 – there is no such thing as a character type in JavaScript. The substring method allows you to extract parts of a string. It takes a starting position and an ending position as arguments, and returns the string that begins at the starting position and ends just before the ending position: web_design.substring(6, 9) is "sig". The length of the substring is equal to the difference between the two argument values.

The indexOf method can be used to search for one string inside another. The string you are looking for is passed as an argument to the method, which is called through the string you are looking in. The result that is returned is the offset of the beginning of the first occurrence of the argument, or −1 if it is not there. So web_design.indexOf("sign") would be 6 but web_design.indexOf("sing") would be −1. It is easy to test for this value to see whether a substring is present. A companion method, lastIndexOf, can be used to search from the end of a string for the last occurrence of a substring. It returns the offset in the same way as indexOf does. For instance, whereas web_design.indexOf("e") would be 1, web_design.lastIndexOf("e") would be 5.

As with numbers, functions, properties and methods returning strings can be used in any context where strings are needed. It is fairly common to combine strings returned by substring and other string methods using the + operator, for example.

Arrays

Strings are sequences of characters; arrays are similar, but they are sequences of values of any type. We have met something similar already: the NodeList values returned by document.getElementsByTagName, for instance, are sequences of objects, which are accessed using the item method. Arrays are similar sequences, but their items are accessed using a more compact notation. If a is an array, and i is an integer, a[i] is the item at position i in the array. This operation is called array indexing, and i is said to be the index of the item in the array. Like NodeLists, arrays have a length property, indexes begin at 0, and cannot be negative. In fact, the similarities are no coincidence. DOM NodeLists are implemented in JavaScript as arrays, and you can, if you like, use array notation instead of the item method, and we will usually do so from now on. (However, in other language bindings for the DOM, this notation is not permitted, so you may prefer to stick with item if you expect to be writing DOM programs in other languages besides JavaScript.)

One way of thinking of an array is as a means of associating numbers with values. If n is a number, a[n] is the associated value. Because of the properties of numbers, the array behaves as a sequence. The values used to index JavaScript arrays do not have to be numbers, though. You can use arrays to associate values with strings instead. For example, you might use an array to store the meaning of certain abbreviations, that is to associate abbreviations with their expansions. The abbreviation could be used as an array index, with its expansion being the value. For instance, abbreviations["DOM"] might have the value "Document Object Model". (In the DOM, a NamedNodeMap is used for this purpose. Like NodeLists, NamedNodeMaps in JavaScript are really just arrays.) When strings are used as array indexes, they are often referred to as **keys**, and we say that the array maps keys to values.

Arrays are also objects, and have their own methods (and a length property). These methods include sort, which arranges the items in the array into ascending order, and join, which is applicable to arrays of strings. It adds all the strings together; if an argument is supplied, it inserts it between the items as a separator. Otherwise, a comma is used. For example, if dom[0] is "Document", dom[1] is "Object", dom[2] is "Model", and dom.length is 3. dom.join(" ") is the string "Document Object Model". The converse operation, of taking a string apart and storing the parts in an array, is performed by the string method split,

---

Technical Detail

Arrays and Objects

JavaScript objects are really arrays, which hold the collection of properties and methods comprising the object. The property and method names are indexes into this array: the notation `obj.property` is simply a convenient shorthand for `obj["property"]`.

---

which takes a separator as its argument, and splits the string at occurrences of it. Thus if `domstring` held `"Document Object Model"`, `domstring.split(" ")` would produce the array of words we started with.

If you need to create an empty array from scratch, you can call the function `Array`, giving it a number as its argument. It will return an array whose length is equal to the argument. Thus `var a = Array(100)` creates an array of 100 items, `a[0]` to `a[99]`.

The sort of data that is naturally exhibited in tabular form has a two-dimensional structure. Two-dimensional matrices of this sort can be stored in JavaScript using arrays of arrays, that is, arrays whose items are themselves arrays. You can think of these as being tabular structures made up of rows and columns. If `m` is such an array, `m[i]` would be one of its rows. Being an array, the row can be indexed, so it makes sense to write expressions like `m[i][j]`, which refers to the object in column `j` of row `i` of the array `m`. We will explain how to build up arrays of arrays later in this section.

Conditions

It is often necessary to compare two values. You can compare any two values to see whether they are equal, but you must use a double equals sign, `==`, to do so. (You will see why shortly, if you don't know already.) As we showed earlier, the inequality operator is `!=`. You can also see whether one value is greater or less than another, using `>` and `<`, or `>=` and `<=`, if you also want to check for equality. For strings, these comparisons are carried out in dictionary order, that is, one string is greater than another if it would appear later in a dictionary organized in a conventional way. The results of tests using these operators are most commonly used in conditional (`if`) statements or `while` loops, such as those we used earlier.

Any of these comparisons produces a value that is either `true` or `false`. Such values are often called **Booleans**, and they may be combined to make more complicated conditions. The `&&` operator combines two Booleans, producing a new value that is `true` if and only if both of them are `true`. For instance, if the variable `web_design` holds the string `"Web Design"` as before, then `web_design.length == 10` is `true`, and so is `web_design.charAt(0) != "w"` (because string comparisons are case-sensitive, so `"w" != "W"`.) Therefore,

```
web_design.length == 10 && web_design.charAt(0) != "w"
```

is `true`. The operator `||` combines two Boolean values, giving `true` if either or both of its operands is `true`. Hence,

```
web_design.length == 10 || web_design.charAt(0) == "w"
```

and

```
web_design.length == 10 || web_design.charAt(0) == "w"
```

are both `true`.

It is also possible to invert the value of a Boolean expression, that is, to turn `true` into `false` and `false` into `true`. This is done using the `!` operator. This operator has a low priority, so it is necessary to put any complicated condition in brackets when it is used. (If you are not familiar with the idea of operator priority, just put brackets round any condition you want to invert. It will never do any harm.) For example,

```
!(web_design.charAt(0) == "w")
```

is `true`.

Assignment

Using operators, we can build up arbitrarily complicated expressions, to perform arithmetic and string manipulation. The values of these expressions can then be stored in variables. We have already used variables several times to give names to values. These names must obey some simple rules: they can only include letters, digits, _ and $ symbols, and cannot begin with a digit. Notably they must not include any spaces.

The value stored in a variable can be produced by any expression. However, a variable need not keep the value that was first stored in it forever: a new value can be stored in it subsequently. This operation is called ***assignment***: we say that a value is assigned to a variable.

Assignment is written as =. For example,

```
i = i + 1;
```

increases the value stored in the variable i by 1, by assigning i+1 to i. This is not an entirely pointless exercise. Consider the following:

```
var i = 1;
var n = 0;
while (i < 10) {
    n = n + i;
    i = i + 1;
}
```

This has the effect of setting n to the sum of numbers from 1 to 10 – not the most exciting computation (there is a simple formula, after all), but a demonstration of the way counting can be implemented by assigning to variables.

Assignments that use the value of the variable being assigned to in order to compute its new value (as both the assignments in the example do) are common, and a convenient shorthand is provided for them. The += operator adds its right hand operand to its left hand operand and assigns the result to the left hand operand, an operation that sounds more complicated than it is: n+=i and i+=1 are the shorthand versions of our two assignments. Similar operators combining arithmetic and assignment are available for the other arithmetic, string and Boolean operations, but addition is by far the most commonly used. Addition of 1 is so common that it has its own, even more condensed notation: ++i is the same as i+=1.

Single variables are not the only things that can be assigned to. Items in an array, and properties of an object can also be used on the left side of an assignment, and the operators that combine arithmetic and assignment can be used with such values, too. More complex things can also be stored using assignment. For example, an entire array may be stored in an array item, possibly to make one row of a two-dimensional array, like this:

```
a[i] = Array(3);
```

Statements

A JavaScript program is a sequence of statements. An assignment is an example of a statement; a method call can also be used as a statement, if it does not return a value, or its returned value is not used in an expression or assigned to a variable. Such simple statements are terminated by semi-colons, as you should have noticed in the examples given so far. Other forms of statement include the conditional statement and loops.

Conditionals

To recap briefly, a conditional statement has the form:

```
if (condition) statement1 else statement2
```

Here, *condition* is any expression that evaluates to `true` or `false`. If it is `true`, *statement1* is executed, otherwise *statement2* is executed. If nothing should be done if the condition is `false`, *statement2* and the `else` before it can both be omitted. Both *statement1* and *statement2* may be either a single statement, such as an assignment or a method call, or a sequence of statements, bracketed together by { and }. Such a sequence is called a **compound statement**, and in general may be used wherever a single statement may.

Note that the values of Boolean expressions may be stored in variables, which can subsequently be used as conditions themselves. Variables used in this way, to remember the result of a test, are often called **flags**. For example,

```
var has_ulist = document.getElementsByTagName("ul").length > 0;
```

Subsequently, this flag might be used like this:

```
if (has_ulist) n = count_lists(); else n = 0;
```

There is a neat alternative notation for circumstances like this where a different value is assigned to a variable depending on some condition. Instead of using the condition to select one of two statements, it can be used as part of an expression to select one of two expressions. The example above could be written:

```
n = has_ulist? count_lists(): 0;
```

The general form of such a conditional expression is:

```
condition? expression1: expression2
```

The syntax is not very pretty but it does the job. Conditional expressions can be used anywhere that any other expression can. They are most commonly found on the right hand side of assignments, but can also usefully be passed to functions or methods.

Loops

We have already shown you the simplest form of looping construct, the `while` loop. This has the form:

```
while (condition) statement
```

where *condition* is something whose value is `true` or `false`. Actually, here and in conditional statements and expresssions, you can use expressions with some other type of value, such as a number, and an automatic conversion will take place. In general, doing so is a fruitful source of errors, and it should be avoided. However, there is one idiom that is so commonly used that you should master it: `null` is converted to `false` and any object that is not `null` is converted to `true`. Hence, to test whether an element with `id` equal to `navbar` existed in a document, most programmers would write

```
if (document.getElementById("navbar")) …
```

rather than

```
if (document.getElementById("navbar") != null) …
```

The statement in the body of a `while` loop may be compound, and usually is.

Many loops are used to iterate through the elements of a list. For example,

```
var i = 0;
while (i < e.childNodes.length) {
    process(e.childNodes[i]);
    ++i;
}
```

A `for` loop allows such iterations to be programmed in a more compact way. The example just given could be written as

```
for (var i = 0; i < e.childNodes.length; ++i)
    process(e.childNodes[i]);
```

The loop is introduced by a header (the highlighted bit) with three components: an initialization, a test and a step. The initialization is done before the loop runs. The test is then evaluated; if it is `true`, the body of the loop is executed, and then the step is performed, and control goes back to the test. You should be able to see how this loop is equivalent to the one originally shown. As usual, the body of the loop may be a compound statement or a single statement.

Programmers often use `for` loops in conjunction with arrays. For instance, one way of constructing a two-dimensional array with four rows and three columns is as follows:

```
var a = Array(4);
for (var i = 0; i < 4; ++i)
   a[i] = Array(3);
```

The items of this array can be given an initial value using a nested `for` loop, that is, a loop within a loop.

```
for (var i = 0; i < 4; ++i)
   for (var j = 0; j < 3; ++j)
      a[i][j] = i*j;
```

Functions

We have shown functions being used, but it is frequently necessary to define your own functions. Dividing the computation performed by a program into functions is one of the best ways of organizing it so that it is easy to understand and maintain. (Defining objects is another, but the examples we will consider are not sufficiently complex to justify a description of how this is done.)

Defining Functions

A function is just a sequence of statements that is executed whenever the function is called. Most useful functions take arguments. The following is a simple example of a function definition:

```
function count_elements(nodes) {
   var n = 0;
   for (var i = 0; i < nodes.length; ++i) {
      var this_node = nodes.item(i);
      if (this_node.nodeType == 1) ++n;
   }
```

```
    return n;
}
```

By now, you should be able to see what is happening between the outer pair of curly brackets. The `for` loop is iterating through all the items in the `NodeList` nodes, skipping the text nodes and adding 1 to the variable n whenever an `Element` node (with `nodeType` equal to 1) is encountered. Since n is set to 0 before the loop is entered, when the loop terminates it will hold a count of all those `Element` nodes.

The highlighted line at the top is what specifies that this is a definition of a function. It begins with the keyword `function`. Following this is the name we are giving to this function, which is the name by which it can be called. In this case, the function is called `count_elements`. The name can be anything you like (provided it obeys the same simple rules, as variable names must), but it helps if it indicates what the function does.

In the brackets after the function name, we provide a name for the argument of this function. When the function is called, the value passed to it will be assigned to this variable. So, for instance, if we call `count_elements(body.childNodes)` when `body` holds the object for the document body, within the function `nodes` will also hold that object, so the function will count the number of `Element` nodes among the children of `body`. A function may have any number of arguments; if there is more than one, their names are separated by commas, the same way as argument values are when the function is called.

The code between { and } following the arguments is called the body of the function. It is executed whenever the function is called, with whatever value has been provided as an argument being used as the initial value of `nodes`. Within a function's body, the `return` statement can be used. This causes execution of the function body to stop, and the value of the expression following the keyword `return` will be the value produced by the function.

This can be demonstrated better with a simpler example.

```
function average(a, b) {
    return (a+b)/2;
}
```

This is a function whose body consists of nothing but a `return` statement – the curly brackets are still needed, though. If we write an expression such as x+average(y, z), the effect is as follows. First, the arguments a and b are assigned the current values of y and z, respectively.

Suppose y is equal to 124 and z to 68. Then, when average is called, the expression (a+b)/2 will have the value 96. This value is returned from the function, so the expression will have the value x+96. Functions are usually called in this way, to produce a value that is used in an expression, or assigned to a variable, or passed as an argument to another function.

Functions as Values

It is important to distinguish between a function, and the value obtained by calling a function. For example, average is a function; average(124,68) is a number. In many programming languages, the only thing you can do with a function is call it, so the distinction is merely academic. In JavaScript, though, you can manipulate the function itself. You can, for instance, store it in a variable, like this:

```
var f = average;
```

Now f is holding the function originally defined as average; in other words, f has become another name for average, and f(124,68) is 96.

Storing functions in simple variables is not often useful, it merely demonstrates the principle. It is more useful to be able to pass functions to other functions, and to store them in other places. For instance, we mentioned earlier that the sort method of an array will sort the items in the array in increasing order. This is only its default behaviour, but other orderings can be used as the basis for sorting an array, by passing a function as an argument to the sort method. Any function used for this purpose must take two arguments and return a value that is either negative, zero or positive. When the sort method looks at two items, a and b, say, to determine which order they should appear in, it passes them to the comparison function, which we'll call cmp. If cmp(a,b) is negative, a comes before b, if cmp(a,b) is positive, b comes before a, and if cmp(a,b) is zero, the two are considered equal, and placed in an arbitrary order.

For instance, suppose m is an array of arrays and you want to sort its rows into ascending order of the value of the first element of each row (m[0][0], m[1][0], etc.). The following function takes two rows as arguments, and compares them in this sense:

```
function cmp(x, y) {
   return x[1] < y[1]? 1: x[1] == y[1]? 0: -1;
}
```

The array of arrays can then be sorted as required by calling `m.sort(cmp)`.

Storing functions in objects is the mechanism whereby methods are created and may be modified – as we explained earlier, functions and methods are essentially the same thing. There is one significant difference between methods and other functions, though. Within the body of a method, the name `this` may be used to refer to the object that the method belongs to.

If you are going to treat functions themselves as values, it isn't always necessary to give them names to begin with. Instead, you can create anonymous functions. An anonymous function is defined just like a named function, except that the function name is omitted. Such a definition has the defined function as its value, and this can be stored, passed to another function, and so on. For instance,

```
var f = function(a, b) {
    return (a+b)/2;
};
```

We will see more useful applications of anonymous functions later.

Dynamic Pages

The point of learning about the DOM and JavaScript is to allow you to write scripts that change elements on a page in response to user input, thereby allowing Web pages to be more responsive and more like desktop applications than they would be if the only way to make changes was by fetching and displaying a new page. If you choose to do this, there are three basic principles that should be observed.

Pages with scripts should degrade gracefully. That is, they should still display acceptably, present all their information and provide all their services, even if scripting is not supported or is disabled in a visitor's browser.

Graceful degradation can more easily be achieved by observing the second principle: *behaviour should be separated from content and structure.* This is sometimes called **unobtrusive scripting**. The principle should sound familiar. We have emphasized that content and structure should be separated from appearance. This is achieved using stylesheets, which are connected to page elements using `class` and `id` attributes, without otherwise interfering with the markup. Scripts can and should be similarly attached to a page without interfering with the markup, and `class` and `id` attributes can be used here to connect scripted actions with elements of the page, in a way that we will describe later.

Our third principle should hardly need stating, but it is frequently neglected. *Scripts should work correctly.* This implies that they must be thoroughly tested, and analyzed to demonstrate their correctness, at least informally. Ideally, scripts should work correctly in all browsers, but because of the legacy of incompatible scripting language implementations and object models, it is difficult to guarantee that every script will work in all older browsers. It is better to insist that scripts work in all browsers that correctly implement the DOM and JavaScript standards, and aim for graceful degradation in others. Basically, this means treating non-standard browsers as if they didn't implement scripting at all.

Adding Scripts to Pages

Scripts are added to XHTML documents using the `script` element. This can be used either to point to a script contained in a file external to the document or to embed a script in the document itself. The former option is usually to be preferred, since it avoids unpleasant problems with & and < characters in the script, and encourages a clean separation of scripts and content. The `script` element's `src` attribute is used to hold the URL of an external script; its `type` attribute must also be used to specify the scripting language it uses. (Although JavaScript is the most common language, there is nothing in the XHTML specification to prevent other languages being used.) A typical script element being used in this way would look like:

```
<script type="text/javascript" src="script.js"></script>
```

Scripts are not attached using `link` elements, the way stylesheets are. Although a `script` element with a `src` attribute is typically empty, it is best to use an explicit end tag, as we have done here, since some browsers do not deal correctly with empty `script` elements written with a combined start and end tag.

The Internet Media Type normally used for JavaScript scripts is, as this example illustrates, `text/javascript`. Formally, this is wrong: a script is something that is executed, so it should be of type `application`, not `text`. Pedantically speaking, the language is ECMAScript not JavaScript. The W3C now advocate using `application/javascript` or `application/ecmascript`, but few browsers correctly interpret these types, so it is best to stick with the historical usage.

Technical Detail

The `noscript` Element

The `noscript` element was intended to provide a way of catering for browsers that do not support scripting. In such a browser, `script` elements should be skipped, and the contents of `noscript` elements should be displayed, whereas in browsers that support scripting, `noscript` elements are skipped, and the contents of `script` elements are executed.

There are two problems with noscript. First, browsers that do not support scripting and do not recognize `<script>` tags don't usually recognize `<noscript>` tags either, so `noscript` only actually caters for users who have disabled scripting in a browser that supports it. More seriously, what can you put in a `noscript` element? A message informing the user that they need to activate scripting is not likely to be welcome: they probably feel they had a good reason for disabling it in the first place.

It is far better to ensure that your page will degrade gracefully in the absence of scripting support. If it does so, there is no need for any `noscript` elements.

If you prefer to keep the script within the document, it can be placed in the content of a `script` element. The main practical drawback of doing so is that JavaScript uses < and & characters for its own purposes, but these must be replaced by character entities anywhere in an XML document. You can, if you like, use character entities in your scripts; they will be replaced by the appropriate character before the script is executed. Your script will, however, be hard to read, and it is easy to forget to substitute character entity references for some characters. To avoid the problem entirely, scripts can be wrapped in a CDATA section, which means any character will be taken literally. To avoid the CDATA being treated as part of the script, it is necessary to insert the characters // in front of the XML at the beginning and end of it, so that it appears to be a JavaScript comment. (Any Web page creation tool worth using will insert this rubric for you.) Thus, an embedded script will usually look like this:

```
<script type="text/javascript">
// <![CDATA[
function count_elements(nodes) {
    var n = 0;
    for (var i = 0; i < nodes.length; ++i) {
        var this_node = nodes.item(i);
```

```
        if (this_node.nodeType == 1) ++n;
    }
    return n;
}
// ]]>
</script>
```

Note that it is still necessary to specify the type attribute of the script element.

Whichever method you use for including your scripts, they are executed when the browser encounters the script element. Any number of script elements may appear anywhere in the head or body of a document, but the principle of separating behaviour from content suggests that you should only place them in the head.

Image Gallery

Click on a thumbnail to see a larger image.

© MacAvon Media Productions 2003

Figure 7.3 An image gallery

Altering Page Elements

We are almost in a position to show some scripts in action on dynamic Web pages. We will begin with an example that has become something of a cliché of DOM scripting: an image gallery. Figure 7.3 illustrates what we mean by this: a page containing a collection of thumbnail images, on each of which you can click to exhibit a larger version of the image. As we will see, the case for using scripting to implement a gallery of this sort is not very compelling, but it does provide a simply understood demonstration of several important principles and techniques.

We aim to separate the behaviour from the markup, so we will begin by creating the XHTML. Each thumbnail image must be enclosed in a link (a element) which points to the corresponding full-sized image. This means that, in the absence of any scripting, clicking on a thumbnail will display the larger image in a new page. This will be the degraded behaviour of the gallery for users without scripting support. It isn't as good as the gallery we will build with scripts, because they need to use the browser's back button to return to the page with thumbnails, but they can still see all the full-sized images.

The thumbnails can be considered to comprise a list, so we will wrap each thumbnail in an li element, and the whole collection in a ul. We are only going to have four thumbnails on the page. For styling and positioning, the ul and some explanatory text are enclosed in a div. The main image is an img element enclosed in a separate div. The img has its id attribute set to the_image, because our script will need to able to find it. To begin with, it will display the full-sized version of the first thumbnail.

The complete XHTML document is as follows:

```
<!DOCTYPE html PUBLIC "-//W3C//DTD XHTML 1.0 Strict//EN"
        "http://www.w3.org/TR/xhtml1/DTD/xhtml1-strict.dtd">
<html xmlns="http://www.w3.org/1999/xhtml" xml:lang="en" lang="en">
<head>
   <meta http-equiv="content-type" content="text/html; charset=utf-8"
/>
   <title>Image Gallery</title>
   <script src="image-swap.js" type="text/javascript"></script>
   <link rel="stylesheet" href="styles.css" type="text/css"
media="screen" />
</head>
<body>
<h1>Image Gallery</h1>
```

```
<div id="thumbnails">
<p>Click on a thumbnail to see a larger image.</p>
<ul>
   <li><a href="Images/sunset-clouds.jpg" title="Sunset Clouds"><img
src="Thumbnails/sunset-clouds.jpg" alt="Sunset Clouds" /></a></li>
   <li><a href="Images/blue-flower.jpg" title="Blue Flower"><img
src="Thumbnails/blue-flower.jpg" alt="Blue Flower" /></a></li>
   <li><a href="Images/orange-flowers.jpg" title="Orange Flowers"><img
src="Thumbnails/orange-flowers.jpg" alt="Orange Flowers" /></a></li>
   <li><a href="Images/sea.jpg" title="Sea"><img src="Thumbnails/sea.
jpg" alt="The Sea" /></a></li>
</ul>
</div>
<div id="main-image">
<img src="Images/sunset-clouds.jpg" alt="Enlarged image" id="the_
image" />
</div>
</body>
</html>
```

A stylesheet is used to lay out the gallery and add the decorative touches seen in Figure 7.3. This introduces no new features, so we will not show it here. The highlighted line in the head element is used to include a script file. All of the JavaScript code is confined to this included file.

The essential functionality is easily scripted. The image displayed in the main part of the screen is determined by the value of the src attribute of the img element. To change the image, all that is needed is to change this value.

Because of the way the links have been set up, if we were somehow able to get hold of an object that corresponded to the link enclosing the thumbnail that had been clicked, we could find the URL of the corresponding full image in the value of its href property. For example, if someone clicked on the thumbnail for the image called blue-flower.jpg, the link enclosing the thumbnail would correspond to the XHTML element

```
<a href="Images/blue-flower.jpg" title="Blue Flower"><img
src="Thumbnails/blue-flower.jpg" alt="Blue Flower" /></a>
```

If the variable me held a DOM Element object corresponding to this element, then its property me.href would hold the string Images/blue-flower.jpg, the URL of the full image.

Hence, to display that image in the `main-image div`, all that is needed is the following three lines of code:

```
var my_image = me.href;
var the_image = document.getElementById("the_image");
the_image.src = my_image;
```

(Actually, you could do it in a single line, but this way is more readable.) When the script runs, the change to the `src` attribute will be reflected immediately in the page – the displayed image will change.

The code is no use unless we can arrange the variable `me` to be set up as required and for the code to be executed when somebody clicks on a thumbnail. To do that requires an additional, extremely important, feature of the DOM.

Events

Whenever a user clicks on a Web page, moves the cursor over an element, submits a form, or does anything else that might cause something to happen on the page, we say that an ***event*** occurs. To add interactive behaviour to a page, it is necessary to associate a script which performs some action, such as changing the `src` attribute of an `img` tag, with an event which we want to trigger that action. In the case of our image gallery, we want to associate a script incorporating the code we just wrote with the event that occurs when a user clicks on one of the thumbnails.

There are several ways of doing this. The preferred method makes use of DOM Event objects; we will describe how these work shortly. However, support for DOM events is not universal among browsers. To accommodate browsers that do not support them, it is necessary to use an alternative technique, of assigning methods to certain attributes of the elements that we want to respond to events. Since Internet Explorer 6 is one of the browsers that does not support DOM events, it is advisable to use this approach to dynamic pages for the time being, even though DOM Events objects are more powerful, so we will describe both techniques of associating scripts with events.

HTML Events

Tables 7.2 lists the names of the events defined in the HTML 4 standard that can be used with scripts attached to HTML, and therefore XHTML, documents. These HTML events are long-established, and supported by most browsers that support scripting. XHTML provides a way of attaching handlers for these events to elements, using specially named attributes.

Event Name	Meaning	Restrictions
load	All the content of a page has been loaded.	body element only
unload	The document has been removed from the window	
click	The mouse was clicked with the cursor over the element.	
dblclick	The mouse was double-clicked with the cursor over the element.	Not a DOM event
mousedown	The mouse button was pressed with the cursor over the element.	
mouseup	The mouse button was released with the cursor over the element.	
mouseover	The cursor was moved onto the element.	
mousemove	The cursor was moved while it was over the element.	
mouseout	The cursor was moved away from the element.	
focus	The element has received the focus, i.e. it will accept input.	a, area and form control elements
blur	The element has lost the focus.	
keypress	A key was pressed and released while the cursor was over the element.	Not a DOM event
keydown	A key was pressed while the cursor was over the element.	
keyup	A key was released while the cursor was over the element.	
submit	The form was submitted.	form elements only
reset	The form was reset.	
select	The user selected some text in a text field.	input and textarea elements only
change	The element has lost the focus and its value has been modified since it received the focus.	input, select and textarea elements only

Table 7.2 HTML events

For each event name in Table 7.2, there is an attribute consisting of the event name, prefixed by on, such as onclick, onload, and so on. The value of each of these attributes is a function that will be called when the named event occurs on the element. If you use the attributes directly inside the XHTML markup, the value has to be a string, of course, but this string is treated as the body of an anonymous function, which is stored as the attribute's value, and called whenever the appropriate event occurs. For instance,

```
<a href="Images/blue-flower.jpg" onclick="swap_image(this); return
   false" … > … </a>
```

would cause the following function to be called whenever a user clicked anywhere in the content of the link:

```
function() {
   swap_image(this);
   return false;
}
```

This function is said to be a **handler** for the click event. Since the attributes of elements become properties of the corresponding DOM objects, the handler becomes a method of the Element object for the element to which it is attached, so it can use the name this to access that object.

It should be evident from the preceding description that, in order to make the main image in the gallery change when one of the thumbnails is clicked on, we need to attach an event handler for the click event to the thumbnail. Which element should it be attached to? The description of the click event states that it occurs when the mouse is clicked over the element, but the thumbnail image is within several elements. It is in the img element, of course, but this is contained in an a element, which is in turn contained in an li element. If the cursor is over the thumbnail on the page, and the mouse button is clicked, we could equally well say the mouse had been clicked on any of the img, a or li elements, or indeed the containing ul, div and even body. A handler attached to any of those elements would respond to a click on the thumbnail.

A little thought will show that it would be foolish to attach the handler to the ul element, or any of its ancestors. It would not then be possible to distinguish between clicks on each of the four thumbnails. The logical place to attach the handler is to the a element, since what it is doing is replacing the default action of following the link that occurs when a user clicks on it. It will turn out that attaching the handler to the link makes it easier to access the URL of the large image, too.

Using attributes to attach handlers to elements isn't actually a good way of doing the job, although virtually every Web creation program generates markup of that form. The scripting is mixed up with the markup, making it hard to maintain. You should also note that, since it is not `swap_image` itself but the anonymous function which is the handler, `swap_image` has no direct access to the object. We therefore have to pass `this` as an argument if we want `swap_image` to be able to access the `href` attribute's value. You will recall from the code fragment shown earlier that this is just what we will need to do in order to swap the image.

Because the DOM provides access to attribute values, either through `getAttribute` and `setAttribute`, or using attribute properties, it is possible in a script to assign functions directly to `onclick` and the other event-related attributes. If a function is assigned directly, it does become a method, so it can use `this` to access the object for the element it is attached to. So if `a` was an object for one of the thumbnails' link elements, we could set the handler in the following way:

```
a.onclick = swap_image;
```

Note that we are assigning the function itself, not calling it. Also note that the setting is part of a script, so we can separate it from the markup. We will describe shortly how to arrange that the assignment of handlers is executed when we need it to be.

We can now write most of a function to serve as a handler for `click` events on the thumbnails. Assuming that we attach the handler to an `a` element using an assignment in our script, we know that it will be called as a method of the `Element` object for that element, so we can access the object as `this`:

```
function swap_image() {
    var me = this;
    var my_image = me.href;
    var the_image = document.getElementById("the_image");
    the_image.src = my_image;
}
```

Since the handler has been attached to the `a` element, the highlighted line of code stores the object for this element in the variable `me`. This was what we assumed earlier when showing how to change the image, so the rest of the function need only duplicate the code we had before.

We will need to attach handlers to each of the thumbnails' enclosing a elements. Since swap_image is able to obtain an object for the element it is attached to, via this, the same function can be used to handle clicks on any of the thumbnails, so all that is necessary is to loop through the a elements inside the div with id equal to thumbnails, attaching swap_image to each of them as a click handler. We will wrap this up in a function of its own:

```
function attach_handlers() {
   var div = document.getElementById("thumbnails");
   var links = div.getElementsByTagName("a");
   for (var i = 0; i < links.length; ++i)
      links[i].onclick = swap_image;
}
```

First we find the div, using its id. When getElementsByTagName is called through an object, it only looks at that object's children, so the second line stores a NodeList containing just the a elements that are inside the div in the variable links. These are precisely the ones that we need to attach our handler to, so the for loop simply works its way through them, assigning to the onclick property of each in turn.

We now face a bootstrapping problem. How is attach_handlers to be called? If the script element that contains our script (or includes the file that does so) is in the head of the document, any call to attach_handlers will fail to do anything. This is because scripts are executed when they are encountered as the document is being read and analysed. Thus, a call to attach_handlers in a script inside the head will be executed before the body of the document has been read; in other words, before the a elements we are trying to attach handlers to exist.

Since we want attach_handlers to be called once the body of the document has loaded, you might be tempted to attach it to the body as a handler for the load event. (See Table 7.2.) This approach runs into the same problem, though, because you would need to attach the load handler to the body before the body existed.

A possible, but inelegant, solution to this dilemma would be to put the script element at the end of the body instead of in the head. Although this works, it mixes the script with the markup, so we prefer a different solution. This has its own drawback: it makes use of an object that is not part of the DOM. This is the window object, which models the browser window. While not part of the DOM, this object is universally supported by browsers. It has several methods that are useful in achieving certain sorts of interactivity, including crude animation, but we will only be concerned with using window to help us over our bootstrapping problem.

Event handlers can be attached to window, in particular, a handler for the load event, which is sent to the window as well as the document body. The window object always exists, so the handler can safely be attached to it in a script contained in the document head. Thus, our complete script looks like this:

```
function swap_image() {
    definition of handler as before
}
function attach_handlers() {
    definition of handler as before
}
window.onload = attach_handlers;
```

The sequence of execution is therefore as follows. When the script element in the head of the document is analyzed, the function definitions are processed and attach_handlers is assigned as a load event handler to the window object. When the document finishes loading, window receives a load event; attach_handlers is therefore called, and in turn attaches click event handlers to all the a elements containing thumbnails. Whenever a user clicks on a thumbnail, the attached handler is called, causing the main image to be replaced.

Unfortunately, the next thing that happens is that the a element receives the click and displays the image in a new page, just as it would have done in the absence of any handlers. To complete the job, it is therefore necessary to ensure that this does not happen.

This is easily done. A handler can return a Boolean value, indicating whether any default action for the event should occur. In particular, if a click handler attached to an a element returns false, the default action of following the link will be prevented. If we modify our click handler in the following way, the image gallery will behave as required – at least, it will do so in any browser that supports DOM scripting:

```
function swap_image() {
    var me = this;
```

```
    var my_image = me.href;
    var the_image = document.getElementById("the_image");
    the_image.src = my_image;
    return false;
}
```

But what about browsers that don't support DOM scripting? Those that don't support script-ing at all will skip the `script` element. Their users will be able to follow links to the images, and see them in their own window. But this still leaves browsers that claim to implement scripting, but don't conform to the DOM standard. We would like such browsers to be treated as if they didn't support scripting at all. We can do this by refusing to attach our event handlers unless the browser supports the `document.getElementById` method. If it doesn't, we know our code isn't going to work; if it does, it almost certainly implements the DOM, and all will be well. Hence, the final modification to our image gallery script is as follows:

```
    if (document.getElementById) window.onload = attach_handlers;
```

Once again, it is the method itself that we are testing here. If the test fails, because the method is `null` (i.e. the browser doesn't implement it), the `load` handler won't be attached to the `window` object, so `attach_handlers` will never be called, and no handlers will be added to any a elements. (Notice here another advantage of attaching handlers using a script. If attributes in the markup had been used, this test would have had to be made when-ever a handler was called.)

Although we have devoted a good deal of space to this example, it is worth spending some time at this stage asking whether it was worth writing this script. Consider an alternative way of making an image gallery. Create four pages, each with the collection of thumbnails down the left, and each with one of the large images on the right. (A template could be used to minimize the effort of making four more or less identical pages, or they could be generated by a program on the server.) Instead of attaching the URLs of the large image files to each of the links on the thumbnails, attach the URL of whichever of the four pages included the large version of the same image. Attach the same stylesheet as we used before to each page, but do not do any scripting.

What happens if a user clicks on a thumbnail on one of the gallery pages? The browser will fetch the page with the corresponding large image. Almost certainly, the thumbnail images will be cached. Any properly written browser will only update the parts of the window that change when a new page is displayed, so in this case, only the large image will be redrawn.

In other words, there will be little discernible difference between an image gallery with four pages and one implemented with a script.

Some additional network traffic will have been generated: the XHTML code of each page must be fetched for each image. Each XHTML document will be less than 1.5kB in size. The images would all have to be fetched anyway, so only this relatively small number of bytes is extra. The script also reduces the number of HTTP requests that the server has to deal with. In cases where the page content was generated dynamically, this might make a non-trivial difference to the load on the server. As we remarked earlier, the case for using scripting for an image gallery is not compelling. We will have to look further to find stronger reasons for using scripts.

Nevertheless, we will return to the image gallery, because it is a suitably simple example for explaining a different way of working with event handlers.

DOM Events

The event handler attributes are part of the HTML and XHTML standards, not part of the DOM. They can be used by scripts in the way we have described because of the way the DOM provides access to attributes. A different method of assigning handlers is defined in the DOM itself. This has the advantage that it does not depend on the definition of XHTML, but works for any XML-based language.

Event Name	Meaning	Restrictions
DOMActivate	The element was activated, by a mouse click or some other means.	
DOMFocusIn	The element received the focus.	Any focusable element.
DOMFocusOut	The element lost the focus.	
textInput	One or more characters have been entered.	
abort	The loading stopped before being completed.	object and body elements only
error	The document loaded, but the page contains some error, such as a script error or an invalid image.	
resize	The window has been resized.	
scroll	The window or an element has been scrolled.	

Table 7.3 DOM events

The DOM provides its own definition of the set of available events. You may have noticed that two of the events listed in Table 7.2 are not actually part of the DOM standard. Apart from these two, however, all of these events are defined in the Level 2 DOM Events Recommendation. This Recommendation defines some additional events, some of which are listed in Table 7.3. The first four events listed here are generalizations of some HTML events. DOMActivate generalizes click, for example, to include activation by any sort of input device. (Actually, a click event is already generated if an element is selected using keyboard navigation, not just by the mouse.) Similarly, textInput generalizes keypress, since it is generated by speech input, pasting from the clipboard, and so on. These new events are not yet generally supported, unlike the remaining events in Table 7.3.

As well as the events in these tables, the DOM also defines a collection of **mutation events**, which occur when the document is changed, usually by a script. For example, a DOMNodeInserted event is generated whenever a node is inserted into the tree. Using these events is tricky, and we will not refer to them again.

In browsers that conform to the DOM Level 2, every Element object has a method called addEventListener. This method takes three arguments: a string consisting of the name of a DOM event, a function and a Boolean value, whose meaning we will explain later. For now, simply assume that it should usually be false.

The effect of a call such as

```
el.addEventListener("click", swap_image, false)
```

is to attach the function swap_image as a handler for click events to the Element el. The handler does not become a method of the object el, but when it is called, it is passed an Event object as its argument. This argument contains some information about the event. For example, if any event generated by the mouse button is received, the Event object will include the screen coordinates of the cursor, and flags to indicate whether any modifier keys were being held down at the time the event occurred. The Event object also has two properties, target and currentTarget, which hold the innermost element which was clicked on, and the element to which the handler is attached, respectively. These may not be the same, as our image gallery example demonstrates: if a handler attached to a link is called when a user clicks on the image, the object corresponding to the img element will be the target, but the currentTarget will be the a element. The handler can therefore use the currentTarget property of its Event argument to get at the attributes of the a element, in the same way as it used this previously.

One other change is needed to the handler. It can no longer return a Boolean to specify whether the default action is to be performed after it finishes handling the event. However, every Event object has a method called preventDefault for just this purpose. If DOM events are being used, the swap_image function must therefore be changed slightly, like this:

```
function swap_image(ev) {
    var me = ev.currentTarget;
    var my_image = me.href;
    var the_image = document.getElementById("the_image");
    the_image.src = my_image;
    ev.preventDefault();
}
```

The rest of the script must also be changed to use addEventListener:

```
function attach_handlers() {
    var div = document.getElementById("thumbnails");
    var links = div.getElementsByTagName("a");
    for (var i = 0; i < links.length; ++i)
        links[i].addEventListener("click", swap_image, false);
}
if (document.getElementById)
    window.addEventListener("load", attach_handlers, false);
```

Making these changes is enough to implement the image gallery using DOM events. There is no need to alter the markup or stylesheet in any way, demonstrating that we have success-fully separated the behaviour from the structure and appearance of the page.

The DOM event version of the script is more verbose, and probably looks more clumsy, than our first version using HTML events. For such simple scripts, the HTML approach is at least as good as the DOM approach, and we will use it in subsequent examples, because of its simplicity and its wider support in browsers. However, DOM events are more powerful in some ways. For example, more than one handler can be attached to an element for the same event, handlers at different levels in the tree can be invoked for a single event, and the Event objects passed to the handlers contain information that can be useful for handling events in more elaborate ways. In any case, you must understand DOM events, because they are likely to supersede HTML events in future versions of XHTML and other XML-based languages on the Web.

Technical Detail

Event Bubbling and Capture

The DOM event handling model is actually more complicated than we have described it here. When an event occurs, the browser passes it down the tree towards its target. Each node in the tree corresponding to an ancestor of the target has a chance to handle the event, a process known as 'event capture'. If you want a handler to capture events directed at its children, set the third argument of addEventListener to true when setting up the handler.

If a handler captures an event, it can choose to prevent any of its descendants handling it by calling the Event object's stopPropagation method. If it does not do so, the event continues to pass down the tree towards the target, so it may be handled more than once.

Once the event reaches the target, it is passed back up the tree. This phase of the event handling is called bubbling. As an event bubbles back up, it may again invoke handlers on the target's ancestors. In our image gallery, since the target of a click event is the img element containing the thumbnail, the event is handled as it bubbles up to the enclosing a element. If we had specified that our handler should capture the event, it would have been invoked as the event moved down the tree instead – which would have been marginally earlier.

Capturing and bubbling mean that event handlers can be combined in a flexible way, but for most simple Web scripts, it is adequate to attach a single handler to one element and rely on the default behaviour to invoke it at a suitable time.

Applications of DOM Scripting

Regardless of its merits as a way of displaying images, the Web gallery example is useful because it demonstrates a pattern of scripts that can be applied to many tasks. An event handler for the load event on the window object is used to attach handlers to other elements of the page. These handlers respond to events caused by users' input, and by altering the value of some attributes they make changes to the page displayed in the window.

Emerging Technology

XML Events

XHTML2 will incorporate a new way of setting up event handlers. Elements will no longer have event attributes, such as `onclick`. Instead, the `listener` element defines an association between an element (the observer), an event and a handler. As well as attributes for each of these components, the `listener` element has extra attributes controlling detailed aspects of the event handling. In particular, the `defaultAction` attribute may be set to `cancel` or `perform` to specify whether or not a default action, such as following a link when an `a` element is clicked on, should be performed.

The `event` attribute is the name of a DOM event; the `observer` is the id of the element to which the handler is being attached, and `handler` is a URL (usually a partial one) identifying the handler code. An example might look like this:

```
<ev:listener event="DOMActivate" observer="thumb1"
defaultAction="cancel" handler="#swap_image />
```

(The element's name is `ev:listener` because XML events are not in the default XHTML namespace; `ev:` is the conventional namespace prefix for XML events. See Appendix B for more information about namespaces.)

The XML Events specification also allows the `ev:handler` attribute to be used to attach a handler directly to an element, and the `ev:observer` attribute to be used to attach observers to handlers. To attach handlers dynamically, `addEventListener` is still required.

Before we describe some more examples of this pattern, we will offer some practical advice for your own scripting.

Testing and Debugging Scripts

Books that describe programming – including this one – are usually misleading about how programs are written. They present a program in a logical order, to best explain its structure and the way it works. This presentation tends to give the impression that programs are written in a similarly logical and well-organized way, as if the correct code fell out inevitably. Of course, this is not the way real programs get written. There are many false starts and slip-ups. Code usually needs to be re-organized and tidied up before it exhibits the clean logical structure it ought to have. Often, first attempts fail to work at all.

It is important to recognize that scripts used on Web pages must work correctly. As far as possible they should be flexible, that is, it should be possible to add some extra functionality, or improve their performance, with a minimum of effort and disruption. They should also be organized in such a way that they can be understood easily, because in future some other programmer may have to take over responsibility for them.

JavaScript does not provide as much in the form of linguistic features to help ensure correctness as some other languages do. If you make a mistake in a script you will often get no warning about this before the script is executed. Hence, careful and extensive testing is required. Browsers can provide some assistance in this.

Most browsers provide a facility for viewing any messages generated as a result of errors in a script. In most cases, this takes the form of a special window that displays all messages of this sort. This window is usually called the JavaScript Console. A menu command is provided to display the console, although there is no agreement about where this command should be placed. For example, in Firefox, there is a `JavaScript Console` command on the `Tools` menu, in Opera the same command is on the `Tools>Advanced` sub-menu, and in Safari it is on the `Debug` menu, which has to be specially activated as it is not displayed by default. Internet Explorer does not have a full console, but it can be made to display error messages in a pop-up window, by setting an appropriate preference.

Some messages relate to straightforward syntactical errors, such as leaving out a bracket or mis-spelling a keyword such as `function`. These errors can usually be easily corrected with the help of the message, which should tell you which line the error was detected on. Other messages concern more obscure errors, which are only detected when the script runs. For example, if you try to access a property using a variable whose value is `null`, you will get an error message telling you that you have tried to do so. Your problem then is to discover why that value was `null` when you thought it was going to be an object. Did a call of `getElementById` return `null` because you gave it the wrong argument, or failed to set the `id` attribute of an element in your markup, perhaps? The real source of errors of this sort is often to be found in a different part of the script from the one where the error message is generated, or even in the markup.

You should never ignore an error message, even if the script seems to be working correctly anyway. The message is telling you something. It is also important to run scripts on as many different browsers as possible, in case some of them are more forgiving of errors than others. For instance, if s is a string, the correct way to access a character within it is to use the charAt method, for example, s.charAt(i). A surprising number of browsers allow you to use array indexing notation instead, for example s[i]. This is not, however, allowed by the JavaScript standard[†] and will fail in some browsers. Hence, you must test as widely as possible, and make sure that you comply with the strictest browser you can find. (At the time of writing, Opera seems to be the least tolerant of deviations from the standard.)

One way of tracking down obscure errors is to display the values of key variables at critical points in the script. This can be done fairly simply by making use of a method of the window object, called alert. This takes a string, and displays it in a pop-up window. Hence, a typical debugging call would be something like:

```
window.alert("In function compute_value, argument is " + n);
```

It is tiresome having to insert these statements, but browsers do not provide interactive script debuggers analogous to those you may be familiar with from using other programming languages. It is very important to remember to remove all your debugging alerts before your site goes live.

Another aid to tracking down problems with scripts is a facility for examining the structure of the DOM tree. Many browsers provide such a facility, allowing you to see which nodes are present and how they are inter-related. This can be helpful in cases where you have overlooked the presence of text nodes for new lines, for instance.

Some programmers advocate a style known as 'defensive programming'. In this style, you essentially assume that if anything can go wrong, it will, and ensure that your program is equipped to deal with it. For example, whenever you call getElementById, you should check the returned value and see whether it was null. This is a sensible approach on projects created by a team, where the programmer writing the script will not have produced the markup. For smaller projects, where the markup and script are produced by the same person, or by members of a small team who communicate closely, it is better to make any assumptions implied by the code explicit, and then verify that they are satisfied. This is because, if you adopt the defensive approach, you are left with the problem of what to do if one of your tests fails. During debugging, you can emit an informative message and then go and fix things, but once the site is live, such messages serve only to confuse visitors – because they

---

† Actually, there is no JavaScript standard, it is the ECMAScript standard that forbids this notation.

should never happen. They are no more helpful to users than the error message the browser would have generated anyway.

If you do feel that you have to leave such tests in place, then when they fail a page should be displayed apologising, making clear that the mistake has been made by the site's developer, and asking the user to report the circumstances. To display a new page using a script, you can assign a URL to the `window.location` property. Ideally, in the case of error pages, the URL should be that of a server-side script that can automatically log the error and notify the developer. (A query string appended to the URL can be used to pass details of the error to the script.) If, as a developer, you ever receive a bug report from a user, you should always investigate it, and provide a fix if necessary.

Changing Classes

A particularly powerful application of DOM scripting results if handlers change the value of `class` attributes, because this controls how stylesheets are applied.

Collapsible Lists

As a first script that works by changing `class` attributes, we can return to the problem that we used to introduce this chapter: implementing collapsible lists.

As before, since we wish to separate the behaviour from the content and structure, we can begin by writing the XHTML. We will only show the markup required to create the lists themselves. A useful page would have more information, and in the most likely scenario, the items of the inner lists would have links attached to them. Adding this detail would obscure the presentation without adding anything to the discussion of scripting, so we will leave it out.

The structure clearly consists of nested unordered lists, so a first version of the document would contain the following:

```
<ul>
  <li>Fruit
    <ul>
    <li>Apples</li>
    <li>Oranges</li>
    <li>Kiwi Fruit</li>
    </ul>
  </li>
```

```
      <li>Vegetables
        <ul>
        <li>Carrots</li>
        <li>Broad Beans</li>
        <li>French Beans</li>
        <li>Asparagus</li>
        <li>Potatoes</li>
        </ul>
      </li>
      <li>Oils
        <ul>
        <li>Olive</li>
        <li>Sesame</li>
        <li>Sunflower</li>
        </ul>
      </li>
    </ul>
```

This will display all the lists using the default styling, so it works well for users without CSS or scripting.

Our approach to making the list change its appearance when clicked will be to switch between two different CSS rules, by changing the value of the `class` attribute of selected elements. The next stage, therefore, is to add a stylesheet. Assuming that `triangle-up.gif` and `triangle-down.gif` are images of the right-pointing and downward-pointing triangles, stored in a sub-directory called `images` of the directory containing the document, we can use the triangles as bullets for `li` elements. Those belonging to the class `open` will have the downward-pointing triangle inserted in front of them, those belonging to the class `closed` will get the right-pointing triangle, and no default bullet will be used for any list if the following rules are in the stylesheet:

```
li {
   list-style-type: none;
}
li.open {
   list-style-image: url(images/triangle-down.gif);
}
li.closed {
   list-style-image: url(images/triangle-up.gif);
}
```

More importantly, we can hide any lists that occur inside a closed li element, and display any inside an open one, by setting the display property.

```
li.closed ul {
    display: none;
}

li.open ul {
    display: block;
}
```

We also need to make sure that the inner list items do not inherit the triangle bullets. This only has to be specified for li elements inside open li elements, because if the enclosing li element is closed, the inner ones won't be displayed anyway.

```
li.open li {
    list-style-image: none;
}
```

To ensure that users whose browsers do not support scripts see all the information in the lists, the outer li elements must all have their class attributes set to open in the markup.

```
<ul>
  <li class = "open">Fruit
    <ul>
      li elements for the list of fruit
    </ul>
  </li>
  <li class = "open">Vegetables
    <ul>
      li elements for the list of vegetables
    </ul>
  </li>
  <li class = "open">Oils
    <ul>
      li elements for the list of oils
    </ul>
  </li>
</ul>
```

The inner li elements do not need any class attribute. This list displays with all the sub-lists visible.

Since the lists must respond to clicks, a handler for click events will be needed. It should be easy to see that the following handler will change an element's class from closed to open or from open to closed:

```
function toggle() {
    this.className = this.className == "closed"? "open": "closed";
}
```

The code assumes that the handler has been attached to one of the outer li elements, so that is what we must do. The way the document has been marked up, the li elements that need handlers are the only ones that have their class attributes set (to open) to begin with, so we can set up the handlers by looping through all the li elements in the document, and attaching toggle as a click handler to any whose className property is not null. For users whose browsers do support scripts, we want the lists to be displayed in their closed state to begin with. We can arrange this at the same time as setting the handlers, by setting the className of the relevant elements – the same ones as we are attaching handlers to – to closed. We wrap this initialization up in a function:

```
function setup() {
    var lis = document.getElementsByTagName("li");
    for (var i = 0; i<lis.length; ++i) {
        var li = lis[i];
        if (li.className) {
            li.onclick = toggle;
            li.className = "closed";
        }
    }
}
```

A NodeList of all the li elements in the document is retrieved and stored in the variable lis (intended as the plural of li). The script then uses a for loop to run through this list, setting li to each element in turn. If the element's class attribute has been set (its className property isn't equal to null), its value is reset to closed and toggle is assigned to its onclick property.

Figure 7.4 Fancy style

All that is needed to make this work is to call `setup` when the document is loaded, which is done by making it into a `load` event handler for the `window` object (but only if the browser supports the DOM):

```
if (document.getElementById) window.onload = setup;
```

There is a minor drawback to this using setup to close down all the lists, which is that the lists are shown momentarily in their open state before being closed. This seems to be an acceptable price for ensuring that no data is hidden from people whose browsers do not support the script.

Style Switching

Switching `class` attributes can have far-reaching effects, as Figures 7.4 and 7.5 illustrate. Making changes to the styles applied to an entire page is not an entirely frivolous exercise. Fancy styles with backgrounds and tasteful fonts may look nice, but for people with poor eyesight they can be a strain to read. By providing a way of switching to a plainer, more readable

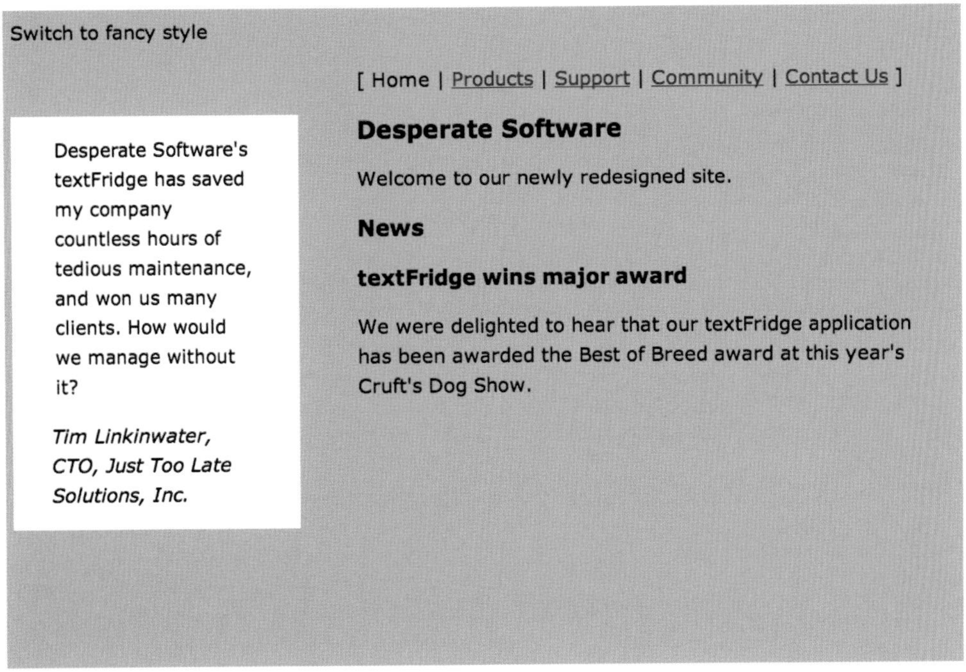

> Switch to fancy style
>
> [Home | Products | Support | Community | Contact Us]
>
> Desperate Software's textFridge has saved my company countless hours of tedious maintenance, and won us many clients. How would we manage without it?
>
> Tim Linkinwater, CTO, Just Too Late Solutions, Inc.
>
> **Desperate Software**
>
> Welcome to our newly redesigned site.
>
> **News**
>
> **textFridge wins major award**
>
> We were delighted to hear that our textFridge application has been awarded the Best of Breed award at this year's Cruft's Dog Show.

Figure 7.5 Plain style

appearance, we help such people, while at the same time providing a more interesting page design for those who have no difficulty reading small type on a fussy background.

The change in the page's appearance is brought about by executing a single assignment:

```
body.className = style;
```

Most of the work is done in the stylesheet attached to the document. The XHTML code is simple, but it provides plenty of hooks, in the form of `class` and `id` attributes, for applying CSS rules.

```
<!DOCTYPE html PUBLIC "-//W3C//DTD XHTML 1.0 Strict//EN"
        "http://www.w3.org/TR/xhtml1/DTD/xhtml1-strict.dtd">
<html xmlns="http://www.w3.org/1999/xhtml" xml:lang="en" lang="en">
<head>
   <meta http-equiv="content-type" content="text/html; charset=utf-8
/>
   <title>Switchable Styles</title>
```

```
<script src="switcher.js" type="text/javascript"></script>
<link rel="stylesheet" href="switch.css" type="text/css"
media="screen" />
</head>
<body class="plain">
<div id="switch">
</div>
<div id="navigation">
<ul>
    <li class="current first">Home</li>
    <li><a href="prods.html" title="View products">Products</a></li>
    <li><a href="support-main.html" title="Product support
services">Support</a></li>
    <li><a href="forums/index.html" title="User forums">Community</
a></li>
    <li><a href="contact.php" title="Customer feedback form">Contact
Us</a></li>
</ul>
</div>
<div id="sidebar">
<blockquote>
<p>Desperate Software's textFridge has saved my company countless
hours of tedious maintenance, and won us many clients. How would we
manage without it?</p>
</blockquote>
<p class="attribution"> Tim Linkinwater, CTO, Just Too Late
Solutions, Inc.</p>
</div>
<div id="main">
<h1>Desperate Software</h1>
<p>Welcome to our newly redesigned site.</p>
<h2>News</h2>
<h3>textFridge wins major award</h3>
<p>We were delighted to hear that our textFridge application has been
awarded the Best of Breed award at this year's Cruft's Dog Show.</p>
</div>
</body>
</html>
```

Because we have assigned a class to the body element, we can write a stylesheet using contextual selectors in such a way that the entire appearance of the page depends only on the body's class. Most of the work can therefore be done in the stylesheet, without any scripting. Setting the class to plain in the markup means that users whose browsers do not support scripting will be shown the page in its plain incarnation. We won't reproduce the entire stylesheet, but the following samples should demonstrate how it works.

Global aspects of the appearance are set in rules for the body element. We provide two of these, one for a body element of class fancy, another for one of class plain:

```
body.fancy {
   color: #894A42;
   font-family: "Lydian MT",Georgia,serif;
   font-size: medium;
   line-height: 180%;
   background-color: #EEF3F5;
   background-image: url(faded-logo.gif);
}
body.plain {
   color: black;
   font-family: Verdana,Arial,sans-serif;
   font-size: large;
   line-height: 150%;
   background-color: silver;
}
```

If the class of the body is plain, sans serif fonts at a large size are used, instead of the smaller, relatively ornate serifed fonts specified if it is fancy. The tonal contrast between text and background is increased in the plain case, and the background image is taken off.

For the plain case, the unsolicited testimonial is simply printed on a white background to make it stand out:

```
.plain #sidebar { background-color: white; }
```

In the fancy layout, much more elaborate styling is used:

```
.fancy #sidebar, .fancy attribution {
   color: #7A7D7E;
   font-size: 95%;
}
.fancy.blockquote {
   padding: 2em;
}
```

```
.fancy blockquote p:before {
   content: url(openquote.gif);
}
.fancy blockquote p:after {
   content: url(closequote.gif);
}
```

The important thing to notice here is that the use of contextual selectors means that the appearance of the `blockquote` element depends on the value of the `class` attribute of the body, just as the properties set directly in the rules for `body` do. Contextual selectors are used in a similar way to make the appearance of the headings and the list of links depend on this one attribute.

Some aspects of the layout are the same in both versions, so some rules in the stylesheet do not use contextual selectors. For instance, the size of the main layout regions is set the same way in both cases, although the use of `em` units means that they will appear larger on the screen when the plain layout is used, since the font size does depend on the class of the body:

```
#main {
   padding: 0 0 0 18em;
   width: 30em;
}
#sidebar {
   width: 15em;
   display: block;
   float: left;
}
```

It should be clear that assigning to the `className` property of the `Element` object for the body will indeed change the appearance of this page. The interesting part of the job done by the script is arranging for that assignment to be executed.

The user needs to be able to click on something in order to switch the styles. The first idea that comes to mind is to add something like the following to the XHTML document:

```
Choose your preferred style: <span id="plain">Plain</span> |
<span id="fancy">Fancy</span>
```

and then attach click handlers to the two spans, which assign the appropriate class.

This is unsatisfactory in several respects, though. First, when they arrive at the site, users have no way of knowing whether they are seeing the plain or the fancy version. The fancy could be even fancier, or the plain even plainer. Therefore, it will be necessary to indicate somehow which style is currently being used and which can be chosen instead. If you have ever found yourself turning the subtitles of a DVD on when you thought you were turning them off, you will recognize that indicating which of two options is active in an unambiguous fashion is not easy. Another problem with adding markup to do the switching is that users with no scripting support will be bewildered at apparently seeing an option to switch styles, but finding that it does nothing.

A foolproof way of ensuring that only users whose browsers can execute the style switching script will see the controls for switching styles is to use a script to create that part of the page. We saw earlier that the DOM allows scripts to modify pages by creating tree nodes on the fly. If we create our controls this way, we can be sure that they will never be seen unless scripts can be executed.

This suggests a solution to the problem of confusing controls, too. Instead of creating a pair of controls to select either of the styles, simply create one control to select whichever style is not currently in force. When styles are switched, the control is changed appropriately.

Having arrived at this strategy, we can start writing our script. We will start out with a bit of wishful thinking. If we assume that there is a function called switch_style, which takes a string which is either "plain" or "fancy" as its argument, switches to the style with that name and creates a control for switching back, the rest is easy:

```
function plain() {
    switch_style("plain");
}
function fancy() {
    switch_style("fancy");
}

if (document.getElementById) window.onload = fancy;
```

We have reduced the problem to one of calling plain or fancy at an appropriate time. Since we have arranged for the page to be displayed in its plain state if no script is used, an appropriate time to call fancy is when the page loads, so that most users will see it using the fancy styles.

We know that `switch_style` has to change the class of the `body` element, so we can write that function with a little more wishful thinking. Assuming that `set_up_switch` can set up the control and handler for changing to the other style, `switch_style` can be defined like this:

```
function switch_style(style) {
    var body = document.getElementsByTagName("body")[0];
    body.className = style;
    set_up_switch(style);
}
```

If you look back at the XHTML source for the page, you will see that we have included a `div` with `id` equal to `switch`, with no content. This is there to serve as a placeholder for the control the user must click on to change styles. (Which demonstrates that the separation of behaviour from content cannot always be as clean as we might hope.) For now, we need not worry about what that control will be. If we assume that a function `create_control` will return an object that will do the job, we can write `set_up_switch` to place that object in the right position in the tree:

```
function set_up_switch(style) {
    var switch_div = document.getElementById("switch");
    while (switch_div.firstChild)
        switch_div.removeChild(switch_div.firstChild);
    var the_control = create_control(style);
    switch_div.appendChild(the_control);
}
```

First, we obtain an object for the `div` in question. Although this element starts out empty, once the page has been displayed it will have some content, so we need to remove this before inserting the new control. This is done in the `while` loop, which keeps removing the element's first child until it has none. After this, we just create the new control and insert it as a child of the `div`.

What remains to be done is write the function to create the control. This is now a fairly simple job. We first have to decide what the control will look like. We chose to use a `span` just containing the text `Switch to plain style` or `Switch to fancy style`. The style mentioned here is the one that is not being passed as an argument to `switch_style` and thence to `set_up_switch` and `create_control`. We also need to attach a handler to this span element, which will be either the plain or fancy function, depending on which direction the style is being switched.

Our new function begins by setting up the text and choosing a handler to attach. All it then needs to do is create a text node and an element node, add the text node to the element node's children and set the handler:

```
function create_control(style) {
    var other = style == "plain"? "fancy": "plain";
    var other_f = style == "plain"? fancy: plain;
    var t = document.createTextNode("Switch to " + other + " style");
    var the_span = document.createElement("span");
    the_span.appendChild(t);
    the_span.onclick = other_f;
    return the_span;
}
```

Remember that when the page is loaded, the function fancy is called, since it is the window's load event handler. It will immediately call switch_style with "fancy" as its argument. This will change the body's class and then call set_up_switch, still passing "fancy" as the argument; set_up_switch will call create_control and then insert the resulting span containing Switch to plain style into the div. The span will have the function plain attached to it as a click event handler, so if a user clicks on the text, plain will be called, and a similar chain of events will occur, leading to the page being displayed in the plain style, with a control to switch back to the fancy style.

Scripts and Forms

The use of scripts in conjunction with forms is long-established. Scripts are used in two ways: to provide assistance with filling in the form and to validate input. We will illustrate both types of use in relation to the form shown in Figure 7.6. The form is designed to allow users of Desperate Software products to report problems to the customer support department. Several fields of this form are compulsory: a name and email address are required, to ensure the request is from a genuine person and to allow the support team to contact the user. A customer ID number is required, since we assume that only registered users are eligible for support, and the description of the problem is also required, otherwise the form is pointless. Other fields are optional: the user's country of residence would be used in case local arrangements were available for dealing with problems, and their phone number could be used for urgent contact, if they were willing to provide it.

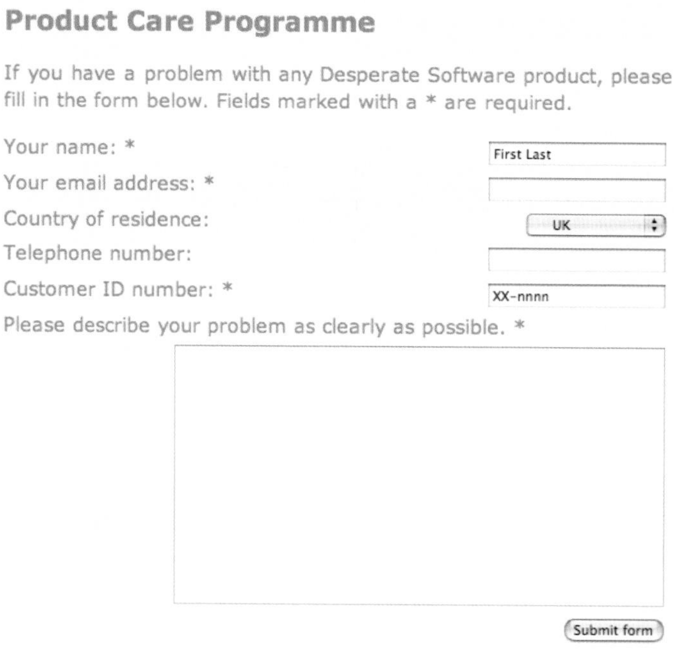
Product Care Programme
If you have a problem with any Desperate Software product, please fill in the form below. Fields marked with a * are required.
Your name: *
First Last
Your email address: *
Country of residence:
UK
Telephone number:
Customer ID number: *
XX-nnnn
Please describe your problem as clearly as possible. *
Submit form

Figure 7.6 A simple form

The XHTML source for the form is as follows. We will expand on the highlighted parts of the code later.

```
<form action="support.php" method="get" id="theform">
<p>
<label for="custname" class="required">
Your name:
</label>
<input name="Custname" id="custname" type="text" value="First Last"
/>
</p>
<p>
<label for="email" class="required">
Your email address:
</label>
<input name="email" id="email" type="text" />
</p>
```

```
<p>
<label for="country">
Country of residence:
</label>
<select id="country" name="country" >
<optgroup label="Europe">
<option label="UK" value="uk">UK</option>
<option label="France" value="fr">France</option>
<option label="Germany" value="de">Germany</option>
<option label="Netherlands" value="nl">Netherlands</option>
<option label="Spain" value="es">Spain</option>
</optgroup>
<optgroup label="N America">
<option label="United States" value="us">United States</option>
<option label="Canada" value="ca">Canada</option>
</optgroup>
<option label="Other" value="oth">Other</option>
</select>
</p>
<p>
<label for="phone">
Telephone number:
</label>
<input name="phone" id="phone" type="text" />
</p>
<p>
<label for="custid" class="required">
Customer ID number:
</label>
<input name="custid" id="custid" type="text" value="XX-nnnn" />
</p>
<p>
<label for="msg" class="required">
Please describe your problem as clearly as possible.
</label>
<br />
<textarea id="msg" name="msg" rows="16" cols="55">
</textarea>
</p>
<p id="submitp">
<input name="submit" id="submit" type="submit" value="Submit form" />
</p>
</form>
```

As you can see from the screenshot, the initial values of the Custname and custid fields provide an indication of the format of data that is required. These values are set by the markup, as indicated by the highlighted value attributes for these fields. Whereas these hints might remove some uncertainty about how the fields should be filled in, it is a nuisance for the user to have to select and erase the default values before filling in the field. A handler can do it for them. We can define a trivial function to clear any text field (i.e. an input element with its type set to text), by setting its value attribute to the empty string. We will pass an Element object for the input element as an argument:

```
function clear_field(ie) {
    ie.value = "";
}
```

We want to call this function when the user places the cursor in the field (either with the mouse or by tabbing) preliminary to typing a value. That is exactly when the focus event occurs, so we need to set handlers for that event for the fields with default values. In due course, we will create a function set_up_handlers to be used as a load event handler for window, in the familiar way. The following assignments will be part of the body of that function. (The arguments to getElementById are the values of the id attributes of the relevant input elements.)

```
var cname = document.getElementById("custname");
cname.onfocus = function() {
    clear_field(this);
}
var custno = document.getElementById("custid");
custno.onfocus = function() {
    clear_field(this);
}
```

We have used anonymous functions for the handlers, a common idiom.

There is another way in which we can help users with filling in their customer ID number. As the default is intended to show, the first two characters must be upper-case letters. Many users don't bother with the shift key, though. We can use the toUpperCase method of strings to normalize the case when they have finished typing, that is, when a blur event occurs. This is done by assigning a handler as follows:

```
custno.onblur = function() {
    this.value = this.value.toUpperCase();
}
```

There is one final useful piece of assistance we can give. Desperate Software is a company based in the UK, so if a customer gives their phone number, it will help if they include the international dialling code, unless they are in the UK too. We can't always do this for them, but if they select a country from the limited number on the pop-up menu labelled Country of Residence (which is a select element, with id set to country), we will be able to insert the code in the phone field when it receives the focus. Again, this is done by assigning an anonymous function as the focus handler for the phone field, whose id is phone:

```
var phone = document.getElementById("phone");
phone.onfocus = function() {
   var c = document.getElementById("country");
   set_phone(this, c.value);
}
```

The value property of the country field holds a country code as specified in the mark-up. The function set_phone, called from the handler, must map the country code to the international dialling code. This is done here just by looking it up in an associative array:

```
function set_phone(the_phone, country) {
   var codes = Array();
   codes["uk"] = "0";
   codes["fr"] = "0033 ";
   codes["de"] = "0049 ";
   codes["nl"] = "0031 ";
   codes["es"] = "0034 ";
   codes["us"] = "001 ";
   codes["ca"] = "001 ";
   codes["oth"] = "";
   the_phone.value = codes[country];
}
```

For UK numbers we insert the leading zero, required for calls within the country, in the hope of preventing people entering the UK dialling code. For countries not on the short list provided on the pop-up, we do not automatically insert anything.

Users whose browsers do not support scripts can still use the form, although it may be a little more inconvenient for them. So far, then, our script does degrade gracefully.

When we turn to the question of validating input, we also have to consider the possibility that the script may not actually be run by some visitors to the page. It is also important to remember that it is possible for a POST request to be generated by some program other than a Web browser, either for legitimate purposes, or in an attempt to cause mischief on the server. The implication of both of these considerations is clear: whatever script handles the form data on the server is going to have to perform careful validation on the data it receives in the request. Any validation performed by a script in the browser is only a convenience to users, allowing them to correct errors without having to send a request and wait for a reply.

Validation has to be done carefully, because you do not want to create a situation where users cannot submit a form containing legitimate values because your validation code is incorrectly rejecting it. In general, client-side validation should err on the lax side, leaving stricter checking to server-side scripts.

The question of what to do if validation fails must inevitably arise. We will defer a full answer, but it is conventional to display erroneously filled-in fields in some distinctive fashion, so we can assume that it will be necessary to set their class attribute to a special value. We can begin, therefore, with a little function that does this, which will be called whenever some necessary condition is not fulfilled by the value in a field. If you look back at the XHTML document, you will see that each form control is enclosed in a paragraph, together with its label. We need to highlight the control and label, and the simplest way to do so is by setting the class attribute of the enclosing p element. This element will be the parent of the control itself, so if we pass the Element for the control to our function, it should be defined as follows:

```
function mark(ctl) {
    ctl.parentNode.className = "invalid";
}
```

Another simple function can be used to determine whether a text field has been filled in. The defaultValue of a control's Element object holds its initial value. We need to determine whether the current value is equal to this, or equal to the empty string. Either condition might hold if a user had not entered anything in the field.

```
function has_been_filled(ie) {
    return ie.value != "" && ie.value != ie.defaultValue;
}
```

We can use these two functions to check that all the required fields have been filled in, and to mark those that have not. There is a complication here caused by the way the document has been marked up. The required fields are not themselves assigned to any class;

it is the attached `label` elements which have their `class` attribute set to `required`, since these are what needs styling. Therefore, to determine which elements to check using `has_been_filled`, we need to find all the labels whose `class` is `required`, and then find the associated control. This is identified in the markup by the `for` attribute of the label. The corresponding property of the `Element` node for the label is called `htmlFor`, to avoid a clash with the use of `for` as a keyword in loops.

Our function works as follows. First it finds the form, then all the `label` elements within it. It loops through these, checking to see whether the `class` is set to `required`. If it is, we get the `Element` identified by the `for` attribute (i.e. the `htmlFor` property of the object). This is checked to see whether it has been filled in. If not, it is marked. The flag `valid` is used to remember whether any field was missing. Its value is returned from the function – it will only be `true` if all the required fields have been filled in.

```
function check_required_fields() {
   var valid = true;
   var the_form = document.getElementById("theform");
   var the_labels = the_form.getElementsByTagName("label");
   for (var i = 0; i < the_labels.length; ++i) {
      var this_label = the_labels[i];
      if (this_label.className == "required") {
         var the_control = document.getElementById(this_label.
htmlFor);
         if (!has_been_filled(the_control)) {
            mark(the_control) ; valid = false;
         }
      }
   }
   return valid;
}
```

We can usefully perform some checks beyond making sure that all the required fields have been filled in. The customer ID number must conform to a fixed format, so we can check whether the value entered looks right, even though we can't possibly tell whether it is a legitimate customer's ID. (This check has to be made on the server.) We can also check whether the email address supplied looks feasible. The allowable syntax of email addresses is quite complex, and many real email addresses are not actually strictly legal, so making a rigorous check is quite difficult and often done wrongly. We will just settle for making sure that there is an @ symbol and at least one dot in the address, to exclude random gibberish and catch simple typing errors.

A depressing number of people apparently find pleasure in typing randomly into online forms, so we will also check that the name and message fields have a value that might be legitimate. Again, we have to be careful not to reject legitimate values, so we will simply make sure that the name has at least three characters in it, the first being a letter, and that the message has more than ten characters.

Checking the message and email according to our simple criteria is easy:

```
function feasible_message(m) {
    return m.length > 10;
}
```

```
function feasible_email(e) {
    return e.indexOf("@") > 0 && e.indexOf(".") > 0;
}
```

To perform the checks on names and customer IDs, we will need to be able to determine whether a string consists of all letters or all digits. To make these checks neater, we define a more general function, which takes two strings, s and t, and determines whether every character in s occurs in t. This in turn makes use of a function that determines whether its first argument, a character, occurs in its second, a string:

```
function chars(c, s) {
    return s.indexOf(c) > -1;
}

function all_chars(s, t) {
    for (var i = 0; i < s.length; ++i)
        if (!(chars(s.charAt(i), t))) return false;
    return true;
}
```

It is now easy to define functions that determine whether their string argument consists entirely of letters or of digits:

```
function digits(s) {
    return all_chars(s, "0123456789");
}
```

```
function letters(s) {
   return all_chars(s,
"ABCDEFGHIJKLMNOPQRSTUVWXYZabcdefghijklmnopqrstuvwxyz");
}
```

We can now check the name:

```
function feasible_name(n) {
   return n.length > 2 && letters(n.charAt(0));
}
```

Checking the customer ID is a bit more complicated. It must have the form of two letters followed by a hyphen and four digits. We approach the check by using the split method to break apart the string at the hyphen. We can then check that only two components resulted from the split (there was only one hyphen), that each component is the right length and consists of the right sort of characters:

```
function valid_custno(v) {
   var vv = v.split("-");
   return vv.length == 2 && vv[0].length == 2 &&
         vv[1].length == 4 &&
         letters(vv[0]) && digits(vv[1]);
}
```

We are now almost ready to put our tests together into a single validation function for the form. We need to incorporate a further decision about what should happen if any test fails, though. We have set the class of paragraphs enclosing invalid fields to invalid. We may decide that we also want to change the appearance of valid fields when the form is presented for correction, so we will also need to set the class attributes of fields which have been verified. The easy way to do this is to set all the classes to an appropriate value (we will use the class name validated) before doing the checks. The submit button represents a special case – it should always be displayed in the same way. We need to skip its enclosing paragraph when setting classes (that is why it has an id attribute). Once the class attributes have been initialized, verification is a simple matter of calling the functions we have just defined to carry out the tests, and marking the elements that fail. As before, we use a flag to remember whether any tests are failed, and return it as the value of our function verify:

```
function verify() {
   var the_form = document.getElementById("theform");
   var paras = the_form.getElementsByTagName("p");
```

```
    for (var i = 0; i < paras.length; ++i)
      if (paras[i].id != "submitp")
        paras[i].className = "validated";
  var valid =  check_required_fields();
  var name_field = document.getElementById("custname");
  if (!feasible_name(name_field.value)) {
    valid = false;
    mark(name_field);
  }
  var email_field = document.getElementById("email");
  if (!feasible_email(email_field.value)) {
    valid = false;
    mark(email_field);
  }
  var custno_field = document.getElementById("custid");
  if (!valid_custno(custno_field.value)) {
    valid = false;
    mark(custno_field);
  }
  var msg_field = document.getElementById("msg");
  if (!feasible_message(msg_field.value)) {
    valid = false;
    mark(msg_field);
  }
  return valid;
}
```

Now it's time to decide exactly what to do if validation fails. By setting the classes of paragraphs containing valid and invalid data to different values, we have allowed ourselves to determine the final appearance of the page in the stylesheet. Whatever it is, though, we will need to insert some message into the page, informing the user that they need to correct their input. It would be nice if we could make the text of this message independent of the appearance as determined by the stylesheet, but this is somewhat impractical. If the stylesheet turns invalid entries red, the text will have to refer to red items. We therefore need to decide how we want to highlight invalid input.

One approach, which makes it unambiguously clear which fields need fixing, is to hide the valid fields. This can be done very easily, using the following stylesheet rules:

```
.invalid { color: red; }
.validated { display: none; }
```

Invalid fields are shown in red, valid ones simply disappear. Although setting the display property to none prevents any boxes being created on the screen for these elements, they are still there in the DOM tree and their values are still sent to the server when the form is submitted.

We can now formulate our warning message and write a function to insert it into the page. The only thing to watch out for is the possibility that this is not the first time the user has failed to submit the form. A warning might already have been inserted. If so, we just leave it alone, otherwise we create a new paragraph and insert it before the form. While we are creating the paragraph, we set its id property, so we can find it again if necessary, and assign it to a class, so we can apply some conspicuous styling to it:

```
function insert_warning() {
   var old_warning = document.getElementById("warning");
   if (!old_warning) {
      var the_body = document.getElementsByTagName("body")[0];
      var the_form = document.getElementById("theform");
      var the_warning = document.createTextNode("You seem to have
left out some required fields, or entered invalid data. Please check
and amend the fields below.");
      var the_para = document.createElement("p");
      the_para.id = "warning";
      the_para.className = "warning";
      the_para.appendChild(the_warning);
      the_body.insertBefore(the_para, the_form);
   }
}
```

Finally, we can combine the verification and the insertion of the warning into a handler for the submit event on the form, and set up all the handlers:

```
function check_form() {
   var ok = verify();
   if (!ok) insert_warning();
   return ok;
}

function set_up_handlers() {
   set up focus and blur handlers as before
   var the_form = document.getElementById("theform");
   the_form.onsubmit = check_form;
}
```

Product Care Programme

If you have a problem with any Desperate Software product, please fill in the form below. Fields marked with a * are required.

You seem to have left out some required fields, or entered invalid data. Please check and amend the fields below.

Your name: * | First Last |

Your email address: * | |

Customer ID number: * | XX-nnnn |

Please describe your problem as clearly as possible. *

| |
| |
| |
| |
| |
| |
| |

(Submit form)

Figure 7.7 Indicating invalid input

Figure 7.7 shows what happens if a user tries to submit the form without filling in any of the fields at all.

Embedded Applications

The examples of DOM scripting we have described so far are concerned with using relatively simple scripts to manipulate DOM objects. A different class of scripts relies on JavaScript's abilities to carry out more complex computations in the browser, using the DOM to manipulate a Web page that serves as the user interface to what amounts to a small application program.

Simple Interactive Applications

The simplest applications of this sort perform all their input and output through the Web page. They are therefore very limited in what they can do, having no access to persistent data in files on either the server or client machine. Nevertheless, an example of such a script is

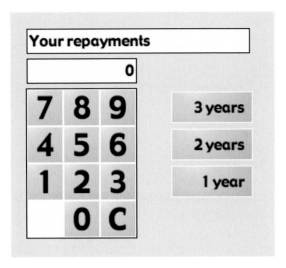

Figure 7.8 A repayment calculator

worth studying as a preliminary to considering a more powerful class of applications that do access data from the server.

Figure 7.8 shows a little application for computing loan repayments, which has a user interface based on the metaphor of a calculator. Users can enter the amount of a loan using the numeric keypad, and then click on one of the buttons labelled with the duration of the loan to learn the amount of each monthly repayment over that period.

The XHTML markup is trivial:

```
<div id="calculator">
<div id="keypad">
   <div id="one" class="button">
   1
   </div>
   nine similar divs for the other numeric keys
<div id="clear" class="button">
   C
   </div>
</div>
<div id="result">
0
</div>
```

```
<div id="answer">
Your repayments
</div>
<div id="years">
   <div id="year1" class="yearbutton">
   1 year
   </div>
   two similar divs for the other loan periods
</div>
</div>
```

The outer div elements group together the parts of the calculator; the inner divs isolate each of the input and output elements of the application – the calculator keys and the result fields. A simple stylesheet is used to select suitable fonts, apply some backgrounds and to arrange the keypad in a grid, using absolute positioning. We will not go into the detailed rules here.

The id attributes of the div elements are not only used by the stylesheet to position them. They also provide hooks for the script to access the elements, in order to read from and write to them.

When you press a number key on a calculator, the corresponding digit is appended to the number displayed in the window at the top. We want the number keys in our interface to work in the same way. It seems easier to work with numbers than with strings (although some might prefer to do it the other way), so whenever one of these keys is pressed, we want to multiply the existing value in the field at the top (with id equal to result) by 10, and add the value of the key's digit. This function will do exactly that if it is attached to each number key as a click event handler:

```
function key_handler(ev) {
   var kv = this.firstChild.data;
   var n = get_result();
   n = 10*n + Number(kv);
   set_result(n);
}
```

The handler is attached to the div element for a key, so its first child is the text node containing the character for that key's digit. The data property of a text node holds the node's contents as a string, so the variable kv is declared to hold a string containing the digit's character (and perhaps some white space). By passing this string to the built-in Number function, we obtain the corresponding number. This handler uses two functions (shown highlighted) to get and set the value of the result – which is displayed at the top of the calculator – in the div element with id equal to result. The assignment in between the getting and setting performs the necessary arithmetic described earlier. (The entire body of this handler could in fact be written as a single statement.)

Thinking ahead a little, it should be evident that after doing all the calculations we will need to write a string in the div element with id equal to answer. This suggests that instead of writing a function to set the value of the result, we would do better to write a more general function that puts a string into a div element, given the id of that element. Here it is:

```
function set_text(id, v) {
    var res = document.getElementById(id);
    var value = res.firstChild;
    value.data = v;
}
```

Notice that this overwrites any existing string.

Once set_text is written, we can easily write functions to write the result and answer. We can also write a handler for the C key, which clears everything down:

```
function set_result(v) {
    set_text("result", v);
}
function set_answer(a) {
    set_text("answer", a);
}
function clear() {
    set_result(0);
    set_answer("Your repayments");
}
```

The function get_result, which we used in the key handler, is simple:

```
function get_result() {
    var res = document.getElementById("result");
    var value = res.firstChild;
    return Number(value.data);
}
```

The functions we have written so far handle the communication of values between the script and the elements on the page. We still need to write some code that actually calculates loan repayments. It will be called after a user clicks on one of the three buttons at the right, labelled with the proposed loan period.

The algorithm we will use to compute monthly repayments is as follows. We will compute the total amount owed, by adding compound interest over the period of the loan, and then divide that total by the number of months. There is a formula for computing compound interest, but since this is a computer program, it is easier and not much less efficient just to use a loop which adds the interest every month. The following function takes a number of months and an amount borrowed and returns the value of the monthly payment. To do this, it needs the interest rate to be applied. We will use a fixed value, but store it in a variable called `rate`, which will make it easier to find if we ever wish to modify it. We'll use a deceptively modest-sounding rate of 0.75% per month.

```
function compute_payment(m, amount) {
    var rate = 0.0075;
    var total = amount;
    for (var t = 0; t < m; ++t)
        total *= (1 + rate);
    return total/m;
}
```

All that apparently remains is to write a handler for the loan period buttons, which calls this function, using the amount presently shown in the result field, and the number of months corresponding to the period indicated on the button. We use a slightly lazy technique to get the latter value. By giving these buttons `id` values of `year1`, `year2` and `year3`, we have embedded the number of years in the `id`, so we can use a single handler for all three buttons, and find out the period by looking at the fifth character of the `id` of the object the handler is attached to. It works and it cuts down the amount of code you have to read, but we must admit that it isn't very maintainable:

```
function do_payments(ev) {
    var the_id = this.id;
    var m = 12*Number(the_id.charAt(4));
    var payment = compute_payment(m, get_result());
    set_answer(m + " payments of " + payment);
}
```

That would seem to be all that is required, apart from setting up the handlers, which can be done in much the usual way. First we loop through all the `div` elements within the keypad `div`, setting their `click` handlers to `key_handler`, except for the clear key, which is a special case. Then we look for each of the year keys and set its handler to `do_payments`:

```
function setup_keys() {
   var keypad = document.getElementById("keypad");
   var keys = keypad.getElementsByTagName("div");
   for (var i = 0; i < keys.length; ++i) {
      var ki = keys.item(i);
      var h = ki.id == "clear"? clear: key_handler;
      ki.onclick = h;
   }
   for (var i = 1; i <= 3; ++i) {
      var y = document.getElementById("year"+String(i));
      y.onclick = do_payments;
   }
}
if (document.getElementById) window.onload = setup_keys;
```

If you do all this and try it, you'll discover that it isn't quite finished yet. Entering 555 on the keypad and choosing a period of two years causes the following to be written as the answer:

```
24 payments of 27.667062867204383
```

This is not acceptable, so we have to amend `do_payments` slightly. The penultimate line must be changed to

```
var payment = format_amount(compute_payment(m, get_result()));
```

and we need to define `format_amount` to trim its argument to just two digits after the decimal point. This can be done with a little grubby arithmetic, which we won't dwell on.

```
function format_amount(n) {
   var i = String(Math.floor(n));
   var f = Math.round((100*n)%100);
   f = f<10?" 0"+String(f): String(f);
   return i + "." + f;
}
```

This now produces the intended output, such as:

```
24 payments of 27.67
```

As well as demonstrating how a script can perform non-trivial computation and use elements of a Web page as its user interface, this little example shows that doing so presents a major problem: it completely fails to degrade gracefully. If a browser doesn't support DOM scripting or a user has disabled it, the calculator does nothing at all. To provide the same functionality to users without scripting, it would be necessary to provide an alternative implementation of the calculator on the server. As before, to ensure that only users who could take advantage of the client-side script would see it, it would be necessary to use additional scripts to write the calculator page dynamically.

Fetching Data

Although it is not part of the W3C DOM, an object called an XMLHttpRequest is implemented by almost all Web browsers. This object can read an XML file from a server, parse its contents and return a DOM tree, which can be manipulated in the same way as any other DOM tree. This provides a way for scripts to obtain data from a remote location and incorporate it into the page currently being displayed. In other words, it allows a page to be updated in place, instead of requiring the browser to load a new page. Starting in 2005, there has been an upsurge of interest in this way of updating pages, as part of the so-called AJAX approach to providing rich user interfaces to Web applications.

As a simple example of how this works, we will return to the image gallery. In the version we developed earlier to introduce dynamic pages, clicking on a thumbnail caused a large version of the same image to be displayed. Suppose now that we also want to display some information about the image, but that we still don't want to create a separate page for each picture in the gallery. Instead, we want to keep the information in an XML file, and load and display it using a script that is activated when the user clicks on a thumbnail.

In order to keep the example relatively simple, we assume that the data for each image is kept in a separate XML file. (In practice, it is perhaps more likely that the XML data would be generated by a script, but that does not affect what happens in the browser.) We further assume that the XML files are kept in the same directory as the large images, and that the name of the XML file is the same as the name of the image file, except that it ends in .xml instead of .jpeg. This assumption is made simply to remove the need for some extraneous detail from our example script, as you will see later.

For each image, we will display a title and some metadata: a descriptive category to which the image belongs, the date on which the picture was taken, and a star rating, summarizing its quality. A typical data file will look like this:

Image Gallery

Click on a thumbnail to see a larger image.

© MacAvon Media Productions 2003

Blue Flower

[2003 | Flowers | ***]

Figure 7.9 An enhanced image gallery

```
<picture>
    <ptitle>Blue Flower</ptitle>
    <category>Flowers</category>
    <date>2003</date>
    <rating>***</rating>
</picture>
```

Figure 7.9 shows how an image is displayed with its data.

The markup in our XHTML document hardly needs to be changed. We just add a div element to serve as a placeholder for the data. (Even this is not strictly necessary, since it could be created dynamically, but matters are slightly simplified if we can assume that this element always exists.)

```
<div id="info"></div>
```

The structure of the script remains more or less the same, too: a function called swap_image will be attached to each thumbnail as a click event handler. However, the body of this function is augmented with a call to a new function, which we define so that it fetches and inserts the data about the image. (We have also taken the opportunity to eliminate a superfluous variable, me, which we introduced for expository purposes earlier.)

```
function swap_image() {
    var my_image = this.href;
    var the_image = document.getElementById("the_image");
    the_image.src = my_image;
    swap_data(my_image);
    return false;
}
```

Before we can write swap_data, we need to describe how XMLHttpRequest objects are created and used. This is made complicated by the fact that XMLHttpRequest is implemented using ActiveX in Internet Explorer (prior to IE7), but is an ordinary object in every other browser. Hence, we need to write some conditional code that creates an object in an appropriate fashion depending on the browser's capabilities. This requires a further short digression about objects in JavaScript.

The DOM objects we have been using so far are all created by the browser. When an object has to be created explicitly in JavaScript, we use the new operator, which is followed by the name of the object, followed by any values needed to create it, in brackets. For example,

```
var the_request = new XMLHttpRequest();
```

No values are needed to create an XMLHttpRequest object.

The expression following new looks like a function call, and in fact XMLHttpRequest is a function, of a special sort, called a **constructor** – because it constructs new XMLHttpRequest objects. (When we talk about an Element object, and so on, what we mean is precisely an object created by the Element constructor.) In JavaScript, functions are really methods belonging to the window object. Therefore, to find out whether it is possible to create an XMLHttpRequest object using the constructor, we need only test whether window.XMLHttpRequest is null, much as we tested for DOM support by checking the value of document.getElementById. If it is null, we need to create the object using ActiveX, which is done using the ActiveX constructor, which takes a special string as its argument, to indicate what sort of control it should build:

```
var the_request = new ActiveXObject("Msxml2.XMLHTTP");
```

To keep everything in one place, we define a function that returns a new object, created using the appropriate constructor:

```
function getRequestObject() {
   return window.XMLHttpRequest?
      new XMLHttpRequest():
      new ActiveXObject("Msxml2.XMLHTTP");
}
```

Calling this function just creates the object; it won't do anything until we call some of its methods. The first thing we need to do is set up an HTTP request to some URL. This is done by calling the open method. Its first argument is a string containing the method for the request line, which will usually be "GET" or "POST". The second argument is the URL to which the request is to be sent. An optional third argument is a Boolean that indicates whether the request should be processed synchronously or asynchronously. If the value supplied is false, the request is processed synchronously, which means that the script cannot do anything until the response is received. If the value is true, when the request is sent, control returns immediately, so that the script can do something else while the data is being fetched. An event is used to signal the conclusion of the operation.

Calling open doesn't send the request. This is done by calling another method, send, which takes as its argument any data to be sent in the body of the request. In the case of a GET request, this will be null. When the request is returned, the responseXML property of the XMLHttpRequest object holds the data, in the form of a parsed XML document tree.

To see how this works, we can return to our specific example. The swap_data function is passed the name of the image file as its argument (this being the easiest value to get hold of). Before we can fetch any data, we will need to change the extension on this filename to obtain the name of the XML file that goes with it. This is easily done, since we know that the final dot in the filename will be the one before the extension.

```
function change_extension(f, ext) {
   var dot_pos = f.lastIndexOf(".");
   var root = f.substring(0, dot_pos);
   return root + "." + ext;
}
```

Now we can fill in the body of `swap_data`. It must create an `XMLHttpRequest`, and then use it to fetch the XML file obtained by changing the extension of its argument. To begin with, we will fetch the data synchronously. When control returns from `send`, we will pass the `XMLHttpRequest` object to a separate function `handle_data`, which will extract the returned data for incorporation into the original document.

```
function swap_data(img) {
    var the_request = getRequestObject();
    var data_file = change_extension(img, "xml");
    the_request.open("GET", data_file, false);
    the_request.send(null);
    handle_data(the_request);
}
```

The `handle_data` function must extract the XML data returned in the HTTP response and replace the existing `div` with `id` equal to `info` with a new one built from it. If we hand over the creation of the new `div` to a separate function, which we'll call `build_new_div`, `handle_data` can be defined like this:

```
function handle_data(the_request) {
    var d = the_request.responseXML;
    var old_body = document.getElementsByTagName("body")[0];
    var old_div = document.getElementById("info");
    var new_div = build_new_div(d, "info");
    old_body.replaceChild(new_div, old_div);
}
```

What `build_new_div` must do is create a `div` element for each of the elements in the XML document. We can usefully break this task down, by writing a function that creates a single `div` element. It will need the object for the XML document and the name of the XML element from which the data is to be extracted. We will set the class of the resulting `div` to the name supplied, to provide a hook for applying styling to the inserted data. The function does not introduce any new ideas.

```
function make_div(doc, s) {
    var el = doc.getElementsByTagName(s)[0];
    var t = document.createTextNode(el.firstChild.data);
    var d = document.createElement("div");
    d.className = s;
    d.appendChild(t);
```

```
      return d;
   }
```

It's simple to combine several calls to make_div to create build_new_div. The resulting elements are inserted into an enclosing div, which is returned and will then be used by handle_data to replace the existing information, as shown previously:

```
function build_new_div(d, id) {
   var new_div = document.createElement("div");
   new_div.appendChild(make_div(d, "ptitle"));
   new_div.appendChild(make_div(d, "date"));
   new_div.appendChild(make_div(d, "category"));
   new_div.appendChild(make_div(d, "rating"));
   new_div.id = id
   return new_div;
}
```

All that remains is to make sure that the right data is displayed when the page first loads. This can be done by calling the click event handler for the first thumbnail explicitly at the end of attach_handlers. There is nothing to stop you calling handlers yourself if you attached them by assigning to the event properties – they are just methods.

```
function attach_handlers() {
   attach click handlers to the thumbnail links, as before
   links[0].onclick();
}
```

A few extra stylesheet rules, which we won't show here, are needed to format the div elements created from the loaded data. (We chose to set the display property of most of them to inline.)

All of this works fine, provided everything goes well with fetching the XML data. However, the high-level abstraction of the XMLHttpRequest object conceals the fact that when send is called, an HTTP request is sent and the data comes back in a response. That is, the_request.send causes network transfers to take place, and things can go wrong with network transfers in ways that they cannot go wrong with local computation. In particular, a network connection can go down, so that the expected response is never received. If the XMLHttpRequest is operating synchronously, the script will be blocked while it waits for the response to arrive; if the response fails to arrive, the script will hang up, and so, in turn, will the browser.

This possibility can be prevented if the XMLHttpRequest object operates asynchronously. Once the transfer has been started, control returns to the script. It's true that often the script won't be able to do anything useful until the data arrives, but it can periodically check the time that has elapsed since the request was sent, and if it exceeds a reasonable value, conclude that something has gone wrong and take appropriate action.

When an asynchronous request is set up, by passing the value true as the third argument to the open method, a function must be designated to be called when the data has arrived. This is done by assigning it to the onreadystatechange property of the XMLHttpRequest object. In our case, this means making the following assignment:

```
the_request.onreadystatechange = handle_data;
```

This looks as if the handle_data should become a method of the object – in JavaScript, methods are just proeprties whose value happens to be a function – but bizarrely it is not called in that way. In particular, within the function, you cannot use this to refer to the XMLHttpRequest object. This is awkward, because it is necessary to have access to this object inside handle_data, in order to find the data.

We are therefore forced to do something we normally avoid, and make the_request into a global variable. That is, we put the declaration

```
var the_request;
```

at the top of the script, outside any function definition. This makes the variable accessible inside all functions. We must now make a few more small changes, as follows:

```
function swap_data(img) {
    var data_file = change_extension(img, "xml");
    the_request = getRequestObject();
    the_request.onreadystatechange = handle_data;
    the_request.open("GET", data_file, true);
    the_request.send(null);
}
```

Notice that we no longer declare the_request inside swap_data, because we need to use the global that we declared earlier. The changes to handle_data itself are also minor.

```
function handle_data() {
    if (the_request.readyState == 4 &&
            the_request.status == 200) {
        proceed as before
    }
}
```

Again, we are now using the global variable `the_request`, instead of passing it as an argument. There is only one other change here. The function assigned to the `onreadystatechange` property of an `XMLHttpRequest` object is called whenever some state change occurs. There are several events that can cause a state change, but the only one of interest to us is completion of the data transfer. This is indicated by the `readyState` attribue of the object being set to the value 4, so we check this before trying to extract the data. We also check the object's `status` property, which holds the HTTP response status. As always, a value of 200 indicates OK. If any other value occurs, there is nothing much we can do, so we just skip the processing of the data.

Nothing else in the script has to change for asynchronous operation. Despite the additional complexity of the code, asynchronous requests are generally to be preferred, both because they do not hang up the browser if a network error occurs, and because they allow a script to do some extra computation while waiting for the data to arrive, if that is appropriate.

Drawbacks

The use of scripts that fetch data has caused a good deal of excitement in the Web design community since the term **AJAX** (Asynchronous JavaScript and XML) was coined in early 2005 to describe the use of applications embedded in Web pages to provide users with an experience similar to that provided by desktop applications, by avoiding the requirement to load new pages every time some data was fetched from the server. Although the techniques were not new at that time, the arrival of a handy acronym appears to have provided a focus for talking about them, which allowed isolated experiments to coalesce into a coherent approach to implementing responsive user interfaces in Web pages. On the face of it, this is a more significant and worthwhile use of scripting than the tricks and visual effects produced under the name of Dynamic HTML when browsers first started supporting scripting.

Such applications are not without their problems, though. First and foremost, they depend entirely on scripting support in the browser. Users who turn off scripting, or who are viewing sites on mobile devices or using assistive technology that does not support scripting, are locked out of such sites. In order for scripts of such complexity to degrade gracefully, it is generally necessary to provide a server-based alternative implementation of the same functionality. Having done that, you might wonder whether it is worth the effort of duplicating it on the client, simply to avoid loading pages.

AJAX also creates usability problems. If the data is fetched asynchronously, it may arrive at unpredictable times, so a page might update itself at an arbitrary time after the user has done something. This is potentially confusing in itself, but by that time, they might have scrolled down the page to look at another part of it. If new content is added higher up the page, the display will change in a very strange manner.

More fundamentally, the possibility of updating a page with data that has been fetched by a script breaks the connection between a page and a URL. Consider, for example, a possible extended version of the image gallery, with tens or hundreds of images. At any time, only four thumbnails would be displayed, but back and forward buttons could be provided to move through the collection. If these buttons triggered scripts which fetched the new thumbnails, rather than fetching a new page, every page of the gallery would have the same URL, even though the images displayed would be different. This makes it impossible to bookmark any single set of images, or link to it: going to the URL would always bring you to the first page of the gallery. Similarly, the history list and back button would not work as expected. Users have become accustomed to thinking of the Web in terms of discrete pages. Anything that disrupts this expectation can cause problems.

A third problem is the state of standardization of scripting support. Although the DOM specifications are now generally implemented, there are large areas which they do not cover. Operations that a rich client application might need, such as drag and drop, or animation, depend on objects that are not defined in the DOM – rightly so, since the DOM is only a model of a document, and these objects belong to the browser. There are *ad hoc* Browser Object Models, but these are not standardized.

At the time of writing, the W3C has established a Working Group to consider 'Rich Web Clients', which should address these areas, and hopefully remove this objection. One of this group's first tasks has been to create a specification of the XMLHttpRequest object – despite the fact that the Level 3 DOM includes an object called an LSParser, which duplicates the function of XMLHttpRequest. It appears that there is likely to be some confusion over standardization of the features required by AJAX applications for some time.

In view of these potential problems, any sites that depend on AJAX should be subject to extensive user testing.

Key Points

Fundamentals

Writing scripts is a form of programming.

A program can be composed from the interaction of objects.

An object consists of a set of values, called properties, together with a set of operations, called methods.

If o is an object, o.p is the value of its property p, and o.m() is a call to its method m.

Variables are named containers that can hold objects and values.

The DOM

The W3C Document Object Model (DOM) provides a standard way of modelling Web pages as a collection of objects.

The Core DOM models any XML document. The HTML DOM adds additional objects which are specific to HTML and XHTML documents.

The DOM allows programs to alter documents and change their appearance in the browser.

The structure of a document's element hierarchy is modelled as a tree, containing element nodes and text nodes.

Element objects correspond to the element nodes. Their methods include getAttribute, setAttribute and appendChild. They have a childNodes property, which holds a NodeList object; other properties include firstChild and LastChild.

The document object represents the entire document. Its methods include createElement and CreateTextNode, for making new objects, as well as getElementById and getElementsByTagName, for accessing individual Element objects and all elements of a specific type, respectively.

In the HTML DOM, every Element object has properties corresponding to the element's attributes. Assigning to the property changes the attribute's value.

The property for the class attribute is className.

JavaScript

Numbers can be combined using conventional arithmetic notation.

Strings may be written between double or single quotes, and can be concatenated using the + operator. A string's length property holds the number of characters it contains. The charAt method returns the character at the specified position, the substring method is used to extract parts of a string, while the indexOf method can be used to search for one string inside another.

Arrays are sequences of values.

If a is an array, and i is an integer, a[i] is the item at position i in a.

Arrays can also be indexed by strings, when they map keys to values.

Arrays have a length property and methods for sorting and joining all their elements.

The Array function creates a new array.

Boolean values (true and false) are returned by the ==, !=, <, >, <= and >= operators. They can be combined using && (and) and || (or). ! negates a Boolean value.

Assignment is written as =.

Shorthands such as += are used to combine assignment with another operation. ++ is used to add 1 to a variable.

A JavaScript program is a sequence of statements, including assignments, method calls, conditional statement and loops.

A conditional statement has the form

```
if (condition) statement1 else statement2
```

A conditional expression has the form

```
condition? expression1: expression2
```

A `while` loop has the form

```
while (condition) statement
```

A `for` loop has the form

```
for (initialization; condition; step) statement
```

Dividing the computation performed by a program into functions is one of the best ways of organizing it.

A function definition has the form function `name(arguments) { body }`

The value of the expression in a `return` statement will be returned by the function when it is called.

Functions may be stored in variables, passed to other functions or stored in objects, where they become methods.

An anonymous function is defined just like a named function, except that the function name is omitted.

Dynamic Pages

Pages with scripts should degrade gracefully.

Behaviour should be separated from content and structure.

Scripts should work correctly.

Scripts are added to XHTML documents using the `script` element.

The `src` attribute holds the URL of an external script; the `type` attribute specifies the scripting language (`text/javascript`).

Scripts are associated with events to trigger actions interactively.

Event handlers can be attached to elements by assigning functions to properties corresponding to attributes whose names begin with `on`, such as `onclick`.

If a handler returns `false`, any default action will be prevented.

Code for attaching handlers to page elements can be included in the `window` object's `load` event handler.

Event handlers should only be attached if `document.getElementById` is defined, implying that DOM scripting is supported.

Applications of DOM Scripting

Using handlers to change the value of some elements' `class` attributes is a powerful method of making changes to the appearance of a page.

If a stylesheet specifies different values for the `display` property of elements according to their class, changing the class can make elements appear or dispapear.

Dramatic changes in the appearance of a page can be implemented with a script that changes the body element's class, if suitable contextual selectors are used in the stylesheet.

> A stylesheet switcher implemented in this way can be used to allow users with poor eyesight to select a more easily readable version of a page.

Using a script to create controls that trigger handlers ensures that only users whose browsers support scripting will see them.

Scripts are used in conjunction with forms to provide assistance with filling in the form and to validate input.

Handlers for the `focus` event can be used to delete default values or set values based on those already entered in another field.

Validation of form data must be done carefully. Users must never find themselves unable to submit a form with legitimate values.

Invalid fields can be indicated by changing a `class` attribute.

Embedded Applications

Simple applications can be embedded in Web pages, using JavaScript to perform calculations, and the DOM to provide access to a user interface on the page.

Values can be read from and written to form elements by the script.

The `XMLHttpRequest` object can read and parse XML files stored on a server and return a DOM tree.

`XMLHttpRequest` objects are created either by calling the corresponding constructor, or calling the `ActiveXObject` constructor with the argument `"Msxml2.XMLHTTP"`.

The object's `open` method sets up an HTTP request, and its `send` method sends it.

When the request is returned, the `responseXML` property of the `XMLHttpRequest` object holds the data, in the form of a DOM tree.

Requests may be processed either synchronously or asynchronously.

Synchronous processing means that the script may be blocked if there is a network problem, so asynchronous processing is preferred.

For asynchronous requests, a function must be assigned to the object's `onreadystatechange` property.

AJAX applications use `XMLHttpRequest` to fetch data without refreshing the page, in order to provide a smoother interface and improved user experience.

AJAX applications may present usability problems, so they should be adequately tested.

Exercises

Test Questions

1. Give some examples of features of Web pages that are implemented using scripting. (Examine the page source if you cannot tell any other way.) Can any of these features be implemented in another way? For those that cannot, explain why not.

2. How would you obtain a collection of objects corresponding to all the `img` elements inside a `div` element with `id` equal to `navbar`?

3. A Web designer writes the following code to remove all the children of an `Element` node `el`:

```
for (var i = 0; i < el.childNodes.length; ++i)
  el.removeChild(el.childNodes.[i]);
```

It doesn't work as intended. Explain why not.

4. The `for` loop is a redundant construction. Demonstrate this by writing a `while` loop that is equivalent to the general form of the `for` loop. Why do you think the `for` loop is provided?

5. Explain carefully why a handler for the `load` event attached to the body of a document cannot be used to attach event handlers to other elements.

6. Give an example of a situation in which it would be necessary to detect separate `mousedown` and `mouseup` events, instead of just the combined `click` event.

7. How would you add event handlers to the controls of a form so that the element which has the input focus is highlighted?

8. Give two reasons why a Web application should not rely on JavaScript alone to validate data from a form.

9. Why do we say that giving the buttons in our repayment calculator `id` values of `year1`, `year2` and `year3` and letting our script determine the period by examing the fifth character is not very maintainable? How would you improve on this approach?

10. Would it be sensible to attach `click` event handlers to all the links on a page to use `XMLHttpRequest` to fetch a new page instead of letting the browser send a request in the usual way?

Discussion Topics

1. How would the model of the sandwich shop outlined at the beginning of this chapter be altered if there was more than one assistant working behind the counter?

2. It is often the case that, when a page loads and a handler for the window's `load` event runs, the page's appearance changes, as occurred in our collapsible list example. How might you prevent users seeing this happen? (That is, how could you ensure that they only saw the page in the state following the execution of the `load` event handler?)

3. JavaScript is becoming an increasingly important component in Web-based applications, with the widespread adoption of AJAX. At the same time, there is a rapid increase in the number of mobile devices,

which often don't support JavaScript, being used to access the Web. How can these developments be reconciled?

Practical Tasks

1. Write a JavaScript function that takes three strings, t, s1 and s2 as its arguments, and returns a new string made from t by replacing every occurrence of a character in s1 by the corresponding character in s2. That is, if s1 was "abc" and s2 was "xyz", the function would return the string obtained by replacing every a in t by x, every b by y and every c by z. Do not assume that s1 and s2 are the same length. Create a Web page that will enable you to test your function by entering a range of values for its arguments in a form.

2. Write a script that operates on a document with a navbar consisting of a list of links, and moves the first link to the end of the list.

3. Create a navbar consisting of links each of which is an a element, whose content is a small image, perhaps just some text rendered in a suitable style. For each image, create a second, suitably modified version, to be displayed when the cursor rolls over the link. (Change the background colour, apply a drop shadow, etc.) Write a script to make this rollover effect occur. Try to use as little code as possible; it will probably help to use a systematic naming scheme for the set of images.

4. Create a two-level navbar. For each entry in the top level, there should be a set of second level entries. (Nested lists would be suitable as the markup.) Write scripts and stylesheets to make the corresponding second level entries appear as a drop-down menu when the cursor rolls over a top-level entry, and disappear when it is moved away. The navbar links should still work in browsers that do not support JavaScript or CSS.

5. As an alternative to our approach of using a script that changes the body's class attribute, together with contextual selectors in a stylesheet, a script can change a page's appearance by altering the link element that points to an external stylesheet so that it points to a different one. Implement a stylesheet switcher that works in this way.

Web Applications

8

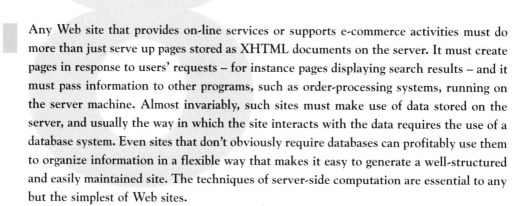

Any Web site that provides on-line services or supports e-commerce activities must do more than just serve up pages stored as XHTML documents on the server. It must create pages in response to users' requests – for instance pages displaying search results – and it must pass information to other programs, such as order-processing systems, running on the server machine. Almost invariably, such sites must make use of data stored on the server, and usually the way in which the site interacts with the data requires the use of a database system. Even sites that don't obviously require databases can profitably use them to organize information in a flexible way that makes it easy to generate a well-structured and easily maintained site. The techniques of server-side computation are essential to any but the simplest of Web sites.

In Chapter 2, we outlined how data entered into forms can be sent to the server in a GET or POST request, and how that data is then passed to a script, which processes it and generates the response. (You may wish to review the section of that chapter headed *Dynamically Generated Pages*.) If you are attracted by the AJAX approach, you should also realize that the data fetched by a client-side script using an XMLHttpRequest object will also, in most cases, be produced dynamically on the server.

Server-Side Technologies

Whereas client-side technologies – markup, stylesheets and scripting – are specified by a small number of standards, there is a much greater variation among the technologies employed at the server end of the Web. This is not in itself a problem: when you create a Web application, you usually know in advance which platform will be used to host it, so you do not have to worry about using standards to create applications that run on any platform, in the way that you have to worry about using standards to ensure compatibility with different browsers. However, the range of technologies available does present a bewildering choice.

Mechanisms for Passing Data

The passing of data from an HTTP request to a program that creates a response dynamically can be done in several ways.

CGI

The oldest and most primitive mechanism is known as the **Common Gateway Interface (CGI)**, as we mentioned briefly in Chapter 2. All that CGI specifies is the mechanism for passing data from an HTTP request to a separate program invoked by the HTTP server. Implicit in the specification is the assumption that this program will run as a separate process, which will be started up by the server. Most values sent in the request, including form data and the request headers, are copied into environment variables, which can be accessed by the program. Any data sent in the body of a POST request is passed in the standard input stream. The standard output from the program is normally passed back to the server process, where HTTP response headers are added to it before it is sent to the client.

Environment variables and standard input and output streams are system-dependent concepts. The CGI specification appears to assume that all HTTP servers run on Unix, so on some other platforms these mechanisms must be faked. This has been done successfully, and programs written according to the CGI specification – usually simply called **CGI scripts** – can run on almost any platform and interact with almost any HTTP server.

CGI places most of the onus of deciphering the data from the request on the CGI script. Any query string appended to the path of a GET request is passed exactly as it is in a single environment variable. The script must take the string apart to access the name/value pairs sent by a form. POST data is similarly sent to the CGI script's standard input exactly as it is received by the server, and so this must be deciphered in the same way.

Because almost any CGI script must decipher query strings, programming languages commonly used for CGI scripting usually provide a higher-level interface to the CGI data. Generally, an object or associative array is created, either automatically by the run-time system or explicitly using some library call, which allows the script to look up the value of any variable sent in the request.

More Efficient Mechanisms

CGI is defined in terms of environment variables and standard input and output, so the obvious way to implement it is by creating a new process every time a request for a script is received. This is inefficient: the overhead of creating and destroying processes is considerable.

An additional overhead is incurred if the script has to be recompiled every time it is run, which is commonly the case with CGI scripts written in the most popular languages used for this purpose. Since the processes for each request are separate, a great deal of memory may be allocated to running multiple copies of the same script. If, as is usual, the script is written in an interpreted language, each process will need a copy of the interpreter. A script that is part of a popular site may be requested many times a second, so the overheads may place a considerable load on the server machine.

FastCGI is an extension to CGI, which avoids this overhead. Instead of processes starting up when a request is received and terminating when they have dealt with it, FastCGI processes are created when the HTTP server is started, and continue running all the time. When a request is received by the HTTP server, it opens a connection to the appropriate FastCGI process. On Unix systems this connection will often take the form of a pipe, but FastCGI allows for the possibility of processes running on different machines from the server, so a TCP connection can also be used. This connection is used to pass the information that a CGI process would receive in the environment and its standard input. The FastCGI process sends its output back over this connection to the server, which passes it on to the client in the form of an HTTP response. After sending the output, the FastCGI process closes the connection and then waits for another. FastCGI can be significantly faster than CGI, but this additional speed is obtained at the expense of keeping a pool of running processes, one for each Web application hosted on the server. Although FastCGI has been around since 1996, it has recently attracted a new wave of attention, because of the current interest in Web application frameworks such as Ruby on Rails (see below).

The widely-used Apache Web server provides another way of avoiding the overhead of creating and destroying processes incurred by CGI. It supports the use of dynamically loaded modules. Rather like browser plug-ins, these are loaded into the server itself when they are needed. A module of this sort can include an interpreter, so that instead of spawning a new process with its own copy every time a CGI script is requested, the script can be run inside the server, thus avoiding the overhead of starting up the process and the memory requirement associated with it. Once a script has been compiled, it can be kept in memory for subsequent requests. An extra advantage of this approach to implementation is that it makes it possible to provide additional ways for the script to interact with the server.

A script running inside an Apache module does not have access to environment variables – these are created for a process, and the script is running as part of the Apache process, so the actual CGI mechanism cannot be used to pass data to the script. However, various expedients are available to make it appear to the script as if the environment variables had been set up, so that CGI scripts can run more efficiently in a module with little or no modification.

Microsoft's **ASP.NET** framework does something similar. ASPX documents, the equivalent of scripts, can be compiled into dynamically loaded libraries (DLLs), which are then loaded into the server. Typically, compilation occurs the first time a document is requested, and then the compiled version can be executed rapidly on subsequent requests. One of the strengths of ASP.NET is that it allows almost any programming language to be used, although Visual Basic and C# tend to be preferred by programmers using this technology.

Most other modern server-side technologies work in a broadly similar way, by providing some mechanism whereby compiled versions of scripts can be executed inside the HTTP server's process. However, such approaches are server-dependent, and including modules complicates the business of deploying a server. For this reason, FastCGI (and similar technologies, such as SCGI) are sometimes preferred.

Languages

Certain programming and scripting languages are favoured for server-side programming. Most of these languages are dynamically typed – variables do not need to be associated once and for all with a certain type when they are declared; in fact they do not need to be declared at all. Dynamic typing usually goes hand in hand with interpretive implementation, and most of the languages we will describe are implemented by some sort of interpreter, which helps make programs portable. (No machine code is ever generated.) Automatic memory management ('garbage collection') is usually built in, which can help prevent certain sorts of fatal errors, as well as ensuring that memory is properly de-allocated when it is no longer required. Support for pattern matching based on regular expressions is generally provided, which helps with the text processing that is often required in Web applications. Extensive libraries which include interfaces to databases are usually available. The most popular Web programming languages are released under some variety of Open Source licence.

Web applications are often developed by Web designers and system administrators who are not primarily programmers, and languages which have been devised or adopted for this type of programming are usually designed with the intention of making programming easier. This often means that language features such as strong typing are omitted; this eases learning, but in the long run may make programming of large-scale software more difficult. Most Web applications are relatively small in scale, or composed of small pieces, so this is not a great problem. Because of their intended use, some of the most popular Web programming languages were developed outside the mainstream of programming language design, with the result that they generally appear quite eccentric to programmers accustomed to mainstream languages.

Embedded Scripts

Normally, a program consists of a sequence of definitions and statements which can be executed. In the case of server-side scripts, the program produces some output, which is sent to the client. For many languages used for writing server-side scripts, a mechanism is provided for embedding executable statements in an XHTML document. The statements are interspersed with the markup; when the document is processed, these statements are executed and replaced by any output that they generate, which should, therefore, be a legitimate fragment of XHTML. Since the program code is replaced by its output, the result will be an XHTML document that can be sent to the client. We showed a simple example of such an embedded script in Chapter 2. (An alternative way of looking at what is going on is that the script includes some XHTML, which is treated as if it was the argument to some function that sent it to the output stream.)

Perl

Although popularly identified with CGI scripting, Perl is a general-purpose programming language that has been used for many things besides server-side Web scripting. Perl was not the first programming language to include pattern matching facilities based on regular expressions, but it was the first such language to achieve widespread acceptance. Combined with powerful built-in data types, such as associative arrays, Perl's text processing facilities made it suitable for many of the tasks typically performed by CGI scripts, and for a while it was the most popular language used for that purpose. Perl's syntax is highly unconventional – at least, it was when the language was first released, but it has now influenced several other languages. For instance, the names of variables must begin with a non-alphabetic character, such as $, @ or %, and the initial character indicates the general type of the variable. The meaning of certain operators and other constructs may depend on the context in which they appear. Perl's detractors consider the language unreadable, while its enthusiasts claim that it is more natural and closer to the way most people think than the more mathematical notations used in mainstream languages.

Like most software, Perl has gone through a number of versions. Perl 5 introduced modules and object-oriented facilities of a sort. This made it possible to encapsulate the interface to HTTP requests in a convenient form, as an object with properties corresponding to the request data, and methods for constructing a response. Modules also provide convenient access to databases.

Server-side Perl scripts can now be executed efficiently, by way of an Apache module, `mod_perl`, or within the ASP.NET framework. Various expedients exist for using Perl as an embedded language.

Python

Python shares many of Perl's characteristics, especially built-in high-level data types and an extensive library, but lacks some of its more extreme syntactical peculiarities, although it has a few of its own. It does not share Perl's reliance on punctuation characters, and its variable names look like JavaScript names, but Python is one of a small number of languages that rely on indentation to express program structure. Compound statements are not surrounded by curly brackets, as they are in JavaScript and most other programming languages, but are simply indented.

Regular expression pattern matching is not part of the language, but is provided in the form of a library module. Python's object-oriented features are more fully developed and integrated than Perl's. Like Perl, Python is a general-purpose language; Web programming is only one of many things it is used for.

Python's library includes a module for CGI programming, which presents the data from a request in a convenient form. An Apache module is available for more efficient execution.

As well as Python itself, there is an alternative implementation known as Jython, which is Python implemented in Java and using the Java Virtual Machine. Jython code may be embedded in XHTML documents, using the PSP (Python Server Pages) scripting engine.

While it would be misleading to talk about rivalry between programming languages, it is the case that Perl and Python do much the same job, but in different ways, and each has its own advocates and detractors. Subjectively, it appears that Perl is declining in popularity, while Python is becoming more popular, especially in Europe.

Ruby

Ruby was invented in Japan in the early 1990s. It only became widely known in the West a few years later, with the translation of the documentation into English, and the publication of English-language books. Since then, it has become increasingly popular around the world, because of its powerful object-oriented features and simple expressive syntax – which avoids the worst eccentricities of Perl – combined with the support for high-level data structures and regular expression found in Perl and Python.

Whereas Perl and Python are basically procedural languages with object-oriented features, Ruby is object-oriented through and through. Everything in a Ruby program is an object, including basic data types like numbers and strings; regular expressions and functions are also objects. Everything is accomplished through method calls; even the arithmetic operators are technically methods. New control structures can be created out of the basic method-calling mechanism by passing blocks of code to methods.

Once again, we find an extensive library, including modules for querying databases and a module for interfacing with HTTP request data to facilitate CGI programming. There is also an Apache module, for efficient execution of Ruby scripts inside the server, and a pre-processor, `eruby`, for allowing Ruby code to be embedded in XHTML documents.

Heightened interest in Ruby was sparked by the release in 2005 of a Web application framework known as ***Ruby on Rails***, which was used to create several high-profile 'Web 2.0' sites.

PHP

The languages described so far are all general-purpose languages that have been heavily used in Web applications, for which some mechanism for embedding scripts in Web pages has been devised after the event. In contrast, **PHP** (which fatuously stands for PHP: Hypertext Processor) was designed from the start as an embedded language. Although it can be used from a command line, most PHP scripts are executed using a server module, or at a pinch, via CGI or FastCGI. Nearly all Apache installations come with the `mod_php` module included, so PHP support is almost ubiquitous.

Considered as a piece of programming language design, PHP is inelegant and crude. It shares some of Perl's quirks, such as the use of variable names that begin with $ signs, but lacks the shorthands and syntactical alternatives that allow Perl to support different styles of programming. The object-oriented features are basic.

PHP's strengths are its simplicity (and hence ease of learning), its vast library, and the ease with which it can be embedded in Web pages. It is an Open Source project, and can be used in conjunction with almost any Web server. Many Web hosting providers make PHP available at little or no charge, which means that sites that are dependent on such services can generally rely on PHP, whereas some other server-side technologies may be supplied at a premium cost, if at all. (However, hosting providers are notoriously slow at updating their software, and so the most widely available version of PHP is PHP 4, although the later PHP 5 offers improved support for objects.)

Java

Unlike most languages used for server-side programming, Java is statically typed, which means that all variables must be declared and permanently assigned a type. Only values of that type may then be stored in the variable. Java has extensive support for defining classes of objects; the type associated with a variable is usually a class, so that there is a well-defined set of operations that can be applied to any value which can be stored in the variable. This allows the compiler to perform many checks which otherwise must be deferred until run-time, so that many errors can be caught before a program is actually executed. This makes the language more verbose than a dynamically typed language like Perl, and requires that programmers think carefully about the classes required by any program. There is sharp disagreement between those who claim that this makes programs more reliable, and those who maintain that it forces programmers to do extra work to satisfy the requirements of the language, instead of just getting on with the job in hand. In the end, it is probably a matter of temperament, and will depend upon whether you are happier writing programs in a statically typed or a dynamically typed language.

Java programs are, as you probably know, compiled to the instruction set of a virtual machine, whose instructions are executed by an interpreter. In theory, all Java Virtual Machines (JVMs) interpret the instructions identically, so that Java programs can run without change or recompilation on any machine that provides a JVM. Reality falls a little way short of this ideal, but as a general rule, Java programs are highly portable. The language is heavily used in the enterprise environment, and in embedded systems.

When it was first introduced, though, one of Java's main applications was in client-side Web programming. A Java program can take the form of an ***applet***, which is a compiled program that can be downloaded and executed in a Web browser, using the JVM on the client machine. Applets can be embedded in Web pages, using the `object` element (or the deprecated `applet` element). Because implementations of Java are not as uniform as they are supposed to be, applets sometimes fail to work on all platforms. For many purposes, including animation and rich interactivity, they have been superseded by the use of plug-ins and AJAX.

Applets are still often preferred for carrying out secure transactions through Web sites; they are especially popular for on-line banking.

Java is now more often used on the server side. Because of the way it is implemented, Java programs cannot be executed using CGI or the equivalent mechanisms used for other languages. Instead, a special type of server, called a *servlet container*, is used, which is capable of loading and executing certain compiled Java programs, called *servlets*. Servlet containers may be self-contained programs, such as Jakarta Tomcat, or extensions to conventional HTTP servers. Servlets run inside the container, they are not executed as separate processes, so they are more efficient than CGI scripts.

Technically, a servlet is an object belonging to a class that implements the `javax.servlet` interface. What this means is that it must belong to a class that has a set of methods for handling requests from a client. Each such method receives an argument that supplies it with the usual collection of request data, as well as a means of writing its output to an HTTP response to be sent back to the client.

Because servlets are just Java programs, they can make use of the extensive Java APIs. In particular, they can use JDBC to access databases. Since Java is widely used in large enterprises, servlets make it easy to integrate Web applications with other systems, and make corporate information and services available through the Web.

Like CGI scripts, servlets often contain many print statements that write XHTML to the output stream. *Java Server Pages (JSP)* provide a form of embedded servlet. JSP does not simply allow the embedding of Java code amongst XHTML markup, though. Instead, a programmer can create a Java class implementing the `javax.servlet.jsp.tagext.SimpleTag` interface and associate it with an XML element type, by way of a configuration file. A collection of such classes is called a *custom tag library*; it defines a namespace for all the XML element types associated with the classes it contains. A JSP document that uses a custom tag library can contain ordinary XHTML elements together with XML elements from the library. The document will be well-formed XML. When the document is processed, objects of the appropriate class are created for the custom elements. These objects will have a standard collection of methods, defined by the interface that they implement, which are executed at certain points in the processing of the page. In particular, the `dotag()` method is executed when the element is encountered. The values of any attributes of the element and its content are made available to this method. It can write output, which is substituted for the element in the processed document.

A *Standard Tag Library (STL)*, which provides facilities for most commonly required tasks is available to JSP programmers. Simple Web applications can be created using just the elements of the STL, without the need for any Java programming. In addition, JSP 2.0 has a rudimentary scripting language, called simply *Expression Language*, which can be used for embedding dynamically computed values in a JSP page. Finally, if all else fails, it is possible to embed arbitrary Java code directly in a page.

JSP is commonly combined with servlets. The servlets deal with data sent in HTTP requests, and pass their results to JSP pages, which are processed to create the corresponding response, in the form of an XHTML document.

ECMAScript

On the face of it, ECMAScript (i.e. the JavaScript core language that you use to manipulate the objects of the DOM) is an ideal candidate for use as a language for server-side scripting. Because it is designed to accommodate different host systems, via host objects, it can be adapted to this purpose by the use of a Server Object Model (SOM). Such a SOM would be analogous to the DOM, and comprise objects suitable for server-side scripting, including objects containing the request data. Since Web designers are likely to be familiar with ECMAScript from using it for DOM scripting, less learning will be involved than if a different language was used.

Nevertheless, ECMAScript is rarely used in this way. Netscape's Enterprise Server supports 'server-side JavaScript', that is, ECMAScript with a SOM. Mozilla Rhino provides a way of allowing ECMAScript to manipulate Java objects, which can provide a sort of Server Object Model; it has been incorporated into various Java-based servers, and can be made available to Apache via a module, but ECMAScript, in the guise of JavaScript, is used much more for client-side than for server-side scripting.

Frameworks

Most Web applications have to do many of the same things: query and update databases, handle request data, format and display results, and so on. This makes Web application development somewhat repetitive. An obvious step is to produce a framework for applications, which incorporates all the commonly required code, and allows the developer to plug in only those parts which are specific to a particular application.

Many Web applications conform to what is known as the *Model-View-Controller (MVC)* design pattern. That is, logically they consist of three components: the *model* is concerned with organizing and manipulating the application's data; the *view* with presenting it to the user; the *controller* interacts with the model and view, in response to user input. In Web applications the data is usually held in a database, so the model comprises the code for updating and querying the database. Data is presented in the form of Web pages, so the view is concerned with building XHTML documents incorporating values obtained from the model. The controller will consist of code that takes data from incoming HTTP requests, and invokes the model and view to retrieve information and send it back to the user.

This three-way division into model, view and controller tends to fall out naturally in Web applications that are written by hand. It is used more formally in the design of Web application frameworks. These provide a means of creating a model by mapping rows of a database to objects, and creating a view by embedding code or tags in XHTML documents. Typically, the logic that is specific to a particular application resides in its controller. A framework will provide scaffolding in the form of code that ties together the model and view, and a means of extending and customizing it to create the complete application.

In theory, Web application development frameworks should save a lot of time and effort by removing the need to write the repetitive code for interacting with databases and so on, leaving the developer free to concentrate on the necessary coding. In practice, their benefits are offset by the requirement to master the requirements and conventions of each framework. The documentation for some frameworks runs to hundreds of pages, and although the amount of code that must be written tends to be relatively small, many frameworks require you to conform to a precise directory structure and to provide configuration files. These are usually XML documents, conforming to a DTD specific to the framework, which describe how the various components of your application fit together and interact. For small applications, it may be quicker to write everything by hand.

Among the well-known application frameworks in use for Web development are *Jakarta Struts*, *Zope* and *Ruby on Rails*, which work with Java, Python and Ruby, respectively.

Ready-Made Applications

The easiest, and often the best, way to implement a Web application is by using somebody else's code.

Web applications are particularly well served by the **Open Source** movement. Although the central tenet of Open Source is the distribution of source code so that it can be debugged and enhanced by its users, for many people the overriding attraction of Open Source software

Terminology

LAMP

Many Open Source projects are built on the combination of the Linux operating system, Apache Web server, MySQL database management system and PHP, collectively known by the acronym LAMP. The P can also stand for Perl or Python (or Ruby, though this last possibility presents certain orthographical problems). LAMP is not really a platform: PHP scripts can work with almost any Web server and DBMS; none of the A, M and P components is tied to Linux. LAMP is more of an ideological statement, since all four elements are released under some form of Open Source licence (whatever you take the P to stand for). LAMP effectively stands for freely distributed, collaboratively developed Web application software that is not tied to any corporation or proprietary formats.

is that it is free of charge. Whereas commercial packages may offer superior functions or be better supported, their cost is often prohibitive for individuals and small organizations. Open Source software, on the other hand, presents no financial barriers.

Open Source applications are available for tasks as simple as adding a guestbook to a site or as complicated as a complete on-line shop, complete with catalogue, special offers, shopping basket and checkout facilities. Image galleries, Web-based project management tools, e-learning systems, Web portals, blogs, forums and wikis can all be obtained free, without the need for any programming.

Almost all systems of this sort provide some means for each Web site built from them to customize aspects of their appearance, so that it is not the case that every site based on a particular system looks just the same. Usually, the site's pages are built from templates, consisting of markup interspersed with variables that represent values generated by the underlying server-side programs. These templates can be customized to a greater or lesser extent by somebody who understands the markup. Styling and layout should be done using CSS, so the surface appearance of the pages can easily be changed by editing stylesheets.

There are disadvantages to using ready-made Web applications. The most serious problem is that the documentation accompanying these systems is often poor, incomplete or even non-existent. Frequently, there are excellent detailed installation instructions, and lengthy descriptions of how to write extensions to the system, but almost nothing on how to use it for its intended purpose. (This seems to be a characteristic failing of Open Source projects, where more effort is devoted to making the program accessible to the rest of the developer community than to making its operation comprehensible to end users.) In an effort to make the system useful to as large an audience as possible, programs tend to acquire extensive lists of features that will only be of use to a few people.

As well as this, using somebody else's code means relying on them to do a good job. Even though you may not feel adequate to the task of writing complicated server-side programs, you may feel that you know plenty about XHTML markup and CSS stylesheets. You may find, though, that you do not have any control over the quality of the generated code, and end up with a site that uses non-standard markup or fails to meet accessibility criteria, because the application's developer does not share your concerns about these matters and does not provide ways of customizing the code adequately.

Basing an entire Web site on a single third-party application may be fairly straighforward, especially if you are happy with the default layout, but integrating something like a Web forum using an Open Source package into a hand-coded site can present problems. The degree to which the package can be customized may not make it possible to blend the forums in with the layout of the rest of the site. It might make extensive use of icons, for example, while the rest of the site avoids them; or it may use colours with a significance which they lack elsewhere. This sort of divergence of design ideas cannot be solved simply by hacking a stylesheet.

Because of the potential problems, and the sheer range of systems on offer, choosing a ready-made Web application can be a difficult business, requiring extensive research. If possible, local test sites should be set up to evaluate different systems before a commitment is made that will tie a production site to the final choice of system.

Content Management Systems

Content Management Systems (CMS) are among the most powerful Web application packages that are available. Their job is to create Web pages dynamically from content (text, images and so on) that is stored and organized in a database. Content is retrieved from the database and combined with templates to create the pages of the site. A typical page template will consist of some XHTML boiler-plate, and placeholders for navbars, breadcrumbs and blocks of content. When the page is generated, these placeholders are filled in with values from the database. If you find it helpful, you can think of a CMS as an MVC framework in which only the view can be modified.

The model of site development and maintenance behind Content Management Systems is that a designer creates the templates, thereby determining the site's appearance, and then the content is added by one or more editors, whose only concern is with writing text and choosing images and other embedded media. A site built on a CMS separates content from presentation, and provides a way for non-technically minded editors to contribute to the site. A CMS therefore presents two interfaces: a visitors' interface, and an editors' interface. The visitors' interface consists of the generated pages containing the site's content. The editors' interface consists of form elements for adding new content and specifying how it is to fit into the site's structure.

Blogging systems are a very successful special case of Content Management Systems. Here, the blogger takes on the editor's role, and the templates and logic of the system present entries in a chronological order, and also provide classification, searching and archiving facilities.

The functions of a CMS can be summarized as follows.

Content Creation

The editors' interface provides a means of writing content that is not, in itself, valid XHTML, but just text. Often, styling controls are supplied in the manner of word processors, to control typography, alignment, and so on. Their effect is to insert appropriate markup or class attributes, so that when the content is converted to XHTML it will have the appropriate styling. For some systems, a desktop client can be used instead of a Web page for creating the content. This is a program that runs on the editor's machine, and communicates with the CMS proper on the server. Such clients allow the editor to create, revise and proof-read their content before sending it to the CMS for incorporation into a site.

Uploading

Implicit in the content creation function is the ability to upload material to the server. Normally, files must be uploaded to the server using FTP. This requires the user to be able to use an FTP client, and to understand the directory structure of the site. With a CMS, uploading is usually done using HTTP. The data is sent, either by submitting a form or from a desktop client, to a server script, which stores it in a database or an appropriate location in the site's directory structure. This is more convenient for the editor, who will in general not be technically knowledgeable, and it also prevents any possibility of accidentally overwriting files or otherwise corrupting the site.

Presentation

The fundamental job of a CMS is to combine content with markup to generate Web pages. As well as markup and styling, various features may be added to the pages, such as calendars (for chronologically organized sites), and email links. The CMS may also support site features, such as searching, commenting, and RSS feeds.

Archiving

Most Content Management Systems offer facilities for archiving. Archives may be visible to visitors to the site, as is usually the case for blogs, or they may just be used to preserve out-of-date content, in case it is ever required again. Advanced systems may use the archive to provide a means of rolling back the site, that is, undoing recent changes.

Collaboration

Few large Web sites are created and managed by a single person. A CMS can support collaboration among teams of contributors. Users of the system can be registered and granted different privileges. Some will not be allowed to post content directly, but only to submit it for approval; others will only be allowed to change certain parts of the site. There must be a system administrator with the power to register new users and grant them privileges. Usually, an administrative interface for performing such functions is provided as part of the CMS.

Databases

Almost all Web sites that use server-side programs make use of data stored on the server. For all but the most simple sites, this data is organized as a **relational database**, and the program must interact with a **database management system (DBMS)** in order to store data in and retrieve it from the database. MySQL and Postgresql are Open Source DBMSs which are commonly used in Web applications. Commercial systems used by enterprise sites include Oracle, IBM's Informix products and Microsoft SQL Server.

As well as providing facilities for storing data, a DBMS must also provide a means of retrieving data that satisfies certain conditions. Retrieval of data is performed using a **query language**: a simple language designed for the purpose. Query languages also provide ways of creating and administering the database and entering, changing and deleting data. DBMSs must also provide a way of defining the structure of a database – how the stored data is organized. This is done using a **data definition language**.

All serious DBMSs, including those mentioned in the first paragraph of this section, use **SQL**, an ANSI/ISO standard combined query language and data definition language.

Web applications that interact with databases need some interface to SQL. This is usually provided in a programming language by library functions or methods; Web application frameworks often disguise the interface, by mapping values stored in the database to objects.

Maintaining large databases can be demanding: they must be kept secure, backed up safely, and configured to optimize performance. Constraints on the integrity of the data must be enforced. Where a Web application is heavily dependent on a large database it may be necessary to appoint a database administrator to take responsibility for the design and day-to-day maintenance of the database.

Modern database management systems use the client/server model, just as the Web does. The hard work is done by a database server, which handles the efficient storage and retrieval of the data. For small applications, the database is usually stored on the machine on which the server is running, but for sites that need to store large amounts of data and process many requests it may be distributed across several machines. Clients establish connections to the server and then send requests for various services, such as storing some values, or retrieving data from the database. These requests take the form of SQL statements. Users only interact with the database indirectly through a client. Clients may run on the same machine as the server, but often they will run on the user's own machine and send requests to the server over a network. If a Web application interacts with a database, the server-side script must be able to send requests to a database server, so in effect it is a database client whose user interface is provided over the Web.

We will briefly review some database concepts, in a suitably simplified form, before looking at how databases are used in Web applications.

Relational Database Concepts

Almost all modern database management systems employ the relational model of data. The database is organized as a collection of tables, each of which contains rows of data.

title	date	category	rating
Sunset Clouds	2005	Sky/Clouds	****
The Sea	2002	Sea	*****
Orange Flowers	2002	Flowers	****
Blue Flower	2003	Flowers	***

Figure 8.1 A database table

title	date	category	rating
Sunset Clouds	2005	Sky/Clouds	****
The Sea	2002	Sea	*****
		Blue-grey	
Orange Flowers	2002	Flowers	****
		Orange	
Blue Flower	2003	Flowers	***
		Blue-grey	

Figure 8.2 A table with multiple values

(Formally, the rows are tuples of values, so a table corresponds to the mathematical notion of an *n*-ary relation, hence the name of the data model.) Figure 8.1 shows part of a typical database table. (Compare this with the representation of the same data in XML used in Chapter 7.) As in a table used for displaying information, the columns have names, which can be used to identify each of the elements of any row. For example, the rating value of the third row of this table is the string ****.

An important property of the tables used in relational databases is that each cell contains a single value. The values which can be stored in systems that implement the SQL standard may be integers or floating point numbers with different numbers of bits and degrees of precision, strings of various sizes, dates, times, and 'blobs' – binary large objects, which can be used for storing arbitrary collections of bits, such as digital images. Values may also be null. There is, however, no provision for storing lists of values in a single table cell, and nothing equivalent to the column- and row-spanning cells available in XHTML tables. Every cell must either be null or contain a single value of one of the available types.

This restriction can sometimes lead to a counter-intuitive representation of information. Suppose, for instance, an image could potentially belong to more than one category. For example, we might want to classify some images according to their dominant colour, as well as their subject. The obvious way of representing this in a table would be as shown in Figure 8.2. You might imagine that the computer representation of the data would use something like an array for the category, to accommodate multiple values, but this is not permitted in relational databases. Instead, the data must be represented as shown in Figure 8.3.

The table shown in Figure 8.3 exhibits some undesirable characteristics, though. Most obviously, the information that the image entitled *The Sea* was made in 2002 and is rated *****

title	date	category	rating
Sunset Clouds	2005	Sky/Clouds	****
The Sea	2002	Sea	*****
The Sea	2002	Blue-grey	*****
Orange Flowers	2002	Flowers	****
Orange Flowers	2002	Orange	****
Blue Flower	2003	Flowers	***
Blue Flower	2003	Blue-grey	***

Figure 8.3 A relational database table with multiple values

is duplicated, as is the corresponding information about two other images. This doesn't necessarily mean that the values are actually stored twice: the tables of a relational database represent the logical organization of the data, so it may be stored on disk in quite a different way. However, operations on the database must respect this logical organization, and duplication can lead to problems. For instance, if the rating of *The Sea* is changed to ****, the value must be changed in two places, or the database will become inconsistent. If *The Sea* is assigned to yet another category, a complete row must be added, with the same date and rating values. Again, if this update is performed incorrectly, the database will become inconsistent. Deleting data from this table can have unintended effects. If the row for *Sunset Clouds* is deleted, the fact that there is a category *Sky/Clouds* is no longer represented in the database, although removing either of the rows for *Blue Flower* does not cause any category to disappear. Conversely, we cannot record the fact that there is a category *Pink*, because no image belongs to it. By rearranging the data, these possibilities can be eliminated.

Figure 8.4 shows how the data from Figure 8.3 can be redistributed among three tables. The images table collects together information that uniquely depends on the particular image: its title, date and rating. This means that there is no need for duplication. (In fact, there is no possibility of it. A relation is a set, which means that no two rows can be identical.) The categories have their own table. The names of the categories are recorded independently of any image, so deleting the row for an image will never cause a category to be lost from the database, and categories can be added before any image belongs to them. To record the assignment of images to categories, a third table is used. This pairs off images with categories. To make this easier and more efficient, each image and category has been assigned a unique identifier. The categorization table consists of pairs of these identifiers. If an image's identifier appears next to a category's identifier, the corresponding image belongs to that category. You should satisfy yourself that any data that could be recorded in the single table

images

id	title	date	rating
1	Sunset Clouds	2005	****
2	The Sea	2002	*****
3	Orange Flowers	2002	****
4	Blue Flower	2003	***

categories

id	name
1	Flowers
2	Sky/Clouds
3	Sea
4	Orange
5	Blue-grey

categorization

imgid	catid
1	2
2	3
2	5
3	1
3	4
4	1
4	5

Figure 8.4 Normalized tables

of Figure 8.3 can also be recorded using these three tables, and that this improved representation can be updated without the risk of inconsistency or loss of information.

A database that is organized so that insertion, deletion and modification operations can be performed without such risk is said to be **normalized**. The concept of a normalized database can be given a precise formal meaning; if you are likely to be designing databases, you should consult a specialized text for more details on this subject. In general, whether or not a particular collection of tables is normalized will depend on constraints on the data – such as whether or not an image can belong to more than one category – that cannot be deduced from the data alone. It may be worth noting that tables with only two columns are always normalized, but this is not a necessary condition.

A description of the structure of a database, in the form of a list of the names of all the tables, together with the names of their columns and the type of data that may be stored in each column, is called a **database schema**.

SQL

Although SQL stands for Structured Query Language, it allows you to do more than submit queries (statements that retrieve data) to the database. It is also used as a data definition language for defining a database schema by creating tables, and provides facilities for creating databases, inserting, updating and deleting rows, registering users and controlling their privileges, setting options to optimize performance, and other administrative tasks. Normally, though, the creation of tables and all the administrative functions are performed by the database administrator, using a client program (which may use a Web page as its interface) that provides a graphical user interface, so that the details of the SQL syntax for these operations need not concern casual users or writers of Web scripts. However, server-side programs that manipulate data in a database must use SQL to insert, delete and change stored values and to retrieve data.

SQL is a relatively verbose language, which uses English keywords with approximately their colloquial meanings to construct statements that describe the operation to be performed. This makes it easy to see roughly what is meant by any statement, but you should remember that SQL is a computer language with its own very specific semantics; do not be deceived by the similarity to natural language – sometimes the words don't mean exactly what they appear to.

Despite appearances, SQL is extremely powerful, and permits data to be combined and retrieved according to complex and subtle conditions. Space does not permit anything like a full description of the language here. We will describe the bare minimum to enable us to make use of SQL in our example Web applications. If you need to know more, consult a good textbook on databases.

Retrieval

The simplest SQL queries retrieve specified columns from a single table. They take the form

```
select columns from table ;
```

where *columns* is a list of column names separated by commas, and *table* is the name of a table. For instance, referring to the normalized images database illustrated in Figure 8.4, we could retrieve the names of all the images with the following query:

```
select title from images;
```

If we wanted their dates as well, the following query would be used:

```
select title, date from images;
```

The abbreviation * is used to stand for all the columns, so

```
select * from images;
```

retrieves the entire `images` table.

The result of a `select` query like this is itself a table. Where queries are performed using a graphical interface or a command line processor, the resulting data is usually displayed in tabular form. We will describe later how the results of a query are passed to a program.

Although we stated earlier that a relation is a set and could not contain duplicate rows, tables returned by select queries do not respect this restriction. For instance, with the data in Figure 8.4, the query

```
select catid from categorization;
```

returns a table with seven rows, containing the values 2, 3, 5, 1, 4, 1 and 5. To obtain a table consisting of the category ids which had been applied to some image, the keyword `distinct` must be used before the column names, like this:

```
select distinct catid from categorization;
```

which returns the desired table of five rows, each containing a different value.

There is no intrinsic ordering to the rows of a table. In practice, they are often ordered according to when they were added to the table, but this cannot be relied on. If it is important that the rows retrieved by a query be in some particular order, this can be specified explicitly, by adding `order  by`, followed by a column name, to the end of the query. For instance,

```
select * from images order by date;
```

will retrieve the rows of the `images` table in chronological order. (If you wish to reverse the order, you can add the keyword `desc`, for descending, right at the end of the query.)

Often, you only want to retrieve certain rows, which satisfy some condition. This is done by adding a clause of the form

```
where condition
```

after the table name in a `select` statement. The condition can take many forms. For our purposes, we only need to consider ones that compare the value in a column with either a constant or the value in some other column. For these, the usual comparison operators are available. Unlike JavaScript, SQL uses the conventional = operator for testing equality, and <> for inequality. The query

```
select * from images where date = 2002;
```

will retrieve the rows from all those images made in 2002, while

```
select title, rating from images where date <> 2002 order by date
desc;
```

will retrieve the title and rating for images made in any other year, in reverse chronological order. Note that the date column can be used for ordering the rows, even though it does not appear in the final result of the query.

Because normalization usually requires logically connected information to be distributed among several tables, it is often necessary to combine data from more than one table in a query. This is done by specifying a list of tables instead of just one following the `from` keyword in a `select` query. For example, to select the title of each image together with the id of any category it was assigned to, the following query could be used:

```
select title, catid from images, categorization where imgid=id;
```

One way of understanding queries involving two tables is to imagine that they are executed by creating a new table by combining each row of the first table with each row of the second. Any condition following the `where` keyword is then applied to this combined table, and specified columns are picked out to produce the result. This operation is loosely referred to as a *join* of the two tables. (Various different types of join are formally defined.)

Figure 8.5 shows how this would work for the query just given. The complete table shown in the figure is created by pairing off the rows of `images` and `categorization`. (It has 28 rows,

id	title	date	rating	imgid	catid
1	Sunset Clouds	2005	****	1	2
2	The Sea	2002	*****	1	2
3	Orange Flowers	2002	****	1	2
4	Blue Flower	2003	***	1	2
1	Sunset Clouds	2005	****	2	3
2	The Sea	2002	*****	2	3
3	Orange Flowers	2002	****	2	3
4	Blue Flower	2003	***	2	3
1	Sunset Clouds	2005	****	3	1
2	The Sea	2002	*****	3	1
3	Orange Flowers	2002	****	3	1
4	Blue Flower	2003	***	3	1
1	Sunset Clouds	2005	****	4	1
2	The Sea	2002	*****	4	1
3	Orange Flowers	2002	****	4	1
4	Blue Flower	2003	***	4	1
1	Sunset Clouds	2005	****	2	5
2	The Sea	2002	*****	2	5
3	Orange Flowers	2002	****	2	5
4	Blue Flower	2003	***	2	5
1	Sunset Clouds	2005	****	3	4
2	The Sea	2002	*****	3	4
3	Orange Flowers	2002	****	3	4
4	Blue Flower	2003	***	3	4
1	Sunset Clouds	2005	****	4	5
2	The Sea	2002	*****	4	5
3	Orange Flowers	2002	****	4	5
4	Blue Flower	2003	***	4	5

Figure 8.5 Joining two tables

title	name
The Sea	Blue-grey
Blue Flower	Blue-grey
Orange Flowers	Flowers
Blue Flower	Flowers
Orange Flowers	Orange
The Sea	Sea
Sunset Clouds	Sky/Clouds

Figure 8.6 The result of a join query involving three tables

since `images` has 4 and `categorization` 7.) The highlighted rows are those satisfying the condition `imgid=id`.

Joins are not restricted to just two tables, and they can be embellished in the same way as simpler queries, to order them or remove duplicates. To find the titles of all the images together with the names of the categories each was assigned to, and order them according to category, the following query could be used.

```
select title, name from images, categories, categorization
where images.id = imgid and categories.id = catid
order by name;
```

The table that results from executing this query on the data in Figure 8.4 is shown in Figure 8.6.

This query illustrates a couple of extra points. Since both images and categories have a column called `id`, it is necessary to distinguish between the two in the query. This is done using a dot notation, similar to that used for objects' properties in JavaScript: `images.id` refers to the `id` column of the `images` table, and `categories.id` to the `id` column of the `categories` table, so each is being compared with the appropriate row from `categorization`. Column names can always be disambiguated in this way, but where they are unique within the query, as in the case of `imgid` and `catid` here, the table name can be omitted, as we have done.

The second point to notice about this query is that the `categorization` table must be specified, even though no columns from it are actually being selected. All tables used in computing the result must be specified after `from` in this form of query. (There is an alternative way of formulating join queries which may be more intuitive in this respect, but for our present purposes we prefer to stick with queries in one style only.)

Inserting, Deleting and Updating Rows

Editing stored data is somewhat simpler than retrieval. Once again, we will only describe the simplest ways of performing these operations. More elaborate variations are possible, but the simple methods suffice in most cases that are likely to be required in server-side scripts.

To insert a new row into a table, an SQL statement such as the following may be used:

```
insert into categories values (6, "Pink");
```

The list of values comprising the row to be inserted is given in brackets; the syntax of the rest of the statement should be self-explanatory.

Deleting rows is done with a `delete` statement, which uses a `where` clause, like that of the `select` statement, to specify the rows to be deleted. Any rows that satisfy the condition will be removed from the database. Hence, to remove the row we just added, we might use the following statement:

```
delete from categories where name = "Pink";
```

Again, the meaning should be self-evident, even if the phrasing is clumsy. A condition might well be satisfied by more than one row, in which case all the rows for which the condition is true will be removed.

It is sometimes necessary to update some values in one or more rows. It is always possible to delete the affected rows and insert new ones, but it may be more convenient or efficient to do the updating in place. Simple `update` statements take the following form:

```
update table set column = value where condition;
```

The effect is to change the value in the named column to the given value in all rows of the table that satisfy the condition. For example, to move all the images in the *Orange* category to the *Pink* category, we could update the `categorization` table in the following way:

```
update categorization set catid = 6 where catid = 4;
```

(The category id for *Orange* is 4, that for *Pink* is 6.)

If the condition is omitted, the update is applied to all the rows of the table. The value may be specified literally, or it may be an expression. If, for some reason, we wished to add 100 to all of the image id values, it could be done like this:

```
update images set id = 100 + id;
```

Notice that doing so would destroy the link between images and categories, which could only be restored by applying a similar update to the `categorization` table. Although advanced DBMSs allow constraints to be specified and enforced, simpler systems like MySQL do not, and rely on programmers and the database administrator to ensure that the integrity of the data is maintained, and the database remains an accurate model of the real world.

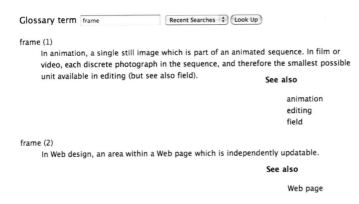

Figure 8.7 The interface to the glossary application

Dynamically Generated Pages

Earlier, we briefly described some of the technologies and languages available for generating Web pages dynamically, using server-side programs. To make this description more concrete, we will now develop a simple example of a Web application. We will use PHP as our implementation language, because of its widespread availability and relative simplicity. Any of the other languages described earlier in this chapter could have been used equally well.

The example is a version of the online glossary from `www.webdesignbook.org`. Figure 8.7 shows the user interface we will provide. At the top of the page is a display of the most popular terms that have been looked up in the glossary. This display takes the currently fashionable form of a 'cloud', with the size of the glossary terms indicating their relative popularity. Below the cloud is a text entry field, for typing a term to be looked up. This is supplemented by a pop-up menu, showing the glossary terms most recently looked up by this user, from which a term may be chosen for looking up again.

When a term is looked up, its definition or definitions are shown at the bottom of the page. As the example shown here demonstrates, some glossary terms have more than one meaning, and this will have to be accommodated in our database as well as in the presentation of definitions. Glossary terms are cross-referenced. We have chosen to pull out cross-references into a separate list, headed **See also**, rather than try to embed links in the text of the definitions. These cross-references will also need to be represented in the database.

Before we start to design the Web application behind this interface, it is worth considering whether it would be possible to provide the same service using static Web pages. A page for each glossary term's definitions presents no problems, but how would a user access them? There are hundreds of terms in our glossary, so putting a set of links on each page would result in a very cluttered interface. You could put intra-page links for each letter of the alphabet to help organize the links for the actual terms, and use imaginative layout to present them in a perspicuous fashion, but you can't get away from the fact that two or three hundred links on a page is too many. To keep the interface manageable, it would be necessary to split it among several hierarchically organized pages, which would require extra clicks from the user, and extra HTTP requests from their browser.

A text input field, like the one in Figure 8.7, could be used in conjunction with some client-side scripting, if each page with a definition had a URL based on the term being defined. (For instance, the definition of bandwidth would be in `definitions/bandwidth.html`.) A script could then create a URL from the text entered, and assign it to `window.location` to fetch the corresponding page. There is no way to make such a script degrade gracefully: users without scripting support would be left out in the cold. In addition, entering a term that was not in the glossary would lead to a URL with no corresponding page, which would result in a standard 404, 'Page not found' error. This is not very helpful to the user.

In principle, the recent searches feature could be implemented on the client side too. A script could be used to store a user's recent searches in cookies, although this is not a very sensible way of keeping the information. When we come to the glossary term cloud, however, there is no way to provide the feature without the use of computation on the server. It relies on storing information about the history of all visits to the page. This information is not tied to any single user; it can only be saved on the server, where the searches of every user are seen.

This last feature can therefore only be provided with the assistance of server-side scripting. The other features could in theory be made to work using scripts running in the client, but if they are implemented on the server instead then they will work for all users, even if their browsers do not support scripting, and can be realized more elegantly and efficiently.

PHP Syntax

Because they both draw on the same influences, notably the C programming language, the similarities in syntax between JavaScript (as described in Chapter 7) and PHP are greater than their differences. They both use the same symbols for common operations on numbers and Boolean values. They use the same syntax for conditional statements and expressions, `while` loops and `for` loops.

There are some differences, though. Most obviously, variables in PHP must have names that begin with a $ sign. The main reason for this would appear to be to make life easier for PHP's implementors, but it also permits variables to be combined with strings in a convenient fashion. If a string in PHP is delimited by double-quote characters, any variable names that appear inside the string are replaced by the variable's current value. For instance, if the variable $i had the value 77, the string

```
"The value of \$i is $i"
```

would have the value

```
The value of $i is 77
```

Notice that we have put a \ character in front of the first $ in the string, to prevent its being interpreted as the start of a variable name. Note also that **_variable interpolation_** – as the replacement of variables inside a string by their values is known – only occurs if a string is delimited by double quotes. Single quotes may also be used as string delimiters, but if they are, no interpolation takes place.

Variables cannot be declared in PHP. When you need a new variable, you just use it. (So you had better be careful that you always type variable names correctly, otherwise you may introduce new ones into your program by accident.)

A minor difference between PHP and JavaScript is that in PHP the operator used for sticking two strings together is ., not +. The difference is minor, but may trip you up. You will appreciate that since this operator exists, variable interpolation is simply a notational convenience.

PHP provides arrays to hold sequences of values. As in JavaScript, arrays are associative, so that the indexes can be numbers or strings. PHP provides some special constructs for iterating over arrays. We only need one of these, the `foreach` loop. If `$a` is an array with numerical indexes,

```
foreach ($a as $x) statement
```

has the effect of executing _statement_ once for each element of `$a`. Within _statement_, the variable `$x` holds the value of the current element. Similarly, if `$aa` is an array with string indexes,

```
foreach ($aa as $k => $v) statement
```

executes statement repeatedly, with `$k` and `$v` holding the key (index) and value of each element of `$aa` in succession.

Functions are defined in PHP in the same way as in JavaScript, and they are usually called in the same way. However, there is a variant form of call: if the function name is prefixed by an @ sign, any errors that occur within the called function will be ignored. Normally, certain types of error cause PHP to write an error message to its standard output. This can be undesirable, since these messages will get mixed up with the script's real output, and may invalidate it. If these messages are suppressed using @, the script can perform its own, more appropriate, error handling.

Unlike JavaScript, PHP provides a way to define named constants. That is, you can define a name for a value, and use the name wherever the value is required, but unlike a variable, you can never change the value associated with the name. Defining constants makes scripts more readable, and makes it easy to change the values of parameters – such as the number of recent searches to include in the pop-up menu in our glossary application – without having to search for them throughout the script. By convention, the names of constants consist entirely of upper-case letters. They are defined using the appropriately named define function, which takes two arguments. The first is a string comprising the constant's name, the second is its value. For example, the following definition will be used in the glossary application to set the number of recent searches:

```php
define("HISTLEN", 10);
```

It can be convenient to divide PHP applications into separate files. For instance, one file might contain the definitions of all the functions used in the application, another might contain definitions of configuration constants, while another would contain XHTML markup, interspersed with calls to the functions. The require function is used to include external files. It takes a string containing the URL of the file to be included as its argument. In the example just given, the markup file would use require to include the function definitions, which in turn would use it to include the configuration file. You will see this pattern used in our example Web application.

PHP deals with objects in quite a different way from JavaScript. Its object-oriented facilities only really matured with the release of PHP 5, so objects do not play an important role in most PHP scripts. There is nothing comparable to the concept of host objects, or the DOM. The bulk of the extensive PHP library takes the form of functions, not objects. Probably the majority of PHP programmers still favour a procedural style of programming, based on passing values to functions rather than calling methods through objects. To avoid burdening you with the details of PHP's object support, we will develop our example Web application in a procedural style.

As we mentioned earlier, a PHP script is a document with PHP code embedded in it. The PHP must be enclosed between the characters <?php and ?>. In all our examples, everything outside these delimiters will be XHTML. The embedded PHP code is executed and replaced by anything it writes to standard output. Most PHP installations also allow a shorter syntax for an important special case. A sequence of the form <?= *expression* ?> is replaced by the value of the expression. (If your PHP installation has not been configured to allow the shorthand form, use <?php echo *expression* ?> instead.)

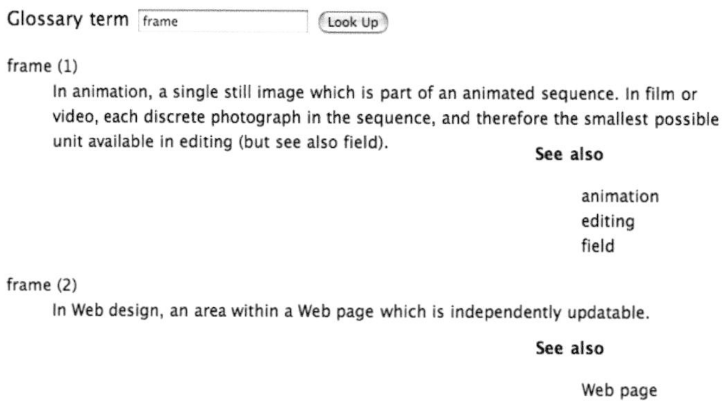

Glossary term [frame   ]   (Look Up)

frame (1)

    In animation, a single still image which is part of an animated sequence. In film or video, each discrete photograph in the sequence, and therefore the smallest possible unit available in editing (but see also field).

        See also

            animation
            editing
            field

frame (2)

    In Web design, an area within a Web page which is independently updatable.

        See also

            Web page

Figure 8.8 The interface to the simplified glossary application

The Glossary Database

We will begin with a simplified version of the glossary application, which only provides a basic interface, consisting of a text entry field for entering a glossary term and a submit button, and looks up the term, displaying its definitions with any cross-references. (We will add the glossary term cloud and recent searches menu in later sections.) Figure 8.8 shows this simplified interface.

All that the database for this first version needs to do is record the definition or definitions of each term, and the corresponding cross-references. As we pointed out when originally describing the glossary application, some terms will have more than one definition, and the cross-references are associated with a definition, not with a term. (In theory, two glossary terms might have identical definitions, so it would be more correct to say that the cross-references are associated with a combination of term and definition.) For example, *frame* has two distinct meanings, one in the context of animation and video, the other in the context of Web pages. Cross-references to glossary terms such as *animation* and *field* are only relevant to the first meaning.

The database schema must therefore associate terms with their definitions, and definitions with cross-referenced terms. Figure 8.9 shows how this can be done. The `term` and `definition` columns of the `glossary` table create the required association between terms and their definitions. The `id` column identifies a particular definition of some term. The `xrefs` table then provides the cross-reference association. (This is not the only possible schema. You might prefer to give each term its own `id` as well, for example.)

glossary

id	term	definition
96	font	A collection of glyphs sharing the same basic design so that they are visually related and work well together for the display of text.
97	fps	Frames per second. The units in which frame-rate is usually measured.
98	frame	In animation, a single still image which is part of an animated sequence. In film or video, each discrete photograph in the sequence, and therefore the smallest possible unit available in editing (but see also field).
99	frame	In Web design, an area within a Web page which is independently updatable.
100	frame-rate	A way of specifying the speed of playback of a sequence of video, film or animation.

xrefs

id	term
96	glyph
97	frame
97	frame-rate
98	animation
98	editing
98	field
99	Web page
100	animation

Figure 8.9 Database tables for the simple glossary application

Before the glossary application can be run, a database must be created according to this schema, and the terms, definitions and cross-references must be entered into it. How this is done is not the concern of the Web application. Ultimately, somebody will have had to type all the data.

With the database set up, the following query will retrieve the id and definitions of the term *frame*:

```
select id, definition from glossary where term ="frame";
```

and the following will retrieve an alphabetically ordered list of all the terms cross-referenced from the definition with `id` equal to 98:

```
select term from xrefs where id = 98 order by term;
```

Queries with these general forms will be needed in our PHP script when it comes to looking up definitions and cross-references.

Accessing the Data from PHP

The PHP library includes functions for passing queries to a DBMS and carrying out other operations on a database. Unfortunately, each DBMS has its own set of functions, which means that a script must be targeted at some particular DBMS. We choose to store our glossary database using MySQL, and use the corresponding functions to interact with it. (PHP 5 provides an alternative object-oriented interface to MySQL, but this is not universally available.) We will wrap the calls to the raw library functions in our own functions, to provide an extra layer of abstraction that conceals some details.

Recall that DBMSs use the client/server model. Before a script can send queries to MySQL, it must establish a connection to the MySQL server and select a database. (A single MySQL server can support several different named databases.) The functions `mysql_connect` and `mysql_select_db` are used for these two preliminary operations. Either one may fail – the server may be down or inaccessible, authentication may fail, the selected database may not exist, and so on.

To connect to a MySQL server, three pieces of information must be supplied: the host name or IP address, a user name, and a password. Access to the database must have been granted to the named user by the database administrator. This is an operation that lies outside the scope of our script; we will assume that it has been done. On security grounds, it is highly advisable to create a database user with the minimum privileges for carrying out database operations in a script. In particular, the user whose name a script uses to connect to the DBMS should not be able to grant privileges to other users or to create new users.

For convenience, the host name, user name and password can be defined as constants in a separate configuration file, together with the database name that will be needed when `mysql_select_db` is called. This file may be kept in a directory outside the HTTP server's document hierarchy, to add an extra measure of security. The values of the constants will depend on the configuration of the particular database, but the file will look something like this:

```php
<?php
define("HOST", "127.0.0.1");
define ("USER", "dbuser");
define("PASSWORD", "secret");
define("DBNAME", "webinfo");
?>
```

The file containing these definitions, which we will call config.inc, will be included in our main script using require. Whenever PHP starts processing a new file, it starts out by assuming that it contains marked-up text which will be used unchanged as the output; it only starts treating text as PHP code when it encounters an opening <?php sequence. This rule applies to any file. In particular, when a file is included using require, PHP reverts to its markup processing mode. Hence, if such a file consists only of PHP code, as config.inc does, it must begin with <?php and end with the matching ?>. It is important that no blank lines precede or follow the PHP code.

Instead of embedding calls to the raw MySQL functions in our code we will write our own functions, thereby isolating the dependency on MySQL, and allowing us to confine the necessary error handling to one place. This forces us to confront the question of what to do if something goes wrong when the script is executing. To begin with, we assume that there is a function called give_up, which takes an error message as its argument and does something appropriate if we have to abandon an attempt to look up a glossary term as a result of some error we cannot recover from.

Assuming give_up exists, we can use the following function to connect to the MySQL server and select a database:

```php
function db_connect() {
  $link = @mysql_connect(HOST, USER, PASSWORD );
  if (!$link) give_up("could not connect to the database server");
  $select = @mysql_select_db(DBNAME, $link);
  if (!$select) give_up("could not select the database");
  return $link;
}
```

The constants defined in `config.inc` are used by `db_connect`, so a line such as the following must appear in the file in which it is defined:

```
require("config.inc");
```

(If, as we recommend, the configuration file is kept outside the document hierarchy, a more complicated path will be needed.)

If it succeeds, the library function `mysql_connect` returns a value referred to as a link identifier, which is used by some other library functions. If it fails, it returns `false`, so in the second line of `db_connect` we test the returned value, which we have assigned to the variable `$link`, and if it is not `true`, we give up. Notice that the call to `mysql_connect` is prefixed by an @ sign; this prevents any failure causing PHP to issue its own error message, as we explained earlier.

If the connection attempt succeeds, the link is passed to `mysql_select_db`, another library function, which also takes the database name as an argument. Once again, we suppress any PHP error messages. The function returns a Boolean value to indicate whether the database was successfully selected. As before, we test this value and give up if it is `false`. If everything goes well, we return the value of the link, in case it is required. (In fact, we will never do anything with it in this example script.)

There is no need to close the connection to the database explicitly. It will be closed when execution of the script terminates.

We will define a second function to execute database queries, and catch any errors. This is exceedingly simple. The library function `mysql_query` takes a string, which it treats as an SQL query, and sends it to the MySQL server to be executed. A connection must have been established, and a database selected, beforehand. If the query is successful, `mysql_query` returns a special value, called a resource, which can later be used by other functions to access the rows of the query's result. If it fails, it returns `false`, which is all we are concerned with at present. Our function will take a string, pass it to `mysql_query`, check the return value, call `give_up` if it is `false`, and return the resource otherwise.

```
function db_query($q) {
    $result = mysql_query($q);
    if (!$result) give_up("a database query ($q) failed");
```

```
      return $result;
}
```

Simple Error Handling

Since we have admitted that things might go wrong, we have to decide what to do if they do so. In other words, we need to write the `give_up` function before going any further. Since it will only be called when events beyond our control cause something to fail, we can really only display an apologetic message, and do as the function's name suggests: give up. The easiest way to display a message, without complicating the logic of the glossary script itself, is to redirect the client to a different page. This is done by sending an HTTP response with a code indicating that the resource has moved, and specifying a new URL with a `location` header. (This is similar to the technique of assigning to `window.location` in a client-side script.) The PHP function `header` can be used to send raw HTTP headers; it takes a string consisting of the header exactly as it will be sent by the server. As a special case, if the header begins with `location:`, the response code will be modified as well, to redirect the browser as required.

To begin with, we will simply use a static page to display our apologetic message. We will call this page `error.html` and keep it in the same directory as the main glossary script. The location header needs a full absolute URL to this page. It would be a bad idea to embed the host name and full path in our code, but fortunately we can extract them from an associative array called `$_SERVER`, which PHP sets up when the script is invoked. This array holds information about the environment in which the script is executing. Two elements are relevant here. `$_SERVER["HTTP_HOST"]` holds the host name and `$_SERVER["PHP_SELF"]` holds the path to the script itself, so `"http://".$_SERVER["HTTP_HOST"].$_SERVER["PHP_SELF"]` is the absolute URL of the script. But this isn't what we want: we want the URL of the directory in which the script is stored, so that we can add `"/error.html"` to the end of it to obtain the URL of the error page. The library function `dirname` takes a path and returns the directory part of it, which is exactly what we need to do.

Putting these ideas together gives the following first attempt at a definition of `give_up`:

```
function give_up($mess) {
   header("Location: http://" . $_SERVER["HTTP_HOST"] .
        dirname($_SERVER["PHP_SELF"]) . "/error.html");
   exit();
}
```

After sending the header, the script calls another library function called exit, which terminates its execution. If this was not done, control would return from give_up, as from any other function call, and execution of the script would attempt to continue, with unpredictable results. Notice that this version of give_up does nothing with the message it is passed as an argument, so only a generic apology can be displayed. Later, we will modify the function so that it does something more useful.

The apparently innocuous decision to send a response with a location header if anything goes wrong has momentous consequences. It means that anything that might cause a fatal error leading to a call of give_up must have been done before the server starts sending any HTTP response. As soon as a script has to generate some of the body of the response – usually because PHP has encountered something not enclosed in <?php and ?> – the response headers are sent. If an error occurs subsequently, it would cause the location header to appear in the middle of the body of the response. This would mean the redirection was ineffectual, and would corrupt the document being sent to the browser. PHP therefore refuses to do this, and exits with an error if an attempt to send any HTTP headers is made once a response has been started.

The benefit of this restriction is that it encourages a clean separation between the logic of the program and the presentation of the results, which fits in nicely with the MVC pattern of organization.

Presentation of the Results

It's time to consider the way in which our application is organized and invoked. The URL for the glossary points to a PHP script which generates the form controls. We'll call it glossary.php. Because the form is displayed again along with the definition after a glossary term has been looked up (see Figure 8.8), the only sensible way to organize the application is to have the action attribute of the form element that the script generates point back to glossary.php. The script therefore has to determine whether any values have been sent in the HTTP request that invokes it, in order to find out whether it must look up a term and display its definition. This is a very common way of organizing simple Web applications.

Although, as we will show, it does not affect the way the script is written, we must decide whether to send values to it using the GET or POST method. A general guideline that is often advocated is to use GET for requests that just retrieve data from a database, and POST for requests that update the database. This suggests that we should use GET as the method here. This has the additional advantage that it allows us to use URLs with query strings to look up terms directly, without requiring a user to enter anything in a text box. This means that we can put links to their definitions on the cross-references.

Looking back at Figure 8.8 and thinking about how each part of the page is generated, you should be able to see that we can achieve the required effect using a script that consists of static XHTML, except for the term that appears in the text box and its definition and cross-references. To separate the presentation as cleanly as we can from the computation, we will use a pair of variables to hold strings containing the required content for these two parts of the page. These variables will be initialized by calling functions, which we will define in an external file called actions.inc. Clearly, the definition depends on the term being defined, so the result of the first function needs to be passed to the second.

This leads to the following glossary.php:

```php
<?php
require("actions.inc");
$the_term = get_term();
$the_definition = do_definition($the_term);
?>

<!DOCTYPE html PUBLIC "-//W3C//DTD XHTML 1.0 Strict//EN"
  "http://www.w3.org/TR/xhtml1/DTD/xhtml1-strict.dtd">
<html xmlns="http://www.w3.org/1999/xhtml" xml:lang="en" lang="en">
<head>
   <title>Glossary</title>
   <link rel="stylesheet" href="styles.css" type="text/css"
media="screen" />
</head>
<body>
<form action="glossary.php" method="get">
<div id="form">
<label for="term1">Glossary term</label>
<input name="term1" id="term1" type="text" size="20" value = "<?=
$the_term ?>"/>
<input name="lookup" id="lookup" type="submit" value="Look Up" />
</div>
</form>
<div id="definition">
<?= $the_definition; ?>
</div>
```

```
</body>
</html>
```

Apart from the highlighted material, this is just an XHTML document. In fact, if you removed all the highlighted parts, it would display the data entry form. By adding the two highlighted sequences in the body of the document, we insert the dynamically generated content. The PHP code at the top of the file is used to obtain this content. Note that the only place fatal errors can occur is within the functions called in this preamble, so we have avoided any risk of calling give_up after the legitimate response headers have been sent.

It only remains to implement the two functions that we need to call.

Accessing Request Data and Database Records

Looking again at the form element that glossary.php generates, you should be able to see that, when the form is submitted, requests like the following will be sent to the server:

```
GET /glossary.php?term1=frame&lookup=Look+Up HTTP/1.1
```

That is, the term to be looked up is sent in the query string as the value of the variable term1. Our script does not need to extract the value from the query string. It does not even need to be aware that the data has been sent in a query string and not in POST data. PHP handles all that, passing the values of all query variables to the script, irrespective of the HTTP method used by the request, in an associative array called $_REQUEST, which is indexed by the variables' names. Thus, $_REQUEST['term1'] is the term, if any, entered by the user. The function get_term could just return this value, but we can try to clean up the user's input a little. The library function trim will remove any white space characters from the beginning or end of its argument. By using this, we can prevent any problems arising from users inadvertently (or perhaps maliciously) inserting spaces, tabs, and so on, before or after the glossary term they want to look up. Hence, get_term is defined as follows:

```
function get_term() {
   return trim($_REQUEST['term1']);
}
```

The result of this function is assigned to the variable $the_term, which is used in glossary.php to set the value of the text box so that it matches the term being defined (no matter whether the term was entered by the user or passed in a query string attached to the URL on a link). The value is also passed to the function do_definition, which is the heart of the application. Its job is to query the database for the definition or definitions of its argument and related cross-references, and to format the results it obtains. We also need to ensure that if its argument is the empty string – which means that the script was invoked without a query string – do_definition returns an empty string. Finally, if the database query returns no result, which implies that the term is not in the glossary, we need to make sure that a suitable message is returned instead of an empty definition.

For easier understanding, we will break down the task of retrieving and formatting the definitions into several subsidiary functions. (If you don't like so many function calls, you can easily combine them into a single function.) To begin with, we will just deal with the trivial case, and pass the general case on to another function:

```
function do_definition($term) {
    return $term == ""? "": get_definition($term);
}
```

If get_definition is called, we know that its argument, which we will also call $term, is not empty, and that we need to look up a definition. Looking at the sample query we had earlier for retrieving the definitions of *frame*, you should be able to see that, if we pass the following string to db_query, which we defined earlier, it will retrieve any definitions for the term that is the current value of $term:

```
"select id, definition from glossary where term = '$term'"
```

However, there is danger in executing any query that incorporates text that has been supplied by a user. Suppose, for example, a malicious user were to type the following into the text box:

```
Web'; insert into glossary values (999, 'halibut', 'a flightless
pomegranate');#
```

If this string was interpolated into the query, the result would be:

```
"select id, definition from glossary where term = 'Web'; insert into
glossary values (999, 'halibut', 'a flightless pomegranate');#'"
```

In MySQL, a semicolon can be used to separate two SQL statements, and the # sign is used to introduce comments: anything from the # to the end of the line is ignored. If we pass this string to MySQL, therefore, it will first execute a harmless look-up and then insert a bogus definition into the database.

You may object that this will never happen, because it requires that the malicious user has an understanding of the form of query string that the script is building and a knowledge of the database schema. It would, however, be easy for anyone with some knowledge of PHP and MySQL to guess roughly what the query string must look like. It would probably only take a couple of guesses to arrive at a string that would sabotage the database in the way we have described. While it is true that a bogus definition could only be added by somebody who knew something about the database schema, there are other queries that could be injected in the same way which are independent of the schema, but could do worse damage. In particular, if you had been foolish enough to write a script that connected to the database with a user name that gave it administrative privileges, a cleverly written query term could grant full access to the database to anybody.

This technique of sabotaging databases by injecting SQL into URL query strings is well known, and so ways of preventing it from doing any damage are available. PHP can be configured with an option, 'magic quotes', which will automatically insert \ characters in front of any double or single quote characters in data sent in an HTTP request. This prevents malicious users from closing any strings prematurely, as happened in our example, and therefore prevents them from slipping in extra queries. If your installation of PHP has not been configured with magic quotes, or you don't know whether it has, you can perform the same operation explicitly using the library function `mysql_escape_string`. In the case of input that should be numerical, you should check that it really is of the right form, by calling `is_numeric`.

Our function `get_definition` must escape its argument in this way, form the query string and then pass it to `db_query`. The result of the query is then passed on to another function, `extract_definition`, which will take the resource returned from `db_query` and use it to access the actual data in the query result. Hence, `get_definition` is defined as follows:

```
function get_definition($term) {
   db_connect();
   $term = mysql_escape_string($term);
   $definition_query = "select id, definition from glossary where term
                                                     = '$term'";
   return extract_definition($term, db_query($definition_query));
}
```

Notice that the first thing this function does is call db_connect. We can't make any queries until that has been done.

If we get as far as extract_definition we know that our query was executed successfully, because of the way db_query was defined, but we don't know that it retrieved any data: the term entered by the user might not be defined in the glossary. The library function mysql_num_rows takes a resource and returns the number of rows retrieved. This is a useful piece of information. In particular, if it is zero, we know that no definition was found. Otherwise, we need to format the rows that were retrieved in a suitable form for displaying. Hence extract_definition calls mysql_num_rows and returns a suitable message if there are no rows, or passes its arguments, together with the number of rows, to yet another function for processing:

```
function extract_definition($term, $definition_records) {
    $n = mysql_num_rows($definition_records);
    if ($n == 0)
        return "<p>No definition for <strong>$term</strong> was found</
p>";
    else
        return make_definitions($term, $definition_records, $n);
}
```

Finally, we are in a position to access the stored data. To do this, we use another PHP library function, mysql_fetch_array. This takes a resource obtained by executing a query and returns an associative array, whose keys are the names of the columns in the query result ("id" and "definition", in our current query) and whose values are the corresponding values in one row of the result. A sequence of calls to mysql_fetch_array will retrieve each row of the query result in turn. We already know how many rows there are, so we can write a loop that calls mysql_fetch_array the appropriate number of times. We will pass the resulting arrays to a function we will call format_definition, together with some other values, which will add some XHTML tags and the cross-references to the definition.

We will build up the string to return from make_definitions, which will propagate back through our function calls and end up being inserted into the XHTML document, by sticking together all the values returned from format_definition. (Most of the time there will only be one, but we have to be prepared to deal with terms that have more than one definition.)

At this point we have to decide how to mark up the definitions. (We don't have to worry about their appearance. An external stylesheet is used to lay out the glossary.) The result of looking up a term in a glossary is obviously a definition list, so we will use a dl element. The make_definition function therefore starts out by assigning an opening <dl> tag to a variable. It then loops through all the rows of the query result, appending a formatted version of each to the string. Finally, it adds the closing </dl> tag, and returns the complete result.

```
function make_definitions($term, $definition_records, $n) {
   $definition = "<dl>";
   for ($i = 1; $i <= $n; ++$i)
      $definition .= format_definition($term,
             mysql_fetch_array($definition_records), $i, $n);
   $definition .= "</dl>";
   return $definition;
}
```

Remember that in PHP, strings are combined using the . operator.

Formatting a single definition is pretty trivial if we assume that there is a function format_xrefs which will return a formatted list of cross-references. If that is so, all we need to do is insert the appropriate <dt> and <dd> tags, once we have extracted the definition from the array passed as an argument. To add a little bit of finesse, if there is more than one definition we insert a number in brackets after the term. That is why, in make_definitions, we passed $i and $n to format_definition. The information is there, so we may as well use it.

```
function format_definition($term, $definition_array, $i, $n) {
   $q = $n > 1? " ($i)": "";
   $def = $definition_array["definition"];
   $xrefs = format_xrefs($definition_array["id"]);
   return "<dt>$term$q</dt><dd>$def$xrefs</dd>";
}
```

All that remains is to find and format the cross-references for this definition. This doesn't introduce any new ideas, so we will only describe the function briefly. The id from the current row of the glossary table is passed as an argument to format_xrefs. This is interpolated into a query string which retrieves the cross-references. If there are any, we iterate through the rows, as before, setting them as items in an unordered list. Each cross-referenced term is made into a link, which points to glossary.php with a query string setting the variable term1 to the term itself. Thus, clicking on an item in the list of cross-references will cause its definition to be retrieved.

```
function format_xrefs($id) {
   $xref_query = "select term from xrefs where id = $id order by
term";
   $xref_records = db_query($xref_query);
   $xrefs = "";
   $n = mysql_num_rows($xref_records);
   if ($n > 0) {
      $xrefs = "<div class = \"xrefs\"><h1>See also</h1><ul>";
      for ($i = 0; $i < $n; ++$i) {
         $refa = mysql_fetch_array($xref_records);
         $ref = $refa["term"];
         $xrefs .= "<li><a href=\"glossary.php?term1=$ref\" title =
\"look up $ref\">$ref</a></li>";
      }
      $xrefs .= "</ul></div>";
   }
   return $xrefs;
}
```

To clarify how this all fits together, we will examine what happens when a user visits the glossary and looks up the term *bandwidth*. (You might find it helpful to download the complete script from www.webdesignbook.org and refer to it in conjunction with the following description.)

We will assume that, to begin with, the glossary is first accessed using a URL with no query string, perhaps by the user typing it into the address bar. When PHP begins to process glossary.php, the first thing it does is call get_term, which returns $_REQUEST['term1']. This will be the empty string, which is assigned to $the_term, and then passed to do_definition, which tests its argument and immediately returns the empty string. After processing the closing ?> of the block of code at the top of the file, PHP starts sending the HTTP response. This comprises the remainder of glossary.php, with empty strings interpolated where the variables appear in the code. This only affects two elements:

```
<input name="term1" id="term1" type="text" size="20" value = ""/>

<div id="definition">
</div>
```

The form is therefore displayed, with nothing in the text box and no definition.

The user next types the word *bandwidth* into the text box and clicks on the Look Up button. An HTTP request is sent, with the following request line:

```
GET /glossary.php?term1=bandwidth&lookup=Look+Up HTTP/1.1
```

On receiving the request, before processing glossary.php, PHP sets up the $_REQUEST array, in particular it sets $_REQUEST['term1'] to "bandwidth". As before, processing begins with the call to get_term, which this time, therefore, returns "bandwidth" and assigns it to $the_term. When do_definition is called, since its argument is not empty, it passes it on to get_definition, which connects to the database and executes the query

```
select id, definition from glossary where term = 'bandwidth'
```

which retrieves a single row from the glossary table.

The resource for the query result is passed to extract_definition, which determines that the number of rows is greater than zero, and passes it on to make_definition.

The loop in the body of this function will only be executed once, since the query result only comprises a single row. This row is fetched into an array and passed to format_definition, where the text and id of the definition are extracted. The id, whose value is 23, is sent to format_xrefs, where it is interpolated into the query string, so that the query

```
select term from xrefs where id = 23 order by term
```

is executed.

This query returns a single row, so the test on the fifth line of format_xrefs succeeds, and $xrefs is initialized with the markup for the heading of the block of cross-references. The following for loop will only be executed once, with $ref being assigned the string "data transfer rate", which is the value of the item column of the row retrieved by the query, which has been fetched into an array. This value is interpolated three times into the string for the list item corresponding to this cross-reference, which becomes

```
<li><a href="glossary.php?term1=data transfer rate" title = "look up
data transfer rate">data transfer rate</a></li>
```

That is, the list item contains a link back to glossary.php itself, with a query string that will cause *data transfer rate* to be looked up if the text is clicked on. This string is appended to $xrefs.

The necessary closing tags are added to the end of the $xrefs, so the function returns a string comprising all the markup that is needed to display the cross-references. Back in format_definition, this string is inserted into a string consisting of the markup for a dt element containing the term and a dd element which contains the definition and cross-references. This is returned to make_definitions, where it is added to the string containing the opening dl tag for the definition list. On exiting the loop in that function, the matching closing tag is added to the end of the string, which is returned, via extract_definition and get_definition all the way to do_definition, whence it is assigned, back at the beginning of glossary.php, to the variable $the_definition.

This time, both $the_term and $the_definition have non-empty strings as their values, so when the input and div elements in the body of the document are processed, these dynamically computed values are inserted, giving the following, which – when displayed in the browser – shows the defined term, definition and cross-references as required. (We have added some line breaks to make the markup more readable.)

```
<input name="term1" id="term1" type="text" size="20" value =
"bandwidth"/>

<div id="definition">
<dl><dt>bandwidth</dt>
<dd>A measure of the maximum possible data transfer rate available
over a communication channel.
<div class = "xrefs">
<h1>See also</h1>
<ul><li><a href="glossary.php?term1=data transfer rate" title = "look
up data transfer rate">data transfer rate</a></li></ul>
</div>
</dd></dl></div>
```

(A dd element may contain other block-level elements as well as character data so, despite possible appearances, this is valid XHTML.)

Using Persistent Data

The version of the glossary that we just described treats the database as a fixed repository of definitions, from which it only ever reads data. Many Web applications must also write data to a database, storing it there for later retrieval. By extending the script to add the glossary term cloud shown in Figure 8.7 to the glossary, we can demonstrate how this is done.

In terms of the MVC pattern, changes are needed to the model, the view and the controller. Changes to the model are needed to record the number of times a term has been looked up. Changes to the view are required in order to display the cloud, and changes to the controller are needed to tie the other changes together. We will deal with these in order.

The required change to the database is obvious. We simply need to add a new table with two columns, term and count. The count value in each row records the number of times that the term in that row has been successfully looked up. Rather than initialize the table with a row for each term in the glossary table, each with its count set to zero, we will start with an empty table and add a row the first time each term is looked up. This means that we will have to make a special case of recording the first look-up.

The glossary.php file does not require much change either. We need to add a call to a new function, which we will call do_cloud, and save the result to a variable which will be interpolated into a new div element. We have chosen to move some initialization into a separate function called set_up, which is called at the very beginning. Hence, the script now looks like this:

```php
<?php
require("actions.inc");
set_up();
$the_term = get_term();
$the_definition = do_definition($the_term);
$the_cloud = do_cloud();
?>
```

The new function set_up is simply defined like this:

```php
function set_up() {
   db_connect();
}
```

This is more by way of preparation for the more elaborate set-up that will be needed in the next version of this application than a necessary change to the code. In the previous version, it would not have been appropriate to connect to the database at this point, because it was possible that the script would be invoked without a query string, in which case it would not have been necessary to connect to the database at all. Now that we are going to display a glossary term cloud, we know that we will always need to look at the counts, at least, so it makes sense to establish the connection at the start. The original call to db_connect is removed from get_definition.

As well as defining do_cloud, to display the glossary term cloud, we must also take steps to ensure that the counts table holds the correct information. That is, each time a term is successfully looked up, we must add one to its count. The point at which we know that a look-up has been successful is in the function extract_definition, at the point where it has been determined that the number of rows retrieved by the query is greater than zero. We will add a call to a function to add one to the appropriate count at this point:

```
function extract_definition($term, $definition_records) {
    $n = mysql_num_rows($definition_records);
    if ($n == 0)
        return "<p>No definition for <strong>$term</strong> was found
</p>";
    else {
        add_to_count($term);
        return make_definitions($term, $definition_records, $n);
    }
}
```

Here is how we define add_to_count. For the first time, the script writes data to the database. As we mentioned before, we have to determine whether there is a row for the term in the table already. The only way to find out is to try to retrieve it. If there is such a row, an SQL update statement is used to add one to the count, otherwise, an insert statement is used to create a new row.

```
function add_to_count($term) {
    $records = db_query("select * from counts where term='$term'");
    if (mysql_num_rows($records) == 0)
        db_query("insert into counts values('$term', 1)");
    else
        db_query("update counts set count = count + 1 where
```

```
      term='$term'");
   }
```

Now that we have made sure that the `counts` table holds the correct data, we just need to retrieve it and present it in the desired form. Before we can go into the details of the code, we need to explain how the glossary term cloud is formatted.

Each term that appears in the cloud is actually a link, which points to its own definition. That is, the `href` attribute of the a element enclosing the term has as its value the URL of `glossary.php` with a query string setting `term1` to the term itself. Additionally, each of these elements has a class attribute, which assigns it to one of the classes 10 to 15, depending on how frequently the term has been looked up. The terms least often looked up will belong to the class 10 (short for level 0); those most often looked up will belong to the class 15. Thus a typical link for a relatively unpopular term in the cloud will look like this:

```
<a href="glossary.php?term1=Web browser" class="l1" title="Look up
Web browser">Web browser</a>
```

The actual sizing of the text is controlled, like all the other formatting, by a stylesheet, which includes the following rules, as well as other layout and formatting rules:

```
a.10 { font-size: 75%; }
a.11 { font-size: 80%; }
a.12 { font-size: 90%; }
a.13 { font-size: 100%; }
a.14 { font-size: 120%; }
a.15 { font-size: 135%; }
```

The font sizes are chosen somewhat arbitrarily to convey a sense of the relative importance of the different terms.

To allocate terms to their classes, we need to map the count values to numbers in the range 0 to 5. We have chosen to use a (roughly) linear mapping, since we imagine that that is how most people will interpret the relative sizes of the terms. This means that we have to divide the range from zero to the highest count into six intervals, and then determine which interval each retrieved count belongs to.

The following little function performs this mapping using arithmetic:

```
function normalize($v, $n1, $n2, $m) {
   return round((($v - $n1 + 1) * $m)/($n2 - $n1 + 1));
}
```

The first argument is a value retrieved from counts. The next two are the lowest and highest count values, and the last argument is the highest level to be used – we have implemented a general mapping, although in this script the function will only ever be called with a fourth argument of 5. The PHP library function round takes a real number and returns the nearest integer. That is, round(3.1) is 3 and round(3.6) is 4, for instance. You should be able to verify that this function will always return a number between 0 and $m, which maps $v to the nearest number to its proportion of the range of values ($n2 - $n2+1). This is what we needed to do.

To use this function, we need to retrieve the counts and find their maximum. Since there is a limit to how many terms we can reasonably display, we also need to discard any unpopular terms beyond a certain number. It is sensible to define a constant for that number – a certain amount of trial and error is needed to determine a value that produces a display that fits nicely on the page, so we want to make it as easy as possible to change the value. Therefore, the following is added to config.inc:

```
define("MAXCLOUDSIZE", 45);
```

What we will do in the do_cloud function is read all the rows from the counts table. We will get MySQL to order them in descending order for us at this stage. Next, we will take the first MAXCLOUDSIZE rows, or all the rows if there are not that many, and pull the data out into an array, which maps terms to their counts. We then pass the resulting array to another function, make_cloud, to be turned into the markup for the glossary term cloud.

```
function do_cloud() {
   $records = db_query("select * from counts order by count desc");
   $n = mysql_num_rows($records);
   if ($n > MAXCLOUDSIZE) $n = MAXCLOUDSIZE;
   for ($i = 0; $i < $n; ++$i) {
      $record = mysql_fetch_array($records);
      $counts[$record["term"]] = $record["count"];
   }
   return make_cloud($counts);
}
```

After the call of `mysql_fetch_array`, `$record["term"]` holds the term from the current row and `$record["count"]` the count, so the highlighted assignment adds an element to the array `$counts`, whose index is the term and whose value is its count, as required.

The main job of `make_cloud` is to replace these raw count values by the corresponding levels, computed by the `normalize` function we defined earlier. To do this, it needs to find the minimum and maximum values in the array it has been passed as an argument. The way this is done may be a little confusing – if so, blame the way PHP implements associative arrays.

Although their indexes are strings, not numbers, associative arrays are considered to be ordered, with a first, second, …, last element. When we added the values to `$counts`, each was added to the end of the array. Since the query retrieved the counts in descending order, the elements of the array are also in descending order, so the maximum and minimum counts can be found in the first and last element of the array respectively. Every array is considered to have an 'internal pointer', and when a `foreach` loop is used to iterate through the elements of an array, what happens is that this internal pointer runs through each of the elements in turn. Two functions operate on the internal pointer: `reset` sets it to point to the first element in the array, and `end` to the last. What makes these useful to us is that each of these functions returns the value of the element it sets the internal pointer to point to, so `reset($counts)` and `end($counts)` will be the maximum and minimum count values that we need to pass to `normalize`.

After looping through the array and normalizing the count values, we still have an array ordered from largest to smallest count. If we were to generate the glossary term cloud by running through this array in a `foreach` loop, all the popular terms would come first, then the less popular, and so on. That is, the words in the cloud would start out large and decrease in size, which does not provide the nice graphic effect that characterizes this way of presenting the popular glossary terms. We therefore pass the array to the library function `ksort`, which sorts it alphabetically by key. (Actually, it sorts it according to the ASCII codes, so words beginning with upper- and lower-case letters are sorted in separate sequences, as you can see in Figure 8.7. This doesn't seem terribly important, since all we're really trying to do here is break up the ordering by frequency.) The sorted array is passed to a function called `encloud`, which just iterates through it, creating the link elements.

```
function make_cloud($counts) {
    $max = reset($counts);
    $min = end($counts);
    foreach ($counts as $k => $v)
```

```
        $counts[$k] = normalize($v, $min, $max, 5);
    ksort($counts);
    return encloud($counts);
}



function encloud($a) {
    $s = "";
    foreach ($a as $k => $v)
        $s .= make_link($k, $v) . " ";
    return $s;
}
```

The function make_link called here just wraps up its first argument, the term, in an a element, with an appropriate href attribute pointing to its own definition, as described earlier. The second argument is used to construct the class name for this link: if the argument is 0, the class will be l0, and so on.

```
function make_link($t, $n) {
    return "<a href=\"glossary.php?term1=$t\" class=\"l$n\" title=\
"Look up $t\">$t</a>";
}
```

Using Cookies

To implement the Recent Searches pop-up menu, it is necessary to associate information stored in the database with a particular visitor to the page. This means that we need to be able to identify visitors. We don't need to know who they are, we just need to be able to recognize the same visitor when he or she returns. Hence, there is no need to allocate user names and implement a login system – it's hard to believe that many visitors would think it worth while registering to use an on-line glossary in any case. All we need to be able to do is allocate a unique identifier to each new visitor to the glossary, and store their recent search terms in the database alongside that identifier. We also need some way of ensuring that each time the visitor returns, their identifier is presented to the script.

If you read the section about cookies in Chapter 2, you will recognize that we only have to store a visitor's identifier in a cookie for it to be sent in any request that their browser sends to the glossary. Conceptually, therefore, the implementation of the Recent Searches menu

user	term	n
43ce71a611a9c	accessibility	1
43ce71a611a9c	aliasing	8
43ce71a611a9c	broadband	6
43ce71a611a9c	frame	3
43ce71a611a9c	quicktime	9
43ce71a611a9c	software	4
43ce71a611a9c	Web page	2
43ce71a611a9c	Web site	5
43ce71a611a9c	World Wide Web	0
43ce71a611a9c	XHTML	7
43ce8d24906ec	jpeg	0
43ce8d34bc3da	Web page	0
43ce8d51b7ac1	XHTML	0
43e35e318115a	bandwidth	0
43e35e318115a	broadband	3
43e35e318115a	tag	1
43e35e318115a	Web page	2

Figure 8.10 Some typical history data

should be straightforward. As before, we will need to make fairly small changes to the model and view, and add some new code to the controller.

The database must be extended with a new table, which we will call histories, with three columns: user, which contains a visitor's identifier; term, which holds a term that they successfully looked up in the glossary (we assume that they won't want to remember unsuccessful searches); and n, which indicates how far back in history the search took place. The most recent search has n equal to 0, the one before has n equal to 1, and so on. We will place a limit on the number of entries in the Recent Searches menu, and hence on the number of searches that have to be recorded in the database for each user, and hence in turn, on the maximum value of n. Figure 8.10 shows some typical history data.

The changes to `glossary.php` are a little more elaborate than those we made to add the glossary term cloud, because of the way the visitor's identifier and history have to be passed around among the various functions.

We chose to incorporate the code for obtaining the visitor's identifier from the cookie into the `set_up` function, which now returns the identifier as its result. This is passed to `get_history`, which is a new function that looks up the rows for that visitor from the `history` table. These will be returned in an array, which we can pass to `do_recent_searches`, a function to build the Recent Searches pop-up menu from it. Less obviously, we must pass both the visitor's identifier and the history to `do_definition`, because they are both needed to add the latest search to that visitor's history, if it is successful. (Once again, we are presenting the code as if it was logically inevitable and obvious, but in practice these modifications to the view component evolved in parallel with the writing of the modified controller.) The addition of the Recent Searches menu does not affect the glossary term cloud in any way.

The block of PHP code at the beginning of `glossary.php` now looks like this:

```php
<?php
require("actions.inc");
$the_visitor = set_up();
$the_term = get_term();
$the_history = get_history($the_visitor);
$the_recent_searches = do_recent_searches($the_history);
$the_definition = do_definition($the_term, $the_visitor, $the_history);
$the_cloud = do_cloud();
?>
```

The new pop-up menu must be incorporated into the body of the document. Since some users will be visiting the page for the first time, the chance that there are no recent searches, and hence no need for a menu, must be allowed for. We cannot, therefore, put any static code for the menu control in the document, we must generate it all dynamically and just interpolate the result returned from `do_recent_searches`.

```html
<div id="form">
<label for="term1">Glossary term</label>
<input name="term1" id="term1" type="text" size="20" value = "<?=
$the_term ?>"/>
<?= $the_recent_searches ?>
<input name="lookup" id="lookup" type="submit" value="Look Up" />
</div>
```

With this new organization, once it has connected to the database, the set_up function has to determine whether the current request has been sent by a returning visitor. As we explained, the information can be deduced from the presence of a cookie. Cookies are made available by PHP in an associative array called $_COOKIE, which contains elements for each cookie in the request. Because of the way cookies work, these will be all the cookies originally sent by the domain of the glossary. Each cookie has a name, and the names are used to index the $_COOKIE array, so finding the value of any particular cookie in a PHP script is trivial. The glossary script will use userid as the name of the cookie it uses to remember visitors, so $_COOKIE['userid'] will hold its value, if any. (This name is determined by the script, not by any external factors.) If it turns out that there is no such value, we know that this is a new visitor (or a previous visitor who has deleted the relevant cookie from their browser), and must generate one. The PHP library function uniqid generates strings based on the current time in microseconds. For our application, this is good enough for us to be confident that each such string will be unique, so we can use uniqid to generate our users' identifiers. (The function takes a string to be prefixed to its result as an argument, but we don't need to use that, so we will just pass the empty string.) Once this value has been generated, we need to send it back to the user's browser in a Set-Cookie header. PHP provides a set_cookie function to do just that.

Since the point of using this cookie is to remember visitors, we need to specify an expiry date for it. (Recall that if no expiry date is sent in a Set-Cookie header, the cookie is deleted at the end of the current browsing session – that is, when the user quits the browser.) If you look at the cookies stored in your own browser, you will probably see that a lot of sites set an expiry date a long way into the future. This seems unreasonable, and we prefer to set the date just thirty days ahead, but renew it every time the user returns to the page. This means calling set_cookie, whether or not this is a new visitor. Hence, we re-define set_up as follows:

```php
function set_up() {
   db_connect();
   $user_id = $_COOKIE["userid"];
   if ($user_id == "")
      $user_id = uniqid("");
   setcookie("userid", $user_id, time()+30*24*60*60);
   return $user_id;
}
```

The third argument to set_cookie is the time at which the cookie expires, in seconds; the library function time returns the current time in seconds, so the value we have set here causes the cookie to expire after thirty days, as required.

Having obtained an identifier for this visitor, the next job is to retrieve their history, if any. This presents no problems. An SQL query retrieves the relevant rows of the histories table, and then the data is transferred to an array.

```
function get_history($user) {
    $query = "select term from histories where user = \"$user\" order
by n";
    $records = db_query($query);
    $n = mysql_num_rows($records);
    if ($n == 0) return null;
    for ($i = 0; $i < $n; ++$i) {
        $record = mysql_fetch_array($records);
        $hist[$i] = $record["term"];
    }
    return $hist;
}
```

Turning this array into a select element is straightforward and introduces no new ideas. Each value from the array is wrapped up in an option element.

```
function do_recent_searches($history) {
    if ($history == null) return "";
    $s = "<select id=\"term2\" name=\"term2\">";
    $s .= "<option label=\"Recent Searches\" value =\"\" selected=\
"selected\">Recent Searches</option>";
    foreach ($history as $h)
        $s .= "<option label=\"$h\" value=\"$h\">$h</option>";
    $s .= "</select>";
    return $s;
}
```

The select element that encloses these option elements has its name and id set to term2. This means that if a user selects their search term from the menu, it will be sent in the query string of the HTTP request as the value of the query variable term2, not term1, as it would be if they had typed it in the text box. Hence, get_term needs modifying slightly.

```
function get_term() {
   $t2 = $_REQUEST['term2'];
   return $t2 != ""? $t2: $_REQUEST['term1'];
}
```

The menu selection thus takes precedence over anything typed in the box. Later, we will see how to resolve any confusion this may cause (at least, in most cases).

If all of this is to work, we need to update the histories table every time a glossary term is successfully looked up. This means adding a call to a new function add_to_history to the body of extract_definition, whose declaration must also be modified.

```
function extract_definition($term, $definition_records, $user,
$history) {
   as before
   else {
      add_to_count($term);
      add_to_history($term, $user, $history);
      return make_definitions($term, $definition_records, $n);
   }
}
```

To get these additional values into extract_definition, the declarations of – and calls to – the other definition handling functions must also be changed to pass the extra arguments. This change is trivial, so we won't show the details.

Our approach to add_to_history is a bit crude. We simply delete the user's old history, and then insert a new collection of rows, starting with the newly looked-up term, then adding values from the $history array. We ensure that if this user already had a full history, one value will drop off, so that the Recent Searches menu does not expand unboundedly. A little care is needed to make sure that duplicate menu entries are not generated if the same glossary term is looked up more than once.

```
function add_to_history($term, $user, $history) {
   db_query("delete from histories where user=\"$user\"");
   db_query("insert into histories values (\"$user\", \"$term\",
0)");
   if ($history != null) {
      $i = 1;
      foreach ($history as $h) {
```

```
              if ($h != $term && $i < HISTLEN) {
                  db_query("insert into histories values (\"$user\", \"$h\",
   $i)");
                  ++$i;
              }
          }
      }
  }
```

Suppose a user looks something up or clicks on a glossary link, and then, after the definition has been displayed, chooses an entry from the Recent Searches menu. The term they looked up first will still be in the text entry field, while a different term is shown as the value on the menu. This may be confusing. It is easily fixed by adding a little client-side script that transfers any value chosen from the pop-up menu to the text field.

```
<script type="text/javascript">
if (document.getElementById) window.onload = function() {
   var sel = document.getElementById("term2");
   if (sel)
      sel.onchange =
         function() {
            var t = document.getElementById("term1");
            t.value = sel.value;
         }
}
</script>
```

This doesn't work for users who have disabled scripting or whose browsers don't support it. You may perhaps take the view that this does not matter much, but a more gracious approach is not to provide the Recent Searches menu unless client-side scripting is supported and activated. (The application's service is degraded, but gracefully – they won't know that they are missing anything.) This can be done using a technique we demonstrated in Chapter 7: use a script to create the relevant elements of the document. For a Web application, this means writing a server-side script that writes a client-side script that modifies the DOM tree. We will leave this as an exercise.

Sending Mail

Although we hope that errors won't occur when this script is run, the possibility cannot be ruled out, and the error handling that we have provided so far is not really adequate. Recall that the function give_up, which is called when an irrecoverable error occurs, takes an error message as its argument, but doesn't do anything with it. It simply causes a standard error page to be displayed. Now that we know something about how PHP deals with query data, we can do better than this.

Instead of using a static XHTML document as the error page, we can use a PHP script, and pass the error message from `give_up` in a query string. That is, we can rewrite `give_up` like this:

```
function give_up($mess) {
    header("Location: http://" . $_SERVER["HTTP_HOST"] .
        dirname($_SERVER["PHP_SELF"]) . "/error.php?mess=$mess");
    exit();
}
```

A minimal `error.php` could have the following body:

```
<body>
<h1>Sorry</h1>
<p>An error occurred, the message was:
 <em><?= $_REQUEST['mess']; ?></em></p>
</body>
```

This is an improvement; the user has now got some idea of what has happened. It would be possible to be more helpful, by adding extra arguments to `give_up`, indicating the severity of the error, and whether it might be worth while trying again (if we suspected a transient problem), but apologizing to the user is only part of the necessary response to an error's occurring. If possible, errors should be fixed, which means that the site's developer should be notified.

The simplest way to do that is by sending an email message. PHP makes it very easy to do this. The `mail` function takes at least three arguments: the first is the address to which you wish to send a message, the second is the subject (which will appear in the subject line in the recipient's email client), and the third is the message itself. Things could hardly be simpler.

Most ISPs, though, impose certain restrictions on mail messages sent by scripts running on their servers. For instance, it is common to require that the email address to which the message is being sent has the same domain name as the page from which it is being sent. For instance, if the URL of the error page was `www.desperatesw.co.uk/error.php`, error messages could only be sent to addresses of the form *user*@desperatesw.co.uk. Also, it is common to require that every message has a valid sender's address (the `From` field in the message). To do this, you must add a fourth argument to `mail`. This takes the form of a string comprising any number of mail headers. (These are like HTTP headers, and defined in the relevant standards.) The sender is the value of the `From` header, so this argument must take the form `"From: "` followed by the sender's email address. But what should this address be, since the message isn't actually from anybody? A popular option is `noreply@domain`, where *domain* is the domain name of the page.

An improved error handling script could therefore take the following form:

```php
<?php
$message = $_REQUEST['mess'];
mail("webmaster@desperatesq.com.uk", "A Glossary Error Occurred",
$message, "From: noreply@desperatesq.com.uk");
?>
DOCTYPE and document head as before
<body>
<h1>Sorry</h1>
<p>An error occurred, the message was: <em><?= $message ?></em></p>
</body>
</html>
```

If you intend to use a script to send messages from a site that is hosted by an ISP, you should check which restrictions, if any, are imposed by your particular service provider.

The `mail` function is not restricted to being used for error reporting, of course. It can be used whenever a script needs to send email. For simple applications, like Web surveys and customer feedback forms, this may be all that the script needs to do.

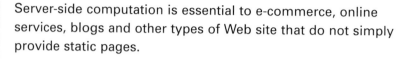

Key Points

Server-side computation is essential to e-commerce, online services, blogs and other types of Web site that do not simply provide static pages.

Server-Side Technologies

CGI (the Common Gateway Interface) specifies a mechanism for passing data from an HTTP request to a separate program.

Programming languages commonly used for CGI scripting usually provide some convenient means of accessing the values contained in the request.

FastCGI is an extension to CGI, which avoids the overhead associated with creating a new process for every request that invokes a script.

Apache modules allow scripts to run inside the server process. ASP.NET uses a similar approach employing dynamically loaded libraries.

Programming languages used for server-side scripting are usually dynamically typed, and provide automatic garbage collection, regular expression pattern matching and libraries giving access to databases.

Several languages provide a mechanism for embedding executable code among the markup of an XHTML document.

Popular languages for server-side scripting include Perl, Python, Ruby and PHP. PHP is almost always embedded in XHTML.

Java can be used to write servlets, which execute within a servlet container, not a conventional HTTP server. JSP (Java Server Pages) is a form of embedded servlet.

Web application frameworks incorporate all the repetitive code for tasks common to most applications, allowing a developer to plug in only the code specific to a particular application.

Most Web application frameworks are based on the Model View Controller (MVC) pattern.

Jakarta Struts, Zope and Ruby on Rails are frameworks for Java, Python and Ruby, respectively.

Ready-Made Applications

Open Source Web software which can be customized for individual sites is available for most classes of Web application.

Content Management Systems (CMS) are used to create Web pages dynamically from content that is stored in a database.

The functions of a CMS are content creation, uploading, presentation, archiving and supporting collaboration.

Databases

Data stored on a server and used by a Web application is usually organized as a relational database, and accessed by programs interacting with a database management system (DBMS).

SQL is a standard query language and data definition language.

A relational database is organized as a collection of tables, each of which contains rows of data. Each table cell contains a single value.

Databases should be normalized to prevent inconsistencies resulting from insertion, deletion and modification operations.

A database schema is a description of the structure of a database.

An SQL select query of the form

```
select columns from table where condition;
```

is used to retrieve values in specified columns that satisfy a given condition.

Duplicates are removed if `distinct` appears after `select`.

Results can be ordered by adding `order by` *column* at the end of the query.

Join queries, where more than one table name appears after `from`, can be used to combine data from several tables.

Data can be added to tables with an `insert` statement, deleted with a `delete` statement and modified with an `update` statement.

Dynamically Generated Pages

PHP's syntax resembles JavaScript. Arithmetic and Boolean operations, conditionals, loops, function definitions and calls are the same in both languages, but string concatenation is written with a `.` instead of +.

Variable names must begin with a $ character.

This allows variables to be interpolated into double-quoted strings.

The `foreach` loop is used to iterate over arrays. It has the form

    foreach ($a as $x) *statement*

for numerically indexed arrays and

    foreach ($aa as $k => $v) *statement*

for associative arrays.

The `define` function is used to give names to constants.

The `require` function is used to include external files.

PHP statements within an XHTML document must be enclosed between the characters `<?php` and `?>`.

A sequence of the form <?= *expression* ?> is replaced by the value of the expression.

The PHP library includes functions for passing queries to a DBMS and carrying out other operations on a database.

The functions mysql_connect and mysql_select_db are used to set up a connection to a MySQL database and choose a database.

The library function mysql_query takes a string, which it treats as an SQL query, and sends it to the MySQL server to be executed. If any rows are retrieved, mysql_query returns a resource.

The function header is used to send raw HTTP headers. If the header begins with location: it causes the browser to be redirected to a new page (for error messages, etc.)

PHP passes the values of all query variables to the script in an associative array called $_REQUEST, which is indexed by the variables' names.

Setting the magic quotes option or explicitly calling mysql_escape_string prevents SQL injection attacks.

The library function mysql_num_rows takes a resource returned by mysql_query and returns the number of rows retrieved.

A sequence of calls to mysql_fetch_array with the resource as argument will return each row of the query result in turn, in the form of an associative array, whose keys are the names of the columns in the query result and whose values are the corresponding values in one row.

The associative array $_COOKIE contains elements for each cookie in the request. The set_cookie function is used to send a Set-Cookie header.

The mail function can be used to send email from a script, to report errors to a site's developer, for example.

Exercises

Test Questions

1. What features are usually found in programming languages for server-side computation but not in mainstream programming languages, such as Java and C++? What makes these features appropriate for Web application programming?

2. Give an example of a type of Web site that could be based on a CMS, and an example of one that couldn't.

3. Are there any circumstances under which it would be a good idea to use a database that was *not* normalized?

4. Why is is customary to use a single script to generate a form and the response generated from data entered into it?

5. Why is it important to ensure that any function calls that might generate error messages are placed before the beginning of the XHTML mark-up in a PHP script?

6. Explain how using the `mysql_escape_string` function can prevent malicious users from corrupting a database or accessing confidential information. What other steps should you take to ensure that a Web application's data is secure?

7. Suppose you thought it was important to order the terms in the glossary's term cloud alphabetically, instead of separating terms beginning with lower-case letters from those beginning with upper-case letters, as our code does. Outline how you would do this.

Discussion Topics

1. If you were in charge of creating a new Web application from scratch, what considerations would determine your choice of language for implementing the server-side programs?

2. Most Web application frameworks automatically map database tables to classes and rows to objects. Some, such as Ruby on Rails, rely on the developer following a convention about how columns are named, in order to identify relationships between data in different tables (such as our use of `imgid` and `catid` in the `categorization` table to join `images` and `categories`). Other frameworks require this information to be specified explicitly in a configuration file. Discuss the relative merits of these two approaches.

3. One way of organizing a Web site's navigation is by using a database to record all the pages and the relationships between them, and generating navbars dynamically. What are the advantages of this approach compared to using navbars that are part of the pages? Would it make sense to use this approach on a site where no other server-side computation was required?

4. Some people set their Web browser to refuse cookies. Is this sensible? How might you go about determining in a script whether cookies were being accepted? What could you do if they weren't and your script depended on them?

Practical Tasks

1. Find some sites that use the phpBB system to power a forum. How successfully is the forum integrated with the rest of the site? Download phpBB and see how easy you find it to customize the appearance of a forum.

2. Modify the glossary application in the way outlined on page 489, so that the Recent Searches menu is only provided if scripting is enabled on the user's browser.

3. Write a script in PHP, or some other language of your choice, which accepts the data from the form you designed for Practical Task 3 in Chapter 3, and returns a page with the information from the form laid out in the style for a job application you developed for Practical Task 1 in Chapter 4. Modify the form document to invoke the script.

4. Modify your script from the previous exercise to store the data from the form in a database. (You will have to create one or more suitable tables to hold the data. This can be done outside your script using whatever administration tools your DBMS provides.) Test this script by submitting data for yourself and several co-students or fictitious people. Add a separate form and script to allow a prospective employer to retrieve a résumé for a job candidate by entering their name.

   Further extensions to this script are possible. Consider adding a registration system, so that only registered employers can retrieve résumés. You could also add a facility for employers to post job specifications. The script could also be extended in the direction of allowing people to retrieve the résumés according to other criteria, such as educational qualifications. This might require a redesign of your database and possibly the data entry form. As a final embellishment, you could add a facility to email invitations to interviews to selected candidates.

Web Accessibility

9

It is vital to the success of any Web site that its designers never lose sight of the fact that it exists to communicate with and provide services to the people who visit it. If it fails to do so, it will also fail in any other purpose it may have, such as making money for its owners, providing information, or enhancing the reputations of its designers. No amount of programming or design virtuosity can compensate for a site's being hard or impossible to use.

Just about everybody will have come across sites that are so poorly presented and organized that it is a struggle to figure out what you have to do to use the site, but you may find it hard to imagine a site that is actually *impossible* to use. If so, you probably have good vision and motor control, and no cognitive disabilities. For people who do not share your good fortune, it is quite conceivable that Web sites might be literally unusable. Because this is such a fundamental shortcoming of any site, we will devote this chapter to methods of avoiding it.

Problems with Access

If a Web page is equally usable by everybody, irrespective of any physical or mental limitations they may suffer from at the time, it is said to be **accessible**. Following the latest draft guidelines of the W3C Web Accessibility Initiative (see below), we can refine this definition, by saying that a page is accessible if and only if its content is *perceivable* by every user, any interface components it contains are *operable* by every user, the content and controls are *understandable* by every user and the content is *robust* enough to work with current and future technologies. These four principles of accessibility are sometimes collectively referred to by the acronym POUR.

Table 9.1 summarizes some of the problems that people might experience when using the Web. The range is broad, and each may create different barriers. However, none of these conditions

	Typical Conditions	Problems with Web Access	Assistive Technology
Vision	Blindness	Inability to perceive graphical interface	Screen readers, Braille displays
	Low vision	Extreme difficulty seeing and reading	Screen magnifiers
	Colour defects	Inability to perceive information represented by colour	Browser option to set stylesheets
Hearing	Deafness	Inability to perceive information conveyed by sound	Signing avatars
Movement	Repetive Strain Injuries	Inability to use pointing device and/or conventional keyboard	Alternative devices simulating keyboard input, voice input
	Limb injuries		
	Effects of stroke		
	Cerebral palsey		
	Motor neurone disease		
Cognition	Dyslexia	Difficulty perceiving information conveyed in text	Screen readers
	Attention deficit disorders	Difficulty concentrating	
	Lack of sleep		
	Autism	Difficulty understanding content, problems with orientation and navigation	
	Down's syndrome		
	Effects of stroke		
	Alzheimer's disease		
Age-related	Presbyopia	Difficulty reading small text	Browser option to increase text sizes
	Loss of coordination	Difficulty making selections with pointing device	
	Short-term memory loss	Loss of orientation	

Table 9.1 Some conditions affecting the accessibility of Web sites

Terminology

People With Disabilities

Most of the literature and legislation concerning Web accessibility is couched in terms of enabling access for 'people with disabilities'. This is an emotive expression, which tends to suggest people with relatively severe disabilities, perhaps in wheelchairs or being led by guide dogs. It establishes people with disabilities (or, worse, 'the disabled') as a separate category, who need looking after by 'normal' people. Not only is this wrong in itself, but many of the limitations that interfere with people's access to the Web can in fact afflict anybody. An athlete who has sprained her wrist and cannot therefore use a mouse is unlikely to consider herself a 'disabled person'. Nor are the millions of people whose ability to read small print has declined during middle age, or a young Web designer suffering repetitive strain injury from too much computer use. And yet all of these people, as well as those with more severe limitations, need Web sites to be accessible .

Accessibility is an issue for just about everybody at some time in their lives. For this reason, we will try to avoid referring to 'people with disabilities' in this context, as if they were a distinct group of people who have been set apart. Instead of disabilities, we will consider all those limitations that might interfere with people's use of the Web.

makes it impossible to use a computer. In fact, as we mentioned in Chapter 1, many conditions can be mitigated by computers and access to the Internet, with the aid of assistive technology such as screen readers. It is a Web designer's responsibility to ensure that they do nothing to erect additional barriers to acessibility. There are relatively simple steps that can be taken to improve and maximize accessibility, and all Web designers should be aware of them and use them.

Making Web sites accessible benefits a wide range of people, but it most obviously and effectively helps people with physical and mental disabilities. If this doesn't make you feel a social obligation to maximize the accessibility of your sites, you should be aware that in many countries there are legal requirements to do so. Legislation forbidding discrimination against people with disabilities is increasingly common around the world. Although there is considerable variation among the laws in different countries, generally, where disability legislation is in force, either Web sites are explicitly required to provide certain sorts of services to be made accessible – according to some specified criterion – or general prohibitions against discrimination are interpreted by lawyers as applying to Web sites.

For instance, in the United States, amendments made in 1998 to Section 508 of the 1973 Rehabilitation Act require that any 'Electronic and Information Technology' procured, maintained or used by Federal departments and agencies must be accessible to federal employees with disabilities and members of the public with disabilities seeking information from Federal agencies. This last provision includes information from Web sites maintained by Federal agencies.

In the UK, the Disability Discrimination Act of 1995 makes it unlawful for a 'service provider' to treat disabled people less favourably for a reason related to their disability, and explicitly states that 'access to and use of means of communication' and 'access to and use of information services' are both examples of services which would be covered by the Act. Although in respect of such things as providing wheelchair access, the Act acknowledges circumstances under which it would require an unreasonable effort to comply with its requirements, and leaves it to a court to judge what constitutes a reasonable effort, we will see in this chapter that the effort required to make Web sites accessible is not especially unreasonable, so although at the time of writing the applicability of this Act to Web sites has never been tested in court, it is generally understood to require Web sites to conform to the accessibility standards we will describe later in this chapter. (Similar legislation in Australia *has* been tested in court, where the Organizing Committee for the Sydney Olympic Games was found guilty of failing to provide access for a blind person to its Web site's ticket reservation system.)

We would expect most Web designers to feel that making sites accessible is the right thing to do, irrespective of the legal position. However, the existence of laws that effectively require sites to be accessible provides a lever for convincing clients that it is worth the extra effort and cost to maximize accessibility. Another argument is provided by the number of people affected by accessibility issues.

It is not possible to arrive at an accurate value for the number of people in the world facing barriers to Web access. Not all problems are reported; the only figures that are readily available are those for people who are officially registered as disabled, but definitions of what qualifies as a disability vary from country to country. A broad picture can be obtained for some conditions, though.

There were, for instance, 359,000 people registered as blind or partially sighted in the United Kingdom in 2005 (out of a population of roughly fifty eight million). RNIB (the Royal National Institute for the Blind) estimated that there are a further 750,000 people who are eligible to register. In the United States, according to the latest census statistics, 1.5 million people over the age of 15 suffered from blindness.

An often-cited statistic is that 1 in 12 men and 1 in 200 women suffer from some defect in their colour vision, usually an inability to distinguish clearly between reds and greens. Figure 9.1 illustrates approximately how this affects the appearance of colour images that contain a lot of red and green. Since colour defects are largely genetically determined, their prevalence varies among different populations, and the figures quoted only apply to people of European origin. People from other parts of the world do not suffer as commonly from colour defects: among Asians the figure is estimated at 1 in 20 males, and among people of African origin it is as low as 3%, and the common form of deficiency is different from that found among Europeans.

Determining how many people suffer from repetitive strain injuries (more accurately known as cumulative stress disorders) is problematical, because of the difficulty in diagnosing the condition accurately – or even defining it. The US Bureau of Labor Statistics has reported that 60% of all reported occupational illnesses are RSIs; in 2001, a study reported that 10% of Canadians (an estimated 2.3 million people) had suffered some form of RSI 'serious enough to limit their normal activities' in the preceding year. Both these studies concluded that the incidence of RSI was increasing.

Figure 9.1 A simulation of the effect of defective red/green colour vision

The developed world presently has an aging population. That is, the proportion of people over the age of 60 is increasing steadily. With increasing longevity comes an increase in age-related conditions, such as deteriorating vision, arthritis, loss of muscular coordination and lapses in short-term memory.

Taken together, the total number of people who might be having trouble using a computer in the conventional way is considerable. All of these people are potential visitors to Web sites. For commercial sites they are potential customers, so failing to make sites accessible means turning away customers in large and growing numbers. Whatever other considerations might apply, this is poor business practice.

Even if we add together all of the people who might possibly be suffering from some permanent or temporary condition that interferes with their access to Web sites, we still underestimate the potential benefits of making sites accessible. People who work in noisy environments cannot always hear anything on their computers, so they are presented with the same barriers to using the Web as deaf people. Anybody who uses a mobile device, such as a PDA or a Web-equipped mobile phone to access Web sites may experience the same problems as somebody with limited vision or an injury that prevents them from using a mouse. The small screens of these devices often prevent an entire page being displayed at once: a similar problem is faced by people who use screen magnifiers (see below). The revenue models and low bandwidth of current mobile connections makes downloading large images expensive and slow, so users may prefer to turn off image loading, so that they need to be able to understand and use pages without images, just as blind people using screen readers do. Mobile devices usually lack any pointing device, so sites that rely on the use of a mouse are as inaccessible to mobile users as to RSI sufferers. Finally, mobile devices rarely support scripting and the full range of plug-ins used by desktop browsers, so mobile users may be denied interactivity and multimedia content, in the same way as users who are blind or deaf. Thus, increasing accessibility does not just benefit users with physical or cognitive problems, it also benefits users with with mobile devices (who tend to have relatively large disposable incomes, if you insist on viewing accessibility in commercial terms).

There is one final benefit from increasing accessibility. The robots and spiders that crawl the World Wide Web on behalf of search engines cannot see, hear or use a mouse. Any information that is embedded in a bitmapped image cannot be indexed; any links that can only be activated by a mouse click (perhaps because they are implemented using a script) cannot be followed. In other words, by making your site accessible, you increase the amount of information that can be extracted from it automatically, and thus you increase the site's visibility to search engines.

Assistive Technology

To understand what is required to make a Web site accessible, you need to know some-thing about the devices that people use to help them overcome their limitations. ***Assistive technologies*** are software or hardware products that allow users to interact with computers in ways they would find difficult or impossible without them. In the context of Web use, assistive technologies provide alternative forms of input and output for people who cannot use the conventional mouse, keyboard and screen.

Screen Readers and Refreshable Braille Displays

Among assistive technologies, the devices used by people who are blind or have very limited vision probably present the biggest challenge to Web designers. These devices alter what psychologists call the 'modality' of the interaction with the computer. This means that the information is transmitted via a different sense – hearing or touch instead of sight – and processed in the manner appropriate to that sense.

Screen readers are programs that use speech synthesis to speak the contents of Web pages. Simple screen readers in effect scan a window, reading whatever they encounter in the order it appears. Simple programs of this type are sometimes called 'screen scrapers', since they simply take the text off the screen. More sophisticated programs work at a deeper level, rendering actual data as text. In the context of the Web, programs of this type are able to interpret the structural information contained in XHTML documents, and use it to create a more meaningful verbal rendering of the page. For instance, if a page is laid out in two col-umns, using absolutely positioned `div` elements, a screen scraper might read straight across the columns, whereas a screen reader that could interpret the markup would distinguish the contents of the two `div` elements correctly.

As well as their obvious benefits to blind people, screen readers are also of use to people who are dyslexic or illiterate.

Screen readers may be independent programs, they may be built in to the operating system, or they may be implemented as browser extensions. The leading screen reader program, which is often taken as a *de facto* standard of screen readers' behaviour, is called ***JAWS***. (It only runs on Windows and is obscenely expensive.) Less powerful screen reading capabilities are built into MacOS X 10.4 in the form of ***VoiceOver***, while ***FireVox*** is a free extension that adds screen reading to the Firefox browser on Windows, MacOS X and Linux.

Braille is a system of representing text as patterns of raised dots that blind people can learn to read with their fingers. Refreshable Braille displays use pins that can be dynamically raised or lowered to present a changing Braille representation of the text on a computer screen. Such displays are particularly useful to people who are both blind and deaf, and cannot therefore use a screen reader.

Screen readers and refreshable Braille readers both alter their users' perception of Web pages in two ways. First, they reduce them entirely to text, so that any information that is conveyed by images alone is lost. Second, they turn browsing Web pages into a time-based experience. The elements of each page are read out or translated into Braille in order, over time, and it makes sense to talk about its duration. So, for example, if every page of a site has a navbar across the top, a blind person using a screen reader might have to wait to hear all the navbar's links before getting to the page's main content.

It is possible to get some idea of how somebody using a screen reader will experience a site by viewing it with a text-only browser, such as Lynx. The only way for a sighted person to get an accurate impression is by dimming the screen and trying a screen reader.

Screen Magnifiers

People with poor eyesight who can nevertheless see to some extent may need to increase the size of text on their screens in order to read it. Middle-aged and elderly people who suffer – as almost everybody over a certain age does – from the hardening of their eyes' lenses known as presbyopia find it difficult to focus at short distances, so they cannot read small print or text in a small font on a screen. For them, increasing the font size in their browser by a factor of up to two is usually sufficient to make text readable without the use of reading glasses (which are not very satisfactory for use with a computer screen). Almost all Web browsers now provide a means of doing this. The effect on the layout of pages not designed to accommodate changes in font size may be highly disruptive.

People with more severely impaired vision may need to magnify the contents of their screen to a much greater extent. Screen magnifiers perform this function. As Figure 9.2 shows, this may lead to an almost complete loss of context, especially on pages with a lot of empty space. (Both shots in this figure show the same area of the screen, at normal magnification on the left, zoomed on the right.) A certain amount of trial and error will be needed for the person viewing this page to get back to the navbar, for example.

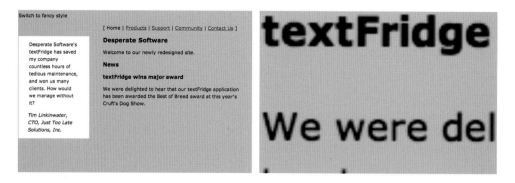

Figure 9.2 Zooming in with a screen magnifier producing a loss of context

Alternative Input Devices

Mice and trackballs are among the main culprits in cases of RSI, so there are many people who must avoid using them. In that case, and if the injury does not prevent it, sufferers use the keyboard for all input. Blind people cannot use a mouse, since they are unable to see what they are pointing at, so they too must rely on keyboard input. Many physical and cognitive disorders can make it difficult for people to point accurately with a mouse. Mobile devices often lack any pointing device, leaving their users in the same situation as people who are physically unable to use mice and trackballs.

Anybody who cannot use a mouse or an equivalent pointing device must use keys to move around the screen: sometimes the arrow keys can be used as a direct substitute for a mouse to control the cursor, but more often in Web browsers some designated key or combination of keys is used to move from one element of a page to the next. Normally, the tab key is used to move between form elements. A browser option is often available to include all elements, including links, among those that can be reached by tabbing, although some browsers require a modifier key to be held down, or use a different key for this purpose.

People who are unable to use conventional keyboards may need to use a variety of alternative devices. If they can use the mouse or an equivalent device, they can select keys by pointing at a virtual keyboard on the screen. If the use of a mouse is impossible, a keypad consisting only of over-sized arrow keys can be used to move the cursor to make selections from the virtual keyboard or other controls, such as input elements. (Interaction with these devices is rather like using the arrow keys on a remote control to select options from a DVD menu.) In cases of severely impaired movement, switches controlled by blowing and sucking through a tube, or by eye movements, can be used in a similar way.

The common property of all these alternative input methods is that they generate the same input as a keyboard. That is, a Web browser receives keystrokes, even though they were not generated by pressing keys. In most cases, the function of a pointing device cannot be simulated, so the fundamental action of pointing at something, such as a link, and clicking is not possible.

It is a simple matter for any Web designer to find out whether someone who cannot use a mouse would experience difficulty navigating a site: just unplug the mouse.

Making Sites More Accessible

XHTML includes features that can be used to enhance Web pages' accessibility. By using these features and avoiding others which may have the opposite effect, Web pages can be made accessible to everybody, not just to those able-bodied young people with good eyesight, perfect colour vision and no cognitive impairments who are able to use a conventional keyboard and mouse.

If you have read the previous chapters in this book you should not have too much difficulty in making your sites accessible, because some of the most important steps you can take towards maximizing accessibility are things that we have been recommending all along. Equally, many of the things that make sites inaccessible come from using language features and techniques that we have avoided discussing, because they are deprecated or no longer considered good practice.

WAI Content Accessibility Guidelines

The *Web Accessibility Initiative (WAI)* of the World Wide Web Consortium takes responsibility for ensuring that W3C technologies support accessibility, and for developing guidelines to be followed in order to maximize accessibility. WAI has developed guidelines in three areas: content, authoring tools and user agents. It is the first of these areas that most directly concerns Web designers, since Web content is what they design. The other two areas have a significant impact on accessibility, but lie almost entirely beyond the control of designers. (Note, though, that any system that allows people to create Web pages should conform to the Authoring Tool Accessibility Guidelines. This includes Web-based blogging systems implemented with scripting.)

Version 1.0 of the *Web Content Accessibility Guidelines (WCAG 1.0)* provides the most widely recognized set of guidelines for making Web pages accessible. Legislation in many countries explicitly or implicitly requires some level of conformance to these guidelines.

WCAG 1.0 is a W3C Recommendation, which comprises fourteen simple pieces of advice that should be followed by Web designers. Under each of these fourteen guidelines, several checkpoints which may apply to a Web page are listed. These are specific requirements, which can be checked. Each checkpoint has a priority: priority 1 checkpoints *must* be satisfied, otherwise some groups of users will find it impossible to access the Web page; priority 2 checkpoints *should* be satisfied, otherwise some groups of users will find it difficult to access the page; priority 3 checkpoints *may* be satisfied, and doing so will make it easier for some groups to access the page. If a page satisfies all the applicable priority 1 checkpoints, it may claim Level A conformance to WCAG 1.0; if it satisfies all the applicable priority 2 checkpoints, it may claim Level Double-A conformance, and if it manages to satisfy all the priority 3 checkpoints, it may claim Triple-A conformance. Where accessibility legislation is based on WCAG 1.0, it usually requires Level A conformance, but some countries (notably Canada) require Level Double-A. (Triple-A conformance is a demanding requirement, but one that can be aspired to.)

The guidelines for Section 508 conformance in the United States closely resemble the Priority 1 checkpoints of WCAG 1.0, although they differ in detail and do not make explicit reference to WCAG.

You should appreciate, as you read the rest of this chapter, that accessibility is not a property of a Web site that can be checked completely automatically, the way that validity of XHTML markup can. For instance, one of the features that is required of accessible sites is that all non-textual content should have a meaningful textual alternative. (We discuss this requirement more fully later on.) It is simple for a program to check that all non-textual content has a textual alternative, but only a human being can determine whether the alternative is meaningful. There are programs and online services that carry out accessibility checks, and they can be valuable for those aspects of accessibility that are amenable to mechanical checking, but it is important to realize that the automatic checks must be supplemented by manual checking.

We won't provide a detailed account of every checkpoint in WCAG 1.0, but we will describe the key principles of accessibility that they embody. Every Web designer should read the WCAG 1.0 Recommendation and the associated documents which provide advice on HTML[†] and CSS techniques for satisfying the checkpoints. These are short and understandable documents, which are much easier to read than some of the other W3C Recommendations.

---

† WCAG 1.0 predates XHTML.

WCAG 2.0

Although WCAG 1.0 has been highly influential and effective in raising awareness about Web accessibility, and although it forms the basis of accessibility legislation in some parts of the world, it has been subject to criticism. In the main, this criticism centres on the extent to which the guidelines are specific to W3C technologies, specifically HTML and CSS, and neglect other widely used formats, such as PDF and Flash. Additionally, WCAG 1.0 is becoming outdated – it was adopted as a W3C Recommendation in 1999 – and contains some inconsistencies.

A successor, in the form of the Web Content Accessibility Guidelines 2.0 has been in preparation since early 2001, but at the time of writing, five years later, it has not yet become a Recommendation but is in the Last Call Working Draft phase. It is an attempt to make the Guidelines less dependent on W3C technologies, and uses a subtly different approach from WCAG 1.0. Instead of providing checkpoints specifying actions which must be taken, it provides 'success criteria': statements about a page which can be true or false, and must be true if the criterion is to be satisfied. WCAG 2.0 also incorporates a notion of 'baselines', which specify a set of facilities which may be assumed to be supported by user agents. Conformance can only be specified relative to a baseline.

Some of the innovations in WCAG 2.0 are controversial, and its attempt to be independent of specific technologies makes its criteria somewhat abstract and harder to verify than the very specific checkpoints of WCAG 1.0. On the whole, even in draft form, WCAG 2.0 provides a more mature approach to accessibility than WCAG 1.0, but it may also be an approach that is less readily taken up by the Web design community.

Alternative Pages

Many people's initial reaction to the issue of accessibility is to provide an alternative version of their site for the benefit of people who cannot access the original version. Usually, they imagine that stripping out all images to create a text-only version is adequate. Indeed, WCAG 1.0 Checkpoint 11.4 is: 'If, *after best efforts*, you cannot create an accessible page, provide a link to an alternative page that uses W3C technologies, is accessible, has equivalent information (or functionality), and is updated as often as the inaccessible (original) page.' (Our emphasis added.) The emphasized text is significant, though. The alternative page is a last resort, after all other efforts have failed. Why is this so?

It reflects the experience and sensibility of disabled people, who (usually rightly) see alternative pages as a second-rate substitute for the real page. Asking people to use a text-only page is often the Web's equivalent of telling wheelchair users to go in through a freight entrance at the back of a building instead of providing a ramp to enable them to use the main entrance. Furthermore, equating accessibility with an absence of images is incorrect. There is a range of problems that interfere with people's use of the Web. For example, removing images does little for people who cannot use a mouse; it may positively interfere with accessibility for people who are dyslexic.

If you provide an accessible alternative to a page, you give yourself two versions to maintain. It is almost inevitable that the accessible version will be updated less frequently than the other, which will tend to be considered the main version. It is likely that the accessible page will not, in fact, provide an equivalent experience, but instead will provide a minimum of information and functionality that the site's owners feel will satisfy their accessibility obligations. These problems are ones of organization and attitude, which could be overcome to fully satisfy checkpoint 11.4, but in almost all cases alternative pages are simply unnecessary. By using appropriate techniques, it is possible to produce a site that is accessible to everybody, without compromising its design. This is what you should always aim for.

Structural Markup

Probably the most important steps towards accessibility through graceful degradation are the use of valid markup and the separation of structure from presentation. Assistive technology is not always as forgiving as a graphical Web browser when presented with invalid documents, so validators should be used to ensure that your markup conforms to the relevant standards. A `DOCTYPE` declaration should, therefore, be included, and all the compulsory page elements, such as `title`, should be provided. As we remarked earlier, you should be doing all this already.

Validators can only determine whether documents conform to the rules in a DTD or schema specifying which elements may appear where. They cannot tell whether elements are being used for their intended purpose, but if a page is to be accessible then they always must be. Don't, for example, use `blockquote` elements to make indented paragraphs, but do use them for lengthy quotations. Similarly, use an `address` element for the page author's contact details, but don't use it for setting text in a small font. Put a meaningful title in the content of the `title` element. (Almost all Web creation software will put the default 'title' `Untitled`; don't just leave it there.) Using elements suitably in this way will make it easier for assistive software to determine the meaning of the document, and present it in an appropriate way.

It is particularly important to use heading elements (`h1`, `h2`,...) correctly to mark the main divisions of a page. Screen readers usually include a means of presenting all the headings on a page, which provides their users with a quick summary of the page's contents and structure, similar to the overview that sighted users obtain by scanning the page quickly for distinctively styled headings. Screen readers can only create their list from correctly marked up headings. It is also important to nest headings properly, and not, for example, to jump from a level 1 heading (`h1`) to a level 3 heading (`h3`), with no intervening level 2 heading, since the heading levels convey the hierarchical structure, and an omitted level may lead users to think that they have missed something.

Another important special case is the use of the `label` element in conjunction with form controls. As we explained in Chapter 3, this element is used to associate labelling text explicitly with a control. By using a `label` instead of just placing the text in the vicinity of the control, you make it possible for programs to discern the relationship between label and control. Some screen readers have a special form-filling mode, which depends on being able to do this in order to tell their users about each control. In the absence of proper `label` elements with correct `for` attributes, screen reader users may hear nothing except the words `Text Field`, with no indication of what the field is for. You should therefore always use `label` elements in the way we described, and never rely on proximity alone for labelling the controls in a form.

By using CSS for controlling presentation you can provide layout and typography that is as rich and sophisticated as you like for the benefit of visitors who can see, without interfering with the information about structure which is embodied in the XHTML markup. Users who find it difficult to see the page displayed using your stylesheets can use their own to present it in a way that is suited to their needs. For instance, an aural stylesheet which describes how a screen reader should speak the page can be used by blind people. People with low vision can specify a stylesheet that uses large easy-to-read fonts, and provides high contrast between foreground text and the page's background. People with defective colour vision can use a stylesheet to specify a colour scheme that does not use combinations of colours that they find confusing. You should do nothing to interfere with this capability, such as using deprecated HTML attributes to specify presentation in the markup. We assume that you are unlikely to do such a thing deliberately, but many Web creation programs do so, in the interests of compatibility with obsolete browsers. Since such browsers are now rare, it is better to use pure CSS, and ensure that your page displays acceptably without it. This is simply to say again that you should maintain a clean separation between content and presentation.

All modern Web browsers allow their users to specify a stylesheet on their own computer to over-ride any stylesheet provided by the designer who created a page. However, not all users know how to do this, and most will not know how to write their own stylesheets. Web designers can help by providing stylesheet switchers, as described in Chapter 7, to allow users to choose larger fonts and a simplified style of presentation. By using @media rules in style elements, they can provide stylesheets for different types of output device, which should be selected automatically (although support for @media rules remains patchy, and the range of media supported in CSS 2.1 does not cover all cases).

Most screen readers will read the elements of a document in the order they appear in the source file. If CSS is used to position the elements absolutely, this order need bear no relation to the order in which elements are displayed on the screen. Remember that somebody using a screen reader must listen to everything in the order it is presented to their software; they cannot, in general, skip to something that looks interesting. So, if every page on a site has a navbar at the top, and the documents making up the site are arranged in the obvious way, with the navbar at the beginning, such a person will have to listen to all the navbar links being read out before they get on to the page's content. By using absolute positioning, it is possible to put the important content of the page at the top, so that it will be the first thing that a screen reader speaks. If you use pseudo-WYSIWYG Web creation software instead of writing XHTML by hand, you may not be able to control this order, though. You should inspect the output of such programs, and fix it up manually if necessary. (An alternative strategy for dealing with navbars at the top of pages is described later.)

Where floating is used to position such things as sidebars, sets of related links, and so on, the ordering of elements is determined by the demands of the float properties. In general, a floated element must appear before the content that flows round it. This can make it impossible to re-order the content to place the most important elements first (although there are tricks involving negative margins that can help). As a rule, therefore, it is advisable to use absolute positioning for layouts wherever possible. (We will describe techniques for multi-column layouts in Chapter 10.)

Accessible Content

Making most types of page content accessible is simple, provided you have used valid structural markup, and have not introduced unnecessary barriers to accessibility by misusing elements or by using deprecated features.

Textual Alternatives

Screen readers can only read text, but the majority of Web pages include some non-textual elements. Images appear on most Web pages, but time-based media, including animation, and applets are also fairly common. If these non-textual elements are to be accessible, some way of making them evident to screen readers and similar technology is required.

Still Images

As we explained in Chapter 5, the `img` element has an `alt` attribute, which allows a short textual alternative (often abbreviated to *alt-text*) to be provided for images. If no `alt` attribute is provided, screen readers will normally speak the entire URL of an image. This usually conveys no useful information, and is exceedingly tiresome to listen to. In XHTML the `alt` attribute is compulsory, so checking the validity of a document will verify that every `img` has its `alt`. It cannot, however, determine whether the alt-text is a proper alternative to the image. A document will validate even if the values of all the `alt` attributes it contains are empty strings or pure gibberish, like `"dkfgdhjag"`. Some Web page creation programs set the alt-text of images to their URLs by default. This is entirely pointless and does not constitute an alternative to the image.

What does constitute a suitable textual alternative depends on how the image is being used. An image might convey information, as in the case of a pie chart, it might be functional, as in a graphical button, it might be there simply to be looked at, as in a reproduction of a painting or a photograph of scenery, or it might not be any of these, as in a small image used as a marker for unordered lists. Each of these cases must be treated differently.

To start with the easiest case, images such as list markers, which are largely decorative in nature, should be given `alt` values of `""` (the empty string). This will cause screen readers to ignore the image entirely. Since the image provides no information or functionality, this is the best thing to do. It allows the screen reader to get on to the meaningful content, without distracting, or possibly confusing, the person listening to it. Note that it is necessary to add the attribute with its empty string value explicitly. Simply leaving it out, apart from invalidating the markup, will cause the screen reader to read the image file's URL.

If an image is there to be looked at, the experience it evokes is not going to be provided for people using screen readers (or text-only browsers). The standard advice for such images is to provide alt-text with a short description of the image, so that such users can know what it is that has been encountered. Without this minimum of information, they might become confused. People who have turned off image loading in their browser (because they are using a mobile device and paying for bandwidth used, for example) may use the alt-text to decide whether they want to load a particular image. Hence, alt-text should provide a clear indication of what the image shows. For example, a news photograph might be given the alt-text 'The Prime Minister eating asparagus'. Remember also that people using screen readers will hear this text spoken. While it should be short, so that it does not take too long to convey its meaning, it should not be so short that it may be missed. 'PM pic' would not be a good alt-text for the example just given.

Including articles ('the' and 'a') in the alt-text, instead of adopting a telegraphic style without them, allows the reading to be more natural and provides the spaces for orientation that occur in normal conversation. Screen readers typically prefix the alt-text of an image with the word 'Image', so there is no point including that word, or a synonym, among the alt-text, as in 'A photograph of the Prime Minister…'.

Where images are used as links, the alt-text effectively becomes the text of the link for these users. Screen reader users often create lists of all the links on a page as a way of obtaining an idea of where they can get to. This means that link text, and thus alt-text for linked images, must make some sense out of context. For this reason, if no other, you should avoid simply setting the `alt` attribute of all your images to `"An image"` or something similar.

As we noted in Chapter 5, the `area` elements which make up an image map must also have `alt` attributes, and these are used in the same way as for `img` elements. It is even more important to provide alt-text for areas in an image map than for images, since image maps contain links. Without alt-text, there is no way for a screen reader to identify these links. If you use `a` elements to define the areas of the image map, there is no problem, since the alternative textual links are provided automatically.

Some images convey information. An example would be a pie chart showing, for instance, the distribution of browsers among the visitors to a Web site. Such information can usually be presented in an alternative, purely textual, way. In this example, a list of browsers, with the percentage values for each could be given. However, such a list would be too long to be used as alt-text for the image, and could benefit from some markup, which cannot be applied within alt-text.

Many pictures can be described in words for the benefit of people who cannot see. For instance, a photograph of an ancient artefact might show what the object was like to somebody who can see it. A skillfully written description can convey a similar impression in words. It is trickier with something like a reproduction of a painting, or even a scenic photograph, but some attempt to describe it in a way meaningful to those who cannot see should still be made.

XHTML provides the `longdesc` attribute of the `img` element as an intended means of providing lengthy textual alternatives. Its value is a URL which points to a separate document containing the alternative descriptive text. Although this attribute has been provided in versions of HTML for a long time, it has not proven to be a very successful mechanism. Almost all graphical browsers simply ignore it, even if image loading is turned off. Only the high-end screen readers implement `longdesc` in such a way that a user can access the long description of an image.

You might well ask yourself why you should hide the long description from most users (which is what `longdesc` does, in effect). If you have gone to the trouble of writing a description, why not let everyone read it if they want to? Redundant information is not a bad thing in itself; people often benefit from being told the same thing in different ways. Rather than use `longdesc`, it makes more sense to provide an ordinary link, with a suitable label, that points to a long description. If space allows, there is much to be said for putting the long description right next to the image it describes.

Images that provide functions, such as graphical buttons and links, should have alt-text that clearly describes their function, not their appearance. For instance, the popular icon used for links to the home page of a site should have alt-text `Go to the Home Page`, not `A cute drawing of a little house`. The use of images in this way should be avoided if possible. If clearly labelled textual links are used instead, their meaning will be clear to everybody. CSS rollovers, possibly involving background images, can be used to give the links a pleasing appearance for sighted visitors.

Images that are used as backgrounds, by way of the CSS `background-image` property, cannot have alt-text attached to them in any way. Normally, this is not a problem, because backgrounds are decorative elements which a screen reader can safely ignore without losing any of the content or function of the page. There are, however, some CSS tricks involving background images which are sometimes used in ways that do affect functionality. For instance, graphic buttons can be produced by applying a background image to a `span` element. This allows designers to produce buttons with a greater range of appearances, and when used in conjunction with the :hover pseudo-class, many rollover effects can be achieved. Care should be taken when using such tricks to ensure that there is some text associated with the button. The usual way of doing this is to put a text equivalent in the content of the span, and then use CSS positioning to hide it, for example by moving it off the top of the window.

Time-based Media

Time-based media require textual alternatives at least as much as still images do. Since video and animation often include soundtracks, and sound is sometimes used alone on Web pages, when considering time-based media we must take account of the needs of people who cannot hear, either because they are deaf or hard of hearing, or because they are using devices that do not support audio. Such people require written text alternatives. For video and animation, we still need to consider people who cannot see. Their needs may be met by an audio equivalent to the visual content, such as a spoken commentary track. Any controls for starting and pausing playback, and so on, should not require the use of a pointing device. This is usually a property of the plug-in being used, which cannot be controlled by the designer, but Flash movies with embedded controls must take account of the needs of people who cannot use a mouse.

Ideally, time-based media should be provided with a synchronized textual alternative, in the form of captions or sub-titles, comprising a transcript of any dialogue or commentary and representations of any significant sounds that occur, interspersed with a description of what is happening in the scene being displayed. This is a tall order, especially for live video, and a lesser compromise may be required. On the other hand, even providing synchronized captions does not satisfy the needs of all users. Some people who are deaf, especially those who were born deaf, are more fluent in sign language than they are in written language, so, to provide the best experience for such people, a sign language interpretation should be supplied (as it often is for televised transmissions of important political events, for instance). Since the sign languages used in different countries are different, this presents considerable problems, and is a task that would usually require the services of a specialist agency.

XHTML provides no means for attaching synchronized text tracks to video, but all the major Web video formats do. Hence, adding these tracks is part of the video post-production process. Plug-ins do not always make it possible to turn captions on and off, so it may be necessary to provide two versions of a video clip, and allow users to choose which one to play.

Software tools for creating caption text and adding timecode to it in order to synchronize it with video are available. Advice on how to write captions so that they convey their information most efficiently can be obtained from various organizations concerned with captioning – a considerable body of experience has grown up from the use of captions in television.

To augment the synchronized captions, a complete transcript should also be supplied. This can be an XHTML document, which can be pointed to by a link. Whereas captions that are part of the embedded video may not be accessible to screen readers, a transcript of this sort always would be, so it can serve as an alternative for blind users. Transcripts can also benefit people with cognitive difficulties, who may have trouble following what is going on in a video, and people who are learning the language used on the soundtrack. As with captions, the transcript should include a description of significant actions and sounds, as well as any spoken content.

If it is not feasible to supply a synchronized textual alternative or a full transcript for embedded time-based media, you must at least provide a short alternative, as you do for images. (This is your only real option for animated GIFs.) Ideally, the description should give some indication of what happens, but if this is not possible in a few words the text should state the subject of the video or animation. As we explained in Chapter 6, the content of an

Emerging Technology

SMIL

The Synchronized Multimedia Integration Language (SMIL) is an XML-based language, defined by a W3C Recommendation, for specifying the structure of time-based multimedia presentations consisting of text, images, sound and video. Different components may be played back in sequence or in parallel. Its facilities can be used for combining synchronized captions and audio commentary tracks with video. Although SMIL was first defined in 1998, browser support for it remains weak, and the most widely available implementation is the Real Player, described briefly in Chapter 6.

If and when support for SMIL is added to mainstream browsers, it will become a viable method for adding synchronized textual alternatives to time-based media that does not require editing of the original media. Hopefully, since SMIL is just XML, it should also be possible to make text tracks visible to screen readers.

`object` element is displayed if the media it embeds cannot be, so a textual alternative can be placed there. If you must use the `embed` element, it has an `alt` attribute that can be used in the same way as for `img` elements. These ways of providing alternatives are not entirely satisfactory, because they require users to disable the display of video in order to allow the alternative text to be displayed.

All of this may tempt you to simply forget about using time-based media on your Web pages. You should bear in mind, though, that a short animation or video clip may convey information more clearly than pure text, especially to people who suffer from some sorts of cognitive problem, so by banishing time-based media you may actually decrease the accessibility of your site in some ways. It is certainly the case that you should not abandon the use of images, since these can undoubtedly communicate efficiently, and making them accessible with alt-text presents no substantial problems.

Colour

If colour is used unwisely, people with defective colour vision may be unable to distinguish some of the content of a Web page. To take an extreme – and, we hope, unlikely – example, if you use green text on a red background of the same brightness (or vice versa), people who are red/green colour-blind will be completely unable to read it – indeed they will probably not even realize that there is text on the page. The top row of images in Figure 9.3 shows such an example, together with the way it is likely to appear to someone who is red/green colourblind (centre image), and the version they would see if they switched their screen to greyscale in an attempt to avoid the problem. In situations where colour is used to convey information, as when red is used to highlight compulsory fields in a data entry form, people who cannot distinguish colours may fail to perceive the necessary information.

You can use programs that simulate what people with various colour defects see in order to find out whether a particular combination is likely to cause problems. More simply, you can just switch your display to greyscale – although few people are unable to distinguish any colours at all, this will show you the tonal contrast present in your colour scheme. As the lower row of images in Figure 9.3 illustrates, tonal contrast can compensate effectively for an inability to distinguish between different hues. Somebody who is red/green colour-blind will be able to read red text on a green background, provided the red and green differ enough in tone. (Just as anybody can read red text on a red background, if one red is light and the other dark.) Maintaining high tonal contrast between text and its background will ensure that information can be perceived by the maximum number of sighted users, and is generally to be recommended in all cases.

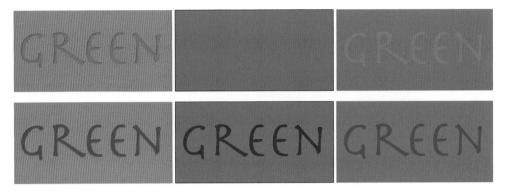

Figure 9.3 Green text on a red background may not be visible at all

As Figure 9.4 demonstrates, it is not always immediately obvious what precise colour combinations in the red and green areas of the spectrum will work and which will not. The apparently bold contrasts in the plain version of the page on the left disappear almost completely, leaving the links invisible to somebody with a red/green vision defect, even if they switch to greyscale. Notice that it isn't the red in itself that is a problem – the red-coloured text can easily be read against the white background on the left, even though the actual hue cannot be perceived. You might think that the version of the page on the right would be altogether less readable, because the background is fussy and there is a green cast over it all which might cause problems with the dark red text. But in fact, because of the high tonal contrast, this page is perfectly readable without its full colour, or indeed any colour.

Where diagrams or other created graphics are used, colour schemes should also be chosen to maintain good tonal contrast. For instance, in a pie chart, the colours of adjacent slices should contrast in tone. High contrast is, in itself, of great benefit to anybody with low vision, so maintaining it wherever possible contributes to accessibility for a much larger group of people than those who have problems distinguishing different colours.

If a page uses a patterned or textured background, you should make sure that there is even more tonal contrast between it and any text that is superimposed on it. Your own eyes should tell you if a background texture is interfering with the legibility of text, but if in doubt, avoid the use of textured backgrounds.

You should always use CSS to apply backgrounds and set colours, so that users who know how to do so can apply their own stylesheets if they need to because of problems caused by your choices. You should consider providing a style switcher, such as the one we described

Figure 9.4 Red/green confusibility and the effect of tonal contrast

in Chapter 7, to allow users who do not know about stylesheets to remove a background or change colours.

The WCAG 1.0 guidelines also require you to ensure that all information conveyed with colour is also available without colour. Context or additional styling should be used to supplement any colour coding. For instance, where a colour is used to denote which of the fields in a form the user is required to complete, an asterisk, or the word *required*, can be placed next to the field's label, or the label can be set in bold or italic. The classic example is the default style of displaying links. They are shown in blue and underlined, so anyone who cannot perceive the colour will see the underlining. (However, by default, colour alone is used to distinguish between visited and unvisited links, which violates this guideline.) A different approach is to add icons and other ornaments that do not depend on colour to augment information conveyed in colour. For instance, some sites append a little icon to links.

As before, it is not colour in the wide sense that causes problems, just hue, so variations in brightness can be used to convey information. For instance, if a background highlight is used to indicate the presence of a link, it is only necessary to ensure that it contrasts with the link text and the page background.

Motion

Probably all Web users have been irritated at some time or other by distracting moving elements on a page, such as flashing icons or blinking text. For some people these elements are more than a minor annoyance. In individuals with what is known as a 'photosensitive seizure disorder', epileptic-like seizures may be triggered by flashes at certain frequencies. These seizures are serious and can lead to hospitalization; potentially they can lead to injury or death. Flashes of a saturated red colour are most likely to trigger photosensitive seizures.

There are detailed technical definitions of flash thresholds that must be avoided to prevent the possibility of seizures being triggered, but there is a simple and safe way of guaranteeing that your Web site will never be responsible for them: never use blinking content. This means avoiding the value `blink` for the `text-decoration` property in CSS. It also means never creating animations that use strobe-like effects or other rapid alternations of images.

Another, less dramatic, reason for avoiding blinking is that it has a distracting effect. Most people can cope with this, but people suffering from certain cognitive problems, including attention deficit disorders, may find blinking elements so distracting that they are unable to use the site. If you are certain that your blinking will not be dangerous and you are convinced that its function of attracting attention is necessary, you should arrange that nothing blinks for more than about three seconds.

Moving elements generally can be difficult for people with various sorts of cognitive problems. In particular, people who have difficulty reading will find it even harder, or impossible, to read moving text. The fashion for using crawling and rolling text on the Web has more or less passed, although it is still seen on some sites. If you have found a compelling use for

Technical Detail

Flashing Content Thresholds

The draft of WCAG 2.0 replaces WCAG 1.0's blanket interdiction against blinking and flashing content by success criteria that do not allow such content to exceed a flash threshold. There are two flash thresholds. The *general flash threshold* is exceeded by a sequence of flashes or rapidly changing image sequences where both the following occur:

1. The combined area of flashes occurring concurrently (but not necessarily contiguously) occupies more than one quarter of any 335×268 pixel rectangle anywhere on the displayed screen area when the content is viewed at 1024×768 pixels.

2. There are more than three flashes within any one-second period.

Here a flash is defined as an increase of brightness of more than 10% of the maximum brightness, followed by a matching decrease of brightness. (And brightness is defined precisely in a reference colour space.)

Since red flashing is most likely to cause seizures, the *red flash threshold* is defined as *any* transition to or from a saturated red where both of the above conditions occur.

It still remains safest to avoid blinking and flashing entirely, and we strongly recommend that you do so.

this effect, you should, in the interests of accessibility, provide a way for users to pause the movement of the text to give themselves a chance to read it.

Text

Properly marked-up text is accessible to screen readers and should cause no problems to people who cannot hear, but the textual content of Web pages may nevertheless present accessibility problems to some people.

In the first place, text that is an integral part of an image is not accessible to screen readers. Some designers cannot learn to live with the way in which Web browsers may substitute fonts for those they have carefully chosen. To prevent this happening, they set type in a graphics program and export it as a GIF image, which is then embedded in the page in an img element.

There are three situations in which GIF text is commonly used. Company logos frequently feature a distinctive font. To substitute a different one would destroy the logo, which is unlikely to be acceptable to the site's owners. Here, using a graphic for the entire logo and providing suitable alt-text is acceptable.

More contentious is the use of images as buttons, especially in navbars, as illustrated in Figure 9.5. Using images in this way allows more varied graphic effects to be applied to buttons, allowing the controls on Web pages to be less austere than text decorated with CSS in a straightforward way. In Chapter 10 we will outline some CSS techniques that make it possible to produce navbars and buttons with some of the desirable characteristics of images, which will often be more accessible. Nevertheless, most screen readers can cope adequately with images used in this way, provided that meaningful alt-text is provided.

Occasionally, it may be considered necessary to use a special font for headings, and GIF text is employed for this purpose. The result can be striking and can make a page stand out, but it does present accessibility problems.

Providing alt-text for any textual image makes the text available to screen readers again, but alt-text is not treated the same way as the text content of elements. Consider, for instance, Figure 9.6. The heading has been set in a font that most users probably will not have on their machines, so the designer has incorporated it as a GIF image to make sure that no other font will be substituted to ruin the effect. The relevant markup is as follows:

```
<h1><img src="heading.gif" alt="Medieval Web Design"></h1>
```

Screen readers normally identify images when they encounter them, so this text would be read out as 'graphic Medieval Web Design' or 'Medieval Web Design image', either of which might, in itself, be a possible heading. This problem does not necessarily occur with images

Figure 9.5 Using images in a navbar

Figure 9.6 Using GIF text to avoid font substitution

within a elements, since intelligent screen readers recognize that the alt-text should be treated as the link's text, and do not flag it as being an image.

A second serious problem with using GIFs as text is that users cannot change the font size, or use a stylesheet to replace it with something they find easier to read. For some people, the ability to do this is essential, so a site that resorts to GIF text is effectively excluding them.

As a general rule, you should assume that at least some visitors to your site will want to use a type size bigger than the one you originally selected, whether it is because they are too old to read small type easily or because they are using a high screen resolution. You need to construct your page layouts accordingly. In particular, you should be aware that if you set the width of div elements to a fixed size in absolute units, text will have to rewrap if somebody changes the type size. This can have a disastrous effect on navbars in particular. We will consider the problem of designing layouts to accommodate changes in font size in Chapter 10, but for now we strongly recommend that you always try increasing the font size when previewing your page designs to see what happens to the layout. With the dishonourable exception of Internet Explorer 5, all Web browsers provide a menu command for increasing or decreasing the type size, and you can implement a stylesheet switcher as an alternative and to make other changes to improve readability.

A quite different kind of barrier to accessibility lies in the natural language used on a page. If a screen reader cannot identify whether the text, or part of it, is in Finnish, say, or in English, it will have trouble reading it out. Software is not usually intelligent enough to determine the language of a piece of text automatically, so some annotation is required to communicate this information.

We described in Chapter 3 how the natural language used on page is indicated by the `lang` and `xml:lang` attributes of its `html` element. As we explained, it is advisable to use both of these attributes in XHTML documents, to allow them to be served as either HTML or XML. These attributes can be used with almost any element to indicate a change of natural language, such as a French word or phrase embedded in a paragraph of English:

```
<p>Creating successful Web applications requires business <span
lang="fr" xml:lang="fr">savoir faire</span> as well as technical
skill.</p>
```

It has to be confessed that not all screen readers cope with foreign languages even in the presence of these attributes. (VoiceOver's French accent leaves a lot to be desired, for example.) However, you should use them for the sake of those that do, and to help search engines.

Tables

Tables present a particular problem for screen readers, because the way they display information depends crucially on the two-dimensional arrangement into rows and columns. People who can see are able to get a good idea of what the relationships among the values are by looking at the row and column headers, and can understand what each value represents because of its position in the table. Stylistic effects, such as row and column borders or distinctive fonts for headers, are often used to emphasize these relationships. All of this information is lost when a table is turned into a linear sequence of spoken words. For example, Figure 9.7 shows one of the tables we originally displayed in Chapter 3. If you can see, you will almost certainly be able to understand it. However, a screen reader might read it like this:

```
kbps (theoretical) 6kB text page 100 kB text page 4 MB movie Modem
56 1 sec 15 secs 10 mins ADSL (typical) 512 0.1 sec 2 secs 1 min
```

	kbps (theoretical)	6kB text page	100 kB text page	4 MB movie
Modem	56	1 sec	15 secs	10 mins
ADSL (typical)	512	0.1 sec	2 secs	1 min

Figure 9.7 A table

If the heading cells are marked up properly using th elements, the better screen readers will make use of this information to associate headings with the values. For instance, the first row of this table might be read as

```
Modem kbps (theoretical) 56 6kB text page 1 sec 100 kB text page 15
secs 4 MB movie 10 mins
```

This is certainly an improvement in making the table understandable, but readers may become confused by cells that span more than one column (defined using the colspan attribute). If each heading cell is given an id attribute, any data cell may have a headers attribute, whose value is a list of these heading identifiers. For instance,

```
<tr>
    <td></td>
    <th id="speed" abbr="kbps">kbps (theoretical)</th>
    <th id="text" abbr="short text">6kB text page</th>
    <th id="big text" abbr="long text">100 kB text page</th>
    <th id="movie" abbr="movie">4 MB movie</th>
</tr>
<tr>
    <th id="modem">Modem</th>
    <td headers="speed modem">56</td>
```

And so on. By no means all contemporary screen readers can take advantage of these attributes, but it is as well to include them, especially in complicated tables, for the sake of future technology.

You may have noticed in the example markup that we had also added an abbr attribute to the column headings. To understand the purpose of this, imagine that the table contained twenty or more rows. Now imagine listening to a synthesized voice saying 'kbps (theoretical)' and each of the other headings for every row. You will probably agree that this could get tedious. The abbr attribute of the th element is used to provide a short alternative to the heading, which should be sufficient to orientate the listener, but short enough to be less trying to listen to repeatedly. Once again, though, not all screen readers yet take advantage of this attribute.

Providing as much information about the table as possible helps people who cannot see it understand it better. For this reason, if no other, you should include a caption element inside the table, to convey an idea of its content or purpose. You can supplement this information by adding a longer summary, using the summary attribute of the table element. Where the table's structure is complicated, this summary can also be used to explain how the rows and columns relate to each other. For our simple table, the following would be adequate:

```
<table summary ="This table shows the typical download times
for different sized documents using different types of Internet
connection">
    <caption>Download Times</caption>
```

The table summary is not displayed by graphical browsers, but may be read out by screen readers.

Accessible Function

Ensuring that all the content of a site is accessible is only half the job. It is also necessary that any function that the site provides is available to all users. This means in particular that it must be possible to operate any controls without demanding the use of a pointing device. It also means that it must be possible for all users to move around the site without getting lost.

Keyboard Access

The ease with which users who are unable to use a mouse or other pointing device can move around Web pages is partly beyond the control of Web designers. All graphical browsers support the use of the tab key to move between controls on a form, but the extent of further support for keyboard navigation varies. In some cases, an option is provided to change the behaviour of the tab key so that it causes the cursor to move between links as well as form controls; in other browsers, this is the default behaviour. Still others require a modifier key, and some require the use of a modifier key and the arrow keys instead of tab. There are also browsers that provide no means at all of navigating to links using the keyboard. At the operating system level, there may be options for using keyboard keys to control the movement of the mouse cursor.

Typically, once a user has tabbed to a link, pressing return or enter has the same effect as clicking on it. This includes the triggering of any handlers for the `click` event that may be attached to the link, even though no click has actually occurred.

Because the tab and return keys (and perhaps the arrow keys) are used in the ways just described, it is not helpful to use `keydown` or `keypress` event handlers that trap them and cause something different to happen. In particular, any event handler that is triggered by the tab key and returns `false` will prevent users from tabbing out of the element the cursor is in.

Another consequence of the fact that some users will activate elements using the keyboard and not by pointing with a mouse is that the concept of mouse or cursor coordinates will not always make sense. Any function that depends on sensing the current position of the mouse may behave unpredictably if the cursor is not being used in the conventional way. For instance, if a user is activating links by tabbing and pressing return, the cursor need not be anywhere near any link. Formerly, the main feature that depended on mouse coordinates was image maps where the map was processed on the server. These have now largely been superseded by images maps of the form we described in Chapter 5, which are processed in the browser, so this is rarely a problem. However, the recent interest in using client-side scripting to provide dynamic user interfaces to Web applications means that scripts are once again using mouse coordinates, for example, to implement drag and drop. You should provide an alternative to such features. For instance, if your interface supports drag and drop editing, you should make sure that it also supports cut and paste, and that selection is possible using the keyboard as well as the mouse.

XHTML provides a feature to allow users to activate links and move the cursor directly to form controls by pressing a key, thereby avoiding the need to tab through every preceding link or control and, in the case of screen reader users, avoiding the need to listen to them all. Any a element, form control or `label` element may have an `accesskey` attribute, whose value is a single letter. For example,

```
<a href="support.html" title="product support" accesskey="2">
```

The idea is that by pressing the 2 key, a user can follow the link to `support.html`. In practice, browsers usually require a modifier key to be pressed at the same time, which is not helpful to RSI sufferers and other people who have trouble using their hands. An additional problem with using this feature is that few, if any, browsers provide a means of finding out which access keys have been defined on a page, and what they do. (It is possible to write

Key	Meaning	Key	Meaning
S	Skip navigation	6	Help
1	Home page	7	Complaints procedure
2	What's new	8	Terms and conditions
3	Site map	9	Feedback form
4	Search	0	Access key details
5	Frequently Asked Questions (FAQ)		

Table 9.2 A conventional assignment of access keys

scripts to provide this facility.) It is therefore advised that such information should be provided explicitly somewhere on the page or site. If access keys are used consistently across a site – for instance, to activate the links on a site-wide navbar – an accessibility statement can include a list of available keys and their function.

There is no standard for assigning access keys. An informal convention that is recommended for use on UK government sites is listed in Table 9.2. These assignments are applicable to many sites, and should be used unless there is a good reason to do otherwise. Note that almost all of the access keys are numeric. This is to minimize the risk that the key combination required to use them will conflict with other keyboard shortcuts in some browsers and screen readers.

Navigation

Almost all Web sites have some links, and the idea of moving the cursor over some text or an image that constitutes a link and clicking on it is a fundamental part of most people's experience of using the Web. Because pointing and clicking is central to this idea, people who use screen readers and those who cannot use a pointing device have particular problems with navigation.

Whether you are conscious of it or not, the links on a page give you an immediate overview of the structure of the site it is part of, and may also give you an idea of its content. A sighted person can obtain this overview at a glance, because the links stand out – they can be found in navbars or else they are distinctively styled. A person who cannot see does not have the chance to obtain this immediate information. Screen reader software almost always provides a facility for constructing a list of all the links on a page, which can then be read in order to provide a similar overview of the site.

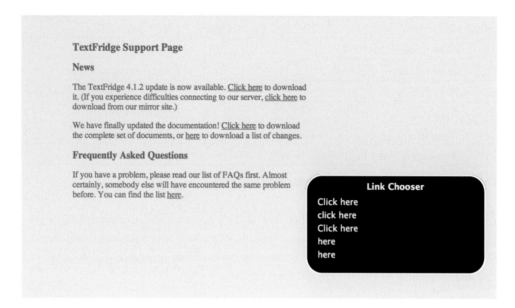

Figure 9.8 Poorly written link text

Figure 9.8 shows a page that utilizes a common style for the text of its links. The inset panel shows what a screen reader user would hear read to them as the list of links on that page. A similar situation would occur on a typical blog front page, where the abstract of each article was followed by a link labelled More.... The user has no clue what any of these links mean or what they might point to. To make pages accessible this lazy approach to link text must be abandoned, and the page must be rewritten so that the links make sense out of context. Usually, this results in a more natural and readable page, as well as making lists of links useful. Figure 9.9 shows how this example page might be rewritten, and the list of links that results.

While it is essential that link text works out of context, it is also desirable to keep it short. Remember that screen reader users have to listen to everything being read out to them. Notice in this example that we have not included the words Download the in the text of the first link. It will be clear to most users that activating the link will cause the update to be downloaded. Additional information about the link can be added using the title attribute of the a element. Some screen readers will read this extra information on request. We could usefully clarify the slightly obscure second link on this page as follows:

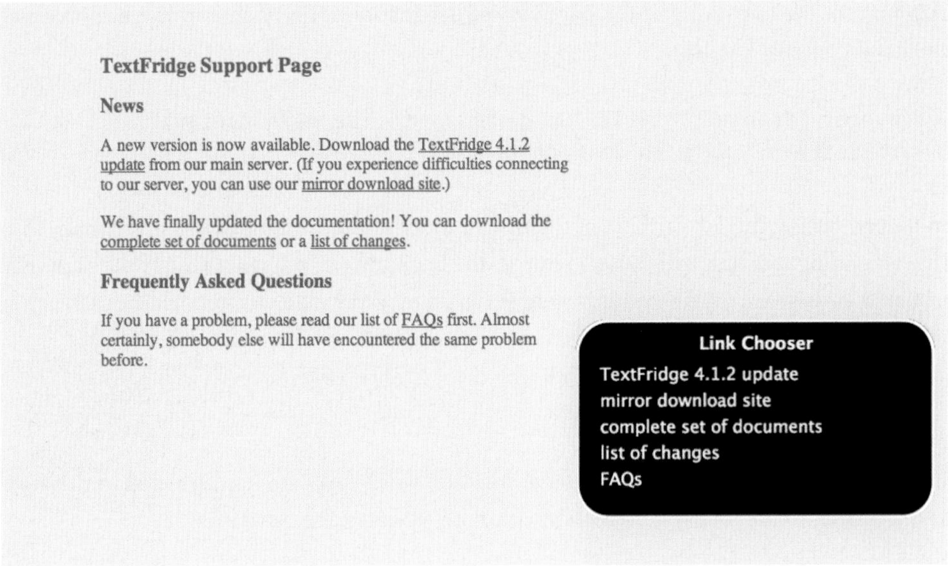

TextFridge Support Page

News

A new version is now available. Download the TextFridge 4.1.2 update from our main server. (If you experience difficulties connecting to our server, you can use our mirror download site.)

We have finally updated the documentation! You can download the complete set of documents or a list of changes.

Frequently Asked Questions

If you have a problem, please read our list of FAQs first. Almost certainly, somebody else will have encountered the same problem before.

> **Link Chooser**
> TextFridge 4.1.2 update
> mirror download site
> complete set of documents
> list of changes
> FAQs

Figure 9.9 Improved link text

```
<a href="http://downloads2.desperatesw.co.uk/textfridge/tf412.tar.
gz" title="Download the update from our mirror site">mirror download
site</a>
```

Not all screen reading software understands `title` attributes, though, so you cannot rely on this mechanism to make up for meaningless link text.

All of a site's visitors benefit from the presence of navbars on its pages. Normally, the navbar appears at the top or the left, which usually means that it is the first thing in the XHTML source document for the page. For screen reader users, this means that they must listen to all the links in the navbar being read on every page before they hear any of its main content. As we explained elsewhere, it is possible to reorder the source and use CSS absolute positioning to move the navbar to the top of the page, but there is empirical evidence that a substantial number of screen reader users value having the navigation links read out at the beginning of a page, and they just want a way of skipping past them when they choose.

This ought to be a user agent's problem, and when XHTML 2's navigation list element becomes widely available, it is to be hoped that browsers and screen readers will provide means of jumping past such lists. In the meantime, it is up to the Web designer to provide a means of skipping navbars. This is usually done by placing a link, often referred to as a *skip link*, at the beginning of the page, whose destination is an anchor at the beginning of the main content, like this:

```
<a href="#content" title="Go directly to the main content"
accesskey="S">Skip to main content</a>
```

In theory, setting the id attribute of the first element of the content is enough to make sure that activating this link will cause a jump to the beginning of the main part of the page. For instance, if the page's main content were enclosed in a div element, it could be marked up with the following start tag:

```
<div id="content">
```

In practice, some browsers do not behave correctly when links are implemented in this way, and it is safer to use an explicit anchor with both id and name attributes.

```
<a name="content" id="content"> </a>
```

To be more precise, when a link is activated, the display focus – the part of the page at the top of the window, or the part that will be read next by a screen reader – is transferred to its destination. At the same time, the tab focus – the notional point from which the tab key moves forward – should also be moved to the same place, so that the next time a user presses the tab key, the first link within the main content should be activated. In practice, some commonly used browsers do not transfer the tab focus, which makes skip links almost useless to people using those browsers. Nevertheless, since screen readers usually do follow skip links correctly, they should be included if there is a substantial number of links on a page before its main content. Hopefully, newer browser versions will correct the problem with tab focus.

Providing a site map consisting of links to all the site's pages is a valuable contribution you can make to helping people get to parts of the site with a minimum of the sort of interaction that they might find difficult. Most sites, except for the smallest, should in any case provide a site map for the benefit of all users, but you should be aware that site maps are especially welcomed by users with accessibility problems, since they allow them to go directly to the pages of most interest to them.

There is one page that users with accessibility problems may find especially interesting, and that is the site's accessibility statement, if it has one. The information in such a statement will not be of much interest to most users, so it would be inappropriate to include it on the

Technical Detail

Flash and Accessibility

Sites that make extensive use of Flash must make extra efforts to ensure accessibility. Recent versions of Flash do have some features for interacting with screen readers, but these only work on Windows. To ensure maximum accessibility, it is necessary to use Flash itself to provide voice alternatives and so on. Separate Flash accessibility guidelines are available from Adobe. The fundamental principles are the same as those behind WCAG, but their implementation is specific to Flash.

home page. Not all sites need such a statement, but sites that make extensive use of access keys, or whose owners want to make a point of emphasizing their accessibility can easily and usefully provide one. It would include any claims of conformance to WCAG or Section 508 guidelines, to give users an idea of whether they would expect to encounter problems using the site, together with a list of access key bindings, if any were used throughout the site, and information about any special accessibility features, such as a stylesheet switcher or skip links, that the site provides. A link to this page should be provided in an place that makes it easy to find, especially by new visitors to the site.

It is possible that a site designed with accessibility in mind may feature a skip link, a link to the accessibility statement, a link to the site map and a stylesheet switcher control on every page. The skip link, at least, must appear very near the beginning of the page if it is to be of any use. Incorporating these elements into a page design is a challenge in itself. Some designers advocate using various CSS techniques to make these links invisible, on the grounds that they are only of interest to people accessing the site with screen readers. As we have demonstrated, this is a mistaken belief, since these features can be of benefit to others, including people with restricted mobility.

An alternative approach is shown in Figure 9.10. Rather than trying to hide the accessibility links, we have emphasized their presence, but in so doing we have clearly separated them (by the contrasting background and bottom border) from the navbar and the page's content. It is clear that these controls are not part of the page, in the same way that it is clear from the way browser windows are laid out that the browser's toolbar is not part of the page. (Something like this style is used on the WAI's own pages.) There is ample evidence that users do not look at areas of a page which they are expecting, from their past experience of many sites, to contain something of no interest to them. (In particular, they do not look at anything that resembles a banner ad across the top of the page.) If the convention just described for including accessibility links in a strip across the top of the page is widely adopted, it seems likely that users who are not dependent on accessibility features will similarly learn that it is of no interest to them, and, in effect, fail to see it. We therefore hope that the convention will be used on as many sites as possible.

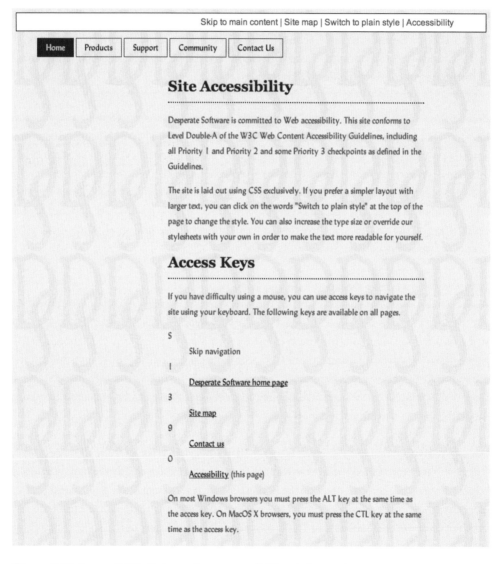

Figure 9.10 Accessibility links and an accessibility statement

Key Points

Problems with Access

A Web page is accessible if it is equally usable by everybody, irrespective of physical or mental limitations.

Content must be perceivable, interface components must be operable, content and controls must be understandable and content must be robust.

In many countries there are legal requirements to make Web sites accessible.

A substantial number of people suffer from blindness, defective colour vision, repetitive strain or other injuries, and age-related conditions that can interfere with their ability to use Web sites.

Users of mobile devices are faced with many of the same problems as people with disabilities. Search robots behave as if they were blind and unable to use a pointing device.

Assistive Technology

Assistive technologies provide alternative forms of input and output for people who cannot use the conventional mouse, keyboard and screen.

Screen readers are programs that use speech synthesis to speak the contents of Web pages for the benefit of blind, partially-sighted or dyslexic people.

Refreshable Braille displays present text as Braille. They are especially useful for people who are both blind and deaf.

Screen readers and Braille displays reduce pages entirely to text and add a time dimension.

Increasing font size to make small text more easily readable may disrupt page layout unless the page has been designed to accommodate changes in font size.

Screen magnifiers make text big enough to be read by people with low vision, but they can produce a loss of context.

RSI sufferers, blind people and other people who cannot use a mouse must use the keyboard, or some device that generates keyboard input by some other means.

Making Sites More Accessible

The W3C's Web Accessibility Initiative develops guidelines for maximizing accessibility.

Web Content Accessibility Guidelines, version 1.0 (WCAG 1.0) provide the most widely recognized set of guidelines for making Web pages accessible, and form the basis of most Web accessibility legislation.

Alternative pages should only be used as a last resort, since they rarely provide a truly equivalent experience and tend to become neglected.

The use of valid markup and the separation of structure from presentation greatly assist in making pages accessible.

Correct use of headings makes it possible to present a summary of the page's structure and contents.

Using `label` elements in conjunction with form controls will make it possible for programs to match labels with controls.

Using stylesheets to control presentation makes it possible for other modes of presentation to be specified by supplying alternative stylesheets.

Stylesheet switchers can be provided to make it easy for users to alter the presentation.

Accessible Content

Textual alternative must be supplied for non-textual elements.

The `alt` attribute of `img` elements must contain a suitable alternative to the image: the empty string for purely decorative elements, a short description of images that are purely visual, a clear description of function for images that provide functions, such as buttons.

The `longdesc` attribute of an `img` can point to a detailed description of an image that conveys information, but it is usually better to make such a description available as part of the page.

Time-based media should be provided with a synchronized textual alternative, in the form of captions or sub-titles.

A complete transcript should also be supplied.

The content of an `object` element can provide a short textual alternative.

Ensure high tonal contrast between text and its background, especially for red and green.

Ensure that all information conveyed with colour is also available without colour.

Never use blinking or flashing content that might trigger seizures.

Provide a way for users to pause moving text.

Alt-text must be supplied for any images used as text or links.

Avoid using GIF text unnecessarily, because it cannot be resized and may lead to confusing screen reader output.

Use the `lang` and `xml:lang` attributes to identify the natural language of pages and any changes in language, to assist screen readers.

Use th elements with id attributes for table headers, and header attributes for dt elements in complicated tables. Include a caption element and use the summary attribute to summarize the content and structure of tables.

Accessible Function

It must be possible to operate any controls without a pointing device.

Event handlers that are triggered by the tab key should never return false and prevent the default behaviour of tabbing between fields.

Always provide alternatives to any interaction that depends on sensing the cursor coordinates.

If access keys are used consistently across a site, an accessibility statement can include a list of available keys and their function.

Use short link text that makes sense out of context so that it can be understood in a list of links created by a screen reader.

Additional information about links can be added using the title attribute of the a element.

Use skip links to allow screen reader users and people who cannot use a pointing device to jump over navbars.

Site maps make navigation easier for users with accessibility problems.

Group together accessibility links so that they can be easily identified.

Exercises

Test Questions

1. If you suffered a repetitive strain injury in your wrist, how would it affect the way you used your computer? What features of Web sites might present difficulties that you had not encountered before you suffered the injury?

2. Why do you think the higher conformance levels for WCAG 1.0 are called Double-A and Triple-A instead of AA and AAA? What level of conformance should you aim for when designing Web sites?

3. When is providing alternative pages the best way of ensuring that a Web site is accessible?

4. What benefits in accessibility result from separating markup from presentation?

5. Write suitable alt-text for the photograph on the left of Figure 9.1 and the diagram Figure 2.5 in Chapter 2. When would you omit the `alt` attribute from an `img` element?

6. Is avoiding the use of time-based media necessary or desirable in ensuring Web sites are accessible?

7. What is the best way to ensure that a Web site will not cause problems for people with defective colour vision? How can you test whether a Web page will be readable by someone with defective colour vision?

8. How would you explain to a client who wanted to include blinking buttons on the home page of their site that it was not a good idea?

9. If you need to use a special font for the links in a navbar, how would you make sure that no other font was substituted for it? What potential accessibility problems would result, and what could you do to minimize them?

10. Suppose a blog site's front page consists of the opening paragraphs of the twelve most recent entries, each with a link to the full entry. What would you use as the text of the links, and why?

Discussion Topics

1. If you advocate accessibility in Web design, sooner or later you will hear somebody arguing along the following lines: 'There are some things disabled people just have to accept that they cannot do. Blind people can't drive cars, for instance. Using our Web site is one of those things. There's no point worrying about accessibility.' How would you refute this argument?

2. Some designers advocate hiding skip links until they are activated (i.e. until the cursor moves over them or a user tabs to them), at which point they appear. Discuss whether this is preferable to having skip links visible at all times. What other options might there be for presenting skip links?

Practical Tasks

1. Create an XHTML version of Table 9.1, incorporating all the necessary markup required to make it as accessible as possible.

2. Choose a fairly prominent Web site, such as a medium-sized online retailer or your college's site, and write a report on its accessibility. Begin by checking how many WCAG guidelines it follows – use an automated checker if you find it helpful – and then try to carry out some typical tasks at the site, such as finding some information and contacting the site's owners using or simulating assistive technology. (You can approximate the effect of using a screen reader by visiting the site with a text-only browser, and simulate a colour blind person's experience either by using a simulator or by switching your screen to greyscale. To appreciate the problems of people who cannot use a pointing device, disconnect or deactivate yours.) Finally, if the site is unsatisfactory in any way, produce a set of recommendations for improving its accessibility.

Web Page Design

10

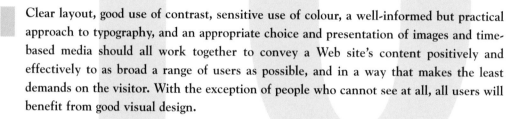

Clear layout, good use of contrast, sensitive use of colour, a well-informed but practical approach to typography, and an appropriate choice and presentation of images and time-based media should all work together to convey a Web site's content positively and effectively to as broad a range of users as possible, and in a way that makes the least demands on the visitor. With the exception of people who cannot see at all, all users will benefit from good visual design.

No Web designer can afford to ignore the basic principles of visual design and visual communication, because every Web page implements them – some very badly, with the result that the site fails to convey its content or is hard to use – and some very well, with the result that the site is easy to use and understand, popular with users, and likely to attract repeat visits. Above all, visual design should work to make Web sites more usable, more accessible and more successful. Very often, the principles which lead to the achievement of these goals also result in more attractive sites.

It is not the purpose of this book to teach graphic design, partly because space does not allow us to cover this specialist subject anything like adequately here (that would require a whole book in itself), and partly because many Web designers will have little to do with graphic design in practice. We therefore limit our coverage to those general principles of usability, visual communication and visual design which are fundamental to the practice of good Web design as a whole, and which are implemented in markup and stylesheets. Even if you never do any visual design work yourself, but work as part of a team with specialist graphic designers, it is important to be able to understand what their requirements are and why. In turn, you also need to be able to communicate to the graphic designers how and why their visual ideas may or may not be appropriate for implementation on a Web page.

Remember that, on the Web, structure and content should be separated from presentation. Whereas graphic designers working in print media are accustomed to developing a structure visually, on the Web structure is already explicitly present in markup, and so – in addition to ensuring usability and the effective communication of content – it is also the job of visual design to express that inherent structure clearly, through CSS rules that control the layout and appearance of the elements of the page. The hierarchy which is already defined by the page's markup should be expressed through the appearance and position of elements on the page, by the use of such attributes as size, colour and spacing. Ideally, this visual presentation and the explicit structure will work hand-in-hand. This ideal situation falls down in the face of the limited repertoire of elements provided by XHTML, which are not always adequate to express the appropriate structure of a page. The use of `class` and `id` attributes to provide hooks for styling is a way of getting round this shortcoming and, at the same time, creating ad hoc markup to express the true structure, so in a sense, the visual design does contribute to the development of the structure.

Visual Communication

The basic principles of visual design have been developed through hundreds of years' accumulated experience in print media. But, as we have repeatedly stressed, the Web is a new medium, with profound differences from printed media. This unfortunately renders many of the practices of print-based visual design inappropriate or impractical, above all because the size and shape of a Web page, and the appearance of many elements in it, may be determined by the browser and the user in ways which the designer cannot foresee. Nevertheless, some of the fundamental principles of visual design apply in all contexts where content is being conveyed visually, and the use of stylesheets allows the designer at least to indicate, if not to determine absolutely, the way that they wish the page to appear.

Visual Design for Usability

The notion, prevalent in some circles, that visual design is just concerned with trivial ornamentation which is not really necessary – 'eye candy' as it is disparagingly referred to – is wholly mistaken. Neglect of visual design is one of the main factors that lead to Web sites being hard to use.

An enormous amount has been written about **usability** in the context of Web design, and a great deal of advice has been put forward by self-proclaimed experts on the subject. Some of this advice is valuable, some is trite; some of it is based on ideas that are almost certainly wrong, or on inadequate models and invalid statistical analyses, whereas some is based on common sense and ideas that most people would agree are right. So how do you sort out the useful guidelines from the rest?

Usability is a vague term which relates to something that cannot be quantified. Furthermore, owing to substantial variation among users in the global community, a site that is usable for some may be quite unusable by others, so it makes no sense to talk about the usability of a Web page or site as though it were an absolute fixed measure. Nor does it help to think of an average user. As we asked back in Chapter 1, what gender is the average user? We can go much further and ask, what educational level have they achieved? What physical difficulties or limitations do they experience? How familiar are they with the conventions of the World Wide Web? What language do they speak? The list of potential questions is long, but the answer is clear: there is no average user, and there is no such thing as a Web page or site which is usable in the abstract. The most beautifully designed and functional site might be completely unusable by someone in Africa for the simple reason that it is written entirely in Japanese. And yet in Japan that same site might be considered particularly easy to use. Even if we eliminate language entirely and rely solely on images, there will be some people who cannot see those images, and some who do not understand them.

All usability experts advocate user testing, but they generally draw their test group from their own nation, and often from a very much smaller community of people – perhaps only a handful. While the results of a small test may provide broad qualitative results that may be adequate for certain types of commercial or corporate enterprise with a restricted target audience, there are many other types of site for which they will be a very poor guide. (Published claims that tests on no more than twenty participants are sufficient to produce quantitatively meaningful results are based on hopelessly naive statistical analyses, and should not be taken seriously.)

Usability is concerned with several aspects of Web design, notably function, structure, accessibility, and visual presentation. Once again we must stress that – so far as it is possible to ensure – a Web site must work properly and without errors on all browsers, it must be navigable and coherent, and it must be made accessible to all potential users. Clearly, if a site fails in any of these respects then it is not fully usable, but we deal with these aspects of Web design in other chapters of this book. In this chapter, therefore, we will only look at the way usability may be controlled by visual design.

Experience in the field of interface design in general has shown that both familiarity and memory play an important role in usability, and visual design plays an important role in ensuring that page elements are familiar or memorable. Although some usability guidelines suggest that the purpose of functional features should be intuitively obvious, that is clearly an inappropriate objective. For example, without previous experience or instruction we cannot intuit that an underlined piece of text is a link to another document; there is no inherent reason why it should be, and no precedent. On the contrary, in printed and hand-written media, underlining has traditionally been used for emphasis – even to the extent that it is conventionally used by students to draw attention to important passages in books they are studying – so a Web novice would probably make a completely wrong assumption about underlined text on a Web page. But the widespread establishment of this type of textual formatting as a convention for links ensures that it quickly becomes familiar in the context of the Web once the user has learned the convention. And this convention is visual – we see the underlining, and instantly recognize its meaning. It is a wholly visual sign. We can understand this better when we realize that assistive technologies do not tell their users that a piece of text is underlined; instead, they simply say what it is, for example 'link'. In an XHTML document, the fact of something's being a link is determined by mark-up, but it is conveyed to the user by visual or spoken convention. We will return to the role of signs shortly, in the section on *Gestalt Principles and Semiotics*.

Many different visual factors work together to make a site usable. One look at a Web page should be sufficient to convey to a sighted user where the navbar is and where the links will lead; where the search box is and how to use it; who owns the site; what type of content is being presented; and – if the site has a specific function such as e-commerce – how to operate all aspects of that function (for example, how to order goods and services, how to check what has been ordered, and how to pay). It is not sufficient that all of these elements are present somewhere on the page; it is necessary that they are presented in a way that makes each one easy to find, identify or use.

Figure 10.1 shows a simple, usable Web page, which draws both on current conventions and fundamental visual design principles to present all its elements in a clear and obvious way. The company logo appears at the top of the page, because the top of the page will always be seen. The logo identifies the owner of the site and should tell the user something about what kind of site it is (for example, it might be the logo and name of a university). Whether it is positioned on the right or left should be determined by the reading conventions of the language in which the site's content is written. The search box also appears at the top of the page, with the box in which search terms should be entered distinguished from the search button by use of contrast and colour. It has become conventional to place the search box at the top because it provides a function which is so frequently used. A white background was chosen for this top area, to keep it simple, legible and apart from the rest of the page whose function is different. It also works to create a visual balance and link with the large

| | | | | | | Search |

link   link   link   link   link   link

Lorem Ipsum

Rud min hendiam, qui tet praesto duis dolore faciliquis am, vulputatio odit wis aliquat wis eraesequisi ea faci blaore tisi.

Ure conullandrem zzriustrud duipsum dolum dolor iniat adiat iurero er ad ming esectet nonsectet ipit, veraestie Rud min hendiam, qui tet praesto duis dolore faciliquis am, vulputatio odit wis aliquat wis eraesequisi ea faci blaore tisi.

Na aliquis eu feu feuipisl dignisisi blaoreet nulput eliquis adiam dip ex eu facidunt ut del enit do dolorem irit adipism olorting ea core modignit accum zzrilit luptatue delent doluptatem quisl etum ea augiametue dunt laoreet, sim iusto do consed eugiam, commy num dolorper sed tate tet at pratisse ex eu feuguero odiat. it, veraestie.

Ectet, verostrud magna faccum quatem ea faccumm odipis adio odipit lore magna faccum iril iuscincipsum do et ulla consenim zzrilla con essi.

Figure 10.1 A usable Web page

white area lower down, so that the parts of the page do not become too detached from one another.

Immediately below the logo and search box we find the navbar. This is set apart from the rest of the page by being placed on an area of contrasting colour and tone, to ensure that users with all levels of vision can easily identify it. (It also scales up cleanly to a very large size, without wrapping, when magnified – unlike the logo, which is a GIF image.) We will

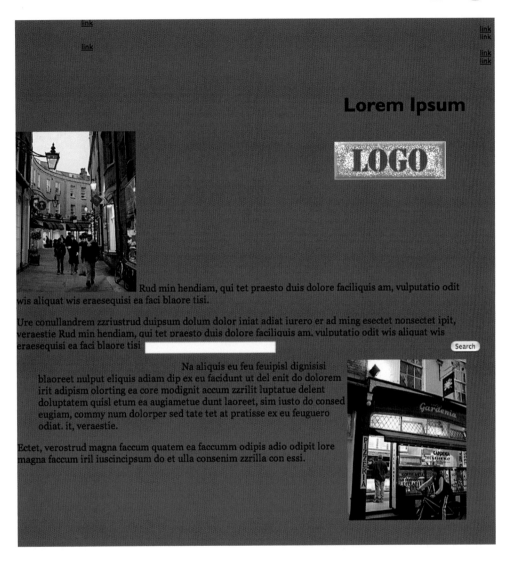

Figure 10.2 A less usable Web page

discuss the composition and presentation of the navbar itself further in the next section, but its position as a bar across the page near the top has become a matter of convention. It is usual now either to position the navbar in the way shown in Figure 10.1, or down one or other side of the page.

For this example we have chosen a centred design for the main content of the page. There is no strong inherent virtue in this choice, but it is a popular means of presentation at the time of writing, and has the benefit of looking the same whether users are accustomed to organizing their screens from right to left or from left to right. It also means that the content is displayed in the centre of the window, no matter how wide or narrow that window may be. (It would not be such a good choice, however, where the amount of content to be presented required a multi-column layout.) The box which contains the content has a white background as this provides the highest contrast with the black text (and thus maximum legibility) and makes the photographic images stand out well without any risk of colour clash. As we will see later on, however, it is not necessary to use quite such a stark contrast as this in order to achieve good legibility. Within the white box, the content has been laid out on a simple grid, aligning the photographs and the blocks of text in a way that makes it easy to see which elements go together. The heading has been set apart at the top of the page, in a larger size, to make it clear that it is the heading for the content below.

Finally, the main background to the page has been set to a fairly dark tone which harmonizes pleasantly with the other colours, and which acts to make the white content box stand out and 'advance' visually towards the user. The choice of the same colour that is used for the search box and navbar text works to make the whole page more visually coherent and to indicate to the user that all the elements are part of a single whole, and allows the background to remain unremarkable, as it should do. The choice of a radically different background colour – bright pink or sky blue, for example – would have acted to break up the parts of the page and suggest that there might be something special about the background (some particular reason for choosing bright pink), which sends a misleading message to the user.

To illustrate what might happen if all the visual design principles that governed the design of the page in Figure 10.1 were ignored, we created a second, unusable page, shown in Figure 10.2. Functionally the two pages are identical. They both have the same links, a search box and a company logo, and they both present exactly the same information. But one is clear and simple to use (if not very exciting) and the other is not. The markup for the two pages is essentially the same. The only difference between them is their visual design, which is controlled by different stylesheets.

The way in which elements are visually organized and grouped on the page, familiarity with visual conventions and signs, the use of visual hierarchies to make it clear which elements are the most important on a page, the use of alignment, the avoidance of confusing visual complexity, the choice of suitable colours with adequate tonal contrast where appropriate, and the choice of suitable fonts (so far as that can be controlled), all play a role in making our simple Web page usable and visually coherent. We discuss each of these design issues in turn in the rest of this chapter.

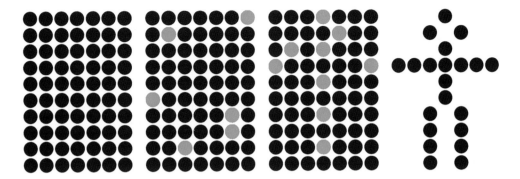

Figure 10.3 Gestalt principles of visual perception

Gestalt Principles and Semiotics

Gestalt

Gestalt principles of visual design are derived from the theories of gestalt psychology, which were applied to the study of visual perception in the 1930s and 1940s in order to investigate how the human brain tends to organize the visual information that reaches the eyes. Although we are able to identify the parts of a visual image separately – for example, we can see that each of the four images in Figure 10.3 is actually composed from individual dots – we nevertheless tend to organize visual information into patterns and structures, rather than concentrating on each piece of discrete information – each object – in the visual field. Looking again at Figure 10.3 the image on the far right immediately stands out, because the we see that the arrangement of dots forms a crude drawing of a human figure, a symbol which is likely to be recognizable by almost all people and cultures. This universal recognition of the human figure is so strong that it is almost impossible to see this image simply as a collection of dots.

In the image on the far left of Figure 10.3, however, we can discern no symbolic pattern. Here we simply see a field of dots, but we percieve that they are aligned into a perfectly regular grid. If we stare at this image for a while we may perhaps see the regular lattice pattern formed by the negative white space between the dots, rather than that formed by the dots themselves.

The perception of patterns and structures is determined by various factors, but particularly by the grouping of objects in a visual field. Our recognition of grouping is in turn determined by the proximity of elements, by similarity between elements, by symmetry, by the distinction between figure and ground, and by closure – that is, by the brain's ability to infer a complete visual pattern or image from incomplete information. These gestalt principles of visual perception are often summed up by the adage that the whole is greater than and different from the sum of the parts.

In the field of black dots on the left of Figure 10.3, we perceive grouping as a result of the similarity between the elements (the dots are identical), proximity (the dots are close to one another, and the whole group is set apart from its surroundings by some white space), and a distinction between figure (black dots) and ground (white background) – although with some effort we can make the white lattice pattern (the ground) seem dominant. We can organize this particular image no further, but this sort of non-symbolic ordering is not without value in itself. Figure 10.4 shows how these Gestalt principles work in a tiled background for a Web page, composed from the repetition of a logo. When the logo is repeated many times we perceive it simply as a pattern. Like the field of black dots, the background is composed of a collection of identical objects laid out in close proximity in a structured grid. We therefore perceive the result not as a collection of parts but as a whole pattern.

In the second and third images in Figure 10.3 (counting from the left), some of the dots have been coloured red. Looking at these two fields of dots we immediately attempt to organize the red ones into some kind of visual structure or pattern. In the second image, however, there is no pattern to be found – there is neither any meaningful symbol nor any discernible abstract pattern to be seen in this particular arrangement. The human brain works in such a way that this can make this image the most frustrating of the four; we try in vain to find a visual structure, and may expend unwarranted time and effort on this attempt.

The third image is more satisfying, however. With a little effort we can see a symbol in this image, composed from the arrangement of the red dots. This demonstrates one of the most interesting principles of gestalt theory: closure. Almost half of the dots in the arrow shape are in fact black and not red – nearly half of the visual information that says 'arrow' to us is in fact missing. And yet we can see the arrow without much difficulty, and do not try to arrange the red dots into another visual pattern. The brain completes the pattern implied by the dots that are coloured red in such a way that we can almost see a complete red arrow if we stare at this image.

The gestalt visual principles illustrated in Figure 10.3 are of considerable importance to the Web desginer. First, we need to realize that the user's brain is going to be looking for patterns. This means that a user will find a Web page easy to use if its elements are arranged in accordance with gestalt principles, and difficult and frustrating to use if no visual structure or order can be perceived. Some social networking sites presently allow the creation of personal

Figure 10.4 The whole is different from and greater than the sum of its parts

pages by their users, without imposing any design guidelines. Without sufficient attention to design principles, some of these pages can be very difficult to use, like the example shown in Figure 10.5. (This particular page extends downwards below the part illustrated for some considerable distance.) While it is up to the individual to determine how they wish to represent themselves on a personal Web page (after all, chaos might be a deliberate choice), this sort of design can make pages unusable (and in this type of case, probably inaccessible too). The fault does not lie in the separate elements that comprise the page, but in the way that they are arranged (or not) into a whole. In this particular case the design fails not only with respect to gestalt principles, but also on grounds of legibility as a result of poor colour and contrast, and over-complexity. In this case the whole is greater than the sum of the parts only in achieving a sense of chaos and confusion which the parts themselves lacked. The result acts in a way that actually detracts from any merits which the individual parts might have had.

Even the component parts of a Web page may themselves be constructed according to gestalt principles. We have seen how this might work in a background (in Figure 10.4) but it is often most obvious in the navbar. The convention has become so well established that users are unlikely to stop to think about this, which is as it should be. However, as we saw in Figure 10.2, there is no structural reason why a navbar should appear as a coherent whole. The types of menu and navbar that we are used to seeing and constructing owe their concept to gestalt principles of visual design. In a contemporary navbar, links are usually all presented in the same font, in the same size and colour, in close proximity to one another, and organized into an ordered structure. In the case of complex multi-level navbars, additional use of the principles is usually made in order to make it clear which upper-level element relates to which lower-level ones. The use of a coloured tab metaphor, adapted from office filing

Figure 10.5 Design chaos

Technical Detail

Navbars, Gestalt and Markup

The navbar is an excellent example of gestalt principles in operation which also illustrates the relationship between document structure and visual structure.

The very earliest Web sites had no navbars; HTML had (and XHTML 1.0 has) no element type suitable for grouping together a set of links. But designers seeking to make the links that define the top-level structure of a site conspicuous and easy to find soon came up with the idea of grouping them together in a distinctive style and a consistent position. This is a pure application of the gestalt principles of visual design.

This purely visual grouping led to the emergence of the navbar as a concept. This led Web designers to start using ad hoc markup to delimit navbars: first, a table, then a `div` element, finally a consensus has emerged that navbars should be marked up as unordered lists. They aren't, though. It is only with the inclusion of the `nl` (navigation list) element in the XHTML 2 proposal that markup has been provided to specify navbars as structural elements. The relationship between document structure and visual structure is not just one way.

conventions, has become very popular for this purpose. We recognize the pattern easily, and understand that each tab is a separate link to a collection of pages (or even other links) which belong together in some way. Although the navbar is made up of many separate parts, we recognize it as a whole; we visualize a navbar as a single object because of the way that the parts are presented visually.

In the same way, the designer should ensure that any visual components of a Web page that are linked conceptually will also seem linked visually, as this makes the page much easier to comprehend. If a weather forecasting site offers a set of predictions for temperature, precipitation, wind speed, etc., then these should be presented and organized on the page in a way that is visually coherent. This may be so intuitively obvious that few people will stop to think about it, but imagine how confusing it would be if the symbol for 'heavy rain' was a different size, a different colour, or even of a different design each time it appeared. To simplify matters further, suppose the forecast was provided in text only, set out in a table with a row for each of the next seven days (which we assume will be very wet), but that the font

Monday	**Heavy Rain**
Tuesday	Heavy Rain
Wednesday	HEAVY RAIN
Thursday	**Heavy Rain**
Friday	**Heavy Rain**
Saturday	*Heavy Rain*
Sunday	*Heavy Rain*

Figure 10.6 Confusing absence of similarity

for 'heavy rain' was different almost every time it appeared, as in Figure 10.6. Users would assume that there was some reason for the difference – that one day's heavy rain was going to be somehow different from the next, and that the two occurrences of the same font signified some similarity. But if every occurence of heavy rain was in the same font, size and colour, users simply recognize the pattern.

Semiotics

Because the human brain so readily organizes visual information into patterns, it is important to understand when these patterns may have meaning, and to avoid the accidental creation of visual patterns or signs that could have some unintended meaning. For example, it would be inappropriate to arrange a set of images on a page in a single column which crossed a single row in the centre, unless you intended to make use of the sign of the cross for some specific reason. Gestalt theory tells us that users will see the cross sign because of the grouping of the images; *semiotics* (or semiology, as it is known in Europe) tells us that those who recognize it will interpret that sign in a particular way and infer some meaning from it.

Semiotics was originally concerned with the way in which natural language is built up out of meaningless phonemes into whole words that have meaning. For example, the word 'elephant' is understood by all who know English and are familiar with the relevant creature to refer to the animal 'elephant'. When they hear or read the word, they think of an elephant. In the terminology of semiotics we say that the word is the *signifier*; the elephant itself is what is *signified*. The relationship between the signifier and the signified is arbitrary, and we only understand it through knowledge of the specific system within which it operates – in this case, the English language. (The word for 'elephant' in languages other than English is of course quite different, and yet the same animal is signified.)

This approach to the understanding of how meaning is created was extended to cover visual language and the way that we understand images and graphic signs. The analysis of images is of considerable importance in graphic design, but it is not directly relevant to the work of most Web designers, although it is useful to have some familiarity with this when designing sites whose content includes images. (Those who are interested in this field of study will find suggestions for further reading on the book's supporting Web site.) But the meaning of signs and symbols does concern Web designers. One of the simplest examples is the use of underlining to indicate hypertext links. As we observed earlier in this chapter, the association between the underline and the function of linking to another document (or another part of the page, perhaps) is entirely arbitrary, and has been established by convention. In semiotic terms the underline is the signifier, and the act of jumping to somewhere if we click on that underlined term is what is signified. In this case the situation is slightly complicated by the text that is involved; the text that is underlined should tell us something about what we are likely to find if we click, so the text acts in conjunction with the underlining symbol. The problem with underlining links, however, was that it used an existing signifier – the underline – for a new purpose. Underlining in hand-written and printed media had long been used to signify emphasis, and in the early years of the Web some designers continued to use it for this purpose, carrying on a long-established convention. But it soon became clear that using the same signifier to signify two completely separate things just could not work. Users were quite naturally confused. So usability experts started to prescribe that underlining must *only* be used for links to avoid confusion, and this has now become standard practice.

Not all of the uses of signs in Web design have become so well defined, however. Consider the simple arrow – the basic sign that we recognized in the third image in Figure 10.3. Arrows of various designs (though not usually made up of dots) are quite often used on Web pages, most frequently in the vestigial form of arrowheads. It is not enough that the user recognizes the sign; if a page is to be usable it has to be absolutely clear what that sign means. It is confusing to the user if the same signifier – an arrowhead – relates to several different signifieds, that is, if it has several different meanings. However, this is quite often seen in practice. For example, the use of arrowheads pointing to the right and left at the bottom of a page probably mean 'go to next page' and 'go to previous page' in a sequence of pages, and clicking on the arrow will perform that function. Arrowheads used to separate breadcrumbs indicate the page's place in the site's hierarchical structure; in this case clicking on an arrow will achieve nothing at all as it serves only as a sign, not as a link. Arrowheads used in the context of a time-based media player are conventionally connected with player controls, but the symbols for these differ. It is not always obvious what clicking on each sign using an arrowhead in this context will achieve, but it is very unlikely to link to another document. In a quite different context, arrowheads are frequently used for pop-down menus, in which case

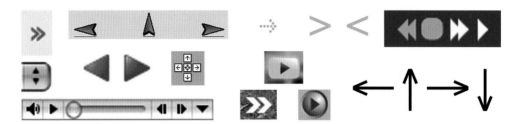

Figure 10.7 Arrows, signifying

the user is expected to click on the arrowhead beside a menu item to reveal the sub-menu. And, at the time of writing, at least one major European e-commerce site is using arrowheads in menus simply to point to each of the menu items. Figure 10.7 illustrates some of the many forms this sign can take on the Web.

In each of the cases above the designer of the page (or the media player) is relying upon a combination of convention, context and user experience to convey the meaning of the sign accurately to the user. But all three of these factors require that the user has some pre-existing knowledge to draw on, which might not always be the case. It is important to remember that the connection between visual symbols and what they signify is arbitrary (just like the connection between the word 'elephant' and the animal). We cannot expect a user to intuit or guess what a sign will mean, except on the basis of experience. An arrow may mean many things; at any time it could come to be associated with a new meaning. For this reason usability experts are now trying to insist upon standard symbols for particular purposes, but this seems both overly prescriptive and slightly desperate. It would also require that every user is able to distinguish clearly between a range of different arrows, for example, and that all designers world-wide adhere to this 'code', which in practice is unlikely to happen.

The use of symbols in Web design is therefore both contentious and subject to change. If we look back over the past few years we can see that a number of symbols once commonly used have already been largely (though not completely) abandoned. It used to be common to see a simple graphic of an envelope used on a navbar as a link for 'contact us', and a crude graphic of a house for 'home'. Simplified drawings of shopping carts or baskets are still very widely used on e-commerce sites to signify 'view my shopping basket', and variations on this theme can be found, from almost indecipherable graphic of a large, bright pink bag to an elegantly simplified line drawing of a wire basket of the kind commonly used in supermarkets. When a designer uses one of these signs they are relying upon the user's recognizing what it is and what it means. But once again it is vital to remember that the connection between the sign and what is signified is arbitrary. After all, in almost every case the basket or cart is illustrated empty, when in fact it is a link to view the contents. The sign is therefore positively misleading if interpreted literally.

Current thinking about good design practice tends to the view that designers should avoid the use of symbols of the sort we have been discussing above. Although the reasons for avoiding signs which may be potentially confusing are clear, there are two good reasons for retaining at least some of them in Web design. The Web is a global community of people who speak many different languages, and who will therefore have difficulty understanding links that are only in text form. The use of a symbol such as a shopping cart, if sufficiently widely established as a convention, transcends language barriers (it is, for example, the only understandable link on the Japanese version of a well-known online bookstore's site, if you cannot read Japanese or the very few labels in English). And there are some cases where it is virtually impossible to think of an adequate alternative for a sign or symbol. The underlining of hypertext links is one; certainly it would be possible to think of an alternative, such as putting a circle around each link, but that is simply to change to the use of a different sign. The use of arrowheads for pop-down menus is another. It is difficult to see how to indicate that a menu can be popped down without the use of some symbol, and again the symbol serves to transcend barriers of language.

So although signs should always be used cautiously and with due thought, it is not necessarily the case that they should simply be avoided.

Layout

Even if you just place images and blocks of text randomly on a page, people looking at it will see them as being visually related to each other, simply because they are all presented within the space of their browser window. As we have seen, some relationships work to convey an impression of order, but others convey a disorganized or chaotic effect which interferes with usability. Some elements need to be visually grouped together, while others require to be clearly separated. It is therefore important to pay attention to every Web page's layout – how the elements are placed on the page, which can be controlled, as we described in Chapter 4, by CSS positioning properties.

Layout Grids

Graphic designers frequently use a *layout grid* to help organize the elements of a page in a way which is visually structured and coherent, and this device is also of value in Web design, even though Web pages have no fixed dimensions. A layout grid is a geometrical division of the page that can be used to control the placement of text blocks and images. Figure 10.8

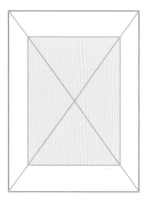 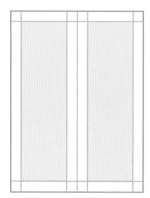 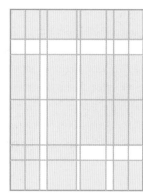

Figure 10.8 Layout grids

shows some examples. Simple grids, such as the two on the left, divide the page into areas, such as text blocks and margins. More complex grids, such as the one on the right, define a framework, into which different-sized blocks can be placed. But a grid does more than define alignments. As the example on the left of Figure 10.8 shows, elements can be aligned but still look untidy and not clearly grouped. For example, we cannot tell by a quick glance whether the text between the images belongs with the image above or below it – to discover this we either need to read the text or check the top or bottom image. The way in which the images appear on the right-hand side but the text is aligned to the left interferes further with our ability to recognize grouping. The eye also has to move repeatedly backwards and forwards across the page from image to text. Contrast this with the example on the right of Figure 10.9. Even though the images are not all of the same width, the strict left-alignment of the images and text blocks in two columns is sufficient to make the page look ordered, while the top-alignment of each block of text with the relevant image, combined with their proximity, makes it possible for us to recognize without difficulty how the blocks of text and images are grouped – that is, to see at a glance which bit of text belongs with which image. As in earlier examples, the two pages in fact present the same information and have the same function; the only difference lies in their appearance, which makes one more usable (and more pleasing to look at) than the other. (You will note that the more usable page is also a lot shorter; a good layout grid often helps make the most efficient use of space.)

Although alignment is of great importance in creating visual coherence, the grid's additional function of defining regions is what makes it such a powerful tool for visual organization. As long as the same grid is used throughout a Web site's design, different combinations of images and text blocks can be used on different pages, while preserving a feeling of uniformity throughout. Users will recognize the same overall pattern and groupings, even though the

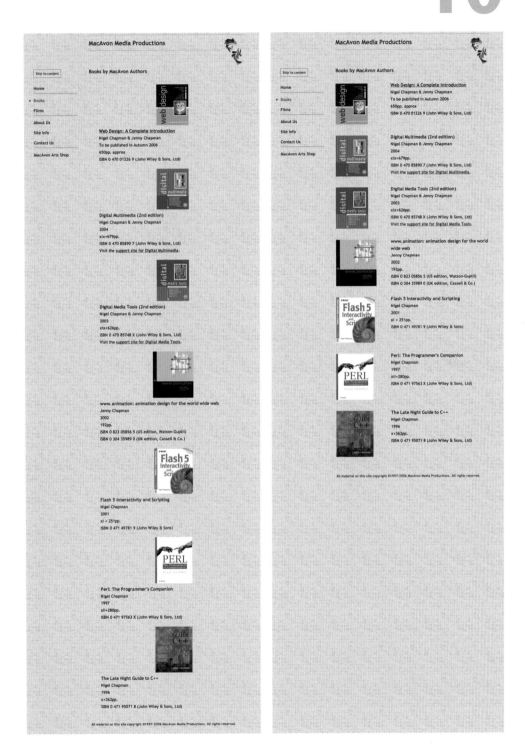

Figure 10.9 Alignment and a grid

Units	Changing font size	Changing window size
px, pt, pc, mm, cm, in	No effect	No effect
em, ex	Lengths change proportionally	No effect
%	No effect, unless the parent element's length is specified in em or ex	Lengths change proportionally, unless the parent element's length is specified absolutely or in em or ex

Table 10.1 Units in flexible layouts

elements change, and this helps give the site a particular identity. It also makes it easier to use, as we remember where particular types of elements were placed on previous pages and look for them in the same place again.

Although the grid is a powerful design element, the grid itself normally remains invisible – we see only the resulting visual structure that it imposes on layout, and not the supporting structure itself. The grid is exceptional, therefore, in that it is an abstraction – unlike visual design elements such as typography or colour.

Grids are often based on ratios, such as $\sqrt{2}$ or the Golden Ratio, to create elements with pleasing proportions. Many books have been written on the subject of creating layout grids to create harmonious pages. However, there is a serious problem in applying established guidelines for layout grids to the design of Web pages: we never know how tall or wide a page will be, because users have screens of different sizes and they can resize their browser windows. Nor do we necessarily know how big any element on a page will be, because sizes might be defined in relative units, which depend on the font size or window dimensions. Trying to create a fixed grid layout based on the geometry of a page is not going to work for the Web. (This hasn't stopped designers trying, and creating pages that force some users to scroll horizontally, others to see vast areas of blank space, and others to see a mess of overlapping text and images.)

However, all is not lost. Grids aren't an end in themselves, they are just a means of creating alignment and grouping, and enforcing uniformity. If you abandon rigid geometrical constraints, it is possible to employ a modified type of grid that accommodates the dynamic dimensions of Web pages, while maintaining a framework for vertical and horizontal alignments. This leads to flexible – or 'fluid' – layouts.

Flexible Layouts

A flexible layout abandons the idea of the elements on a page having fixed width and height in favour of allowing them to change their dimensions to accommodate changes in the size of the browser window and font. The way in which elements behave when either of these changes occurs depends on the units that have been used to specify their size. Table 10.1 summarizes the behaviour of lengths specified using the various units available in CSS.

The case of percentage units perhaps requires a little explanation. When a width or height is specified as a percentage, it is interpreted as a percentage of the corresponding dimension of the containing box. If the containing box is the entire window, the element will shrink and expand proportionally when the window is resized, but it will be unaffected by changes in font size. If, however, the containing box is itself defined in absolute terms, so that it doesn't change size, the enclosed box which is defined as a percentage will not change either. Similarly, if the containing box is defined using em or ex units, so that it changes size when the font size changes, the enclosed box will do so too, maintaining its proportion. A box which is not at the top level, and whose dimensions are specified using percent, might change size when the window is resized only if it is enclosed in another box defined using percentage units.

To make matters more complicated, many Web pages contain a mixture of textual elements and images, with perhaps some embedded time-based media objects. It is normally a bad idea to use anything other than absolute units to define the width and height of images, because if the size changes – when the window is resized or the font size altered – the image will be resampled to scale it to the new size. Web browsers make an appalling job of resampling. Even if a new generation of browsers were to employ better resampling algorithms, they would still have to work with the image at screen resolution, whereas most images are originally prepared at higher resolution, and only downsampled to screen resolution when they are exported for the Web. If you care at all about image quality, you will want to ensure that the size of all bitmapped images is fixed in absolute units to the size at which the images were originally saved. Embedded animations and video often cannot be resized at all, because the plug-ins used to play them are not capable of resizing. As a result of these considerations, many pages consist of a mixture of liquid elements, whose size can change, and fixed elements, whose size cannot change.

Lorem ipsum dolor sit amet, consectetur adipisicing elit, sed do eiusmod tempor incididunt ut labore et dolore magna aliqua. Ut enim ad minim veniam, quis nostrud exercitation ullamco laboris nisi ut aliquip ex ea commodo consequat. Lorem ipsum dolor sit amet, consectetur adipisicing elit, sed do eiusmod tempor incididunt ut labore et dolore magna aliqua. Ut enim ad minim veniam, quis nostrud exercitation ullamco laboris nisi ut aliquip ex ea commodo consequat.

Lorem ipsum dolor sit amet, consectetur adipisicing elit, sed do eiusmod tempor incididunt ut labore et dolore magna aliqua. Ut enim ad minim veniam, quis nostrud exercitation ullamco laboris nisi ut aliquip ex ea commodo consequat. Lorem ipsum dolor sit amet, consectetur adipisicing elit, sed do eiusmod tempor incididunt ut labore et dolore magna aliqua. Ut enim ad minim veniam, quis nostrud exercitation ullamco laboris nisi ut aliquip ex ea commodo consequat.

Figure 10.10 The default display of a single column layout

Single-Column Layouts

There is much to be said on grounds of simplicity for adopting a layout consisting of a single column. Understanding how single-column layouts behave also provides an insight into more complex layouts.

You will get a single-column page if you do nothing about layout in your stylesheet. It will look terrible, like Figure 10.10. (The coloured background shows the extent of the page in a browser window 800 pixels wide.)

There are many things wrong with the way browsers display XHTML documents by default in the absence of stylesheets, but in the context of layout, there are two in particular that make the result unacceptable. The lines are too long and they go too close to the edge of the window. Both are easily rectified.

People find it hard to read text that is laid out in very long lines. There is a great deal of experimental and anecdotal evidence to suggest that, for continuous text, lines must be short enough to be read without excessive eye movements so that after reading each line it is easy to find the beginning of the next. While there is some doubt about the effect on reading speed of long lines presented on screen – some research suggests that it is actually increased – there is no doubt that most people feel more comfortable with shorter lines. In accordance with our guideline of making it nice, therefore, we advocate avoiding long lines of text.

There is no agreement on a precise definition of what constitutes an excessively long line. The size at which a line becomes too long to be read comfortably can depend on the font family, type size, leading and margins, as well as on the user. Style guides advocate various measures: one traditional formula is 'an alphabet and a half', that is, 39 characters, but 72 characters is also often quoted. Some recommendations express the length as 10 to 12 words, which (in English) equates to around 50 or so characters. A broad consensus is that any

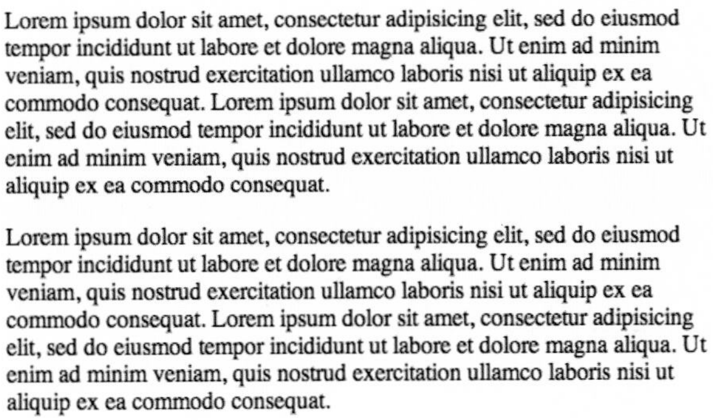

Lorem ipsum dolor sit amet, consectetur adipisicing elit, sed do eiusmod
tempor incididunt ut labore et dolore magna aliqua. Ut enim ad minim
veniam, quis nostrud exercitation ullamco laboris nisi ut aliquip ex ea
commodo consequat. Lorem ipsum dolor sit amet, consectetur adipisicing
elit, sed do eiusmod tempor incididunt ut labore et dolore magna aliqua. Ut
enim ad minim veniam, quis nostrud exercitation ullamco laboris nisi ut
aliquip ex ea commodo consequat.

Lorem ipsum dolor sit amet, consectetur adipisicing elit, sed do eiusmod
tempor incididunt ut labore et dolore magna aliqua. Ut enim ad minim
veniam, quis nostrud exercitation ullamco laboris nisi ut aliquip ex ea
commodo consequat. Lorem ipsum dolor sit amet, consectetur adipisicing
elit, sed do eiusmod tempor incididunt ut labore et dolore magna aliqua. Ut
enim ad minim veniam, quis nostrud exercitation ullamco laboris nisi ut
aliquip ex ea commodo consequat.

Figure 10.11 Restricting the column's width

value between 40 and 60 characters is likely to work, depending on the associated factors we
just mentioned. The lower end of this range will usually look more elegant than the higher,
which will, of course, be more efficient at fitting text into a given amount of vertical space.

In 16pt Verdana, a fairly generous font for a Web page, a line containing 55 characters is
about 450 pixels wide. Most laptop screens and desktop monitors are at least 1024 pixels
wide, and it is unlikely that many users will use browser windows that narrow by choice, so
for most people, the default layout of a page will be too wide – usually much too wide. We
must therefore constrain the width using a stylesheet.

In CSS there is no unit that allows you to express a length in characters, but em is fairly
closely related in most fonts. 1em is usually between 1.5 and 2 characters. Therefore, a line
length of 30 em should give you the required 40 to 60 characters in any conventional font.
Figure 10.11 shows the effect of the following CSS rule on the width of our text:

```
body { width: 30em; }
```

This sets the width in terms of the size of the default font. Any elements, such as headings,
set at a larger size will have fewer characters per line.

Setting the *measure* (as the text width is technically called) in em units means that it will
scale with the font size. In other words, blocks of text will get wider on the screen if the
font size is increased, and narrower if it is decreased. If a large font is used, or the user has
opened a narrow window, text may grow to occupy an unreasonable proportion of the window. It may even exceed the width of the window, requiring horizontal scrolling to read.

One way of preventing this is to set a maximum width, expressed as a percentage. If the maximum is set in a rule for the body element, it will be computed as a percentage of the window. Hence, a better rule would be:

```
body {
    width: 30em;
    max-width: 85%;
}
```

The measure is constrained to a reasonable number of characters, but if it begins to fill the window, text will reflow in shorter lines so that horizontal scrolling is avoided. (The value of 85% is essentially arbitrary; any value below 100% will avoid the scrollbars.)

A different approach to setting the measure is to concentrate on the proportion between the text and the window, instead of the number of characters in each line. From this point of view, it makes sense to define the body measure as a percentage. The text will then occupy a constant proportion of the window's width. If the font size is increased, the text will reflow, but the boundary of the box containing it won't jump around. If the measure is a large proportion of the window, there is a risk that lines will get too long to be comfortably readable, as happens if no width is specified. To prevent this, a maximum width can be specified, this time in em units. For instance,

```
body {
    width: 50%;
    max-width: 40em;
}
```

On the face of it, very narrow windows will cause a layout of this sort to break, especially if a large font size is used. In practice, browsers prevent their users making windows so narrow that no text will fit in them.

The third way of specifying the measure is in absolute units, such as px.[†] The line length never accommodates itself to any changes in font size or window width. In the case of a single column layout, this may be acceptable behaviour, provided the width is chosen so that it will accommodate reasonable font sizes and windows, but it is an increasingly risky strategy, as more devices with small screens, such as PDAs, are being used to access the Web.

[†] Technically, px is a relative unit in CSS, but on any particular monitor it behaves as an absolute unit as long as the resolution is not changed.

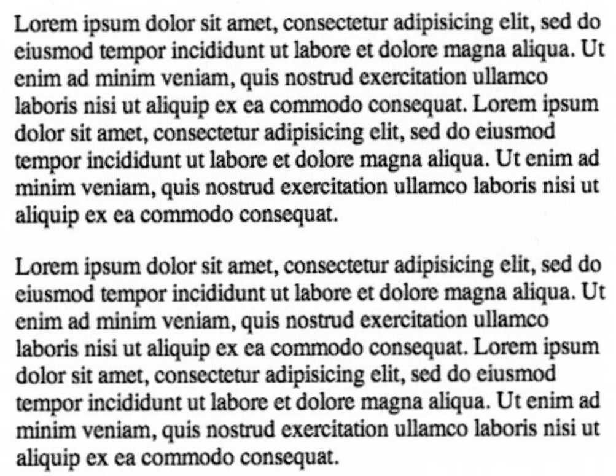

Lorem ipsum dolor sit amet, consectetur adipisicing elit, sed do eiusmod tempor incididunt ut labore et dolore magna aliqua. Ut enim ad minim veniam, quis nostrud exercitation ullamco laboris nisi ut aliquip ex ea commodo consequat. Lorem ipsum dolor sit amet, consectetur adipisicing elit, sed do eiusmod tempor incididunt ut labore et dolore magna aliqua. Ut enim ad minim veniam, quis nostrud exercitation ullamco laboris nisi ut aliquip ex ea commodo consequat.

Lorem ipsum dolor sit amet, consectetur adipisicing elit, sed do eiusmod tempor incididunt ut labore et dolore magna aliqua. Ut enim ad minim veniam, quis nostrud exercitation ullamco laboris nisi ut aliquip ex ea commodo consequat. Lorem ipsum dolor sit amet, consectetur adipisicing elit, sed do eiusmod tempor incididunt ut labore et dolore magna aliqua. Ut enim ad minim veniam, quis nostrud exercitation ullamco laboris nisi ut aliquip ex ea commodo consequat.

Figure 10.12 Centring the column with auto margins

At present, though, fixed absolute widths seem to be the most commonly encountered, probably because Web authoring software usually generates them by default.

Any of these methods will set the text width to a more readable size than the default, but they all leave the text jammed against the left edge of the window.

To fix this, we can add either padding or margins to the `body` element. It doesn't really matter which we use at this stage, although using the `margin` properties avoids some potential problems with early versions of Internet Explorer. One option is to set the left and right margins to `auto`. This divides any horizontal window space shich is not occupied by text equally, so that the text block is automatically centred in the window, no matter how wide the window is. (At the time of writing this type of layout is quite commonly seen on the Web.) For instance, the following CSS rule leads to the display illustrated in Figure 10.12:

```
body {
    width: 50%;
    max-width: 40em;
    margin: 0 auto;
}
```

A popular variation on this approach, much favoured by bloggers, uses slightly more elaborate markup, and takes advantage of the fact that margins are transparent, to centre the page's content on a contrasting background. An extra, semantically unnecessary, `div` element is placed around the content, so the outline of the document looks like this:

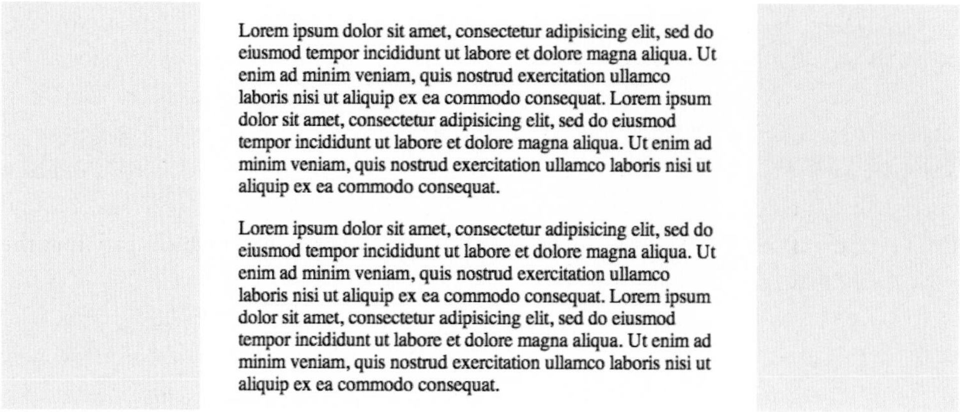

Lorem ipsum dolor sit amet, consectetur adipisicing elit, sed do
eiusmod tempor incididunt ut labore et dolore magna aliqua. Ut
enim ad minim veniam, quis nostrud exercitation ullamco
laboris nisi ut aliquip ex ea commodo consequat. Lorem ipsum
dolor sit amet, consectetur adipisicing elit, sed do eiusmod
tempor incididunt ut labore et dolore magna aliqua. Ut enim ad
minim veniam, quis nostrud exercitation ullamco laboris nisi ut
aliquip ex ea commodo consequat.

Lorem ipsum dolor sit amet, consectetur adipisicing elit, sed do
eiusmod tempor incididunt ut labore et dolore magna aliqua. Ut
enim ad minim veniam, quis nostrud exercitation ullamco
laboris nisi ut aliquip ex ea commodo consequat. Lorem ipsum
dolor sit amet, consectetur adipisicing elit, sed do eiusmod
tempor incididunt ut labore et dolore magna aliqua. Ut enim ad
minim veniam, quis nostrud exercitation ullamco laboris nisi ut
aliquip ex ea commodo consequat.

Figure 10.13 Centring the column as a div

```
<body>
    <div id="content">
    page content
    </div>
</body>
```

The automatic margins are then applied to the div, which is thus centred in the window. A little padding is also added, to prevent the text jamming against the edge of the div's box, which will now be visible. Contrasting background colours are applied to the div and body, and the body's margin is set to zero, producing the result shown in Figure 10.13:

```
#content {
    background-color: #FCE5D2;
    width: 50%;
    max-width: 40em;
    padding: 1em 2em;
    margin: 0 auto;
}

body {
    margin: 0;
    background-color: #B6D6ED;
}
```

You could use a background image for a more elaborate effect, and a non-zero body margin if you didn't want the content to butt up against the top of the window.

However, there is no particularly good reason to centre the content area of a page; you may prefer to use asymmetrical margins. (Our thesaurus lists the following synonyms for asymmetrical: lopsided, unsymmetrical, uneven, unbalanced, crooked, awry, askew, skew, misaligned; disproportionate, unequal, irregular; informal, cockeyed, wonky. This suggests that asymmetry may be perceived in a somewhat negative manner, but in visual design this is not necessarily the case.) Generally, pages which read from the left will seem more readable and more pleasing if the right margin is wider than the left, whereas pages which read from the right should have a wider left margin.

The margins' width may be specified in any of the units available in CSS, depending on how you want them to behave when the window is resized or the font size is varied. There is a case for not using em units for margins: if the margin gets wider when the font size is increased, even less text will fit within the window. Using percentage margins maintains their proportions; using absolute sizes maintains a fixed distance around the text. Either may be desirable depending on the rest of the page design.

Although we have illustrated the possibilities for margins with the content width set as a percentage, the same techniques are applicable to widths defined as ems or using absolute units.

Two- and Three-Column Layouts

Single-column layouts are simple to design and implement and can be elegant, but they do not make efficient use of the available space, and they impose a monolithic structure on the page which is not always appropriate. Adding extra columns helps to overcome these limitations.

Before considering how to place columns side by side, we need to look at how they might be used. In books, magazines and especially newspapers, columns are often used to allow type to be set on narrow measures within a wide page. The text flows from one column to the next, so each column is read from top to bottom in turn, as indicated in Figure 10.14. This is rarely an effective use of columns on a Web page. Although the wide windows typical of browsers appear to lend themselves to this arrangement, there is no way of knowing how deep a window will be, so there is no way for the user to know where the bottom of a column will be found. The darker background area in Figure 10.14 shows a probable extent of a window on a conventionally shaped monitor. Here, having the text laid out in imitation of a multi-column magazine spread requires the user to scroll to the bottom of each column

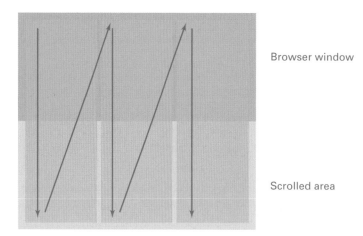

Browser window

Scrolled area

Figure 10.14 Linked text columns

and then back up to the top of the next. This frequently happens when several columns are used to hold linked text like this.

Columns in Web pages are therefore better used in a different way, generally with a main column carrying the body text or main content, and others holding material that is relevant to, but separate from, it. This material might consist of a separate story, illustrative images, hypertext links to related material, called-out quotes from the main text, digressive material (like traditional sidebars), advertisements or navigation aids. The columns should break up the horizontal space in a proportion which is pleasing, appropriate to their content, and which assists in making the page more usable by separating elements in a visually clear way. In most cases the main column will be significantly wider than subsidiary columns, both to indicate by its scale that it contains the main content, and to convey an appropriate visual balance to the page. However, this is not to say that a narrow column necessarily contains material of lesser importance. A vertically oriented navbar is hardly unimportant, but it fits conveniently into a narrow width, and a narrow navbar, with compact buttons or text, conforms to user expectations and is likely to be more usable. Users without sight impairment will often quickly recognize a feature such as a navbar by its typical layout; diverging from the norm may be interesting in some contexts, but it will compromise usability.

In practice, the proportion of the page which each column occupies can only be judged by eye once typical content has been added, but arithmetic can provide some starting points. Figure 10.15 shows some typical ways of dividing up a page horizontally. The first two examples use columns of equal width, a design which is only really suitable for cases where the

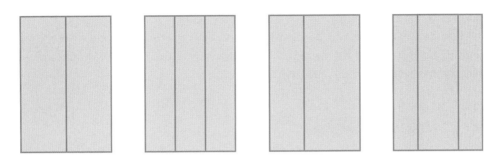

Figure 10.15 Column ratios

content of each column has equal importance, because identity in size conveys a sense of identity of importance to the user. The two asymmetrical cases are based on division by the Golden Ratio (approximately 1.618), which has long been held to produce a visually pleasing proportion. (It is also mathematically pleasing, since, in the two-column case, the ratio of the width of the larger column to the whole page is the same as the ratio of the widths of the smaller and larger columns.)

We'll begin by considering two-column layouts that use a separate div element for each column. That is, the document has the following structure:

```
<body>
    <div id="left">
    contents of left column
    </div>
    <div id="right">
    contents of right column
    </div>
</body>
```

With each column isolated in its own div, it is easy to set their widths and apply distinctive backgrounds to each, if that is desired. An explicit separator between the columns can be provided by setting a border on the right edge of the left column (or the left edge of the right), and CSS rules using contextual selectors can be used to style the contents of the two columns separately. All we need to do is place the two columns side by side, instead of one after the other, as they would be displayed by default.

There are two ways of achieving the desired placement.

Conceptually, the simpler way is to use absolute positioning – just set the location of the two columns so that the left edge of the right column butts against the right edge of the left column. A first attempt to lay out two columns that divide a page of any width into the Golden Ratio might use the following rules:

```
#left,#right {
    position: absolute;
    top: 0;
    margin:0;
    padding:0 2%;
}
#left {
    width: 34%;
    left: 0;
}
#right {
    width: 58%;
    left: 38%;
}
```

Both the elements are absolutely positioned. We have added a little padding to separate their contents, and rounded up the percentage values for the Golden Ratio to whole numbers, since most browsers fail to deal correctly with percentages that are not integers. The total width of the wider right column should thus be 62% of the page, leaving 38% for the left column, so the left property of the right column is set to that value. Subtracting the padding, the content widths of the two columns are 58% and 34%, since each has left and right padding of 2%, making 4% in all. (Recall from Chapter 4 that both content width and padding expressed using percentage units are calculated as a percentage of the enclosing box.)

The widths of the two columns can be expressed in any CSS units, depending on how you want them to behave when the font or window size is changed. There is nothing to stop you mixing units – a fixed width column for images and a zoomable text column in ems, for instance – but the left property of the right hand column has to be computable from the dimensions of the left column. This means, for instance, that you can't apply a fixed 12px of padding to a left column whose content width is 25%. There is no way in CSS2 to set the left property to 25%+24px. (In CSS3 there will be.)

For cases where you want to combine a fixed-width column with one that flexes when the window is resized, you can use the value auto for the width of the latter. For example, the following rules will give you a left column that is always 250px wide, with 10px of padding on each side, and a right column whose width adjusts itself to fill the rest of the window, no matter how big or small the window is:

```
#left,#right {
    position: absolute;
    top: 0;
    padding: 0 10px;
    margin:0;
}
#left {
    width: 250px;
    left: 0;
}
#right {
    width: auto;
    left: 270px;
}
```

These techniques using absolute positioning can be extended in a trivial way to layouts with three or more columns. Notice that because the elements are being absolutely positioned, it doesn't matter what order they appear in the source document. It will always be possible to place the most important content first, so that skip links will not be necessary for screen reader users.

The alternative way of creating a two-column layout is to float one column to the left or right, leaving the other in the normal flow. As we explained in Chapter 4, the margin on the element that is not floated should be set to a wide enough value to accommodate the floating element. For instance, the last example could be implemented using the following rules:

```
#left,#right {
    padding: 0 10px;
    margin:0;
}
#left {
    width: 250px;
    float:left;
}
#right {
    width: auto;
```

```
        margin-left: 270px;
    }
```

The code is slightly simpler than the previous version, and floats work more reliably in more browsers than absolute positioning does. It would, of course, be possible to float the right column to the right, instead of floating the left column to the left.

It is important to remember that the floated material must come before the material it floats by. This may sometimes force you to put less important elements, such as navbars, before the main content, leading to a requirement for skip links. If you need to place material, such as a page footer, below both columns, it will be necessary to set its clear property.

As with the absolute positioning techniques, any units can be used, and units can be mixed, providing it is possible to obtain a value for the left margin from the dimensions of the left column.

Note that a column is a visual component of the laid-out page. Each column may or may not correspond to an element of the source document. Hitherto, we have used a div to group together some elements to form a separate column; it is also possible for several floated elements to be aligned so that they appear to be placed in a column. Since, by default, the top of a floated box is aligned with the first line of text that follows it, using floats provides a way of adding horizontal alignment to the vertical alignment of columns. Consider, for instance, a document with the following outline:

```
<body>

<p>
<img class="left" src="url1" alt="first image"/>
    Text of first paragraph
</p>
<p>
<img class="left" src="url2" alt="second image"/>
    Text of second paragraph
</p>
<p>
    Text of third paragraph
</p>
<p>
<img class="left" src="url3" alt="third image"/>
    Text of fourth paragraph
```

Browser Quirks

Floats, Margins and Internet Explorer

There is a strange and nasty bug in versions of Internet Explorer for Windows, at least up to IE6. If a block element (for example, a `div` or `p`) is floated and has a non-zero (positive or negative) margin, the width of the margin on the side that the element is floated to is doubled. (That is, if the element is floated left, its left margin is doubled.) Although this won't affect the floated layouts described in the text (`img` is an inline element) it would have a disastrous effect on any similar layouts using floated `div` elements, for example, as pull-quotes.

The workround is as strange as the bug. Set the `display` property of the floated element to `inline`. When the element is floated, it is converted to a block irrespective of the value of this property, so correct browsers are not affected. In IE, though, the margin is no longer doubled.

```
    </p>
    <p>
        Text of fifth paragraph
    </p>
```

We can easily define a CSS rule that floats all the images to the left. Provided all the images are the same size, we can also set their width explicitly, and add a negative left margin, so that they are all moved leftwards from the place they would normally occupy. That would be the left edge of the content region of the box for the body element. If we add a margin to the body sufficient to accommodate our floated images, all the images will move out into this margin to form a column. Figure 10.16 shows how the elements of the page would be placed by the following CSS rules:

```
    .left {
        padding: 0;
        width: 250px;
        float:left;
        margin: 0 0 10px -270px;
    }
    body {
        margin: 0 0 0 270px;
    }
```

Figure 10.16 Floating several elements into a left column

Extending the float techniques to three columns is not straightforward, except for the simplest cases. For instance, three fixed-width columns, defined in absolute units, can be created by applying wide margins to both sides of the page, floating one column to the left and one to the right, leaving the third one alone to occupy the middle. Considerable ingenuity has been expended in devising ways of using floats for three-column layouts that allow you to use a mixture of units for the columns' dimensions. We will not describe the solutions that have been put forward, since they are elaborate and do not seem to offer any improvement over the use of absolute positioning, unless, perhaps, you need to support some older browsers.

Arbitrary Grid Layouts

Grids with more than three columns are best treated as a framework which can be used to align elements on the page, horizontally as well as vertically. Broadly speaking, there are two ways of using a grid for layout of this sort, which we will call dense and sparse. These possibilities are illustrated in Figure 10.17.

In a dense layout, most of the grid cells are filled with text or images (or embedded time-based media objects). The widths of these elements are chosen so that they occupy one or more grid cells, with standard margins around them. The result is similar to some newspaper layouts. Using a dense layout will tend to create a cluttered effect, but it does allow you to pack a lot of information into a small space. Sometimes, clutter might be appropriate or necessary, for instance in a classified ad site or a gallery of thumbnail images.

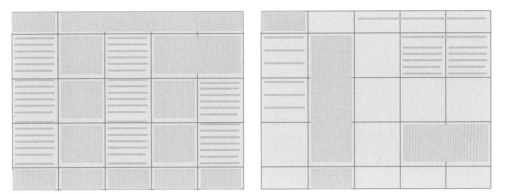

Figure 10.17 Dense and sparse grid layouts

A sparse layout leaves many of the cells empty, creating negative spaces around the elements in the filled cells. By placing those elements on the grid, though, related elements can be connected visually by their alignment and proximity. For example, in the sparse layout in Figure 10.17, the tall narrow image (indicated by an orange rectangle) naturally leads downwards to the small image at the bottom below it.

If you don't care about what happens when users resize their browser window or increase the font size, grid layouts can be implemented very easily using absolute positioning, some simple arithmetic and a bit of trial and error. Web authoring programs, such as Dreamweaver, allow you to lay out blocks on a grid just by dragging out rectangles on the screen. They then generate stylesheet rules that set the position and size of div elements that correspond to each box you have drawn in px units.

This approach to layout is paper-based thinking, and cannot be recommended, except for pages consisting of nothing but images, which, as we explained before, should never be resized. Once textual elements are incorporated, as they almost always are, you should start thinking about flexible layouts, otherwise a user with poor eyesight will find that when they increase the font size, text overflows its box, and users who prefer narrow windows will be forced to scroll horizontally.

There is no totally satisfactory solution to creating flexible complex grid layouts. One way to approach the problem is by breaking it into two: a layout for narrow windows and small screens, and a layout that accommodates font size changes. A stylesheet switcher can be used to select one or the other, as described in Chapter 7. Multiple columns are never going to fit

Figure 10.18 A zooming layout

in a narrow window, so one style should remap the grid to a single-column layout. This leaves the style for wide screens with the problem of accommodating font size changes only.

If all the widths and heights of the elements on the grid and their horizontal and vertical coordinates are specified in em units, you will end up with a zooming layout. That is, when the font size is increased, all dimensions are increased and objects are moved, so that the entire page is bigger in both directions but maintains the same proportions. (See Figure 10.18.) Images must be placed inside some other element, usually a `div`, so that the space around them can be zoomed while the image itself remains the same size. It is advisable to allow some space around each image at its default size (that is, using your default font settings) in case somebody makes the font smaller and causes the layout to shrink.

If your page was wide to begin with, letting it expand in both directions may lead to users' needing to scroll horizontally, which is unpopular. Vertical scrolling, on the other hand, is something that most people accept as necessary, so it may be preferable to design your layout so that it only ever expands vertically, while remaining the same width.

This is done by using absolute widths for all the elements and their horizontal coordinates (i.e. their `left` or `right` property), reserving relative units for the heights and vertical coordinates (`top` property). When the font size is increased, text boxes will get higher to accommodate the extra lines that will result when the larger text reflows. (See Figure 10.19. Both pages are exactly the same width.)

CSS3 Template-Based Layouts

There are very good reasons for not using `table` elements to lay out Web pages, but it cannot be denied that tables provide a good approximation to grids – they consist of rows and columns, after all – which absolutely positioned elements don't really. The CSS3 *Advanced Layout Module* Working Draft proposes a new positioning scheme for CSS that provides a simple mapping of a grid layout to rows and columns, without requiring the abuse of markup that table-based layouts lead to.

In brief, the `display` property can be set to a template that defines a collection of grid cells, named by letters. The `position` property for elements of the document can then be set to one of these letters, with the effect of positioning the element inside the corresponding cell of the grid. The following simple example shows how this will work:

```
body { display: "aaa"
                "bcd"; }
#navbar { position: a; }
#left { position: b; }
#main { position: c; }
#right { position: d; }
```

The page is divided into a 3×2 grid. The three cells of the top row are merged into a single region, because all three cells have the same letter. The element with `id` equal to `navbar` is then placed in that row, with the three cells of the lower row being filled with three other elements.

It is possible to specify the size of some or all of the cells in any CSS units. If no sizes are given, the cells are all set to the same size.

The proposed display model will simplify the construction of grid-based layouts considerably if and when it is correctly implemented in browsers, but, given the record of browsers' implementing CSS2, that may be some way off.

Figure 10.19 A stretching layout

Whether you choose to have a zooming layout or one that stretches vertically only, you will need to work out the dimensions and heights of all your elements in order to use absolute positioning. This can only be done by measurement: you must lay out the boxes and fill them with the actual text of the page, using the font at the size specified in your stylesheet. This can conveniently be done in a Web authoring program, or mocked up in a graphics program. You will have to convert the measurements, which will be in absolute units, to em units, using the font size.

Why can't you just set the boxes' widths to a pre-determined value, and set the `height` property to `auto`, so that the boxes will be as tall as they need to be? If you do so, and therefore don't know the actual height of any particular box, you cannot know where to position any boxes that lie below it. Allowing what you believe to be plenty of space is a risky business – few things look worse on a Web page than text crashing into material that is supposed to be below it.

To use automatic box heights, you need a layout based on floated elements instead of absolute positioning. The float algorithm means that, if several elements are floated to the left, they will line up next to each other. Any following element that has its `clear` property set to `left` will be positioned below all the floated elements. Hence, a row of a grid can be made by floating all the cells in it to the left, and then the next row can be started with an element that clears its left edge. For sparse layouts, extra margins can be applied where necessary to create gaps in the rows. Each row will be as high as the tallest cell it contains. There is no need to know how tall each row is, but the elements must appear in the same order in the XHTML source as they are to appear on the grid (reading left to right, top to bottom).

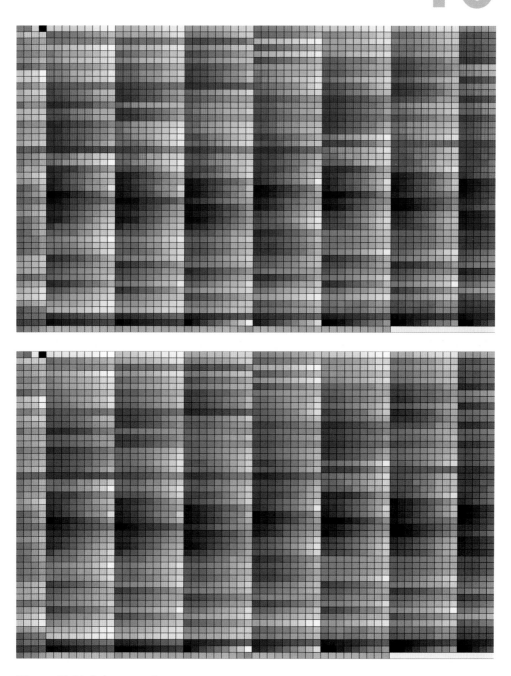

Figure 10.20 Colours and tones

This method lends itself well to columns whose widths are defined as percentages of the window, where that is possible. If any other units are used, then it is essential that the width of the body is also specified, otherwise there is a possibility that the rows will wrap within the window, if it is not wide enough to accommodate them. This will completely ruin the layout.

Colour and Tone

We have discussed many aspects of colour for Web design in Chapters 5 and 9, so we will not repeat here what has already been said. However, when thinking about the visual design of Web pages, colour obviously plays an important role which has to be considered by the designer. Every element on a Web page, including the text, will be assigned some colour, even if it is only black or white; there can be no such thing as a visual element which is colourless. (There will always be some other coloured element underneath transparent areas.)

Colour in Web Page Design

As we saw in Chapter 5, computer displays use an RGB colour space which includes millions of different colours. However, in reality it is improbable that anyone can perceive the subtle distinctions between all these possible colours. Even in the much more limited table of just a few thousand colours shown in Figure 10.20 it is difficult to distinguish many of the colour samples from one another, although in fact no two are identical. When we consider that it is also impossible to know how any colour we might specify in a stylesheet will be seen on a user's computer (different screens and personal settings result not just in slight variations but in completely different colours being seen), we realize that it is not worthwhile being too particular about chosing one subtle shade of a colour in preference to another. This can be very frustrating to graphic designers who are used to having much tighter control over colour in print media, but on the Web this problem is unavoidable and there is no way round it, nor will there ever be for as long as people view Web pages from different machines and have control over display settings.

In practice this means that although we need to think carefully about colour, we should do so in fairly broad terms, and not worry about minor distinctions between hues or tones. Even then, however, it can be very difficult to choose colours. Figure 10.21 shows the same Web page with a range of different coloured backgrounds (please check the example pages on the supporting Web site to see the actual colours). On a Web page like the simple one illustrated here, which has only two small graphics and fairly sparse text, there is a great deal of screen space available between the elements conveying the content. This means that when we fill

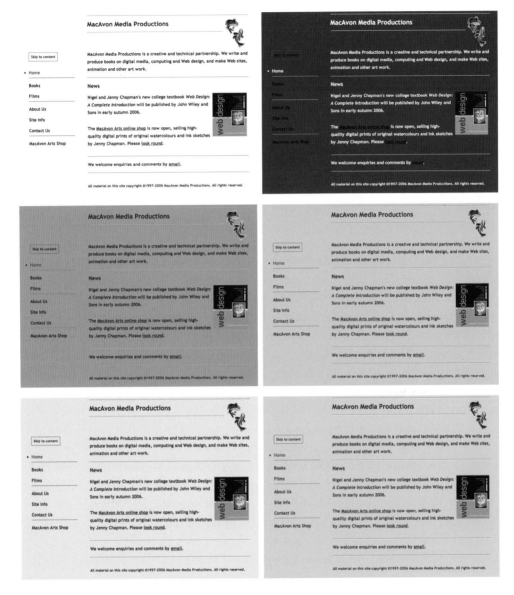

Figure 10.21 The effect of different background colours

that space with colour, that colour is the dominant visual element in our browser window – it occupies by far the largest proportion of the page's available space – and it will therefore have a significant impact on any viewer who does not suffer problems with vision.

With the exception of the change of text colour for greater legibility in the example at top right of Figure 10.21 there is no difference between the six pages other than the background colour. Why does a change of colour seem to give the page a different character? If we viewed them all in greyscale there would be little discernible difference in character, despite the variations in tone, except for the page (top right) with the very dark background. (Grey is generally perceived as 'neutral' which is why it is used by designers who wish to avoid imparting any particular character – other than neutrality – to their sites.) Colours other than greys, however, generally evoke some kind of emotive response. Various theories about this have been put forward, but we will not discuss them here because many are contentious, and most are culturally insensitive. (For example, when it is suggested that black is a funereal colour it exhibits ignorance of the fact that in many cultures black does not play this role, whereas other colours do).

So it is impossible to discuss colour differences like those illustrated in Figure 10.21 without reference to personal taste, aesthetics, cultural differences and fashion, and these are imprecise factors upon which to base colour decisions. However, they are also powerful influences upon personal responses to visual material, and cannot simply be ignored. The one thing you can be certain of is that, given a wide enough sample of people around the world, there will be a full range of different opinions about which colour works best, or which colours and colour combinations they like or hate, and this will tend to vary between cultures as well as between individuals. Despite what anyone might claim to the contrary, there is no right answer when it comes to colour (apart from issues affecting accessibility). And yet the colours chosen affect not only how easy it is to use a page, but how people will respond to it, because responses to colour are often emotive – and for a site that requires to get its message across, or to be effective in selling something, emotive responses may be very important. On top of personal taste, fashion and convention play a role. (Why do we roll out a red carpet for VIPs to walk on and not a green one? Why do bankers wear dark grey suits and not yellow ones?) And once again, there are wide differences between different cultures. On a Web site, what seems a garish riot of many colours to users in one part of the world may seem a normal colour scheme in another; what seems the epitome of muted good taste in certain countries may seem excessively dull and boring elsewhere.

As there is so much variation both culturally and personally in response to colours it is impossible to arrive at any general guidelines for the choice of colours in Web design, and any that are proposed must be liable to change as fashions and conventions change. It is therefore prudent to be wary of people or services which claim to tell you right answers about colour choices. For example, there are a number of 'colour schemers' available online or even to purchase. You may find some helpful, but the colour schemes they provide are of very variable quality, give no consideration to cultural or emotive feelings about colour, and usually ignore the necessity for the use of good tonal contrast in Web design. (And because the RGB colour space is not perceptually uniform, it is not possible just to lighten or darken a colour without altering the perceived hue, so to be useful a scheme must actually specify the colours in the precise tones you require.)

There is one aspect of human response to colour that we can consider more precisely, however. As human brains and eyes work in roughly the same way the world over, we can investigate how colour combinations are perceived (in people with standard colour vision) – how the presence of one colour affects perception of another, and so on. Painters in the late 19th century experimented with placing dots of colours side by side to create optical mixing – that is, new colours mixed in the brain rather than on the canvas. In the same way that if you actually mix blue and yellow paint together you will get green, if you put sufficient small dabs of pure blue and pure yellow paint on a canvas in very close proximity you will see not blue and yellow but green.

You are probably also familiar with the concept of the afterimage: if you stare at an area of pure colour for a while and then look away you will 'see' an area of the same shape but in the *complementary* colour. For example, if you stare hard at a yellow patch you will see a violet one, or if you stare at a something light blue you will see an orange afterimage, and so on. If you place small grey squares on strong plain-coloured backgrounds (of equal brightness to the grey) and look at them for a while each grey square will seem to take on a tinge of the colour which is complementary to the background, although of course they do not change in fact.

In other words, the brain plays some funny tricks on us. For example, the yellow and red squares in Figure 10.22 are all of exactly the same size, but they don't look it. (The black and white frames are of identical sizes too.) We say that a colour seems to advance or recede, according to whether it looks nearer and larger, or further away and smaller. (Unfortunately,

Figure 10.22 The effect of colour combinations on perception of size

however, while most people experience this phenomenon to some extent, there does not seem to be universal agreement on which colours advance and which recede in particular circumstances, so once again be wary of anyone offering prescriptive rules about this.)

Figure 10.23 illustrates the way in which the same colour is perceived differently when combined with a range of other colours. The colour of the red frame shape is identical in all three cases, and yet it not only seems to have a different hue when superimposed upon different coloured backgrounds, it also seems to be brighter or duller and more lifeless, according to the colour upon which it is superimposed. You may also find that the size of the red shape seems to vary too.

When using colour in Web design, therefore, there are many factors to consider, and no easy answers. The only aspect of colour which we can be reasonably confident of exploiting to good effect for all users is tonal value.

Contrast and Tonal Values

We have already discussed the implications of colour choices for accessibility in Chapter 9, and advised that to make pages more accessible for people with any kind of vision problems – and more usable for all – good tonal contrast should be used. But what is good tonal contrast? Two colours are said to have high contrast if there is a great difference between their brightness; the greatest contrast, therefore, is between black and white. They will have low contrast if their brightness is very similar, regardless of their hue. It is conventional to refer to colours with the highest levels of brightness as 'light', and colours with the lowest levels as 'dark'. (In RGB representation the darkest tones in each colour component have the lowest numerical values, and the lightest have the highest values.) While it is certainly not always necessary to use maximum contrast on a Web page, it is advisable to use high

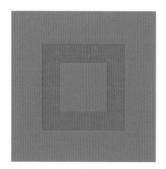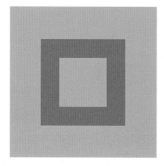

Figure 10.23 The effect of colour combinations on perception of colour

3. very high contrast

2. high contrast 5. high contrast

4. low medium contrast 6. high-medium contrast

7. low contrast

1. very low contrast

3. very high contrast

2. high contrast 5. high contrast

4. low medium contrast 6. high-medium contrast

7. low contrast

1. very low contrast

1. very high contrast 7. very high contrast

4. high contrast

6. low-medium contrast

5. low contrast

2. very low contrast 3. very low contrast

1. very high contrast 7. very high contrast

4. high contrast

6. low-medium contrast

5. low contrast

2. very low contrast

Figure 10.24 Tonal contrast

contrast between text and background, and at least medium contrast between any other elements which need to be readily distinguished from one another.

However, it isn't always easy to judge the tonal values of colours, and some people naturally find this much more difficult than others. In the lower part of Figure 10.19 we showed an approximation of the tonal values of the several thousand colours above, by converting the colour chart to greyscale. You will notice that most colours convert to a grey which is neither very light nor very dark. Just as we cannot perceive the subtle nuances of hue that distinguish one colour in the upper chart from another, we cannot always see differences in tonal value either, and can even completely misjudge the relative brightness of colours.

Figure 10.24 shows seven colours presented as text, first on a light apricot background and then on a dark blue background. As we have observed, the same colour may look different when presented in conjunction with certain other colours, so to make it clear which colours are in fact the same in the two cases, each one has been assigned a number from 1 to 7. (Colours with the same number are identical.) Each fully-coloured version in this example (the first and third bands in the figure) has then been reproduced in greyscale to show the tonal values more clearly (in the second and fourth bands respectively). Many people will find some of the results surprising. For example, people with good colour vision may feel that the red text (5) and the bright blue text (6) stand out quite well against the dark blue background, while in fact the tonal contrast is not good. The red colour (5), in particular, offers almost no contrast with the dark blue. And on the light apricot-coloured background the bright blue text (6) seems really quite striking, but the contrast is only moderate. In this case the red (5) offers significantly better contrast than the bright blue, even though both hues are very clearly differentiated from the apricot background. On this light background the orange (4) seems to stand out quite well against the pale apricot colour, but in fact the contrast is barely adequate for good legibility. For text on this background a darker tone of the same colour would have been a much better choice, but if the two colours were each being used as background for two different areas on a page, such as the main body text and the navbar, the contrast would be acceptable. The level of contrast required will therefore vary with the purpose of the element to be coloured.

In all cases, however, it is prudent to test the tonal contrast of any colour scheme by converting either your display or your colour space (in Photoshop or a similar program) to greyscale. If, having done this, you can easily read or distinguish the different elements on your Web page, then your tonal contrast is adequate for good usability and accessibility.

Typography

Many of the subtle points that distinguish fine typography in print are largely irrelevant to Web designers, because they depend on being able to use specific fonts. Unless and until the downloading feature of CSS Web fonts is widely implemented, it will not be possible to assert that any particular font will be used when a page is displayed. It will depend on whether the user has got that font installed on their system. (Even if font downloading is a possibility, it will also depend on whether the user has overridden your stylesheets with their own.) There is thus little point in carefully adjusting inter-word spacing and tracking by hand, even though CSS provides means of doing so. What works for one font probably won't work for a different one, so for some visitors to your site, such adjustments may do more harm than good.

There are, however, some typographical adjustments that should be considered. They provide ways to express the structure of a page visually, by the use of contrasting typographical properties. Font size and weight have a natural ordering, from smallest to largest and from lightest to heaviest, respectively, which provides one possible way of arranging type hierarchically. This hierarchical arrangement will reflect the structure of the page as expressed in its XHTML markup.

Typography for Reading

It would be quite possible to set an entire page in a single font family, style, weight and size and – provided you paid attention to line length and leading – the result would be perfectly readable. However, text can convey its message more clearly with the aid of typography. For the most part, this means using typographical contrasts to mark out different elements that serve particular functions. In particular, emphasis can be denoted typographically. We can also use the same style for different pieces of text which serve the same purpose on a page, in accordance with gestalt principles of similarity.

Before considering variations in type properties, we must look at the question of which font settings to use for the bulk of the text on a page – the standard values from which any changes will differ. A simple choice is the user's defaults. This choice would mean that you do not specify any font family, size, weight or style, except for elements, such as headings, that you want to distinguish typographically. The reasoning behind this would be that, although you don't know what the page will look like in any particular user's browser, you can be sure that it will respect any choices they have made about fonts.

There are two flaws in this reasoning. First, many users do not know how to change their default fonts, or can't be bothered to do so. The defaults do not represent a choice that these users have made, but one made for them by a browser designer. (And for the majority of users, this is Microsoft, not a company known for its aesthetic sense.) Second, as a designer, you ought to know more about fonts and typography than ordinary Web users do. Even if a user has made a deliberate choice of font, it may not have been a good choice. Even if it was a good choice in general, it may not suit a particular page.

We therefore recommend that a `font-family` declaration should be used to set a default font for use in all elements. As we described in Chapter 4, the value of the `font-family` property is a list of fonts. It should begin with the font that you think should ideally be used for the page. This may be followed by a more widely available approximation, then one of the fonts listed in Chapter 4 that are almost universally available, and finally a generic font family. For instance,

```
font-family: "Lucida Grande",Univers,Verdana,sans-serif;
```

The question of whether to specify a font size is a more difficult one to answer. Although it is probably true (there is no real way of knowing for sure) that the majority of users leave the browser default settings alone, and have not made a deliberate choice of font size,

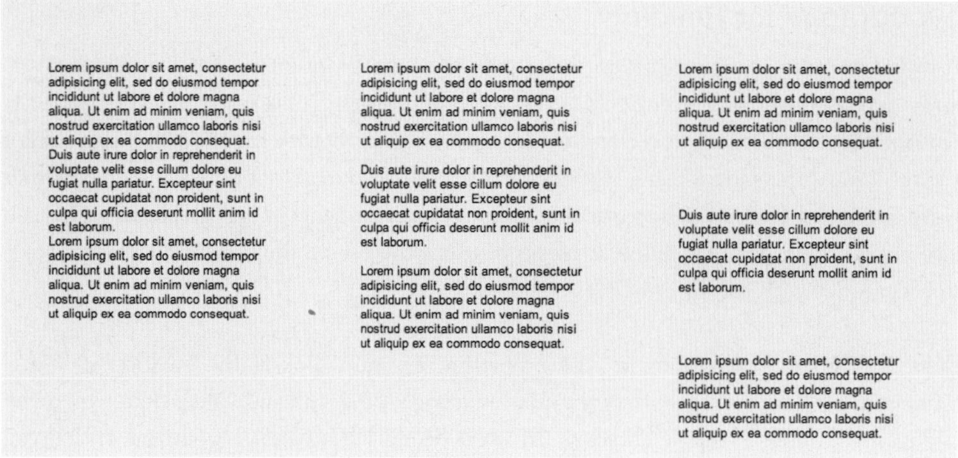

Figure 10.25 The effect of varying the vertical space between paragraphs

there will be some people who have changed the default to suit their eyesight and display resolution. Should you then take the view that you, as a designer, know better, as we recommend that you do in the case of font families? No definitive rule is possible, but generally the answer is 'probably', provided that your choice is informed by considerations of users' likely needs, and not just by the superficial appearance of the page. In particular, don't use tiny text. (On a Web page, unlike a book, 10pt is tiny. 14pt or 16pt will display without seeming particularly huge at most common resolutions. Even 21pt only looks fashionably chunky.) You must remember that many people do not have perfect vision, and others may be using very small screens, so users may need to increase or decrease the font size in their browsers. You therefore need to devise your layout accordingly, as we discussed earlier.

You can set default font characteristics for all elements using a CSS rule with * as the selector. The font family, size and other settings will be used for all elements, unless a specific rule overrides them.

The reason for overriding the default font characteristics is to provide contrast that distinguishes different types of element. We have several typographical attributes at our disposal for emphasizing (and de-emphasizing) text: spacing, position, font family, style, size and weight. All of these, as we showed in Chapter 4, can be controlled by CSS.

To begin with, consider the use of vertical spacing. Figure 10.25 shows the same three paragraphs, set with different amounts of vertical space between them. (This is done in the

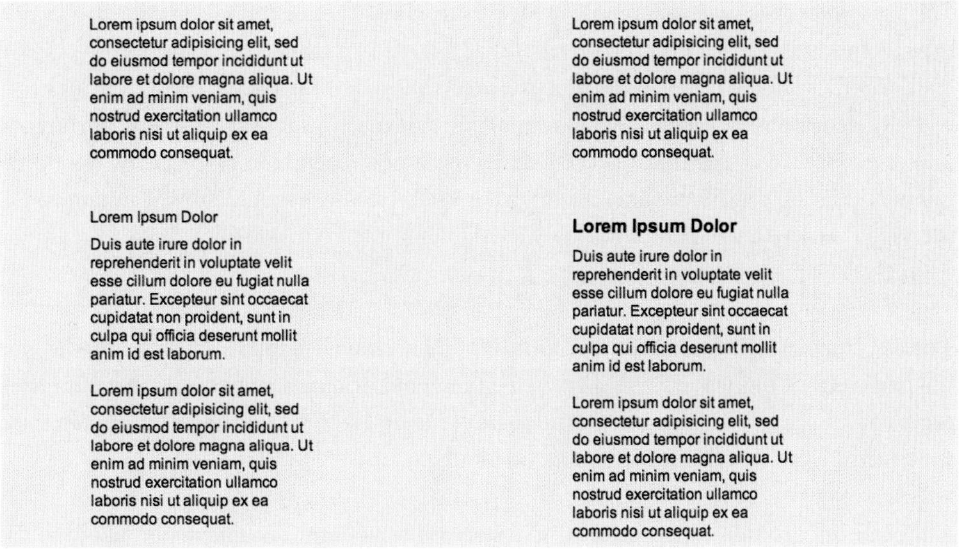

Lorem ipsum dolor sit amet, consectetur adipisicing elit, sed do eiusmod tempor incididunt ut labore et dolore magna aliqua. Ut enim ad minim veniam, quis nostrud exercitation ullamco laboris nisi ut aliquip ex ea commodo consequat.

Lorem Ipsum Dolor

Duis aute irure dolor in reprehenderit in voluptate velit esse cillum dolore eu fugiat nulla pariatur. Excepteur sint occaecat cupidatat non proident, sunt in culpa qui officia deserunt mollit anim id est laborum.

Lorem ipsum dolor sit amet, consectetur adipisicing elit, sed do eiusmod tempor incididunt ut labore et dolore magna aliqua. Ut enim ad minim veniam, quis nostrud exercitation ullamco laboris nisi ut aliquip ex ea commodo consequat.

Lorem ipsum dolor sit amet, consectetur adipisicing elit, sed do eiusmod tempor incididunt ut labore et dolore magna aliqua. Ut enim ad minim veniam, quis nostrud exercitation ullamco laboris nisi ut aliquip ex ea commodo consequat.

Lorem Ipsum Dolor

Duis aute irure dolor in reprehenderit in voluptate velit esse cillum dolore eu fugiat nulla pariatur. Excepteur sint occaecat cupidatat non proident, sunt in culpa qui officia deserunt mollit anim id est laborum.

Lorem ipsum dolor sit amet, consectetur adipisicing elit, sed do eiusmod tempor incididunt ut labore et dolore magna aliqua. Ut enim ad minim veniam, quis nostrud exercitation ullamco laboris nisi ut aliquip ex ea commodo consequat.

Figure 10.26 Spacing and styling of headings

stylesheet by using different values for the `margin-bottom` property, with `margin-top` set to zero.) The example on the left shows the effect of setting the space to zero. In the absence of any gap between them, it is hard to perceive the paragraphs as separate elements. In the middle, we show the effect of a space equal to the line height (1.2em in this case). That is, we have left a single blank line between paragraphs. The elements are clearly separated visually, but remain sufficiently close together to be perceived as a connected series. In contrast, when the space between paragraphs is increased to the equivalent of four lines, as it is on the right, the visual connection between the paragraphs is diminished, and the individuality of each one is emphasized. For text intended to be read continuously, this is undesirable, but where each paragraph may stand alone, using exaggerated spacing like this can be a simple and effective way of isolating each one and deliberately preventing their being perceived as a connected sequence.

It follows that two elements can be visually combined by making the space above the first greater than that below it, as shown on the left of Figure 10.26. The single line `Lorem Ipsum Dolor` is clearly attached to the following paragraphs and separated from the first. The relevant CSS rules used here are:

```
p { margin: 0 0 1.2em 0; }
h1 { margin: 3em 0 0.6em 0; }
```

This pattern of spacing is commonly used with headings (hence the selector for the second rule). A heading belongs with the material that follows it; it marks the beginning of a logical division which should be separated from the preceding one. The spacing does that, but headings also demand some emphasis. There is ample evidence to suggest that much of the time most users skim Web pages instead of reading them from beginning to end. Any important information should therefore draw attention to itself. Headings should provide a summary of the page's content and organization. By making them stand out, you allow users to grasp the essence of the page at a glance.

The first things that probably come to mind for emphasizing headings are increasing the type size and weight. You will doubtless have seen big bold headings many times, both on Web pages and in print. The example on the right of Figure 10.26 shows the effect of increasing the heading's size by a factor of 1.2, and using a bold font.

Although only certain sorts of scientific paper and some legal documents are likely to use the full range of six levels of heading provided by XHTML, many pages will need two or possibly three levels. For two levels of heading, it is appropriate to use two sizes, reflecting their relative importance. For a third level, it may be better to use some other typographical effect, as we will describe later.

Making them big and bold is not the only way to make headings stand out, however. If the body text is set left-aligned with a significant margin, using a negative text indent on headings will make them stand out from the body, drawing attention to themselves. If the body text is justified, headings can be centred or right-aligned. These three possibilities are illustrated in Figure 10.27. There is a risk in either centring or right-aligning, that if the heading is roughly the same width as the following paragraph, its alignment will not be visually distinctive. In accordance with gestalt principles of grouping, instead of being clearly demarked, the heading may look as if you had meant to line it up with the following paragraph and had failed. This is particularly likely to happen if the body text is set with a ragged right margin, or if the first line of the paragraph following the heading is indented, so you should combine centred and right-aligned headings with justified text without indented first lines. Centred headings tend to look old-fashioned, although they remain popular in North America. (The technique sometimes used in print of altering the tracking to make the heading fit exactly over the paragraph cannot be applied on Web pages, because it will fall apart if a different font is substituted in the browser.)

This is by no means the end of what can be achieved with spacing. Where a wide left margin is being used, headings can be pulled out into it to line up with the following paragraph,

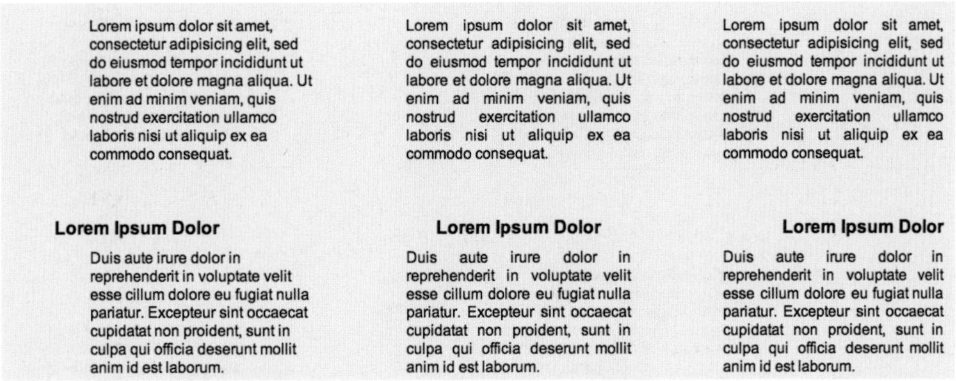

Figure 10.27 Exdented, centred and right-aligned headings

just as images can. The following rule is one way of achieving this effect. (As we showed in Chapter 4, similar effects can be achieved by floating the heading.)

```
h1 {
    font-weight: bold;
    font-size: 220%;
    line-height: 115%;
    margin: 3em 0 -2.2em -6.5em;
    width: 6em;
    color: white;
}
```

Note that it is necessary to set the width of the heading, as well as its margins, to ensure that it wraps within the margin area.

Use of negative bottom margins but a smaller exdent allows a heading to overlap the following paragraph. This may sound undesirable, but with a suitable choice of colour and type size, it can provide a visually striking style of heading, which is nonetheless readable and effective at drawing readers' attention to itself.

Colour should, as we explained in Chapter 9, never be used as a signifier on its own, but it can effectively be used in conjunction with other properties to distinguish headings. Tonal contrast will help to make the heading stand out. In Figure 10.28, which also illustrates the two preceding examples, the neutral background allows both the body text in black and the heading in white to be read easily, and the contrast immediately distinguishes the heading.

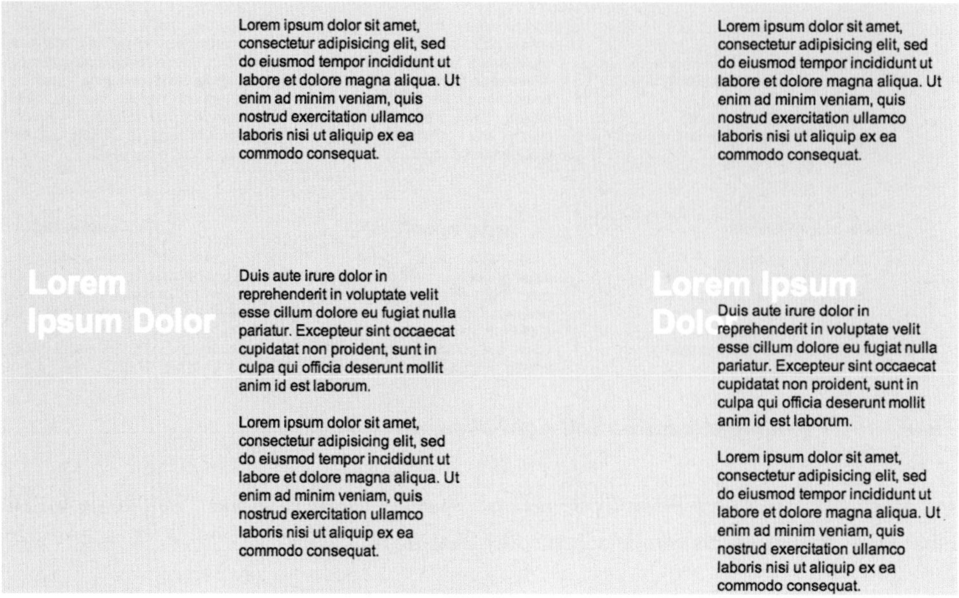

Figure 10.28 Pulled and overlapped headings

Font style also provides a means of denoting headings: they can be italicized. However, on its own, italicization provides only a minor contrast, so it does not often work for important distinctions. But it may be appropriate for lower level headings (h3 and perhaps h2 elements).

Italics are more often used when inline text must be emphasized. In XHTML, the em and strong elements provide the markup for two intensities of inline emphasis. The conventional rendering of these elements uses an italic version of the body font for emphasis and a bold weight for strong emphasis. For sites with a serious character and for purely informative prose these conventions are appropriate and safe, although if you find that italic text does not work well on screen, bold can be used for both, since the distinction between emphasis and strong emphasis is rarely meaningful. (It is unknown in print typesetting.)

Colour can be used for textual emphasis, but only with care. In the first place, the same considerations apply here as to the use of colour in headings. You should choose colours that provide good tonal contrast, and possibly augment the colour with some other distinction, such as bold or italic. Additionally, you should be aware that many users are likely to assume that coloured text denotes a link, and will therefore try to click on it. Most Web designers reserve coloured text for this purpose and so avoid using it for emphasis. For the same reason, underlining and background highlighting are best avoided for this purpose.

be achieved hierarchy
may changing size and
visual through weight

be achieved
hierarchy may
changing **size** and
visual through
weight

Figure 10.29 Expressing hierarchical emphasis through type size

In less conventionally typeset pages, font size can be used as an indicator of emphasis. This approach might lend itself to the two levels, `em` and `strong`, being manifested as two sizes, but more levels can be used to good effect. Figure 10.29 shows how changing the size of words within a word cloud places them into a visual ranking, which is absent when the words are all the same size. You will probably find it necessary to increase the leading to allow for larger words, and you will also find that the mixture of type sizes interferes with justification, so this approach is best used with ragged margins or, as we have done here, centred text.

The way in which we perceive the relative importance of elements on a page – that is, the visual hierarchy – does not depend on size and weight alone in an obvious way. The examples in Figure 10.30 show that the interaction between size, colour and space is sometimes complex. In the version at the top left, the big bold text is clearly the most important, but simply by adding a colour, as in the version at the top right, the smaller word, in its vast blank space, acquires more importance and draws the eye towards it (but only providing you have good colour vision). The two lower examples show that by partitioning the space or altering the contrast between the text and backgrounds, subtle shifts in emphasis can be achieved.

We have implicitly assumed so far that each page is typeset using a single font family. This is a safe and reliable but dull approach to typographic design. All the members of a font family are designed to work well together visually, so there is no risk of creating undesirable visual conflicts, as there can be when fonts from different families are combined. However, by restricting yourself to a single font family you are denying yourself a dimension of contrast and interest, which, when used appropriately, can provide a valuable design element. In particular, it is common practice in print design, to use a display font (see Chapter 4) for headings. In books, headings are often set in a sans serif font, with a serifed font being used

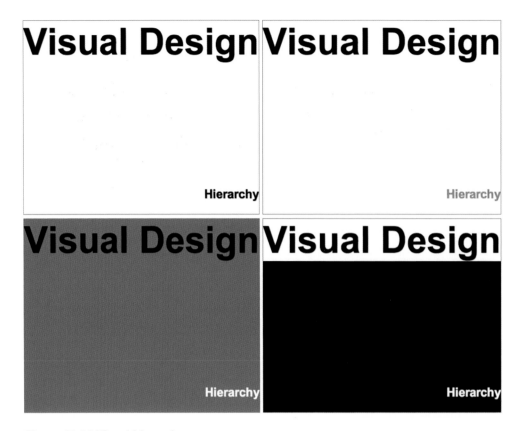

Figure 10.30 Visual hierarchy

for the body text. In addition to the basic contrast of glyph shapes created by using different fonts, differences in x-height and other font metrics can cause elements set in different faces to appear to have different size and weight, even though they don't.

We have repeated *ad nauseum* that on the Web you cannot be sure which fonts a user will see. It isn't even the case that the generic families serif and sans-serif will necessarily produce serifed and sans serif fonts on the user's screen – most browsers allow their users to choose any font to be used for each generic family. The majority of users probably don't know how to do so, however, so although it is the case that if you specify that headings should be set in Officina Sans with body text in Bembo, there is not much chance that they will be, if you add sans-serif and serif to the font list for those elements, you can reasonably expect that some of the distinction between the font families will be retained. For the benefit of those users who do set both the serif and sans-serif generic families to a font like Verdana, say, you should also use colour, size or weight to ensure that headings can still be distinguished.

Alternatively, you can employ the more drastic expedient described in the next section.

GIF Text

In graphic design, type is considered to be a visual element, albeit one of a special kind because it can convey meaning through its linguistic content. The same text set in different fonts may be more or less readable or attractive and may alter the balance and appearance of a complete page for better or worse. For these reasons, the careful choice of fonts has been a major part of the job of the graphic designer and book designer. But as we have repeatedly explained, on the Web you cannot dictate the precise fonts that will be used.

There is a way round this problem, but it is not one that should be used casually. Type may be prepared in a graphics application and saved as a GIF image, which can be embedded in a Web page. In Chapter 9 we pointed out that GIF text should only be used where really necessary, because the use of images for text can present accessibility problems.

In Chapter 9 we showed a naive way of using GIF text as a heading:

```
<h1><img src="heading.gif" alt="Medieval Web Design"></h1>
```

This produces the desired result, but the alt-text is not treated in the same way that the text content of an h1 element normally is: screen readers may read it in a special way, and search engine robots may not index it properly.

There is a more elaborate way of using GIF text that – while not 100% satisfactory – does avoid these problems. The basic idea is to use the GIF as a background image for the element it replaces. For this example, the heading would use conventional markup, with no img element, but it would be given an id attribute to hang some special styling on:

```
<h1 id="head">Medieval Web Design</h1>
```

In the associated stylesheet, the image originally used in the content of the heading is applied as a background. The size of the heading is explicitly set to match that of the image. Here, the use of absolute units is essential.

Figure 10.31 Using GIF type as a background

```
#head {
    background-image: url(heading.gif);
    width: 191px;
    height: 26px;
}
```

The result of applying this rule is the horrible mess shown on the left of Figure 10.31. To achieve the desired result, it is necessary to hide the text of the heading, leaving only the background image.

Several different ways of doing this have been devised. The most obvious is to set the `display` property to `none`. This has the effect of generating nothing for the content of the `h1` element. Unfortunately, most popular screen readers therefore do not speak the content, so this approach is actually worse from an accessibility point of view than using an `img` element inside the `h1`. A better approach is to add the following declaration to the rule for `#head`:

```
text-indent: -50em;
```

The effect is to move the text `Medieval Web Design` so far to the left that it moves off the page, leaving the element's background behind, as it were, giving the result shown on the right of Figure 10.31. By using em units here, we guarantee that the displacement will always be big enough, no matter how much the font size is increased or decreased.

This is an improvement over the other approaches. Despite the physical displacement, screen readers and robots will treat the heading in the normal way on the basis of the markup, but sighted readers will see the text displayed in the special medieval font. There is, unfortunately, one fairly unlikely combination of circumstances under which the heading is not displayed in any form. We leave it to you to determine what this is as an exercise.

GIF text is often used for buttons and the elements of navbars. The usual approach is to place an `img` element inside an `a` element, as we originally did for headings. JavaScript is frequently used to create a rollover effect by replacing the image with a different one – perhaps with some effect, such as a drop shadow, applied to it. However, the CSS technique just described can also be used for links and buttons. Applying a large negative `textindent` does not change the area of the element that receives `click` and other events; this is still the visible area occupied by the element, so the GIF text will respond to mouse events as required. You can only apply a `textindent` to a block element, but buttons and links in navbars usually are blocks, or else are floated, in which case their `display` property can safely be set to block. (The element will be treated as if it was anyway.)

A background GIF will never scale, so readers with poor vision will not be able to blow up GIF text. You should therefore never use a GIF for small type. The technique is not really suitable for extended pieces of text. Here, the content is paramount, and the ability to scale text and to allow it to reflow within a liquid layout is valuable, so it makes sense to use ordinary CSS styling – if you wish to insist that all text be typeset exactly as the designer envisaged, the Web is not the medium for you.

GIF text is therefore best reserved for headings, navbar links, logos and those Web pages where the type is being used less as a medium for language than as a graphic, visual object in its own right. In such cases, vector graphics programs such as Illustrator can be used not only to set type in whatever esoteric font you choose, but also to apply kerning and tracking with precision and to set the type on a path or inside a shape. Type can also be combined with other graphic objects, before being rasterized and exported as a GIF image. (Possibly, in the future, SVG will be used to create such effects, while still making the text accessible.)

Key Points

Visual Design

Neglect of visual design is one of the main factors that lead to Web sites being hard to use.

Usability is concerned with function, structure, accessibility, and visual presentation.

Familiarity and memory play an important role in usability; visual design can ensure that page elements are familiar or memorable.

Elements must be presented in a way that makes each one easy to find, identify or use.

Gestalt principles of visual design are derived from theories about how the human brain organizes visual information.

The perception of patterns and structures is determined by by the grouping of objects in a visual field.

Proximity, similarity, symmetry, the distinction between figure and ground, and closure all contribute to our perception of grouping.

Closure is the brain's ability to infer a complete visual pattern or image from incomplete information.

The whole is greater than and different from the sum of the parts.

Semiotics is the study of systems of signs.

The relationship between the signifier and the signified is arbitrary, and can only be understood through knowledge of the system within which the sign operates.

Web pages incorporate signs, such as underlining for links, whose meaning depends on convention.

Web designers rely on a combination of convention, context and user experience to convey the meaning of signs accurately to the user.

Layout

A layout grid is a geometrical division of the page, used to control the placement of text blocks and images.

Grids create alignment and define regions, which can be used for similar purposes on all pages to help create an impression of uniformity.

Web pages must use flexible layouts, since the height and width of the page and regions within it are not fixed.

The way in which elements behave when the window is resized or the font size is changed depends on the units that have been used to specify their dimensions.

The length of lines of text should be restricted to roughly 30em using a stylesheet.

> A max-width expressed in % will restrict the width to avoid the need for scrollbars if very large fonts are used.

Setting the measure in % units maintains the proportion between text and the window.

Setting left and right margins to `auto` centres a single column in the browser window, however wide it is.

> Centring a `div` within the `body` can produce contrasting margins.

Multi-column layouts on the Web usually have a main column holding the primary content, with separate columns used to hold separate related material or images.

> Layouts with multiple linked columns of text are awkward to read on Web pages.

Two-column layouts can be created either using absolute positioning or by floating one of the columns beside the other.

There is no totally satisfactory solution to creating flexible complex grid layouts.

Specifying the dimensions and coordinates of the elements on a grid in em units results in a zooming layout.

Specifying the width and x-coordinates in absolute units results in a stretching layout.

Colour and Tone

Because of the characteristics of computers and Web pages, precise control over colours is not possible.

Colour may influence users responses to Web pages; an individual's reponse to particular colours may be emotive and/or determined by cultural conventions, personal taste and fashion.

There is therefore wide personal and cultural diversity among the responses to any particular colour or combination of colours.

Combinations of colour affect the way the size of coloured objects and colour itself is perceived. The same colour will not look the same in every context.

Good tonal contrast makes pages more accessible and usable, but tonal values are not always easy to see.

Tonal contrast should be checked by converting to greyscale.

Typography

Web designers can never rely on particular fonts being available to all users, so many fine points of typography are irrelevant to Web design.

A `font-family` declaration should be used to set a default font for use in all elements, since users' defaults may not be appropriate.

If a font size is specified for the body text, it should not be very small.

The vertical space between paragraphs determines whether they are seen as individual elements or as a sequence.

Placing a heading close to the following paragraph makes it clear that the heading belongs with what follows it.

Increased font weight and size can be used to emphasize headings.

In order to set them apart from body text, headings may be exdented, centred, right-aligned, pulled out into the margin or overlapped with the following text.

Contrasting colour can also be used to draw attention to headings.

Italic and boldface are conventional indicators of emphasis.

Type size can impose a hierarchy on textual elements.

Visual hierarchy can be expressed in more subtle and creative ways.

GIF type allows the designer full control over fonts and typography, but must be used judiciously to avoid accessibility problems.

CSS rules can be used to allow GIF type to co-exist with ordinary markup for better accessibility.

Exercises

Test Questions

1. Why is visual design so important a factor in determining the usability of a Web page?

2. What is the probability that a randomly chosen group of twenty people will include somebody with defective red-green colour vision? (State any assumptions you make about what constitutes a random selection.) What can you deduce about the reliability of usability studies based on groups of that size?

3. List all the visual design faults evident in the Web page illustrated in Figure 10.2.

4. In what ways are gestalt theories of visual perception relevant to the design of Web pages? List at least two common elements in Web design that depend on these principles and explain how they utilize them.

5. Explain what is meant by the signifier and the signified in semiotic terminology. Under what circumstances do Web designers need to take the meaning of signs into account?

6. On page 566, we remarked, 'This hasn't stopped designers trying [to create fixed grid layouts], and creating pages that force some users to scroll horizontally, others to see vast areas of blank space, and others to see a mess of overlapping text and images.' Explain how each of these problems might come about.

7. Suppose you have a div inside a div inside a div at the top level. For all combination of em, % and mm widths, what will happen to the inmost div when (a) a user increases the font size, (b) a user stretches the browser window? Note any adverse effects that may occur.

8. Explain how you would centre a navbar that was twice as wide as the text measure across a centred one-column layout.

9. What factors may influence a user's response to the colours on a Web page?

10. If you specify colours for page elements in a stylesheet, what will determine whether a user will see the same colours that you see when you preview the result on your screen?

11. Why is good tonal contrast important in the visual design of Web pages? Which elements on a Web page should contrast most strongly with each other, and why?

12. What can you do to make one piece of text stand out from the rest of a page?

13. What will happen to a heading with GIF type as its background and a negative text indent if a user with a browser that supports CSS turns images off? Is this likely to happen?

Discussion Topics

1. If search engines returned a thumbnail-sized screenshot of each Web page when you conducted a search, how would that affect your approach to the visual design of Web pages?

2. When should iconic symbols, such as arrows, icons for home page and email, and so on, be used on Web pages? Give reasons for your answer.

3. Can you think of use for a layout with three columns not all of the same width, where the widest was not in the middle?

4. Should a Web designer be concerned with colour?

5. It is said that Web users frequently skim the text of pages, instead of reading them carefully from beginning to end. How would you ensure that when they do so, they see the essential textual content on the page?

Practical Tasks

1. Find a Web page or site that you believe makes good use of the principles of visual design we have discussed in this chapter. Analyze how each aspect of the design works, and explain why. If there is some room for improvement, make suggestions for ways to improve the design further.

2. Find a Web page or site that you think is very poorly designed, and identify all the ways in which the design could be improved. If the page is not too complex, create a simple working version of your improved design with mocked-up content.

3. This exercise should be done by a group. Each person should look at the six screenshots in Figure 10.20, and, without consulting the others, rate them in order of prefered colour. Then, all members of the group should compare their preferences and explain what they like and dislike about each background colour. Is there a consensus, either about which colours are preferable, or about why?

4. Find a page on the World Wide Web with lots of different colours on it. Write down a list of the colours according to their tonal value, in order from lightest to darkest. Put your screen into greyscale and see if your assessment was correct.

5. Design a two-level navbar, with at least seven items on the upper level, which exhibits good visual coherence and usability.

6. Design a Web page for displaying advertisements for job vacancies. Each job should be described in a few short sentences. For example, 'Contract Web designer required for three month project in insurance sector. PHP experience vital. CSS preferred. Payment negotiable.' Your page should display several such announcements in such a way that each is clearly delimited and readable. Devise some way of classifying the types of job, and use suitable visual devices to make the classification clear to somebody reading the page.

Web Site Design

11

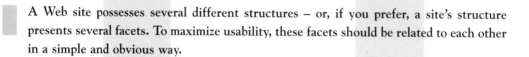

A Web site possesses several different structures – or, if you prefer, a site's structure presents several facets. To maximize usability, these facets should be related to each other in a simple and obvious way.

Each visitor to a site will construct a mental model of its structure. On the basis of the visible navigational structure, they will gain an idea of how pages in the site are connected. Most experienced Web users will begin to construct such a model as soon as they see the site's home page. The model may then be modified as they explore the site. This modelling process will usually be an unconscious one.

The process of building an accurate conceptual structure can be assisted by the use of metaphor. If a site resembles something whose structure is familiar, structural knowledge can be transferred. For instance, a blog is like a diary or journal. It has entries, which are arranged chronologically. This suggests that there is an ordering to entries, so you should be able to look at them in chronological order. It also suggests that you should be able to look at all the entries for a given time period. A blog site's designer can exploit the metaphor by making sure that these expectations are satisfied by providing links that enable the entries to be viewed in these ways.

Increasingly, experienced Web users will find their metaphors in other Web sites. A blog site may be like a journal, but it's even more like another blog site. Similarly, although online shops are consciously designed around metaphors from bricks and mortar shops – shopping baskets and checkouts, for example – these metaphors have taken on a life of their own. Users' expectations of online shops are shaped more by their experience of online shopping than their knowledge of the high street.

What this means in practice is that, where there are conventions about site structure, navigation and labelling, it is foolhardy to defy them without good reason. (Not liking them is not a good reason.) In some areas of page design, originality is desirable and will improve users' experience of your site. In structural matters, though, originality is no virtue. You must always remember that any site you design is part of the whole Web, and that visitors will come to it bringing experience from a host of other sites. If they have to adjust their experience to cater to your site's idiosyncratic conventions, they will most likely leave instead.

Logical Structure

The fundamental structure is something that only exists in the mind of the site's designer, or on paper. It comprises the logical relationships among the pages of the site. Arriving at a logical structure means breaking the information to be presented and the functions to be performed into chunks which can be presented on a page, and then examining how the chunks can be organized. The logical structure of all but the most trivial sites will be a complicated affair, but it will be composed by combining smaller components of the site, each organized according to one of a small number of simple structural arrangements.

Hierarchy

The most common and familiar structural arrangement is the hierarchy. Pages are grouped into larger units, which we will call categories, and the categories may be grouped into larger units, and so on, until at the top of the hierarchy is a single unit which contains the entire collection, as shown in Figure 11.1. In a pure hierarchy, information will only appear on pages at the lowest level. Pages at higher levels, corresponding to categories, will only serve a structural function, collecting together the pages they contain. They would be collections of links. In practice, this is a wasteful and inelegant way of building sites, and pages at all levels in the hierarchy usually contain information or perform functions.

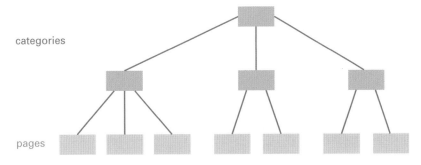

Figure 11.1 A pure hierarchy

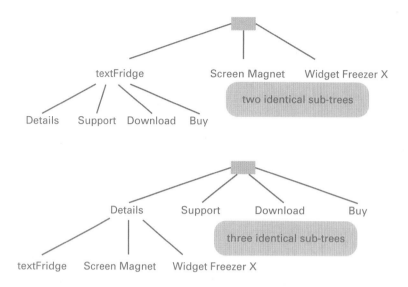

Figure 11.2 Alternative hierarchies

In most cases, there will be more than one possible hierarchical arrangement for a site. Suppose, for example, our fictitious small software company makes three programs, and for each of these programs its Web site provides a support page, a page of product details, a page from which to download a demo and a page to buy a licence key. Figure 11.2 shows two equally logical ways of arranging these pages hierarchically. The choice between the two should be made on grounds of usability. Which arrangement allows users to perform common tasks and find information with the minimum of effort? As a result of thinking about usability and perhaps performing some tests with sample users, it may turn out that a hybrid arrangement, with some consolidation, such as that shown in Figure 11.3 is better than either of the two uniform arrangments that suggested themselves at first.

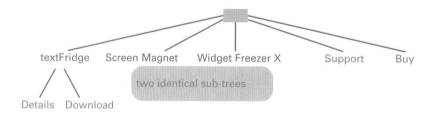

Figure 11.3 A consolidated hierarchy

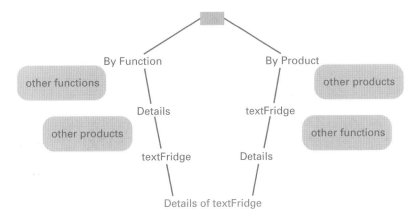

Figure 11.4 Superposed hierarchies

Alternatively, it may be appropriate to support both arrangements, in effect allowing individual pages to occupy a place in more than one hierarchy. Figure 11.4 illustrates such an arrangement.

Sequences

The most common alternative to the hierarchy is the sequence, in which pages follow each other linearly. Normally, the pages making up a sequence are traversed in order, one after another. Sometimes, a sequence may be traversed in either direction; other sequences may be unidirectional, with no way of going backwards.

Sequences crop up in two major guises. First, where there is a collection of material, broken into discrete pieces, that makes sense when viewed in order. One example is a long article on some topic. Any extended piece of writing has a natural reading order – from beginning to end. If an article is too long to fit comfortably on a single page, it is often broken into sections which are assigned to separate pages. These then form a natural sequence. A slide show is another example: a sequence of pages, each of which has an image on it. The images are intended to be looked at in order – perhaps they tell a story or describe a process – so the pages have a sequential logical structure.

The other context in which sequences are found is where a task is broken down into steps. Almost always when this is done, the order in which the steps must be performed is rigid. The classic example is checking out from an online shop. First you must confirm your order, then supply shipping details, then credit card details, then confirm your payment.

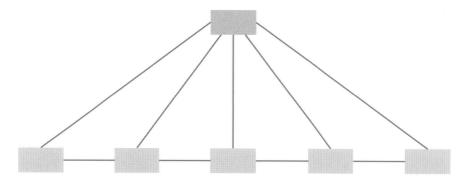

Figure 11.5 A randomly accessible sequence

It makes no sense to carry out these steps in any other order, or to carry out some but not all of them. Tasks made up of steps give rise to the most rigid sort of sequential structure.

In less rigid cases, it may make sense to jump in to a sequence at an arbitrary point. Figure11.5 shows a structure with elements of both sequence and hierarchy that expresses this organization. Blogs provide a familiar example of a type of site that has such a structure. For each entry (except the first and last) there is a next entry and a preceding entry, so it certainly makes sense to see the set of entries as a sequence. However, not everyone always wants to look through a blog's entries chronologically, so it is necessary that the entries have another structure, which allows them to be accessed randomly. In the case of a blog, there might be several levels of hierarchy indexing the sequence. For instance, commonly a blog will provide an index for each month's archives.

Another very familiar example of randomly accessible sequences is the set of pages of results returned by a search engine. Usually, this will be a long sequence of pages of links, ordered by relevance. It is customary to provide a set of numbered links, allowing users to go straight to another page in the sequence, in effect jumping over any that may lie in between. Messages to online forums and comments on blogs are also sometimes organized in this way.

URL Structure

A Web site, as we explained in Chapter 2, comprises a collection of resources. Each resource making up the site has a URL, and the relationship between these URLs defines a structure based on the organization of the site on the server. We will call it the site's **URL structure**. (There is, in fact, a more fundamental file structure below the URL structure, since Web servers must map URLs to files on hosts, which they can do in elaborate ways, but we will treat this mapping as transparent.)

At first sight, the URL structure is irrelevant to the site's visitors. It is a direct reflection of the directory structure on the server within which the files making up the site are stored, and the naming scheme used by the site's designer for these file. Both of these can be arbitrary without affecting the working of the site.

Suppose, for instance, that the `desperatesw.co.uk` site includes pages with product details for each of the company's three programs, textFridge, Screen Magnet and Widget Freezer X. Two possibilities immediately suggest themselves for organizing the XHTML source for these. You could put three files in the same directory as the site's home page, leading to URLs such as `http://desperatesw.co.uk/textfridge.html`,`http://desperatesw.co.uk/screenmagnet.html` and `http://desperatesw.co.uk/widgetfreezerx.html`. Alternatively, you could create sub-directories for each product, and call each file `index.html`, giving the URLs `http://desperatesw.co.uk/textfridge/index.html`,`http://desperatesw.co.uk/screenmagnet/index.html` and `http://desperatesw.co.uk/widgetfreezerx/index.html`. Does it matter which you choose?

To the person administering the site, it certainly does. Using separate sub-directories may make it easier to keep material relating to each product organized. For instance, each sub-directory could include a folder for images that related to that product. On larger sites, if there was so much information for each product that it was desirable to assign separate designers to each one, each designer would only need access to one sub-directory. They would not need to worry about name clashes with other designers' files, and so on. Putting all the files into a single directory might be preferable for a small site, however, where such problems are unlikely to arise. Such a flat organization is the simplest conceivable structure, and simplicity is always desirable.

Where a site has a hierarchical structure, there is some sense in choosing a URL structure that reflects this hierarchy, but it is not necessary to do so. A logical structure can be mapped onto any URL structure. The URL structure does not alter the efficiency of the server, and URLs within the site will usually be invisible to most users, so it is not apparent that the URL structure matters to users. There are, however, at least three aspects of the URL structure that can affect them.

The first is trivial. Almost everybody sometimes just types a domain name, such as `www.desperatesw.co.uk`, into their browser's address bar in order to get to a site. The precise page that is returned when they do so depends on how the Web server has been configured, but usually it will have one of a small set of names, including `index.html` and perhaps some other index files with other extensions. If you decided that `homepage.html` was a more sensible name for the home page then – unless you have access to the server configuration file and know how to change it appropriately – users will get an error message if they just type the domain name, and probably conclude that the site does not exist. Hence, the choice of URL affects the site's usability and whether users will actually succeed in reaching it. Ironically, this is because the site will be more usable if the final component of the home page's URL has been chosen so that it can be invisible.

Second, remember that users will often arrive at a site from the results page of a search engine, which may take them to a page inside the site, not to its home page. Very often, if a page with a long URL, such as `www.desperatesw.co.uk/textfridge/support/faq.html`, turns out to be interesting, a visitor will hack the end off the URL in the address bar, to move up in the hierarchy. In this case, they might delete the last two components, leaving `www.desperatesw.co.uk/textfridge`, on the assumption that that is where they would find an overview of the textFridge product. It is therefore helpful to arrange the URL structure so that this works as the user expects, with `index.html` files in each directory at an intermediate level in the hierarchy. In other words, mapping a hierarchical logical structure onto a hierarchical URL structure has practical advantages for users.

Third, even though users may never type or even look at a URL, they may add it to their bookmarks or email it to a friend. (Most modern browsers provide commands for doing either of these things automatically, without cutting and pasting.) Now, suppose Desperate Software grows into a large enterprise and posts copies of all its press releases to its Web site. One approach to maintaining the site would be to have recent press releases kept in one place, say `/recent`. After a document was more than two weeks old, it would be archived to a different directory. This may be convenient for people creating press releases – they know they always drop a new release into the `recent` directory – but it would mean that a bookmark pointing to `www.desperatesw.co.uk/recent/140106.html`, for instance, would become invalid after a fortnight. Because they are kept and exchanged, URLs should be as nearly permanent as is feasible; documents should not be assigned to locations according to time-dependent criteria. In this case, directories could be created for each month, named according to the date, for example `0106`. The date on which a document was written is never going to change, so if a document from January 2006 was placed in the `0106` directory it would stay there. The `recent` directory could contain an `index.html` file that pointed to the most recent press releases.

There are some additional complications affecting URL structures. If frames are used, as we explained in Chapter 3, a URL may identify a frameset. As new documents are loaded into the individual frames, the URL doesn't change. The URL structure can only capture part

Terminology

Permalinks

Despite the excellent arguments for never using URLs that may not always point to the same page, there are occasions when this is unavoidable. The most commonly encountered examples are those blogs where the home page of the site contains the latest entries. After a while, these entries will be pushed off the home page by later ones, and will be archived. In the meantime, people who encounter the entry on the home page may want to bookmark it or send the URL to somebody else, but if they send the entry's current URL, at some unknown time in the future it will become invalid.

Permalinks – a contraction of 'permanent links' – are used to deal with this difficulty. A permalink is attached to each article, in the form of a conventional hyperlink, whose text is either the word `permalink` or a conventional icon. The URL is guaranteed always to point to the same blog entry. It may be a pointer to an archival location, where a duplicate copy of the entry is kept, or it may be a specially encoded link that the server-side program used to generate the blog site is able to translate into wherever the entry is currently held. If somebody wants to bookmark the entry, they use the permalink.

of the structure of the site, therefore. This is another way of saying that framesets break the mapping between URLs and pages, which is why their use is discouraged.

Where pages are generated dynamically by a server-side program, URLs only identify scripts. Although a single script may generate several different pages, depending on the data sent in an HTTP request, the URL always identifies the same resource. Hence, as far as the URL structure is concerned, any collection of pages generated by a single script must be considered as a single entity.

Navigational Structure

The connections between a site's pages constitute a structure that determines how visitors to the site can move around it. From the visitors' point of view, this is the most important structure the site possesses. To understand it better, we need to look generally at the connections that enable us to move between pages on the Web.

The Structure of the World Wide Web

When you browse the Web, you can go from page to page by clicking on links. The Web is therefore sometimes portrayed as a collection of pages connected by links. Using terminology from computer science, we could say that the pages are nodes in a directed graph, whose edges are the links that connect them. A **directed graph** is defined as a finite set of **nodes** – which can be anything, provided you can make a finite set of them which is not empty – connected by **edges**, which are just ordered pairs of nodes. That is, an edge connects the two nodes it consists of. (See Figure 11.6. As is conventional in pictures of directed graphs, the circles represent the nodes, the arrows the edges.) Directed graphs provide simple abstract models of any network-like structures and a great deal is known about their mathematical properties. If the Web is a directed graph, and Web browsing amounts to traversing the graph by moving between nodes along the edges, we could deduce facts which would help us design better Web sites from theorems about directed graphs.

Unfortunately, the Web is not a directed graph consisting of pages and links, but it is instructive to consider why not.

A relatively trivial point is that the source anchor for a link can occur anywhere within a page, and may point to a destination anchor anywhere on another page or the same page. That is, links don't actually connect two pages, but two points within pages. This is just a technicality, though. Since the navigational structure is only concerned with the connections between pages, and not their content, for our present purposes links can only connect pages.

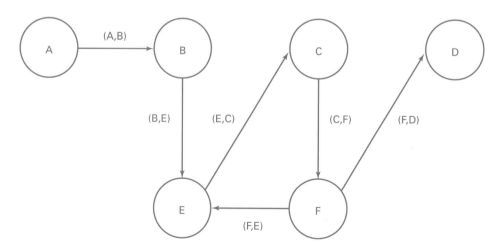

Figure 11.6 A directed graph

It is true that treating internal links as edges whose start and end nodes are the same page loses the point of such links, but this is a relatively minor defect of the model.

It is when we try to incorporate dynamically generated pages that the flaws in the simplistic directed graph model of the Web become apparent.

When you consider pages that are generated as the output of server-side programs, such as those we described in Chapter 8, it becomes clear that the connections between pages do not consist simply of links implemented as a elements. If you press the submit button on a form, you will see a new page displayed in your browser, but you haven't followed a link. Not only that, but the page that you see displayed depends on the data that is included in the HTTP request sent by the browser – as a query string appended to a GET request or included in the body of a POST request, or even in a Cookie header. There is clearly a connection between the page with the form and the page that displays the results, but it is different in kind from the connection between the source and destination anchors of a link.

To rescue the directed graph model of the Web, we need to change our interpretation of the nodes and edges so that dynamically generated pages can be incorporated into the model. In fact, we need to re-examine our ideas of what a Web page is.

Until now, we have identified a page with a collection of resources, as described in Chapter 2. This makes sense when you are creating pages: you do so by assembling such a collection of resources. However, from the user's point of view, a page is what a browser displays between page refreshes. That is, a page is what you see until the window clears and the browser loads a new one. The fact that pages can be generated dynamically on the basis of request data means that a page in this sense cannot be equated with an XHTML document together with a collection of images, scripts, stylesheets and other resources. Nor can it be identified with a script on the server, since a single script may generate many different pages, depending on the data in the request that invokes it. A page as seen by a user is a state of the browser, and when a user moves between pages, what is occurring is a change of the browser's state.

If the nodes of our directed graph are states of the browser, the edges must be HTTP requests, since it is the combination of the destination URL and request data that determines the new state. Sometimes, there will be no such data, and we will be left with our original notion of a network of static pages connected by links. Figure 11.7 shows a modified directed graph, where some of the edges, shown as heavier orange arrows, carry data. (Technically we now have a labelled directed graph.) We can also distinguish two types of node, those which are generated dynamically, also shown in orange, and those which are static. Note that it is not

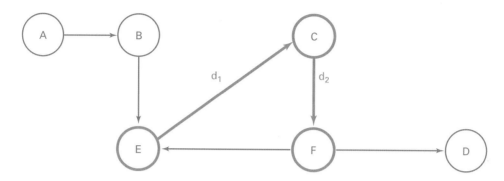

Figure 11.7 Transitions between browser states

necessary to send data in order to reach a dynamically generated page: a script may generate a default page if there is no data in the request. This graph does not represent relationships between resources on the Web. It is a state transition graph, which represents the way in which users can move between pages, considered as states of their browser.

In Figure 11.7, the pages E, C and F might all be generated by a single script. When a GET request for this script is sent with no data, a form is generated (page E). When this form is submitted, a request with data d_1 is sent. This data is processed, causing a second form (page C) to be sent. When the data d_2 from the second form is received and processed, page F is sent, which contains links to E and D. No data is associated with these links.

Figure 11.8 shows a concrete example of this structure. If a user was signing up for some online service, page E could be a request for their name and email address. The contact details from the filled-in form would be sent back to the original script, which would generate a form requesting credit card details. When these were sent, it would generate a confirmation notice, with links back to the original form, to let them sign up for another service, and on to some other page where they could carry on enjoying the site.

The arrows in Figure 11.8 represent entire classes of transition, comprising arrows labelled with any possible legitimate data for those requests. Each such transition may lead to a slightly different page. For instance, the payment page may incorporate the individual user's contact details. Hence, each of the page nodes shown in orange also represents a whole class of individual pages. Although the number of such arrows and nodes may be very large, it is always finite. However, it should be remembered that there is another large set of arrows labelled with data that is not legitimate. For example, a user might enter contact details that do not include a syntactically valid email address. Such erroneous data ought always

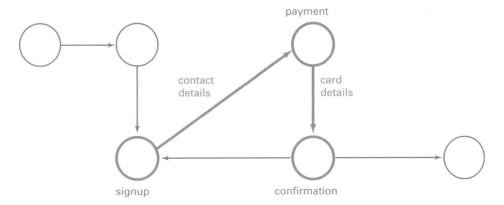

Figure 11.8 State transitions during a sign-up process

to lead to some page, usually one that displays a message pointing out that the data was not valid. Failure to take account of such transitions will lead to program errors, and may pose security risks. Figure 11.9 shows the additional pages and transitions necessary for the sign-up processing example.

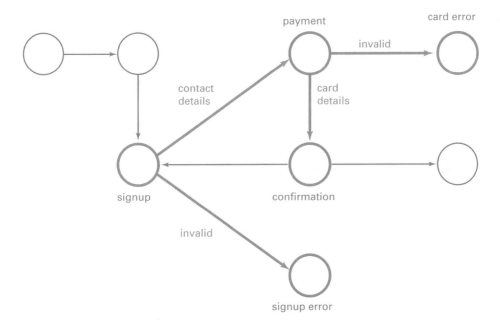

Figure 11.9 Additional transitions caused by erroneous input

Emerging Technology

Structure and AJAX

The use of the XMLHttpRequest object, as outlined in Chapter 7, means that parts of the page can be refreshed independently. That is, what is displayed in the browser window can change without the normal page refresh occurring. This undermines our idea of what constitutes a page, and has implications for site structure: if it is no longer possible to identify a page, it is no longer possible to fit it into a structure.

Sites that use AJAX to implement a rich user interface to a Web application do not face this problem. It makes perfect sense to consider an application with an AJAX interface as a single element within a site's structure. It is only sites that use XMLHttpRequest as a way of avoiding page refreshes that disrupt site structures.

You can see from the foregoing discussion that, although it does not make sense to model the structure of the resources making up the Web as a directed graph, we can use a similar structure, with the refinement of different types of node and edge, to model navigation through the Web. Since this is the basis of the user's experience, it provides an appropriate reference point for looking at the internal navigational structure of the pieces of the Web that make up individual sites.

Navigational Structure and Logical Structure

As we remarked before, a site's logical structure only exists in the mind of its designer, or as a sketch on paper. It must be turned into a navigational structure that allows users to move around the site along routes that make sense within the logical structure.

In the case of sequences, this mapping can be carried out in a straightforward way. Each page must have a transition to its successor in the sequence: a link or button labelled Next, for instance. If the elements in the sequence are stages in a computation, so that the pages are generated dynamically, a button will be required, and some data may have to be sent in the request to generate the next element. If the sequence only consists of static pages, a link would normally be used instead. Where the sequence can be navigated in either direction, a transition to the predecessor in the sequence, in the form of a link or button labelled Previous, is also needed. The other connections between sequence elements discussed earlier can be mapped to links or buttons in an obvious way.

Hierarchies may be more problematical. In a pure hierarchy, such as the one illustrated in Figure 11.1, each page needs transitions to each of its children, if it has any, and, except for the root, to its parent. In practice, this is not sufficient, though, since it forces the user to back up all the way to the root of the hierarchy in order to visit a different branch. A more usual arrangement is therefore to provide for transitions from any page to the root and any of its children. Where the hierarchy encompasses a whole site, these will correspond to the home page and the major divisions of the site. These transitions are provided by way of the familiar site-wide navbar. For sites with more than two levels of hierarchy, the navbar may have a two-level structure, with the contents of the second level changing, depending on which area of the site the page is in. Alternatively, drop-down menus attached to navbar entries can be used to reduce further the number of pages that must be visited when moving between pages deep in the hierarchy. Figure 11.10 shows the transitions added to a hierarchy by the presence of a site-wide navbar. (We have only shown the extra transitions from the two highlighted nodes, to avoid cluttering the diagram excessively.)

Shallow, broad hierarchies (or sub-hierarchies) often lend themselves to a pattern known as **master-detail pages**. If there are just two levels, and there are many pages at the lower level, the top-level (master) page can contain short summaries of each of the lower-level (detail) pages. The transitions down from master to detail may be links labelled Read More... or words to that effect, or each summary may have a heading that also serves as a link. This latter option is preferable for accessibility, since the links should make sense out of context.

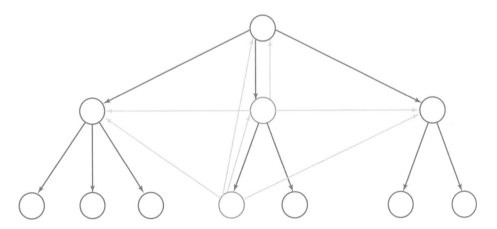

Figure 11.10 Navigational structure for a hierarchy

When the site is being built, it will often become evident that rigid adherence to sequential and hierarchical structures does not capture all the connections that exist among the information on different pages. The transitions that correspond to the fundamental structural relationships may well need to be augmented with *ad hoc* connections to arbitrary pages. These will often occur as run-in links in the page's main text, or they may be called-out in some fashion, for example by placing a collection of them in a separate column. While some such connections are often required, the presence of a large number of them usually indicates a fundamental misconception in the site's design.

Sites whose logical structure consists of superposed hierarchies are an exception to this general observation. If a page belongs to two hierarchical structures, it may need to provide links for navigating in both of them. Consider a blog where entries are classified by their subject, with subjects being grouped according to some classification scheme, and arranged chronologically, with all the entries for a particular month grouped together, and the groups arranged by year. Here there is a subject hierarchy with topics containing sub-topics containing the entries, superposed on a chronological hierarchy with years containing months containing entries. Any entry has its place in both hierarchies, and it would normally make sense for a visitor to be able to move around within both of them.

A single navbar cannot provide the necessary links. Where there are only two hierarchies which are conceptually distinct, like a subject classification and a chronology, it is usually possible to provide two navbars. Typically, one of these will be placed at the top of the page, to serve as the primary navigation, while the other will be placed down the left or right side. Alternatively, a way of allowing visitors to choose whether to browse by subject or by date could be provided. If the site is being generated dynamically, it is relatively trivial to arrange to generate one navbar or the other depending on which means of navigation has been chosen.

The navigational structures of some large complex sites just cannot be accommodated with navbars, not even two two-level navbars, which seems to be the maximum level of complexity that can sensibly be accommodated. One response to such a site is to break it into distinct sub-sites, each with their own navigational structure, with a link back to the home page of the entire site providing an indirect connection between the sub-sites. It is fairly common to find that where a site is used for selling something as well as providing information, the pages dealing with sales are separated into a distinct shop or store, for instance.

If the site cannot be broken into sub-sites, then various *ad hoc* navigational schemes can be employed. An ugly but effective technique is the use of a pop-up menu (implemented using a standard `select` control) with a list of destinations within the site. This serves as a navbar in circumstances where there are too many links to fit within the space of a conventional bar. Typically, this occurs in a wide, shallow hierarchy. (It may be possible and preferable to rearrange the structure into a narrower, deeper hierarchy, which does not present the same navigational problems.) For the special case of chronologically organized pages, a neat and attractive way of allowing visitors to access the pages for a particular date is by providing a calendar, with controls to go forward and backwards by month or year. The numbers for dates for which there are entries are highlighted and have links attached, as shown in Figure 11.11. A calendar of this sort effectively adds links to the site between archive pages for each month, which are then accessed using the individual dates as links.

Site Maps and Searching

We have shown that, in general, the navigational structure of a site will consist of not just the essential connections in its logical structure (next and previous in a sequence, child and parent in a hierarchy) but also shortcuts (such as a site-wide navbar) and *ad hoc* connections that provide additional routes through the site. Additionally, there will usually be a site map and search facility that permit direct access to any page.

Every site, except for the smallest and most simply organized, should have a site map, which is usually a page containing nothing but links. These may be classified, thereby showing the entire site hierarchy in one place, or arranged alphabetically. Short simple annotations may be added to help visitors understand what each link points to.

CALENDAR

August 2006

Sun	Mon	Tue	Wed	Thu	Fri	Sat
		1	2	3	4	5
6	7	8	9	10	11	12
13	14	15	16	17	18	19
20	21	22	23	24	25	26
27	28	29	30	31		

Figure 11.11 A calendar as a navigational aid

The site map stands outside the logical structure of the site, giving direct access to every page that can be reached without requiring a user to enter data to be sent in the HTTP request. This is not the same as every page in the site. For instance, it would not make sense to include a page for entering credit card details in the site map if this page was normally accessed only after an order had been confirmed.

The site map is not the only way in which users can access pages directly without reference to the logical structure. Most sites also provide a search facility, allowing visitors to find pages according to some criteria. The search box, if there is one, must appear on every page and be clearly identifiable. The label Search should be used on the button that initiates searching, or applied to the text box in which terms are entered, in which case the button can be labelled Go. A widespread, but not universal, convention is to place the search box in the top right corner of each page. Usually, after entering some keywords and perhaps other parameters to the search and pressing the search button, the user is taken to a page of results, which contains links to the actual pages returned by the search. (The relationship between these pages is an example of the master-detail pattern described earlier.)

Users tend to take site searching for granted, but it can be problematical to implement. If we consider sites consisting entirely of static pages, a naive approach to searching would consist of looking for the search term in the text of every XHTML document in the site. This would be very inefficient, not so much because of the volume of text to search as because of the need to open and close many files. It is usual, therefore, to build an index of the site, which can then be searched efficiently. There are freely available scripts for indexing and searching static sites, but a popular alternative is to send the query to one of the Web-wide search engines, as we noted in Chapter 1. These will have already indexed the site as part of their task of indexing the entire Web.

Where pages are generated dynamically, a complete index can only be constructed if there is some expedient available for generating every possible page that a script might produce as its output. This is not the best approach here, though, because the data from which pages are created will usually be available in a database, and databases can be searched efficiently. The problem is that a database search works best when you know where to search. For instance, consider the tables in Figure 8.4 on page 454, which we used in the image gallery example in Chapter 8. If you were looking for an image with a particular title, you would need to use a query that selects according to the title attribute of the images table, but if you were looking for the images made in a particular year, you would need to select on the date attribute. These two searches would be implemented using different SQL queries.

If you are looking at this as a developer, you would probably think it was a good idea to provide something like a pop-up menu alongside the search box, from which users could select the sort of thing to search for. (You have probably seen such menus on many sites.) Users, on the other hand, generally just want to enter some words and hit the search button. In order to allow them to do this, the search function must operate in one of three ways. First, it can search everywhere. This will be inefficient, and may be hard to code. Second, you can provide a pop-up menu, as outlined earlier, but make searching everywhere its default entry. (This solution can be seen at large e-commerce sites, where the default is to search all of the site, but a pop-up menu allows you to restrict the search to books, electronics, popular music, kitchen appliances etc.) Lazy users will then have to put up with slow searches, but those who can be bothered will be able to restrict the scope of their search, which will therefore usually return results faster. Third, you can try to analyze the form of the search terms that are entered, and guess where the most profitable part of the database to search would be. This is likely to be a somewhat haphazard procedure, but it does reflect what the user wants you to do.

Expressing Navigational Structure

The structure of a site that is seen by its visitors consists of the connections that can be followed between its pages. In other words, the site's visitors see the state transition graph of the site. Therefore, it is necessary that there are elements on each page that indicate clearly which transitions exist from that page, and where they lead to.

The first requirement is for some means of identifying links. These may occur either run in to some text or set apart in some distinctive way, such as in a navbar. As we explained in Chapter 10, conventions based on semiotic and gestalt principles have been developed to distinguish links. Some usability experts further advocate distinguishing visited links by using a darker tone of the colour used for unvisited links. There is, however, no universal convention about what a visited link looks like. This greatly diminishes the utility of any visual distinction, so that the practice of identifying visited links is falling into disuse. It is not customary to distinguish between visited and unvisited links in navbars, and it may, in fact, be confusing to do so.

Figure 11.12 illustrates some possible navbar styles. All of these examples were done with CSS, which can also be used to add rollover effects, by changing backgrounds, for example, as we described in Chapter 4. Because of the need to make navbar entries distinctive, it is common practice to use GIF text or icons instead of styled text, allowing a wider range of navbar styles to be employed. (Providing the GIF text in navbars is large, there need be no

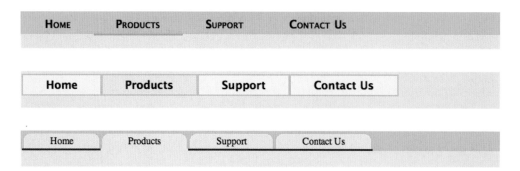

Figure 11.12 Navbar styles

accessibility problem associated with this use of images as text, as long as alt-text is supplied.) CSS rollovers can be used in conjunction with the technique described earlier for using GIF text as a background image, but most navbars that are created in popular Web design programs use the long-established technique of JavaScript image swapping and img elements for navbar rollovers.

You will notice that in each of the examples in Figure 11.12, one entry is styled differently from the others. This is to indicate the location of the current page within the hierarchy expressed by the navbar. Breadcrumbs, as described in Chapter 4, can be used to add extra orientation, if this seems necessary.

As we mentioned earlier, drop-down menus can be attached to navbar entries to add an extra level of connections. In a simple hierarchy, each navbar entry identifies a top-level category; a drop-down menu attached to it will identify the sub-categories within that category, so that users can jump directly to the second level as well as the first. Figure 11.13 shows an example. Drop-down menus can be implemented using CSS rollovers, or with JavaScript, but there are drawbacks to their use. It is not always easy to integrate a drop-down menu into a page or navbar design, or to provide a suitable space for the menu to drop down into. Menus that are implemented with JavaScript can also present accessibility problems. As an alternative, therefore, navbars may simply be split onto two levels, as shown in the lower example in Figure 11.13. The second level only changes after a top-level entry has been selected. Thus, the direct connections between pages at the second level in different parts of the hierarchy – which are provided by drop-down menus – are lost.

No matter how the navbar is laid out and styled, it is important for good usability that it occupies the same position on every page of the site.

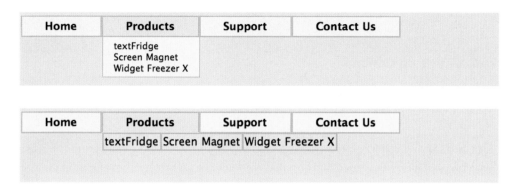

Figure 11.13 Adding a second level

Navbars are not the only places where links occur outside a continuous text flow. It is often convenient to collect together a group of links and set them off in some way. A commonly encountered example is a set of links to other sites relevant to the topic of a blog entry or news item. The cross-references in the glossary application of Chapter 8 provide another example. While it would be acceptable to set such a collection as a paragraph or list at the end of the main text, it is often more effective to apply some of the gestalt principles we introduced in Chapter 10, and place them in a separate box, usually positioned in a separate column. Readers' attention can be drawn to this box by giving it a different background colour from the rest of the page. Within the box, especially if it has an unambiguous heading, such as See Also or Related Links, it is not necessary to use the same styling as for links within the text. A more subtle indicator – perhaps just a highlight on rollover – can suffice.

Compared with identifying source anchors, identifying buttons that cause a transition by sending an HTTP request with some data is usually trivial. The default appearance of submit buttons is standard and determined by the browser, and resembles the appearance of buttons in desktop applications, so any computer user should recognize them as something to be clicked that will cause something to happen. The limited amount of styling that is sometimes possible using CSS should not interfere with this recognition. It is only if JavaScript is used to submit form data using some non-standard trigger that confusion may result. This, coupled with accessibility concerns and the possibility of user agents that do not support scripting, is sufficient reason always to rely on the standard mechanism for submitting form data, and thereby effecting a transition to a dynamically generated page.

In the case of sequences that are built out of steps in a process, such as checking out from an online shop, it can be useful to supplement the buttons with an indication of the current position in the sequence. This can take the form of a little road map, showing each step in

1 Confirm Selections **Gift Wrap Options** Delivery Address Payment Details Billing Address Confirm Order

2 Gift Wrap Options

Figure 11.14 Providing orientation in a sequential operation

order, with an indication of which step is currently being executed. Numbering the steps reinforces the notion of sequencing and makes it easy for users to see how far along in the process they are. Figure 11.14 illustrates such a road map. Note that the elements within the map must not be links; the map is provided for information only. As the sequence must always be carried out from beginning to end (or abandoned), there should never be a way of going directly to one of the steps.

Making links readily identifiable is necessary for users to comprehend the navigational structure of a site, but it is not sufficient. They must also be able to form an idea of where each link will take them. Here again, we must consider the case of links that occur within continuous text separately from links in navbars and called-out boxes.

Links within continuous text generally present the easier case, because there is context available as well as the text of the link itself. Furthermore, this text is not constrained to fit in a small space, in the way that navbar links usually are, so the page's author has more scope for writing meaningful link text. You should always try to write link text that succinctly describes the destination of the link, and – for the benefit of screen reader users – works out of context. That, of course, is a tall order (especially the last part), but it is achievable with some care and thought. The `title` attribute can be used to provide a tool-tip with more information about the link's destination, as described in Chapter 9, if it is thought that the link text on its own is not sufficient.

Where a link must stand alone, in particular in a navbar, the most useful thing you can do to help users understand the purpose and destination of links is to make use of conventional labels wherever possible. For instance, the link to the home page should be labelled `Home`, rather than, for instance, `Root` or `Top`. Information provided in the form of questions and answers should be accessible using a link labelled `FAQs` (whether or not the questions are really asked frequently, or at all), and so on. You may not like these labels, but usability will be greatly enhanced if you stick to established conventions. Only when a site is intended to be novel and challenging and original does it make sense to depart from the conventions which users will readily recognize and understand.

Creating Web Sites

Somebody wants a Web site. They may be a large established enterprise, a new Web startup, a local guest house, a university department, your mother-in-law or yourself, but the starting point is their wish for a Web site. The task of making their wish come true usually falls to a Web design agency. Agencies vary in size, from one-person operations to international organizations who, as one such agency's own Web site tells us, 'develop creative communication solutions across all media formats' for large corporations. Whereas a lone designer will need to be a master of all elements of Web design, the larger agencies will employ a range of specialists including graphic designers, usability and accessibility experts, copy writers and programmers – and project managers to coordinate their activities.

The first step in design is refining the client's wish, so that instead of some vague idea of an abstract site it becomes a wish for a specific site. Here, the key question is: What exactly is this site going to be for? There are as many answers to this question as there are Web sites, and a first answer may need additional refinement until it can serve as a basis for a site design. This process of refinement must be done in consultation with the client.

Sometimes a client will have very clear ideas about what they want from the site. For instance, an artist who paints watercolours may want to sell reproductions on-line; the owner of a guest house may want a Web version of their existing printed brochure; a college may want to publicize their research activities and provide information about application procedures to prospective students. In other cases, though, the client may just feel that they should use the Web to 'get information to their customers', or that they ought to 'have a Web presence'. In such cases, the Web designer must try to tease out some more concrete wishes from the client: What information do they want to get to their customers? Will the Web do anything that existing forms of communication are not doing? What purpose will a Web presence serve? It may turn out that there really isn't much purpose, in which case the professional thing to do is try to discourage the client from proceeding. Not everybody needs a Web site.

Once the designers and the client have a clear idea of what the site is for, the design work can begin. It may be helpful to write down an agreed statement about the site's purpose, which can serve as a reference point in later stages of the design process and – where such documents are used – the basis of a brief for the designers. Proposed features can be tested against the statement, and rejected if they do not further the purpose. (We are not offering advice about professional practice, but such a statement can be useful as an annexe to a contract, as it can provide the designer with a means of rejecting unreasonable demands for extra features that a client might make at a late stage in the site's development.)

Classifying Site Content

Knowing the intended purpose of a site makes it possible to make sensible decisions about what it should include. In most cases, it will be necessary to begin by constructing a list of contents. Again, this will need to be done in consultation with the client. If the client is a large organization, several different people may want to provide input at this stage, and it may be necessary to arbitrate between their requirements. Resist the temptation to try and structure the site at this stage. It may be that once a description of all the content has been compiled, connections among it will emerge that were not evident beforehand. Be especially wary of allowing the client to impose (or 'suggest') an organization that reflects their internal structures or power relationships within their enterprise. The content must determine its own organization.

In cases where the organization is not obvious, some experts advocate the use of *card sorting* exercises to determine how potential users of the site perceive the contents as being classified. The methodology is simple: a representative set of users is provided with a stack of cards, each bearing an item from the contents list. The users are asked to sort the cards into piles, each containing items that they consider to be related. With luck, a consensus will emerge from among the test users about how items should be grouped together. As a next step, the users can be asked to suggest a title for each pile, thereby naming the categories into which the items have been classified. These category names could serve as labels for use in navbars. Card sorting is not infallible – no consensus may emerge – and, like all user testing, it does beg the question of how to select test subjects who adequately represent the diversity of the Web community. However, the results can be suggestive, and can perform a useful function in undermining preconceptions based on irrelevant factors, such as the division of a large corporation into departments.

As a working example of the early phases of site design, we will consider building a support site for this book. Its purpose is to help students with learning, and to assist teachers with teaching, in the context of courses based on the book. We know, from our publisher's market research and our experience with other textbooks, that students and teachers value certain things in a support Web site for a course text. These include answers to exercises, lecture slides, code for examples, some demonstration pages and links to relevant Web sites. Based on the site logs and feedback concerning the support site for our older books, we also know that some superficially attractive features are not used or wanted. These include discussion forums and a space to exhibit examples of work done by students using the book. These features can therefore be rejected for inclusion. The publisher's marketing department tells us that a form which instructors can use to request evaluation copies is essential, and that sample material from the book is helpful in encouraging new courses to adopt the book. In the past we have found that an interactive glossary is widely appreciated, so we want to include that, and we have also been asked to provide some notes on teaching. As well as these specific items, the site also needs to provide information about itself and a means of contacting us.

These considerations led us to draw up the list in Figure 11.15. The order is of no significance at this point – the topics were simply written down as we thought of them. In this preliminary stage of site design, it is not necessary to be specific about how these headings map to pages, although it is evident that it will be possible to accommodate some topics on a single page, whereas other will end up occupying several pages.

Once the content has been decided on, a first attempt can be made to arrange it to form the skeleton of the site's logical structure. Here, we begin to look at the relationships between the topics, to see how they fit in to the fundamental logical structures we identified at the beginning of this chapter. This entails consideration of the entities in the real world to which the site's contents are related, and any processes that are reflected in the site or implemented by it. In this case, that means that we need to consider the book itself, and the way people use it for teaching and learning.

Home

Site info

Accessibility statement

Site map

Contact

Evaluation copy request form

About us

Links

Code examples

Sample Web pages

Lecture slides

Answers to questions

Teaching notes

Interactive glossary

Sample material

Table of contents for book

Errata and updates

FAQs

Figure 11.15 A list of topics for the book's support site

There are some topics that can be grouped together on the basis of their intrinsic semantics alone. For instance, the site map, site info and information about the authors fall together naturally into an information category. On the other hand, the organization of material derived from the book's contents needs to take account of the way the book is organized into chapters.

Take the lectures slides, for instance. These are based on the key points at the end of each chapter, so they already form a sequence, based on the sequence of the chapters. We could therefore create a category for lecture slides, within which the collection of slides would form a sequence. We could do the same thing for teaching notes, answers to questions, and so on. However, because we have several parallel sequences, it would be equally valid to organize the material according to category, with the material within each category arranged as a sequence in order of chapter. These two possibilities are illustrated in Figure 11.16. Which is better?

Unfortunately, neither is better. We know that some instructors only use certain chapters from a textbook, and given its breadth of coverage, we guess that this book may sometimes be used in that way. Also, it makes sense to want to look at all the material related to the chapter you are studying. However, a lecturer preparing a course might want to look at all the teaching notes, and a student revising for an exam might want copies of all the lecture slides, and in either case it would be tiresome to have to visit each chapter in turn in order to get them. It looks, therefore, as if this site will have superposed structures. As we explained earlier, this means that some expedient will be required to enable visitors to navigate through the material by chapter or by category. Since the number of chapters is known and finite, it seems possible that two orthogonal navbars can be provided, but that decision need not be made at this stage, so long as we understand the structure we wish to use.

The two arrangements shown in Figure 11.16 by no means exhaust the possibilities for organizing this site. For example, the top-level category The Book might be eliminated, and the items underneath it could be promoted to the top level. In the end, there will almost always be an element of arbitrariness about the precise way in which a site's material is organized. One of the potential benefits of user testing is the check it provides on decisions about organization. If users cannot find their way around the site, something is probably wrong with its organization.

You will recognize a similarity between the shape of the diagrams in Figure 11.16, and the layout of multi-level navbars. In general, a diagram of a site's organization will suggest the content of navbars. For example, the decision about whether or not to group together the

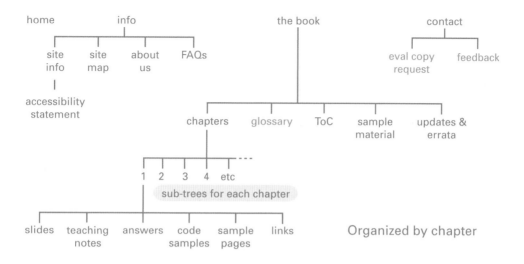

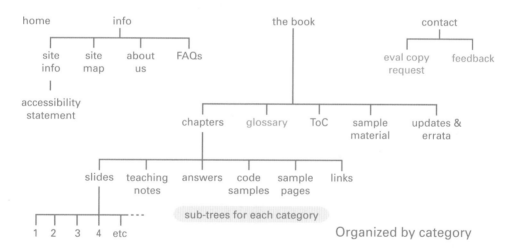

Figure 11.16 Alternative ways of organizing the support site

sub-topics of The Book in our example may be based on the space available for a navbar. Looking at the organization as if it was a navbar may help clarify your understanding of the implications of arranging material in a certain way.

Terminology

Information Architecture

During the late 1990s, the term information architecture began to be used to describe the structural design of Web sites and other computer systems. Information architecture is largely concerned with the inter-related topics of classification, labelling and navigation.

Should information architecture be considered a separate discipline or just part of Web design? On the face of it, analyzing information structures requires different skills from designing the visual appearance of pages, so it might seem to be more efficient to separate the activities, and allocate them to different specialists. In practice, Web designers do a pretty good job of analyzing structure, and separating the functions leads to communication problems and an excess of documentation. Designers often feel resentment at being confined to rigid specifications drawn up by information architects who do not have to implement them.

It remains to be seen whether information architecture will prosper as a distinct profession. For now, information architecture is a convenient shorthand for those aspects of Web site design concerned with classification, organization and navigation.

Dynamic Pages

By examining the site's content and the structural framework, it will be possible to determine which parts of the site – if any – must be dynamically generated. For our book's site, we know that the parts to be dynamically generated are the items shown in orange type in Figure 11.16. The glossary must be generated from a database, for reasons explained in Chapter 8. We also know that the contact and evaluation copy request forms must be handled on the server: we certainly don't intend to expose our email address to spam-harvesting robots, and we need to ensure that lecturers requesting an evaluation copy send the information which is needed by the publisher's marketing department, so we can't just provide email links and let people compose messages as they see fit. There is therefore an unambiguous need for server-side scripting. Given that this is so, we would next consider whether it would be more effective to generate other parts of the site dynamically. For instance, should we generate classified lists of links from a database instead of creating static pages of links?

In general, once you have determined that some scripting is required, you may find that it makes sense to create the entire site dynamically. This gives you great flexibility in the way you combine information. For instance, it would be relatively easy to allow visitors to the support site to choose whether to browse by chapter or by topic, and to generate the appropriate pages and navbars on the fly on the basis of that choice.

If a site does require server-side computation, can it be done using a content management system, or some other Open Source or third-party package? It's always tempting to let somebody else do the work, but this route should only be taken if everybody, including the client, is satisfied that the package does the job that is required, that it conforms to relevant standards and accessibility guidelines, that its capacity for customization does not unduly restrict the possibilities for page design and site structure, and that it is properly documented. If all these criteria are met, much of the design work will be confined to customizing templates and stylesheets. If these criteria are not met, however, a large part of the creation of the site will consist of the writing of server-side scripts and the design and construction of the database.

Determining whether pages are to be dynamically generated has considerable repercussions. There is a qualitative difference between a site, such as a typical brochure site, that just presents static information and needs no server-side scripting, and one that creates pages dynamically in response to input from users.

A static site is relatively easy to create. Much of the work lies in designing its appearance to convey its information effectively. As a rule, static sites have a simple structure, so making the site navigable does not present many challenges. Creating accessible pages using valid markup should be routine. No programming skill is needed, unless JavaScript is being used to enhance the user interface, but static pages offer few opportunities to do much in that line.

Dynamically-generated sites present more challenges. (In return, they are usually more useful and interesting.) Most obviously, somebody will have to write the server-side code. A design agency that does not have any programmers may be unable to make sites of this sort, or may have to make arrangements for sub-contracting programming work. If there are server-side scripts, it tends to be desirable to use extensive scripting on the client-side as well, if it is appropriate to create a rich interface for visitors. This requires an additional, slightly different, set of programming skills.

A dynamically-generated site will have to be served from an environment that supports scripting. This requirement will generally rule out free and budget-priced shared hosting services.

If any shared hosting package is to be used, there will probably be restrictions on which languages and frameworks can be used. Many hosting providers currently limit users of such packages to Perl, Python and PHP, and rarely offer the latest versions or any application frameworks. If, on the other hand, the site is to be hosted on a corporate client's own servers, constraints may be imposed by the IT department. Quite possibly, only certain technologies (very likely Java-based ones) will be approved and supported.

Only by using a dedicated server can you be sure that you will have a free choice in the matter of languages and frameworks. This choice comes at the cost of having to install software and administer the server yourself – not a task to be undertaken lightly by a Web designer with limited resources. But if the primary purpose of the project is the implementation of a Web-based application or service, the setting up of one or more dedicated servers might be seen as part of the job.

Additional Requirements

Sometimes, it is not possible for a site's functions to be fulfilled entirely by computers. For instance, for an e-commerce site selling physical goods, although a script can record orders when they are placed, it is necessary for a person to pack and despatch the goods. Some mechanism can be implemented for informing them when new orders are made, but it is essential that the appropriate steps have been taken to ensure that somebody has been given responsibility for dealing with orders, and that the necessary infrastructure is in place to enable them to do the packing and despatching.

Such matters of procedure should be the client's responsibility, but if the client does not have any experience doing business over the Web, they may overlook requirements of this sort. This is more likely to be the case with smaller clients, so a designer should make sure, before implementing an online room booking system for a guest house, for example, that somebody will regularly check whether any bookings have been made, and that there is a mechanism in place to ensure that bookings made over the telephone will not conflict with bookings made through the Web site.

Accessibility issues create their own requirements. All Web sites should be accessible, as we discussed in Chapter 9, but some clients will have more stringent requirements than others. In particular, government departments and agencies may be legally bound by specific accessibility criteria, and may require extensive testing with disabled users. In the UK, the Disability Rights Commission's *Guide to good practice in commissioning accessible websites* (usually referred to as PAS78) lays down procedures for accessibility testing during the development of Web sites. It is important for designers to be aware of any such requirements and to allocate the necessary resources. If it is not possible to recruit test users with a range of disabilities, it would be wise not to accept the commission. (We must emphasize that we are only referring to specific requirements about testing. All designers should make the necessary effort to ensure that any site they create is accessible.)

Page Templates

Once the structure of a site has been decided on, it is time to move on to the design of the features that will be common to all pages. These include navbars – which can now be created, since the structure is known – colour scheme, layout and typography, which should be used consistently and in accordance with the principles described in Chapter 10.

The first step in a visitor's establishing a mental model of a site's structure is seeing it as a unified entity. To facilitate this step, all the pages on a site should use repeated design elements that emphasize their unity. It is not necessary to be dogmatic about using an identical layout for every page; the demands of the content must determine the details of layout. However, unless there is a reason for diverging from it, a standard layout should be used throughout. The consistent use of colours and page backgrounds provides another effective means of establishing a coherent site identity.

Even if it is not practical or desirable to lay out every page in the same way, certain elements should be treated uniformly throughout the site. In particular, the navbar should always be in the same place on every page, and every page should carry some form of site identification, also in a fixed position in some part of the page (usually the top) which users are bound to see. (It is customary for the site identifier to be a link to the home page.) A logo or the site's name normally serves as identification. Although we do not generally recommend the use of GIF text, it helps to use a distinctive font if the sole identification consists of the site's name, and GIF text ensures that this font will always be used. (Alt-text is needed for users who cannot see images.) Many corporate clients will require that their company logo be reproduced precisely, so the use of an image for the logo is often unavoidable.

To avoid undue repetitive work and reduce the risk of inconsistency, *page templates* should be used as the basis of the markup. These are XHTML documents that contain two types of region: fixed regions and editable regions. As the name implies, fixed regions do not change. These are the regions which will contain the elements that are common to all pages. Editable regions are those which contain the content that is specific to each page. The individual pages making up the site are created, in effect, by copying a template and

Figure 11.17 A template and a Web page built from it

replacing the contents of its editable regions with the material that is unique to the page being constructed. Templates can include any type of element that can appear in an XHTML document, including img elements for embedding images in the same place on every page. They can also include link elements for including a site-wide stylesheet. Figure 11.17 shows a typical template, which includes the site identification and navbar, and a page built from it by adding some text and images.

Simply taking copies of templates does not provide all the potential benefits of a template-based approach. Ideally, you will want to maintain the relationship between a page and the template it was built from, so that, if global changes are required, such as the addition of a new item to the navbar, they can be made just once to the template and will propagate to all the pages based on it. Dreamweaver (see Appendix A) has built-in support for the use of templates of this sort. If you prefer to use a text editor to create documents, several advanced editors support the inclusion of snippets, which may include executable code, which can be used to provide equivalent functionality.

Where the pages are to be generated dynamically, provided the server-side application follows the MVC pattern described in Chapter 8, the views will naturally serve the function of page templates. The only difference between views and page templates as we have just described them is the time at which the pages are generated from them. In the case of views, this will not happen until the controller is executed in response to an HTTP request, whereas with templates the page is generated before it is uploaded, and only re-generated if the template is altered.

Technical Detail

Template Implementation

Templates are usually implemented by an inelegant but effective trick. XHTML documents may include comments, delimited by the strings `<!--` and `-->`. These are intended to allow designers to annotate their documents, but are rarely used for this purpose – well-constructed XHTML needs little comment. However, comments provide a mechanism for embedding information in documents that can be used by programs that process them. In particular, by adding comments of a prescribed form, Web authoring programs can manage templates and the documents created from them.

Dreamweaver, for example, adds a comment of the form

```
<!-- TemplateBeginEditable name="region name" -->
```

at the beginning of each editable region, and

```
<!-- TemplateEndEditable -->
```

at the end. When a template is edited, the program can scan the documents that have been built from it, and update them, leaving the editable regions alone.

Similar mechanisms based on special forms of XHTML comment are used by other programs that provide page templates, although there is no standard that would allow templates created in one program to be used in another.

As well as basing the site's markup on templates, you will, in accordance with the principle of separating appearance from content and structure, use site-wide stylesheets to ensure uniformity of layout and styling. Where pages must diverge from standard layouts, stylesheets can easily be overridden. Page templates can be tested and validated without any stylesheets, to ensure that the markup works on its own. This can be done by instantiating a template with placeholder text and images.

The markup in the site's page templates defines the internal structure of each page. The layout and styling are the visual attributes of the pages. Whereas the markup can be designed without reference to the pages' final appearance, the visual aspects necessarily require design in a visual medium. Many designers are still most comfortable sketching their initial ideas for layouts on paper. Others prefer to create mock-ups in a graphics program, while still others are happiest working with XHTML and CSS as early as possible in the site design process, previewing pages to check their appearance.

Mock-ups can be valuable, especially as a way of communicating ideas and presenting different proposed versions to the client or other members of a design team, but it is important to remember the distinctive characteristics of Web pages. A page mocked-up in Photoshop will have fixed dimensions, and type will not be resizable. Once the general idea of a design has been agreed on, it is essential to implement it in CSS, and to test real pages, albeit with nonsense text and stock images, to make sure that they behave acceptably when fonts and windows are resized. If any of the material for the real site is available, some actual pages can be created, to show to clients and test users, and to see how the material fits and whether the design is appropriate to it. Early implementation in CSS also provides a check that the design can actually be made to work on the Web – it is easy to be tempted to use nice effects in Photoshop that cannot be readily transferred to real pages.

The job of designing the server-side part of a Web application is largely independent of the design of the site's appearance. Determining the sites's structure, on the other hand, is intimately bound up with it: the structure determines how requests must be sent to and from the server-side scripts. Once this has been decided, though, and page templates have been created to serve as views for the application, the job becomes one of program design and implementation. This has its own established methodologies, although for some simple applications the code may not be sufficiently complicated to require any systematic use of formalized processes and notations.

In all cases where a database is used, its design must occur early in the coding. Analysis of the data that must pass between the server and client will show what needs to be stored. It is common practice to construct an *entity-set relationship model* of the data, which shows how the values are grouped together to model entities in the real world, and what relationships exist between those entities. A proper description of data modelling is beyond the scope of this book, but any good account of relational databases should include the full details. Creating normalized tables from an entity-set relationship model is a largely mechanical process.

The database can be populated with dummy data for testing purposes. Once the tables have been constructed, it is sensible to create a simple script that allows them to be queried and updated through a Web interface. Most Web application frameworks are able to do this automatically. Since the page templates constitute the views, and the interface to the database is the model, all that remains is to implement the controllers. Programming is rarely straightforward, but with the other pieces in place, writing controller code should not be terribly arduous.

One aspect of the site remains to be dealt with. If JavaScript is being used, the scripts must be developed at some point. Since pages ought to work without scripts, it makes some sense to defer the development of scripts until the site is working without them. However, if JavaScript is used to provide interface elements such as drop-down menus, the scripts will affect the page's appearance, so they must be specified, if not necessarily implemented, in parallel with the stylesheets. The unobtrusive scripting approach that we have advocated requires the use of `id` and `class` attributes to allow elements to be found so that handlers can be attached to them, so the scripting also has a minor impact on the markup. Thus, it is likely that specifying what scripts will do at an early stage, and implementing them later, will be the most successful approach to incorporating JavaScript into a site. If a Web application framework is being used, though, it may impose its own way of adding JavaScript to the generated pages, in which case the developers will have to work with the framework.

With the completion of page templates, stylesheets and scripts, the actual design of the site is finished. It is highly unlikely that the phases of design will proceed in an orderly fashion one after the other. Implementation concerns may require some early design decisions to be reconsidered. When working pages become available, deficiencies may appear that need to be rectified. When the site is tested on users, it is very likely that usability problems which the designers had overlooked will surface. Likewise, accessibility testing may reveal unforeseen problems. Thus, the design is likely to proceed erratically and require several iterations. In order to allow the designers to go back to earlier versions, to facilitate collaboration and to avoid the risk of losing work, it is advisable to use a version control system of some sort, either one that is built in to a Web authoring tool or a general-purpose system such as Subversion, to organize files.

Sooner or later, an acceptable working design will be arrived at. This will rarely be the end of the job, though. Web designers are usually expected to be site creators, which means that it will be their responsibility to insert the real data into the database, and to instantiate page templates and add the content of all the pages. On some projects, operational tasks, particularly optimizing the performance of the database and server, may also be considered a requirement.

In fact, since site maintenance and updating may also be required, some Web design jobs are never finished.

Epilogue

Like programming, creating Web sites is an activity that is rarely carried out in a neat logical sequence. Ideas about colours, layout and typography may start flowing as soon as a project starts, even before all the content has been considered. A site's structure may remind you of other sites, which may trigger ideas about navigation before the logical structure has been sketched out.

It's foolish to try to cope with too many things at once or to try to do things before decisions have been made that might affect them, but it's also foolish to let good ideas escape. If you have an idea before it's needed, write it down or make a sketch. Do something to make sure you don't forget it. It may turn out that when its time comes, the idea turns out to be no good. But you never know: it may come in useful later on another project.

So keep a notebook. A real physical, preferably hard-backed, notebook, in which you can record your all ideas, keep your sketches and rough diagrams, record the URLs of sites that you find interesting. Some people like to use big sketchbooks, others prefer small notebooks that fit into a pocket. It doesn't really matter. You might think it's better to use a computer-based organizer, to make things easier to find, but you'll lose the chance to do a quick sketch or to jot something down on a bus.

And on the fly leaf of your notebook, write the following:

Get it right
Make it nice

Key Points

Logical Structure

A site's logical structure comprises the logical relationships among pages.

In most cases, a large site's structure is composed of smaller sub-structures.

The fundamental logical structures are the hierarchy and the sequence.

Hierarchies arise from grouping pages together into categories.

Sequences arise when material needs to be viewed in a set order, or where steps in a process must be carried out one after another.

URL Structure

The relationship between the URLs of a site's pages reflects the way they are stored on the server.

A logical structure can be mapped onto any URL structure.

Using a conventional name for the home page allows viewers to enter the domain name instead of the complete URL.

Using URLs whose structure reflects the hierarchy of the site allows users to move up the hierarchy by removing components from the end of URLs.

Choosing URLs that do not alter over time is necessary to avoid bookmarks and links becoming invalid.

Navigational Structure

A site's navigational structure is made up of the connections between its pages.

The structure of the Web can be modelled as a directed graph, with nodes representing pages, considered as states of the browser, and the links representing HTTP requests.

The links must be labelled with any data sent in the request.

Sequences give rise to simple navigational structures: Next and Back links or buttons between the pages in the sequence.

Hierarchies require extra links from any page to the root and all of its children for convenient navigation.

Master-detail pages can often be used to navigate through shallow, broad hierarchies.

Additional ad hoc links run in to the text or in a separate box may be needed.

Superposed hierarchies require a way of navigating within two structures at once.

Large sites may need to be broken into sub-sites, or they may make use of pop-up menus to provide links between pages.

Chronologically organized sites can use a calendar for navigation.

Every site, except for the smallest and most simply organized, should have a site map.

Most sites provide a search facility, but this is not always straightforward to implement, especially where pages are generated from a database.

Links and navbars must be easily identifiable, to allow visitors to perceive the site's navigational structure.

Distinctive styling of the current navbar entry, breadcrumbs and road maps help users orient themselves within the site's structure.

Using conventional labels for navbar links helps make their purpose and destination clear.

Creating Web Sites

The site's purpose should be clearly established at the outset.

A list of contents should be constructed in conjunction with the client, and arranged to form the outline of the logical structure.

Classification must consider the entities and processes in the real world to which the site's contents are related.

Alternative organizations will usually be possible.

The need for server-side computation should be determined. If pages must be dynamically generated there will be implications for the facilities and resources required to construct and host the site.

Any external requirements should be determined and specified.

Resources should be allocated to any mandatory accessibility testing.

All the pages on a site should use repeated design elements that emphasize their unity.

Page templates should be used to avoid repetitive work and reduce the risk of inconsistency.

In an MVC application, views serve the function of templates.

Use site-wide stylesheets to ensure uniformity of layout and styling.

Mock-ups and dummy pages can be used to check and communicate ideas about appearance.

The design of server-side programs can be largely independent of the site's visual design, but is bound up with its structure.

Databases must be designed at an early stage in the coding.

Client-side scripts may be specified in parallel with the design of stylesheets.

The site design may require several iterations.

Exercises

Test Questions

1. Why do Web sites rarely exhibit a purely hierarchical structure?

2. Give an example of a sequential structure you might encounter on the Web that can be traversed in either direction, and one that must always be traversed from beginning to end.

3. What problems would be caused by using the file name `homepage.html` for a site's home page? When would these problems *not* occur?

4. Can an automated link checker determine whether every page in a site can be reached from the home page?

5. Explain why links between pages and their children in a hierarchical structure are normally augmented with additional links when creating the corresponding navigational structure.

6. Should a site map contain a link to every page in the site?

Discussion Topics

1. One possible way of organizing a site consists of writing a script that selects the contents on the basis of the data in an HTTP request. That is, every page is generated by the script index.php, which looks at its parameters and serves an appropriate page. Discuss the advantages and disadvantages of this approach.

2. Do plumbers need Web sites? If not, why not? If so, specify a design for a plumber's Web site that takes into account all of their needs.

3. Under what circumstances, if any, would it be sensible to give responsibility for the design of a site's structure and navigation to a specialist information architect?

4. Should the home page of a Web site conform to the standard layout and styling used on the rest of the site?

Practical Tasks

1. Make a list of the navbar link labels common to most sites you visit.

2. Revisit some of the sites you have looked at for previous chapters, and analyze their structures. Identify hierarchies, sequences and sub-sites, if any. Look at the URLs of pages as you explore each site, and see how they relate to the logical structure. Does the navigational structure express the logical relationships you have identified?

3. Create an online labour exchange – a site where employers can post details of jobs, and people seeking work can post their résumés. Each group can scan the items posted by the other, and make contact with the poster for further details. You will need to provide facilities for people to register as either an employer or a job-seeker, and separate interfaces for the two groups, enabling each kind of visitir to the site to find the information they need. This project will draw on work you did for previous chapters, but you should be prepared to adapt to the requirements of the site as a whole.

4. Create a Web site to serve as an online brochure for a small business. This should present information about the goods or services they provide (including prices where appropriate), as well as some information about the company, such as its history, location and the people involved, and contact details. All of this should be presented in as attractive a way as possible – the purpose of the site is to generate business. If you can, get in touch with a real local business who can act as the client for this job, and try to fulfill their requirements.

Software for Web Designers

It is possible to create rudimentary Web pages using nothing more than a basic text editor, such as Notepad or TextEdit, since XHTML documents and CSS stylesheets are nothing more than text files. In reality, most Web designers employ a substantial collection of software for the creation and editing of XHTML, CSS, JavaScript and server-side programs, for site maintenance, and for the preparation of graphics and other media to be included in their pages.

Most tasks in Web design are served by a choice of commercial applications, shareware and Open Source programs. Some commercial programs have the status of industry standards, and every Web designer will be expected to have some knowledge of these. This does not mean that they are always the best tool for every job, though, and professionals should be familiar with a wide range of software.

In this appendix, we will briefly survey some of the more important programs, to give you an idea of the tools that Web designers have at their disposal. We make no attempt to be exhaustive, nor to teach the use of any of these tools here; we just indicate their capabilities.

Web Pages and Sites

There is a spectrum of programs for creating Web pages, ranging from raw code editors, which let you enter tags, attributes, CSS rules and so on by hand, to 'code-free' page creation software, which completely hides the code and lets unskilled users create pages visually using a graphical interface. The most popular professional tools lie between these extremes and combine elements of both approaches.

Code Editors

You can use any text editor to create XHTML documents, CSS stylesheets and JavaScript scripts, but there exist many editors which reduce the drudgery of typing tags and attributes, and provide additional help in ensuring that your documents do not contain errors. Some of these are specialized Web editors, but most are general-purpose text editors, which also provide similar help in creating programs in a range of languages. The most powerful of these editors provide extension mechanisms, allowing modules to be added for specific languages, and their Web programming support is provided in this way.

No single program in this class can be identified as a market leader or standard. Most of them are confined to a single platform. The notable exceptions are Emacs and vim, which are available on nearly every platform, although they betray their Unix origins. On MacOS X, BBEdit has long been popular with Web designers who prefer writing code by hand. TextMate is a newer alternative with a powerful extension mechanism that allows new commands to be added by the use of scripts. Crimson Editor, UltraEdit-32 and HomeSite+ are among the capable options available to Windows users.

All code editors provide syntax colouring of XHTML and CSS documents, to enable you to identify tags, attributes, strings and so on at a glance. The main document window in Figure A.1 shows the syntax colouring of an XHTML document in a popular editor. In addition, some means of inserting tags without having to type them explicitly is usually provided. This may take the form of menus, tool bars or palettes, such as the ones shown at the right of Figure A.1, with entries for the most commonly used elements. As this shows, similar means are provided for adding CSS properties. Selecting an entry from a palette – or its equivalent – will cause a dialogue to be displayed, such as the one in Figure A.2, where relevant options may be set. Some editors, which are primarily aimed at programmers, use a different approach, providing keyboard shortcuts for adding the boilerplate for inserting tags.

The best code editors provide a context-sensitive way of adding attributes. For example, a context menu like the one shown in Figure A.3} may be available, from which an attribute may be chosen when the cursor is inside a start tag, causing it to be added to the tag. If `class` was chosen here, then

```
class = ""
```

would be added to the start tag, and the cursor would be placed between the quote marks, so you could just type the attribute's value. Alternatively, the dialogue invoked when inserting a tag may provide a means of adding attributes at the same time.

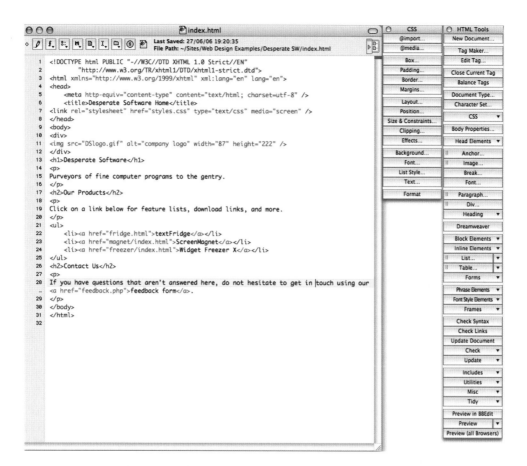

Figure A.1 A typical code editor

Figure A.2 Setting options for an element

Figure A.3 Inserting attributes with a contextual menu

Valid XHTML documents include a lot of red tape, such as the DTD and namespace declarations. A good editor will provide a way of inserting all this for you automatically. The usual method makes use of document templates, which consist of a framework containing all the fixed elements, to which you add the specific elements of a particular document. Usually, a selection of templates corresponding to different DTDs is available. A typical XHTML 1.0 template has the following content:

```
<!DOCTYPE html PUBLIC "-//W3C//DTD XHTML 1.0 Strict//EN"
        "http://www.w3.org/TR/xhtml1/DTD/xhtml1-strict.dtd">
<html xmlns="http://www.w3.org/1999/xhtml" xml:lang="en" lang="en">
<head>
   <meta http-equiv="content-type" content="text/html;
      charset=utf-8" />
   <title>Untitled</title>
</head>
<body>

</body>
</html>
```

When a document is created from this template, the cursor is placed on the blank line between the opening and closing tags for the body element.

One of the most valuable facilities provided by Web code editors is a means of validating documents. This may be done either within the editor itself or by sending the document to an online validation service, such as that provided by the W3C. Most editors also offer some way of previewing pages. There may be a command to pass the current document to one or more browsers running on the designer's system, or the editor may have a previewing function built in to it, allowing you to switch between a window in which you edit the code and another that displays it as it would be in a browser. (This may be quicker and more convenient, but it is no substitute for previewing in a range of browsers.)

As well as XHTML and CSS, code editors often have modes for editing programs in JavaScript, PHP and other languages used for server-side computation.

Semi-Visual Editors

When people who were not programmers started to create Web pages, a need arose for a more visual approach than raw code editors provide. The first attempts at satisfying this need used the well-established paradigm of the word processor as their inspiration. Web pages were to be created in the same way as word processor documents, by applying styling commands to text typed into a document window, which displayed the page as it would appear, in a WYSIWYG fashion.

As you should appreciate, the WYSIWYG concept – what you see is what you get – does not fit well with Web pages, where you never know what you will get, since it depends on the user's browser settings and window size. Furthermore, the complexity of CSS and its use of selectors mean that simply clicking an appropriate button to apply styling to the current selection is not adequate. As a result, programs of this type have evolved to incorporate elements of code editing, and interface features that are more appropriate for creating and applying styles using CSS.

Dreamweaver is the most widely used example of this type of program, so we will concentrate mainly on that. Nvu is a less well known Open Source alternative, which offers many of the same facilities.

Both of these programs incorporate a code editor – in Dreamweaver's case, a very powerful one, with most of the functions provided by the programs described in the previous section. However, they also offer an alternative mode of working. In Dreamweaver this is called design mode, in Nvu, normal mode. In this mode, the page is shown in roughly the way it

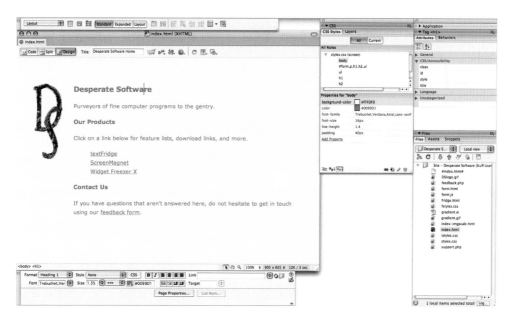

Figure A.4 Dreamweaver's workspace in design mode

will be displayed by a browser, and editing is carried out directly on this view of the page, without reference to the tags.

Figure A.4 shows Dreamweaver's workspace when it is in design mode. The left part of the screen looks similar to a word processor, with the document itself, a toolbar above it, from which elements like images and links can be added to the document, and a context-sensitive inspector below, where properties of the currently selected object can be set. So, for example, to add a link, you would select the text of the source anchor, click on the link icon in the toolbar, and set the destination and other parameters in a simple dialogue with fields for the link text and attributes of the a element, including href. For links within the site, you can browse to the appropriate file instead of entering the URL by hand. Subsequently, when the text of the link is selected in the document window, its parameters are displayed in the inspector, where they can be changed if necessary.

A similar style of interaction is used for adding most elements to the page. Absolutely positioned div elements (which Dreamweaver insists on calling layers, after an obsolete non-standard Netscape tag) can be created by dragging out a rectangle with an appropriate tool. Images and other content can then be added to the div, so arbitrarily positioned layouts can be created interactively with ease and without the need to work out any coordinates or

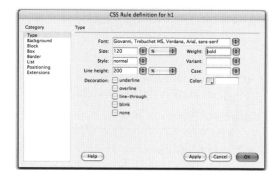

Figure A.5 Defining a CSS rule in Dreamweaver

sizes arithmetically. However, Dreamweaver will use pixel units, which is not always what is required.

CSS rules can be defined easily: Figure A.5 shows the succession of dialogues that are used to define a new rule. The second dialogue allows you to set values for just about every CSS property, using standard dialogue controls. All the CSS syntax is handled for you by Dreamweaver. The CSS styles palette that you see towards the right of Figure A.4 allows you to inspect all the CSS rules in scope, or all those that are applied to the currently selected element, and change the values of their properties without using a modal dialogue. The tag inspector in the top right of the screen provides a similar means of inspecting and changing the attributes of any selected element.

It is probably inevitable that code generated automatically by a program will not always be as good as you could write by hand. In that case, you will want to edit and improve it yourself. As we mentioned earlier, Dreamweaver incorporates a powerful code editor that has all the features of dedicated editors, including syntax colouring and assistance with tag and attribute insertion. The main document window can be switched between its default design view, which we illustrated before, and code view, in which it displays the code. There is also a split view that shows the code in the upper half of the window, with the design view below it. Code view can be used for editing programs written in JavaScript, PHP, Java, C# and other languages.

Dreamweaver is a powerful application, with many more features than we have space to describe here. As well as simple page creation, it supports integration of pages with server-side scripts. It also has extensive support for reusable page fragments, templates and site management, and provides a library of behaviours – packaged JavaScript routines for performing common tasks.

Given all these features and the possibility of mixing page creation in design view with raw code editing in code view, why would anyone not use Dreamweaver or a similar application? When most of a site's pages are generated dynamically, the design view model of page creation doesn't make much sense. Although Dreamweaver does have support for certain types of dynamic page, it cannot comfortably accommodate most Web frameworks or complex patterns of interaction. Similarly, although there are behaviours for some simple sorts of JavaScript interaction, elaborate interaction of the sort routinely found in Web 2.0 sites cannot be produced in that way. (In any case, the scripting is not unobtrusive and does not always conform to standards.) Hence, designers of ambitious modern sites will spend most of their time in Dreamweaver's code view. In that case, it may be preferable to use a less complex, single-purpose editor – it will certainly be less expensive.

Visual Page Creation

There will always be a demand for purely visual page creation programs from people who want to create Web pages but don't want to learn XHTML, CSS and the other Web technologies. You should be able to appreciate that, because of the way Web technologies work, such an approach is always going to be limited, and for the most part, programs that take the approach of completely hiding all the code are only suitable for casual use by amateurs. A possible exception to this rule is SoftPress Freeway, which presents an interface that resembles that of a desktop publishing application, such as Quark Xpress, and allows designers to build pages by drawing frames on the page and adding content to them. Freeway could generate adequate code in this way in the past, but its approach has failed to keep up with developments in Web technology. However, graphic designers may still find it the best way to turn their ideas into Web pages.

Most other visual page creation programs use an approach based on templates. A user selects a template, which defines the layout and appearance of a page and possibly includes some fixed features, customizes it, and adds their own content, by dragging and dropping images and typing new text to replace the template's placeholders. Often wizards are used to guide the user through the process. Web professionals are unlikely to use such programs to create Web sites, but they may find themselves having to create templates.

Content Management Systems and blogging systems could also be thought of as applications for creating Web pages without writing code. Once again, the Web professional's main role in connection with such systems is in creating the templates for other users – although if Web designers want to keep a blog, they would be well advised to use the same sort of software as everybody else.

Site Management

Web designers rarely need to create single pages in isolation. Pages are usually combined into sites, which must then be deployed on a server accessible over the Internet. Software can assist with maintaining consistency among the pages of a site. The usual way this is done is by allowing users to create templates, which are XHTML documents that include two types of area: fixed and editable. New documents can be created from a template. Within the document, only the editable areas can be altered. (If you have used a desktop publishing program, such as InDesign, you will see a parallel with master pages.) If a fixed area of a template is changed, then all documents that have been created from the template will be updated to reflect the change. Templates are a feature of Dreamweaver and they are supported by some code editors.

Programs can also help with the maintenance of links. They routinely include functions for checking that all the links in a site are valid (i.e. that the links point to documents that actually exist). It is also customary for semi-visual design programs to provide site maps, which display the structure of links between pages. It may also be possible to make changes, for example to a URL, in every page of a site. If your preferred editor does not provide link-checking facilities, there are dedicated utilities that can be used to perform these checks outside the editor.

Files are normally uploaded to their server using FTP. Most Web design programs of all types have an FTP client built in to them. This means that, once the necessary details for a site – such as the FTP server's URL and a user name and password – have been entered, the files can be uploaded with a single command which causes the program to open a connection and upload the files. Usually, the programs are intelligent enough to upload only files that have changed. (That is, if a version of the same file is already on the server and is no older than the version on the designer's machine, no new version will be uploaded.)

Although the FTP clients built in to Web design programs are usually adequate, it may be more convenient to use a separate program dedicated to FTP transfers. Such programs may offer additional facilities or a more convenient interface, and can sometimes cope with non-standard behaviour from FTP servers.

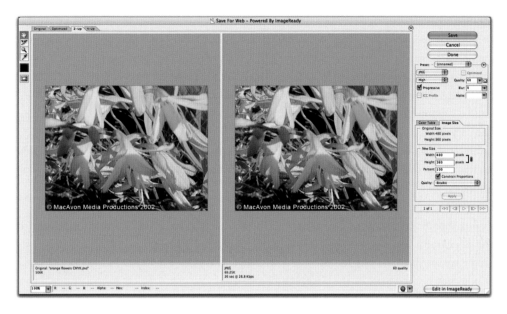

Figure A.6 The Save For Web dialogue in Photoshop

Graphics

Web designers are usually expected to be able to prepare the graphic elements of pages. Photographs and artwork may originate with somebody else, but it is part of a Web designer's job to convert them to a format suitable for the Web, and perform any downsampling and resizing necessary. They may also have to perform some image correction.

Bitmapped Images

Anybody who works professionally with bitmapped images must be familiar with Photoshop. For those who believe strongly in the Open Source/Free Software philosophy, there is an alternative known as The Gimp, but it lacks some essential features, and has nothing approaching Photoshop's status as an industry standard.

One of the features of Photoshop that is of most use to Web designers is the Save For Web command. This opens a dialogue box illustrated in Figure A.6, in which a Web graphics format – GIF, JPEG or PNG – can be chosen, and any appropriate parameters can be set. As you see in the illustration, a preview of the optimized version being saved may be shown next to the original image. It is also possible to view the original with three candidate optimized versions, to allow you to compare different settings.

Another feature intended for Web designers is image slicing. You can break up an image into rectangular pieces called slices, either by using a tool to draw the divisions or by assigning the elements on different layers to slices. When you save the image for the Web, each slice is saved to a separate file, and an HTML file that puts them together on a Web page is generated at the same time. Some slices can be designated as `No Image` slices, and marked-up text can be supplied as their contents. When the slices are exported, this text is used instead of the part of the image that corresponds to the slice. This can provide a way of creating pages entirely within Photoshop for graphic designers who have little or no knowledge of Web technologies. However, it naturally leads to fixed layouts using absolute units, which is rarely desirable, and the quality of code generated is poor.

A less direct way of using Photoshop for Web design is for creating rough mock-ups of the appearance of pages. These can then be translated into real Web pages fairly easily. Dreamweaver has a facility for importing an image into a document as a tracing background. It does not become part of the page, but can be used as a guide for laying out the real page elements. This can only be a starting point, though, because an image has fixed dimensions, so it cannot directly form the basis of a fluid layout or one that uses relative units.

Photoshop has a companion program called ImageReady, which was originally designed as a dedicated Web graphics editor. As such, it can only work with RGB images at screen resolution, and it lacks some of Photoshop's more sophisticated facilities, as well as all of its features that are related to print. ImageReady also has some features intended specifically for Web designers, such as tools for creating rollover buttons and image maps. Over the years, other Web-related features have migrated into Photoshop itself, and ImageReady is now virtually redundant, but it may sometimes be more convenient than having to deal with the full complexity of Photoshop.

Vector Graphics

Vector graphics are rarely found on the Web as still images, SVG notwithstanding, but vector graphics applications can be useful to the Web designer nevertheless. If a program can export finished artwork in a Web graphics format, it doesn't matter how the image was created originally. Vector tools are much more convenient than bitmapped image editors for some tasks, such as creating icons and buttons with simple geometrical shapes.

Illustrator is the most mature vector graphics application in use. As well as the standard vector tools for creating and transforming shapes and paths, it allows complex strokes to be applied to paths, creating the impression of natural media drawing. Recent versions also include rudimentary support for 3-D effects.

Illustrator provides a `Save For Web` command that is identical to Photoshop's. This makes it easy to turn vector graphics into compressed bitmapped images suitable for the Web. It is also possible to slice an image, assigning different objects to different slices. Objects can be used as image map areas, with URLs attached to them.

Like Photoshop, Illustrator can be effectively used to create mock-ups of Web pages.

Illustrator is essentially a PDF-based program, but it can also export SVG. For those who are primarily interested in SVG there is an Open Source program called Inkscape, which uses SVG as its native format. This is, however, an immature program compared with Illustrator.

Vector graphics are of course most frequently seen on the Web in the form of animation, and Illustrator may be used for creating Web animation in the form of SWF files.

Time-Based Media

Animation, video editing and sound production require specialized skills and complicated software. Although some Web designers may have professional skills in these media, most will need to leave these jobs to people who are trained and experienced in them. However, in small companies it may sometimes be necessary for a Web specialist to do some simple animation.

For somebody with experience using mainstream graphics applications, the easiest way to create animation is in Illustrator or Photoshop. Illustrator allows the layers of a document to be exported as frames of an animation in SWF format. Photoshop has more elaborate support for animation. In its `Animation` palette, frames can be defined as a combination of layers, so some layers can be reused in more than one frame. Animations can be exported as animated GIFs; from ImageReady they can also be exported as SWFs.

Image rollovers, a form of limited duration time-based media, can be created within ImageReady in a similar way to animations. They can also be created in Dreamweaver, simply by specifying a set of images for each of the different possible states of the rollover.

Anyone who is a Web animator will have to learn Flash itself, but that program is too complex and specialized to describe here.

Testing

Every Web designer needs a collection of browsers with which to test their pages and sites. It is hardly practical to have a copy of every single browser in existence, but at the very least, it is necessary to test on the most popular desktop browsers. Currently these are Internet Explorer, Firefox, Safari and Opera. Since it is only the rendering of pages that is of concern, there is no need to test using browsers which use the same layout engine. For example, if you test on Firefox, there is no need to test on Mozilla.

Since Internet Explorer only runs on Windows (the Mac version, which is no longer supported, used a different layout engine) and Safari only runs on MacOS X, it follows that some means of running both operating systems is needed, whether it is a virtualization system, such as Virtual PC, a dual booting arrangement, or separate machines.

Ideally, you should be able to test several versions of each browser, but this presents problems. In their different ways, both Internet Explorer and Safari are integrated into their respective operating systems. In the case of Internet Explorer, it is virtually impossible to run two versions at the same time. For Safari, operating system updates may prevent older versions running. Ironically, this means that users who do not want to update their systems may continue to run older versions of browsers, while at the same time Web designers with up-to-date systems cannot test these older versions. It may therefore be necessary to keep an old machine, running obsolete systems, for the purpose of testing.

As well as testing pages on the mainstream graphical browsers, it is advisable to test them using a text-only browser, to get a broad idea of their accessibility to people using screen readers. The most widely used text-only browser is Lynx.

It is sometimes useful to be able to inspect the HTTP requests and responses sent between a Web browser and server. This can be especially helpful for sites that use AJAX. There are many traffic watching utilities available, which provide this service. The most basic of these simply provide a transcript of the data sent between client and server, while more sophisticated programs provide additional information and extra control. Figure A.7 shows a session window in Charles, a cross-platform traffic watcher written in Java. As well as showing the headers and data in individual HTTP requests and responses, Charles provides a structural view of a sequence of messages, showing how the URLs are related. This is shown in the

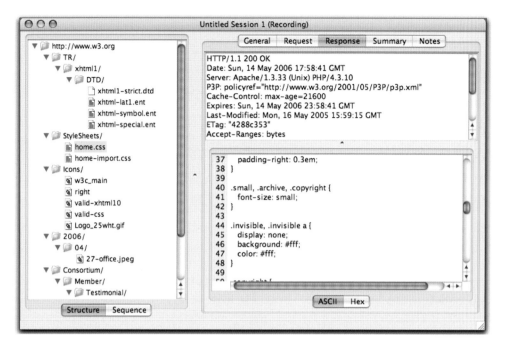

Figure A.7 Watching HTTP traffic with Charles

left pane of the session window. The program also provides tools for manipulating cookies, throttling bandwidth to simulate different types of connection (modem, broadand, etc.), disabling caching and overriding IP addresses, as well as providing summaries of the message data, its size and the data rate achieved.

Web designers should also have access to a utility that simulates the appearance of pages to people with colour vision defects. There are several such utilities available as freeware for all platforms.

A final piece of software that can help with testing is a font manager. By successively turning off any fonts that you have explicitly used in a `font-family` declaration in a stylesheet, you will be able to see how the page degrades if users do not have the necessary fonts installed on their systems.

XML Namespaces

By writing a DTD or schema you can create a specialized markup language for a particular class of documents, but this is not always the most sensible thing to do. For instance, XHTML is a markup language for Web pages, and MathML is a markup language for mathematics. If you wanted to make a Web page containing some mathematical equations, it wouldn't be very efficient to create a new markup language for mathematical Web pages. You would want to be able to combine XHTML and MathML instead. Since they are both XML-based languages, this would seem to be a reasonable thing to do, but in general, combining different XML-based languages raises some issues which must be addressed before this can be done safely.

The most serious problem is the potential for name clashes. That is, the languages you wish to combine may use the same name for element types, but with different meanings. To see how this might come about, and how the problem is resolved, consider a simplified version of a possible real scenario.

Imagine that an XML-based language called BiblML has been devised for recording bibliographical data. (Several such languages do exist, but none is standardized.) A BiblML document might look like this (omitting the prologue):

```
<bibliography>
  <article>
    <author>H.Z. Hackenbush</author>
    <title>Bilaterally anomalous hypertension in wealthy
females</title>
```

```
   <journal>Veterinary Dissimulation</journal>
   <volume>23</volume><pages>14-16</pages>
   <date>1939</date>
 </article>
 elements for other items in the bibliography
</bibliography>
```

Now suppose that an academic institution sets up documents containing the personnel records of its staff, using another XML-based language, StaffML. A typical staff record might be similar to the following:

```
<member>
   <surname>Hackenbush</surname>
   <forenames>Hugo Z</forenames>
   <title>Dr</title>
   <post>Head of Sanitarium</post>
</member>
```

Finally suppose that it became necessary to produce a document listing the publications of all the members of staff. The natural way to do this would be by adding a bibliography element to each member element, like this:

```
<member>
   <surname>Hackenbush</surname>
   <forenames>Hugo Z</forenames>
   <title>Dr</title>
   <post>Head of Sanitarium</post>
   <bibliography>
     <article>
       <author>H.Z. Hackenbush</author>
       <title>Bilaterally anomalous hypertension in wealthy
females</title>
       <journal>Veterinary Dissimulation</journal>
       <volume>23</volume><pages>14-16</pages>
       <date>1939</date>
     </article>
     elements for other publications by Hackenbush
   </bibliography>
</member>
```

As you can see, we now have two `title` elements, shown highlighted, performing quite different functions. Such name clashes will always be possible when the vocabularies of separately developed languages are combined. It is easy for a human reader to see what is going on, but a computer program needs some explicit indication that these two elements are different. The solution is to allocate names to *namespaces*, which are just identifiable collections of element and attribute names, and to add a mechanism for indicating which namespace a name belongs to.

Although it is not practical to demand that names used in XML documents are unique, there is a mechanism in place that allows us to generate unique identifiers. Domain names are unique, and the method by which they are administered ensures that they will remain so. It is reasonable to suppose that organizations or individuals that register a domain name can maintain control over the path components of any URLs belonging to that domain. In other words, URLs can safely be assumed to be unique. Thus, if a namespace is associated with a URL, element and attribute names could be prefixed with this URL, and they would, in turn, be guaranteed to be unique. URLs are, however, long and unwieldy to use in this way; they also may include characters that are not allowed in names in XML. The solution is to allow an arbitrary short prefix to be defined, which stands in for the full URL. A colon is used to separate a namespace prefix from the rest of a name.

To make this clearer, suppose that the developers of BiblML use the URL `http://www.biblml.org/bibns` for the BiblML namespace. In our document that uses BiblML with StaffML, we might decide to use the prefix `b` to designate names from the BiblML namespace. The journal element's name would be written `b:journal`, and the `title` element, for the title of the article, would become `b:title`. To associate a prefix with the namespace's URL, it is necessary to declare the namespace by assigning the URL as the value of an attribute with a special name, consisting of the string `xmlns` followed by a colon and the chosen namespace prefix, which can take the same form as any XML name, but cannot contain a colon. (Remember that XML names cannot begin with the three letters x, m, l, so `xml` is not a valid prefix name. There are, to confuse matters, some predefined names that use the `xml` prefix, but these are not actually in a namespace, but defined by the XML standard, with fixed meanings.) Hence in this case, we need to assign the BiblML namespace URL to the attribute `xmlns:b`. If we preferred to use the prefix `bbl`, we would have to assign the URL to `xmlns:bbl`, and so on.

This attribute can be used with any element. Its effect extends throughout that element. In our example document, a good place to declare the namespace is the `bibliography` element, since all the BiblML names are contained within it. Thus, the publication details could be written like this:

```
<b:bibliography xmlns:b="http://www.bibml.org/bibns">
  <b:article>
    <b:author>H.Z. Hackenbush</b:author>
    <b:title>Bilaterally anomalous hypertension in wealthy
females</b:title>
    <b:journal>Veterinary Dissimulation</b:journal>
    <b:volume>23</b:volume><b:pages>14-16</b:pages>
    <b:date>1939</b:date>
  </b:article>
  ...
</b:bibliography>
```

Notice that we have used the b prefix on the bibliography element itself; the start and end tags are part of the element, so the prefix is defined within them.

If, at the same time, the developers who created StaffML had chosen to use the URL http://www.staffml.com/staffns for their namespace, we could use a prefix p for the StaffML element names, so that there would no longer be a clash between the two uses of title. The combined document would now look like this:

```
<p:member xmlns:p="http://www.staffml.com/staffns">
  <p:surname>Hackenbush</p:surname>
  <p:forenames>Hugo Z</p:forenames>
  <p:title>Dr</p:title>
  <p:post>Head of Sanitarium</p:post>
  <b:bibliography xmlns:b="http://www.bibml.org/bibns">
    <b:article>
      <b:author>H.Z. Hackenbush</b:author>
      <b:title>Bilaterally anomalous hypertension in wealthy
females</b:title>
      <b:journal>Veterinary Dissimulation</b:journal>
      and so on
  </b:bibliography>
</p:member>
```

It is the author of the document who decides what prefixes to use, so these can always be chosen to be unique within a document. If prefixes were chosen by the developer of the language, we would still have the possibility of name clashes, since language developers working independently might chance upon the same prefix and the same element or attribute name. By using URLs to identify namespaces, this possibility is avoided; by letting the author of the document choose prefixes to stand in for namespace URLs, a manageable notation is achieved, which still guarantees freedom from name clashes.

There is one additional complication to the use of namespaces. Where a document is predominantly or entirely marked up with elements from a single namespace, it is tiresome to have to add a namespace prefix to every name used in the document. This can be avoided by declaring a ***default namespace***. Any names that do not have a namespace prefix are taken to belong to this namespace. A default is set by assigning its URL to the attribute `xmlns`, with no suffix. Thus, if we wanted to use the names from the BiblML namespace without prefixes within the bibliography element, we would use the following start tag:

```
<bibliography xmlns="http://www.bibml.org/bibns">
```

Within the bibliography element, `title` would then mean the `title` from the BiblML namespace, and so on.

When URLs are used for namespaces in this way, there is no implication that there is anything at the location which the URL points to. In particular, you cannot assume that the URL points to some description of the namespace, such as a list of the names it contains. It is possible that this will be the case, but there is nothing in the XML namespaces standard that requires it. Namespaces use URLs because they are unique.

We have stressed the use of namespaces to avoid name clashes, but you can also think of them as a way of tagging names to indicate their generic function. For instance, the XLink Recommendation defines a collection of attributes, which can be used by any element type that performs a linking function. The names of these attributes are contained in a namespace, so any document that uses them must declare this namespace. The effect is that any program that processes such a document can easily recognize the XLink attributes and process them accordingly.

Where does this leave the DTD? There is an apparent conflict between the namespace and document type definition mechanisms. The DTD defines the collection of elements and their attributes for a particular type of document. Technically, this is different from defining a collection of names, which is all that a namespace does, but in practical terms it is necessary to reconcile the two sets of definitions, and this is not as easy as it might be.

Emerging Technology

Modules

A related issue to that of combining different XML-based languages is that of breaking existing XML-based languages into reusable parts, or modules. This allows well-defined subsets of a language to be implemented in software that runs on restricted hardware, such as PDAs. It also offers greater opportunities for creating languages by combining modules in a 'mix and match' manner, using only certain features of an existing language. XHTML has been modularized in this way, and various combined languages have been built out of its modules and modules from other languages, such as SMIL. As before, there are certain technical difficulties associated with decomposing languages in this way, mostly connected with DTDs. Because a document can only have one document type declaration, referencing a single DTD, it is necessary for the DTDs for modules to be combined. This is somewhat messy. Generally, though, Web designers do not need to be aware of it, and can treat the combined DTD as if it were a traditional, monolithic definition.

The fundamental problem is that the DTD mechanism is inherited from SGML, which has no namespaces, and as a result, DTDs and namespaces do not fit together very comfortably.

In the case of a single XML-based language, there is no real problem, since declaring a default namespace allows you to use the undecorated element names as found in the DTD. The namespace declaration becomes another piece of housekeeping syntax, which will usually be inserted into your documents automatically by any editor used to create them. This is the usual state of affairs with simple XHTML Web pages. Where languages are combined, the situation gets more complicated, because there is no way to declare a namespace inside a DTD, so various unsatisfactory expedients must be employed. The only satisfactory solution is to move to schemas for this situation. Whereas DTDs and namespaces have an uneasy relationship, schemas and namespaces have been integrated from the beginning. The full details lie beyond the scope of this book, but the important fact is that the author of a schema may define (within the schema itself) a target namespace, to which all the names defined in the schema are allocated. A document that uses the schema can then declare the namespace and use all the names from the schema.

Index

A

a element 123–124
  in image maps 274–275
AAC 328
abbr attribute 532
Abilene 91
abort event 383
absolute positioning 194–198, 576–577
absolute units 172, 195
  and text measure 570
accessibility 16, 504–540, 640, 645, 664
  and Flash 539
  legislation 506–507
  via alternative pages 515–516
  via structural markup 516–518
  via textual alternatives 519–526
accessibility statements 535, 538
accesskey attribute 534
access keys 534–535, 539
access points 88
action attribute 127, 472
ActionScript 303, 342
:active pseudo-class 200
ActiveX controls 288, 420

addEventListener method 384
additive primary colours 227, 234
address element 72, 116, 517
ADSL 18, 84–85
Advanced Audio Coding 328
:after pseudo-element 208
age-related conditions 509
AIFF 329
AJAX 27, 418, 425–426, 436, 624, 664
alert method 389
alphabets 76
alpha channels 253
alt attribute 269, 274, 519
alt-text 519–521, 529, 630
anchors 123, 126
  named 127
animated GIFs 300–302
animation 296–306
  as video 307
  by program 306
  see also animated GIFs; Flash; toons
anti-aliasing 257
Apache 438, 441
appendChild method 354, 356
applets 443

application layer 47
area element 273, 520
arrays
  in JavaScript 361
  in PHP 464, 486
ASCII 76, 77
ASP.NET 439, 441
assignment 363
assistive technology 505, 510–512
Asymmetric Digital Subscriber Line, see ADSL
Asynchronous JavaScript and XML, see AJAX
Atom 14
attributes 104–105, 117–118
  and properties 355
  Boolean 105
  ID type 105, 117
  inserting 653
audio, see sound
AVI 319
axes 255

B

B-frames 313
back button 8
background-attachment property 190